Exchanges

A Global History Reader
Volume II, from 1450

TREVOR R. GETZ
RICHARD J. HOFFMAN
JARBEL RODRIGUEZ

ALL OF SAN FRANCISCO STATE UNIVERSITY

PEARSON

Prentice
Hall

Upper Saddle River, New Jersey 07458

Library of Congress Cataloging-in-Publication Data

Getz, Trevor R.
  Exchanges: a global history reader / Trevor R. Getz, Richard J. Hoffman, Jarbel Rodriguez.
    v. cm.
  Contents: v. 1. To 1500
  ISBN 978-0-321-35508-9 (alk. paper)
  1. World history—Textbooks.   2. World history—Sources.   I. Hoffman, Richard
J. (Richard Joseph)   II. Rodriguez, Jarbel   III. Title.
  D21.G45 2008
  909—dc22   2008031900

Executive Editor: Charles Cavaliere
Editorial Director: Leah Jewell
Editorial Assistant: Lauren Aylward
Project Manager: Rob DeGeorge
Senior Marketing Manager: Laura Lee Manley
Marketing Assistant: Athena Moore
Senior Managing Editor: Ann Marie McCarthy
Production Liaison: Fran Russello
Permissions Supervisor: Sherry Hoesly/The Permissions Group
Senor Operations Supervisor: Mary Ann Gloriande
Cover Design: Margaret Kenselaar
**Cover Illustration: Volume II: The front cover image was taken from *Transit Maps of the World* by Mark Ovenden
(Penguin Books, 2007). Used by permission of Mark Ovenden.**
AV Project Manager: Mirella Signoretto
Illustrator/Cartography: Maps.com
Manager, Rights and Permissions: Zina Arabia
Manager, Visual Research: Beth Brenzel
Manager, Cover Visual Research & Permissions: Karen Sanatar
Image Permission Coordinator: Jan Marc Quisumbing
Composition/Full-Service Project Management: Elm Street Publishing Services
Printer/Binder: RR Donnelley & Sons Company

Credits and acknowledgments borrowed from other sources and reproduced, with permission, in this textbook appear
on pp. 343–344, which constitutes an extension of the copyright page.

Pearson Education LTD., London
Pearson Education Singapore, Pte. Ltd
Pearson Education, Canada, Inc.
Pearson Education–Japan
Pearson Education Australia PTY, Limited

Pearson Education North Asia, Ltd., Hong Kong
Pearson Educación de Mexico, S.A. de C.V.
Pearson Education Malaysia, Pte. Ltd.
Pearson Education, Upper Saddle River, New Jersey

10 9 8 7 6 5 4 3 2 1

ISBN-(10):   0-321-38748-1
ISBN-(13): 978-0-321-38748-6

Contents

Preface

We originally wrote this textbook for our students. Although we were trained in different fields of history, we have shared many of the same experiences in teaching undergraduate courses in western civilizations, world history, classical history, and area studies courses. In so doing, we have found that many of our students, both history majors and nonmajors, understood history largely as a set of dates and facts, within which there were several subsets categorized by geography and chronology. Students generally agreed that history was largely known and its stories all told. Many of them further felt that history was mostly irrelevant to their day-to-day experiences.

Yet we gradually became aware that in most cases, our students' surface disenchantment with history as a discipline masked a hunger to understand the historical roots of the world around them and of their own individual and collective heritage. Moreover, it became clear that many students understood that these histories were interpreted differently not only by various historians but also by the people who lived them. In fact, we found that most students who enrolled in our survey courses were ready to be guided beyond the "history as fact" stage to an understanding of "history as debate." They were also increasingly ready to see the world around them not as the end of history but as part of an unguided, ongoing global human experience. The 9/11 terrorist attacks in the United States and subsequent events around the world especially emphasized the significance of global history. Students wanted to know *why* these events were happening—to understand the relationships between events and trends in different times and in different parts of the world. This textbook is the result of the challenge our students gave us to rethink our approaches to teaching history.

We also wrote this textbook for ourselves and for other instructors like us who have watched the discipline of world history evolve. In many cases, we were the first generation of history students to have taken classes that featured the relationships between societies as their main themes. Many of us have discovered world history on our own. We were usually trained as regional specialists, but in conducting research in small rural communities or great capitals we have ascertained that we cannot tell our stories without reference to the influence of factors originating *outside* of our research area. Or we stumbled upon world history through being required to teach world history surveys, especially if we were trained in "non-western" fields. Our shared discovery is that the history of the world is as much about the relationships *among* societies as it is about transformations and continuities *within* societies. It is about diffusion as much as invention. This is not to say that invention doesn't happen, just that replication, exchange, confrontation, and diffusion are more prevalent and probably more important in the history of the world. This has led us to reinterpret invention more as the result of long collaborative and competitive processes than the spark of a moment. It is an interpretation that seems obvious to some of us today, but if so it is a secret kept by professional historians and only rarely shared with undergraduate students. It is disappointing that, while monographs and texts aimed at graduate students have embraced a new sense of interaction in the past and present, most world history readers still cling to the notion of *civilizations* as rigidly defined, isolatable aggregations of tradition, a notion that we challenge in the introduction to this text.

Instead, this reader is underpinned by three axioms. They are axioms that every student should understand at the conclusion of a world history survey. They are concepts that we believe will help students achieve academic success, as well as comprehend the world around them. The first is that any event in history can be interpreted differently even by two people who witness it directly. Thus the sources in this text are not intended to impart truth to the students, but rather to be interrogated as flawed and biased accounts that reveal as much about the author as the subject. It is for this reason that we have written a great deal of guiding text in each chapter and have developed questions that link sources, chapters, and parts. The second, related idea is that history is both created and debated by historians. It is for this reason that we hope instructors will direct students to read the sources together rather than separately. In each chapter, polemical works are matched with documentary evidence and with contrasting interpretations so that students will learn to disassemble and to question the work of scholars and nonscholars alike.

Finally, world history is much more than just comparative history or "big" history. It is not merely the sum of nation-state or civilizational histories. It is something all its own, a field made up of attempts to understand the relationships among regions, states, and societies. This text asks students to investigate the flow of people, things, and ideas between societies. In this perspective, borders become zones of interaction as well as exclusion. Distinctions between "tribes," "nations," and "races" become opaque instead of polarizing. Societies are connected, rather than merely compared.

This reader is designed as an introduction to world history as a discipline. Its scope is the period from around 1450 to the present. Geographically it covers the world, bounded only by the availability of sources and the limits of space. The structure is geared toward achieving coherence: Not all regions are covered evenly in every part, nor do all periods receive the same attention. The goal of the text is to help students look beyond strictly delineated regionalism and chronological structures to understand history as a product of ongoing debates. Thus the text is structured as a series of interconnected themes and debates. Each part revolves around a global inquiry investigated and debated by world historians, defined partly by chronology but also by topic. The parts are divided into chapters, each of which highlights an issue or approach within the part-level topics. Within each chapter are both secondary and primary sources, matched to each other in an opposing, supporting, and/or evidentiary relationship. Although the distinction between primary and secondary sources is useful, we found in writing the two volumes that make up this series that it is sometimes problematic to try to rigidly distinguish between them. This is true not only because it leads students to miss the role perspective plays in historians' accounts but also because some sources can easily be considered to fit into both categories. Thus we have not sought to identify between them. In combination, the sources provide students with the tools not only to question assumptions and arguments but also to understand historians' methods. Each chapter contains significant introductory material, and each source is accompanied by explanatory text. The chapters conclude with two types of questions: Mastering the Material questions, which help students to analyze, evaluate, and compare the sources, are suitable for assigning as homework or chapter exams. Making Connections questions ask students to connect sources both across chapters and across parts. These questions are designed to be used for midterms, unit exams, and final exams.

Scholars at the center of the study of interaction claim for their work the title "the new world history" because they feel their approach is truly a breakthrough. Perhaps instructors and students will question just how revolutionary the transformation from nation-state–based history to the new world history really is. Nevertheless, world historians convey a certain sense of excitement at these attempts to explain the why the human experience has been shaped as it has. We hope that excitement will rub off on students.

This textbook would not have been possible if not for the input of friends, students, and peers. We would especially like to thank our colleagues at San Francisco State who helped us to identify sources in areas of history about which we knew little. Julyana Peard, Abdiel Oñate, Maziar Berhooz, Frank Kidner, and Sarah Curtis were particularly obliging in pointing us in the direction of obscure texts and major works. Christopher Chekuri, Anthony D'Agostino, and William Issel helped to shape our understanding of world history, but not always by agreeing with our approach. Trevor Getz would particularly like to thank mentor Paul Longmore for imparting an understanding of at least a little American history. None of the errors or failings of this text are their fault, but many of the important features are to their credit. In addition, several former students made contributions to this text. Debra Greco's interpretation of the debates on the origins of the world wars and the Holocaust formed the basis for three chapters of unit four. Jon Brooke and John Corbally helped with research, and Hillary Lazar spent part of a winter vacation tightening up the first two units. We were further assisted by the contributions of historians and history instructors who read and commented on portions of the text: Theodore Kallman, San Joaquin Delta College; Patricia A. Mulvey, Bluefield State College; Richard Mahon, Riverside Community College; Denis Paz, University of North Texas; David Christian, San Diego State University; Ken Faunce, Washington State University; Roger Schlesinger, Washington State University; Charles Mercieca, Alabama A&M University; Mark Jones, Central Connecticut State University; Esperanza Brizuela-Garcia, Montclair State University; Kristina A. Boylan, SUNY Institute of Technology; Lesley Mary Smith, George Mason University; A. Martin Wainwright, University of Akron; Carolyn R. Dupont, Eastern Kentucky University; Aiqun Hu, University of Central Arkansas; and Amy Floss, Metropolitan Community College. These scholars helped us to avoid egregious errors and to identify pertinent points.

There are three historians to whose work this book owes an especially large intellectual debt. William H. McNeill's 1963 *The Rise of the West* introduced the thematic approach to world history. His 2003 *The Human Web,* co-written with J.R. McNeill, reflects the advances made over the past 40 years and places him once again at the front of the pack. Patrick Manning's *Navigating World History* is the field's concise and authoritative defining text. Ross E. Dunn's edited volume, *The New World History: A Teacher's Companion* is an instructor's delight. Many other scholars have contributed to the creation of a truly global discourse on world history, but the input of these three scholars stand out. Although none of them saw this text in production, it could not have existed without them.

Finally, it is hardly possible to give sufficient credit to our editors at Pearson: Janet Lanphier, who shepherded this project for four years, and Charles Cavaliere, who saw it to fruition. Without their patience, perseverance, and belief in this project we could not have succeeded.

Trevor R. Getz
Richard J. Hoffman
Jarbel Rodriguez

A Note on Spelling

Because of the wide diversity of human languages and texts, the transliteration of terms and names into the English language and the Roman alphabet is not a simple matter. As authors, we recognize that these words can be transliterated in a variety of ways. Our two guiding principles in this book have been to respect schemes recognized by the major scholars of and from each region on the one hand, and to adopt transliterations that are most useful for students.

Sometimes these goals are in conflict with one another, and we have had to try to forge a compromise.

Several of these compromise solutions deserve somewhat more explanation. In the interests of students, in cases where terms are very recognizable we have stuck to familiar formulations like "Rome," rather than the more strictly correct "Roma." We have also decided strictly not to use diacritical symbols and accent marks that are unfamiliar to most of our readers. Thus, for example, we write "Timur" for the name of the great Turkic leader rather than the more Europeanized "Tamerlane" or the phonic "Tīmūr" or "Temür". Chinese terms present a unique problem, as the sources in this book variously adopt two different systems of transliteration. In our commentary and discussion of sources, we have chosen to adopt the Pinyin system, which was developed in China and which became the international standard in 1979. Where our sources use the older Wide-Giles system of transliteration developed in late nineteenth century Britain, we preserve the integrity of the texts by presenting the terms as spelled in the source followed by the Pinyin spelling in brackets.

About the Front Cover Illustration

The front cover image was taken from *Transit Maps of the World* by Mark Ovenden (Penguin Books, 2007). ISBN 978-0-14-311265-5. Ovenden's book is the first and only comprehensive collection of official urban-rail system maps on earth. Reflecting the style of the famous London Underground diagram, this image links all cities that either already have, or that are planning to build, a rapid transit system. The map was prepared by Ovenden to help readers visualize the interconnectedness of disparate world cities by the similarities of graphic design and the universal recognition of this style of cartographic imagery. To order a copy, visit http://www.metromapsoftheworld.com. The map reflects many of the ideas embodied in this book.

Introduction

What Is World History? An Introduction for Students of the Recent Past

The field of world history developed as a new way to seek answers to questions that were beyond the scope of regional specialists. As the globalization of the world became increasingly evident in the second half of the twentieth century, scholars came to recognize the importance of global trends and events in shaping the national histories on which they were working. They began to search for global answers to questions that they had only previously contemplated on local levels. World history is a relatively new field, although it is closely related to a number of other evolving approaches to human history and to existing disciplines in the social sciences and humanities. In arguing that there are many different perspectives on history, world historians are in agreement with many of their colleagues in the humanities. In their emphasis on trade and exchange they are like economists. In their investigation of the way humans have shaped the world they owe a debt to sociologists and anthropologists. In seeking to tell stories of global change on a massive scale, world historians have sometimes found that the biography of a single individual is a useful tool.

The underlying premise of world history is that the interaction among human societies resembles not the relationships among building blocks or billiard balls, but rather among bacteria. Building blocks can be stacked next to or on top of each other, but they rarely if ever affect their neighbors' shapes or composition. Similarly, billiard balls careening around the table may collide and affect each other's trajectories, but they do not actually change each other: The eight ball is an eight ball even after it is struck by the cue ball. Societies act more like billiard balls than building blocks in that they interact with each other. However, in doing so they do not just collide and move off, they also fundamentally shape each other. In this way their relationships are somewhat like those among bacteria. The membranes covering bacteria are full of pores. Thus when bacteria touch, they can exchange genetic information and can even fundamentally alter each other's basic make-up. Similarly, human societies in contact deeply affect each other's development. World historians, recognizing this, seek to understand human history through studying both developments within societies and the way in which they relate to each other. They look at not only the process of invention but also the key role played by the diffusion of people, things, and ideas around the world. Their work does not, however, invalidate the work of historians who take a more regional approach. Rather, it adds a new layer of complexity to our understanding of the histories of societies, states, and cultural groups around the world.

Questions and Connections: The World Since c. 1450 C.E.

Why did western Europe industrialize first? How did the United States and the Soviet Union become great powers? What caused the First and Second World Wars? Investigations of these issues on an intercontinental level led historians to explore wider issues. Why are some societies wealthy and others impoverished? How did the great empires manage to conquer much of the world? Why do wars happen? How do complex societies rise, and why do some fall? What is the role of identity—ethnicity, gender, race, age, class status, and group affiliation—in influencing the decisions people make? Admittedly, these questions were not entirely new: Professional social scientists of previous generations had conducted a limited number of analyses of world "civilizations." However, their work had been framed by the nation-state, which was considered the principal unit of analysis for historians. For example, although the widespread roots and intercontinental impact of the French Revolution was immediately obvious, historians of French history almost uniformly analyzed it as a French national event. Similarly, the transformation of the British Empire and global decolonization were obvious contexts of Indian independence, but the main line of scholarly inquiry for decades was that of Indian nationalism. World historians, on the other hand, emphasize the transatlantic commerce and Anglo-French rivalry as causes of the French Revolution. They look closely at the relationships between Indian nationalists and anticolonial movements elsewhere.

As globally oriented regional analyses began to proliferate, some scholars began to assemble a theoretical framework that tied them together. The result was the gradual evolution of the cohesive field that world history has become today. World history survey courses at the university level now outnumber Western civilization courses. The World History AP exam has recently been introduced. Practitioners have organized themselves in the World History Association. Journals like *World History Connected* and *The Journal of World History* have begun to enjoy sizable readerships. Guidebooks to pedagogy and research in world history have appeared, most notably Patrick Manning's *Navigating World History: Historians Create a Global Past* and *The New World History: A Teacher's Companion* edited by Ross E. Dunn. Finally, world history textbooks that stress the interrelationship among societies have begun to appear for undergraduate and even high school courses.

World historians, like their colleagues who focus on regional or even local history, are heavily influenced by both the humanities and the social sciences. On the one hand, historians develop narratives—they tell stories and interpret other peoples' stories. On the other hand, historians are involved in a quest to understand how and why things happen, to analyze evidence as accurately as possible. Neither of these two approaches dominates the other. Rather they are interrelated processes in the search for the past.

The authors of the sources in this textbook give many different explanations for these great issues in human history. These explanations generally fall into one of several categories that we call themes. Some sources suggest that geography and differences in environment account for the paths taken by human societies. Others focus on economic approaches, cultural structures, population density, or political institutions and opera-tions. Many scholars look within societies for answers, but most recognize that evidence can be found in the relationships among societies: competition for resources, military alliances, and most important, the movement of people, ideas, and things across state borders that has been taking place throughout human history. Others debate the signif-icance of the immediate versus the distant past: whether events are more the products of local, recent history or of long trends. Still others debate the role of intention versus process: whether most events are planned or they are just the outcome of human reac-tion to their environments and experiences. Finally, some observers note in the same event both global and local causes and effects.

Periodization

Most two-semester world history courses divide at about 1500 C.E. (Common Era). Thus well over 5,500 years of recorded human history is usually covered in the first semester, and merely 500 in the second. Although chronologically uneven, this division of the world into a long premodern period and a much shorter modern period starting around 1500 is so widespread that it sometimes seems almost incontestable. Not only do we know a great deal more detail about the recent than the distant past, but there is also some sense of a real historical divide around the end of the fifteenth century. Consider the experience of Christopher Columbus. In a single year, 1492, he not only departed on his journey to the Americas but also personally witnessed the expulsion of the Muslims from their last stronghold in western Europe and the beginning of the Spanish Inquisition, which seems an antecedent of the persecution of Jews and other minorities in the following centuries. Yet for East Asia the year 1492 was relatively insignificant. A more defining set of events for this world region may have been the late-fourteenth-cen-tury expulsion of the Mongols from China. For West Africans, the first crossing of the Sahara by camels more than half a millennium earlier was an enormously important event. The subsequent exchange of ideas and products with the Muslim world helped to bring about massive social and economic changes. Thus Columbus's expeditions seem far less significant to the inhabitants of regions on both sides of this desert. It is evident, therefore, that it is a great challenge to develop a common chronology of world history.

Yet it is possible to make a case for the late 1400s and early 1500s as a transitional period of great global significance, if it is done carefully. For millennia prior to the 1500s the Americas were not in sustained contact with the so-called "Old World" continents of Europe, Africa, and Asia. Large sections of Oceania and the Polynesian island chains were also essentially isolated. Even within the Old World, regions far outside the principal trade routes were sometimes only in intermittent contact with distant regions. Yet over the next 500 years this situation was transformed, until only a very few regions could be meaningfully termed remote or isolated. The evolution of this close relationship between societies that defines the modern world is the topic with which this volume begins.

This text makes use of benchmarks commonly accepted by many researchers. Scholars often term the last 500 years the modern era because it gave birth to many of the things and ideas we consider to define modernity: industrialization, rapid global communication, and multiparty democracies. In addition, this period saw the creation of a global network of two interacting types of political structures: the multicontinental **empire** (in which a large proportion of the population were deprived of political rights and seen as noncitizens), and the **nation-state** (in which each citizen was theoretically imbued with political rights). Ironically, many modern states were both nation-states and empires at the same time.

Historians further divide this period into the "early modern" and "modern" periods based largely on events in Europe such as the industrial and French revolutions, events addressed in Part 2. Part 3 looks at the late-nineteenth-century establishment of large-scale, industrial, maritime empires, a trend that had clear significance for Asia, Europe, and Africa but was also a shared, global experience. The First and Second World Wars have also been proposed as the beginning or end of an era, a debate that is explored in Part 4. The topic of globalization addressed in Part 5 begs the question whether the "modern era," which encompasses the last 500 years, has in fact recently ended. In each case, the division of world history into periods, while useful for this text, remains problematic and should not be accepted unquestioningly. While it is sometimes useful to highlight dramatic transformative events and trends, very often much of what came before survives them. In history, continuity is as important as transformation.

Sources

In this book the student is asked to explore historical events and trends by analyzing the writings of both contemporary observers and formally trained scholars. Historians call these texts sources. The sources in this book have been chosen because they relate to what historians do: They use these materials as evidence to reconstruct what happened in the past and to attempt to explain why it happened that way rather than some other way.

Sources can include written texts, archaeological and scientific data, oral histories such as songs and stories, and images such as paintings and photographs. In this volume we deal mainly with written sources. Some of these are primary sources: official documents, letters, diaries, records, and other accounts written or recounted by people who experienced or witnessed the events being studied. Historians use these sources as evidence in writing books and articles that seek to interpret the past. These books and articles are in turn called secondary sources. Together, the primary and secondary sources form a body of knowledge that other scholars and historians can consult. Previous generations of historians often saw the two types of sources as being very different. They believed that historical (primary) sources were more subject to the biases and perspectives of the author than secondary sources by professional historians who they saw as being subject to scientific and factual rules. In this book we do not usually distinguish between the two types of sources for two reasons. First, many sources are both primary and secondary. Some of the most significant sources of the past 500 years can be studied both as professional histories and as sources of information about the period in which they were written. This is true of the work of Adam Smith, V. I. Lenin, and a number of other authors whose work is excerpted in this book. Second, we now know that the work of historians, like all other authors, is always affected by their perspectives and biases. Thus the distinction between the two types of sources often (although not always) confuses matters more than it simplifies them.

Through this textbook, the student becomes the historian. Students are given the sources, as well as accompanying text intended to introduce the subject, to guide their investigations and to aid them in the evaluation of the arguments and ideas put forth by the sources. Students will quickly perceive that none of the sources is definitive. Rather, they are all part of debates between scholars, observers, and other commentators on the human past. Thus the sources and scholars in this book disagree or contradict each other at times. Sometimes these debates are obvious within a chapter in which the analyses of scholars are presented alongside some of the evidence used in their work. Sometimes they are evident within the larger structure of each part in which a period of world history is addressed. Finally, some debates appear in sequential parts in which scholars discuss similar themes for different periods of time.

Our hope in this textbook is that students will see part of the process that historians use to write history and explain the past. This process usually begins with primary sources. Marc Bloch, an important twentieth-century historian, commented that "the past does not change; but our knowledge of the past is constantly being transformed and perfected." New sources, whether written or archaeological, are always being discovered, and old sources are constantly being reinterpreted, often by asking new questions and applying new analytical techniques to materials that have been around for millennia. Historians thus make a number of choices in interpreting source material. First, from all of the materials available, they choose certain documents and certain details from those documents to include in an analysis. Second, historians sometimes reject information in a document as either inaccurate or wrong—this is part of the art of source criticism. And third, historians not only reject information they consider to be in error but also gather meanings that are not specifically stated in a document. Part of the task of the historian is to make reasoned deductions from information within a given source. In the end, documents contain a great deal of interesting material that is often organized in very unhelpful ways. The historian takes this information, subjects it to criticism and analysis, and then reorganizes it to present a particular understanding of the past. The end result is a new history and the continuation of a debate that is age old. History is not actually the past itself, but it is our understanding of that past. As Marc Bloch suggests, that understanding changes with each individual and each generation.

The principal goal of this textbook is to present theories and evidence about the human experiences. This textbook does not seek to impose on you a single interpretation of history or to guide students toward perceiving the "truth." Rather, through questions that connect different sources, chapters, and periods of time, this textbook helps students to evaluate the very notion of historical truth. Nor does this textbook claim to be a complete human record. The sources have been selected to inform each other and to enable students to develop a deep understanding of a few major questions, rather than to superficially survey many different facets of the human experience.

In reading the primary and secondary sources in the following units, keep in mind both the **perspectives** of each author and the information available to the author. Both primary and secondary sources should be read with equal skepticism. Even with the benefit of hindsight, historians have a great deal of difficulty interpreting the past. Things are much more difficult for participants in an event. Frequently, their information is not complete. They may also feel passionately about the events. For historians, as well, it is difficult to place objective evaluation before personal ideology and perspective. History is colored by perspective—the perspective of the writer and the perspective of the audience. Our job, as historians, is to understand that perspective. By looking at history from the view of the author, we can better understand the meaning of a document.

Understanding perspective is also an important tool in evaluating sources for historical accuracy. In the questions contained in each chapter, you will frequently be asked to compare theories and accounts. Your task is to interpret meaning as well as to assess precision. Only infrequently will you be entirely convinced by one account. Often, you may decide that conflicting arguments all have value or are all flawed. This will give you the opportunity to construct your own theories, based on the evidence in the sources. Through this process, you will come to understand history as debate, as perspective, and as a body of knowledge. That is your first step toward becoming an historian.

Themes in Modern World History

The sources in this book have been chosen because they inform a series of debates about the relationships among societies and between trends and events. The sources are organized into five parts, each of which focuses on a different core question:

1. Why was it western Europe that forged a permanent connection with the Americas at the end of the fifteenth century?
2. What were the origins of the revolutions and reforms of the sixteenth through nineteenth centuries in the Americas, France, the Ottoman and British Empires, and elsewhere?
3. Why did certain European states, alongside the United States and Japan, embark upon a period of empire building in the last quarter of the nineteenth century?
4. What caused the First and Second World Wars, and how did they become globalized?
5. What forces are shaping the world today?

In each case, the answers tend to be more global than might initially be thought. Even actions and ideas that seem to have been driven solely from within one society or region turn out to have roots in other parts of the world. This acknowledgement of the global nature of local history is one of the major contributions of world history.

Terms to Know

empire   *(p. 4)*

nation-state   *(p. 4)*

perspective   *(p. 5)*

Part 1 | Debating the "Great Opening": 1450–1600

Most history textbooks and world history courses divide the human past into two sections at around 1450–1500 C.E. This division emphasizes the significance of the voyages of Christopher Columbus and fellow explorers, voyages that connected the two largest landmasses: the **"Old World"** of Eurasia and Africa and the **"New World"** of the Americas. Proponents of the fifteenth-century dividing point maintain that it was this age of exploration and subsequent exploitation of the Americas that elevated western European states—especially France, Britain, Spain, Portugal, and the Netherlands—from minor countries in a small, western region of Eurasia to a position of global preeminence. Other researchers, however, have downplayed the importance of these events. The versatile historian and economist Andre Gunder Frank, for example, has asserted that there was no great break in 1500. In *ReORIENT?*, a book that explicitly questions the notion of western European ascendancy, Frank argues that "the voyages of Columbus and Vasco da Gama should probably be regarded as expressions of [an ongoing] *world* economic expansion, [in] which Europeans wanted to attach themselves to Asia." Columbus, after all, was searching not for a new world but merely for a new way of accessing the spices and manufactured goods of East and South-East Asia. In other words, the voyages of exploration were just a further stage in the centuries-long cycle of Old World interaction.

Certainly, all evidence indicates that Columbus was unaware of the two American continents when he embarked upon his much-celebrated voyage of exploration, and admittedly his happening upon them resulted in few *immediate* changes for much of the world's population. Yet the fact remains that the connecting of the two great landmasses coupled with the opening of new, permanent maritime routes around Africa and (after 1517) across the Pacific marked a major development in world history with long-term repercussions for humans everywhere. Millions of humans flowed across these new ocean routes as settlers, both willing and unwilling. They brought with them technologies and culture to be shared and merged. Similarly, after Columbus the world experienced an unprecedented exchange of organisms. Europeans brought cattle, horses, and pigs to the New World along with wheat and sugarcane and diseases like cholera and smallpox. In return, they brought to the Old World American crops like maize (corn) and potatoes and, less profitably, syphilis. Historian Alfred W. Crosby, Jr. has labeled this process the **Columbian Exchange.** Since it was western Europeans who made these lasting connections, it was they who profited most from them in the following centuries.

Most world historians, therefore, acknowledge the period 1450–1650 as one of great and important changes that had repercussions for the entire human community. Even if the importance of the gradual occupation of the Americas and the new maritime dominance of western Europeans is generally acknowledged, however, many debates about the process remain. Indeed, the topic remains one of the most highly disputed issues among both world historians and regional specialists. Why did some western European rulers and merchants choose to undertake long-distance maritime voyages of discovery and trade at this point in time, and what factors enabled them, for the first time, to do so? Why did the inhabitants of other regions not do so to the same extent? Why were Europeans able to conquer and settle large parts of the Americas and to dominate maritime trade even in regions, such as the Indian Ocean, that were bordered by equally or more sophisticated societies? Finally, what was the impact of this new global connectivity not only for various groups of Europeans but also for inhabitants of the world's other regions?

The starting points for answering these questions are the themes of geography and **demography,** or population, introduced in Chapter 1. A number of theorists, most prominently the physiologist and biologist Jared Diamond, suggest that Eurasians (Europeans and Asians) were more likely to make large-scale sustained voyages of exploration and settlement to another continent than were Africans, Americans, or Australians because they possessed more favorable environments, geographic configuration, and domesticatable plant and animal species. Moreover, the shape and orientation of Eurasia facilitated the sharing of goods, species, and ideas among Eurasian societies. Three zones especially enjoyed these environmental advantages, and thus came to have the largest and densest populations of any region of the world: Europe, India, and China. This denser demography was arguably an advantage for Eurasia and helps to explain Eurasian states' generally more sophisticated production techniques and maritime technology, levels of literacy, and governmental organizations.

Yet within Eurasia, western Europe did not appear to be exceptional. Indeed, China and India were in many ways the world's leading economic powers and—along with the Islamic states of central Asia and northern Africa—had historically tended to larger and better unified political units than Europe. What was it that led European states at this moment in history to disproportionately plan for and support maritime exploration and exploitation?

There are three broad explanations given by scholars for western European merchants' and mariners' particular will and abilities to embark on such undertakings in the late fifteenth century. The most simplistic argues for the "superiority" of western European inhabitants or societies, whether in political organization, economics, or culture—an approach called **eurocentrism.** The second suggests instead merely divergent choices: that the inhabitants of India, China, and Europe poured their resources into different strategies for dealing with the shared problem of resource and land allocations. The third approach is more integrative. It suggests that it was *global* relationships, rather than factors within Europe or any other region, that propelled western Europeans in a direction different from others. These three theories are examined in Chapters 2–6, expressed through the themes of environment, culture, technology, politics, and economics.

Before 1500, Europe was a moderately populous peninsula without any real distinction from other Eurasian regions. After 1500, some of its states were on their way to becoming the world's leading political, economic, and military entities. Arguably, it was the western Europeans' discovery and exploitation of maritime trade routes around Africa and Asia and to the new colonies in the Americas that was the principal factor behind this change. The transition would be gradual and impermanent, and it is important to view the connection of the Old World and New World as a global event and not exclusively a European one. Nevertheless, this is the first period in the posited "rise of the west." Through the debate herein students should be able to develop their own perspectives on the importance, mechanisms, and repercussions of the new maritime age.

Part 1 Timeline

1405–1433	Chinese admiral Zheng He commands great fleets that traverse the Indian Ocean to India, Arabia, and East Africa.
1430–1480	Black Death plague, spreading from Asia to North Africa and Europe, leads to the breakdown of long-distance trade between these regions.
1453	Ottoman armies capture Constantinople.
1492	Italian explorer Christopher Columbus, sailing under the Spanish flag, lands in the Americas. He was searching for a better route to East Asia.
1503	Portuguese explorer Vasco da Gama, having besieged several East African and Arabian ports, fights a major battle against the fleet of the Indian state of Calecut.
1511	A Portuguese-led force captures the key Asian trading port of Malacca.
1527	Wang Yang-ming [Wang Yangming] writes "Inquiry on the Great Learning" in China.
1532	Spanish explorer Francisco Pizarro defeats an Inca army at Cajamarca.
c. 1540–1560	Spanish intellectuals and priests, including Bartolomé de las Casas and Juan Ginés de Sepúlveda, debate Spain's role in the Americas.
1579	The Portuguese and Spanish, with local allies, unsuccessfully invade the Angolan kingdom of Ndongo.

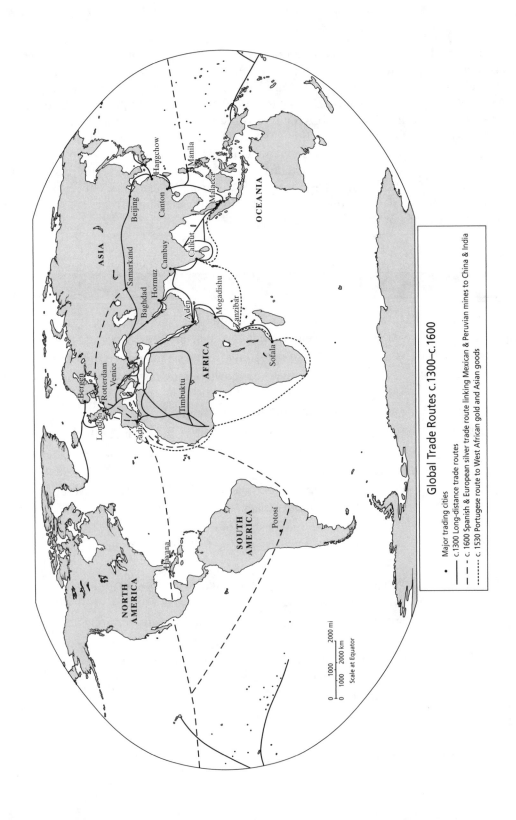

Global Trade Routes c.1300–c.1600

- Major trading cities
- —— c.1300 Long-distance trade routes
- – – – c. 1600 Spanish & European silver trade route linking Mexican & Peruvian mines to China & India
- – · – · c. 1530 Portugese route to West African gold and Asian goods

NORTH AMERICA

SOUTH AMERICA
Potosí
Havana

ASIA
Samarkand
Beijing
Baghdad
Hormuz
Cambay
Canton
Hangchow
Manila
Malacca
Calicut

AFRICA
Timbuktu
Aden
Mogadishu
Zanzibar
Sofala

Bergen
Rotterdam
Venice
London
Cádiz

OCEANIA

0   1000   2000 mi
0   1000   2000 km
Scale at Equator

Chapter 1

Was There a Eurasian Advantage over Africa and the Americas?

For the greater period of human history—from the end of the last ice age about 12,000 years ago to the relatively recent development of key long-distance travel technologies—several great geographic barriers separated human societies to various degrees. The most important of these were the world's great oceans and deserts. Human societies in the Americas had no sustained contacts with the Old World continents of Africa, Europe, and Asia. Polynesians established a notable trade network across a triangle of the Pacific marked by Hawaii, the Marquesa Islands, and Oceania (Australia and New Zealand) but did not maintain sustained contact with the Americas or most of Eurasia. The Sahara desert, an ocean of sand, all but cut sub-Saharan Africa off from North Africa, Asia, and Europe. Thus while human societies in the Pacific, sub-Saharan Africa, the Americas, and Eurasia/North Africa developed extensive commercial networks *within* their regions, for much of both prehistory and recorded history contact *among* these regions was limited. Extensive connections between sub-Saharan Africa and the rest of the Old World landmass were reestablished perhaps as early as the fifth or sixth century by Arab, Indian, and later African sailors in the Indian Ocean and in about the ninth century by Berber camel caravans that crossed the Sahara Desert. However, the establishment of permanent links between the Old World, Oceania, and the Americas would have to await the European voyages of exploration in the fifteenth century and later.

Modern Western scholars have long noted that most of the concerted efforts to reconnect these different zones were instigated by the inhabitants of Eurasia. They have also suggested that in almost every case the Eurasians were more technologically sophisticated than those they encountered. The earliest "racial" explanations for the apparent advantages of these societies have now been largely discredited. However, in the last few decades a body of scholarship has emerged that argues that inhabitants of Eurasia were exceptionally fortunate in that they lived in an enormous, contiguous, and ecologically advantageous landmass especially conducive to the development of human societies. Underpinning this argument is the theory of **environmental determinism:** the argument that environment and geography are the principal causes of the diverging fates of human societies.

Perhaps the most important work of the past two decades that explores the impact of the environment on the development of human societies is Jared Diamond's *Guns, Germs, and Steel.* In this book Diamond, a physiologist and geographer, looks closely at the European conquest of the Americas, with a starting point of the Battle of

Cajamarca. The primary-source description of this battle, written by Francisco de Jérez, is the starting point of this chapter. In this battle the Spanish explorer Francisco Pizarro, with a band of 168 Spaniards and some local allies, defeated the might of the Inca, which was arguably the greatest of American empires. Diamond argues that "[w]e can identify the chain of proximate factors that enabled Pizarro to capture [Inca Emperor] Atahuallpa, and that operated in European conquests of other Native American societies as well. These factors included Spanish germs, horses, literacy, political organization, and technology (especially ships and weapons)." But why, Diamond asks, did the Spanish possess all of these advantages? The answer he gives is that the Spanish advantages were really Eurasian advantages and that it was the unique environment of the great Eurasian landmass that gave the Spanish a technological and organizational supremacy over the Americans they encountered, rather than any cultural or genetic differences between Spaniards and other people.

According to Diamond, the Eurasian advantage was the result of Eurasia's earlier and easier transition to what is generally called "civilization." Simply put, Eurasia developed more and larger cities and states more quickly than other regions of the world, and these dense, stratified, sedentary societies in turn produced sophisticated technologies. Yet why did Eurasia develop cities first? Diamond suggests that the swiftness of the transition was made possible by Eurasia's favorable environments for cultivation, more easily domesticated plants and animals, and a geography that enabled these crops and animals to spread more easily than any of the other regions inhabited by humans.

Diamond's work is one potential explanation for the disparities in armaments, animals, and vessels between the Portuguese and Spanish conquistadors and the American empires they defeated in battle. Yet critics have questioned both the scope of Eurasian technological superiority and Diamond's explanations for its causes. J. R. McNeill, for example, argues that Diamond goes too far in ignoring culture and society as significant factors, and the groundbreaking linguistic and archaeological work of Africanist Christopher Ehret suggests that the evidence for major innovations in areas *outside* of the Eurasian landmass, specifically in sub-Saharan Africa, has been overlooked.

Rendezvous at Cajamarca

This description of the fight at Cajamarca, written by Pizarro's secretary Francisco de Jérez, is typical of accounts of Eurasian (in this case Spanish) armies meeting those of Americans (described here as Indians). Some of the advantages of the Spaniards are evident: iron and steel for weapons and armor, artillery, and horses. It should be noted that none of these originated in Europe: Iron was probably first forged in southwest Asia, gunpowder originated in China, the cannon was invented by the Arabs, and horses are indigenous to central Asia. Nevertheless, as Eurasians, Europeans had access to all of these materials and technologies. They also had resistance to Old World diseases, of which there were far more than were native to the Americas and which are estimated to have killed 95% of the population of the Americas. Europeans were also heirs to a long legacy of literacy and writing that had been passed down from the first literate societies in Mesopotamia; and they had access to ships that combined Indian, Arabic, and European technology. All these factors combined to give not just Europeans, but Eurasians generally, a significant advantage over the inhabitants of the Americas.

>> 1. Reports on the Discovery of Peru

FRANCISCO DE JÉREZ [1534]

When the Governor [Pizarro] saw that it was near sunset, and that [Emperor] Atabaliba did not move from the place to which he had repaired, although troops still kept issuing out of his camp, he sent a Spaniard to ask him to come into the square to see him before it was dark. As soon as the messenger came before Atabaliba, he made an obeisance to him, and made signs that he should come to where the Governor waited. Presently he and his troops began to move, and the Spaniard returned and reported that they were coming, and that the men in front carried arms concealed under their clothes, which were strong tunics of cotton, beneath which were stones and bags and slings; all which made it appear that they had a treacherous design. Soon the van of the enemy began to enter the open space. First came a squadron of Indians dressed in a livery of different colours, like a chess board. They advanced, removing the straws from the ground, and sweeping the road. Next came three squadrons in different dresses, dancing and singing. Then came a number of men with armour, large metal plates, and crowns of gold and silver. Among them was Atabaliba in a litter lined with plumes of macaw's feathers, of many colours, and adorned with plates of gold and silver. Many Indians carried it on their shoulders on high. Next came two other litters and two hammocks, in which were some principal chiefs; and lastly, several squadrons of Indians with crowns of gold and silver.

As soon as the first entered the open area they moved aside and gave space to the others. On reaching the centre of the open space, Atabaliba remained in his litter on high, and the others with him, while his troops did not cease to enter. A captain then came to the front and, ascending the fortress near the open space, where the artillery was posted, raised his lance twice, as for the signal. Seeing this, the Governor asked the Father Friar Vicente if he wished to go and speak to Atabaliba, with an interpreter? He replied that he did wish it, and he advanced, with a cross in one hand and the Bible in the other. [...]

Atabaliba asked for the Book, that he might look at it, and the Priest gave it to him closed. Atabaliba did not know how to open it, and the Priest was extending his arm to do so, when Atabaliba, in great anger, gave him a blow on the arm, not wishing that it should be opened. Then he opened it himself, and, without any astonishment at the letters and paper, as had been shown by other Indians, he threw it away from him five or six paces, and, to the words which the monk had spoken to him through the interpreter, he answered with much scorn, saying: "I know well how you have behaved on the road, how you have treated my Chiefs, and taken the cloth from my storehouses." The Monk replied: "The Christians have not done this, but some Indians took the cloth without the knowledge of the Governor, and he ordered it to be restored." Atabaliba said: "I will not leave

Source: Excerpt from the chronicle of Francisco de Jérez, in *Reports on the Discovery of Peru,* translated and edited by C. R. Markham (Cambridge: The Hakluyt Society, 1872), 52–55.

this place until they bring it all to me." The Monk returned with this reply to the Governor. Atabaliba stood up on the top of the litter, addressing his troops and ordering them to be prepared. The Monk told the Governor what had passed between him and Atabaliba, and that he had thrown the Scriptures to the ground. Then the Governor put on a jacket of cotton, took his sword and dagger, and, with the Spaniards who were with him, entered amongst the Indians most valiantly; and, with only four men who were able to follow him, he came to the litter where Atabaliba was, and fearlessly seized him by the arm, crying out *Santiago*. Then the guns were fired off, the trumpets were sounded, and the troops, both horse and foot, sallied forth. On seeing the horses charge, many of the Indians who were in the open space fled, and such was the force with which they ran that they broke down part of the wall surrounding it, and many fell over each other. The horsemen rode them down, killing and wounding, and following in pursuit. The infantry made so good an assault upon those that remained that in a short time most of them were put to the sword. The Governor still held Atabaliba by the arm, not being able to pull him out of the litter because he was raised so high. Then the Spaniards made such a slaughter amongst those who carried the litter that they fell to the ground, and, if the Governor had not protected Atabaliba, that proud man would there have paid for the cruelties he had committed. The Governor, in protecting Atabaliba, received a slight wound in the hand. During the whole time no Indian raised his arms against a Spaniard. So great was the terror of the Indians at seeing the Governor force his way through them, at hearing the fire of the artillery, and beholding the charging of the horses, a thing never before heard of, that they thought more of flying to save their lives than of fighting.

Ecological Differentiation

In investigating the Eurasian advantage in encounters like that at Cajamarca, Jared Diamond was not content to merely acknowledge the technology the Spaniards had and the Incas lacked, he also sought to understand the causes of this discrepancy. Diamond contends that Eurasia had four main ecological advantages. The first was simply a matter of timing. Eurasia, fortuitously located close to humanity's origins in Africa, was populated earlier than the Americas or Oceania. The second was a matter of climate. Because they possessed the largest "Mediterranean zone" of dry summers and wet winters in the Fertile Crescent of Mesopotamia, Eurasians could grow the best crops, including 32 of the 56 big-seeded cereals such as wheat and barley. Other regions had at most one or two. Similarly, Eurasia was home to most of the world's domesticatable animal species, including goats, dogs, pigs, oxen, cattle, sheep, and horses. Among the large domesticatable animals, only the llama was absent. By contrast, sub-Saharan Africa, despite its wealth of large game animals, had no easily domesticatable large beasts until they were imported from Eurasia. Finally, as this excerpt explains, Eurasia had long bands of temperate climate that allowed these species of plants and animals to quickly spread to China in the East and Europe in the West, either through human effort or their own migration. No other region of the world possessed these factors in the same combination, and as a result Eurasians had better access to food, transportation, and eventually diseases that would negatively affect the nonresistant populations Eurasians encountered elsewhere. This, Diamond contends, was the Eurasian advantage.

>> 2. Guns, Germs, and Steel:
The Fates of Human Societies

JARED DIAMOND [1997]

Why was the spread of crops from the Fertile Crescent [across Eurasia] so rapid? The answer depends partly on that east–west axis of Eurasia with which I opened this chapter. Localities distributed east and west of each other at the same latitude share exactly the same day length and its seasonal variations. To a lesser degree, they also tend to share similar diseases, regimes of temperature and rainfall, and habitats or biomes (types of vegetation). For example, Portugal, northern Iran, and Japan, all located at about the same latitude but lying successively 4,000 miles east or west of each other, are more similar to each other in climate than each is to a location lying even a mere 1,000 miles due south. On all the continents the habitat type known as tropical rain forest is confined to within about 10 degrees latitude of the equator, while Mediterranean scrub habitats (such as California's chaparral and Europe's maquis) lie between about 30 and 40 degrees of latitude.

But the germination, growth, and disease resistance of plants are adapted to precisely those features of climate. Seasonal changes of day length, temperature, and rainfall constitute signals that stimulate seeds to germinate, seedlings to grow, and mature plants to develop flowers, seeds, and fruit. Each plant population becomes genetically programmed, through natural selection, to respond appropriately to signals of the seasonal regime under which it has evolved. Those regimes vary greatly with latitude. [...]

Animals too are adopted to latitude-related features of climate. In that respect we are typical animals, as we know by introspection. Some of us can't stand cold northern winters with their short days and characteristic germs, while others of us can't stand hot tropical climates with their own characteristic diseases. [...]

That's part of the reason why Fertile Crescent domesticates spread west and east so rapidly: they were already well adapted to the climates of the regions to which they were spreading. For instance, once farming crossed from the plains of Hungary into central Europe around 5400 B.C., it spread so quickly that the sites of the first farmers in the vast area from Poland west to Holland (marked by their characteristic pottery with linear decorations) were nearly contemporaneous. By the time of Christ, cereals of Fertile Crescent origin were growing over the 8,000-mile expanse from the Atlantic coast of Ireland to the Pacific coast of Japan. That west–east expanse of Eurasia is the largest land distance on Earth.

Thus, Eurasia's west–east axis allowed Fertile Crescent crops quickly to launch agriculture over the band of temperature latitudes from Ireland to the Indus Valley, and to enrich the agriculture that arose independently in eastern Asia. [...]

Contrast the ease of east–west diffusion in Eurasia with the difficulties of diffusion along Africa's north–south axis. Most of the Fertile Crescent founder crops reached Egypt very quickly and then spread as far south as the cool highlands of Ethiopia, beyond which they didn't spread. South Africa's Mediterranean climate would have been ideal for them, but the 2,000 miles of tropical conditions between Ethiopia and South Africa posed an insuperable barrier. [...]

Similarly, the spread southward of Fertile Crescent domestic animals through Africa was stopped or slowed by climate and disease, especially by trypanosome diseases carried by tsetse flies. The horse never became established farther south than West Africa's kingdoms north of the equator. The advance of cattle, sheep, and goats halted for 2,000 years at the northern edge of the Serengeti Plains, while new types of human economies and livestock breeds were being developed. [...]

Source: Jared Diamond, *Guns, Germs, and Steel: The Fates of Human Societies* (New York: W.W. Norton, 1997), 183–187, 190.

Contrast also the ease of diffusion in Eurasia with its difficulties along the Americas' north–south axis. [...] A few crops, notably Mexican corn, did indeed spread to the other region in the pre-Columbian era.

But other crops and domestic animals failed to spread between Mesoamerica and South America. The cool highlands of Mexico would have provided ideal conditions for raising llamas, guinea pigs, and potatoes, all domesticated in the cool highlands of the South American Andes. Yet the northward spread of those Andean specialties was stopped completely by the hot intervening lowlands of Central America. [...]

Continental differences in axis orientation affected the diffusion not only of food production but also of other technologies and inventions. For example, around 3,000 B.C. the invention of the wheel in or near Southwest Asia spread rapidly west and east across much of Eurasia within a few centuries, whereas the wheels invented independently in prehistoric Mexico never spread south to the Andes. Similarly, the principle of alphabetic writing, developed in the western part of the Fertile Crescent by 1500 B.C., spread west to Carthage and east to the Indian subcontinent within about a thousand years, but the Mesoamerican writing systems that flourished in prehistoric times for at least 2,000 years never reached the Andes.

Critique of *Guns, Germs, and Steel*

Diamond's work immediately attracted the attention of some of the leading global historians, including J. R. McNeill. McNeill, whose work placed a greater emphasis on culture and the relationships between cultures than on environmental factors, wrote a generally positive review of Guns, Germs, and Steel *in which he nevertheless suggested that Diamond had overstated the significance of geographic and environmental disparities between regions of the world. In particular, while admitting that Eurasia was fortunate to possess many of the most favorable plant and animal species for domestication, he took issue with the idea of continental axes of orientation as major determinants in the ease of species spreading. In this excerpt from his 2001 review of* Guns, Germs, and Steel, *he suggests that Diamond errs in ignoring human choice and effort in purposefully spreading, or choosing not to spread, certain crops and animals.*

>> 3. The World According to Jared Diamond

J. R. McNeill [2001]

Diamond's argument exceeds its limits on another point as well, that of the "tilting axes." Throughout the book Diamond argues that the East-West axis of Eurasia provided an advantage in the dispersal of useful, mainly domesticated, plants and animals. [...] With respect to the lengths of days and the importance thereof for flowering plants, the argu-

ment makes fine sense. Maize's spread northward from Mexico was, Diamond persuasively argues, slowed by the necessity of genetic adaption to different day lengths at different latitudes. Maize could spread much more easily East-West than it could North-South. But with respect to animals the argument must be made in more general climatic and ecological terms, and here it gets weaker. Eurasia's East-West axis could not have been much help in the spread of cattle or goats. Its extreme variety of climatic conditions, its high

Source: J. R. McNeill, "The World According to Jared Diamond," *The History Teacher* 34 (2001).
Permanent URL http://www.historycooperative.org/journals/ht/34.2/mcneill.html.

mountains, deserts, and tropical forests posed a considerable challenge for the spread of most animals (and I should think, plants). From the Gulf Stream-induced equability of western Europe, to the continental climate extremes of Kazakhstan, to the monsoon rhythms of Korea, temperature and moisture regimes show tremendous variation. A given line of latitude within Eurasia might embrace conditions as diverse as those of Shanghai, Lhasa, Delhi, Basra, and Marrakesh, all of which are very close to thirty degrees north (North Africa accounts for most of Diamond's purposes as part of Eurasia) [. . .]. Beyond this, since North Africa counts as part of Eurasia, then Africa deserves an East-West axis like Eurasia's, because it is much farther from Dakar to Cape Gardafui than it is from the Cape of Good Hope to the Sahara. And Australia, which does not get an axis on the map, extends further East-West than North-South. In Australia, I should think rainfall isohyets would correspond better to the migration history of plants and animals than do lines of latitude and longitude. All this, I think, casts some doubt on the explanatory power of the axis argument.

Indeed, the successful spread of crops and livestock (not to mention the writing, wheels and other inventions that Diamond mentions in this argument) is surely determined in large part by factors other than geography, and the role of geography is much more complex than the axes suggest. The role of other geographical factors I alluded to in reference to Eurasia. But the spread of useful species was usually a conscious act (weeds were different). They could not, of course, flourish where ecological conditions did not permit, but where they went when was largely a human affair, determined by trade links, migration routes, and happenstance. Coffee, an Ethiopian native, eventually made its greatest impact in southern Brazil, not at Ethiopian latitudes within Africa. Cattle domestication spread from its point of origin (in southwest Asia) to South Africa and Sweden, flourishing in between in circumstances as diverse as Sudan's and Switzerland's. Along the East-West axis of Eurasia, cattle became important in Europe, fundamental in India, yet inconsequential in China. This is not because Chinese environmental conditions were inhospitable to cattle, but because Chinese social and economic conditions were. The diffusion of cattle as of AD 1000 was along a North-South axis more than an East-West one, partly because cattle can cope with both heat and cold, but also because cattle-raising fit in with the ideological, cultural, social, and economic systems of some societies better than others, regardless of geography.

For these reasons I think Diamond has oversold geography as an explanation for history. I find the best part of his geographic determinism to be the biogeographic part. The business about the distribution of potentially domesticable species was new to me, and I think to historians generally, and I accept the importance of these facts. The differential ease of plant and animal diffusion as determined by continental axes strikes me as less persuasive. But that, on Diamond's scale, may be only a quibble. However the spread of useful species was governed, who had them and got them first was indeed important.

A Conversation with Christopher Ehret

It is often startling to those just starting to read world history that Europeans, despite having circumnavigated Africa in the early fifteenth century, made remarkably little headway in conquering African states or overcoming African armies until late in the nineteenth century. In fact, it has become increasingly evident to scholars over the past four decades or so that African societies in the fifteenth century were in many cases highly stratified and sophisticated, utilizing their sometimes difficult environments to cultivate and herd animals, and building cities and nations in many areas. Moreover, the eastern coast and western interiors of sub-Saharan Africa had been in contact with Asia and North Africa via Indian Ocean and Saharan trade routes for some centuries. Thus, unlike the inhabitants of the Americas, most Africans were resistant to Eurasian diseases. Christopher Ehret has been a leader in re-envisioning African history before 1500 both in his African history textbook, The Civilizations of Africa, *and in his monograph,* An African Classical Age. *In this excerpt from an interview from the journal* World History Connected, *Ehret both suggests Africans were far more successful cultivators than has previously been acknowledged and explains some of the unique difficulties scholars have had in dealing with historical evidence in Africa.*

>> 4. A Conversation with Christopher Ehret

TOM LAICHAS [2004]

World History Connected: What are the most important things world history teachers might teach their students about Africa?

Ehret: Africa sometimes seems to students off the edge of the world. The first thing is to realize is that it's an integral part of what's going on in the rest of the world. If you are going to integrate Central Asia into your history, you can absolutely integrate sub-Saharan Africa into your history.

You just can't *talk* about the Indian Ocean unless you talk about eastern Africa. And you can't talk about Mediterranean history unless you know what's going on in West Africa. You can't talk about the Red Sea and the Middle East unless you're talking about Ethiopia actually, for the Middle East, you need West Africa and East Africa too. If you're doing world history, you need to connect up all these places.

And then too, students just do not know that Africa is a seminal area of innovation in world history.

WHC: Describe that innovation.

Ehret: You can of course begin with the fact that all our ancestors were fully human before any of those ancestors left Africa 60,000 years ago. The first places that you see artistic or symbolic representation are in eastern Africa. You

see the first backed stone tools, the first shaped and reshaped bone tools. It's after 60,000 BCE or so that real humans finally leave the continent. So we're all Africans. Face up to that fact.

But people who do world history usually begin with the origins of agriculture. There are at least seven or eight maybe eleven to thirteen world regions which independently invented agriculture. None in Europe, by the way. One, of course, is in the Middle East, and many people still believe that this was the first, from which all the others developed. The idea of diffusion from the Middle East still lingers.

That idea really can't be sustained.

You have, for instance, one independent invention of agriculture in East Asia, maybe two. You have it more widely accepted now that there's an independent invention of agriculture in the interior of New Guinea. People argue about what to make of the Indian materials, but certainly India saw one of the three separate domestications of cattle; there are enough uniquely Indian crops that we might end up with India as another center of independent agricultural innovation. There are different ideas about the Americas, but I think we have two for sure: Mesoamerica and the Andes. There may also be a separate lowland tropical South American development. It also seems that there might be a few things domesticated in the southeastern United States even before there was Mesoamerican stimulus of diffusion. So that makes four.

Source: Tom Laichas, "A Conversation with Christopher Ehret," *World History Connected* 2 (2004). Permanent URL http://worldhistoryconnected.press.uiuc.edu/2.1/ehret.html.

Here's the point: agriculture was invented in Africa in *at least* three centers, and maybe even four. In Africa, you find the earliest domestication of cattle. The location, the pottery and other materials we've found makes it likely that happened among the Nilo-Saharan peoples, the sites are in southern Egypt. There is an exceptionally strong correlation between archaeology and language on this issue.

A separate or distinct agriculture arose in West Africa around yams.

A third takes place in southeastern or southern Ethiopia. I've got a student working this year in Ethiopia to see whether we can pin this down more precisely. The Ethiopians domesticated a plant called *enset*. It's every unique: Ethiopians use the lower stem and the bulb; not the tuber, the fruit, or the greens. Enset grows in a climatic zone distinct from that where cattle were first domesticated; that was further north.

The possible fourth area of agricultural invention would involve people who cultivated *grain* in Ethiopia. They seem to have begun cultivation of grain independently, but adopted *cattle* from the Nilo-Saharans of the middle Nile region. To pin this down, we need archaeology from a whole big area, but so far it's missing.

There's another really interesting innovation in Africa: pottery. There are two places in the world which develop pottery really early. One is Japan, where you find pottery before 10,000 BCE, going back to at least 11,000 or 12,000 BCE. And then you've got pottery by 10,500 BCE in the eastern Sahara, and it spreads widely in the southern Sahara. Unlike the Middle Eastern ceramics, where you can see the development of pottery at every stage, the stuff we find in the southern Sahara is *already* great pottery. So there's probably 500 years we're missing from the archaeological record. So let's say that pottery develops in the southern Sahara 2,500 years *before* Middle Eastern pottery. The Middle Eastern stuff *does* look like it was developed independently of the African, but hey, this is really interesting! Africa is not too far away; there may have been some diffusion. [...]

WHC: Why [is there not more evidence of agriculture in Africa]?

Ehret: Because wood tools would not have survived. And because yams don't have seeds which might be burnt and preserved so that we could know that they're domestic rather than wild cultivars. Also, there's a stage it might have lasted 2,000 years when African peoples moved between the wild and the cultivated crops. You don't necessarily go straight to domestic seeds; it's an uneven transition.

Well, the language evidence says that there *was* early agriculture. You go back to the word for "cattle-raising" in Nilo-Saharan. It's not in the proto-language, it's in one of the branches. A few hundred years later, you get words for "cultivation," so you know they're cultivating, not long after they begin to raise some cattle. All we have after the first cattle are some sorghum seeds, and people argue whether those were domestic or wild. But the *language* evidence says that they were cultivating sorghum. And the archaeology indirectly supports the language evidence. The Nilo-Saharans have granaries, we know that. By 7200 or 7300 BCE, they've got sedentary sediments. Yeah, you can have people collecting wild grasses really intensively and putting the grasses in a granary. However, the intensive grass collectors we know about didn't have granaries this big. So the language evidence and the archaeology both provide evidence of cultivation.

In the case of the rainforests of West Africa, you have the language evidence and the development of polished stone axes. It looks like they're having to clear the land; the yams they're raising need the sunlight. There are yams in the rainforest that don't need much light, but the yams they're cultivating at this stage are from the savannah. There's a verb to "cultivate" pretty far back, so, yeah, we've got the evidence there, and we've certainly got the words for "yams," though they could be wild yams.

>> Mastering the Material

1. According to Diamond, what was the Eurasian advantage? How convincing is his argument?

2. On what basis does McNeill criticize Diamond?

3. How does Ehret's discussion of the multiple sites of agricultural invention affect your opinion of Diamond's argument as to a Eurasian environmental advantage?

4. How does de Jérez's account of the "Rendezvous at Cajamarca" support Diamond's claims?

Chapter 2

Why Not Ming China?

For reasons that are still widely debated, fifteenth-century Eurasian societies were clearly better prepared to undertake and support projects of long-distance exploration and trade over the world's oceans than their counterparts in the Americas and sub-Saharan Africa. Among Eurasia's societies, however, the consensus among historians is that China, rather than Europe, was the best technologically prepared and most commercially sophisticated region in the fifteenth century, and in many ways the most likely to have assumed the lead in global exploration.

The first Western depictions of China in the early modern era came from overland explorers—merchants and ambassadors from European courts of kings and the Pope. The most famous, and one of the most controversial, was Marco Polo. In 1298, after returning from a seventeen year journey across Asia to Venice, Marco Polo was captured in a battle with the rival city-state of Genoa and imprisoned. While incarcerated, he wrote *La Meraviglie del Monde* with a fellow war captive, a story that was quite rapidly reprinted in many languages. Polo was followed by Jesuit missionaries and papal ambassadors, all of whom found the court of the Ming Emperor a baffling place, full of technology far in advance of that in Europe but rejecting the specific conception of science then increasingly appearing in Europe. Some modern European scholars have interpreted these travelers' accounts as proof of the backwardness or stagnation of the Ming court. In fact, however, a careful reading of both European and Chinese sources of the fifteenth century describe China, emerging from Mongol rule under the Ming emperors, as an exciting and innovative place with its own special social rules, regulations, and opportunities.

The Ming emperors came to power in the waning years of the Mongol Empire, whose power had stretched from the very edge of Europe across central Asia and the Middle East and all the way to the eastern edge of the continent. The rule of the Mongols in China (known as the Yuan Dynasty) had at times been oppressive but had also exposed the great cities of the Chinese seaboard to influences from other parts of the world and had left relatively intact its **meritocratic system.** Under this system, which advanced the most capable administrators through a system of examinations, China had for centuries produced the world's most effective bureaucrats.

The first Ming emperor, a peasant and former Buddhist monk who had led rebellious forces against the Mongols, came to power in 1368. Over the next half-century, he and his successors reestablished both China's internal stability and its influence over much of southeast Asia. Thus, unlike Europe or India at the time, Ming China was largely politically unified. The Ming treasury was probably the richest in the world during this period, and advances such as the extension of the Grand Canal far into the interior made China a trading giant. Fleets of ships and caravans of camels and horses sustained the far-flung outposts of the Ming Empire.

The question remains, then, why Ming China did not explore and settle the Americas before western Europeans. Clearly, China had the technological capacity to do so. This is the theme of the first two readings in this chapter, Kuei-Sheng Chang's "The Maritime Scene in China at the Dawn of Great European Discoveries" and his supporting document, Ku P'o's [Gu Po] Afterword to Ma Huan's *The Overall Survey of the Ocean's Shores* from 1433. Since China's maritime and commercial *capacity* has been so well established, some Western scholars have argued that Ming China must have been culturally deficient in some way, lacking the *will* to explore and exploit overseas regions. We will encounter this argument in Chapter 3. Most modern interpretations, however, suggest that the Ming government made a *choice* to turn away from maritime exploration and to concentrate instead upon internal problems. Some proponents of this theory have suggested that the Chinese landowners were more powerful than the merchant class during this period and influenced the Ming emperors to focus on agrarian policies to the detriment of external trade. Others, like Kenneth Pomeranz, posit that China's expanding population demanded that the Ming emperors concentrate on developing new cultivating technologies rather than on expanding outward. Chinese historian Li Ung Bing argues that the ever-present Mongol threat to the northwest dominated the Ming emperors' attention. Finally, some critics of eurocentrism suggest that, unlike Western Europe, the manufacturing powerhouse of China produced most of what it needed and thus did not have to look overseas for finished goods. Pomeranz and others point to the fact that Columbus left Spain to look for finished products in high demand in Europe—especially Asian spices and Chinese silks and porcelains. Europe, on the other hand, may have possessed little that China needed.

The Impact of Zheng He's Voyages

In the early fifteenth century, Ming China was the greatest naval power the world had ever seen. Some sources suggest that the Emperor's navy included 3,500 ships, including 1,700 warships and about 400 armed transports. The largest of these were 400 feet long. By contrast, the Spanish armada that threatened to conquer England in 1588 consisted only of 130 ships, the largest being the 22 fighting galleons of about 140 feet in length. In 1405, Chengzu, the third Ming emperor, dispatched a great fleet of over 300 ships crewed by 27,000 sailors, marines, merchants, and ambassadors to visit the trading nations of the Indian Ocean world. Not only did China enjoy profits from its trade with southeast Asia, India, Arabia, and the east coast of Africa, but Chengzu wanted to demonstrate the power of a resurgent Ming Dynasty to the rest of the known world. The admiral of this fleet, Zheng He, was a Chinese Muslim and a court servant, a eunuch. In four voyages, Zheng He visited most of the important Indian and Arabian ports and even brought ambassadors from Egypt and eastern Africa back to China. In 1433, however, the fourth Ming emperor ordered the imperial shipyards destroyed and all great voyages to end. By 1500, there was little Chinese naval presence left in the Indian Ocean. Fortunately, at least two of Zheng He's entourage documented their experiences on one of the fleet's journeys. The more significant is Ma Huan's Ying-yai Sheng-lan [Yingyai Shenglan], *or* The Overall Survey of the Ocean's Shores. *As Ku P'o's [Gu Po] Afterword makes clear, Ma Huan's account of the voyage had a great impact on educated Chinese scholars.*

>> 5. Afterword, in Ying-yai Sheng-lan [Yingyai Shenglan], or The Overall Survey of the Ocean's Shores

Ku P'o [Gu Po] [1433]

Some time ago The Grand Exemplar The Emperor issued an imperial order that the grand eunuch Cheng Ho [Zheng He] should take general command of the treasure-ships and go to the various foreign countries in the Western Ocean to read out the imperial commands and bestow rewards for meritorious service; and these two gentlemen, being skilled interpreters of foreign languages, received appointments in this [capacity].

Three times they accompanied [Cheng Ho's] train, travelling ten thousand *li*. They started out from Wu hu in Min; first they put in to Chan city, then Chao-wa and Hsien Lo, then again Old

Haven, A-lu, Su-men, Nan-p'o, His-lan, and Ko-chih; most distant of all, A-tan and the Heavenly Square were visited—in all more than twenty countries. In each country they stayed and travelled for many a day.

As to the extent of the earth's surface, they noted the difference in distances. As to the diversity of customs, they noted the difference in morals. As to the appearance of the people, they noted the difference in their attractiveness. As to the products of the land, they noted the difference in their importance. All these things they recorded in writing. Their record completed, they made a book. They certainly expended care and industry.

Their task completed, the two gentlemen returned to their native villages, and constantly went out to enlighten other people, to enable everybody to acquire knowledge about conditions in foreign regions, and to see how far the majestic virtue of our imperial dynasty extended—far-flung as in this [book].

The Fifteenth-Century Maritime Scene in China

Taiwanese historian Kuei-sheng Chang's research on fifteenth-century Chinese maritime history is based largely on documentary evidence such as that left by Ma Huan. In this selection, Chang illustrates the extensive technology and navigational skills that were available to Chinese sailors such as Zheng He. These compared favorably with the resources available to Iberian (Portuguese and Spanish) sailors half a century later. However, Zheng He's fleet was burned at its docks in 1433 and the Ming administration failed to press forward with the process of crossing the Pacific to the Americas or exploring up the western coast of Africa. Chang gives two explanations for this policy decision: the reassertion of antimaritime "traditionalist" parties within the Ming government and the lack of an economic impetus for overseas exploration and commerce.

Source: Ku P'o, "Afterword," in *Ying-Yai Sheng-Lan, or The Overall Survey of the Ocean's Shores,* edited by Feng Ch'eng-Chün and J. V. G. Mills (Cambridge: The Hakluyt Society, 1970), 179–180.

>> 6. The Maritime Scene in China at the Dawn of Great European Discoveries

CHANG KUEI-SHENG [1974]

Type	Number of Masts	Length in feet[*]	Width
Treasure ship	9	444	144
Horse Ship	8	370	150
Supply Ship	7	280	120
Billet Ship	6	240	94
Combat Ship	5	180	68

[*]A Ming foot is longer than the English foot by 2%.

At the outset it should be noted that when the new momentum was generated in Iberia at the turn of the fifteenth century, China's maritime operations had already reached a stage of considerable sophistication by pre-industrial standards. This was fully demonstrated during what might be called the zenith of Chinese maritime power, epitomized by the seven voyages (1405–1433) under the Ming eunuch commander-in-chief Cheng Ho [Zheng He]. His last voyage to Africa actually preceded that of Vasco da Gama by more than half a century. This gap in time alone, while indicative of the lack of direct challenge to and therefore response from China, may not be significantly accountable for the ineptness or inability of the Chinese to explore new routes beyond the Indian Ocean. The contrast is overwhelming when one recalls that precisely as the Portuguese were probing the Coast of Guinea, China had begun to look eminently inward resulting in a near-complete abandonment of its maritime endeavor.

The actual capability of early Ming China in distant voyaging may be evaluated on the basis of the voyages of Cheng Ho [Zheng He] and their many ramifications. The scale of operation on which records abound can be summarized by a few quantitative references. The size of the crew in the various voyages ranges between 27,000 and 37,000 men. To carry the crew and material, as many as 249 and 317 ships were used on two occasions. To meet every possible contingency, the flotillas consisted of five major types of vessels, their carrying capacity and functions can be seen in the following table.

While most of these ocean-going vessels were constructed at the official dockyard near Nanking, the total ship-building capacity should have been easily three times the largest number of ships used in a single voyage, as evidenced by the completion of 1,622 ships in less than two years preceding the first voyage.

Besides the impressive size of the ships and the number of masts in use, several other important features may be worth mentioning. From the very beginning of ship-making, the Chinese had been inspired by the resiliency and buoyancy of bamboo from which the use of transverse bulkheads for the building of ship hulls was developed. It was the concept of the bulkhead derived from the septa in the bamboo stem that enabled the Chinese to build elongated ships with large and separate compartments. With strong and evenly distributed support by the thick bulkheads, the construction of multi-storied ships known as *lou ch'uan* dated to pre-Han times. [...]

Along with these distinctive features in early Chinese shipbuilding, certain unique aspects in navigational skills may be worth noting. At the time when interregional trade across the South China Sea was in full swing in the twelfth century, several nautical techniques for distant voyaging were in general use according to a brief description by Chu Yü, author of *P'ing-chou k'e-l'an* published in 1119:

Vessels generally sailed out from Canton by northerly winds in November and December and returned by southerly winds in May and June. They are squarely built like grain

Source: Kuei-Sheng Chang, "The Maritime Scene in China at the Dawn of Great European Discoveries," *Journal of the American Oriental Society* 94 (1974): 347–348, 350–353, 357.

measures. If there is no wind, they stand still, for the masts are firmly planted and the sails hang sidewise—one side attached to the mast around which they move like door leaves. They are called chia t'u, *which is a local term. At sea, they can use not only a favorable wind but also winds off or on shore. It is only the head wind that drives them back. In such a way they can use winds from three directions. The captains can ascertain the ships' position at night by looking at the stars, and in the day time by looking at the sun. In dark weather, they look at the south-pointing needle.*

In this passage, the use of the magnetic needle, familiarity with the effect of the monsoons and the traditional ship design are clearly evident. [...]

With all its resources and capabilities, the Ming fleet at the apogee of Chinese maritime power did not, however, extend its voyages beyond the Indian Ocean. What seems even more significant is the suddenness and completeness of China's withdrawal in the decades that followed with no evidence of economic calamity or technological collapse. It is logical, therefore, that we turn to the institutional and cultural backdrop for answers. [...]

The time during which the Ming voyages took place was one of the most unorthodox periods in Chinese socio-political history when eunuchs, notably Cheng Ho and his able lieutenants, wielded unprecedented power and influence. Emperor Yung-lo's (1402–1424) ascension to power through usurpation owed much to the loyal service of these men whose social status offered them little choice. It was also a time when the matter of legitimacy in the Confucian tradition was in question. [...]

When tradition was temporarily restored before the last voyage, it was not surprising that the eunuchs and their followers were shabbily treated. What was once perhaps the world's greatest shipyard in Nanking sank into oblivion. [...]

Up to Cheng Ho's time, China's foreign trade, however voluminous by existing standards, still weighed insignificantly with reference to the nation's total economy which was basically self-sufficient except for luxury items from tropical lands. Even as late as Lord Macartney's mission to China in 1793 to open up trade on behalf of the British Crown, the response typical of the Chinese thinking, though expressed by a Manchu emperor, was heard: "There is nothing we lack, as your principal envoy and others have themselves observed. We have never set much store on strange or indigenous objects, nor do we need any more of your country's manufactures." Indeed, in contrast with southern Europe, never was there any pressing need or driving impetus on the part of China to search for a new route around Africa.

A Twentieth-Century Chinese Historian's View of the Early Ming Dynasty

Li Ung Bing's history of China was written in the early twentieth century, a period during which Western-trained Chinese scholars began to embark on histories of their own nation that followed European rather than Chinese notions of how history is produced and written. These were often superior to the textual treatments of Chinese history written by Westerners in the previous decades. In these excerpts from his Outlines of Chinese History, *Bing explains both the sophistication of the Ming bureaucracy and the continuing Mongol challenges to China. The dates and important figures correspond to the decline of China's maritime expeditions. Chengzu (here written as Cheng Tsu), the third Ming emperor, was the sponsor of many of Zheng He's voyages and was quite successful in his campaigns against the Mongols. His successors were less fortunate, and the Mongol threat became highly pronounced once more by the middle of the fifteenth century.*

>> 7. Outlines of Chinese History

Li Ung Bing [1914]

Chu Yüan-chang, the founder of the Ming Dynasty, was canonized as T'ai Tsu; but better known by the name of Hung Wu under which he reigned. We must not suppose that his sway extended over the whole of China, when he ascended the throne at Nanking. On the contrary, the western provinces, notably Szechuan and Yünnan still held out against him, while the Mongols beyond the Great Wall continued to menace China. [...]

The China of the Ming Dynasty was divided into thirteen provinces, viz., Shantung, Shansi, Shensi, Honan, Chekiang, Kiangsi, Hukuang, Szechuan, Fukien, Kuang-tung, Kuangsi, Yunnan, and Kuei-chow; the present province of Chihli being known as the north metropolitan province while the provinces of Kiangsu and Anhui, the south metropolitan province. [...]

Besides the provinces, there were nine frontier cities where strong garrisons were maintained. [...] The Treasurer was the highest authority in a province; the offices of governor and viceroy were not created until the dynasty drew towards its close; and these existed only at places near the northern frontier, or where there were military operations. [...]

In 1409, Ch'iu Fu, a Ming general, invaded Mongolia but was defeated. His defeat by no means discouraged Ch'eng Tsu. On the contrary, he took the field himself, in the following year, at the head of 500,000 men and dispersed the Mongols on the bank of the Onon. [...]

After Ch'eng Tsu's death (1424), his successors were never able to maintain their authority in Mongolia. Toghan, the successor of Mahmud, taking advantage of their state of confusion prevailing in Mongolia and the weakness of China, created quite an empire for himself. On his death (1443) his throne fell to Essen, his son, who was no degenerate successor. Having extended his sway to Hami in the west and Ulianghai in the east, he was ready to measure strength with the Emperor of China, hitherto his overlord. [...] Because of the ill-treatment accorded to the tribute-bearing envoys from Essen, the Mongols began to make inroads into China. In the beginning of 1449, the fourteenth year of Ying Tsung's reign, they were before the city of Ta Tung. An army of half a million men was raised and despatched under Wang Chên to the rescue of the city. Against the wishes of his council, Ying Tsung was induced to accompany the expedition. On arriving at Yang Ho, it was discovered that the army was in no condition to fight; and at the entreaties of the generals, a retreat was at once ordered. But at Tu Mu, the imperial army was attacked by the Mongols; and, being taken by surprise, the Chinese were easily routed with great slaughter.

Shared Problems in Early Modern China and Europe

In this forward-looking piece, Kenneth Pomeranz argues that China and Europe were more similar than dissimilar in 1500 and that only a few minor factors drove Chinese society into developing skilled intensive land-use practices while western Europeans instead searched for new resources overseas. He suggests that many Western-trained historians have misunderstood and misrepresented the origins of

Source: Li Ung Bing, *Outlines of Chinese History* edited by Joseph Whiteside (Shanghai: The Commercial Press, 1914), 232–235, 238–239.

Ming China's choice to not undertake significant overseas expansion as being due to "cultural" shortcomings or deficiencies. Instead, he argues, both China and Europe (and to a lesser degree, India) had to respond to the same problem: a need to gain access to more resources, including foodstuffs, to feed rapidly growing populations. Pomeranz contends that China—unlike western Europe—chose to focus on feeding its citizens through new technologies and intensification of land use. He further suggests that Europe would have followed a similar path if not for the fortuitous discovery of the Americas. In the long run, the skills and practices China developed contributed to its development of dense, urban populations while western Europe's path led to overseas empires.

>> 8. The Great Divergence: China, Europe, and the Making of the Modern World Economy

KENNETH POMERANZ [2000]

The literature that incorporates the "fall of Asia" tends to do so with the aid of an oversimplified contrast between an ecologically played-out China, Japan, and/or India, and a Europe with plenty of room left to grow. [. . .]

In an attempt to move beyond such impressionistic claims, this text offers a systematic comparison of ecological constraints in selected key areas of China and Europe. This inquiry shows that although some parts of eighteenth-century Europe had some ecological advantages over their east Asian counterparts, the overall pattern is quite mixed. Indeed, key Chinese regions seem to have been better-off than their European counterparts in some surprising ways, such as available fuel supply per capita. Moreover, Britain, where industrialization in fact began, had few of the underutilized resources that remained in various other parts of Europe. Indeed, it seems to have been no better-off than its rough counterpart in China—the Lower Yangzi Delta—in timber supply, soil depletion, and other crucial ecological measures. Thus, if we accept the idea that population growth and its ecological effects made China "fall," then we

would have to say that Europe's internal processes had brought it very close to the same precipice—rather than to the verge of "take-off"—when it was rescued by a combination of overseas resources and England's breakthrough (partly conditioned by geographic good luck) in the use of subterranean stores of energy [coal]. [. . .]

In making this argument this book parallels some of the arguments in work on global development by Sugihara Kaoru [. . .]. Sugihara emphasizes, as I do, that the high population growth in east Asia between 1500 and 1800 should not be seen as a pathology that blocked "development." On the contrary, he argues, this was an "East Asian miracle" of supporting people, creating skills, and so on, which is fully comparable as an economic achievement to the "European miracle" of industrialization. Sugihara also emphasizes, as I do, the high standard of living in eighteenth-century Japan and [. . .] China, as well as the sophistication of institutions that produced many of the beneficial effects of markets without the same state guarantees for property and contract that many Westerners believe is the precondition of markets. He also argues—a point consistent with my argument though beyond the scope of this book—that in the long run it has been a combination of western European and east Asian types of growth, allowing Western technology to be used in societies

Source: Kenneth Pomeranz, *The Great Divergence: China, Europe, and the Making of the Modern World Economy* (Princeton: Princeton University Press, 2000), 12–13.

with vastly more people, which has made the largest contribution to world GDP, not a simple diffusion of Western achievements.

Sugihara does, however, suggest that a basic difference between these two "miracles" is that as far back as 1500, western Europe was on a capital-intensive path and east Asia on a labor-intensive path. By contrast, I argue [...] that Europe, too, could have wound up on an "east Asian," labor-intensive path. That it did not was the result of important and sharp discontinuities, based on both fossil fuels and access to New World resources, which, taken together, obviated the need to manage land intensively.

>> Mastering the Material

1. Evaluate the relative power and capabilities of Chinese naval power and technology during the early Ming Dynasty based on the sources in this chapter. Are you convinced by the arguments that it was a lack of will, rather than ability, that turned China away from active government support of overseas exploration, commerce, and settlement during this period? Why or why not?

2. How do Chang and Li explain the Ming Dynasty's rapid shift away from naval activity and the emperors' failure to pursue overseas exploration and conquest in the fifteenth century? In your opinion, how important was the continued threat from Mongols and other groups of the Asian interior?

3. According to Pomeranz, in what ways were Europe and China similar around 1500? What factors caused their divergence? What does he consider the "East Asian miracle," and why was it significant?

4. Consider Pomeranz's argument that China solved its need for resources through improved agricultural practices while Europe came to rely on goods from the American colonies. Also consider Chang's comment that "never was there any pressing need or driving impetus for...a new route around Africa" for the Ming emperors. Is it arguable that China's "stagnation" and "fall" resulted in fact from its self-sufficiency and success? Was the incentive for transoceanic ventures actually western European societies' relative backwardness and lack of key resources?

>> Making Connections

1. How does environmental determinism (Chapter 1) feature in Pomeranz's argument?

Chapter 3

Theories of Cultural Exceptionalism

The scholars who wrote the reading in the previous chapter argue that China had the technology and organization to undertake the great enterprises of establishing maritime empires in the Americas and along the African and Eurasian coastline. Other densely populated, technologically sophisticated societies in India and the Middle East may have as well. Yet none of these societies pursued an ongoing course of overseas exploration and colonization, whereas western Europeans did. Was there in fact something "different" or exceptional about western European societies—especially Portugal and Spain—that caused this divergence?

Among the explanations put forth for western Europe's rise to maritime preeminence, perhaps the most controversial is that of culture. It is also the oldest and most enduring. The modern European academic tradition emerged alongside the conquest of the Americas, and the experience of conquering and ruling others heavily influenced early European scholars. Many of the most important Spanish scholars of the sixteenth century, for example, were at one time or another caught up in the debate over Spain's "rights" and "duties" toward the Native American societies that they had conquered. The dispute on this topic between Juan Ginés de Sepúlveda and Bartolomé de las Casas is perhaps the most famous exchange within this debate. Although these two great Spanish thinkers disagreed on the duty of Spain toward its new subjects, they both believed that Spanish society was culturally superior to Native American societies.

Champions of Western cultural superiority still exist today. They variously suggest that fifteenth-century European cultures were uniquely curious, or practical, or logical. Certainly one of the most important proponents of this theory is the economic historian David Landes. In his best-selling book *The Wealth and Poverty of Nations,* Landes compares the cultural attributes of various rigidly defined states over a long period of history. For the early modern era, he depicts Ming China as stagnant and despotic, bound by a Confucian ethic that placed morality and hierarchy above economic striving and innovation. By contrast, Landes describes European cultures as distinctly vibrant, tolerant, fluid, inventive, capitalist, and intellectually curious, and thus uniquely suited to undertake overseas exploration and conquest.

While not always expressed in terms of "superiority," the division of the world into cultural blocks with distinct and dissimilar attributes underpins the Europe-centered argument that it was the expansion of European culture that created the modern world. In this interpretation of history, western Europeans are single-handedly credited with the invention of science, free-market economics, and democracy. These innovations on the part of the Portuguese, Italians, and Spanish—and later the British, French, and Dutch—are usually attributed to the inventiveness and flexibility of their national cultures. Yet the very idea of distinct national cultures—and of attaching values to culture—has become increasingly questioned by critics such as William McNeill, who argue for a more interactive, inclusive view of world history. Their critiques are represented by the last reading in this chapter.

Justifying the Spanish Conquest of the Americas

In Spanish philosopher and theologian Juan Ginés de Sepúlveda's sixteenth-century Just War Against Barbarians, *culture is used to justify the Spanish conquest and oppression of American populations. This work was just one treatise in an open exchange between Sepúlveda and Bartolomé de Las Casas, an outspoken critic of the Spanish treatment of the indigenous American population. Their audience was the Spanish Habsburg Emperor Charles I, the Council of the Indies, and the Spanish educated classes generally. Significantly, both Sepulveda and de las Casas accepted Spanish rule and the duty of Spain to bring Christianity to the New World. They differed only over the correct treatment of the indigenous population. De las Casas argued that the Spanish had a duty to treat the Americans as they treated themselves, according to Spanish law and Catholic morality. Sepúlveda's response was strident, staunchly defending the right and indeed responsibility of the Spanish to treat their conquered subjects harshly and to contemptuously eradicate their cultures and customs. Although in this debate the specific cultural comparison being made is between the Spanish and the Aztec, similar assessments of other people around the world appeared in this and later centuries to justify such processes as the transatlantic slave trade and nineteenth-century European imperialism and colonialism.*

>> 9. Just Causes of War Against the Indians

JUAN GINÉS DE SEPULVEDA [C. 1544]

It is established then, in accordance with the authority of the most eminent thinkers, that the dominion of prudent, good, and humane men over those of contrary disposition is just and natural. Nothing else justified the legitimate empire of the Romans over other peoples, according to the testimony of St. Thomas in his work on the rule of the Prince. St. Thomas here followed St. Augustine, who, in referring to the empire of the Romans in the fifth book of *The City of God,* wrote: "God conceded to the Romans a very extensive and glorious empire in order to keep grave evils from spreading among many peoples who, in search of glory, coveted riches and many other vices." In other words God gave the Romans their empire so that, with the good legislation that they instituted and the virtue in which they excelled, they might change the customs and suppress and correct the vices of many barbarian peoples. [...]

Turning them to our topic, whether it is proper and just that those who are superior and

Source: Juan Ginés de Sepulveda, *Just War Against Barbarians,* in *The Spanish Tradition in America,* edited by Charles Gibson (New York: Harper & Row, 1968), 115–120.

who excel in nature, customs and laws rule over their inferiors, you can easily understand, […] if you are familiar with the character and moral code of the two peoples, that it is with perfect right that the Spaniards exercise their dominion over those barbarians of the New World and its adjacent islands. For in prudence, talent, and every kind of virtue and human sentiment they are as inferior to the Spaniards as children are to adults, or women to men, or the cruel and inhumane to the very gentle, or the excessively intemperate to the continent and moderate. […]

As for the Christian religion, I have witnessed many clear proofs of the firm roots it has in the hearts of Spaniards, even those dedicated to the military. The best proof of all has seemed to me to be the fact that in the great plague that followed the sack of Rome, in the Pontificate of Clement VII, not a single Spaniard among those who died in the epidemic failed to request in his will that all the goods stolen from the citizens be restored to them. And though there were many more Italians and Germans, no non-Spaniard, to my knowledge, fulfilled this obligation of the Christian religion. And I, who was following the army and was in the city observing it all diligently, was a witness to it. […] What shall I say of the Spanish soldiers' gentleness and humanitarian sentiments? Their only and greatest solicitude and care in the battles, after the winning of the victory, is to save the greatest possible number of vanquished and free them from the cruelty of their allies. Now compare these qualities of prudence, skill, magnanimity, moderation, humanity, and religion with those of those little men [of America] in whom one can scarcely find any remnants of humanity. They not only lack culture but do not even use or know about writing or preserve records of their history—save for some obscure memory of certain deeds contained in painting. They lack written laws and their institutions and customs are barbaric. And as for their virtues, if you wish to be informed of their moderation and mildness, what can be expected of men committed to all kinds of passion and nefarious lewdness and of whom not a few are given to the eating of human flesh.

Do not believe that their life before the coming of the Spaniards was one of Saturnine peace, of the kind that poets sang about. On the contrary, they made war with each other almost continuously, and with such fury that they considered a victory to be empty if they could not satisfy their prodigious hunger with the flesh of their enemies. This form of cruelty is especially prodigious among these people, remote as they are from the invincible ferocity of the Scythians, who also ate human bodies. But in other respects they are so cowardly and timid that they can scarcely offer any resistance to the hostile presence of our side, and many times thousands and thousands of them have been dispersed and have fled like women, on being defeated by a small Spanish force scarcely amounting to one hundred.

So as not to detain you longer in this matter, consider the nature of those people in one single instance and example, that of the Mexicans, who are regarded as the most prudent and courageous. Their king was Montezuma, whose empire extended the length and breadth of those regions and who inhabited the city of Mexico, a city situated in a vast lake, and a very well defended city both on account of the nature of its location and on account of its fortifications. It was similar to Venice, they say, but nearly three times as large both in extent and in population. Informed of the arrival of Cortés and of his victories and his intention to go to Mexico under pretext of a conference, Montezuma sought all possible means to divert him from his plan. Failing in this, terrorized and filled with fear, he received him in the city with about three hundred Spaniards. Cortés for his part, after taking possession of the city, held the people's cowardliness, ineptitude, and rudeness in such contempt that he not only compelled the king and his principal subjects, through terror, to receive the yoke and rule of the king of Spain, but also imprisoned King Montezuma himself, because of his suspicion that a plot was on foot to kill some Spaniards in a certain province. This he could do because of the stupor and inertia of the people, who were indifferent of the situation and preoccupied with other things than the taking up of arms to liberate their king. And thus Cortés, though aided by so small a number of Spaniards and so few natives, was able to hold them, oppressed and fearful at the beginning, for many days. They were so immense a multitude that he seemed lacking not only in discretion and prudence but even in common sense. Could there be a better or clearer testimony of the superiority that some men have over others in talent, skill, strength of spirit, and virtue? Is it not proof that they are slaves by nature? For the fact that some of them appear to have a talent for certain manual tasks is no argument for their greater human prudence. We see that certain insects, such as the bees and the spiders, produce works that no human skill can imitate. And as for the civil life of the inhabitants of New Spain and the province of Mexico, I have already said that the people are considered to be the most civilized of all. They themselves boast of their public institutions as if it were not a sufficient proof of their industry and civilization that they have rationally constructed cities, and kings appointed by popular suffrage rather than by hereditary right and age, and a commerce like that of civilized people. But see how they deceive themselves and how different is my opinion from theirs, since for me the foremost proof of the rudeness and barbarism and innate servitude of those people lies precisely in their public institutions, nearly all of which are servile and barbarous. They do have houses, and some rational mode of common life, and such commerce as natural necessity demands, but what does this prove other than that they are not bears or monkeys completely lacking in reason?

I have made reference to the customs and character of the barbarians. What shall I say now of the impious religion and wicked sacrifices of such people, who, in venerating the devil as if he were God, believed that the best sacrifice that they could placate him with was to offer him human hearts? [...] Opening up the human breasts they pulled out the hearts and offered them on their heinous altars. And believing that they had made a ritual sacrifice with which to placate their gods, they themselves ate the flesh of the victims. These are crimes that are considered by the philosophers to be among the most ferocious and abominable perversions, exceeding all human iniquity. [...] How can we doubt that these people—so uncivilized, so barbaric, contaminated with so many impieties and obscenities—have been justly conquered by such an excellent, pious, and just king, as Ferdinand was and as the Emperor Charles is now, and by a nation excellent in every kind of virtue, with the best law and best benefit for the barbarians? Prior to the arrival of the Christians they had the nature, customs, religion, and practice of evil sacrifice as we have explained. Now, on receiving with our rule our writing, laws, and morality, imbued with the Christian religion, having shown themselves to be docile to the missionaries that we have sent them, as many have done, they are as different from their primitive condition as civilized people are from barbarians, or as those with sight from the blind, as the inhuman from the meek, as the pious from the impious, or to put it in a single phrase, in effect, as men from beasts.

On the Responsibilities of Spaniards in the Americas

If Sepulveda's treatise represents a harsh aspect of Western intellectual development during this period, de las Casas' impassioned rejoinder represents a far more constructive and humanitarian thread, one that would surface later in the Enlightenment and the French and American revolutions. Mobilizing the same historical precedents—the Greeks and the Romans—and informed by the same body of Catholic theological texts, de las Casas came to the opposite conclusion from Sépulveda: that all "men" possess the same capacity for enlightenment. Although he believed that the Aztecs were "rude and uncivilized," de las Casas suggested that they could be redeemed through God. Therefore, he argued, the Spanish had the responsibility to enlighten, rather than oppress, them. Despite its humanitarian tones, however, this argument still holds tightly to notions of European cultural superiority. This concept of a "white man's burden" would reappear to justify oppression in Latin America, Asia, Africa, and Oceania in the coming centuries.

>> 10. Apologética historia de las Indias

BARTOLOMÉ DE LAS CASAS [C. 1550]

From these examples, both ancient and modern, it is clear that no nation exists, no matter how rude and uncivilized, barbarous, gross, savage or almost brutal it may be, that cannot be persuaded into a good way of life and made domestic, mild, and tractable—provided that diligence and skill are employed, and provided that the method that is proper and natural to men is used: namely, love and gentleness and kindness....

For all the peoples of the world are men, and the definition of all men, collectively and severally, is one: that they are rational beings. All possess understanding and volition, being formed in the image and likeness of God; all have the five exterior senses and the four interior senses, and are moved by the objects of these; all have the natural capacity of faculties to understand and master the knowledge that they do not have; and this is true not only of those that are inclined toward good but of those that by reason of their depraved customs are bad; all take pleasure in goodness and in happy and pleasant things; and all abhor evil and reject what offends or grieves them....

Thus all mankind is one, and all men are alike in what concerns their creation and all natural things, and no one is born enlightened. From this it follows that all of us must be guided and aided at first by those who were born before us. And the savage peoples of the earth may be compared to uncultivated soil that readily brings forth weeds and useless thorns, but has within itself such natural virtue that by labor and cultivation it may be made to yield sound and beneficial fruits.

Culture and *The Wealth and Poverty of Nations*

Clearly, the blatant racism and triumphalism of Sepulveda has no place within modern scholarship. However, the notions these early modern scholars helped to instill within Western academia have proven hard to dispel and have been reworked by reputable scholars, especially the idea that culture is the main cause of the "success" or "failure" of societies. One of the most significant heirs to this tradition is Harvard professor emeritus of economics David Landes. In The Wealth and Poverty of Nations, *Landes focuses on culture as the regulator of growth and development. Thus, in explaining the drive of the Portuguese to create the earliest of the great western European maritime empires, he*

Source: Bartolomé de las Casas, *Apologética historia de las Indias,* in *Latin American Civilization: History and Society, 1492 to the Present,* 4th ed., translated and edited by Benjamin Keen (Boulder: Westview Press, 1991), 70.

argues that "[t]he Portuguese achievement testifies to their enterprise and toughness; to their religious faith and enthusiasm; to their ability to mobilize and exploit the latest knowledge and techniques. No silly chauvinism; pragmatism first." Similarly, he proposes that western Europe's conquest of the Americas and the age of modern formal colonialism were the result of features within western European national cultures.

In the selections below, Landes makes a strong case that the western European societies that set out to explore and control maritime trade routes in the fifteenth and sixteenth centuries benefited from the legacies of three cultural strands—Greek, Germanic, and Christian—that fused early modern Europe into a cultural block that embraced competition, protection of private property, economic development, and inventiveness. By contrast, he argues, competing societies in China and India had no such cultural notions of private property. Thus they stagnated. Although Landes admits that some geographic and environmental factors buttressed these differences, it is culture that he puts forth as the principal feature of European exceptionality. Landes argues that these legacies and the openness and innovation they encouraged in Europe, alongside some agricultural innovations, led directly to the sixteenth-century western European predominance in maritime exploration and overseas conquest. He writes, "The discovery of the New World by Europeans was not an accident. Europe now held a decisive advantage in the power to kill. It could deliver its weapons wherever ships could take them; and thanks to new navigational techniques, European ships could now go anywhere." In contrast, however, "...the Chinese lacked range, focus, and above all, curiosity"....

>> 11. The Wealth and Poverty of Nations: Why Some Are So Rich and Some So Poor

DAVID S. LANDES [1998]

[Non-European] societies were falling behind Europe even before the opening of the world (fifteenth century on) and the great confrontation. Why this should have been so is an important historical question—one learns as much from failure as from success. One cannot look here at every non-European society or civilization, but two deserve a moment's scrutiny.

The first, Islam, initially absorbed and developed the knowledge and ways of conquered peoples. By our period (roughly 1000 to 1500), Muslim rule went from the western end of the Mediterranean to the Indies. Before this, from about 750 to 1100, Islamic science and

technology far surpassed those of Europe, which needed to recover its heritage and did so to some extent through contacts with Muslims in such frontier areas as Spain. Islam was Europe's teacher.

Then something went wrong. Islamic science, denounced as heresy by religious zealots, bent under theological pressures for spiritual conformity. (For thinkers and searchers, this could be a matter of life and death.) For militant Islam, the truth had already been revealed. What led *back* to the truth was useful and permissible; all the rest was error and deceit. [...]

The one civilization that might have surpassed the European achievements was China. At least that is what the record seems to show. Witness the long list of Chinese inventions: the wheelbarrow, the stirrup, the rigid horse collar (to prevent choking), the compass, paper printing, gunpowder,

Source: David S. Landes, *The Wealth and Poverty of Nations: Why Some Are So Rich and So Poor* (New York: W. W. Norton, 1999), 54–59. First published in 1998.

porcelain. And yet in matters of science and technology, China remains a mystery. [...]

The mystery lies in China's failure to realize its potential. One generally assumes that knowledge and know-how are cumulative; surely a superior technique, once known, will replace older methods. But Chinese industrial history offers examples of technological oblivion and regression. We saw that horology went backward. Similarly, the machine to spin hemp was never adapted to the manufacture of cotton, and cotton spinning was never mechanized. And coal/coke smelting was allowed to fall into disuse, along with the iron industry as a whole. Why? [...]

Why indeed? Sinologists have put forward several partial explanations. The most persuasive are of a piece:

- The absence of a free market and industrialized property rights. The Chinese state was always interfering with private enterprise—taking over lucrative activities, prohibiting others, manipulating prices, exacting bribes, curtailing private enrichment. A favorite target was maritime trade, which the Heavenly Kingdom saw as a diversion from imperial concerns, as a divisive force and source of income inequality, worse yet, as an invitation to exit. Matters reached a climax under the Ming dynasty (1368–1644), when the state attempted to prohibit all trade overseas. Such interdictions led to evasion and smuggling, and smuggling brought corruption (protection money), confiscations, violence, and punishment. Bad government strangled initiative, increased the cost of transactions, diverted talent from commerce and industry.
- The larger values of the society. A leading sociological historian (historical sociologist) sees gender relations as a major obstacle: the quasi-confinement of women to the home made it impossible, for example, to exploit textile machinery profitably in a factory setting. Here China differed sharply from Europe or Japan, where women had free access to public space and were often expected to work outside the home to accumulate a dowry or contribute resources to the family.
- The great Hungarian-German-French sinologist, Etienne Balazs, would stress the larger context. He sees China's abortive technology as part of a larger pattern of totalitarian control. [...]

The Europeans knew much less of these interferences. Instead, they entered during these centuries into an exciting world of innovation and emulation that challenged vested interests and rattled the forces of conservatism. Changes were cumulative; novelty spread fast. A new sense of progress replaced an older, effete reverence for authority. This intoxicating sense of freedom touched (infected) all domains. [...]

Why this peculiarly European *joie de trouver*? This pleasure in new and better? This cultivation of invention—or what some have called "the invention of invention"? Different scholars have suggested a variety of reasons, typically related to religious values:

1. The Judeo-Christian respect for manual labor, summed up in a number of biblical injunctions. One example: When God warns Noah of the coming flood and tells him he will be saved, it is not God who saves him. "Build three an ark of gopher wood," he says, and Noah builds an ark to divine specifications.
2. The Judeo-Christian subordination of nature to man. This is a sharp departure from widespread animistic beliefs and practices that saw something of the divine in every tree and stream (hence naiads and dryads). Ecologists today might think these animistic beliefs preferable to what replaced them, but no one was listening to pagan nature worshippers in Christian Europe.
3. The Judeo-Christian sense of linear time. Other societies thought of time as cyclical, returning to earlier stages and starting over

again. Linear time is progressive or regressive, moving on to better things or declining from some earlier, happier state. For Europeans in our period, the progressive view prevailed.

4. In the last analysis, however, I would stress the market. Enterprise was free in Europe.

Innovation worked and paid, and rulers and vested interests were limited in their ability to prevent or discourage innovation. Success bred imitation and emulation; also a sense of power that would in the long run raise men almost to the level of gods.

Critiquing *The Wealth and Poverty of Nations*

The last selection in this chapter is a review of David Landes' The Wealth and Poverty of Nations *by one of the masters of world history, William McNeill. When McNeill's seminal* The Rise of the West: A History of the Human Community *was published in 1963 it became an immediate bestseller in the United States but also came under fire for its eurocentrism. Admittedly, it reflected in many ways the dominant, Western perspectives within academia at that date. Yet it still proposed the notion that it is more the relationship between societies, rather than any intrinsic cultural factor within individual societies, that propels trajectories of regional and global change. In subsequent decades McNeill has become a champion of this approach to world history. In his review of Landes' work, McNeill thus critiques Landes' view of world history as a competition between seemingly distinct rival cultures.*

>> 12. How the West Won

WILLIAM H. MCNEILL [1998]

"If we learn anything from the history of economic development, it is that culture makes all the difference." So David Landes sums up the message of his book. The title he chose and the histories of particular nations that he explores with wit and impressive learning are thus part of a sustained criticism of neoclassical economists' faith in the power of free markets to affect all peoples similarly and thus maximize wealth and well-being. Lands, on the contrary, argue that the historical record shows: 1) "The gains from trade are unequal." 2) "The export and import of jobs is not the same as trade in commodities." 3) "The "comparative advantage" a nation may have in international trade "is not fixed, and it can move for and against." 4) "Just because markets give signals does not mean that people will respond timely or well. Some people do

this better than others, and culture can make all the difference." [...]

[Landes'] vision of the human past remains shaped (and I would say skewed) by his apprenticeship in European economic history, because he has been preoccupied with looking for the medieval and early modern roots of the Industrial Revolution, and then pursuing its course and consequences in loving detail while dismissing economic changes elsewhere as trivial for proper understanding of the world's present condition. [...]

[Landes'] sketch of worldwide economic development before the year 1000 is a strange mix of geographic determinism, dubious assertions about the antiquity of European attempts to control population growth (which probably took place in parts of Europe and among some social classes only after the ravages of the Black Death in the fourteenth century), and a rather excessive emphasis on the advantages of animal husbandry. Landes largely

---

Source: William H. McNeill, "How the West Won," *The New York Review of Books* 45 (April 23, 1998).

defines his criteria of what really mattered for understanding how we got where we are by the agricultural expansion and swift rise of urban manufacture and trade that took place in Western Europe after 1000. Here he detects the roots of the Industrial Revolution, whose heirs we are. Nothing else matters much to him, so Landes neglects Muslim economic leadership before 1000 and the extraordinary surge in Chinese economic and technological accomplishment after that date, which anticipated some important European industrial technologies by six centuries and more. A more convincing perspective on medieval times would recognize that what happened in Europe was the extreme Far Western wing of a pan-Eurasian commercial and technological advance of which China was the principal center and driving force.

To be sure, Western Europe in late medieval and early modern times differed from other parts of the world. Accordingly, Landes devoted ten chapters of his book to examining "European Exceptionalism: A Different Path," with special attention to the technology and to the ways that disorderly diversity within Europe prevented priests and rulers from inhibiting disruptive economic innovation. This was not the case in China, where the rapid technological and organizational innovations of the Sung era (960–1279) were damaged and disrupted by Mongol conquest and then contained, and in some cases reversed, by deliberate policy under the Ming dynasty (1368–1644). Landes does not try to understand this (to us surprising) history. He impatiently dismisses it as "a weird pattern of isolated initiatives and sisyphean discontinuities—up, up, up and then down again—almost as though the society were held down by a silk ceiling."

Landes finds much to deplore in European overseas expansion after 1500 in America and Asia, but he does not think much of Amerindian or Asian rulers either. Spaniards and Portuguese "jumped the traces of rationality and turned their land into a platform for empire"; but the worst that Cortez and Pizarro could do, according to Landes, merely matched Aztec and Inca brutality. "They all deserved one another" is his lapidary conclusion. And the net effect of Europe's overseas expansion was to shift economic primacy northward, first to Holland, then to England, thus preparing for the Industrial Revolution, toward which everything that went before had pointed, and on which all that followed depended. […]

Yet it seems to me that there are serious defects in his approach to understanding, as he puts it, "how we have come to where and what we are, in the sense of making, getting, and spending." The first of these is his assumption that only what happened in Europe really mattered, while the rest of the world mostly reacted to innovations Europeans thrust down their throats. This is intrinsically improbable. Most of humankind—four fifths or thereabouts—descend from non-European peoples; and heritages from their differing pasts live on. In particular, local efforts to defend divergent local economic and political ideals never disappeared and continue to influence economic behavior in contemporary Russia, China, and Japan, as well as among Muslims, Latin Americans, and Africans. Lands credits the Japanese with an autochthonous economic history, as we saw; for the others he simply assumes an unchanging "culture" that interferes with efficient use of European (modern) technology and the increase of wealth.

>> Mastering the Material

1. According to Sepulveda, why were the Spanish justified in their conquest of the Americas and any subsequent treatment of the Native American populations?

2. On what points do Sepulveda and de las Casas disagree? On what points do they appear to concur?

3. By what criterion does de las Casas judge the Americans to be "barbarians"?

4. According to David Landes, what inherited social values were key to the "success" of western European nation-states?

5. What common threads run through Sepulveda's, de las Casas', and Landes' pieces on Europe's exceptionality at the beginning of the early modern periods?

6. According to Landes, what were the Islamic and Chinese shortcomings that led to their respective "stagnation"?

7. On what basis does McNeill criticize Landes? How convincing are his arguments?

8. Are you convinced that there were significant cultural differences that led to western Europe states, rather than other Eurasian societies, conquering the Americas? Why or why not?

>> Making Connections

1. Consider Landes' account of China under the Ming Dynasty. How does it compare to the depictions in Chapter 2? At this point in your reading, are you more convinced that early Ming China was a stagnant, despotic empire or a vibrant, technologically advanced society?

2. What do de Jerez's depiction of Pizarro's encounter with the Incas (Reading 1) and other primary accounts such as Sepulveda's and de las Casas' tell us about the Spanish perception of indigenous Americans? What do they indicate about the nature of primary sources?

3. Western (European and American) professional historians emphasize objectivity and scientific detachment as desirable traits in their work. Yet critics have argued that much historical work is eurocentric, in part because the discipline of history emerged during a period of European dominance. What do you think, based on the sources in these first three chapters?

Chapter 4

Theories of Military Superiority

Theories of European cultural superiority have survived in part because both proponents and opponents have found culture to be a difficult factor to measure. While military power may seem easy to quantify—the more powerful states win wars, and the less powerful lose them—in fact, this turns out not to be the case. Disease, geography, finances, and morale all influence the outcome of conflict as much as the size and technology of armies. These complications have not, however, prevented scholars from comparing the military abilities of different states and regions in the era of the American conquest. On the surface, at least, it seems evident that western Europeans had military advantages. After all, in the period 1450–1550 Spain and Portugal carved out empires for themselves in the Americas. The Netherlands, France, and Britain subsequently joined them in doing so. Concurrently, Europeans—the Portuguese especially—won naval battles and captured ports around the African and Asian rims of the Indian Ocean, including perhaps the greatest maritime trading city of them all: Malacca on the Malaysian coast of Southeast Asia. In subsequent centuries they would extend these victories to conquer almost all of Africa and a sizeable chunk of Asia.

Looking backward, it is easy to attribute these early successes to a European superiority of arms and organization. However, there are dangers to this analysis. For instance, there is little evidence that during this early maritime age European militaries were either better officered and organized than their Asian and African opponents or that their technology was superior. In fact, Asian armies had been defeating European armies with some consistency for several centuries, beginning with crusades of the eleventh to thirteenth centuries. The subsequent expansion of the Ottoman Empire into Europe was only barely checked by Europeans. Following their 1453 victory over the defenders of Constantinople, including a body of Venetians and western Europeans, the Ottoman Turks continued their march westward, conquering much of the Balkan peninsula. In the west, by contrast, European forces managed over the course of several centuries to evict Muslim armies from Spain, but the Muslim states on the Iberian peninsula existed at the very limit of Islamic power.

The lack of a clear-cut advantage for either Christian European or Islamic armies reflects the relative parity of technology across Eurasia and northern Africa. Europeans simply did not have the martial advantages over Asians that they had over Americans. Asian societies had equal or higher levels of literacy, access to iron, and large numbers of horses. It was Asians, probably the Chinese, who invented gunpowder, and the Ottomans who first made use of siege cannons. Almost all Asian societies made use of horses and metal armor. Moreover, the great Asian and Eurasian empires could mobilize well-organized military forces of a size unheard of in Europe. Against Asians, then, any European military advantage must have been specific and limited, rather than general.

It is perhaps surprising to us that sub-Saharan African societies were also generally able to match European expeditions in combat. Although many parts of the continent were unsuited to horses, these tended to include large areas of dense forest that gave an advantage to experienced locals. In addition, African armies had access to iron technology that was probably independently discovered in western Africa and had by this period spread through most of the continent. Moreover, across much of Africa disease was a disadvantage for European invaders who had no resistance to tropical illnesses. Finally, both large African states and smaller societies harnessed sophisticated military organizations to respond to outside threats. John Thornton, a leading Africanist whose expertise includes military history, suggests that in this period Europeans both taught and learned from the peoples they encountered and fought against in Africa, in a reciprocal process in which neither had a consistent advantage.

So western Europeans did not possess a general advantage in the size or capabilities of their armies against Old World opponents such as they enjoyed in the Americas. But did they have a specific naval advantage? The contrasting evidence from land and naval battles tends to suggest they may have. In the first reading in this chapter, we see a description of a land battle that resulted in the defeat of European forces and the capture of Constantinople by the Ottomans. The second source is an account of the invasion of Malacca by the Portuguese, an amphibious attack in which the Portuguese naval vessels supported their expeditionary force and were only barely victorious. The third source, a retelling of the Portuguese admiral Vasco da Gama's decisive victory over the navy of the Indian state of Calecut, is something of a contrast to the first two documents. Da Gama's naval forces were, in fact, consistently successful in pirating, holding ports to ransom, and winning naval battles across the Indian Ocean, as were those of later European expeditions.

It is interesting to note that the famed European galleons used by da Gama were built on technology available across Eurasia. Their cannons were European refinements of Arab weapons technology based on the Chinese invention of gunpowder. They navigated using a compass invented in China and known for decades to Arabs who in turn taught European mariners. Yet it was Europeans who developed the immensely useful technique of combining square sails (such as were used on the Atlantic coast of Europe) with the lateen or triangular sails adapted from Arab ships. This technique gave them a combination of speed and the ability to sail almost against the wind. It was also Europeans who constructed sail-powered ships that could carry batteries of guns and ocean-going vessels capable of withstanding the recoil of heavy cannon. These ships did not allow Europeans to conquer large inland territories in either Asia or Africa, but they may have enabled them to control commerce through seizing ports and sinking ships. In fact, without this military advantage Europeans could not have controlled the Indian Ocean trade, as most of the merchant shipping they relied upon continued to be built and managed by Asians until at least the nineteenth century.

But how did this European naval advantage arise? Historians suggest a variety of reasons: Europe's two relatively small inland seas—the Baltic and the Mediterranean—were safe zones in which they could develop sailing technology. Both were also militarized seas, the scenes of arms races between various Muslim and Christian states as well as independent pirates. Western Europe was arguably also fortunate in that it possessed vast forests of timber for building ocean-going vessels. Yet these theories must be closely questioned. According to historian P. J. Marshall, the European military advantage was so slight, and so specific, that any single overarching explanation seems suspect.

Ottoman Military Supremacy at the Siege of Constantinople

Nicolo Barbaro was a Venetian who participated in the defense of the Byzantine capital of Constantinople against an immense Ottoman army in 1453. The city of Constantinople, once the seat of the Eastern Roman Empire, had built in an easily defensible position. Nevertheless, its strategic importance and wealth had attracted to its walls numerous invaders in the centuries prior to the Ottoman assault, including Germanic groups, Persians, Russians, and western European crusaders. In this description of the ultimately successful 1453 Ottoman siege, Barbaro describes the Ottoman advantages of a large, well-equipped army and unmatched heavy artillery that ultimately defeated the Byzantines and their contingents of European allies.

>> 13. Diary of the Siege of Constantinople

NICOLO BARBARO [1453]

Since I happened myself to be in the unfortunate city of Constantinople, I have decided to put in writing the following account of the attack by Mahomet Bey, son of Murat the Turk, which gave him the mastery of it. And so that it may be understood exactly how it was taken, I shall first say how the war began between the Turks and the Greeks, and then you shall hear in order of all the attacks made from day to day, and know what happened from the beginning until its final savage and grievous capture.

In March, 1452, Mahomet Bey the Turk set about building a fine castle six miles from Constantinople towards the mouth of the Black Sea. It had fourteen towers, of which the five principal ones were covered with lead and very strongly built. And when he came to build it, he came from Gallipoli, with six galleys fully equipped and 18 *fuste* and 16 *parandarie,* and came into the waters of Constantinople and built it six miles from the city on the Greek coast near the old castle. All through the month of August, 1452, this castle was being built, and it was made for the express purpose of taking the city of Constantinople. [...]

On the eleventh of April the Sultan had his cannon placed near the walls, by the weakest part of the city, the sooner to gain his objective. These cannon were planted in four places: first of all, three cannon were placed near the palace

Source: Nicolo Barbaro, *Diary of the Siege of Constantinople 1453,* translated by J. R. Jones (New York: Exposition Press, 1969), 1, 30–31, 62–64.

of the Most Serene Emperor, and three other cannon were placed near the Pigi gate, and two at the Cressu gate, and another four at the gate of San Romano, the weakest part of the whole city. One of those four cannon which were at the gate of San Romano threw a ball weighing about twelve hundred pounds, more or less, and thirteen *quarte* in circumference, which will show the terrible damage it inflicted where it landed. The second cannon threw a ball weighing eight hundred pounds, and nine *quarte* in circumference. These two cannon were the largest that the Turkish Khan had, the other cannon being of various sizes, from five hundred pounds to two hundred pounds, and smaller still. […]

On the twenty-ninth of May, 1453, three hours before daybreak, Mohamet Bey son of Murat the Turk came himself to the walls of Constantinople to begin the general assault which gained him the city. The Sultan divided his troops into three groups of fifty thousand men each: one group was of Christians who were kept in his camp against his will, the second group was of men of a low condition, peasants and the like, and the third group was a janissaries in their white turbans, these being all soldiers of the Sultan and paid every day, all well-armed men strong in battle, and behind these janissaries were all the officers, and behind these the Turkish Sultan. […]

When the second group had come forward and attempted unsuccessfully to get into the city, there then approached the third group, their paid soldiers the janissaries, and their officers and their other principal commanders, all very brave men, and the Turkish Sultan

behind them all. This third group attacked the walls of the poor city, not like Turks but like lions, with such shouting and sounding of castanets that it seemed a thing not of this world, and the shouting was heard as far away as Anatolia, twelve miles away from their camp. This third group of Turks, all fine fighters, found those on the walls very weary after having fought with the first and second groups, while the pagans were eager and fresh for the battle; and with the loud cries which they uttered on the field, they spread fear through the city and took away our courage with their shouting and noise. The wretched people in the city felt themselves to have been taken already, and decided to sound the tocsin through the whole city, and sounded it at all the posts on the walls, all crying at the top of their voices, "Mercy! Mercy! God send help from Heaven to this Empire of Constantine, so that a pagan people may not rule over the Empire!" […]

The Turks were attacking, as I have said, like men determined to enter the city, by San Romano on the landward side, firing their cannon again and again, with so many other guns and arrows without number and shouting from these pagans, that the very air seemed to be split apart; and they kept on firing their great cannon which fired a ball weighing twelve hundred pounds, and their arrows, all along the length of the walls on the side where their camp was, a distance of six miles, so that inside the barbicans at least eighty camel-loads of them were picked up, and as many as twenty camel-loads of those which were in the ditch. This fierce battle lasted until daybreak.

Sejara Melayu, or the Portuguese Conquest of Malacca

This Malayan account of Afonso d'Albuquerque's conquest of Malacca in 1511 is illustrative of the balance of military power in this region. The description of the battle between the Portuguese expeditionary force (whom the writer calls "Franks" in typical Muslim fashion) and the forces of this city-state illustrates the decisive impact of the

Portuguese navy, in terms of both mobility and firepower, in what was otherwise a very close battle. The text was probably originally written around 1536, but the original version did not survive. The translation here is based on a 1612 revision. [c. 1536/revised c. 1612]

>> 14. A Malay Account of the Conquest of Malacca

[c. 1536]

Here now is a story of Fongso d'Albuquerque. At the end of his term of office as viceroy he proceeded to Pertugal and presenting himself before the Raja of Pertugal asked for an armada. The Raja of Pertugal gave him four carracks and five long galleys. He then returned from Pertugal and fitted out a fleet at Goa, consisting of three carracks, eight galleasses, four long galleys and fifteen foysts. There were thus forty (sic) craft in all. With this fleet he sailed for Malaka. And when he reached Malaka, there was great excitement and word was brought to Sultan Ahmad, "The Franks are come to attack us! They have seven carracks, eight galleasses, ten long galleys, fifteen sloops and five foysts." Thereupon Sultan Ahmad had all his forces assembled and he ordered them to make ready their equipment. And the Franks engaged the men of Malaka in battle, and they fired their cannon from their ships so that the cannon balls came like rain. And the noise of the cannon was as the noise of thunder in the heavens and the flashes of fire of their guns were like flashes of lightening in the sky: and the noise of their matchlocks was like that of ground-nuts popping in the frying-pan. So heavy was the gun-fire that the men of Malaka could no longer maintain their position on the shore. [...] And the Franks shouted from their ships, "Take warning, you men of Malaka, tomorrow we land!", And the men of Malaka answered, "Very Well!" [...]

When day dawned, the Franks landed and attacked. And Sultan Ahmad mounted his elephant Juru Demang, with the Sri Awadana on the elephant's head and Tun 'Ali Hati balancing the king of the packsaddle. The Franks then fiercely engaged the men of Malaka in battle and so vehement was their onslaught that the Malaka line was broken, leaving the king on his elephant isolated. And the king fought with the Franks pike to pike, and he was wounded in the palm of the hand.

Vasco da Gama's Defeat of the Calecut Fleet

Gaspar Correa was a secretary in the service of Alfonso d'Albuquerque, conqueror of Malacca and governor of the Portuguese Indies. He based his history of Vasco da Gama's expeditions, written around 1561, largely on the diary of a priest who accompanied the admiral. This excerpt describes a 1503 battle between da Gama's ships and a fleet gathered by the ruler of the Indian state of Calecut. Previously, da Gama had bombarded Calecut without provocation, and it is of little surprise that upon his return he found that resistance had hardened. The following narrative, in which the forces of Calecut are described as "Moors" in the language typical of Europeans at the time, aptly illustrates the weaponry advantage of the European ships over even the fleet of so powerful a trading state as Calecut. Although Correa calls the Calecut sailors Moors, a term usually reserved for Muslims, in fact the population of Calecut included Hindus, Muslims, and even some Christians.

Source: "A Malay Account of the Conquest of Malacca," translated by C. C. Brown, *Journal of the Malayan Branch of the Royal Asiatic Society* 25 (1952): 167–169.

>> 15. The Three Voyages of Vasco da Gama and His Viceroyalty

GASPAR CORREA [c. 1561]

One morning they sighted the fleet of Calecut, which was coming along the coast with a light land breeze; there were so many sail that our people did not see the end of them. [...] When Vicente Sodré saw the fleet he ordered the caravels to edge in close inshore, one astern of the other in a line, and to run under all the sail they could carry, firing as many guns as they could, and he with the ships remained behind. Each of the caravels carried thirty men, and four heavy guns below, and above six falconnets, and ten swivel-guns placed on the quarter deck and in the bows, and two of the falconnets fired astern; the ships carried six guns below on the deck and two smaller ones on the poop, and eight falconnets above and several swivel-guns, and before the mast two smaller pieces which fired forwards; the ships of burden were much more equipped with artillery. [...]

Ahead of the Moorish flagship came many paraos, which are like fustas, and they remained to seaward, so that their ships might shelter them from the guns of the caravels; these, with the instructions under which they sailed, could only use their two guns on the seaward side, which in all the caravels would be ten guns. When they had reached as far forward as the Moorish ships, all recommending themselves to the Lord, discharged their guns, all firing at the flagship; and those which passed forward went against the other ships, for it was not possible to miss; and they made such haste to load again that they loaded the guns with bags of powder which they had ready for this purpose made to measure, so that they could load again very speedily. But with this first discharge our men made such good work that they brought down the mast of the flagship, which fell over and stove in the ship and killed many Moors; and another shot hit it full and passed through near the poop, which it shattered much and killed and wounded many people; of the other large ships there were stove in low down, so that they foundered and went to the bottoms, many people remaining on the water swimming, who betook themselves to the paraos and caught hold of the oars, so that they could not row, and they could not get out of the way of their own ships, which came against them and capsized them, so that they so much embarrassed one another that they all remained stuck close to each other, and our ships fired into them for a considerable time, for they fired into the thick with their heavy guns, so that they shattered many in pieces, killing many people, on account of which there were shrieks and cries amongst Moors.

Was There a Naval Arms Gap in the Indian Ocean?

P. J. Marshall was one of several world history scholars who began in the early 1980s to question the assumption that western Europeans had a naval advantage in Asia in the sixteenth century. His work was in part a response to historians like Carlo Cipolla who had argued that, while naval technology was relatively even across Eurasia, European cultural attitudes led them to make a sustained commitment to the military sciences. By contrast, Cipollo had portrayed Asians as more concerned with stability, refusing to commit to new technologies and forms of organization. Throughout the modern era, Western academics had portrayed societies outside of Asia as less willing to improvise, and not

Source: Gaspar Correa, *The Three Voyages of Vasco da Gama and his Viceroyalty,* translated by Henry E. J. Stanley (New York: Burt Franklin, 1869), 367–369.

only in the military field. Although not entirely willing to reject some sense of difference between Asia and Europe, Marshall was one of the first to question the evidence that suggested Asians were indisposed to innovate, to learn, and to make sustained efforts to produce naval forces equal to those of Europeans. Instead, he suggests, Asian merchants and maritime powers in the Indian Ocean either accepted Portuguese control of their trading networks because it suited them to do so, or they became smugglers, evading Portuguese patrols. However, this view has a number of critics, some of whom suggest that Marshall does not sufficiently account for Portuguese naval victories such as the one over the Calecut fleet. Nor, critics say, does he definitively dispose of the fact that through force of arms the Portuguese managed to siphon much of the maritime commercial profit of the Indian Ocean into their own pockets.

>> 16. Western Arms in Maritime Asia in the Early Phases of Expansion

P. J. MARSHALL [1980]

By the fifteenth century it may well be possible to generalize about entities called 'Europe' and 'Asia' which have distinct patterns of development in cultural, social and other respects. European expansion brought these entities into a competition, whose outcome no doubt reflected their respective strengths and weaknesses. But this paper will try to make the case that, in the special circumstances prevailing in maritime Asia before the nineteenth century, more limited explanations are extremely important in determining the outcome of military competition. Western military successes are striking, but there is no uniform pattern of success and they are not necessarily the occasions on which differences between the two societies manifest themselves in inevitable European triumph. [...]

The reputation of the Portuguese as military innovators seems [...] secure. There can be no doubt that the systematic use of force by the Portuguese on a continental scale for ostensibly commercial ends was entirely new to Asians. But the weapons at their disposal were only partially new. The Portuguese certainly did not introduce cannon or small arms to Asia. [...]

The Ottomans and the Mamluks used cannon extensively in the later fifteenth century, Turkish guns being considered as good as any available to the Portuguese. Artillery was also being used in fifteenth-century India; gunners and musketeers served in the Gujarat fleet in 1482. During the sixteenth-century cannon spread widely in Asia. Some of them were imported from Europe, but many were supplied by the Turks or cast in other parts of Asia. Minuscule Portuguese land forces were not therefore inclined to engage large Asian armies who used much the same weapons as they did. The great Portuguese victories were won at sea in a string of encounters of which the most famous were against the Javanese trading states of Malacca in 1513 and against the Egyptians and Gujaratis off Diu in western India in 1599.

Even at sea, however, the margin of Portuguese superiority was relatively narrow. It was not the case that heavily-gunned Atlantic sailing ships effortlessly demolished oared Asian galleys which relied on boarding and ramming. Ships and galleys were common to both sides and both sides used artillery at sea. [...]

In the western Indian Ocean, Portuguese naval power was largely exerted in default of effective opposition; further east it was increasingly contested. Indians and Indonesians began to build and arm ships on a scale to match

---

Source: P. J. Marshall, "Western Arms in Maritime Asia in the Early Phases of Expansion," *Modern Asian Studies* 14 (1980): 16–19.

the Portuguese. Malacca, the main Portuguese stronghold, was 'harassed on all sides by hostile neighbors' and was incapable of enforcing effective regulation over the trade of its area. Malacca had to contend with Japara in northern Java, with Johore on the same side of the Straits and with Acheh opposite. The Achinese were particularly formidable opponents, who attacked Portuguese Malacca fourteen times. They commissioned large ships to be built in India, obtained guns from the Turks and cast their own. In 1562 the Portuguese encountered an Acheh ship comparable to one of their own Indiamen and armed with fifty guns. From the 1530s the Achinese began to ship pepper and spices to the Turkish dominated Red Sea with little effective opposition from the Portuguese.

Within a few decades of the arrival of Vasco da Gama, Portuguese sea power had enabled them to establish a string of bases from the Persian Gulf to Japan. The geographical outline of European influence in Asia was to change little, except in Indonesia, until the mid-eighteenth century. But neither in commercial nor in military terms was the Portuguese challenge one to which Asians could not respond effectively. Many Asians found it advantageous to do business with the Portuguese, but those who did not wish to stood a reasonable chance of evading the thin network of ships and bases or even of fighting their way through. Well before they came under the hammer of the Dutch, the Portuguese had begun to be absorbed into Asia, participating in its trade and politics but not dominating them.

Warfare in Seventeenth-Century Angola

John Thornton's work on military conflict in Africa is only part of his ongoing contributions to the study of Africa and Africans' contributions to the development of an Atlantic world. In this innovative article, he suggests that European organization, tactics, and equipment were in fact not entirely useful in Angola (on the western edge of central Africa), where indigenous styles of combat and weaponry had developed that were suited to the local environment. In fact, he suggests, the Portuguese only became a potent force in the region when they adopted many local innovations, and even with these changes still only managed to fight such large polities as Ndongo to a draw. Ironically, Europeans were able to put African fighting techniques to good use in the Americas, where African-born slaves were often formed into units to fight independent American peoples in the dense rain forests of the Caribbean and American mainland. On the other hand, many of these enslaved Africans escaped to form independent, or "marroon," communities. Often these former slaves allied to and intermarried with indigenous American populations.

>> 17. The Art of War in Angola, 1575–1680

JOHN K. THORNTON [1988]

European arms in the period before the Industrial Revolution were not always as overwhelming as [some sources] suggest, for in several parts of the world Europeans were notably less successful than they were against the great American empires. One of these regions was Africa, where the Portuguese and Spanish made a substantial effort to conquer the Angolan kingdom of Ndongo in a long series of wars that began in 1579. Although the Portuguese did penetrate into

Source: John K. Thornton, "The Art of War in Angola, 1575–1680," *Comparative Studies in Society and History* 30 (1988): 360–361, 373–378.

the interior and successfully created a colony on the African coast, they never succeeded in conquering the main ruling group of Ndongo, who fought them to a standstill, and were overcome only in the mid-nineteenth century.

The Europeans' inability to make the kind of dramatic, large-scale conquests that had characterized the first half century of Spanish activity in the Americas convinced them that local weapons, tactics, and organization needed to be taken seriously. As a result of this recognition, a new art of war developed that combined European and African arms and strategies. It was gradually adopted by both sides in the confrontation, which had its high point during the long wars between the Portuguese and Queen Njinga (ruled 1624–63) and her successors over control of the highlands region that made up Ndongo heartland, and more or less ended in a stalemate in the early 1680s. [...]

Scholars often assume that firearms have had a revolutionary impact on the battlefield and played a major role in European conquests, even though closer investigation raises some serious doubts. [...] If the Portuguese who fought in Kongo in 1491 carried firearms, they must have been unimpressed themselves with their performance, for the equipment of the 1509 force sent to Kongo included only pikes and crossbows. Indeed, doubts about the utility of firearms in Europe were expressed by as respected an authority as Machiavelli at the same time, and conditions in Angola were less favorable to their employment. The penetrating power of a hand-held firearm, so useful against armored cavalry, was largely wasted on an unarmored foe, and its inaccuracy, moreover, while not such a disadvantage on European battlefields against massed troops, was a major difficulty against the dispersed formations common in Angola. [...]

As with the arquebus and musket, artillery found a limited but prescribed place on the Angolan battlefield. It was worthless for attacking fortifications, its principal use in Europe, in large measure because the Angolan fortifications did not employ high walls, and in fact resembled the earthworks, ditches, and low walls that European engineers built to counteract the cannon. This, when coupled with the difficulty of moving the artillery and the fact that sieges could not in any case be sustained for reasons of logistics, more or less kept the gun as siege engine out of Angolan conflict.

In the seventeenth century, however, Portuguese field artillery did find some use in Angola against attacking formations, even if these troops' relative dispersion meant that the effectiveness of shot would be less. [...] But the Portuguese did put emphasis on the possibility of using cavalry. Members of the early expedition against Ndongo in 1578–79 confidently informed Lopes that one horseman was worth a hundred blacks, perhaps thinking that they might be able to repeat the feats of the Spanish horsemen in Mexico. But although the Portuguese were able to maintain a cavalry force of a dozen or so, these troops were never a significant factor in warfare. They typically fought dismounted, as they did at Cavanga, and even in reconnaissance or pursuit never went faster than the accompanying *pombo*, the quick-footed pedestrian scouts.

Perhaps the most important military advantages the Europeans brought to Africa were, surprisingly, their body armor and skill with the sword. [...]

But the power of these weapons did not come without disadvantages. The armor was heavy, and the troops' mobility was strictly limited because of it. Furthermore, they could not hold the field alone. In situations where they were forced to fight alone because their allies had left them or because the light infantry had fled, they were typically slaughtered, often to a man. [...]

Europeans were remarkably quick to accept African tactics and organization. [...] As early as 1585, Portuguese battlefield organization was set to conform to the patterns of their opponents. Locally recruited archers and soldiers in that year numbered around 9,000 effectives, while the Portuguese force totaled about 300. [...]

The development of a new art of war in Angola reveals some of complexities of military history in the preindustrial world and the difficulties in seeing how the European conquest in Africa were made. Clearly there was no automatic or overwhelming technical or organizational superiority, although military systems of both countries were affected by the contact. It was not until the age of the Maxim gun, in fact, that Africans could be overwhelmed, in Angola or anywhere, by sheer military superiority.

>> Mastering the Material

1. Did Europeans possess a significant military advantage in Asia and sub-Saharan Africa in the period 1550–1650? If so, what was it?

2. According to Marshall, how did the Portuguese come to dominate the Indian Ocean?

3. In light of Correa's account of the naval battle between da Gama and the Calecut fleet, how convincing do you find Marshall's arguments that the Portuguese only held a slight naval advantage over Indian Ocean states?

4. Thornton argues that European arms did not provide them with a decisive advantage over Angolan states. What evidence does he offer to support this? What does he suggest ultimately made them a potent force in the region?

>> Making Connections

1. Compare the military encounters described by Melayu and Barbaro to the battle of Cajamarca (Chapter 2). What advantages did Europeans have over inhabitants of the Americas, but not over Asians such as the Ottomans and Malaccans? Why the difference?

2. Examine Correa's description of the size and armaments of da Gama's fleet, then compare this to Chang Kuei-Sheng's depiction of the Chinese fleet of Zheng He (Chapter 2). If China had continued to send fleets into the Indian Ocean rather than turning away in the mid-fifteenth century, could they have kept the Portuguese from capturing its commerce and major ports?

3. As Marshall and other scholars observe, European weaponry during this period was "only partially new" and based on technology available throughout Eurasia. Yet it is also well established that Europeans improved upon these armaments and techniques. Consider Diamond's concept of East-West diffusion (Reading 2) along with Thornton's argument that the Portuguese incorporation of Angolan military innovations led to their increased military prowess. In light of this, is it arguable that diffusion and "borrowing" was responsible for European naval advancement? If so, does this necessarily imply that culturally they were more willing to improve and adapt? Is there evidence elsewhere in this chapter that suggests other societies also benefited from borrowing?

Chapter 5

Theories of Political Superiority

In part because differences in culture and military prowess could not adequately account for Europe's seemingly unique pursuit of overseas expansion in the fifteenth and sixteenth centuries, a number of scholars have turned to political theory for answers. Proponents of these theories generally suggest that early modern Europe developed unique types of states and a unique system of relationships between these states. Not all historians accept this idea, but as P. H. H. Vries observes in "Governing Growth: A Comparative Analysis of the Role of the State in the Rise of the West," it is a difficult concept to avoid:

> *Almost every text on the subject refers to the peculiarity of Western Europe's states. To be more precise two related points have become stock in trade in the literature on the European miracle. Firstly, Europe was a system of states, not an empire, as was the rule in the other advanced societies in the world. Secondly, states in Western Europe as political entities were structured and governed differently from empires in the rest of the world, to a large extent because they were part of a system of states. The facts of course are undeniable. Europe indeed was a system of states, while the other most advanced economies were not. Europe's states had a different set-up than the empires in the rest of the world. Europe "rose" while "the East" did not. But in itself that does not prove that its state-system and the characteristics of its states were causes of its rise. To make a convincing case one needs to show the mechanism, or mechanisms, which link cause and effect.*

Were European states better suited to overseas exploration and colonization? According to some who support this thesis, fourteenth- and fifteenth-century European states were better able to use their human resources because they were already moving toward democracy. Historians like the medievalist Joseph R. Strayer contend that the institutions and precedents that would later lead to constitutional and representative institutions were already evolving in the medieval era. In his book *On the Medieval Origins of the Modern State,* Strayer explores the formation of the French and English states from the eleventh to the fifteenth centuries. In this period, he argues, these states were already becoming particularly stable and centralized, and this may have enabled them to mobilize resources for exploration overseas.

Even if Strayer is correct, however, the causes of this unique path for western Europe remain to be explored. One answer put forward is that it was the *fragmentation* of Europe into medium-sized kingdoms like England, Spain, and France that promoted overseas commerce by stimulating competition. Historian Paul Kennedy is one of several scholars to emphasize the significance of the lack of a single, centralized European empire in this period. Instead, many small or medium-sized states competed with each other on a relatively even playing field and, if one ever got too strong, the others would band together to bring it down. The Habsburg family, for example, at one time ruled the vast Spanish Empire, the Netherlands, and Austria, yet never managed to overcome France, England, Prussia, Russia, Sweden, and their other opponents. The resulting patchwork of states, Kennedy argues, created a competitive environment that contrasted starkly with the large empires forming elsewhere in Eurasia. Kennedy, along with Jared Diamond, has suggested that the ultimate cause of this disparity was geographic—that Europe's mountain ranges and bodies of water cut it into smaller geographic areas for state building than the vast Asian landmass to the east.

Other political historians locate the origins of European overseas colonialism in the somewhat earlier process by which centralized states acquired outlying regions within Europe. The fourteenth- and fifteenth-century English intensification of its rule over Ireland, the consolidation of Spain, and the French imposition of authority in Languedoc and Provence, for example, could have stimulated the development of institutions and structures that would later prove adaptable to administering American colonies. This process is explored in the first of our primary sources, the letters from English Kings Henry VI to his representative in Ireland.

Collectively, these theories seem quite convincing. Yet they do have their detractors. In an important 1997 article, Victor Lieberman, a scholar of southeast Asia, suggests that the very basis of "west vs. rest" political comparison is flawed. There was, he argues, no clear dichotomy between Western (European) states and Eastern (Asian) empires. Instead, many different parts of Eurasia, of which he selects six, underwent similar processes of state formation and competition throughout the early modern period. Moreover, it is important to note that while modern historians have projected a sense of European exceptionalism upon this period, contemporary Europeans themselves often saw other societies' political systems as admirable and in no way inferior to their own. The Spaniard Juan Gonzalez de Mendoza, traveling in China, was one such observer. Mendoza's often glowing accounts of Chinese governance suggests that China provided for its citizens in a way that most European states did not. Indeed, although China under the Ming emperors has often been regarded by Western scholars as a stagnating state, it is now clear that it possessed quite a vibrant political discourse. As the writing of the great neo-Confucianist scholar Wang Yang-ming [Wang Yangming] demonstrates, China's philosophers were constantly redefining the roles of government and citizen during this period, sometimes with the support of the emperors but more often in opposition to them.

The Emergence of the Nation-State in Europe

In these excerpts from his work on English and French state formation, Joseph Strayer not only sets out the advantages of what he calls the modern state but suggests reasons why it emerged first in western Europe. Strayer's definition of a state is threefold: that it endures in time and space, that it has permanent political institutions that survive the death of individuals, and that it possesses sovereignty. **Sovereignty** *is generally defined as the monopoly the state possesses of legal authority and the exercise of violence. Strayer's work focuses almost entirely on western Europe, and he has been criticized for not exploring whether this type of state was simultaneously emerging in other parts of the world.*

>> 18. On the Medieval Origins of the Modern State

Joseph R. Strayer [1970]

There were periods—not long ago as historians measure time—when the state did not exist, and when no one was concerned that it did not exist. In those times it was the man without a family or lord, without membership in a local community or a dominant religious group, who had no security and no opportunity, who could survive only by becoming a servant or a slave. The values of this kind of a society were different from ours; the supreme sacrifices of property and life were made for family, lord, community, or religion, not for the state. The organizing power of such societies was less than ours; it was difficult to get very many people to work together for any length of time. [...]

Imperfect and spatially limited types of organizations meant that the society could not make the best use of its human and natural resources, that its level of living was low, and that capable individuals were unable to realize their full potentialities. The development of the modern state, on the other hand, made possible such a concentrated use of human resources that no other type of social organization could avoid being relegated to a subordinate role. [...]

The European states which emerged after 1100 combined, to some extent, the strengths of both the empires and the city-states. They were large enough and powerful enough to have excellent chances for survival—some of them are approaching the thousand-year mark, which is a respectable age for any human organization. At the same time they managed to get a large proportion of their people involved in, or at least concerned with the political process, and they succeeded in creating some sense of common identity among local communities. They got more out of their people, both in the way of political and social activity and in loyalty than the ancient empires had done, even if they fell short of the full participation which had marked a city such as Athens.

The distinction between large, imperfectly integrated empires and small but cohesive political units applies fairly well to the Middle East, Central Asia, and India. It fits China (and eventually Japan) less well. But the ability of the European type of state to gain economic and political superiority proved so great that in the end it made the Chinese (or other non-European) experience seem irrelevant. The European model of the state became the fashionable model. No European state imitated a non-European model, but the non-European states either imitated the European model in order to survive or else went through a colonial experience which introduced large elements of the European system. [...]

It is difficult to say what ideas and events revived the process of state-building in Western Europe in the late eleventh century. Certainly the spread of Christianity to unorthodox or heathen Germanic peoples and the improved organization of the Church were important. [...] The Church already had many of the attributes of a state—for example, enduring institutions—and was developing others—for example, a theory of papal sovereignty. The fact that churchmen were deeply involved in secular politics, that no ruler could

Source: Joseph R. Strayer, *On the Medieval Origins of the Modern State* (Princeton: Princeton University Press, 1970), 3–4, 12, 15–17, 24.

function without their advice and assistance, meant that the political theories and the administrative techniques of the Church had a direct impact on lay government. […]

Another, almost equally important factor, was the gradual stabilization of Europe, the ending of a long period of immigration, invasion, and conquest. […] This increased political stability created one of the essential conditions for state-building, continuity in space and time. […]

Perhaps the latest of the stimuli which led to the emergence of the European state was the rapid growth in the number of educated men during the twelfth century.

State Systems and the Advantages of Fragmentation

In the first chapter of his analysis of the development of military and political super-powers, Paul Kennedy puts forth a theory as to why many of the "great powers" of the past 500 years have been European, rather than Asian, states. The main feature he highlights is fragmentation—the development of a network of medium-sized states. He proposes this single factor as the principal cause of European states' commercial domination of the world's maritime trade as well as its military successes.

>> 19. The Rise and Fall of the Great Powers: Economic Change and Military Conflict from 1500 to 2000

PAUL KENNEDY [1987]

The one feature of Europe which immediately strikes the eye when looking at a map of the world's "power centers" in the sixteenth century is its political fragmentation […]. This was not an accidental or short-lived state of affairs, such as occurred briefly in China after the collapse of one empire and before its successor dynasty could gather up again the strings of centralized power. Europe had *always* been politically fragmented. […]

For this political diversity Europe had largely to thank its geography. There were no enormous plains over which an empire of horsemen could impose its swift dominion; nor were there broad and fertile river zones like those around the Ganges, Nile, Tigris and Euphrates, Yellow, and Yangtze, providing the food for masses of toiling and easily conquerable peasants. Europe's landscape was much more fractured, with mountain ranges and large forests separating the scattered population centers in the valleys. […]

The political and social consequences of […] decentralized, largely unsupervised growth of commerce and merchants and ports and markets were of the greatest significance. In the first place, there was no way in which such economic developments could be fully suppressed. This is not to say that the rise of market forces did not disturb many in authority. Feudal lords, suspicious of towns as centers of dissidence and sanctuaries of serfs, often tried to curtail their privileges. As elsewhere, merchants were frequently preyed upon, their goods stolen, their property seized. Papal pronouncements upon usury echo in many ways the Confucian dislike of profit-making middlemen and money-lenders. But the basic fact

Source: Paul, Kennedy, *The Rise and Fall of the Great Powers: Economic Change and Military Conflict from 1500 to 2000* (New York: Vintage Books, 1989), 17–23. Originally published by Random House, 1987.

was that there existed no uniform authority in Europe which could effectively halt this or that commercial development; no central government whose changes in priorities could cause the rise and fall of a particular industry; no systematic and universal plundering of businessmen and entrepreneurs by tax gatherers, which so retarded the economy of Mogul India. To take one specific and obvious instance, it was inconceivable in the fractured political circumstances of Reformation Europe that everyone would acknowledge the pope's 1494 division of the overseas world into Spanish and Portuguese spheres—and even less conceivable that an order banning overseas trade (akin to those promulgated in Ming China and Tokugawa Japan) would have had any effect. [...]

While this competitive interaction between the European state seems to explain the absence of a unified "gunpowder empire" there, it does not at first sight provide the reason for Europe's steady rise to global leadership. After all, would not the forces possessed by the new monarchies in 1500 have seemed puny if they had been deployed against the enormous armies of the sultan and the massed troops of the Ming Empire? This was true in the early sixteenth century and, in some respects, even in the seventeenth century; but by the latter period the balance of military strength was tilting rapidly in favor of the West. For the explanation of this shift one must again point to the decentralization of power in Europe. What it did, above all else, was to engender a primitive

form of arms race among the city-states and then the larger kingdoms. [...]

By the same token, this free-market system not only forced the numerous *condottieri* [mercenaries] to compete for contracts but also encouraged artisans and inventors to improve their wares, so as to obtain new orders. While this armaments spiral could already be seen in the manufacture of crossbows and armor plate in the early fifteenth century, the principle spread to experimentation with gunpowder weapons in the following fifty years. It is important to recall here that when cannon were first employed, there was little difference between the West and Asia in their design and effectiveness. [...] Yet it seems to have been only in Europe that the impetus existed for constant improvements: in the gunpowder grains, in casting much smaller yet equally powerful) cannon from bronze and tin alloys, in the shape and texture of the barrel and the missile, in the gun mountings and carriages. [...]

This is not to say that other civilizations did not improve their armaments from the early, crude designs; some of them did, usually by copying from European models or persuading European visitors (like the Jesuits in China) to lend their expertise. But because the Ming government had a monopoly of cannon, and the thrusting leaders of Russia, Japan, and Mogul India soon acquired a monopoly, there was much less incentive to improve such weapons once their authority had been established.

The Formulation of English Rule in Ireland

Some theorists have suggested that western Europe's states learned the basics of colonization during the period that preceded the early modern period. Medieval examples of colonialism include both the crusader states established in the Mediterranean by western European knights and lords and the process by which centralized European states occupied neighboring regions. For example, England's occupation of Ireland and Scotland, often seen as England's first empire, established the model for subsequent colonies in the Caribbean, North America, and eventually beyond. In this excerpt, we see English King Henry VI's establishment of a colonial governor, called the Lord Lieutenant, in Ireland. The Letters Patent, *delegating his authority to this official, are antecedents of those that would later be granted to companies and individuals to manage the far-flung empire.*

>> 20. Letters Patent from Henry VI to the Lord Lieutenant

HENRY VI [1429]

10 February 1429.

[The earl of Ormond was appointed lieutenant for two years. The king granted him power]

... to guard our peace and the laws and customs of that land and to do all and sundry to bring into our peace both English and Irish of that land and to punish them according to the laws and customs of that land or according as may seem best to him for our profit in the rule of our said land and of our lieges and subjects there. And to summon and convoke parliaments and councils in said land as often as shall seem necessary in places where it seems best to hold them, summoning before him to parliament prelates, magnates and others who ought to come to such parliaments to make statutes and ordinances there for the good rule of the land, according to the custom of the same, by assent of prelates, magnates and others aforesaid.

Also to proclaim in the said land by our writs of the same our royal services and all such services according to the due custom of the same and to punish those who are delinquent. Also to proclaim as often as shall be necessary that all and sundry who have any annuities or fees of our gift or of our predecessors shall be prepared to set forth to ride and to labour with the said lieutenant within the said land for receiving and admitting to our peace both English and Irish who are rebels to our said land and customs....

A Unified Model for Early Modern Eurasia

In recent years, a number of scholars have begun to question the assumption that there is an overriding difference between west and east, Europe and Asia. They have pointed out, among other facts, that Europe is far smaller than Asia, the entirety of Europe being comparable in size and population to India or China alone, and thus that the **east-west dichotomy** *disguises the great variety of different experiences across the Asian continent. One of these critics is Victor Lieberman, a historian of Southeast Asia. In a progression of papers and publications, Lieberman has suggested that it is more correct to look at Eurasia as a variety of different zones rather than merely two. He suggests that many of these zones, both in Europe and in Asia, share certain trends in state formation in the sixteenth century. The regions he selects in this article are three southeast Asian states (Burma, Siam, and Vietnam) as well as France (as the representative for western Europe), the Russian Empire, and Japan. Although each of these six had different experiences in the early modern period, they also shared a number of common processes and can be grouped together in contrast to regions elsewhere in Eurasia that saw the rise of vast empires or in some cases no centralized states at all. One of the processes shared by at least several of these regions was the eroding of the ruler's power*

Source: "Letters Patent from Henry VI to the Lord Lieutenant," *The Empire of the Bretaignes, 1175–1688: The Foundations of a Colonial System of Government,* edited by Frederick Madden with David Fieldhouse (Westport: Greenwood Press, 1985), 113.

and the transfer of some rights to other bodies, usually a group of nobles. This is the very change so often cited as a precursor to democracy in the West. If, as Lieberman's analysis suggests, western Europe was not really unique in this factor, an entire body of scholarship is called into question.

>> 21. Transcending East-West Dichotomies: State and Culture Formation in Six Ostensibly Disparate Areas

VICTOR LIEBERMAN [1997]

The six geographic areas on which I concentrate are discordant, and for that very reason, instructive. [...] That these regions spanned the northern and eastern rimlands of Eurasia, generally had minimal contact with one another, differed profoundly in demography, popular culture, high religion, administrative and economic structures—but nonetheless experienced remarkably synchronized political rhythms illustrates in stark fashion the thesis of Eurasian interdependence.

These six areas were in fact part of a Eurasian subcategory sharing the following features: (a) Lying on the periphery of older civilizations (in India, the Mediterranean, China), all imported world religions, developed urban centers, and underwent [...] 'secondary state' formation during the latter part of the first or the early second millennium C.E. [...] [(b) A] renewed process of political and cultural integration began at some point between 1450 and 1590 and, in key dimensions, continued to gain in scope and vigor well into the nineteenth century. (c) In partial explanation of this accelerating solidity, each polity enjoyed relatively good internal communications and/or an economic/demographic imbalance between districts that was markedly favorable to the capital area. (d) Throughout the period c. 1400–1830 each also enjoyed substantial protection from external invasion, whether overland

from Central Asia or by sea from Europe. In their common possession of such features, these six societies constituted an intermediate category between, on the one hand, China, which experienced a uniquely precocious and durable integration, and on the other, Mughal India and island Southeast Asia, where political integration proved less intense and continuous. [...]

What then were the chief parallels among the areas under consideration?

Most visible was the sustained movement between c. 1450 and 1830 towards the political and administrative integration of what had been fragmented, localized units. Thus in Europe west of the Dniester and Vistula five or six hundred more or less independent polities in 1450 were reduced to some 25 by the late nineteenth century. In northeastern Europe, Siberia, and the Caucasus, over thirty city-states, princedoms, and khanates yielded to a single Russian imperial suzerainty. In mainland Southeast Asia, some 22 genuinely independent states in 1350 were reduced to three—Burma, Siam, and Vietnam—by 1825, when Europeans began to freeze an ongoing process. In Japan a very large, if fluid, number of protodaimyo domains and autonomous religious and merchant communities in 1500 had come under unified rule by century's end. [...]

Notwithstanding [...] differences in geography, structure, and focus, between c. 1400 and 1830 the administrative systems of France, Russia, Burma, Siam, Vietnam, and Japan experienced certain general parallels.

It is convenient to visualize most of these early modern states as closely administered cores, which were privileged demographically or

Source: Victor Lieberman, "Transcending East-West Dichotomies: State and Culture Formation in Six Ostensibly Disparate Areas," *Modern Asian Studies* 31 (1997): 468–469, 473, 476–481.

economically, surrounded by zones of subordinate cities and provinces whose autonomy tended to increase with distance from the center and/or with areas to independent resources. [...] In each polity, as consolidation resumed or began after 1450 or 1500, we find a long-term, if halting tendency for peripheral zones and autonomous enclaves to assimilate to the status of intermediate or core provinces, and for systems of extraction and coordination in the core to improve. Thus, for example, independent kingdoms that fell under Burmese and Siamese rule were converted to governor-ruled provinces, while control of governorships and apanages within the core also strengthened. Supervision in the French *pays d'États* gradually approached that in north-central France. Southern Hokkaido and Kyukshu by 1650 were tied to the center as effectively as outer areas of Honshu had been in 1400. In Vietnam during the era of division the northern and southern seigneuries steadily modified internal operations, while, as noted, from 1830s the new Nguyen dynasty sought to standardize provincial administration.

In this extension of control, moreover, a number of broadly comparable strategies and processes were at work. Before the triumph of the central polity over what eventually would become provincial dependencies, the latter typically had been engaged in independent projects of state building. In Burma, Siam, *ancien régime* France, and Japan (and less commonly in Russia and Vietnam), this triumph typically entailed not the destruction, but the preservation in outlying areas of local institutions: executive agencies, tribunals, armies, tax systems. [...]

But if the state was less autonomous, more subject to faction, negotiation, and paralysis than earlier historians conceded, it is also true that over long term local prerogatives were substantially modified. Most basic, princes and other regional leaders in France, Russia, and lowland Southeast Asia gradually lost the right to tax without permission, to build private fortifications, to run some independent judicial systems, and [...] to employ unauthorized violence against one another or their subjects. [...]

In turn the growing scope of government action, the extension of authority to new territories, the sheer increase in the volume of documents joined with wider literacy [...] to encourage changes in political culture. In all six countries secretariats gradually expanded, the court as it outgrew the ruler's household became more elaborate, and the royal (or shogunal) position became more elevated. In varying degrees, in Burma, Siam, (pre-1600 and post-1800) Vietnam, Russia, and France, the prerogatives of the royal family as a whole were curtailed in favor of those of the paramount ruler. At the same time, most visibly but by no means only in Western Europe, government procedures tended to grow more impersonal, routinized, and professional.

Ming Dynasty Statecraft and Welfare Systems

It is tempting to judge societies merely by the values Kennedy focuses on in The Rise and Fall of the Great Powers: *wealth and success in battles. Yet in the long run, most societies have come to place value on good governance, including social programs to help the people. In this selection from Juan Gonzalez de Mendoza's account of China compiled in the 1580s, the author is frankly admiring the benevolence of the Chinese government, even writing in the margins "I would the like were with us." This type of account has led many academics to question the picture of Asian "despotism" constructed by some modern scholars.*

>> 22. The History of the Great and Mighty Kingdom of China and the Situation Thereof

JUAN GONZALEZ DE MENDOZA [1585]

The towns are great and many, and so full of people, and in infinite number of villages, whereas it cannot be chosen but there are many born lame, and other misfortunes, so that [the justice of the poor] is not idle, but always occupied in giving remedy the necessities of the poor without breaking the law. This judge, the first day that he enters into his office, commands that whatsoever children be born a cripple in any part of his members, or by sickness be taken lame, or by any other misfortune, that their fathers or mothers do give the judge to understand thereof, that he may provide for all things necessary, according unto the ordinance and will of the king and his council. The man child or woman child, being brought before him, and seen the default or lack that it has, if it be so that with the same time it may exercise any occupation, they give and limit a time unto the parents, for to teach the child that occupation ordained by the judge, and it is such as with their lameness they may use without any impediment. This is accomplished without fail. But if it so be, that his lameness is such that it is impossible to learn or exercise any occupation, the judge of the poor does command the father to sustain and maintain him in his own house all the days of his life, if he has the wherewithal. If not, or if he is fatherless, then the next rich kinsman must maintain him. If he has none such, then do all his parents and kinsfolk contribute and pay their parts, or give of such things as they have in their houses. But if he has no parents, or they be so poor that they cannot contribute nor supply any part thereof; then the king maintains them in very ample manner of his own costs in hospitals, very sumptuous, that he has in every city throughout his kingdom for the same effect and purpose. In the same hospitals are likewise maintained such needy and old men as have spent all their youths in the wars, and are not able to maintain themselves; so that to the one and the other is ministered all that is needful and necessary, and that with great diligence and care.

Sixteenth-Century Confucian Intellectual Challenges to the State

Confucianism has been perhaps the most important philosophical school of thought in Chinese history of the last 2,000 years. The first Confucian scholar was K'ung Fu-Tzu [Kong Fuzi], or Confucius, who set down a body of ethical guidelines for citizen and state in the sixth century B.C.E. During the rule of the Ming emperors (1368–1644), Confucianism was again the dominant philosophy. Yet the longevity of Confucianism should not necessarily be understood as stagnation. Confucianism was continually reinterpreted, debated, and commented upon by emperors, philosophers, and scholars in successive dynasties. During the Sung, [Song] and early Ming dynasties, for example, a leading philosopher was the humanist Chu Hsi[Zhu Xi]. Chu[Zhu] believed in the fundamental good of people, but he argued that the state should be ordered in an intelligent and hierarchical manner by highly trained scholar-bureaucrats. Change was deemphasized in favor of stability. Because Chu's[Zhu] work was embraced by the

Source: Juan Gonzalez de Mendoza, *The History of the Great and Mighty Kingdom of China and the Situation Thereof,* translated by R. Parke and edited by Sir George T. Staunton (London: The Hakulyt Society, 1854), 66–67. Translation further edited for this text.

Ming emperors, some Western academics have portrayed Ming China as entirely stagnant and hierarchical. Yet, during the same period students also flocked to hear the rather different messages taught by sages such as the scholar-statesman-general Wang Yang-Ming. Wang suggested that wisdom could be attained by anyone—not just government-tested bureaucrats. Although Wang generally embraced Confucian understandings of hierarchy, he also argued that the "highest good" was a natural revelation of "clear character," or the natural goodness of people, rather than state laws and policies: that is, the purity and learning of the individual rather than obedience to the administration. That such ideas were current in Ming China suggests that Chinese philosophy and approaches to religion and science under the Ming were more vibrant than has been recognized by some Western commentators. In this excerpt from his writings, Wang uses a common rhetorical tool of answering questions he has posed himself on the nature of the "highest good."

>> 23. Inquiry on the Great Learning

WANG YANG-MING [1527]

Question: Why, then does the learning of the great man consist also in loving the people?

Answer: To manifest the clear character is to bring about the substance of the unity of Heaven, earth, and the myriad things, whereas loving the people is to put into universal operation the function of that unity. Hence manifesting the clear character must lie in loving people, and loving the people is the way to manifest the clear character. Therefore, only when I love my father, the fathers of others, and the fathers of all men, can my humanity really form one body with my father, the fathers of others, and the fathers of all men. When it truly forms one body with them, then the clear character of filial piety will be manifested. Only when I love my brother, the brothers of others, and the brothers of all men can my humanity really form one body with my brother, the brothers of others, and the brothers of all men. When it truly forms one body with them, then the clear character of brotherly respect will be manifested. Everything from

ruler, minister, husband, wife, and friends to mountains, rivers, heavenly and earthly spirits, birds, animals, and plants, all should be truly loved in order to realize my humanity that forms a unity, and then my clear character will be completely manifested, and will really form one body with Heaven, earth, and the myriad things. This is what is meant by "manifesting the clear character throughout the empire." This is what is meant by "regulating the family," "ordering the state," and "pacifying the world." This is what is meant by "fully developing one's nature."

Question: Then why does the learning of the great man consist in abiding in the highest good?

Answer: The highest good is the ultimate principle of manifesting character and loving people. The nature endowed in us by Heaven is pure and perfect. The fact that it is intelligent, clear, and not obscured is evidence of the emanation and revelation of the highest good. It is the original nature of the clear character which is called innate knowledge [of the good]. As the highest good emanates and revels itself, one will consider right as right and wrong as wrong. Things of greater or less importance and situations of grave or light character will be responded to as they act upon us. In all our

Source: Wang, Yang-Ming, "Inquiry on the Great Learning," in *Sources of Chinese Tradition*, edited by William Theodore de Bary, Wing-tsit Chan, and Burton Watson (New York: Columbia University Press, 1960), 572–574.

changes and activities, we will entertain no preconceived attitude; in all this we will do nothing that is not natural. This is the normal nature of man and the principle of things. There can be no suggestion of adding to or subtracting anything from them. If any such suggestion in entertained, it means selfish purpose and shallow wisdom, and cannot be said to be the highest good. Naturally, how can anyone who does not watch over himself carefully when alone, and who has no refinement and singleness of mind, attain to such a state of perfection? Later generations fail to realize that the highest good is inherent in their own minds, but each in accordance with his own ideas gropes for it outside the mind, believing that every event and every object has its own definite principle. For this reason the law of right and wrong is obscured; the mind becomes concerned with fragmentary and isolated details, the desires of man become rampant and the principle of Heaven is at an end. And thus the education for manifesting character and loving people is everywhere thrown into confusion.

>> Mastering the Material

1. According to Strayer, what constitutes a modern state and why did this model emerge first in western Europe?

2. What, according to Kennedy, distinguishes European from Asian states? Is this theory a sort of European exceptionalism?

3. What common developments does Lieberman attribute to the six specified European regions?

4. If Lieberman is correct, how does this affect Strayer's argument and his concept of European political exceptionality? Are Lieberman's claims convincing?

5. What do you think the word *peace* means in the Letter Patent from Henry VI to the Lord Lieutenant? What does this tell us about the way in which the English ruled Ireland?

6. Do the institutions described by Mendoza have any analogues in modern nation-states? Does evidence such as Mendoza's account suggest that scholars should consider social policies, as well as political, military, and economic success, in judging successful societies, or is this just "feel-good" history?

7. Ming Dynasty neo-Confucianism stresses "regulating the family," "ordering the state," and "pacifying the world." How does Wang Yang-Ming suggest these goals can be achieved? How does this selection from his work compare to Western interpretations of Confucianism as a philosophy that supported despotism and the suppression of the lower classes?

>> Making Connections

1. To what degree does Kennedy's interpretation of the origins of the Western state system support an ecological determinist history of the world such as that of Jared Diamond (Reading 2)?

2. Kennedy suggests that the fractured nature of Europe's state network was responsible for its military supremacy. In light of the evidence given in Chapter 4, do you find this convincing?

3. Consider Lieberman's challenge to the east-west dichotomy. What other evidence in this chapter supports his argument? What undermines it? How might theories of diffusion fit into the issue? How does this challenge concepts of exceptionality?

4. How does Mendoza's account of the Ming administration of China endorse or contradict Landes' argument for Western cultural superiority? How do the writings of Wang Yang-ming figure as evidence in this debate? What factors do you think have shaped Western scholars' understandings of Ming China?

Chapter 6

Theories of Economic Change

A final, and increasingly popular, way of trying to understand the "rise of the West" is by looking at economic factors, and especially the growing wealth of certain classes in societies both in Europe and around the globe. More measurable than culture or environment, more clearly causative than military strength, economics is increasingly accepted as an important tool for analyzing a period of history that for much of the world was characterized more by commercial competition than military domination.

Was Europe in fact becoming wealthier in the period preceding Columbus' voyage to the Americas? The answer is probably that certain *segments* of the European population were, but others were not. Around 1100, much of western Europe entered a period known as the high, or late, middle ages that lasted until about 1450. This period was characterized by the reemergence of towns, new agricultural techniques, and in some places the liberation of serfs, who became free peasants. As Robert Reynolds illustrates quite colorfully below, one feature of this transition was the reemergence of regional trading systems, linking wool production in England, processing in Flanders, and sale to markets in the Champagne region of France. Reynolds argues that the merchants who participated in this process were capitalists, the predecessors of the merchants who would help pay for the voyages of exploration and colonies of exploitation in the Americas and Asia in the sixteenth century. **Capitalism** is an economic system in which productive and commercial enterprises are privately owned by individuals who invest capital (or money) as well as possibly time and energy. The enterprises compete with each other in pursuit of profits. Capitalism is generally characterized by institutions such as credit and debt, organized banking, and corporations, and Reynolds suggests that these existed in fourteenth-century western Europe.

In arguing that capitalism may have existed in high-middle-ages Europe, Reynolds and other theorists are trying to ascertain the point at which a money-owning class emerged that was distinct from the landowning feudal aristocracy. These money owners, later called the **bourgeoisie,** were generally merchants who used their money to buy goods or land, to invest in projects, and to pay workers. These members of the bourgeoisie have often been depicted as groundbreaking rebels, fighting against the conservative forces of the the landowning aristocracy, including the largest landowner of them all—the Christian Church. Yet in searching for the origins of capitalism in Europe the sociologist Rodney Stark has come to the opposite conclusion. Stark argues that it was in fact the Christian monasteries and theologians of Europe who were the primary instigators of capitalism.

Yet it is not clear to what degree a bourgeoisie existed in western Europe during the high middle ages. A more convincing case can be made for renaissance Italy in the early modern period—after about the middle of the fifteenth century. The renaissance period in Europe is commonly understood in terms of a reawakening of sophisticated artistic and literary techniques, based partly on the rediscovery of Greek and Roman ideas and skills. However, scholars have begun to suggest that the cultural flowering of the renaissance was driven by the emergence of a wealthy class of consumers whose desire for luxury drove them to purchase imported goods, often by borrowing money. This stimulation of trade and debt was reflected in the development of two parallel institutions: the bank and the long-distance trading corporation. The emergence of these institutions can be seen in the documents of the Medici bankers, the financiers of renaissance Florence.

People who point to Europe's economy as key to its expansion argue that the region's renaissance merchant–banking network was a major advantage to the Spanish and Portuguese and the other western Europeans who followed them in exploring and exploiting other regions of the world. The bourgeois merchant-bankers quickly became wealthy and important enough to win support from kings and queens for their commercial undertakings, as evidenced by the sponsorship of Columbus and Vasco da Gama by the Spanish and Portuguese crowns, or the formation under royal charter of the Massachusetts Bay Company and other corporations to colonize the Americas. The merchants contributed much of the funding necessary to undertake these risky investments, promoting Theodore Rabb to admiringly describe them in "The Expansion of Europe and the Spirit of Capitalism":

The thrifty, sober, careful, disciplined entrepreneur was, in the sixteenth and seventeenth centuries, inextricably mixed with the uncontrolled, reckless, idealist. He gained his peculiar strength and capacity from the combination of these two seemingly contradictory sets of attitudes. It would be foolish to call him any less a capitalist than the modern industrialist, but it is clear that he was a different species within the same genus, equally at home with conquistadors or with clerks, both of whom he used.

There are any number of explanations for why capitalism developed in Europe in the renaissance period, if indeed it did. One we have already seen: Kennedy's argument that because Europe was fractured into many states, no one government could halt the commercial enterprises of merchants, unlike in Ming China where Zheng Ho's fleet was impounded and allowed to rot by the fourth Ming emperor. Was it indeed the case that Europe's decentralization meant a greater freedom for merchants in the face of weaker kings and princes, especially when those rulers needed the merchants' support and money to pay for their ongoing wars? If so, Italy, as a supra-decentralized network of city-states linked by trade not only to Europe but also to North Africa and Asia, would have been well-placed for early development of such institutions. Other scholars like David Landes agree with Rodney Stark that western Europe's economic advantage of the fifteenth century had roots far back in the cultural and religious history of the region. Finally, a third argument put forth by scholars like Robert Brenner has suggested that the transition from feudal serfs to free peasants in western Europe, possibly caused in part by the Black Death plague, may have stimulated the economy by creating a consumer class.

However, each of these theories has its critics. Some of the most important are non-European specialists who believe that the institutions of capitalism emerged in regions other than western Europe in or before the same period. Subhi Y. Labib's article "Capitalism in Medieval Islam" is an example of this argument. Focusing on west-central Asia and Egypt, Labib argues that Islam as a religion was able to accommodate capitalism in much the same way as Stark suggests Christianity was able to. Labib's argument is supported by the second primary source reading in this chapter, "The Pilgramage of Kankan Musa."

Renaissance Merchant Capitalists

Proponents of theories that identify an early capitalist society in western Europe generally look at four interrelated transformations: the emergence of the guild system of production, the development of specialization in production, the advent of debt and banking systems, and the transition from serfs to peasants in agriculture. Robert Reynolds considered all four in his text Europe Emerges, *but made his argument most forcefully in this excerpt entitled "Management of Production: The Merchant Capitalist." Reynolds identifies wool merchants in particular, not only as traders in goods but also beneficiaries of specialization in wool processing and as lenders of money. The "capitalist" we follow in this excerpt, for example, is a Flemish wool merchant who plays all of these roles.*

Can we tie these merchants to the overseas traders who helped build the western European overseas empires? Reynolds does not go so far as to propose that merchant capitalists were the exclusive agents of European expansionism, but he does suggest that their money and their skills were indispensable to overseas explorers.

>> 24. Europe Emerges: Transition toward an Industrial World-Wide Society 600–1750

Robert L. Reynolds [1961]

The merchant capitalists were well-to-do merchants dealing in spices, leather, and foreign exchange as well as in cloth, alum, dyestuffs, and other manufacturing supplies. They were the man who went to the fairs of Champagne with several dozen bolts of finished cloth and who carried on transactions at the wholesale level, as described earlier. But in their home towns their main interest lay in the production of the bolts of cloth which were to be taken from that town to those fairs; it was their function to run production by local artisans whose contributions were so well divided in the fabricating processes that they had almost no contact with one another. It was the merchant capitalist who saw to it that the materials moved from the spinsters to the weavers to the fullers.

First of all he saw to it that in England a given amount of wool was bought for him at some Cistercian monastery. Often he made payment in advance, sometimes as much as two or three years ahead of time. [...]

Source: Robert L. Reynolds, *Europe Emerges: Transition toward an Industrial World-Wide Society 600–1750* (Madison: University of Wisconsin Press, 1967), 238–240. Originally published 1961.

The merchant capitalist could be regarded either as the financer of the monastery's debt, taking its promise to repay in wool, or as businessman making sure of his supplies in advance—and incidentally playing the futures in wool.

Once he had obtained the wool, the merchant capitalist had it carried to a port where he had to pay heavy taxes to the king of England for the privilege of exporting it. At the port he placed it on a ship which he and a group of other merchants might either own or have chartered, or on a ship in which another group of merchants had sold him so many of their own places for his wool sacks. The ship carried his shipment to Bruges, and from there the merchant had it transported to his home town.

Here he took the wool to a wool washer, or to several dozen wool washers, who had agreed to cleanse his wool at so much a pound or at so much for the lot. When the washing had been completed, the merchant inspected it, took it back again, and paid off the guildmaster who had done the washing or had it done. The merchant then took the wool to the carders. From the carders the merchant took the wool home, where spinsters came to the door, each to take a few pounds of carded wool home where she would spin it. When it had been returned to him he would then take the yarn to his weavers—several weavers might be working in connection with him—and days or weeks later he got his woven piece from each weaver. He paid the weaver off, the weaver having in turn been paying his own journeymen and apprentices inside his own shop. And so the processing went on, through the fulling or walking of the rough-woven goods, through shearing and dyeing. [...]

Entirely finished, the bolt of cloth, still owned by the capitalist, started on a mule's back or in a wagon toward the fairs of Champagne or, after the later twelve hundreds, back to Bruges to be sold there. It reappeared in the channels of trade as a piece of merchandise.

All of this had called for a great deal of expenditure on the part of the capitalist. He had had to pay for the wool over in England, for the king's export license, for all transportation cost, for the carding, washing, spinning, for the weaving, dyeing, fulling, and shearing and then for transport down to Champagne. It was here that he got something back for the first time, after many months of steadily accumulating costs as each bolt of cloth was made. It had been a long way from his first expense to the liquidation of his cloth venture. Yet even here what he collected was not coined money; it was in turn merchandise—spices, for example. These he had to carry home and pass on to England and keep in trade. It is quite clear from this account that the merchant capitalist needed to have a very considerable reserve of resources in the form of credit, money, merchandisable goods. [...]

It was possible that the merchant capitalist had no more connection with the workers who took care of processing his wool than that which came from making a deal each time he had a job to be done—an individual deal to have that work done and to make a payment for it. In the export industries, such deals were being made all the time. Some of the masters were well enough off so that they did jobs for merchant capitalists just as simple transactions. These masters owned their own small shops, or at least had long-term leases on them, they owned their own tools, they were in a position to make private individual deals, a number of them, in the course of a year. There were men like that at all times

But a very large proportion of all the master fullers, master weavers, and master dyers were not financially and otherwise well enough off to play an independent role as equals with the merchant capitalists. In the big textile cities and in other towns where other industries went on, in considerable measure the merchant capitalist was the person who financed the people who did the work.

This financing went on in the following way. Let us say a merchant capitalist had some work to be done, and a given weaver had illness, a wife who was spending too much, or something like that, and he wanted to get some cash as well as some immediate work. In such a case quite commonly the capitalist paid in advance, or made a part payment anyway, for the work that was being done. So he figured in his interest charges. He might get a reasonable twenty to twenty-five percent per annum or an unreasonable sixty to one-hundred percent per annum for any advances he made, made deductible by one dodge or another when the work was done. Men fell into the hands of merchant capitalists who were quite as much lending usurers as givers of work.

Capitalism and the Church in Medieval Europe

As a leading sociologist studying the relationship between science, economy, and religion in Europe, Rodney Stark has championed the role of the pre-Protestant Christian Church in promoting progress. This line of reasoning is in direct opposition to some previous scholarship that depicted the Church as a conservative force that held Europe back. Stark argues that despite its early injunctions against moneylending, the Church was flexible enough to embrace capitalism as a "fair" way to exchange and pay for goods and services. Moreover, because the Church was the leading landowner and commodity producer in Europe during much of the medieval period, its monasteries were centers of economic progress and innovation. Behind all of this, Stark argues, was the role of the Christian theologian. Many of these thinkers, Stark suggests, believed in the "faith of reason" and built a bridge between religion and logic.

>> 25. How Christianity (and Capitalism) Led to Science

RODNEY STARK [2005]

"It was during so-called Dark Ages that European technology and science overtook and surpassed the rest of the world. Some of that involved original inventions and discoveries; some of it came from Asia. But what was so remarkable was the way that the full capacities of new technologies were recognized and widely adopted. By the 10th century Europe already was far ahead in terms of farming equipment and techniques, had unmatched capacities in the use of water and wind power, and possessed superior military equipment and tactics. Not to be overlooked in all that medieval progress was the invention of a whole new way to organize and operate commerce and industry: capitalism.

Capitalism was developed by the great monastic estates. Throughout the medieval era, the church was by far the largest landowner in Europe, and its liquid assets and annual income probably exceeded that of all Europe's nobility added together. Much of that wealth poured into the coffers of the religious orders, not only because they were the largest landowners, but also in payment for liturgical services—Henry VII of England paid a huge sum to have 10,000 masses said for his soul. As rapid innovation in agricultural technology began to yield large surpluses to the religious orders, the church not only began to reinvest profits to increase production, but diversified. Having substantial amounts of cash on hand, the religious orders began to lend money at interest. They soon evolved the mortgage (literally "dead pledge") to lend money with land for security, collecting all income from the land during the term of the loan, none of which was deducted from the amount owed. That practice often added to the monastery's lands because the monks were not hesitant to foreclose. In addition, many

Source: Rodney Stark, "How Christianity (and Capitalism) Led to Science," *The Chronicle of Higher Education* (December 2005).

monasteries began to rely on a hired labor force and to display an uncanny ability to adopt the latest technological advances. Capitalism had arrived.

Still, like all of the world's other major religions, for centuries Christianity took a dim view of commerce. As the many great Christian monastic orders maximized profits and lent money at whatever rate of interest the market would bear, they were increasingly subject to condemnations from more traditional members of the clergy who accused them of avarice.

Given the fundamental commitment of Christian theologians to reason and progress, what they did was rethink the traditional teachings. What is a just price for one's goods, they asked? According to the immensely influential St. Albertus Magnus (1193–1280), the just price is simply what "goods are worth according to the estimate of the market at the time of sale." That is, a just price is not a function of the amount of profit, but is whatever uncoerced buyers are willing to pay. Adam Smith would have agreed—St. Thomas Aquinas (1225–74) did. As for usury, a host of leading theologians of the day remained opposed to it, but quickly defined it out of practical existence. For example, no usury was involved if the interest was paid to compensate the lender for the costs of not having the money available for other commercial opportunities, which was almost always easily demonstrated.

That was a remarkable shift. Most of these theologians were, after all, men who had separated themselves from the world, and most of them had taken vows of poverty. Had asceticism truly prevailed in the monasteries, it seems very unlikely that the traditional disdain for and opposition to commerce would have mellowed. That it did, and to such a revolutionary extent, was a result of direct experience with worldly imperatives. For all their genuine acts of charity, monastic administrators were not about to give all their wealth to the poor, sell their products at cost, or give kings interest-free loans. It was the active participation of the great orders in free markets that caused monastic theologians to reconsider the morality of commerce.

The religious orders could pursue their economic goals because they were sufficiently powerful to withstand any attempts at seizure by an avaricious nobility. But for fully developed secular capitalism to unfold, there needed to be broader freedom from regulation and expropriation. Hence secular capitalism appeared first in the relatively democratic city-states of northern Italy, whose political institutions rested squarely on church doctrines of free will and moral equality.

Augustine, Aquinas, and other major theologians taught that the state must respect private property and not intrude on the freedom of its citizens to pursue virtue. In addition, there was the central Christian doctrine, that regardless of worldly inequalities, inequality in the most important sense does not exist: in the eyes of God and in the world to come. As Paul explained: "There in neither Jew nor Greek, there is neither bond nor fee, there is neither male nor female, for ye are all one in Christ Jesus."

And church theologians and leaders meant it. Through all prior recorded history, slavery was universal—Christianity began in a world here as much as half the population was in bondage. But by the seventh century, Christianity had become the only major world religion to formulate specific theological opposition to slavery, and, by no later than the 11th century, the church had expelled the dreadful institution from Europe. That it later reappeared in the New World is another matter, although there, too, slavery was vigorously condemned by popes and all of the eventual abolition movements were of religious origins.

Free labor was an essential ingredient for the rise of capitalism, for free workers can maximize their rewards by working harder or more effectively than before. In contrast, coerced workers gain nothing from doing more. Put another way, tyranny makes a few people richer; capitalism can make everyone richer. Therefore, as the northern Italy city-states developed capitalist economies, visitors marveled at their standards of living; many were equally confounded by how hard everyone worked.

The common denominator in all these great historical developments was the Christian commitment to reason.

That was why the West won."

Medici Article of Association

Claims that capitalism existed in thirteenth- or fourteenth-century western Europe are still highly debated, but a much stronger case can be made for the fifteenth century, and especially for northern Italy—the heart of the much-celebrated renaissance. Although now a disputed term, the renaissance has come to encompass a series of economic and cultural transformations that, for some regions at least, seem very real. One of these was the emergence of a highly sophisticated commercial system of corporations and moneylending that was recorded partly in articles of association, or incorporation, by which merchants became partners with each other. Many of these merchant-companies were based on family ties, and some of the families became very rich indeed. As merchants, moneylenders, and later politicians, the Italian family par excellence *was the Medicis of Florence. Numerous records of the Medici family firms are available, and several of them include legal documents of association.*

>> 26. Medici Article of Association

[1434]

In the name of God, Amen, the first day of June, 1434.

Be it known to whomsoever shall see or read the present contract made the year and month mentioned above, that it is declared in the name of God and of profit, that Bernardo d'Antonio de' Medici on the one part, and Giovenco d'Antonio de' Medici on another part, and Giovenco di Giuliano [de' Medici] on the other part, all three Florentine citizens and merchants, have made this present new Company under the *Arte di Lana,* in the *Convento* of San Martino, with this pact and condition and agreement that thus they make a partnership. That is:

In the first place, they are agreed that the capital of the said Company shall be, and must be, 4000 gold florins, and that this shall be contributed in cash within twelve months from now in this wise: the said Bernardo d'Antonio [shall put therein] 2200 florins; the said Giovenco d'Antonio [shall put therein] 1500 florins; and the above-said Giovenco di Giuliano shall put therein 300 for the said term of one year, as stated above, so that in all the sum [shall be] 4000 gold florins. Each one shall put in the above-said amount for the time mentioned, and whosoever shall fail to put in the stated sum within one year for the use of the said Company shall be obliged to make good to the said Company [with interest at] ten per cent of his account at the beginning of the year, according to what he has lacked.

And the said Giovenco di Giuliano promises his person and assistance and service and

Source: "Article of Association Involving Giovenco di Giuliano De' Medici, Giovenco D'Antonio De' Medici, and Bernardo D'Antonio De' Medici, all of Florence," in *Florentine Merchants in the Age of Medici,* edited by Gertrude Richards (Cambridge: Harvard University Press, 1932), 236–239.

usefulness to the said Company and traffic under the *Arte di Lana,* and [he promises] to go to the looms and to other places generally at other times, always in whatever place is necessary, without other provision or salary. And the said Bernardo and Giovenco d'Antonio are not held to any such service in the said shop more than they give voluntarily during the said time. And if it pleases Giovenco d'Antonio to withdraw himself [from the firm] for any reason during the said time, that such absence is possible, providing that it appears to Bernardo d'Antonio and to Giovenco di Giuliano that it is possible; and that such salary [as he may receive] shall be paid into the said shop and Company.

And they are agreed that the said shop and traffic under the *Arte di Lana* shall be conducted in the *Convento* of San Martino in Florence and that the name of this Company shall be Bernardo d'Antonio de' Medici and Company with this sign that appears here on the side. This Company is agreed that they commence and are bound to commence on the 1st day of June, 1434, and are to continue for the next three years and that this contract terminates the 1st day of June, 1437, and at that time the said sign shall remain with the said Bernardo d'Antonio.

And they are agreed that the profit which our Lord God concedes through His mercy and grace will be divided in this manner: that is, that Bernardo d'Antonio shall draw on the basis of 1800 florins, and Giovenco d'Antonio shall draw on the basis of 1300 florins, and Giovenco di Giuliano shall draw on the basis of 900 florins; and similarly during this time if any damage occurs, which God forbid, [each shall contribute on this basis]; and also each may draw out [his share] of their [joint] profits at any time, and at each withdrawal there shall be a balancing of accounts.

And they are agreed that Giovenco di Giuliano de' Medici may draw for his needs 4 florins the month, and similarly Bernardo d'Antonio may draw, and similarly Giovenco d'Antonio may draw, as their necessities demand, such money without paying any costs; and that whoever draws more,

must restore the lack at 10 per cent the florin at the beginning of the year.

And they are agreed that the said Giovenco di Giuliano may not carry on or have carried on any other business or service to another traffic outside of this firm under any [condition] on the pain of paying 200 florins in gold, and if he does so engage, he must pay the said sum to the said Bernardo d'Antonio and Giovenco d'Antonio who may force him if he breaks this agreement. And furthermore, if he engages in any outside enterprise, whether he pays the fine or not, the said Bernardo d'Antonio and Giovenco d'Antonio may claim whatever profits or salary he has made, and he shall be responsible for whatever damages [may be incurred in this other business].

And they are agreed that said Bernardo and Giovenco d'Antonio may manufacture or engage in other traffic of any sort in Florence or out of Florence.

And they are agreed that if any of the said Company shall hold in that Company any amount of money above the original capital, they may receive for it 8 florins the hundred as interest, but that this money may not be put into the Company without consent of all members thereof. And it [the interest] is to be paid from the time when it is deposited as if on interest with a third person, and such money may be withdrawn whenever its owner wishes, providing the others agree.

And they are agreed that the said Giovenco di Giuliano shall not engage any credits outside the business without the express permission of the said Bernardo and Giovenco d'Antonio or at least one or the other of them; and that in case he so does, the fact shall be entered against his account for the day; and the said Giovenco shall not be permitted to extend credit or make any guarantees for the said Company for a sum exceeding 20 florins without permission of both of the senior partners, and that any violation of the above shall incur a fine of 100 florins for each offense.

And they are agreed that when the termination of this Company shall draw near, and if any one of the partners does not wish to continue or reconfirm the traffic, in such case the one or the other must speak; and if he gives six months' notice, the firm shall be discontinued. The said Giovenco di Giuliano shall be obligated to stay in the shop until all the *panni* and samples have been restored to the stock of the said shop. And within two months Bernardo and Giovenco must have cancelled all debts so that within such time

they shall be free of all obligations; and the stock shall be divided among them in this proportion: To Bernardo, 1800 florins in gold; to Giovenco d'Antonio 1300 florins in gold; to Giovenco di Giuliano, 900 florins in gold. And the merchandise shall be divided among them, each receiving according to his share. And whosoever of the partners has taken goods on good security, must pay in money for what is outstanding.

Capitalism in Medieval Islam

Just as some formally trained scholars have sought to paint Ming China as a stagnant culture under the rule of a despotic state unsuited to capitalist commercial development, so Islam too has been portrayed as anti-business and anti-capitalist. The principal evidence given is that the Quran forbids **usury,** *or the charging of exorbitant interest on loans. Many historians of the Islamic medieval world, however, believe that Muslim financiers were central to the long-distance Eurasian commerce of that era, and some scholars have gone so far as to argue that in the eighth- and ninth-century Abbasid Caliphate there had been a "bourgeois revolution" like the one described by historians of early modern Europe. Those who study other regions of Asia, and to some degree Africa, have similarly argued that the western European case was not as unique as it seems, and that capitalism of some type flourished elsewhere. But the Islamic model, here presented by Subhi Labib, is especially useful. Labib identifies the development of wealthy financiers (money owners), long-distance trade, rational decision making, and the development of such institutions as commercial and financial markets: all hallmarks of capitalism as we know it. Labib does, however, acknowledge that parts of Europe were able to "catch up" in the late middle ages for various, largely transregional reasons.*

>> 27. Capitalism in Medieval Islam

SUBHI Y. LABIB [1969]

Islam approved of trading, and not only because of the revelation. Also, trading was enhanced by its milieu. The Islamic merchant was born into an active trading community, and the Prophet himself had engaged in trade. [...]

Arab and Persian traders pushed vigorously to India, Malaya, and Indonesia. Merchants of the

Islamic world became indispensable middlemen because of their contact with the West—either through the Mediterranean of the Baltic—and also the Far East. In consequence of their worldwide trade relationships, the Arabs brought sugarcane from India, cotton to Sicily and Africa, and rice to Sicily and Spain. They learned from the Chinese how to produce silk and paper and took this knowledge with them into all parts of their empire. From China they introduced the use of the compass and from India the so-called Arabic

Source: Subhi Y. Labib, "Capitalism in Medieval Islam," *The Journal of Economic History* 29 (1969): 79–85.

numbers. Everywhere that Islam entered, it activated business life, fostered an increasing exchange of goods, and played an important part in the development of credit. Trading profits formed an important source of income both for states and individuals. [...]

In the early Middle Ages a *Pax Islamica* was the foundation of an economic golden age of which the protagonists in the field of trade were Arabs, Persians, Berbers, Jews, and Armenians. [...]

Oriental and Occidental (Frankish) merchants together created a phase of activity which can be called commercial capitalism, but we should not overlook two essential differences between the Christian West and Islamic East. First, capitalism was able to develop much earlier in the Islamic regions than in the Occident. The process of the reagrarianization and the dismantling of the great exchange economy which began in Europe in late antiquity was intensified in the time of the barbarian invasions and continued beyond the Carolingian period. In the agrarian society of Europe, trade, although it never wholly disappeared, played only a subordinate role. In contrast, the Orient at this time was not affected by any barbarian invasions and a growing trade economy was able there to attain its peak.

The essential difference between the economic development of East and West came about during the late Middle Ages. Internal trade in the entire Islamic area could not keep pace with international commercial developments, for the Islamic lands of Asia, which were affected by the Mongolian invasions, lost much of their productivity, and as a result their business potential diminished. [...]

The cradle of Islamic capitalism was in the main cities of the Islamic world. In the early Middle Ages Baghdad was the commercial metropolis and exerted a marked influence on the whole of Islamic big business. With the tenth century, however, the weight of Islamic commerce was gradually shifted from Iraq and the Persian Gulf to Egypt, the Red Sea, and the harbors of the Arabian Peninsula on the Indian Ocean. Cairo became the leading city. The state fleets of Fatimid Egypt and private ships of its high ranking dignitaries strengthened commercial links in the Mediterranean, above all with Sicily, Tunisia, and Syria.

For Egypt's relations with the West the emergence of the Kārimīs, a unique group of capitalistic entrepreneurs, was of great importance. This group of large-scale merchants, of whom we first hear in the eleventh century, was distinguished by its enterprise and competence, and soon attained wealth and influence in all important eastern markets and—through its considerable financing activities—in the field of politics too. [...]

If one estimated the average capital of a wholesale merchant, either Muslim or non-Muslim, at approximately 30,000 dinars before the Kārimī period in Egypt, the wealth of many Kārimī merchants would amount to at least 100,000 or of a few to 1 million dinars or more. [...]

In addition to their business activity, these houses played an important role in the history of Islamic capitalism thanks to their important financial potential. The financing of great projects was one of their methods of acquiring capital, and they conducted a type of banking institution for loans and deposits. Their best customers were not only Frankish merchants but also Sultans and Emirs, whom they helped with credits and also with soldiers and weapons if necessary.

In the history of Islamic capitalism the Kārimī merchants differ from other entrepreneurs of their time outside of the Egyptian Empire and from the wholesale merchants of this empire before their time (before the twelfth century) in one important way: They were neither landlords nor tax collectors. Their capitalism rested on trade and financial transactions. This remained the basic characteristic of their activity. [...]

Steady traffic and relative safety of the roads contributed considerably to the growth of trade. However, the distance and danger of the route as well as the scarcity of wares influenced prices. Ibn Khaldūn analyzed these things well and arrived at the conclusion that usually the merchants who traded and exchanged their merchandise in distant marketplaces could acquire great wealth. On the other hand, merchants who simply traveled between cities and villages of one province could count on only small profits, since in most cases their merchandise was obtainable in large quantities. Therefore, the more experienced merchants were advised to buy goods through long-distance trade when the goods were in season and in demand. This in turn required a thorough knowledge of the conditions of the wares in their original locations. Traders had to learn whether or not a product might be found there in large or small quantities; whether it was expensive or inexpensive; whether or not it turned out scanty or faulty; and whether or not the routes for import were safe or impeded. Some of this information had to be obtained through inquiries and close questioning of caravans. In other words, business required many rational decisions and preparatory calculations.

Of great significance for the medieval capitalistic trade of Islam was the establishment of the *funduqs*, specialized large-scale commercial institutions and markets which developed into virtual stock exchanges. They dominated the townscape of the great cities in the entire Islamic world.

The Wealth of Mali and the Bankers of Cairo

One of the principal objectives that drove the Portuguese kings to explore the coast of Africa was their search for a maritime route to the western African goldfields that would allow them to outflank the Muslim traders who had been crossing the Sahara for six centuries to buy gold from West African traders. The ties between western African states such as Mali and their counterparts in North Africa and the Middle East were more than merely commercial. Mansa (King) Musa and a number of his subjects were Muslim, and between 1324–1325 Musa undertook a Hajj, or pilgrimage to Mecca, accompanied by a vast entourage and bringing so much gold that he temporarily devalued gold money in the important trading post of Cairo and even in Europe. Musa spent or gave away his money freely as alms for the poor, gifts to establish allies, and incentives to encourage teachers and artisans to return with him to Mali. Thus on his way back from Mecca, he was forced to borrow money from capitalists in Cairo, probably Karimis. A number of these financiers returned with him to Mali to collect the principal and interest.

>> 28. The Pilgrimage of Mansa Musa

IBN HAJAR AL-'ASQALANI [c. 1455]

Musa b. Abi Bakr Salim al-Takuri, king of the Takrur. He came for the Pilgrimage in Rajab 724/July 1324. He was brought into the presence of al-Nāṣir, but refused to kiss the ground, saying: "I shall prostrate myself before God alone!" The Sultan excused him, admitted him into his intimacy, treated him with honour and gave him ample provisions for [the journey to] the Hijaz. There was much gold in the hands of the people [in Cairo which they got] from the people of Takrur (*takarira*), so that the rate of the dinar fell.

He travelled in a caravan of his own. He was held in awe by his people. No one could speak to him except with head uncovered. After the Pilgrimage he stayed three months in

---

Source: Ibn Hajar al-'Asqalani, "The Pilgrimage of Mansa Musa," in *Corpus of Early Arabic Sources for West African History,* edited by N. Levtzion and J. F. P. Hopkins (Cambridge: Cambridge University Press, 1981), 358.

Mecca, and returned. A great number of his men died of cold.

He borrowed large sums of money from the merchants when he returned [to Cairo]. A group of those merchants accompanied him back to his country to collect their money. He was virtuous and pious, and brought many books. It is said that the total money that he had brought with him was 100 loads [of gold], and he spent it all on his way until he ran into debt.

When he returned he settled all his debts. He sent many gifts to a group of Egyptian dignitaries who accompanied him on the Pilgrimage until he arrived [back] at Cairo. His gift to the sultan was 5,000 mithqals. He was very generous and brought to the [Egyptian] treasury a considerable amount of natural unprocessed gold (*al-tibr al-ma'dani'lladhi lam yusna'*). When he returned he sent many presents of the Hijaz to the Sultan. He treated him and his friends gracefully and with kindness and generosity. He did not leave a single emir or official of the Sultan without bestowing upon him a sum of gold.

Mūsā remained in his kingdom for 25 years, then his son for four years, then his uncle Sulaymān reigned.

>> Mastering the Material

1. Robert Reynolds describes some twelfth- and thirteenth-century western European traders as merchant capitalists. What does this term mean? Is it appropriate in the case of the individuals described by Reynolds?

2. What is the significance of the merchant capitalists depicted by Robert Reynolds? How does Subhi Labib challenge the notion that western European merchant capitalists were exceptional?

3. According to Labib, what were the differences between European and Islamic capitalism? What caused the decline of capitalism in the medieval Islamic world?

4. Consider the excerpts from Labib and Rodney Stark. To what degree do they pursue similar goals? What do you think was the relationship between religion and capitalism in the medieval Christian (Catholic) and Islamic worlds?

5. What are the most important terms of the Medici article of association? What is each partner contributing? In what way does this document establish that capitalism existed in fifteenth-century Florence?

6. Consider Reynold's merchant capitalists of the twelfth and thirteenth centuries and the Medici merchants-bankers of the fifteenth century. Do they seem to enjoy the same level of organization and acumen, or has something changed in the intervening period? If so, what?

7. How does the "The Pilgrimage of Mansa Mūsā" support Labib's analysis of capitalism in the Muslim world of the late middle ages?

>> Making Connections

1. Compare and contrast Labib's account of Islamic capitalism with Landes' depiction of Islam (Reading 11).

2. How do Kennedy's concept of political fragmentation (Reading 19) and Diamond's environmental determinism (Reading 2) figure into the theory of economic

exceptionalism? Were western European societies predisposed to competition—a central element in capitalism?

3. Based on the material presented in this chapter, is it possible to determine why western Europeans undertook sustained maritime voyages and overseas exploitation during this period? Can you explain why other Eurasian societies failed to do so? Which theory, or theories, do you find most convincing and why?

4. Consider Question 3 in terms of two contrasting sets of theories. Was the western European exploration, exploitation, and settlement of the Americas more a result of factors *within* western Europe, or of western Europe's place in and relationships with other parts of the world?

5. Should historians continue to think in terms of the "rise of the West" and the "fall of the East" during this period of world history? Why or why not?

6. Based on your analysis of the sources in this chapter, why do you think it was Europeans who established the first lasting, consistent contacts with the Americas? Support your arguments with evidence from these sources.

Part 1 Conclusion

The establishment of the Columbian Exchange around 1500 C.E. ushered in sustained, reciprocal relationships between the Americas on the one hand and Eurasia and Africa on the other. This transformation would shape the modern world in several ways. Most obviously, the ecological exchange of food crops and domesticated animals allowed for a dramatic population increase in many regions. The American crops of potatoes and corn complemented crops already in use in Asia, Europe, and parts of Africa, for example, and animal species such as horses and pigs from Eurasia were quickly adopted by American populations. Conversely, the misguided or unknowing transfer of diseases and pests killed off millions. This was especially true in the Americas, where relatively low levels of genetic diversity and a historic absence of domesticated animals meant that local populations had little resistance to Old World diseases.

Following the establishment of the Columbian Exchange, humans began to move dramatically to new areas, taking with them microorganisms, food crops, and animals. In the sixteenth and seventeenth centuries, this was especially true in the Atlantic region, which saw large numbers of Africans and Europeans moving to the Americas. However, the experiences of these two huge streams of migrants were not equal. Many Europeans came as free individuals and were able to occupy and make use of local land and resources (although some came over as indentured servants). Almost all of the immigrants from Africa, on the other hand, came to the Americas as enslaved captives and labored under harsh conditions of servitude. This meant, in part, that European Americans were able to capitalize on the wealth of the Americas, and much of that wealth came to be transferred to western Europe, which flourished economically in this period. By contrast, many of the African regions bordering the Atlantic suffered terribly from the effects of the transatlantic slave trade and went into economic decline.

Other regions of the world also felt the economic effects of the Columbian Exchange quite rapidly. The Mediterranean zone, for example, found itself cut out of the new global trade. Islamic and Christian societies in the eastern Mediterranean—northern Africa, Turkey and the Middle East, the Balkans and Italy—had long been at the center of a vast Eurasian–African trading zone. Now, with new sea routes being utilized across the Atlantic and Pacific and around southern Africa, these regions became peripheral to global trade. By contrast, China, southeast Asia, and India remained the worlds' great producers until well into the nineteenth century. These regions consumed vast amounts of silver extracted from the Americas by Europeans, fed growing populations on new crops from the Americas, and produced more and more finished goods for global trade.

In the long run, however, nobody benefited as much economically and technologically from the Columbian Exchange as a few western European states. Spain and Portugal are included on this list, but even more their neighbors who followed their lead by occupying parts of the American continents: France, the Netherlands, and Britain. The economies of these states profited from the influx of raw materials—sugar, silver, fur, tobacco, and lumber—from their new colonies. They also profited from the trade in enslaved Africans (and sometimes indigenous Americans). They profited from the new shipping routes established across the Atlantic and Pacific. Ultimately, this new economic reality propelled these European states to the forefront of global technology and wealth.

Yet, if it has become clear in the last few years that the Columbian Exchange was the source of western European wealth, the question remains why it happened this way. Why was it Spanish and Portuguese vessels that first crossed the Atlantic to the Americas and then returned to the Old World? Why not the larger Chinese fleets of the early fifteenth century? Why not the competent sailors of southeast Asia or Morocco? This is the question at the center of this chapter, and no answer has been found; nor will a single cause ever be established. Instead, a multiplicity of factors is being explored by modern scholars. These include environmental factors (wind patterns, the availability of lumber for shipbuilding, the fragmentation of local geography), motive (desire to access far-away markets), and the long-established arguments about culture, economics, politics, and social organization. There may never be a consensus on this question, but as more and more scholars from many parts of the world join in the debate, we are able to explore the richness of this period more than ever before.

Further Readings

The early modern period has been the subject of perhaps the richest collection of world history studies. This is especially true in terms of scholarship dealing with the oceanic connections between continents. For the Indian Ocean, southern Asian scholars have been especially prolific. Two recommended studies are K. N. Chaudhuri, *Trade and Civilization in the Indian Ocean* (Cambridge: Cambridge University Press, 1985) and Sanjay Subrahmanyan, *The Portuguese Empire in Asia 1500–1750* (Longman: New York, 1993). For the Atlantic, perhaps the seminal study of intercontinental connections was the ecological narrative by Alfred Crosby, *The Columbian Exchange* (Connecticut: Greenwood Press, 1972, reprinted in 2003). From the African perspective, an important text is John Thornton, *Africa and Africans in the Making of the Atlantic World* (Cambridge: Cambridge University Press, 1998, second edition). Scholars have also begun to reconceive the complexity and lifestyles of American populations prior to the arrival of Europeans and Africans. A scientific approach to this is represented by Charles C. Mann, *1491: New Revelations of the Americas before Columbus* (New York: Alfred A. Knopf, 2006).

Terms to Know

Old World   *(p. 7)*

New World   *(p. 7)*

Columbian Exchange   *(p. 7)*

demography/demographic   *(p. 8)*

eurocentrism   *(p. 8)*

environmental determinism   *(p. 11)*

meritocracy/meritocratic   *(p. 21)*

sovereign/sovereignty   *(p. 51)*

east-west axis   *(p. 54)*

dichotomy   *(p. 54)*

capitalism   *(p. 61)*

bourgeoisie   *(p. 61)*

usury   *(p. 69)*

Debating the Age of Revolutions: 1600–1870

The story of the world in the early modern period (c. 1450–1850)—as it has been told by generations of American and European historians—is dominated by the **master narrative:** a story that claims to explain the totality of what occurred. This master narrative usually begins with the transformation of Europe from medieval to modern societies. In this recounting, the rest of the world plays only a supporting role as the recipient of European concepts and technologies. The key events featured in this narrative are revolutions that overturn the *ancien regime,* or "old order," in Europe and its colonies: the Reformation, the Enlightenment, the French and American revolutions, and the Industrial Revolution. Each of these events, historians have argued, in turn removed from power one of the major props of the medieval European order: the Catholic Church, the notion of divine rights of monarchs, the manorial economic system, the aristocracy, and the primacy of agriculture. These institutions were replaced, over the course of several centuries, by constitutionalism, limited representative democracy, industry, and capitalism. Historians have traditionally argued that these developments strengthened Europe and turned it into a force the rest of the world would subsequently have to resist or emulate.

However, this eurocentric account of the forging of the modern world has recently come under attack from several directions. Scholars who study regions other than Europe have pointed out major inaccuracies and biases in its depictions of societies in Africa, Asia, and the Americas. These regions were not simply passive recipients of Europeans' attentions in this period, but rather were all undergoing important processes of their own. Within Europe, as well, a new generation of social historians has argued that the master narrative tended to downplay the histories of women, Catholics, and eastern Europeans. Finally, world historians have begun to suggest that the transformations that took place in early modern Europe were really the consequence of increasing interaction among European societies, their colonies in the Americas, and communities around the world with which they traded. Are they right? To what degree *were* these global links important in generating and shaping change in Europe and elsewhere?

This debate over the impact of early modern global commercial networks has been led by historians whose work is based in regions other than Europe. Scholars of the Americas increasingly argue that democratizing revolutions in the Americas preceded and shaped those in Europe. African and Caribbean specialists have suggested that Europe's revolutionary advances were paid for by the labor of Africans and the transatlantic trade in slaves. Historians of Asia have begun to argue that more attention should be paid to reforms and modernization in Japan, China,

Turkey, and elsewhere, and have suggested that events in these countries significantly impacted western Europe.

Without seeking to impose a single understanding of the events of 1600–1870, this part investigates the suggestion that it is no longer possible to investigate events anywhere in the globe during this period without reference to connections and links across regions. This is not to imply that the local context was unimportant: Clearly the Meiji Restoration of the 1860s, the American Revolution of the 1770s, and the British Industrial Revolution that began in the mid-eighteenth century were very different events. Yet they were unique events not only because each region had a different history but also because each occupied a different place in the global system being created after the reconnection of Eurasia and Africa with Oceania and the Americas. How was the world and its regions transformed between 1600 and 1850? We will search for answers by looking at three subsidiary questions.

First, the sources in Part 2 explore the notion that global trade was central to the transformations of the seventeenth, eighteenth, and nineteenth centuries in various regions. Did commerce lead to the political revolutions in France, the Americas, and the Caribbean? Did it create the conditions for Britain's Industrial Revolution? To what degree did profits from this trade create western Europe's riches? To what degree did this the same trade impoverish other regions of the world, especially Africa? Were reforms and revolutions in Turkey and Japan attempts to gain access to the profits of this trade? The second, related question asks whether France and especially Britain were inordinately enriched by global commerce, and if so why? Is it right to suggest that these two states became the center of a global economic and commercial system by the late seventeenth century?

Detractors of global economic models criticize such models for disregarding the importance of local factors as causes of revolutionary change. Therefore the third question addressed in this part is regarding the relative importance of local conditions in shaping developments during this period in many regions. The development of national identity seems to be one of the factors that has shaped the modern world. Its presence can be identified in the American (U.S.), Latin American, Haitian, and French revolutions as well as the Meiji Restoration in Japan. Yet the relationship between the solidification of these national identities, the global expansion of commerce, and revolutions remains disputed.

Part 2 Timeline

c. 1640–1690	The importation of enslaved Africans to the Americas surges as new sugar plantations are put into production around the Caribbean.
1775–1783	Thirteen of Britain's North American colonies revolt, to later form the United States of America.
1776	Adam Smith publishes the Enlightenment economic text, *An Inquiry into the Nature and Causes of the Wealth of Nations.*
1787	Ottobah Cugoano, a former African slave, publishes *Thoughts and Sentiments on the Evil of Slavery.*
1789	The French Revolution begins.
1789–1807	Sultan Selim III of the Ottoman Empire reforms his government.
1792	Conflict in the French colony of Haiti culminates in a successful rebellion by the island's enslaved population.
c. 1770–1790	A number of technological and economic innovations marks the beginnings of the Industrial Revolution in Britain.
1807	Britain and the United States ban the Atlantic slave trade to their countries and for their citizens.
1810	The Hidalgo rebellion begins in Mexico.
1819–1821	Most Latin American colonies achieve their independence from Spain.
1867–1869	The Meiji *Ishin* (Restoration) in Japan replaces the Tokugawa Shoguns with a centralized state that adapted technology as well as military and government organization learned from industrialized states.

Chapter 7

Evaluating the Bourgeois Revolution

From about 1650–1800, the master narrative focuses on a limited group of relatively wealthy *bourgeois* merchants, entrepreneurs, and innovators based in northern and western European states—especially the Netherlands, Britain, and France—whose origins were explored in Chapter 6. From among this group emerged the sponsors of and early participants in the Enlightenment, the Scientific Revolution, the development of capitalism, and industrialization. It is generally posited that other Europeans and European settlers came to be included in this transition only gradually, and non-Europeans played an even more marginal role.

Numerous scholars have tried to account for the decisive role played by this bourgeoisie, and one explanation has stood out. Immediately before the modern era, this account begins, the world was populated largely by rural, agrarian societies. The most developed of these populations lived under political systems in which monarchs (Kings, Shahs, Emperors, etc.) operated through feudal, landowning, **aristocratic** elites (lords, landowners, seigneurs, mandarins). But at some point, probably in the sixteenth century, some European societies transitioned to a system in which the bourgeoisie (merchants, capitalists) became more powerful than the aristocrats. Perhaps many of the northwestern European landowners were even forced to become merchants themselves. Because of this transformation within Europe, a great number of subsequent changes occurred. The Protestant Reformation came about because it legitimized the bourgeoisie lifestyle. The Enlightenment was embraced because it developed notions of popular sovereignty and democracy that expressed the political aspirations of the bourgeoisie. When the bourgeoisie were denied political rights, as in France, the result was the French Revolution. In Britain, the bourgeoisie gained power more gradually and peacefully, in a long process that culminated in **The Glorious Revolution** of 1688 in which the authoritarian King James II was replaced by his daughter Mary and her husband William III of the Netherlands, both of whom agreed to recognize the legislative power of the bourgeois-dominated English parliament. The Industrial Revolution, too, was arguably a revolution that served the bourgeoisie of merchants, financiers, and factory owners. According to this interpretation, the various revolutions really realigned the *class* structures of some European states, and thus created conditions through which the European bourgeoisie could dominate the world by producing cheap goods, by passing laws that facilitated technological innovation, by creating societies that elevated the status of commerce as an occupation, and generally by forcing the state to serve their needs instead of the other way around.

Why, if these theorists are correct, did this small group of the elite in these northwestern European states experience modernity first? One scholar who believes he has the answer is Eric L. Jones. In *The European Miracle,* Jones argues that very long term economic growth trends in this region culminated in a series of leaps in development during the sixteenth through the eighteenth centuries. The specific factors that coincided in early modern Europe but not in other regions of the world included political resiliency, philosophical notions of progress, and specific advances in productivity. These internal factors, Jones argues, can be traced throughout the long-term history of Europe, and merely unfolded themselves in the early modern period. Jones's narrative sounds like the economic arguments for European superiority recounted in Chapter 6, adjusted to suit a slightly later period. In his view, even if Europeans were not clearly capitalist and not uniquely commercially advanced in 1450, they certainly became so in the next few centuries.

Even important critics of theories of early modern European superiority, such as Kenneth Pomeranz, concede that by the mid-nineteenth century some European states—Britain specifically—had clearly achieved a measure of global commercial dominance. Yet they question the explanations for this ascendancy given by Jones and others. In *The Great Divergence,* for example, Pomeranz suggests that Europe's great breakthrough occurred as a result of global developments rather than internal advantages. Chief among these developments were the new European trading routes and colonies. Settlers, slaves, and indigenous populations in the Americas produced consumer goods for consumption or further processing in Europe, and at the same time American metals—specifically silver—allowed Europe to buy their way into Asian trade. The Americas were, Pomeranz argues, an "ecological windfall" for the European colonizing powers. By gaining both resources and labor in the colonies, Europeans were able to divert their own attention to administration, invention, and consumerism.

Pomeranz is not the first to suggest that the American colonies were windfall for Europe. Adam Smith, the celebrated enlightenment economist, wrote about the benefits of the American–European trade at some length. Smith's work is exemplary of the **Enlightenment,** a broad intellectual movement centered in Europe that embraced scientific reasoning and preferenced the search for order in all natural and human worlds. We will see in later chapters that the Enlightenment had an impact on political and social organization across the Atlantic world. It also heavily impacted economics by promoting ideas and practices of economic **liberalism,** also known as *laissez-faire* or free-trade capitalism. Economic liberals believed that the economy worked best when the government stepped back and allowed companies and individuals to trade freely. For much of the early modern period, however, free-trade capitalism did not characterize the relationship between European countries and their colonies. Instead, European governments forced the colonies to trade exclusively with their mother countries through a set of laws called **mercantilism.** Thus Smith argued, in his influential work of political economy *The Wealth of Nations,* that trade with the colonies never reached its potential because of the monopoly system that mercantilism kept in place.

Some modern historians, as well, doubt that the colonies were the principal stimulus of Europe's wealth. Patrick O'Brien, for example, suggests that local commerce may have been more significant because it was in many cases more profitable than long-distance trade ventures. In a fairly balanced article written almost two decades ago, O'Brien managed to capture the skepticism many researchers still feel for theories that purport an external foundation of Europe's prosperity.

A documentary source sometimes used as evidence in debates of this nature is a newsletter from an agent of the Fugger Company placed in Cochin, India, in 1580. The letter is an early example of the development of a commercial infrastructure to gather and share information on overseas trade, in this case by a company headquartered in Spain.

The "European Miracle" Hypothesis

In The European Miracle, *Eric L. Jones sets out to establish the factors that differentiated northwestern Europe from other Eurasian regions in the early modern era. He contends that Europe developed* **responsive commercialism;** *an aspect of capitalism in which the market and even governments responded to consumers' demands for certain goods. What was the cause of this development? Jones avoids singling out any one factor, but does stress the limiting and shaping of the power of the state. Underlying this are political factors familiar from Chapter 5: the rise of the nation-state, the system of medium-sized states, and decentralization. Overseas trade and the colonies, Jones argues, were probably not as important.*

>> 29. The European Miracle:
Environments, Economies, and Geopolitics in the History of Europe and Asia

ERIC L. JONES [1987]

On the face of it a case can be made for seeing the acceleration of European growth as the effect of the bounty of overseas resources brought by the Discoveries. However, what looks more to the point is the existence of economies that could make good use of what was discovered: a native European rather than an imperialist peculiarity. The bounty might easily have been consumed without changing either the social of economic structure. Cheng Ho's distant voyages had not transformed Ming China, neither had the Malagasays or Polynesians, famous voyagers, transformed their homelands, nor, come to that, had the Vikings transformed an earlier Europe by crossing the North Atlantic. Responsive commercialism had emerged in medieval Europe, and it was that which made the Discoveries effective.

This is one area where I would now be more wary. The Discoveries make a brave tale, but before the nineteenth century their total significance was less obvious than it seemed. A paper by O'Brien (1982) provides some rare and much-needed quantification. Although it might be said that the seven percent share of Europe's continental product, which is all he finds contributed by extra-European trade before 1800,

Source: Eric L. Jones, *The European Miracle: Environments, Economies, and Geopolitics in the History of Europe and Asia,* 2nd ed. (Cambridge: Cambridge University Press, 1987), xxviii–xxxi, 238.

may still have been the critical margin for growth, this proportion is infinitely less than implied by writings on Europe's exploitation of the 'periphery.' […]

It is easy, in this species of history, to mistake the forms of development for their essential causes. From the narrowly economic standpoint a more important step, taken in much of Europe after a struggle in the Middle Ages, was probably the curtailing of predatory governmental tax behavior. Beyond that, more problems than we might think could perhaps look after themselves, although disaster management and the provision of other public goods still seem to me great and peculiarly European advances.

Protection from one's own ruler was second in importance only to defence against outside attack. 'Peace and easy taxes' is not an empty first approximation, and Adam Smith was not altogether bigoted when he saw them as preludes to business prosperity, however little flow-on to the average citizen there may have been at first. Political decentralization and competition did abridge the worst arbitrariness of European princes. There were many exceptions, but gradually they became just that, exceptions. Meanwhile freedom of movement among the nation-states offered opportunities for 'best practices' to diffuse in many spheres, not least the economic.

The nation-states that grew up around the better core areas in Europe were consolidated by the attractions of the king's justice and by the centralising power of the king's cannon, both overawing the disorder of lesser lords. It was more important still that the number of states never shrank to one, to a single dominating empire, despite the ambitions of Charlemagne, the Hapsburg Charles V, or Napoleon. Within many states a long process in the history of economic thought conditioned rulers to listen to academics and other wise men. Writers of the seventeenth and eighteenth centuries in central and western Europe dared to offer advice about how to rule, some of which was taken. Compare this with Honda Toshiaki in Tokugawa Japan, who dared not publish, or Pososhkov in Petrine Russia, who did and perished in gaol for his pains.

Humanitarianism and national prudence in much of Europe brought forth the admirable policies of disaster management to which reference has been made, even if other national interests led to many less pretty acts of state. Improvements in welfare or at any rate in the level of risk became matters of national and not merely local concern. At the same time production was being privatised. The enclosure of common fields, dissolution of guilds and abolition of serfdom all seem to express the rise of economic individualism. Yet in the very same breath governments were taking responsibility for fundamental aspects of social provision.

Conditions promoting economic development in Europe formed long ago. Growth in the sense of a sustained rise in average incomes sprouted out of them, slowly but early, perhaps as early as the high middle ages. Pulling this complex of conditions apart does not find us an 'engine of growth.' The pattern, not a single magic change, was what 'brought down the bird.' A relatively steady environment and above all the limits to arbitrariness set by a competitive political arena do seem to have been the prime conditions of growth and development. Europe escaped the categorical dangers of giant centralised empires as these were revealed in the Asian past. Beyond that, European development was the result of its own indissoluble, historical layering. […]

In the present state of knowledge we must resist the notion that any simple model will account for the whole developmental process. We cannot model it, say, as a production function which makes modernisation, eighteenth-century industrialisation, or the sustained rise of real incomes, the output of a handful of stylised inputs, while hoping to retain any sense of the historical complexity involved. Too many parameters shift and dissolve; *very* long-term economic change was much more than the usual conception of an economic process. The model implied by the results of this enquiry resembles a giant combination lock. There is no one key. The parts fit together well enough to work, but perhaps not even in a unique combination: it is difficult to gauge retrospectively what the tolerances of the system may have been. The problem is that economic history has been searching too much in the foreground, in the late eighteenth and nineteenth centuries and among too limited a range of variables, to find all the clues to the process of development. There are many ways of studying the totality, since it is 'not possible to maximise simultaneously generality, realism and precision' […]. For the moment one pays one's money and takes one's choice. Europe's *very* long-term development appears miraculous. Comparable development in Asia would have been super-miraculous.

Adam Smith on the Global Origins of Britain's Wealth

An Inquiry into the Nature and Causes of the Wealth of Nations, *by the English economist Adam Smith, is a product of eighteenth-century thinkers' attempts to establish scientific, rational rules to describe the world around them. This "enlightenment" was caused in part by changes internal to Europe and in part as a response to Europe's growing integration with peoples around the world. Many of the most famous European enlightenment thinkers commented on the very different philosophies and ways of thinking that filtered back to Europe from China, the Americas, and elsewhere. Voltaire, for example, believed that European astronomy was based on Indian sciences. One of the most famous enlightenment theorists was the British economist Adam Smith. In* The Wealth of Nations, *Smith explained the functioning of free-market capitalist economies, in which private enterprises operate for profit by producing goods for both local and distant markets. Smith was one of the first in a long line of economists to comment on the connection between the new-found wealth of the European bourgeoisie and the development of a global trading network including American colonies. According to Smith, however, the benefits of the colonies were limited because mercantilism, which skewed prices, artificially stimulated otherwise unprofitable businesses and diverted the wealth of European states from more profitable ventures.*

>> 30. An Inquiry into the Nature and Causes of the Wealth of Nations

ADAM SMITH [1776]

What are [the benefits] which Europe has derived from the discovery and colonization of America?

Those advantages may be divided, first, into the general advantages which Europe, considered as one great country, has derived from those great events; and, secondly, into the particular advantages which each colonizing country has derived from the colonies which particularly belong to it, in consequence of the authority or dominion which it exercises over them.

The general advantages which Europe, considered as one great country, has derived from the discovery and colonisation of America, consist, first, in

Source: Adam Smith, *An Inquiry into the Nature and Causes of the Wealth of Nations,* Everyman's Library, (London: Dent & Sons, 1904), Vol. II, Book IV, Chapter VII, Part III.

the increase of its enjoyments; and, secondly, in the augmentation of its industry.

The surplus produce of America, imported into Europe, furnishes the inhabitants of this great continent with a variety of commodities which they could not otherwise have possessed; some for conveniency and use, some for pleasure, and some for ornament, and thereby contributes to increase their enjoyments.

The discovery and colonization of America, it will be allowed, have contributed to augment the industry, first, of all countries which trade to it directly, such as Spain, Portugal, France, and England; and, secondly, of all those which, without trading to it directly, send, through the medium of other countries, goods to it of their own produce; such as Austrian Flanders, and some provinces of Germany, which, through the medium of the countries before mentioned, send to it a considerable quantity of linen and other goods. All such countries have evidently gained a more extensive market for their surplus produce, and most consequently have been encouraged to increase its quantity.

But that those great events should likewise have contributed to encourage the industry of countries, such as Hungary and Poland, which may never, perhaps, have sent a single commodity of their own produce to America, is not, perhaps, altogether so evident. That those events have done so, however, cannot be doubted. Some part of the produce of America is consumed in Hungary and Poland, and there is some demand there for the sugar, chocolate, and tobacco of that new quarter of the world. But those commodities must be purchased with something which is either the produce of the industry of Hungary and Poland, or with something which had been purchased with some part of that produce. Those commodities of America are new values, new equivalents, introduced into Hungary and Poland to be exchanged there for the surplus produce of those countries. By being carried thither they create a new and more extensive market for that surplus produce. They raise its value, and

thereby contribute to encourage its increase. Though no part of it may ever be carried to America, it may be carried to other countries which purchase it with a part of their share of the surplus produce of America; and it may find a market by means of the circulation of that trade which was originally put into motion by the surplus produce of America....

The European colonies of America have never yet furnished any military force for the defence of the mother country. Their military force has never yet been sufficient for their own defence; and in the different wars in which the mother countries have been engaged, the defence of the colonies has generally occasioned a very considerable distraction of the military force of those countries. In this respect, therefore, all the European colonies have, without exception, been a cause of weakness than of strength to their respective mother countries....

The advantages of such colonies to their respective mother countries consist altogether in those peculiar advantages which are supposed to result from provinces of so very peculiar a nature as the European colonies of America; and the exclusive trade, it is acknowledged, is the sole source of all those peculiar advantages.

In consequence of this exclusive trade, all the part of the surplus produce of the English colonies, for example, which consists in what are called enumerated commodities, can be sent to no other country but England. Other countries must afterwards buy it of her. It must be cheaper therefore in England than it can be in any other country, and must contribute more to increase the enjoyments of England than those of any other country. It must likewise contribute more to encourage her industry. For all those parts of her own surplus produce which England exchanged for those enumerated commodities, she must get a better price than any other countries can get for the like parts of theirs, when they exchange them for the same commodities. The manufacturers of England, for example, will purchase a greater quantity of the sugar and tobacco of her own colonies than the like manufacturers of other countries can purchase of that sugar and tobacco. So far, therefore, as the manufacturers of England and those of other countries are both to be exchanged for the sugar and tobacco of the English colonies, this superiority of price gives an encouragement to the former beyond what the latter can in these circumstances enjoy. The exclusive trade of the colonies, therefore, as it diminishes, or at least keeps down below what they would otherwise rise to, both the enjoyments and the industry of the countries which do not possess it; so it gives an evident advantage to the countries which do possess it over those other countries....

But the monopoly of the colony trade, so far as it has operated upon the employment of the capital of Great Britain, has in all cases forced some part of it from a foreign trade of consumption carried on with a neighbouring, to one carried on with a more distant country, and in many cases from a direct foreign trade of consumption to a round-about one.

First, the monopoly of the colony trade has in all cases some part of the capital of Great Britain from a foreign trade of consumption carried on with a neighbouring to one carried on with a more distant country.

It has, in all cases, forced some part of that capital from the trade with Europe, and with the countries which lie round the Mediterranean Sea, to that with the more distant regions of America and the West Indies, from which the returns are necessarily less frequent, not only on account of the greater distance, but on account of the peculiar circumstances of those countries. New colonies, it has already been observed, are always understocked. Their capital is always much less than what they could employ with great profit and advantage in the improvement and cultivation of their land. They have a constant demand, therefore, for more capital than they have of their own; and, in order to supply the deficiency of their own, they endeavour to borrow as much as they can of the

mother country, to whom they are, therefore, always in debt. The most common way in which the colonists contract this debt is not by borrowing upon bond of the rich people of the mother country, though they sometimes do this too, but by running as much in arrear to their correspondents, who supply them with goods from Europe, as those correspondents will allow them. Their annual returns frequently do not amount to more than a third, and sometimes not to so great a proportion of what they owe. The whole capital, therefore, which their correspondents advance to them is seldom returned to Britain in less than three, and sometimes not in less than four or five years. But a British capital of a thousand pounds, for example, which is returned to Great Britain only once in five years, can keep in constant employment only one-fifth part of the British industry which it could maintain if the whole was returned once in the year; and, instead of the quantity of industry which a thousand pounds could maintain for a year, can keep in constant employment the quantity only which two hundred pounds can maintain for a year. The planter, no doubt, by the high price which he pays for the goods from Europe, by the interest upon his bills which he grants at distant dates, and by the commission upon the renewal of those which he grants at near dates, makes up, and probably more than makes up, all the loss which his correspondent can sustain by this delay. But though he may make up the loss of his correspondent, he cannot make up that of Great Britain. In a trade of which the returns are very distant, the profit of the merchant may be as great or greater than in one in which they are very frequent and near; but the advantage of the country in which he resides, the quantity of productive labour constantly maintained there, the annual produce of the land and labour must always be much less. That the returns of the trade to America, and still more those of that to the West Indies are, in general, not only more distant, but more irregular, and more uncertain too, than those of the trade to any part of

Europe, or even of the countries which lie round the Mediterranean Sea, will readily be allowed, I imagine, by everybody who has any experience of those different branches of trade.

Secondly, the monopoly of the colony trade has, in many cases, forced some part of the capital of Great Britain from a direct foreign trade of consumption into a round-about one.... The monopoly of the colony trade, too, has forced some part of the capital of Great Britain from all foreign trade of consumption to a carrying trade; and consequently, from supporting more or less the industry of Great Britain, to be employed altogether in supporting partly that of the colonies and partly that of some other countries.... The monopoly of the colony trade besides, by forcing towards it a much greater proportion of the capital of Great Britain than what would naturally have gone to it, seems to have broken altogether that natural balance which would otherwise have taken place among all the different branches of British industry. The industry of Great Britain, instead of being accommodated to a great number of small markets, has been principally suited to one great market. Her commerce, instead of running in a great number of small channels, has been taught to run principally in one great channel. But the whole system of her industry and commerce has thereby been rendered less secure, the whole state of her body politic less healthful than it otherwise would have been.

The Profitability of American Colonies

In The Great Divergence, *Kenneth Pomeranz asks the same basic question as did Eric Jones, yet Pomeranz has a very different approach and opposite conclusions. Pomeranz's strategy is to take a balanced look at Europe and China, striving to understand what might have caused these two populous regions of the world to take very different approaches to similar economic situations. He asserts that China was, in fact, experiencing many of the same problems as Europe in the fifteenth century. Specifically, both were running out of sufficient resources. The Chinese response was to focus on intensifying the efficiency of land use. Western European states, on the other hand, managed to escape the problem by exploiting its new colonies in the Americas. It was this influx of new resources, Pomeranz argues, that propelled Europe for at least a few centuries. Moreover, American resources were especially profitable to Europe because the labor to produce them was in many cases brought in from yet another zone: as slaves from Africa. This situation had several ramifications for parts of Europe. It meant that their labor forces could be diverted to handcrafts or, later, industrial work. It also created a market for European goods, since the slaves and laborers in the Americas had little time to grow or produce for themselves. Finally, slaves were so badly treated that they died in large numbers, necessitating new supplies of human beings be imported constantly to the Americas, to be paid for with American crops and minerals. The result of all of this was a vast expansion of trade in which we see the first* **dependency cycles** *forming: The Americas exported only raw materials to Europe, Africa exported little but slaves to the Americas, Asia exported finished products exchanged by Europeans for silver and gold extracted from the Americas, and Europe carried all of these products around the world. Each leg of these journeys meant a profit for Europeans, and that profit could be invested in innovations and infrastructure within European states.*

>> 31. The Great Divergence:
China, Europe, and the Making of the Modern World Economy

KENNETH POMERANZ [2000]

One core, Western Europe, was able to escape the proto-industrial cul de sac and transfer handicraft workers into modern industries as the technology became available. It could do this, in large part, because the exploitation of the New World made it unnecessary to mobilize the huge numbers of additional workers who would have been needed to use Europe's own land in much more intensive and ecologically sustainable ways—if even that could have provided enough primary products to keep ahead of nineteenth-century population growth. The New World yielded both "real resources" and precious metals, which enquire separate treatment. Let us begin with real resources: they, in turn, begin with plantation products from the Caribbean, northeastern Brazil, and later the southern United States.

The New World's farm exports were largely slave grown. The plantations were almost all either on islands or near the coast. Consequently, exports from the circum-Caribbean plantation zone did not plateau the way that exports from the Chinese interior to Jiangnan and Lingnan did when free laborers ran into diminishing returns and switched more of their efforts to handicrafts. [...]

There were many reasons why African slaves became the principal workforce in so many New World colonies. First and foremost is the astonishing death rates among New World peoples after contact, mostly from disease. Few of Europe's poor, as we have seen, could pay their own passage before 1800, and they were only worth transporting if one could force them to produce exports. With outright enslavement of Europeans unacceptable, this meant indentures that would end with freedom and a grant of land. As survival rates for Europeans (and Africans) in the New World began to improve, this became too expansive for most plantation owners; they preferred to pay more money up front and get a slave who never had to be freed. [...]

Though nearly all bound cash-crop producers in the Old World also grew what was needed for their subsistence, many New World slaves had little or no opportunity for subsistence farming. And since for a long time plantation owners purchased very few women slaves (and manumitted more of them than they did men), many slaves also lacked families, who helped supply the subsistence needs of compulsory cash-crop workers in many Old World settings. Thus, despite their poverty, the everyday needs of slaves created a significant market for imports; in this, slaves were unlike most of the unfree populations in Old World peripheries. These goods (above all cheap cotton cloth for slaves to wear) were a large part of the manufactured imports that took up almost 50 percent of sugar export proceeds in the British Caribbean. Some of these goods were always made in Europe; others came at first from India via Europe but were later replaced by British imitations. [...]

A combination of depopulation and repopulation with slaves made the circum-Caribbean region a perversely large market for imports and a source of land-intensive exports. In fact, it became the first periphery to assume a now familiar "Third World" profile: that of a large importer of both capital goods (in this case, walking, talking, kidnapped ones) and manufactured goods for daily use, with exports that kept falling in price as production became more efficient, capital intensive, and widespread. By contrast, the prices of most forms of energy produced in Europe, including food, rose throughout the eighteenth century, relative to both wages end other goods. Thus the plantation areas of the New World were a new kind of periphery: one that

Source: Kenneth Pomeranz, *The Great Divergence: China, Europe, and the Making of the Modern World Economy* (Princeton: Princeton University Press, 2000), 264–267, 269–271, 273.

would import enough to keep its trade with the core fairly balanced. Moreover, its imports and exports stimulated each other: more sugar exports consistently led to more slave imports, more food and clothing imports, and (often) more plantation debt, which led to selling more sugar next year, at whatever price. [...]

Meanwhile, Mexico, Peru, and later Brazil sent Europe vast amounts of precious metals. Some of this was the direct result of colonial extraction, such as the Spanish and Portuguese kings' cut of all mining in their domains. Legally, this share was at least 27.5 percent—and perhaps as much as 40 percent—of all shipments prior to 1640. Since these rates quickly led to widespread smuggling, the crown's actual share of output was never that high, and the legal rates were gradually lowered to try to reduce contraband; even so, the crown probably received one-tenth to one-fifth of registered output. [...]

One substantial stream of New World gold and silver exports went to various ecologically rich small market zones in the Old World—from Southeast Asia to parts of the Near East to eastern Europe—making it possible for Europe to expand its imports of real resources from these peripheries. [...]

The second stream also helped Europe obtain land-intensive goods, but less directly. This flow was exchanged for various Asian (mostly Indian) manufactured products, which then covered much of the cost of procuring slaves for the Americas. Indian cloth alone made up roughly one-third of all cargo by value exchanged by English traders for African slaves in the eighteenth century and may have made up over half of the goods that French traders (whose industries were slower to produce good imitations of Indian fabrics) used to acquire slaves. Much Portuguese imperial trade went directly from Asia to Africa to Brazil, stopping in the mother country only to deliver New World goods. In other words, this portion of the metals flow facilitated the process we have already described, in which New World slave areas became an important complement to labor and capital rich, land-poor Europe. [...]

Finally, the third stream of metals was for decades the largest of all; but this flow of silver probably did the least to ease pressures on Europe's land. It went to densely populated, heavily commercialized parts of Asia, where it was used as a medium for transactions involving every class in society; and in return, various consumer goods flowed to Europe and to the Americas themselves. This description, as we have seen, may fit some of the Indian trade, but it refers above all to the enormous flow of silver to China, where millions of ordinary people used silver to pay their taxes and for many ordinary purchases. [...]

The transshipment of New World metals did allow western Europe to expand its imports of real resources far beyond what it could have obtained otherwise. Some New World silver may have had to have been converted to cloth, porcelain, or spices to keep expanding the flow of resources from some of the less-monetized Old World peripheries; but thanks to Chinese demand, this option was available, too. And as we have already noted, the combination of New World metals themselves, transshipped Asian goods that had often been obtained with silver, and exotica from the New World itself (such as sugar and tobacco) paid for more of western Europe's imports from the rest of the Old World than did manufacturers created wholly within Europe.

The Importance of Regional Commerce

Patrick O'Brien's 1982 article excerpted here questions the arguments of "globalists" such as Kenneth Pomeranz who depict global trade, both with the Americas and elsewhere, as a driving force in European economic development in the early modern period. Specifically, O'Brien argues that there is little evidence that overseas trade was significant in the first, formative years of this era—the sixteenth and early seventeenth centuries. Thus, he argues, it could not have been external commerce that provided the impetus for Europe's subsequent development, but rather trade and exchange within Europe's borders.

>> 32. European Economic Development: The Contribution of the Periphery

PATRICK O'BRIEN [1982]

According to the new school of development history, the critical period when different parts of the world set off along contrasting paths of economic growth occurred between 1450 and 1750—three centuries within witnessed the emergence and consolidation of "European world economy based upon the capitalist mode of production". The evolution of trade and commerce under this old international economic order [...] created conditions for development and underdevelopment in the nineteenth and twentieth centuries. As they perceive it, the relative backwardness of Asia, Africa, Latin America, and Eastern Europe, which became visible after 1800, originated in the mercantile era when Western Europe turned the terms and conditions for international trade heavily in its favour. [...]

For Europeans international trade at the beginning of the mercantile era meant exchange across the boundaries of states located mainly on the continent of Europe. International trade with Asia, the Middle East, and Africa, although inflated in value terms by silks, spices, jewels, gold, and silver, formed only a tiny percentage of exports and imports. By the late eighteenth century that proportion had definitely increased because trade with the Americas grew rapidly after 1492 to supersede trade with other continents by a large margin. For the 1790s the geographical destination of commodity exports which crossed the boundaries of European states was: to other European states 76 per cent; to North America 10 per cent, to Latin America and the Caribbean 8 per cent, to Asia 5 per cent and to Africa 1 per cent. [...]

A *fortiori,* the importance of such trade would have been far less as we go back in time to the upswing of the "long sixteenth century" and decades of "crisis" during the seventeenth century. National statistics for trades in sugar, tobacco, coffee, tea, slaves, and cotton and the tonnage of ships cleared from European ports indicates that the real upsurge in intercontinental trade occurred after 1650. Although the Americas entered the world economy early in the sixteenth century, flows of commodities across the oceans of the world did not begin to amount to a significant percentage of aggregate European trade before the second half of the seventeenth century. Throughout the mercantile era Europeans sold and purchased far more merchandize from each other than they did from other continents.

Furthermore, external trade formed only a small share of economic activity. Around 1780–90 when something like 4 per cent of Europe's gross national output was exported across national frontiers, perhaps less than 1 per cent would have been sold to Africa, Asia, Latin America, the Caribbean, and the southern plantations of the young United States. A higher but still tiny

Source: Patrick, O'Brien, "European Economic Development: The Contribution of the Periphery," *The Economic History Review,* New Series, 35 (1982): 1–5, 16, 18.

percentage of total consumption by Europeans took the form of imports from these same parts of the world. For particular countries such trade would be more important; especially for smaller maritime powers such as Portugal, Holland, and Britain, where ratios of domestic exports to gross national product probably approached 10 per cent by the second half of the eighteenth century; but less than half of these sales overseas consisted of merchandize sold to residents of the periphery. Imports for maritime economies perhaps fell within a similar range of 10 per cent to 15 per cent of gross national product, again with smaller proportions purchased from the periphery. Interconnexions with the periphery, as they developed during the mercantile era, might on this kind of evidence be dismissed as being of no great importance for the long-run growth of Western Europe. [...]

The claims of the new history of development "founder on the numbers". Some three centuries after the voyage of discovery, Europe's trade with the periphery still formed a very small part of total economic activity. Even for maritime powers, like Britain, closely engaged with Asia, Africa, and Latin America, profits from that commerce probably financed less than 15 per cent of gross investment between 1750–1850. And that percentage must be regarded as far too high an indicator; it refers to the 1780s and 1820s. [...]

As long as oceanic trade remained as a tiny proportion of total economic activity it could not propel Europe towards an industrial society. Global perspectives are not required to comprehend more than a tiny part of the explanation for the progress achieved for three centuries before the Industrial Revolution.

Links across the oceans were built up in the sixteenth century, but to reify the international commerce of the mercantile era into a "world economy" is to misapply a contemporary concept which really has relevance only for our own times. Throughout the early modern era connexions between economies (even within states) remained weak, tenuous, and liable to interruption. Except for a restricted range of examples, growth, stagnation, and decay everywhere in Western Europe can be explained mainly by reference to endogenous forces. The "world economy", such as it was, hardly impinged. If these speculations are correct, then for the economic growth of the core, the periphery was peripheral.

The Difficulties and Rewards of the East Indies Trade

The Fuggers were an important banking and trading family of the Holy Roman Empire who, in the early sixteenth century, established a very profitable relationship with perhaps the most powerful monarchs in Europe: the Habsburgs who at that time ruled the Spanish Empire, the Netherlands, and much of central Europe. Jacob Fugger was the family patriarch who first established a business newsletter around the turn of the century to gather and organize information from the family's business concerns around Europe. By mid-century, his successors were also involved in commerce overseas and collected information from their agents in Asia in much the same way. This excerpt of a letter from an employee sent from Cochin, in modern-day India, reflects the difficulty but also potential rewards of overseas trade. One point made clear by the agent is that the only "European" good in high demand amongst the local populace of Cochin was "money"—silver from the mines in the Americas.

>> 33. The Fugger Newsletters

[1580]

Honourable, most kindly and dear Signor Adelgais! [...]

Here in Cochin we are situated on the ninth degree from this line and on the side of Europe. Lisbon lies thirty-nine degrees off this line. In this place it is rather warm since we are just under the ninth degree. We arrived, thanks and praise be to the Lord Almighty, upon the 10th day of October at the town of Goa, which belongs to the King of Portugal and is the finest capital in this country. Thus we have been on our way here from Lisbon six months and six days, and during that time have seen no land, only the sky and the sea. The Lord God bestows on such journeys His special blessing and mercy, for otherwise it would not be possible to spend half a year between the planks. To sum up, whosoever is well equipped with provisions and a cook, both of which were mine, thanks to the Lord, feels the hardships of such a voyage less than the common people, who suffer great distress from lack of food and drink, especially water, which no money can buy. In such heat one cannot partake of much wine, only water, of which, thanks be to God, I had in sufficient quantity with our food. There were about five hundred persons in our ship of whom not more than twenty-five altogether died on the way from Portugal to India. Some of us, who were well provided with food and drink, extended much help to the poor soldiery. In this half year we have traversed five thousand miles. Although for the direct route from Lisbon to India one counts not more than three thousand miles, one covers at all times for each voyage five thousand miles on account of the head winds. [...]

Our ships have all five arrived from Lisbon, namely, three in Goa and two here. Now all five ships are here in Cochin. I made a sojourn of four weeks in the town of Goa and built me there a house. From thence I travelled one hundred miles onwards by sea. The voyage can be made in ten to twelve days. The ships are loaded with pepper here in Cochin, twenty miles from Calicut, wherefore they all have to come to this place. I shall maintain two establishments, one in Goa and the other here. I have not yet however, resolved upon which shall fall my choice for remaining definitely. Although Goa is the capital in which the Viceroy of Portugal holds his Court, it is wearisome to journey back and forth every year, as I needs must be present in this our pepper store.

Such a pepper store is a fine business, but it requires great zeal and perseverance. It takes six weeks to receive the pepper from the heathen King of Cochin, who is our friend, and to load it into our ships. After the departure of these ships for Portugal I and my servants have but little to do. The pepper business is profitable indeed; when the Lord God grants by His mercy that none of the ships take damage either in coming or going, then the merchants wax rich. With these sailings, all depends upon the right time to take the journey, to wit, during the month of March from Lisbon to this place, and from here to Portugal during the month of January. Also, when this can be arranged, to leave neither place later than upon the 15th day of these months. Then the risk is slight. But it is dangerous to take one's departure later, for then one comes across heavy storms, and has to go by a circuitous route, and often the ships are destroyed. This happens but rarely, provided the ships do not run aground, founder or otherwise come to grief. Great caution has to be practiced in these respects.

This year, in my judgment, we shall not dispatch more than four ships with about twenty loads, although we ought to send thirty. We already possess the money, for so large a sum would not be obtainable by loan. What we are lacking this day can be bought, given a good opportunity, after the

---

Source: "The Fugger Newsletters," from Cochin, 10 January 1580, in *News and Rumor in Renaissance Europe: The Fugger Newsletters,* edited by George T. Matthews (New York: Capricorn Books, 1959), 64–68, 70–71.

sailing of these ships for next year. Of all other spices such as cloves, nutmeg, flour and nuts, cinnamon, maces, and various drugs, this year's supplies are going to Portugal. In precious stones little was dispatched this year on account of the war, which the heathen Kings (of which there are many in this country) waged one upon another. Because of this, precious stones cannot come through from inland into our towns since all of them lie upon the shores of the sea. [...]

Also, I would tell thee that the five ships from Portugal were sent to our master. Thou shouldst know that from the sale of wine, oil, Dutch cheese, fish, paper and other things, usually the greatest profits is derived; this time no gain at all remains. All this has brought in no more than twelve to fifteen per cent., and on the ready cash brought from Lisbon one makes but a profit of twenty-five per cent. The country is no larger as it was formerly, and apart from this, our Viceroy imposes so many new taxes that all commerce diminishes. If he remains here, no good will come of it. I am of the belief, however, that the King of Portugal will send hither another Viceroy when he hears of the doings of this present one. There is no merchandise now that can be sent with profit from here to Portugal.

In precious stones there is nothing this year; in fact this country is not such as is generally imagined. It takes as much trouble to earn money here as in other places. Things are no longer what they were twenty years ago. Buying and selling here is more profitable than sending many wares to Portugal. German merchandise has no market here and is useless for this country. Writing tables split in the great heat; clockwork, or anything else made of iron, deteriorates at sea. This year there is nothing to send to Portugal, for pepper, ginger, maces, cocoa-nut fat have all been brought for the contractors, also cinnamon for the King. One really does not know at this time in what to invest one's money.

The fisher has imported Dutch cheese, but it is not going to derive great profit from it, since much of it was stolen abroad ship. This likewise happened to our stores. In addition, our sales have been bad. Five ships can bring much into port, and thus everything becomes cheap. The Portuguese here are even more diligent than the people in Lisbon. The Pietras de Bezoar are always very dear and not good. After the ships have departed I will try to obtain privately some of these stones that are good, and to send them to thee next year.

>> Mastering the Material

1. Consider the title of Jones's book, *The European Miracle*. Why do you think the author chose that title? What is he trying to tell us?

2. What does Smith suggest were the benefits of the colonies in the Americas to European societies? What does he suggest were the costs of these colonies?

3. What does Pomeranz suggest were the advantages gained by Europe from its colonies in Latin America, the Caribbean, and North America? How convincing is his argument?

4. Consider the excerpts from *The European Miracle* and O'Brien's "European Economic Development." In what way do these two sources complement each other? They each focus on very different data, but are their arguments for internal, rather than global, causes of the European economic transformation more convincing when taken together rather than each separately?

5. Adam Smith is sometimes thought of as the first economic historian. Compare his treatment of the economic impact of the colonies and global trade on Europe with

the work of economic historians Kenneth Pomeranz and Patrick O'Brien. To what degree do they make similar arguments? How are they different?

6. What are the principal products Europeans were seeking to obtain in Cochin, according to the writer of the Fugger newsletter of 10 January 1850? What had they brought to trade in return? Does the fact that they were forced to buy pepper with silver money, rather than bartering European goods, support Pomeranz's assertions?

>> Making Connections

1. Are Jones's arguments similar to any of those put forward by any of the sources in Chapters 1–6? Which ones, and in what way? In what way are they different?

2. Pomeranz suggests that it was the wealth of the Americas, extracted by western European states in the period 1550–1850, that was the principal source of Europe's rise to prominence in the early modern era. This suggests that *none* of the proposed European advantages of the period prior to the opening of the Americas, as expressed by other authors in Chapters 1–6, were in fact momentous. Do you agree with him? Why or why not?

Chapter 8

Locating Nationalism and the Atlantic Revolutions

One of the principal transformations wrought by the European connection with the Americas was the creation of a distinct Atlantic world that, for the first time in history, rivaled the Indian Ocean world in commerce and exchange. European merchants arriving in the Indian Ocean world had been astounded at the thriving trading, diplomatic, and cultural links between East Africans, Egyptians, Arabs, Indians, southeast Asians, Chinese, Philippinos, and others. By contrast, the Atlantic had no such sustained connections prior to 1492, and their development in the early modern period helped to change the world. Unlike in the Indian Ocean, however, one group of peoples—Europeans—quickly came to dominate the Atlantic. In part this was due to the rapid decline of indigenous American populations. Not only were American societies militarily less sophisticated than Europeans, they were also vulnerable to diseases brought from the Old World such as cholera and small pox. In just the sixteenth century alone, the indigenous populations of some parts of the Americas were reduced as much as 95 percent by disease, famine, and warfare. This created a problem for their European conquerors, who desired the raw materials found in the Americas and needed workers to extract them. Although at first they tried to adapt existing labor systems developed by the Aztec, Inca and other American states, they soon found that the combination of diseases and hard labor was literally killing off their workers. In their search to replace the dwindling Native American labor pool, European monarchs and companies turned first to impoverished Europeans brought over as indentured servants, but later began to purchase and ship large numbers of enslaved Africans to American plantations and mines. In fact, in most parts of the European colonies Africans outnumbered Europeans throughout the seventeenth century. Along with these new immigrants came African and European technology, plants and animals, and ideas. The Americas in return introduced to Europe, Africa, and Asia agricultural products like corn, timber, and potatoes as well as a wealth of other resources. This movement of people, goods, species, and ideas among these four continents—Europe, Africa, and North and South America—created the Atlantic world.

In the eighteenth century this Atlantic world underwent a series of celebrated political convulsions that scholars have given the name "the Age of Revolutions." The first sizable upheaval was the rebellion in thirteen of the British North American colonies that we call the American Revolution, for which the start date of 1774 is generally given. This successful rebellion was followed rapidly by an uprising in France in 1789 that overthrew the monarchy there and stimulated revolutions in the French colonies of the Caribbean and even unrest in western Africa. In French-occupied San Domingo (Haiti), an army led by slaves and free blacks expelled French forces and subsequently a British army set to occupy the island. In the second and third decades of the nineteenth century, insurgent forces in Latin America generally led by **creoles**—locally born descendents of European immigrants—similarly defeated Spanish garrisons and gained independence for almost the entirety of the continent. The causes of these convulsions have been widely debated, and this textbook will explore the debate in two parts. In Chapter 9, we will focus on the connections between the revolutions. In this chapter, we will investigate the evolution of modern **nationalism:** the development of a shared identity by a large group of people as a nation. The emergence of this nationalist sentiment was a common theme of the revolutionary movements.

From almost the very beginning of scholarly attention to the Atlantic political revolutions, observers and commentators noted the links between the French and American revolutions. The French philosopher and historian Alexis de Tocqueville wrote texts on both revolutions entitled *De la démocratie en Amérique (On American Democracy)* in 1835–1840 and *L'ancien régime et la revolution (The Old Regime and the French Revolution)* in the 1850s. Similarly, Marxist historians, radical scholars who believed that history was defined by struggles between different socioeconomic classes, in the late nineteenth and early twentieth centuries tended to lump the Atlantic revolutions (with the possible exception of Haiti) together as bourgeois revolutions, serving the political needs of economically empowered but otherwise marginalized capitalists. In the mid-twentieth century, Marxist economic interpretations of both revolutions were gradually superseded by social and political analyses, including works that suggested that revolutions were social diseases that affected states at crucial points. Critics of Marxist theory such as Alfred Cobban even suggested that the French revolution was more a protest against the dominance of capitalism by those who had been left out of the bourgeois revolution than a movement in support of it. These social and political studies tended to be more local than previous economic analyses, and gradually scholars began to focus on the state level and below, emphasizing the importance of a specific factor they identified in big cities like Boston and Caracas, and even rural regions like Champagne. This factor was nationalism.

Late-eighteenth and early nineteenth-century nationalism was something truly new. It was not merely patriotism—the love of one's country—but rather a sense of common identification among the inhabitants of a country, region, or state based on a shared sense of identity. It redefined the population of a state no longer as subjects of a king, but as citizens and full members of a society. In this way, it was deeply rooted in the eighteenth-century philosophical movement known as the **Enlightenment:** a philosophical movement characterized by free inquiry, political and economic experimentation, a focus on rationalism, and a rejection of some forms of authority. The Enlightenment, which was centered in Europe but also manifested in the European colonies overseas, paralleled intellectual developments elsewhere in the world but was also unique in its focus on **popular sovereignty:** the idea that the people at large, rather than any elite class, possessed the exclusive right to exercise authority over the state. There are precedents in history to this notion that government should reflect the general will of the people, but none was carried out as widely. Enlightenment philosophers argued that monarchs and others in positions of authority were responsible to the people that they governed. They also called for the state to recognize the political and legal equality of many, and in some cases all, members of society, and demanded the protection of individuals' freedoms of property and thought. In this way, the Enlightenment is seen as serving the needs of the people, or the "nation." Thus this set of intellectual developments gave birth to modern nationalism.

The Enlightenment has often been seen as *having served* the needs of the bourgeoisie, who often had been restricted from power by their nonaristocratic birth and who desired both greater participation in politics and new protections for their wealth and station. Such evidence as Emmanuel Sieyès French Revolutionary tract "What is the Third Estate?", with its glorification of commoners, is often cited as proof of this. Yet clearly this is not a sufficient explanation for political revolutions to which farmers, urban poor, slaves, and even nobles contributed. Historian Georges Lefèbvres, for example, divided the French Revolution into stages that he argued served first the aristocrats, then the bourgeoisie, and finally the working classes. Other scholars have suggested that the motivations that drove French rural and urban revolutionaries were quite different, and that the two groups cannot be lumped together. Yet these variations only underscore the importance of nationalism as an ideology that could unite people of different backgrounds, classes, and origins. One accomplished historian of nationalism, Liah Greenfeld, illustrates this point in *Nationalism: Five Roads to Modernity*. In the section excerpt in this chapter, for example, she describes how the French revolution was rooted in the particular crises of eighteenth-century France that brought the bourgeoisie and the aristocrats together, if briefly, in the nationalist project.

In fact, however, the French Revolution was not the first nationalist revolution of the Atlantic world. Arguably, that title goes to the rebellion of thirteen of the British North American colonies. This uprising is colloquially known as the American Revolution, although of course it involved only a portion of the British North American colonies. Many scholars have also argued that it was not a revolution at all, but merely a rebellion that replaced one ruling class (the British monarch, parliamentarians, and their bureaucrats) with another (wealthy planter settlers). But it is hard to argue that the inhabitants of what would become the United States had not in fact developed a type of nationalism. In the mid-eighteenth century Britain's colonists were conspicuously loyal to the British Crown. Between 1756–1763 they engaged in a war alongside British imperial forces against French colonists and Native Americans. Ironically, their victory in this Seven Years War led to a worsening of the relationship between the colonists and the British government. The British Crown had gone into debt to fight the war and felt it fair to ask the colonists to repay that debt through new taxes. The colonists, in reply, demanded a voice in government in return for paying the taxes. The Crown's refusal to consider giving the colonists representation in the British government alienated them. T. H. Breen argues that the taxes also helped the colonists forge a sense of a common cause. Their anger at the taxes and legislations, famously echoed in the phrase "no taxation without representation" was in fact an underpinning factor in the emergence of American nationalism. Thus these demands figure prominently in such important revolutionary documents as the *Declaration and Resolves of the First Continental Congress* of 1774.

A similar process seems to have taken place in Latin America. Like their counterparts in British North America, the creoles of Latin America suffered from severe restrictions on whom they could trade with and what goods they could obtain. These restrictions were a result of a growing trend known as mercantilism, in which European governments, seeking to control wealth and trade, restricted their colonies to trading only with the mother country. Along with discrimination in the distribution of political and bureaucratic positions, mercantilism created a sense of anger and eventually of unity within the creole classes of the colonies. In *Imagined Communities*, probably one of the most important books on nationalism to appear in recent years, Benedict Anderson argues that this combination bolstered the rapid emergence of a specifically Latin American form of nationalism in the early nineteenth century.

What Is the Third Estate?

Emmanuel Sieyès was a French monk who was an important participant in many stages of the French Revolution. He helped write several of the chief documents of the revolution, including the Declaration of the Rights of Man and Citizen *and the 1791 constitution. One of his most important publications was the pamphlet "What is the Third Estate?," which appeared in January 1789 and had a great impact on the formation of the national assembly. The title refers to the three estates, or classes, of France: the clergy (first estate), the aristocracy (second estate), and the common people including the bourgeoisie* **(third estate)**. *In this rousting excerpt from the pamphlet, Sieyès suggests that the third estate is the only estate of importance. Its contents were heavily influenced by the work of enlightenment philosophers such as Jean-Jacques Rousseau.*

>> 34. "Qu'est-ce que le tiers état?" or "What Is the Third Estate?"

EMMANUEL (ABBÉ) SIEYÈS [1789]

Chapter 1 The Third Estate Is a Complete Nation

What are the essentials of national existence and prosperity? *Private* enterprise and *public* functions.

Private enterprise may be divided into four classes: 1st. Since earth and water furnish the raw material for man's needs, the first class will compromise all families engaged in agricultural pursuits. 2nd. Between the original sale of materials and their consumption or use, further workmanship, more or less manifold, adds to these materials a second value, more or less compounded. Human industry thus succeeds in perfecting the benefits of nature and in increasing the gross produce twofold, tenfold, one hundredfold in value.

Source: Emmanuel (Abbé), Sieyès, "Qu'est-ce que le tiers état?," or "What Is the Third Estate?" translated and reproduced in *A Documentary Survey of the French Revolution*, edited by John Hall Stewart (New York: Macmillan, 1951), 43–44.

Such is the work of the second class. 3rd. Between production and consumption, as well as among the different degrees of production, a group of intermediate agents, useful to producers as well as to consumers, comes into being; these are the dealers and merchants.... 4th. In addition to these three classes of industrious and useful citizens concerned with goods for consumption and use, a society needs many private undertakings and endeavors which are *directly* useful or agreeable to the *individual.* This fourth class includes from the most distinguished scientific and liberal professions to the least esteemed domestic services. Such are the labors which sustain society. Who performs them? The third estate.

Public functions likewise under present circumstances may be classified under four well known headings: the Sword, the Robe, the Church, and the Administration. It is unnecessary to discuss them in detail in order to demonstrate that the third estate everywhere constitutes nineteen-twentieths of them, except that it is burdened with all that is really arduous, with all the tasks that the privileged order refuses to perform. Only the lucrative and honorary positions are held by members of the privileged order.... nevertheless they have dared lay the order of the third estate under an interdict. They have said to it: "Whatever be your services, whatever your talents, you shall go thus far and no farther. It is not fitting that you be honored."...

···   ···   ···

It suffices here to have revealed that the alleged utility of a privileged order to public service is only a chimera; that without it, all that is arduous in such service is performed by the third estate; that without it, the higher positions would be infinitely better filled; that they naturally ought to be the lot of and reward for talents and recognized services; and that if the privileged classes have succeeded in usurping all the lucrative and honorary positions, it is both an odious injustice to the majority of citizens and a treason to the commonwealth.

Who, then, would dare to say that the third estate has not within itself all that is necessary to constitute a complete nation? It is the strong and robust man whose one arm remains enchained. If the privileged order were abolished, the nation would be not something less but something more. Thus, what is the third estate? Everything; but an everything shackled and oppressed. What would it be without the privileged order? Everything; but an everything free and flourishing. Nothing can progress without it; everything would proceed infinitely better without the others. It is not sufficient to have demonstrated that the privileged classes, far from being useful to the nation, can only enfeeble and injure it; it is necessary, moreover, to prove that the nobility does not belong to the social organization at all; that, indeed, it may be a *burden* upon the nation, but that it would not know how to constitute a part thereof.

···   ···   ···

What is a nation? a body of associates living under a *common* law and represented by the same *legislature.*

Is it not exceedingly clear that the noble order has privileges, exemptions, even rights separate from the rights of the majority of citizens? Thus it deviates from the common order, from the common law. Thus its civil rights already render it a people apart in a great nation. It is indeed *imperium in imperio.*

Also, it enjoys its political rights separately. It has its own representatives, who are by no means charged with representing the people. Its deputation sits apart; and when it is assembled in the same room with the deputies of ordinary citizens, it is equally true that its representation is essentially distinct and separate; it is foreign to the nation in principle, since its mandate does not emanate from the people, and in aim, since its purpose is to defend not the general but a special interest.

The third estate, then, comprises everything appertaining to the nation; and whatever is not the third estate may not be regarded as being of the nation. What is the third estate? Everything!

Identities and French Nationalism

Liah Greenfeld's book Nationalism: Five Roads to Modernity *looks at the emergence of nationalism in England, the United States, France, Russia, and Germany. She argues that the specific form of nationalism that emerged in each location reflected the needs and motivations of the groups that were involved. French nationalism, for example, emerged in France through the coming together of the aristocracy (landowning hereditary lords) and the bourgeoisie. The two classes had different motivations, but both believed the solution to their problems lay in overturning the existing order. Many aristocrats, for example, were undergoing financial crises. They also resented the King's monopoly on political power. Thus they had a common cause with the bourgeoisie, who were frustrated with rigid laws that limited commoners' abilities to achieve high political or social rank or excluded them from certain industries. Together, these groups acted to overthrow the established, royalist regime.*

>> 35. Nationalism: Five Roads to Modernity

LIAH GREENFELD [1992]

The malaise of the French elite was the major factor in the development of the French national consciousness and the emergence of the French nation. It made the aristocracy sympathetic to the idea of the "people" as the bearer of sovereignty and a fundamentally positive entity. This revolution in attitudes was a logical outcome of the situation in which the nobility found itself by the end of the seventeenth century. Its privileges, the significance of which lay in their exclusiveness, were becoming less and less exclusive; of political influence it had as little as any other group in the population; it perceived itself as "degraded," reduced to the "people." There were basically two ways for the nobility to reclaim the status which it was losing: to dissociate itself unequivocally from the "people," or to redefine the "people" in such a way that being of it would become an honor rather than a disgrace. The nobility never committed itself entirely to either one of these solutions, pursuing both all through the eighteenth century. But the second solution, the idea of the nation, had important

advantages over the first, and it is not surprising that in the end it was the one that triumphed. It came with its own stratification, which reflected a new hierarchy of values. Within the community defined as a nation, status was based on service to the nation merit. Unlike the conflicting criteria of birth or wealth, merit made all the groups within the nobility as well as those aspiring to enter it eligible to partake in high status, and unlike culture, service was self-justifiable. [...]

While the elite agonized, French people learned to read. The elite generalized it agony, transforming it into noble indignation with "tyrannies" of all sorts, and fiery patriotic idealism, and as it spared no effort in publicizing the results of these intellectual exercises, it gave the masses food for thought and forged the weapons with which they were to be armed. While the elite was drawn to nationalism, moved by interests peculiar to itself, the rest of at least the literate and semi-literate population in France, the groups that constituted the "bourgeoisie" or the middle class, the denizens of the cities, were also growing more patriotic, realizing that their personal destinies depended on the existence of the nation and earnestly striving to help it on the way to happiness and greatness. But

Source: Liah Greenfeld, *Nationalism: Five Roads to Modernity* (Cambridge: Harvard University Press, 1992), 154–155, 184–186.

the idea of the nation appealed to the bourgeoisie for very different reasons.

If the nationalism of the elite originated in the belief that things had changed for the worse and the desire to arrest this development, to prop and re-found their threatened, but still superior, status, that of the bourgeoisie was aroused by the unhoped-for possibility of improving their lot and acquiring a better status. In a nation, the bourgeoisie could be much more than it was allowed to be in the king's state and the society of orders. A new prospect of dignity opened before it. With the development of the ideology of nationality, the French middle classes found themselves in a potentially advantageous situation which made their members wish to take full advantage of it. They welcomed nationalization of identity. They were receptive to ideas of active membership in the political community, the guaranteed ability to exert influence on public policy which affected their lives, respect for themselves as individuals, liberty and equality in the English sense of these words. A nation defined as a unity of free and equal members both rendered legitimate these heretofore unthinkable bourgeois aspirations and made their realization possible. […]

The writers of the bourgeois *cahiers* would agree that not another nation, but the despotism in France, the class and provincial divisions and privileges, were responsible for its misfortunes, and that not the humiliation of England, but the victory over and abolition of France's own deficiencies would bring the nation happiness. This middle-class nationalism was inward-oriented and fundamentally constructive. The national cause and the cause of liberal individualistic reform were interdependent and seemed identical. Only the elevation of everyone to the lofty position of members of a nation, sharing in the same interests, brothers and equals, would ensure the liberty and dignity of every individual Frenchman. And liberty and equality would contribute to the development among Frenchmen of patriotism, "the secret resource which maintains order in the state, the virtue which is most necessary for its preservation, its internal well-being, and its external force and glory." The surest way to light this sacred fire in the hearts of citizens was "to cater to their interests by rewards" and specifically to offer them equality of opportunity. The glory of France, according to this line of argument, depended on the well-being of its members, not the other way around.

The ideals upheld by elite nationalists, which in their arcane writings tended to assume a different meaning, easily lent themselves to this simple interpretation. Individual liberty could be regarded as "moral liberty found in obedience to general will" and equality as equality of citizens from which the masses of the people were excluded, but to find these notions convincing, one needed to be either very sophisticated (and able to understand them) or stupid (and thus susceptible to indoctrination), and the French bourgeoisie was neither. It consisted of a middling sort of people, smart enough to recognize a good opportunity. The elite forged and armed the middle classes with weapons it had not much use for itself. As the Revolution wrought havoc in the old social structure, and its elite succumbed to the guillotine or self-effaced to escape it, a new elite was recruited from the newly empowered middle classes and blended with the remnants of the old. Its notions were added to the national arsenal of ideas and assumed a prominent, though rarely dominant, place in it—to be used when the chance arose.

Consumption and Identity in the American Revolution

What caused the great bulk of the British colonists in North America to turn against Britain and develop an American nationalism in the 1760s and 1770s? In this insightful article, T. H. Breen suggests that commerce played an important role. Under the strict laws of mercantilism, colonists bought mainly British goods, and Breen suggests that at mid-century this bound them closely to Britain in a shared consumer experience. After the Seven Years War, however, Parliament began to place heavy taxes, or duties, on these goods. The new duties heavily impacted consumers throughout America, who all now shared a common problem. Moreover, inhabitants of Britain were exempt from these taxes, and this difference distanced the colonials from their homeland. The tariffs placed on tea, especially, affected Americans no matter what their class because tea was the most widely consumed imported good. According to Breen, the shared consumer experience of the tea tariffs was one of the factors that brought the colonists together and helped to create an American nationalism.

>> 36. "Baubles of Britain": The American and Consumer Revolutions of the Eighteenth Century

T. H. BREEN [1988]

Something extraordinary occurred in 1774. Thousands of ordinary American people responded as they had never done before to an urban political crisis. Events in Boston mobilized a nation, uniting for the first time artisans and farmers, yeomen and gentlemen, and within only a few months colonists who had earlier expressed neutrality or indifference about the confrontation with Great Britain suddenly found themselves supporting bold actions that led almost inevitably to independence. [...]

Efforts to explain this political mobilization have foundered on an attempt to establish the primacy of ideology over material interest. This is not a debate in which the truth lies somewhere between two extremes. Neither the intellectual nor the economic historian can tell us how Americans of different classes and backgrounds and living in very different physical environments achieved political solidarity, at least sufficient solidarity to make good their claim to independence. [...]

These interpretive issues—those that currently separate the materialists from the idealists—may be resolved by casting the historical debate in different terms. Eighteenth-century Americans, I shall argue, communicated perceptions of status and politics to other people through items of everyday material culture, through a symbolic universe of commonplace "things" which modern scholars usually take for granted but which for their original possessors were objects of great significance. By focusing attention on the meanings of things, on the semiotics of daily life, we gain fresh insight into the formation of a national consciousness as well as the coming of the American Revolution.

The imported British manufactures that flooded American society during the eighteenth century acquired cultural significance largely within local communities. Their meanings were bound up with a customary world of face-to-face relations. Within these localities Americans began to define social status in relation to commodities. This was, of course, an expression of a much larger, long-term transformation of the Atlantic world. And though this process differentiated men and women in new ways, it also provided them with a common framework of experience, a shared language of consumption.

But in America something unusual occurred during the 1760s and 1770s. Parliament managed to politicize these consumer goods, and when it did so, manufactured items suddenly took on a radical, new symbolic function. In this particular colonial

Source: T. H. Breen, "'Baubles of Britain': The American and Consumer Revolutions of the Eighteenth Century," *Past and Present* 119 (1988): 73–77, 97–99, 103–104.

setting the very commodities that were everywhere beginning to transform social relations provided a language for revolution. People living in scattered parts of America began to communicate their political grievances *through* common imports. A shared framework of consumer experience not only allowed them to reach out to distant strangers, to perceive, however dimly, the existence of an "imagined community", but also to situate a universal political discourse about rights and liberties, virtue and power, within a familiar material culture. In this context the boycott became a powerful social metaphor of resistance, joining Carolinians and New Englanders, small farmers and powerful merchants, men and women in common cause.

This interpretive scheme gives priority neither to ideas nor experience. Some Americans undoubtedly boycotted British imports because of political principle. By denying themselves these goods they expressed a deep ideological commitment. Other colonists, however, gave up consumer items because their neighbours compelled them to do so. They were not necessarily motivated by high principle, at least not initially. But the very experience of participating in these boycotts, of taking part in increasingly elaborate rituals of non-consumption, had an unintended effect. It served inevitably to heighten popular awareness of the larger constitutional issues at stake. In this sense, the boycott for many Americans was an act of ideological discovery. These particular colonists may not have destroyed tea because they were republicans, but surely they learned something fundamental about republican ideas by their participation in such events. Questions about the use of tea in one's household forced ordinary men and women to choose sides, to consider exactly where one stood. And over time pledges of support for non-importation publicly linked patriotic individuals to other, like-minded individuals. Decisions about the consumer goods tied local communities to other communities, to regional movements and, after 1774, to a national association. Neither the consumer revolution nor the boycott movement can in itself explain an occurrence so complex as the American Revolution. That argument would amount to a new

form of reductionism. The aim here is more limited: to explore the relation between the growth of national consciousness and the American rejection of the "baubles of Britain". […]

In 1773 parliament stumbled upon an element of mass political mobilization that had been missing during the Townshend protest. By passing the Tea Act, it united the colonists as they had never been before. The reason for this new solidarity was not so much that the Americans shared a common political ideology, but rather that the statute affected an item of popular consumption found in almost every colonial household. It was perhaps *the* major article in the development of an eighteenth-century consumer society, a beverage which, as we have seen, appeared on the tables of the wealthiest merchants and the poorest laborers. For Americans, therefore, it was not difficult to transmit perceptions of liberty and rights through a discourse on tea. […]

Throughout America the ceremonial destruction of tea strengthened the bonds of political solidarity. Once again, we must look to local communities for the embryonic stirrings of national consciousness. It was in these settings that a common commodity was transformed into the overarching symbol of political corruption. By purging the community of tea leaves—an import that could be found in almost every American home— the colonists reinforced their own commitment to certain political principles. But they did more. The destruction of the tea transmitted an unmistakable ideological message to distant communities: we stand together. The Boston Tea Party is an event familiar to anyone who has heard of the Revolution. In many villages, however, the inhabitants publicly burned their tea. Everyone was expected to contribute some leaves, perhaps a canister of tea hidden away in a pantry, a few ounces, tea purchased long before parliament passed the hated legislation, all of it to be destroyed in flames that purged the town of ideological sin. […]

The colonists who responded to Boston's call in 1774 were consciously repudiating the empire of goods. Within barely a generation the meaning of the items of everyday consumption had changed substantially. At mid-century imported articles—the cloth, the ceramics, the buttons—had served as vehicles of Anglicization, and as they flooded into the homes of yeomen and gentry alike, they linked ordinary men and women with the distant, exciting culture of the metropolis. By participating in the market-place, by making choices among competing manufactures, the colonists became in some important sense English people who happened to live in the provinces. By taxing these goods, however, parliament set in motion a process of symbolic redefinition, slow and painful at first, punctuated by lulls that encouraged the false hope that the empire of goods could survive, but ultimately straining Anglicization to breaking-point. Americans who had never dealt with one another, who lived thousands of miles apart, found that they could communicate their political grievances through goods or, more precisely, through the denial of goods that had held the empire together. Private consumer experiences were transformed into public rituals. Indeed many colonists learned about rights and liberties through these common consumer items, articles which in themselves were politically neutral, but which in the explosive atmosphere of the 1760s and 1770s became the medium through which ideological abstractions acquired concrete meaning.

When the colonists finally and reluctantly decided that they could do without the "baubles of Britain", they destroyed a vital cultural bond with the mother country. "The country", explained James Lovell to his friend Joseph Trumbull in December 1774, "... seems determined to let England know that in the present struggle, commerce has lost all the temptations of a bait to catch the American farmer". Lovell may have exaggerated, but he helps us to understand why in 1774 the countryside supported the cities. Consumer goods had made it possible for the colonists to imagine a nation; the Association made is easier for Americans to imagine independence.

Declaration and Resolves of the First Continental Congress

Britain's response to the destruction of tea in Boston and elsewhere in the colonies was to pass a series of acts that came to be known in the colonies as the Intolerable Acts. The acts restricted the power of local legislatures and imposed punishment on Massachusetts especially. This promulgation of the Intolerable Acts mobilized representatives from twelve colonies who met in Philadelphia from 5 September to 26 October 1774, in what later became known as the First Continental Congress. Among other measures, the Congress passed a measure calling for a boycott of British goods. By the following year, open hostilities had commenced. The Declaration and Resolves of the First Continental Congress reflect the principal complaints of the colonists at the outbreak of the revolution.

>> 37. Declaration and Resolves of the First Continental Congress

[1774]

Whereas, since the close of the last war, the British parliament, claiming a power, of right, to bind the people of America by statutes in all cases whatsoever, hath, in some acts, expressly imposed taxes on them, and in others, under various pretences, but in fact for the purpose of raising a revenue, hath imposed rates and duties payable in these colonies, established a board of commissioners, with unconstitutional powers, and extended the jurisdiction of courts of admiralty, not only for collecting the said duties, but

Source: Declaration and Resolves of the First Continental Congress (October 14, 1774).

the trial of causes merely arising within the body of a country.

And whereas, in consequence of other statutes, judges, who before held only estates at will in their offices, have been made dependant on the crown alone for their salaries, and standing armies kept in times of peace: And whereas it has lately been resolved in parliament, that by force of a statute, made in the thirty-fifth year of the reign of King Henry the Eighth, colonists may be transported to England, and tried there upon accusations for treason and misprisions, or concealments of treason committed in the colonies, and by a late statute, such trials have been directed in cases therein mentioned:

And whereas, in the last session of parliament, three statutes were made; one entitled, "An act to discontinue, in such manner and for such time as are therein mentioned, the landing and discharging, lading, or shipping of goods, wares and merchandise, at the town, and within the harbor of Boston, in the province of Massachusetts-Bay in North America;" another entitled, "An act for the better regulating the government of the province of Massachusetts-Bay in New England;" and another entitled, "An act for the impartial administration of justice, in the cases of persons questioned for any act done by them in the execution of the law, or for the suppression of riots and tumults, in the province of the Massachusetts-Bay in New England;" and another statute was then made, "for making more effectual provision for the government of the province of Quebec, etc." All which statutes are impolitic, unjust, and cruel, as well as unconstitutional, and most dangerous and destructive of American rights:

And whereas, assemblies have been frequently dissolved, contrary to the rights of the people, when they attempted to deliberate on grievances; and their dutiful, humble, loyal, and reasonable petitions to the crown for redress, have been repeatedly treated with contempt, by his Majesty's ministers of state:

The good people of the several colonies of New-Hampshire, Massachusetts-Bay, Rhode-Island and Providence Plantations, Connecticut, New-York, New-Jersey, Pennsylvania, Newcastle, Kent, and Sussex on Delaware, Maryland, Virginia, North-Carolina, and South-Carolina, justly alarmed at these arbitrary proceedings of parliament and administration, have severally elected, constituted, and appointed deputies to meet, and sit in general Congress, in the city of Philadelphia, in order to obtain such establishment, as that their religion, laws, and liberties, may not be subverted: Whereupon the deputies so appointed being now assembled, in a full and free representation of these colonies, taking into their most serious consideration, the best means of attaining the ends aforesaid, do, in the first place, as Englishmen, their ancestors in like cases have usually done, for asserting and vindicating their rights and liberties, DECLARE,

That the inhabitants of the English colonies in North-America, by the immutable laws of nature, the principles of the English constitution, and the several charters or compacts, have the following RIGHTS:

Resolved, N.C.D. 1. That they are entitled to life, liberty and property: and they have never ceded to any foreign power whatever, a right to dispose of either without their consent.

Resolved, N.C.D. 2. That our ancestors, who first settled these colonies, were at the time of their emigration from the mother country, entitled to all the rights, liberties, and immunities of free and natural-born subjects, within the realm of England.

Resolved, N.C.D. 3. That by such emigration they by no means fortified, surrendered, or lost any of those rights, but that they were, and their descendants now are, entitled to the exercise and enjoyment of all such of them, as their local and other circumstances enable them to exercise and enjoy.

Resolved, 4. That the foundation of English liberty, and of all free government, is a right in the people to participate in their legislative council: and as the English colonists are not represented, and from their local and other circumstances, cannot properly be represented in the British parliament, they are entitled to a free and exclusive power of legislation in their several provincial legislatures, where their right of representation can alone be preserved, in all cases of taxation and internal polity, subject only to the negative of their sovereign, in such manner as has been heretofore used and accustomed: But, from the necessity of the case, and a regard to the mutual interest of both countries, we cheerfully consent to the operation of such acts of the British parliament, as are bona fide, restrained to the regulation of our external commerce, for the purpose of securing the commercial advantages of the whole empire to the mother country, and the commercial benefits of its respective members; excluding every idea of taxation internal or external, for raising a revenue on the subjects, in America, without their consent.

Resolved, N.C.D. 5. That the respective colonies are entitled to the common law of England, and more especially to the great and inestimable privilege of being tried by their peers of the vicinage, according to the course of that law.

Resolved, 6. That they are entitled to the benefit of such of the English statutes, as existed at the time of their colonization; and which they have, by experience, respectively found to be applicable to their several local and other circumstances.

Resolved, N.C.D. 7. That these, his majesty's colonies, are likewise entitled to all the immunities and privileges granted and confirmed to them by royal charters, or secured by their several codes of provincial laws.

Resolved, N.C.D. 8. That they have a right peaceably to assemble, consider of their grievances, and petition the king; and that all prosecutions, prohibitory proclamations, and commitments for the same, are illegal.

Resolved, N.C.D. 9. That the keeping a standing army in these colonies, in times of peace, without the consent of the legislature of that colony, in which such army is kept, is against law.

Resolved, N.C.D. 10. It is indispensably necessary to good government, and rendered essential by the English constitution, that the constituent branches of the legislature be independent of each other; that, therefore, the exercise of legislative power in several colonies, by a council appointed, during pleasure, by the crown, is unconstitutional, dangerous and destructive to the freedom of American legislation.

All and each of which the aforesaid deputies, in behalf of themselves, and their constituents, do claim, demand, and insist on, as their indubitable rights and liberties; which cannot be legally taken from them, altered or abridged by any power whatever, without their own consent, by their representatives in their several provincial legislatures.

Creole Pioneers and Nationalism in Latin America

Benedict Anderson's Imagined Communities *is a well-known text on the origins of nationalism. Anderson's principal argument is that nationalism is often not based on a real historical unity. Instead, the "nation" is an idea imagined by its participants, who may have differing reasons for unifying but who together create the nation as the symbol and language of their unity. Anderson also argues that the first real emergence of nationalism as a political force took place in the Americas, in the case of Latin American born largely out of creoles' resentment of* **peninsulares** *(Europeans born in Europe and sent out to administer the American colonies). Anderson suggests that the creoles were discriminated against on the basis of the location of their birth, but otherwise shared language and to a large degree culture with the peninsulares. Because of* *this discrimination, they began to identify with other creoles as a group and to resent peninsulares and Spanish and Portuguese rule. Anderson also emphasizes the role of local newspapers, among other tools, in welding colonial populations together and creating a sense of nationalism.*

>> 38. Imagined Communities:
Reflections on the Origin and Spread of Nationalism

BENEDICT ANDERSON [1983]

Of the 170 viceroys in Spanish America prior to 1813, only 4 were creoles. These figures are all the more startling if we note that in 1800 less than 5% of the 3,200 000 creole 'whites' in the Western Empire (imposed on about 13,700,000 indigenes) were Spain-born Spaniards. On the eve of the revolution in Mexico, there was only one creole bishop, although creoles in the viceroyalty outnumbered *peninsulares* by 70 to 1. And, needless to say, it was nearly unheard-of for a creole to rise to a position of official importance in Spain. Moreover, the pilgrimages of creole functionaries were not merely vertically barred. If peninsular officials could travel the road from Zaragoza to Cartagena, Madrid, Lima, and again Madrid, the 'Mexican' or 'Chilean' creole typically served only in the territories of colonial Mexico or Chile: his lateral movement was as cramped as his vertical ascent. In this way, the apex of his looping climb, the highest administrative centre to which he could be assigned, was the capital of the imperial administrative unit in which he found himself. Yet on this cramped pilgrimage he found travelling-companions, who came to sense that their fellowship was based not only on that pilgrimage's particular stretch, but on the shared fatality of trans-Atlantic birth. Even if he was born within one week of his father's migration, the accident of birth in the Americas consigned him to subordination—even though in terms of language, religion, ancestry, or manners he was largely indistinguishable from the Spain-born Spaniard. There was nothing to be done about it: he was *irremediably* a creole. Yet how irrational his exclusion must have seemed! Nonetheless, hidden inside the irrationality was this logic: born in the Americas, he could not be a true Spaniard; *ergo*, born in Spain, the *peninsular* could not be a true American. [...]

What were the characteristics of the first American newspapers, North or South? They began essentially as appendages of the market. Early gazettes contained—aside from news about the metropole—commercial news (when ships would arrive and depart, what prices were current for what commodities in what ports), as well as colonial political appointments, marriages of the wealthy, and so forth. In other words, what brought together, on the same page, *this* marriage with *that* ship, *this* price with *that* bishop, was the very structure of the colonial administration and market-system itself. In this way, the newspaper of Caracas quite naturally, and even apolitically, created an imagined community among a specific assemblage of fellow-readers, to whom *these* ships, brides, bishops and prices belonged. In time, of course, it was only to be expected that political elements would enter in.

One fertile trait of such newspapers was always their provinciality. A colonial creole might read a Madrid newspaper if he got the chance (but it would say nothing about his world), but many a peninsular official, living down the same street, would, if he could help it, *not* read the Caracas production. An asymmetry infinitely replicable in other colonial situations. [...]

By way of provisional conclusion, it may be appropriate to reemphasize the limited and specific thrust of the argument so far. It is intended less to explain the socio-economic bases of anti-metropolitan resistance in the Western hemisphere between say, 1760 and 1830, than why the resistance was conceived in plural, 'national' forms—rather than in others. The economic interests at stake are well-known and obviously of fundamental importance. Liberalism and the

Source: Benedict Anderson, *Imagined Communities: Reflections on the Origin and Spread of Nationalism* (New York: Verso, 1983), 56–58, 62, 64–65.

Enlightenment clearly had a powerful impact, above all in providing an arsenal of ideological criticisms of imperial and *anciens régimes*. What I am proposing is that neither economic interests, Liberalism, nor Enlightenment could, or did, create *in themselves* the *kind,* or shape, of imagined community to be defended from these regimes' depredations; to put it another way, none provided the framework of a new consciousness—the scarcely-seen periphery of its vision—as opposed to centre-field objects of its admiration or disgust. In accomplishing *this* specific task, pilgrim creole functionaries and provincial creole printmen played the decisive historic role.

>> Mastering the Material

1. On what basis does Sieyès suggest that the "Third Estate" is the most important?

2. In what way can Sieyès' "What Is the Third Estate?" be considered a nationalist document? What is the nation to which he refers?

3. According to Greenfeld, what was the role played by the aristocracy and by the bourgeoisie in the French Revolution?

4. How does Breen help us to question the ideological causes of nationalism? Do you accept the notion that economic concerns such as taxes on tea can play a large role in the formation of nationalism?

5. What are the principal complaints of the signers of the *Declaration and Resolves of the First Continental Congress*? As a source for interpreting the origins of American nationalism, what issues does this document suggest bound Americans together?

6. Summarize Anderson's argument. Do you think nationalism can be borne of discrimination? Do you think this argument could be extended or modified to cover the complaints and aspirations of the American and French revolutions?

7. Consider all of these sources together. What factors do you feel made possible the emergence of nationalism in the late-eighteenth- and early nineteenth-century Atlantic world?

>> Making Connections

1. Consider Greenfeld and Sieyès contributions to the study of the French revolution. Do you think the French revolution can be considered a bourgeois revolution, intended to serve the needs of the bourgeoisie discussed in Chapter 7? Why or why not?

2. Analyze Breen's article and the 1774 *Declaration and Resolves of the First Continental Congress*. Based on these sources, do you think the American revolution was a bourgeois revolution? Why or why not?

3. Consider the sources in this chapter and in Chapter 7. To what degree and in what ways do these sources confirm the creation of an Atlantic world in economics, philosophy, and politics? Are these changes significant enough to make the Atlantic world a more significant unit of study than Europe in this period?

4. Some scholars have argued that nationalism was a result of unique political and economic factors within Europe, such as the size of states and the rise of capitalism in earlier centuries (Chapters 5 and 6). Others have suggested that nationalism emerged from the development of the Atlantic commercial world of the sixteenth through the eighteenth centuries. Which perspective do you think is more accurate? Why?

Chapter 9

Connecting the Atlantic Revolutions

Each of the Atlantic revolutions can be explored at a variety of levels—from micro-regional investigations of a single plantation or village to state-level or imperial analyses to global interpretations. The revolutions in Spanish Latin America serve as a good example. It is possible to analyze the events of the early nineteenth century as evidence of transformations within the Spanish Empire. Two major political changes within the empire in this period were the 1808 conquest of Spain by the French Emperor Napoleon Bonaparte and the restoration of King Ferdinand VII in 1814, at the end of the Napoleonic wars. Both of these events had repercussions in Latin America. Napoleon's invasion, for example, gave creole groups in the major cities of the Spanish Latin Americas a justification for declaring independence. Some, such as the council of Caracas, did. Others, however, declared for Ferdinand, and some even chose to support the regime established by Napoleon. Upon his eventual restoration, Ferdinand implemented some reforms aimed at quelling rebellion, but also established a much more intensive oversight of the colonies that is sometimes dubbed a "new colonialism." This reformation of Spanish colonial rule, which brought with it new taxes and mercantile tariffs, inspired a further round of rebellions that this time culminated in the liberation of almost all of Spanish Latin America by 1825.

Yet in the actions of creole in different colonies local, rather than imperial, factors can be seen at play. For example, Mexico alone had experienced a nearly successful rebellion by its oppressed indigenous population and slave class in 1810. Because the rebellion threatened not only Spanish rule but also the privileges of wealthy creoles, this event convinced the Mexican creole class to ally itself with the Spanish Crown. As a result, the bulk of Mexico's creoles did not become rebellious until long after creole groups elsewhere. By contrast, Simón Bolívar led Venezuela's and Columbia's creole elites into rebellion much earlier, and unlike in Mexico his forces largely managed to incorporate the lower classes who subsequently contributed to his military success. Bolívar hoped to unite the former colonies in a state much like the United States to the north, but because of local conditions and divisions this proved impossible.

It is also possible to view the Latin American revolutions at the level of the Atlantic world. Just as the widespread Napoleonic conflict provided an opportunity for creole rebels, the American Revolution provided them with inspiration and the United States later provided them with aid. Britain also assisted the rebels, both to hurt their principal opponent—Napoleon—and in the hopes of capturing Latin American commerce for themselves. Debatably, the rebels were inspired not only by American independence but by the ideas of the French Revolution. As John Lynch shows in

"The Origins of Spanish American Independence," the French, American, and Haitian revolutions each impacted upon the Latin American scene in a different way.

Each of these levels of analysis—imperial, local, and global—therefore helps to give us a more accurate and complete picture of the events and trends of the Latin American revolutions. Much the same is true for the French Revolution. We have already seen in Liah Greenfeld's arguments (Chapter 9) the distinctiveness of French nationalism. Other scholars have pointed out that, because the French Revolution was a reaction to the French monarchy, it must be seen as a uniquely French movement. In 1954, however, the American historian R. R. Palmer suggested that the French Revolution was really one manifestation of "The World Revolution of the West." Palmer linked the French Revolution to the American Revolution as well as movements in Ireland, Switzerland, and elsewhere in Europe. In Palmer's model, the connections were both ideological (through the Enlightenment), political (through the conflict between France and Britain), and economic (as bourgeois revolutions). Palmer was not the first to explore connections between Atlantic revolutions. De Tocqueville himself had much to say on the links between the American and French revolutions, although he was something of a skeptic, as is shown in the extract from *L'ancien régime*.

The Haitian Revolution is perhaps the archetype for analyses of regional pertur- bations as "global" revolutions. Perhaps the first rigorous scholarly text to tie the Haitian Revolution firmly to the French Revolution was C. L. R. James's *The Black Jacobins: Toussaint L'Ouverture and the San Domingo Revolution,* first published in 1938. James pointed to very close intellectual links between the leaders of the French Revolution of 1789 and the Revolution in its San Domingo colony (which would become Haiti) in 1791. However, the situation was more than merely a mirror of the revolution in France. For one thing, the struggles in Haiti involved not only issues of class and politics but also prominently questions of race. The battling parties included both pro-monarchy and revolutionary creole plantation owners, free people of African descent, and slaves. Their struggles culminated in the largest and most successful slave revolution in world history. Yet although the Haitian context was distinctive, the inter- nal conflict soon became intertwined not only in French revolutionary struggle but also the Caribbean arm of the ongoing conflict between Britain and France. As a result, armies of former slaves under the command of Toussaint L'Ouverture found themselves fighting not only French but also British and Spanish forces. These com- plexities are reflected in the Haitian Declaration of Independence, produced in full in Reading 42. As Franklin Knight demonstrates in excerpts from his article "The Haitian Revolution," the revolutionaries' success meant that Haiti became connected to the subsequent revolutions in Latin America.

Linking the Atlantic Revolutions

Palmer's "The World Revolution of the West" exploded into the debate on the French Revolution in 1954. Palmer's wide perspective of the revolution, and his American citizenship, drew the ire of French historians such as Marcel Reinhard and Georges

Lefèbvre. These scholars deplored the idea of the French Revolution as simply one facet of an intercontinental transformation rather than a unique national event. Nevertheless, Palmer made three strong arguments that continue to resonate: that many of the Atlantic revolutions were inspired by common themes of the Enlightenment, that they involved struggles by certain classes against the advantages of others, and finally that they were wrapped up in Britain's and France's political and military rivalry.

>> 39. The World Revolution of the West: 1763–1801

R. R. Palmer [1954]

In the summer of 1798 France was bordered by other revolutionary republics in Holland, Switzerland and Italy. Belgium and the Rhineland had been annexed, and unrest spread through Germany. Ireland was in rebellion, and in Great Britain the government of William Pitt, to use the word of various British historians, was resorting to terror. In Sweden, said the British Foreign Secretary, half the people were Jacobins. In the United States, in July 1798, the same fear of Jacobins, that is of democrats, produced the Alien and Sedition laws; nor were such fears allayed when the democrats won the next election. [...]

The idea that these events constituted a world revolution, that is, a revolution of the Western World, is a very old one, since it dates from the eighteenth century itself. Recently, both in this country and in Europe, historians have begun to revive it. [...]

Such a world revolution may be bounded, for convenience, by the dates 1763 and 1800 or 1801. At the hither end, we have a dramatic close in the election of Jefferson to the American presidency, and the personal triumph of Napoleon Bonaparte in Europe. The two events were not exactly alike, to be sure, but both were followed by a decline of political agitation. At the same time, with the Peace of Amiens and the Concordat both the

British government and the papacy recognized the consequences of international revolutionary republicanism, at least tentatively and pending further developments. [...]

The problem now is to suggest a few unifying themes, running through these years, and more or less common to an Atlantic civilization.

To begin with ideas. To imply that ideas "caused" the Revolution bas long been the signal for controversy, carrying the implication of a conservative approach. Since the Revolution, and indeed before, as in the French Assembly of the Clergy of 1765, there have been warnings that the literature of the Enlightenment made people unruly and filled them with impractical ideas. This is probably true. [...]

The main idea, if we must single one out, seems to have been a demand for self-determination, a sense of autonomy of the personality, a refusal to accept norms laid down outside the self, leading sometimes to a profound subjectivity, or an insistence on self-expression rather than adjustment to preexisting authoritative standards. [...]

Class analysis offers another common theme. Carl Becker once observed of the American Revolution that, with the question of home rule settled by independence, it remained to be seen who should rule at home. Thus the establishment of independence was followed by the heightened democratic agitation of the 1790's. The same pattern can easily be seen in parts of Europe, especially in regions subject to a sovereignty increasingly felt to be foreign. Cases in point are the Lombard and

Source: R. R. Palmer, "The World Revolution of the West: 1763–1801," *Political Science Quarterly* 69 (1954), 2–5, 7, 9–10.

Belgian provinces, under the Hapsburg emperor; or the Swiss territory of Vaud, which belonged to the canton of Berne. […]

In most countries having a middle class a bourgeois phase soon followed the aristocratic protest, and the sub-bourgeois or working classes were often heard from also, not only in France, but in England, Scotland, Holland and elsewhere. […]

Finally it is in the sphere of international relations, and especially in war, that a unifying conception for the era may be formed. […]

The revolutionary struggle, throughout the thirty-odd years, was inseparable from the struggle between England and France. The British government opposed every revolutionary effort— the American, the Irish, the Dutch of 1784 and the Belgian of 1789. It went to war with France in 1793 to maintain the *status quo* in Belgium and Holland, against which many Dutch and Belgians were in rebellion, but which for over a century had been favorable to British naval and mercantile interests. The French, on the other hand, under both the Bourbon and the ensuing republican governments, patronized virtually all revolutionary disturbances.

The French were the only people to make a lasting revolution by their own efforts. All others depended on them. The French shipped 30,000 muskets to America in the year 1777. Nine tenths of all the gunpowder used by Americans before the battle of Saratoga was from foreign sources, mainly French. It is clear that the success of the American revolt depended on France even before France openly intervened. In this respect the American Revolution resembles the revolutions twenty years later which produced the Batavian, Cisalpine and other short-lived republics. The difference lies in the fact that the French withdrew from America, leaving the country independent, whereas they did not, could not, or would not withdraw from Holland or Italy except by abandoning their supporters to the counterrevolution.

de Tocqueville on the American Revolution

Alexis Charles Henri Maurice Clérel de Tocqueville did not in fact live through either the American or the French Revolution. Born in 1805, however, he was one of the first scholars to connect the two. His L'ancien régime *is a standard work on the American Revolution. At the time of its writing in the years just before his death, de Tocqueville was depressed at what he saw as the failure of the French Revolution to achieve any real change in French society. It is thus much more pessimistic than his earlier work on American democracy. In this excerpt, de Tocqueville undertakes a very balanced analysis of the intellectual connections between the American and French revolutions.*

>> 40. L'ancien régime

ALEXIS DE TOCQUEVILLE [1856]

Our Revolution has often been attributed to that of America; the latter had in truth much influence on the French Revolution, but that influence was less due to what was actually done in the United States than to what was thought about it at the same time in France. Whilst to the rest of Europe the American revolution was still nothing but a new and singular fact, to us it only rendered more obvious and

Source: Alexis de Tocqueville, *L'ancien régime*, translated by M. W. Patterson (Oxford: Basil Blackwell, 1952) 155–157.

more striking what we thought we already knew. Elsewhere it astonished; here it secured conviction. The Americans seemed only to have executed what our writers had conceived; they gave the substance of reality to what we were in process of dreaming. It was as though Fénelon had suddenly found himself at Salentum.

This circumstance, so novel in history, of the whole political education of a great people being entirely conducted by men of letters, was that which contributed most perhaps to give to the French Revolution its peculiar character and to produce the results we see.

The writers furnished not merely their ideas to the people who made it, but also their temperament and disposition. As the result of their long education, in the absence of any other instructors, coupled with their profound ignorance of practice, all Frenchmen from reading their books finally contracted the instincts, the turn of mind, the tastes and even the eccentricities natural to those who write. To such an extent was this the case that, when finally they had to act, they transported into politics all the habits of literature. [...]

These new qualities became so thoroughly incorporated with the old basis of the French character that often our nature has been credited with that, which was only the product of this singular education, I have heard it stated that the affection for, or rather the toleration we have shown for sixty years towards general ideas, systems, and grand words, in the political sphere belonged to some quality peculiar to our race, to what was called with a little emphasis the 'French spirit'; as if this pretended attribute could have appeared all at once towards the end of the eighteenth century, after having concealed itself during all the rest of our history!

The Haitian Revolution in an Atlantic Context

San Domingue (Haiti) was just one of dozens of sugar colonies in the Caribbean and the American mainland in which, collectively, millions of slaves worked to produce wealth for European companies and states. It was the crown jewel of French colonies in the eighteenth century, with the largest slave population and highest sugar production of all the Caribbean Islands, as well as producing half of the world's coffee exports. About 40,000 white Frenchmen and almost as many free people of color also populated the French half of the island. These individuals had taken sides in the French Revolution, sending representatives to Paris in 1789 and alternately championing the cause of the monarchy or the Republicans. However, few anticipated the impact the revolution would have on the half-million slaves of the colony. On 22 August 1791, hundreds of slaves launched a coordinated attack on plantations, beginning near the town of Cap François. The rebellion was well organized and spread rapidly as it evolved into a truly revolutionary movement aimed at overturning the slave system of the island. Over the next decade, revolutionary armies battled not only French but also British forces into submission and liberated the French half of the island. Thereafter, it became a base of revolutionary activity and ideology, giving refuge to Simón Bolívar, among others. The slave rebellion in Haiti was undoubtedly the most far-reaching of the Atlantic revolutions, ending slavery and replacing a slave-owning aristocracy with a leadership drawn largely from among the formerly enslaved.

>> 41. The Haitian Revolution

FRANKLIN W. KNIGHT [2000]

If the origins of the Haitian Revolution in Saint Domingue lie in the broader changes of the Atlantic world during the eighteenth century, the immediate precipitants must be found in the French Revolution. The symbiotic relationship between the two were extremely strong and will be discussed later, but both resulted from the construction of a newly integrated Atlantic community in the seventeenth and eighteenth centuries.

The broader movements of empire building in the Atlantic world produced the dynamic catalyst for change that fomented political independence in the United States between 1776 and 1783. Even before that, ideas of the Enlightenment had agitated the political structures on both sides of the Atlantic, overtly challenging the traditional mercantilist notions of imperial administration and appropriating and legitimating the unorthodox free trading of previously defined interlopers and smugglers. The Enlightenment proposed a rational basis for reorganizing state, society, and nation. The leading thinkers promoted and popularized new ideas of individual and collective liberty, of political rights, and of class equality—and even, to a certain extent, of social democracy—that eventually included some unconventional thoughts about slavery. But their concepts of the state remained rooted in the traditional western European social experience, which did not accommodate itself easily to the current reality of the tropical American world. [...]

Without the outbreak of the French Revolution, it is unlikely that the system in Saint Domingue would have broken down in 1789. And while Haiti precipitated the collapse of the system regionally, it seems fair to say that a system such as the Caribbean slave system bore within itself the seeds of its own destruction and therefore could not last indefinitely. [...]

In both France and its Caribbean colonies, the course of the revolution took strangely parallel paths. The revolution truly began in both with the calling of the Estates General to Versailles in the fateful year of 1789. Immediately, conflict over form and representation developed, although it affected metropolis and colonies in different ways. In the metropolis, the Estates General, despite not having met for 175 years, had an ancient history and tradition, albeit almost forgotten. The various overseas colonists who assumed they were or aspired to be Frenchmen and to participate in the deliberations and the unfolding course of events did not really share that history and that tradition. In many ways, they were new men created by a new type of society—the plantation slave society. [...]

With the colonial situation far too confusing for the metropolitan legislators to resolve easily, the armed revolt in the colonies started with an attempted coup by the *grands blancs* in the north who resented the *petits blancs*–controlled Colonial Assembly of St. Marc (in West Province) writing a constitution for the entire colony in 1790. Both white groups armed their slaves and prepared for war in the name of the revolution. When, however, the National Assembly passed the May Decree enfranchising propertied mulattos, they temporarily forgot their class differences and forged an uneasy alliance to forestall the revolutionary threat of racial equality. The determined desire of the free non-whites to make a stand for their rights—also arming their slaves for war—made the impending civil war an inevitable racial war.

The precedent set by the superordinate free groups was not lost on the slaves, who comprised the overwhelming majority of the population. If they could fight in separate causes for the antagonistic free sectors of the population, they could fight on their own behalf. And so they did. Violence, first employed by the whites, became the common currency of political change. Finally, in August 1791, after fighting for nearly two years on one or another side of free persons who claimed they were fighting for liberty, the slaves of the

Source: Franklin W. Knight, "The Haitian Revolution," *American Historical Review* 105 (2000): 106, 109–114.

Plain du Nord applied their fighting to their own cause. And once they had started, they refused to settle for anything less than full freedom for themselves. When it became clear that their emancipation could not be sustained within the colonial political system, they created an independent state in 1804 to secure it. It was the logical extension of the collective slave revolt that began in 1791. […]

The impact of the Haitian Revolution was both immediate and widespread. The antislavery fighting immediately spawned unrest throughout the region especially in communities of Maroons in Jamaica, and among slaves in St. Kitts. It sent a wave of immigrants flooding outward to the neighboring islands, and to the United States and Europe. It revitalized agricultural production in Cuba and Puerto Rico. As Alfred Hunt has shown, Haitian emigrants also profoundly affected American language, religion, politics, culture, cuisine, architecture, medicine, and the conflict over slavery, especially in Louisiana. Most of all, the revolution deeply affected the psychology of the whites throughout the Atlantic world. The Haitian Revolution undoubtedly accentuated the sensitivity to race, color, and status across the Caribbean. […]

Haiti cast an inevitable shadow over all slave societies. Antislavery movements grew stronger and bolder, especially in Great Britain, and the colonial slaves themselves became increasingly more restless. Most important, in the Caribbean, whites lost the confidence that they had before 1789 to maintain the slave system indefinitely. In 1808, the British abolished their transatlantic slave trade, and they dismantled the slave system between 1834 and 1838. During that time, free non-whites (and Jews) were given political equality with whites in many colonies. The French abolished their slave trade in 1818, although their slave system reconstituted by 1803 in Martinique and Guadeloupe, limped on until 1848.

Declaration of Independence of Haiti

The so-called Haitian Declaration of Independence was in fact almost an article of alliance signed by three rebel generals on 29 November 1803, long after the revolution had begun and immediately following the surrender of the commander-in-chief of Napoleon's French armies on the island, Jean-Baptiste Rochambeau. The hero of the revolution, François Dominique Toussaint L'Ouverture, had died earlier in the year and his principal successor was Jean-Jacques Dessalines, a former slave. Dessalines would be succeeded by another signatory of the declaration, Henri Christophe. The third signatory, Clerveaux, was a commander of an independent force that allied with Dessalines against French forces. At the time of its publication, the Haitians had already defeated not only two French armies but also Spanish and British forces. This document itself is militant but also prideful, the product of a long and successful war and an even longer history of oppression.

>> 42. Declaration of Independence of Haiti

[1803]

In the Name of the Black People, and Men of Color of St. Domingo:

The Independence of St. Domingo is proclaimed. Restored to our primitive dignity, we have asserted our rights; we swear never to yield them to any power on earth; the frightful veil of prejudice is torn to pieces, be it so for ever. Woe be to them who would dare to put together its bloody tatters.

Source: "Declaration of Independence of Haiti," in *An Historical Account of the Black Empire of Hayti: Comprehending a View of the Principal Transactions in the Revolution of Saint-Domingo; with Its Ancient and Modern State,* by Marcus Rainsford (London, 1805), 439–441.

Oh! Landholders of St. Domingo, wandering in foreign countries by proclaiming our independence, we do not forbid you, indiscriminately, from returning to your property; far be from us this unjust idea. We are not ignorant that there are some among you that have renounced their former errors, abjured the injustice of their exorbitant pretensions, and acknowledged the lawfulness of the cause for which we have been spilling our blood these twelve years. Toward those men who do us justice, we will act as brothers; let them rely for ever on our esteem and friendship; let them return among us. The God who protects us, the God of Freemen, bids us to stretch out towards them our conquering arms. But as for those, who, intoxicated with foolish pride, interested slaves of a guilty pretension, are blinded so much as to believe themselves the essence of human nature, and assert that they are destined by heaven to be our masters and our tyrants, let them never come near the land of St. Domingo: if they come hither, they will only meet with chains or deportation; then let them stay where they are; tormented by their well-deserved misery, and the frowns of the just men whom they have too long mocked, let them still continue to move, unpitied and unnoticed by all.

We have sworn not to listen with clemency towards all those who would dare to speak to us of slavery; we will be inexorable, perhaps even cruel, towards all troops who, themselves forgetting the object for which they have not ceased fighting since 1780, should come from Europe to bring among us death and servitude. Nothing is too dear, and all means are lawful to men from whom it is wished to tear the first of all blessings. Were they to cause rivers and torrents of blood to run; were they, in order to maintain their liberty, to conflagrate seven-eighths of the globe, they are innocent before the tribunal of Providence, that never created men, to see them groaning under so harsh and shameful a servitude.

In the various commotions that took place, some inhabitants against whom we had not to complain, have been victims by the cruelty of a few soldiers or cultivators, too much blinded by the remembrance of their past sufferings to be able to distinguish the good and humane landowners from those that were unfeeling and cruel, we lament with all feeling souls so deplorable an end, and declare to the world, whatever may be said to the contrary by wicked people, that the murders were committed contrary to the wishes of our hearts. It was impossible, especially in the crisis in which the colony was, to be able to prevent or stop those horrors. They who are in the least acquainted with history, know that a people, when assailed by civil dissentions, though they may be the most polished on earth, give themselves up to every species of excess, and the authority of the chiefs, at that time not firmly supported, in a time of revolution cannot punish all that are guilty, without meeting with new difficulties. But now a-days the Aurora of peace hails us, with the glimpse of a less stormy time; now that the calm of victory has succeeded to the trouble of a dreadful war, every thing in St. Domingo ought to assume a new face, and its government henceforward be that of justice.

Done at the Head-Quarters, Fort Dauphin, 29 November 1803.

(Signed) DESSALINES. CHRISTOPHE. CLERVEAUX. True Copy, B. Aime, Secretary.

The Objectives of the Spanish American Revolutionaries

It is easy to locate the French, American, and Haitian revolutions within the late-nineteenth-century revolutions in Spanish Latin America, but it is difficult to do it well. Not only did the rebellions in mainland Latin America occur some decades later than the other three, but they also generally remained bourgeois revolutions, their leaderships conspicuously avoiding what they saw as the "excesses" of the French and Haitian revolutions. As John Lynch demonstrates very effectively here, the creole classes in the Spanish colonies were concerned that their rebellions not result in the rise of the lower and enslaved classes, as had happened in Haiti and briefly in France. Indeed, most creole revolutionaries sought to emulate the American revolution, which had served mainly the purposes of the bourgeoisie of British North America.

>> 43. The Origins of Spanish American Independence

JOHN LYNCH [1987]

The Enlightenment was brought into political focus by the revolutions in North America and France. In the years around 1810 the influence of the United States was exerted by its mere existence, and the close example of liberty and republicanism remained an active inspiration in Spanish America, one as yet unsullied by misgivings concerning the policy of this powerful neighbour. As early as 1777 a Spanish version of proclamations of the Continental Congress (1774–5) was in the hands of Dr José Ignacio Moreno, subsequently rector of the Central University of Venezuela and participant in the conspiracy of 1797. The works of Tom Paine, the speeches of John Adams, Jefferson and Washington all circulated in the subcontinent. Many of the precursors and leaders of independence visited the United States and saw free institutions at first hand. It was in New York, in 1784, that Francisco de Miranda conceived the idea of 'the liberty and independence of the whole Spanish American continent', Bolivar had an enduring respect for Washington and admired, though not uncritically, the progress of the United States, 'land of freedom and home of civic virtue', as he described it. United States trade with Spanish America was a channel not only of goods and services but also of books and ideas. Copies of the Federal Constitution and the Declaration of Independence, in Spanish translation, were carried into the area by United States merchants, whose liberal views coincided with their interest in the growth of a monopoly-free market. After 1810 Spanish Americans would look for guidance to the republican experience of their northern neighbour in their search for the rights of life, liberty and happiness. Constitutions in Venezuela, Mexico and elsewhere would be closely modeled on that of the United States, and many of the new leaders—though not Bolivar—would be profoundly influenced by North American federalism.

The model of revolution offered by France had less appeal. As Miranda observed in 1799, 'We have before our eyes two great examples, the American and the French Revolutions. Let us prudently imitate the first and carefully shun the second. […] Situated as they were between the Spaniards and the masses, the creoles wanted more than equality for themselves and less than equality for their inferiors. The more radical the French Revolution became and the better it was known, the less it appealed to the creole aristocracy. They saw it as a monster of extreme democracy and anarchy, which, if admitted into America, would destroy the world of privilege they enjoyed. The danger was not remote.

In 1791 the French Caribbean colony of Saint-Domingue was engulfed in a massive slave revolt. […]

To Spanish America Haiti was an example and a warning, observed by rulers and ruled

Source: John Lynch, "The Origins of Spanish American Independence" in *The Independence of Latin America,* edited by Leslie Bethell (Cambridge: Cambridge University Press, 1987), 43–47.

alike with growing horror. The creoles could now see the inevitable result of loss of unity in the metropolis, loss of nerve by the authorities, and loss of control by the colonial ruling class. Haiti represented not only independence but revolution, not only liberty but equality. The new regime systematically exterminated the remaining whites and prevented any white from re-establishing himself as a proprietor; it recognized as Haitian any black and mulatto of African descent born in other colonies, slave or free, and these were invited to desert; and it declared war on the slave trade. These social and racial policies branded Haiti as an enemy in the eyes of all colonial and slave regimes in the Americas, and they took immediate steps to protect themselves, none more vigorously than Spain, which in the course of the Haitian revolution had lost the adjacent colony of Santo Domingo. In November 1791, within three months of the outbreak, Spanish colonial authorities were warned to adopt defensive measures against contagion. Haitian blacks were denied entry to Spanish colonies and even white refugees were suspect. [...]

Spanish American revolutionaries anxiously disassociated themselves from the Haitian revolution. Miranda in particular was concerned about its effect on his reputation in England: 'I confess that much as I desire the liberty and independence of the New World, I fear anarchy and revolution even more. God forbid that the other countries suffer the same fate as Saint-Domingue, scene of carnage and crimes, committed on the pretext of establishing liberty; better that they should remain another century under the barbarous and senseless oppression of Spain. [...]

If Haiti was a warning [...], it was also an incentive. Spanish Americans, too, would soon be faced with a crisis in the metropolis and a failure of imperial control. Then they would have to fill the political vacuum, and they would seize independence not to create another Haiti but to prevent one.

>> Mastering the Material

1. Evaluate Palmer's theory of "world revolutions of the west." What does he argue are the connections between the Atlantic revolutions of the late eighteenth century? Are you convinced by his assertions? Why or why not?

2. To what degree does de Tocqueville believe that the French Revolution is intellectually connected to the American Revolution? Do you agree with him? Why or why not?

3. How does Knight link the French and Haitian revolutions?

4. According to Knight, what was the impact of the Haitian Revolution on other Caribbean slave populations?

5. The writers of the "Declaration of Independence of Haiti" were not members of the bourgeoisie, but largely former slaves and oppressed people of African descent. Is this fact reflected in the document?

6. Do the Latin American revolutions fit into Palmer's model, if at a slightly later time? Why or why not?

7. According to Lynch, which eighteenth-century revolutions did Bolívar and his compatriots in the Spanish colonies seek to emulate? Which did they not? Account for these choices.

>> Making Connections

1. Using the "Declaration of Independence of Haiti" and Knight's article as sources, do you think the Haitian Revolution can be characterized as a bourgeoise revolution? Why or why not?

2. Consider Palmer's thesis and the sources in this chapter and in Chapters 7 and 8. Do you agree that there was an Atlantic world? Were the American, French, Haitian, and Spanish Latin American revolutions in fact part of a wider Atlantic revolution?

3. European settlers and Caribbean slaves of African origin were able to defeat large European armies. What does this suggest about the nature of the Atlantic world in the eighteenth and nineteenth centuries?

Chapter 10

Linking the Industrial Revolution in Africa and Britain

Like political revolutions in Europe and the Americas, some scholars describe the Industrial Revolution as a social and productivity transformation caused by the needs of the rising bourgeoisie. Other theorists, however, consider the Industrial Revolution to be a much more fundamental technological transformation. Robert Marks, in his textbook *The Origins of the Modern World,* suggests that until the eighteenth century the entire world had labored under a **biological regime** in which they relied upon organic sources of energy: human, animal, solar, water, and plant. The Industrial Revolution in Britain, however, enabled that country to harness new sources of energy—particularly a coal/steam combination—that gave it an immediate productivity advantage. "To be sure," Marks writes,

> *the early British "factories" had begun to use water power, but there was a limit to how much that could increase cotton textile production. Indeed, there is every reason to think that cotton textile production would have reached serious limits within the biological old regime, leading not to an industrial revolution but to an economic dead end, had it not been for coal, the steam engine, and iron and steel production that truly launched the Industrial Revolution and allowed Britain to break out of the constraints imposed by the biological old regime.*

It is common for world historians to view the Industrial Revolution in terms of technology or economics, as Marks does in this quote, and there is much to be said for this approach. Certainly, from about the 1720s onward British productivity rose, at least in part because of a rash of new inventions: the improved waterwheel, the steam engine, techniques in refining iron, and machines that vastly sped the production of textiles. These technological innovations were matched by equally significant social developments: urbanization, population growth, and the replacement of artisanship with the factory system. The new technologies also spurred changes in transportation and communication, and ultimately in military technology. These changes gave an enormous commercial advantage to Britain, which as a result was able to outstrip its competitors, especially France. British pride and sense of commercial dominance is palpable in the work of even early eighteenth-century authors such as Daniel Defoe, whose 1726 book *The Complete English Tradesman* is excerpted in Reading 46. Only in the late nineteenth century did other states—particularly the United States, Belgium, the Netherlands, Germany, France, and lastly Japan—really draw alongside Britain.

Historians and social scientists who study Britain, Europe, and the world have long debated why this revolution occurred first in portions of Europe. On the surface, at least, is the argument that the Industrial Revolution was simply another project of the bourgeoisie. Certainly, the ending of the biological old regime in Britain seems to mirror the decline of the political *ancien régime* in France. It seems intuitive that the bourgeois classes who in one country wanted to end rule by royal fiat and aristocratic privilege, would in the neighboring state be served by the development of new production techniques and the building of efficient factories. Thus the traditional account of the emergence of the British Industrial Revolution identifies merchants and capitalists as the agents of innovation. Also significant were changes in food production beginning in the late sixteenth century. Often known as the **agricultural revolution,** new methods of farming and imported crops helped to increase the populations of Britain and other northern and western European states. The agricultural revolution in Britain was accompanied by laws allowing for the "enclosure" of lands. These new enclosures were really vast livestock farms, producing wool for textile merchants. They also had the consequence of creating a large body of potential factory workers by driving peasants off the land. At the same time, new cultivating techniques and new crops enabled more food to be grown on less land, thus providing sustenance for this growing urban working class.

Another proposed cause of the Industrial Revolution, put forward by intellectual and cultural historians, was the increasingly rational, scientific worldview of Europeans as demonstrated by the work of Adam Smith, among others. This new perspective, they ague, was an equally important factor in that it created the potential for scientific and technological innovation. A final part of the dynamic within Britain during this period was its unique geography—flat to facilitate transport but full of raw materials including rich deposits of coal located close to the surface and to convenient transportation facilities. As Peter Mathias argues in *The First Industrial Nation,* it was not one of these factors, but the unique coincidence of all of them, that created the first Industrial Revolution in Britain.

But some differing accounts suggest that the origins of the Industrial Revolution can be found not in the local context but rather in global trends. Kenneth Pomeranz, Robert Marks, and others have posed the question why it was Britain, and not China, that underwent industrialization first, and have suggested again that it was not merely coal or culture but also colonies that made the difference. There are any number of potential connections between the Industrial Revolution and global influences, some of which are merely hypothesized, others of which have been quite firmly established. Was the agricultural revolution that fed the working class in Britain a result of cultivating techniques learned from the Chinese and southeast Asians and of crops introduced from the Americas? Were the British able to concentrate on production of textiles, and to enclose otherwise valuable cultivation land, because they were bringing in foodstuffs and resources from their colonies in the Americas? Was the money that paid for Britain's innovations simply the ill-gotten profits made from the labor of slaves of African descent? Was the market for Britain's industrial goods mainly in Europe, or was it in Africa and the American colonies? One of the most important works to argue that Atlantic—if not global—connections were significant to the emergence of the

Industrial Revolution was Eric Williams *Capitalism & Slavery.* First published in 1944, *Capitalism & Slavery* put forward the theory that British industry was stimulated by profits from the triangular trade in the Atlantic, which in turn was based on slavery. The contradiction is evident: that Britain "developed" capitalism, industry, and free labor only because British merchants and capitalists enslaved people elsewhere.

Indeed, if the Industrial Revolution was a great economic boon for certain groups in Britain, it was devastating to Africa and later much of the world. In *How Europe Underdeveloped Africa,* the Afro-Guyanese historian Walter Rodney argued that the Atlantic slave trade effectively retarded Africa's development. Not only did the trade itself wrack Africa with wars and kidnappings, but it also reduced the African population and denied Africa the labor and ideas of millions of its people. The Industrial Revolution continued this process by making Africans dependent on cheap European goods, to such an extent that many African manufacturing techniques were lost. Much the same happened in India, once the greatest cloth manufacturing region in the world but by the late nineteenth century largely dependent on more cheaply produced British textiles. Likewise, Latin America may have won its political independence from Spain but it soon found itself economically dependent on Britain and, to some extent, the United States. Each of these regions fell into a trap of providing raw materials to the industrialized states at low prices and buying finished products back at much higher prices.

Both Williams' arguments and Rodney's thesis have been subjected to a great deal of criticism. Yet it is clear that the trade in slaves was devastating to at least portions of Africa. By the early nineteenth century, visitors' and inhabitants' accounts tell of regions depopulated by kidnapping and warfare, and it is clear that in some areas productive states were rapidly replaced by slave-raiding societies. Meanwhile, cultivation fell off and large communities were forced to seek the sanctuary of marginal areas like deserts and deep forests. These effects did not go unnoticed by Africans themselves, and are commemorated in oral histories, performances, and stories told about the slave trade. Literate Africans also wrote about them, including several former slaves who were key actors in the movement to abolish the Atlantic slave trade. One of these was Ottobah Cuguano, whose memoir (Reading 48) was an important piece of evidence about the horrors of the trade.

But while Africans may have paid a heavy price for Britain's industrialization, they were not the only people to see its dark side. Before government began to regulate it, industrial labor was devastating for workers everywhere, and this included large numbers of young children put to work in mines and mills. Reading 49 contains the all-too-similar testimonies of two young women employed by the industrial revolution—an English factory girl and a West African child-slave.

Origins of the Industrial Revolution in Britain

In the prologue to his book The First Industrial Nation, *Peter Mathias challenges each of the prominent explanations for the origins of the Industrial Revolution, and suggests that none is sufficient alone. Instead he suggests that industrialization was the result of a complex combination of factors including government and social attitudes toward entre-preneurs, innovations in agriculture and trade, access to resources, and geography. He also compares conditions in Britain to those in other European states in the eighteenth century, although he does not look more broadly at the rest of the world.*

>> 44. The First Industrial Nation:
An Economic History of Britain 1700–1914

PETER MATHIAS [1969]

To search for a single-cause explanation for the industrial revolution is to pose a false analogy with a simple equation governing chemical change. It is less tidy, less satisfying, less simple, but nevertheless more accurate to suppose that there was no one secret key which undid the lock, no single operative variable, no one prime relationship which had to be positive and in terms of which all other aspects of change may be regarded as dependent variables.

To create some confusion, which is always a stimulus to thought, it is worth challenging each factor which has been put forward as a single-cause explanation in its own right. The favourable natural resources position existing in Britain had been existing for a very long time before the mid-eighteenth century. Other countries had been equally bountifully endowed by nature. By itself, therefore, a favourable resource position was not a sufficient, though it may have been a necessary, condition for the industrial revolution. [...]

A rising population is also said to have created the unique context for growth by expanding the internal market and the labour force. But Ireland, and subsequently Norway and Sweden and many other non-European countries, have also experienced rapid population growth without concomitant economic development. In turn, such factors as a bourgeois social structure with attitudes orientated towards trade and economic gain, the extent of trade itself or the plentifulness of capital have each been championed as the

great unique advantages which put Britain in a class by herself. But were any of these things true by themselves? The rate of interest was consistently lower in Holland and capital more abundant there—seeking investment opportunities abroad which were lacking in industry at home. And wealth from foreign trade, the extent of markets in foreign trade, was greater in Holland than in Britain, relative to the size of her economy. The Dutch social structure was also equally fluid; the 'middling orders' in her society were as important as in England. The economic ethic in that bourgeois, merchant society was equally favourable in this sense as social values in England. Wealth and enterprise, particularly trading enterprise, gave status in Holland equally as in England. Holland was also a constitutional state with political power reflecting new wealth there as in England. No one could say that in Holland the extravagances of a lavish court robbed the nation of productive resilience, investment resources or the motivations towards business success, which some have posited in the case of France or Prussia. [...]

Nor can industrialization be explained by any sudden outburst of mechanical ingenuity or inventive genius. France had as impressive a record of scientific advance, of high standards of mechanical contrivance in luxury-market industries like watch-making and automata (performing toys) as England. Much greater positive, deliberate help was given by government to acquiring new industrial skills in France and other continental states than in England. [...]

And if it was just the natural genius of the British people to do these things, there is an onus

Source: Peter Mathias, *The First Industrial Nation: An Economic History of Britain 1700–1914* (New York: Methuen, 1969), 7–11, 13–14.

of proof on explaining just why that genius saw fit to wait until the mid-eighteenth century to throw aside its disguise, and why it faded in relation to that of other countries a brief century later on. [...]

It is much easier methodologically to defend the proposition that, if any *one* prime factor had not been present in eighteenth-century England, if there had developed in any one of half a dozen relationships in the economy absolute resistance, absolute unresponsiveness to change, the whole process of economic growth leading into industrialization might have been held back or slowed down. [...]

Arthur Lewis, when referring to the contemporary world, gave top priority to what he called 'the will to economize'. He meant that there must be a social system and a government which has not got its face turned against economic change, or at least has not got effective power and influence to prevent spontaneous forces for change from acting. [...]

The values of the whole society are not necessarily orientated to economic growth (although momentum will be maximized if these are permissive, responsive to change) but certainly the values of activist minorities must be positive. Social prejudice against enterprise or status won by new wealth, may not prove very significant unless it is institutionalized in law and given sanctions by the state and the juridical system. [...]

In many of these relationships, Britain proved to be fortunately endowed by the early eighteenth century. [...]

A second prerequisite for economic growth was sufficient economic resources to develop new sides to the economy. [...]

Favourable local mineral fuel supplies close to navigable water was, in fact, a key locational advantage for developing a mass-output, low-cost heavy industry. [...] Here Britain enjoyed very considerable advantages when her natural resource position was matched to the technology upon which the early stages of industrialization were based. Plentiful coal and iron ore were conveniently placed with regard to water carriage in many regions of the island; the most important coalfield of all lay close to the north-east coast,

well serviced by loading points along the rivers. A strategic river system, in particular the Trent and the Severn, stretched into the heart of industrial England. [...]

To economic resources must be added inventiveness, applied science or, from some source or other (even if it means importing other people's ideas and skills), a flow of technical innovations through which production and productivity can be increased. Applied science does not seem to have been particularly prominent in this process during the eighteenth century, save in a minority of strategic points in its latter decades. But of the general energetic questing for experiment, innovation, trying new ways of doing things, there is no doubt. [...]

The responsiveness of two sectors in the economy in generations before the decades of the eighteenth century with which the term industrial revolution is usually associated also proved vital conditioning factors to industrialization in Britain: agriculture and foreign trade. [...] Agriculture was not a leading sector in England's industrialization. [...] But even without being a main source of momentum, agricultural development proved a crucial enabling condition—perhaps precondition—for industrialization. The introduction of critical innovations, new crops and rotation techniques characterizing the 'agricultural revolution', long antedated the mid-eighteenth century and agricultural output was growing markedly in the first half of the eighteenth century, if the movement of prices and agricultural exports are a guide. [...]

Foreign trade also provided a vital sector which did see dramatic changes and expansion coming in the century before industrialization. One can also speak of a commercial revolution from 1650 to 1750. Foreign trade proved an important generating source for economic momentum in different ways long before the mid-eighteenth century, affecting levels of wealth, the size of markets available to the industry of a relatively small country, sources of savings, the considerable differentiation of the economy and society in England compared with other countries.

The Profits of the Atlantic Slave Trade for Britain

Eric Williams's theory on the connection between the Atlantic slave trade, slavery, and the development of industry in Britain is so well known that it is often referred to simply as the "Williams thesis." Williams begins with the triangular trade in which Britain, the Caribbean Islands, North America, and Africa were connected. Underpinning this trade were profits from buying slaves in Africa for sale in the Americas, from provisioning those slaves once they were in the Americas, and in selling slave-produced commodities. In the sections excerpted here, Williams explores the connection between these profits and the funds that paid for the Industrial Revolution.

>> 45. Capitalism & Slavery

ERIC WILLIAMS [1944]

Britain was accumulating great wealth from the triangular trade. The increase of consumption goods called forth by that trade inevitably drew in its train the development of the productive power of the country. This industrial expansion required finance. What man in the first three-quarters of the eighteenth century was better able to afford the ready capital than a West Indian sugar planter or a Liverpool slave trader? We have already noticed the readiness with which absentee planters purchased land in England, where they were able to use their wealth to finance the great developments associated with the Agricultural Revolution. We must now trace the investment of profits from the triangular trade in British industry, where they supplied part of the huge outlay for the construction of the vast plants to meet the needs of the new productive process and the new markets. [...]

Many of the eighteenth century banks established in Liverpool and Manchester, the slaving metropolis and the cotton capital respectively, were directly associated with the triangular trade. Here large sums were needed for the cotton factories and for the canals which improved the means of communication between the two towns.

Typical of the eighteenth century banker is the transition from tradesman to merchant and then the further progression from merchant to banker. The term "merchant," in the eighteenth century context, not infrequently involved the gradations of slaver captain, privateer captain, privateer owner, before settling down on shore to the respectable business of commerce. The varied activities of a Liverpool businessman include: brewer, liquor merchant, grocer, spirit dealer, bill-broker, banker, etc. Writes the historian: "One wonders what was covered by that 'etc.'" Like the song the sirens sang, that "etc." is not beyond all conjecture. It included, at some time or other, some one or more aspects of the triangular trade. [...]

Heavy industry played an important role in the progress of the Industrial Revolution and the development of the triangular trade. Some of the capital which financed the growth of the metallurgical industries was supplied directly by the triangular trade.

It was the capital accumulated from the West Indian trade that financed James Watt and the steam engine. Boulton and Watt received advances from Lowe, Vere, Williams and Jennings—later the Williams Deacons Bank. Watt had some anxious moments in 1778 during the American Revolution when the West Indian fleet was threatened with capture by the French. "Even in this emergency,"

Source: Eric Williams, *Capitalism & Slavery* (Chapel Hill: University of North Carolina Press, 1994), 98–99, 102–105. Originally published 1944.

wrote Boulton to him hopefully, "Lowe, Vere and Company may yet be saved, if ye West Indian fleet arrives safe from ye French fleet…as many of their securities depend on it."

The bank pulled through and the precious invention was safe. The sugar planters were among the first to realize its importance. Boulton wrote to Watt in 1783: "…Mr. Pennant, who is a very amiable man, with ten or twelve thousand pounds a year, has the largest estate in Jamaica; there was also Mr. Gale and Mr. Beeston Long, who have some very large sugar plantations there, who wish to see steam answer in lieu of horses." [...]

In the eighteenth century, when the slave trade was the most valuable trade and West Indian property among the most valuable property in the British Empire, the triangular trade occupied an important position in the eyes of the rising insurance companies. In the early years, when Lloyd's was a coffee house and nothing more, many advertisements in the London Gazette about runaway slaves listed Lloyd's as the place where they should be returned. [...]

The triangular trade made an enormous contribution to Britain's industrial development. The profits from this trade fertilized the entire productive system of the country.

The English Tradesman

Daniel Defoe is best known for his tale of the castaway Robinson Crusoe, *but he was also one of the most important commentators of the very early period of the Industrial Revolution in Britain. Defoe wrote prolifically about eighteenth-century England, the most populous of Britain's regions. In his travels, he noted the development of cottage industry—the precursor to the factory system—and also wrote about the role of the English gentry in agricultural innovation, and about the English tradesmen: merchants and shopkeepers. In Defoe's account, the particular skill of the English in commerce— both local and global—pushed Britain to the forefront of European states. Some socio-cultural historians suggest that the glorification of business and trade by social commentators such as Defoe reflected England's emphasis on commercial prowess, one of the factors Mathias puts forward as a leading cause of the Industrial Revolution. However, Defoe also notes the importance of international trade in creating Britain's wealth.*

>> 46. The Complete English Tradesman

DANIEL DEFOE [1726]

The word 'tradesmen,' in England, does not sound so harsh as it does in other countries; and to say a gentleman-tradesman, is not so much nonsense as some people would persuade us to reckon it; and, indeed, the very name of an English tradesman, will and does already obtain in the world; [...] the English tradesman may be allowed to rank with the best gentlemen in Europe. [...]

And hence it is natural to ask, whence comes all this to be so? How is it produced? War has not done it; no, nor so much as helped or assisted to it; it is not by any martial exploits; we have made no conquests abroad, added no new kingdoms to British empire, reduced no neighboring nations,

---

Source: Daniel Defoe , *The Complete English Tradesman,* in *The Novels and Miscellaneous Works of Daniel Defoe,* vol. XVII (Oxford: D.A. Talboys, 1841), 248–250, 252–253.

or extended the possession of our monarchs into the properties of others; we have gained nothing by war and encroachment; we are butted and bounded just where we were in Queen Elizabeth's time. […]

These things prove abundantly that the greatness of the British nation is not owing to war and conquests, to enlarging its dominions by the sword, or subjecting the people of other countries to our power; but it is all owing to trade, to the increase of our commerce at home, and the extending it abroad.

It is owing to trade, that new discoveries have been made in lands unknown, and new settlements and plantations made, new colonies planted, and new governments formed, in the uninhabited islands, and the uncultivated continent of America; and those plantings and settlements have again enlarged and increased the trade, and thereby the wealth and power of the nation by whom they were discovered and planted, we have not increased our power, or the number of our subjects, by subduing the nations which possess those countries, and incorporating them into our own; but have entirely planted our colonies, and peopled the countries with our own subjects, natives of the island; and, excepting the negroes, which we transport from Africa to America, as slaves to work in the sugar and tobacco plantations, all our colonies, as well in the islands, as on the continent of America, are entirely peopled from Great Britain and Ireland, and chiefly the former; the natives having either removed further up into the country, or, by their own folly and treachery raising war against us, been destroyed and cut off. […]

The same trade […] is the cause of the well-living of the people here; for as frugality is not the national virtue of England, so the people that get much, spend much; and as they work hard, so they live well, eat and drink well, clothe warm, and lodge soft; in a word, the working manufacturing people of England, eat the fat, drink the sweet, live better, and fare better, than the working poor of any other nation in Europe; they make better wages of their work, and spend more of the money upon their backs and bellies than in any other country. This expense of the poor, as it causes a prodigious consumption both of the provisions and the manufactures of our country at home, so two things are undeniably the consequence of the part.

1. The consumption of provisions increases the rent and value of the lands; and this raises the gentlemen's estates, and that again increases the employment of people, and consequently the numbers of them, as well those that are employed in the husbandry of land, breeding and feeding of cattle, &c., as of servants to the gentlemen's families, who as their estates increase in value, so they increase their families and equipages.

2. As the people get greater wages, so they, I mean the same poorer part of the people, clothe better, and furnish better; and this increases the consumption of the very manufactures they make; then that consumption increases the quantity made; and this creates what we call inland trade, by which innumerable families are employed, and the increase of the people maintained; and by which increase of trade and people the present growing prosperity of this nation is produced.

The Price of the Atlantic Slave Trade for Africa

The Afro-Guyanese historian Walter Rodney was one of a number of scholars who, in the 1960s and 1970s, began to work on the topic of **underdevelopment.** *Throughout those decades historians and social scientists in the newly independent states of Africa and Asia, alongside revisionists in Europe and the Americas, began to question why* *some regions of the world and some groups were so poor. One of the leading scholars of this movement, Andre Gunder Frank, coined the phrase "the development of under-development" to describe the way in which Asian, Latin American, and especially African states were impoverished by the same transformations—like the development of industrialization—that enriched parts of Europe and the United States. Walter Rodney's text* How Europe Underdeveloped Africa *suggests that the combination of the Atlantic slave trade and industrialization in Europe denied Africa of much of its population, natural resources, and innovative potential. Rodney's arguments have come to be criticized by a number of historians who suggest that Africa had other problems such as a difficult environment, and that Africans participated in the slave trade as enslavers, raiders, and slave sellers. Others, however, continue to come to Rodney's defense.*

>> 47. How Europe Underdeveloped Africa

WALTER RODNEY [1972]

To discuss trade between Africans and Europeans in the four centuries before colonial rule is virtually to discuss slave trade. Strictly speaking, the African only became a slave when he reached a society where he worked as a slave. Before that, he was first a free man and then a captive. Nevertheless, it is acceptable to speak of the trade in slaves when referring to the shipment of captives from Africa to various other parts of the world where they were to live and work as the property of Europeans. The title of this section is deliberately chosen to call attention to the fact that the shipments were all by Europeans to markets controlled by Europeans, and this was in the interest of European capitalism and nothing else. [...]

When one tries to measure the effect of European slave trading on the African continent, it is essential to realize that one is measuring the effect of social violence rather than trade in any normal sense of the word.

Many things remain uncertain about the slave trade and its consequences for Africa, but the general picture of destructiveness is clear, and that destructiveness can be shown to be the logical consequence of the manner of recruitment of captives in Africa. [...]

The massive loss to the African labor force was made more critical because it was composed of able bodied, young men and young women. Slave buyers preferred their victims between the ages of fifteen and thirty five, and preferably in the early twenties; the sex ratio being about two men to one woman. Europeans often accepted younger African children, but rarely any older person. They shipped the most healthy wherever possible, taking the trouble to get those who had already survived any attack of smallpox and who were therefore immune from further attacks of that disease, which was then one of the world's great killer diseases. [...]

No one has been able to come up with a figure representing total losses to the African population sustained through the extraction of slave labor from all areas to all destinations over the many centuries that slave trade existed. However, on every other continent from the fifteenth century onwards, the population showed constant and sometimes spectacular natural increase; while it is striking that the same did not apply to Africa. [...]

African economic activity was affected both directly and indirectly by population loss. For instance, when the inhabitants of a given area were reduced below a certain number in an environment where the tsetse fly was present, the remaining few had to abandon the area.

Source: Walter Rodney, *How Europe Underdeveloped Africa* (Washington, D.C.: Howard University Press, 1982), 95–99. Originally published in 1972.

In effect, enslavement was causing these people to lose their battle to tame and harness nature—a battle which is at the basis of development. Violence almost meant insecurity. The opportunity presented by European slave dealers became the major (though not the only) stimulus for a great deal of social violence between different African communities and within any given community. It took the form more of raiding and kidnapping than of regular warfare, and that fact increased the element of fear and uncertainty. [...]

The changeover to warlike activities and kidnapping must have affected all branches of economic activity, and agriculture in particular. Occasionally, in certain localities food production was increased to provide supplies for slave ships, but the overall consequences of slaving on agricultural activities in Western, Eastern, and Central Africa were negative.

The Evil of Slavery

Ottobah Cuguano was an important figure of the eighteenth-century Atlantic world. A free African enslaved into the Atlantic slave trade, he eventually earned enough money to purchase his freedom and became a leading abolitionist, fighting for the end of slavery. Cuguano was born into a Fante state in the region located in what is today the country of Ghana. He was kidnapped as a young boy and forced to work on plantations on the Caribbean island of Grenada, before being brought to Britain where he managed to free himself and write an attack on the slave system. In his book, Cuguano spent only five pages on his own autobiography. Much of the rest of the book focuses on exposing the rapacity of the system and in countering the racist arguments of pro-slave politicians and writers. In the first part of the following selection Cuguano describes the role of Africans in the procurement of slaves. In the second, he writes about the European slave traders. Finally, he gives us a glimpse into the experiences of the newly enslaved Africans.

>> 48. Thoughts and Sentiments on the Evil of Slavery

OTTOBAH CUGOANO [1787]

These slave-procurers are a set of as great villains as any in the world. They often steal and kidnap many more than they buy at first if they can meet with them by the way; and they have only their certain boundaries to go to, and sell them from one to another; so that if they are sought after and detected, the thieves are seldom found, and the others only plead that they bought them so and so. These kid-nappers and slave-procurers, called merchants, are a species of African villains, which are greatly corrupted, and even viciated by their intercourse with the Europeans; but, wicked and barbarous as they certainly are, I can hardly think, if they knew what horrible barbarity they were sending their fellow-creatures to, that they would do it. But the artful Europeans have so deceived them, that they are bought by their inventions of merchandize, and beguiled into it by their artifice; for the Europeans, at their factories, in some various manner, have always kept some as servants to them, and with gaudy cloaths, in a gay manner, as decoy ducks to deceive others, and to tell them that they want many more to go over the sea, and be as they are. So in that respect, wherein it may be said that they will sell one another, they are only ensnared and

Source: Ottobah Cugoano, *Thoughts and Sentiments on the Evil of Slavery* (London: Dawsons, 1969), 26–27, 94–96.

enlisted to be servants, kept like some of those which they see at the factories, which, for some gewgaws, as presents given to themselves and friends, they are hereby enticed to go; and something after the same manner that East-India soldiers are procured in Britain; and the inhabitants here, just as much sell themselves, and one another, as they do; and the kid-nappers here, and the slave-procurers in Africa, are much alike. But many other barbarous methods are made use of by the vile instigators, procurers and ensnarers of men; and some of the wicked and profligate princes and chiefs of Africa accept of presents, from the Europeans, to procure a certain number of slaves; and thereby they are wickedly instigated to go to war with one another on purpose to get them, which produces many terrible depredations; and sometimes when those engagements are entered into, and they find themselves defeated of their purpose, it has happened that some of their own people have fallen a sacrifice to their avarice and cruelty. And it may be said of the Europeans, that they have made use of every insidious method to procure slaves whenever they can, and that their forts and factories are the avowed dens of thieves for robbers, plunderers and depredators. [...]

The Royal African Company (as it is called, ought rather to be reversed as unworthy of the name) was incorporated 14th Charles II and impowered to trade from Salle in South Barbary to the Cape of Good Hope, and to erect forts and factories on the western coast of Africa for that purpose. But this trade was laid open by an act of parliament, Anno 1697, and every private merchant permitted to trade thither, upon paying the sum of ten pounds towards maintaining the forts and garrisons. This Company, for securing their commerce, erected several factories on the coast; the most remarkable are these, viz. on the North part of Guinea, James Fort, upon an island in the River Gambia, Sierra Leona, and Sherbro; and on the South part of Guinea, viz. on the Gold Coast, Dick's Cove, Succunda, Commenda, Cape Coast Castle, Fort Royal, Queen Anne's Point, Charles Fort, Annamabo, Winebah, Shidoe, Acra, &c. In all these places it is their grand business to traffic in the human species; and dreadful and shocking as it is to think, it has even been established by royal authority, and is still supported and carried on under a Christian government; and this must evidently appear thereby, that the learned, the civilized, and even the enlightened nations are become as truly barbarous and brutish as the unlearned.

To give any just conception of the barbarous traffic carried on at those factories, it would be out of my power to describe the miserable situation of the poor exiled Africans, which by the craft of wicked men daily become their prey, though I have seen enough of their misery as well as read; no description can give an adequate idea of the horror of their feelings, and the dreadful calamities they undergo. The treacherous, perfidious and cruel methods made use of in procuring them, are horrible and shocking. The bringing them to the ships and factories, and subjecting them to brutal examinations stripped naked and markings, is barbarous and base. The flowing them in the holds of the ships like goods of burden, with closeness and stench, is deplorable; and, what makes addition to this deplorable situation, they are often treated in the most barbarous and inhuman manner by the unfeeling monsters of Captains. And when they arrive at the destined port in the colonies, they are again stripped naked for the brutal examination of their purchasers to view them, which, to many, must add shame and grief to their other woe, as may be evidently seen with sorrow, melancholy and despair marked upon their countenances. Here again another scene of grief and lamentation arises;—friends and near relations must be parted, never to meet again, nor knowing to whence they go. Here daughters are clinging to their mothers, and mothers to their daughters, bedewing each others naked breasts with tears; here fathers, mothers, and children, locked in each others arms, are begging never to be separated; here the husband will be pleading for his wife, and the wife praying for her children, and entreating, enough to melt the most obdurate heart, not to be torn from them, and taken away from her husband; and some will be still weeping for their native shore, and their dear relations and friends, and other endearing connections which they have left behind, and have been barbarously tore away from, and all are bemoaning themselves with grief and lamentation at the prospect of their wretched fate.

Working Girls in Great Britain and West Africa

In Britain, the factories and mines of the new industrial society required vast amounts of labor, and children were the cheapest laborers available. Pay was low and dangers were high, but impoverished families often were forced to put their children into employment at very young ages. In West Africa, meanwhile, the Atlantic slave trade had helped to create an enormous market for slaves. Here, children were desired as workers not because they were cheaper but because they were less likely to successfully run away. Some were put to work carrying heavy loads of raw materials to be taken from African coastal ports to factories in Britain and elsewhere. Others were employed in homes. Eventually, reformers began to criticize the conditions and employment of children in both places. In Britain, hearings on child labor were part of a broader reform movement that eventually came to more broadly regulate how employers could treat workers. In West Africa, similar laws were passed by colonial authorities, but were much more seldom enforced. In the two testimonies below, one from Britain and one from the British Gold Coast colony, note the similarities and differences of two young women in different places but around the same time.

>> 49. Testimonies of Elizabeth Bentley and Abina Mansah

[1833/1876]

Elizabeth Bentley, questioned by members of the Commission for Inquiry into the Employment of Children in Factories, Great Britain, 1833

What age are you?—Twenty-three....

What time did you begin work at a factory?—When I was six years old....

What was your business in that mill?—I was a little doffer [machine-cleaner].

What were your hours of labor in that mill?—From 5 in the morning till 9 at night, when they were thronged.

For how long a time together have you worked that excessive length of time?—For about half a year.

What were your usual hours of labor when you were not so thronged—From 6 in the morning till 7 at night.

What time was allowed for your meals?—Forty minutes at noon.

Explain what it is you had to do.—When the frames are full, they have to stop the frames, and take the flyers off, and take the full bobbins off, and carry them to the roller; and then put empty ones on, and set the frames on again.

Source: Testimony of Elizabeth Bentley, Commission for Inquiry Into the Employment of Children in Factories. Second Report. 1833. Testimony of Abina Mansah, in the case of Regina v Quamina Eddoo, Gold Coast, 1876.

Does that keep you constantly on your feet?—Yes, there are so many frames and they run so quick.

Your labor is very excessive?—Yes; you have not time for anything.

Suppose you flagged a little, or were too late, what would they do?—Strap us.

Are they in the habit of strapping those who are last in doffing?—Yes.

Constantly?—Yes.

Girls as well as boys?—Yes.

Have you ever been strapped?—Yes.

Severely?—Yes.

Could you eat your food well in that factory?—No, indeed, I had not much to eat, and the little I had I could not it, my appetite was so poor, and being covered with dust; and it was no use to take it home, I could not eat it.

Abina Mansah, questioned by Judicial Assessor Melton of the Cape Coast Judicial Assessor's Court

Narrates: A man called Yowawhah brought me from Ashantee...He brought me to Salt Pond. Yowawhah went on purchasing goods. On the same day as he finished, he handed me over to defendant to be with him, and said that he was going back and would return.

About ten days after the defendant gave me two cloths and told me that he had given me in marriage to...Tandoe. And the defendant said that if I did not consent to be married to Tandoe he would tie me up and flog me.

Do you [think] then that you were a slave?—Yes, I thought I was a slave, because when I went for water of firewood I was not paid.

Were you placed with any woman to work?—He (defendant) gave me to his sister to live with her, because I am a woman. Eccoah is the name of defendant's sister...

How were you employed during the time you were with Eccoah?—I swept the house, I go for water and firewood and I cooked and when I cooked I ate some. I went to market to buy vegetables I did so by the order of Eccoah.

Did defendant or Eccoah make an agreement with you to pay you any wages for your services?—No I worked for nothing.

Were you...during that time beaten for misconduct or anything like that?—When I was with Eddo Buffoe and did wrong I was flogged and sometimes I was logged [imprisoned by being chained to a log].

>> Mastering the Material

1. According to Mathias, what factors led to the early development of the Industrial Revolution in Britain?

2. Defoe argues that Britain was the greatest commercial state in the world in the eighteenth century. Does his argument seem to better support Mathias' emphasis on internal context or Williams' theory of global trade as the cause of the first Industrial Revolution in Britain?

3. What is the "Williams thesis"? What type of evidence does the author use to try to prove a connection between profits from slavery and the Industrial Revolution? How successful is he?

4. What does Rodney suggest were the effects of the Atlantic slave trade and industrialization in Africa? How convincing do you find his arguments?

5. How does Cuguano's narrative seem to support or refute Rodney's thesis?

6. Cuguano argues that the Africans participating in the slave trade would cease to provide slaves if they knew how terrible conditions were on the American plantations. Do you think this seems likely?

7. What similarities do you see in the testimonies of Elizabeth Bentley and Abina Mansah? What are the differences?

8. Elizabeth Bentley and Abina Mansah worked in different jobs in different parts of the world, but both at the height of the Industrial Revolution. What kinds of connections can we draw between them? How can we study them in the same frame of reference, as world historians would do, rather than separately?

>> Making Connections

1. Does the Williams thesis seem to support Pomeranz' arguments (Reading 31)? How or how not?

2. Consider the state of eighteenth- and nineteenth-century African societies described by Cuguano and Rodney to those of the sixteenth and seventeenth century depicted by Thornton (Reading 17). How do they seem different? What had changed for large portions of Africa in the intervening period?

Chapter 11

Exploring Pathways to Revolution and Reform in Asia

It is ironic that, whereas historians have tended to look for internal causes of Atlantic revolutions first, they overwhelmingly attribute revolutions and reform movements in Asia to the impact of contact with Europe and the United States rather than to internal transformation. This difference illustrates the dominance, until recently, of the traditional European conception of global history: that western Europeans modernized first and that other parts of the world could only modernize by adopting western concepts and technologies. The uncoupling of modernization from westernization is a controversial task, but one that many, especially Asian scholars, have recently undertaken.

In the period studied in Part 2, Asian states underwent a number of important changes that could be termed revolutionary. In southwest Asia (the Middle East) a series of upheavals and reforms gradually propelled the fragmentation of the multiethnic Ottoman Empire into independent nation-states. In Japan two dramatic events unified a fragmented but populous island and resulted in a unique but rapidly developing state. Possibly the largest revolutionary movements in the world during this period were in China. Admittedly, the uprisings in China—including the Taiping Rebellion of 1851–1854 and a series of Muslim separatist revolts—failed to overthrow the Chinese regime. They were nevertheless highly significant episodes. India in the eighteenth and nineteenth century saw a shift away from the Mughal Empire and toward the British Empire, which became the dominant regional power if not yet the sovereign authority throughout India. Yet even here the period was closed by the Indian Rebellion of 1857 (often called the Sepoy Mutiny), which indicated the potential for Indian unity and the coalescing of new senses of Indian identity. All of these events occurred in the context of increased Asian–European interaction, and in each case the major players—the agents of change—were members of local communities. From peasant visionaries to disgruntled colonial soldiers to aristocratic elites, Asians in this period sought to shape their political, economic, and social environments just as did French, Haitian, and Latin American revolutionaries.

Recent scholarship on Asian reforms and revolutions generally acknowledges Asians as the leading actors in these events, but many historians still defend the notion that it was Western influences that touched them off. Western ideas and technology, they argue, catalyzed conflict between traditionalists and reformers in Asia. Exposed to the industrialized, democratizing, scientific west, some Asians responded by seeking to emulate western states in a process often called responsive or **defensive modernization.** Chief among these modernizers were merchants and other members of Asiatic bourgeoisies. In each case they were opposed by entrenched classes who fought to stave off change. As was the case in Europe, these "traditionalists" were often led by landowning aristocrats who believed the changes proposed by the reformers would diminish their power, possibly by increasing the power of the bourgeoisie. Other opponents of reform may have resisted change for cultural or personal reasons.

According to this model of Asiatic revolution and transformation, the major Asiatic upheavals of this period were the result of conflicts between these traditionalist and reformer parties. The outcome of these struggles differed in each state. In some cases—as in China—the traditionalists won and attempts at reform were quashed. In other cases—like Japan—the reformers won. This differing outcome has been used to explain Japan's apparent success at modernization and China's failure. By the late nineteenth century Japan would become an imperial power competing with Europeans and even defeating them in conflict. China, on the other hand, would become partially dismembered by European imperialists. Yet not all researchers admit the primacy of Western influence in the development of reforming classes. In Turkey and Japan especially, Asian scholars and their allies have been successful in demonstrating the causative impact of internal society, culture, politics, and economics. The result has been movement toward a synthesis of internal and external interpretations of the origins of the Meiji Restoration and the Ottoman reforms.

The early nineteenth-century reforms of Sultan Selim III, ruler of the Ottoman Empire, have often been seen purely as a defensive reaction to the growing power of the West represented by the defeat of Ottoman forces by Russian and Austrian forces in a long war (1787–1792), and especially to the successful invasion of the Ottoman province of Egypt by a French army under the command of Napoleon Bonaparte in 1798. Selim consequently undertook a modernization of the army known as the "new order," attempting to replace the empires' slave-soldiers—the *janissaries*—with a modern conscript army. He also tried to reform landownership and taxation. As Thomas Naff shows in "Reform and the Conduct of Ottoman Diplomacy in the Reign of Selim III," some of Selim's most significant reforms were in the area of international relations, where Selim attempted to make alliances with both neighboring eastern European states and the great powers of France and Britain. In their ongoing global war, both of these great powers were eager to contract alliances with the Ottomans, as is illustrated by the Anglo-Turkish treaty of 1799.

Naff treats Selim's reforms as merely one step in Ottoman society's gradual acceptance of the superiority of the west. Not all scholars agree. A leading Turkish historian, Kemal Karpat, has suggested that Selim's innovations were in fact chiefly undertaken in response to the growing power of the Ottoman bourgeoisie, especially represented by the *a'yan*. The *a'yan* were entrepreneurs and local notables who began to replace royally appointed cavalry officers—*sipahis*—as the most powerful rural groups at about the same time as urban commercial classes developed in the great Ottoman cities. In "The Stages of Ottoman History," Karpat argues that in the period leading up to Selim's enthronement the *a'yan* in many regions had begun to assume important legal functions previously monopolized by the agents of the Sultan. Selim III perceived this class as potential revolutionaries, and thus he tried throughout his reign to diminish their power by strengthening the throne. His reforms can therefore be interpreted principally as an attempt to stave off a revolution from the inside, rather than as a response to Western incursions. Yet the role of Turkey's relations with the European powers cannot entirely be ignored, and the reforms adopted by Selim were largely patterned on European models.

The second transformation discussed in this chapter is the Meiji *Ishin* in Japan, alternately labeled the Meiji Restoration. The Ishin was a political event marked by the replacement of a ruling warlord—the Tokoguwa Shogun—by the Japanese emperor, previously merely a figurehead. It made possible changes in policy that allowed Japan's rapid industrialization, its adaptation of Western military organization and technology, and its development of a unique representative political system. For two-and-a-half centuries leading up to the Meiji Ishin, the Tokugawa Shoguns had administered Japan as a relatively decentralized realm with over 300 semi-independent feudal lords, the *daimyo*. The daimyo were the highest level of a hereditary class of landowning aristocrats, the *samurai*. The shoguns generally possessed enough power to keep the peace between the daimyo through their authority over the *bakufu*—the bureaucracy and state administrative bodies—yet did not determine the day-to-day affairs of the provinces.

From the seventeenth century onward the Tokugawa Shoguns maintained a policy of isolating Japan from the outside world. Yet in the nineteenth century this separation became increasingly difficult to sustain. The Japanese were alarmed by European military victories over other Asian states, particularly China's defeat by the British navy and army in the Opium Wars. In addition, some daimyo at the extreme edges of Japan were attracted by the commercial opportunities offered by European merchants, and these daimyo began to contravene the Shogunate's isolationist restrictions. The arrival of an American fleet off the capital of Edo (Tokyo) in 1853 with orders to "open the door" to American commerce merely marked the culmination of the weakening of Japan's isolation. The Tokugawa were forced—literally at canon-point—to make concessions first to the United States and later to European powers. Yet, the Japanese scholar Shibahara Takuji has recently argued that although these ostentatious events closely preceded the Meiji Ishin, their importance should not be overestimated. In "Japan's Modernization from the Perspective of International Relations" Takuji suggests that Japan was able to modernize successfully in part because of a relative *lack* of interest in Japan from the industrial powers. This was especially notable when compared to China, which was the subject of earlier and more sustained Western predatory commerce.

In "The Meiji Revolution and Japan's Modernization," Kuwabara Takeo takes a very different approach. Takeo in fact suggests that the Meiji Ishin was largely the result of Japan's unique geography, experiences, and culture, and was therefore quite unlike any other national revolution. For example, the Ishin was led not by merchants but rather by a group of Japan's powerful daimyo and samurai. Yet their new administration gradually abolished class distinctions and created an egalitarian education system and a true sense of nation, as is illustrated by the Charter Oath of 1868. How did this happen? Some historians have speculated that the new regime needed the aid of peasants to defeat traditionalists who opposed the changes. Others, however, have suggested that Japan, even before the revolution, had already begun to embrace greater egalitarianism. Takeo, for example, cites the high Japanese literacy rates as evidence of this development. The Ishin was also uniquely Japanese in that the emperor was retained as the divine symbol of the state. Some scholars have argued that the Meiji Emperor was merely a powerless figurehead, yet he had symbolic value to the peasantry, at least, and thus came to represent the new Japanese nationalism.

In both the reforms of Selim III and the Meiji Ishin, global and local factors interplayed to give shape and meaning to transformations in Asia. In this, these events are not really different from the rebellions in the Americas, the French Revolution, and the experiences of Britain and Africa at the advent of the Industrial Revolution.

Diplomacy and Modernization in the Ottoman Empire

Selim III took the throne during a conflict with Russia and Austria that ended in Ottoman defeat in 1792. Alongside military defeat came financial difficulties, and Selim therefore moved to reform not just the Ottoman army but also state finances and diplomacy. The Sultan, who considered international relations essential to his revitalization projects, attempted to forge alliances such as those that bound the states of Europe together. This article, written by Thomas Naff, suggests that a realistic assessment of European military supremacy was the driving force behind Selim's diplomatic reforms. Although Naff concludes that the changes eventually failed to accomplish their goal, he does suggest that Selim helped to open the Ottoman Empire up to Western innovations. Naff, while highly critical of the Sultan's reform attempts, is entirely uncritical of the notion of Western superiority.

>> 50. Reform and the Conduct of Ottoman Diplomacy in the Reign of Selim III, 1789–1807

THOMAS NAFF [1963]

In the grand days of the Ottoman Empire, diplomacy had relatively little effect on affairs of state. [...]

But by the end of the 17th century, the Empire had reached the verge of collapse. With their Empire in decay, and with the once splendid Janissaries more often at their throats than at their backs, the Sultans were uniformly unsuccessful in checking either the decline of their state or the advances of their enemies. They were forced, in these circumstances, to negotiate at almost every turn of events, with the result that diplomacy came to be more and more indispensable to the maintenance of their realm. [...]

It was not until the reign of Selim III (1789-1807) that reform was undertaken with determination. Selim was wholeheartedly committed to reform not only to keep his domain intact, but, above all, to restore the Empire to its former greatness. He was intelligent enough to realize that to accomplish his mission he must emulate the technical progress of Europe, and so he attempted to order and modernize some of his state's basic institutions after the pattern of the European powers. The primary objective of his reform program was to regenerate the military might of his Empire. Consequently, it must be emphasized that all other reforms, including those in the sphere of diplomacy, were intended in one way or another to contribute to the attainment of that goal.

Source: Thomas Naff, "Reform and the Conduct of Ottoman Diplomacy in the Reign of Selim III, 1789–1807," *Journal of the American Oriental Society* 83 (1963): 295, 310–311, 315.

However, Selim was aware that "like the wheels of a watch" the affairs of government were interconnected, and reform must be comprehensive if it were to be successful. Given such awareness, and the fact that diplomacy had, by Selim's reign, become one of the vital branches of the Ottoman government, the diplomatic establishment occupied a large place in the remedial schemes of the Sultan and his advisers. [...]

Although Selim's diplomatic reforms were of a technical sort involving the mechanisms of diplomacy, some comment must be made about policy. The formulation of policy remained fundamentally in the hands of the Sultan, the Grand Vizir, and their inner circle of advisers, with the *Reis ūl-Küttab* playing an expanding role. What concerns us here, rather, is a new development in Ottoman foreign policy which was initiated by Selim III. He embraced the principle that sound alliances were essential in the times to acquire strength and security.

For decades it had been apparent that the Ottomans were incapable of defending themselves without foreign assistance. But the only source of effective military support was Europe. Yet the myopic Islamic view toward Europe, and the political rivalries of the European powers themselves, inhibited the Sublime Porte from involving itself in Europe's alliance systems. However, Selim realized he could not preserve his domain by continuing such unrealistic attitudes. Thus, shortly after his accession, even before he embarked upon his reforms, Selim deviated from traditional Ottoman unilateralism by entering into separate defensive alliances with Sweden and Prussia, who, in 1790, were also at war with Russia. But he did not do so without opposition from legal and religious quarters. [...]

Selim's reforms, praiseworthy and courageous as they were, can hardly be said to have achieved even the moderate aims of their promoters. Neither the new techniques, which were adopted, nor the principles which guided Ottoman diplomacy made the Empire appreciably stronger or foreign policy more effective, at least during Selim's reign. Furthermore, while the paraphernalia of Ottoman diplomacy had few strong features to redeem its inherent weakness, the one factor which might have sustained and braced it, the military, remained too corrupt and weak to be effectual. [...]

Selim, in his limited attempts at modernization, retained most of the old apparatus and methods of Ottoman diplomacy, and this fact leads us to the root cause of his failure: Although he was willing to experiment with westernizing reforms, he was unwilling to recast the Islamic mould of the state. [...]

And yet, despite failure, it cannot be concluded that the results of Selim's labors were all negative. Western innovations and particularly western ideas, did not end with Selim's reign. They found in the decayed Ottoman Empire a rich soil in which they eventually took root. Selim's diplomatic reforms made a particular contribution to this process. His establishment of permanent embassies in Europe did enable a few young Ottomans to learn a European language and to inform themselves about some of the revolutionary ideas current in Europe. Some, on their return, "became officials at the Porte, where they formed a Westward-looking minority among the bureaucratic hierarchy, similar to that created among the officers by the military and naval reforms."

Treaty of Alliance between England and the Ottoman Empire

Although he greatly admired Napoleon, Selim III was induced to make his first major diplomatic alliance with the French Emperor's greatest enemy, Britain. There are two reasons for this. First, France was at war with an Ottoman neighbor, Russia, which Selim hesitated to antagonize. Second, Napoleon had invaded a nominal Ottoman province,

Egypt. In this 1799 treaty, note the commitments made by both sides. The treaty required such an extensive commitment on the part of the British government that they kept it secret until it expired in 1808.

>> 51. Treaty of Alliance between England and Turkey, 5 January 1799

[1799]

....ART. I. His Britannic Majesty, connected already with His Majesty the Emperor of Russia by the ties or the strictest alliance, accedes, by the present Treaty, to the Defensive Alliance which has just been concluded between His Majesty the Ottoman Emperor and the Emperor of Russia, as far as the Stipulations thereof are applicable to the local circumstances of His Empire, and of that of the Sublime Porte, and His Majesty the Ottoman Emperor enters reciprocally by this Treaty into the same engagements towards His Britannic Majesty; so that there shall exist for ever between the three Empires, by virtue of the present Defensive Treaty, and of the Alliances and Treaties which already subsist, peace, good understanding, and perfect friendship, as well by sea as land, so that for the future, the friends of one of the parties shall, in like manner, be considered as such by the others. On this account, the two High Contracting Parties promise and engage to come to a frank and mutual engagement, in all affairs in which their reciprocal safety and tranquillity may be interested, and to adopt, by common consent, the necessary measures to oppose every project hostile towards themselves, and to effectuate general tranquility.

II....the two High Contracting Parties mutually guarantee to each other their possessions; [...] His Britannic Majesty guarantees all the possessions of the Ottoman Empire, without exception, such as they stood immediately before the invasion of the French, in Egypt; and His Majesty the Ottoman Emperor guarantees all the possessions of Great Britain, without any exception whatever.

III. Notwithstanding the two Contracting Parties reserve to themselves the full right of entering into negotiation with other powers, and to conclude with them whatever Treaties their interests may require, yet they mutually bind themselves in the strongest manner, that such Treaties shall not contain any Condition which can ever produce the least detriment, injury, or prejudice, to either of them, or affect the integrity of their Dominions. On the contrary, they promise to regard, and preserve, to their utmost, their reciprocal honour, safety, and advantage.

IV. In every case of a hostile attack upon the Dominions of one of the Contracting Parties, the succours which the other is to furnish shall be regulated by the principles of good faith, and in conformity with the· close friendship subsisting between the two Empires, according to the nature of the case. [...]

X. In order to render more efficacious the succour to be furnished on both sides during the war, according to the spirit of the present Treaty of Alliance, the two High Contracting Parties will consult together upon the operations most suitable to be made, in order to render abortive the pernicious designs of the enemy, in general, and especially in Egypt, and to destroy their commerce in the seas of the Levant, and in the Mediterranean; and for this purpose His Majesty the Ottoman Emperor engages not only to shut all his ports, without exception against the commerce of the enemy, but likewise to employ against them, in his dominions, (and in order to prevent the execution of their ambitious projects), an army, consisting at least of 100,000 men,

Source: Treaty of Alliance between England and Turkey, 5 January 1799, in *Documents of Near East Diplomatic History,* edited by J. C. Hurewitz (New York: Columbia University, 1951), 18–20.

and even to augment it in case of need, to the extent of his whole forces. He shall also put his naval forces in a state of preparation, to act in concert with those of his Allies in the seas above mentioned. And His Britannic Majesty, on his part, reciprocally engages himself to employ, in the same seas, a naval force always equal to that of the enemy, to annoy them, and to act in concert with the fleets of his Allies, in order to impede the execution of their plans, and especially to prevent any attack upon the Dominions or Provinces of the Ottoman Empire....

A Reconsideration of Selim III's Reforms

Kemal Karpat is a leading scholar of Ottoman history, especially Ottoman reformism and the evolution of Turkish nationalism. In the following selection of his work, he argues that during much of the early modern period a rural elite called the a'yan *was developing in regions of the Ottoman Empire. Drawn especially from peasant community leaders, the* a'yan *challenged their* sipahi *officials, in some cases by taking over their positions. In this way they tried to shape local government to their own needs. This rural leadership, along with urban merchants, was the greatest threat Selim III had to confront, and Karpat suggests that his reforms were in part an attempt to strengthen the central government against them. Although Selim's reforms were limited, they were carried futher by his successor, Mahmud II.*

>> 52. "The Stages of Ottoman History": A Structural Comparative Approach

KEMAL H. KARPAT [1974]

Provincial Autonomy, and the Ayans, 1603–1789

This is probably the moat important and possibly the most neglected period in Ottoman history during its transition to the modem age. It is important because many of the nineteenth century reforms, as well as the rise of national states in the Balkans, are rooted in the socio-economic developments which occurred at this stage. It is important also because of a drastic change in the criteria for the selection of elites; instead of an elite status decided by the ruling authority, there was a self-status-seeking effort by lower class people based on their economic power. [...]

The emergence of the *ayans* as the most important social group outside the government is the outstanding mark of this period. Functionally speaking, they were a new group, but used some of the ancient titles common in the Middle East, such as *ayan-esraf* given to communal leaders or notables; hence the mistaken idea of social continuity defended by some scholars. The *ayans* were neither the heirs of the *sipahis*, as far as land ownership was concerned, nor were they former *sipahis* who usurped the state lands and thus emerged as a new proprietary group. [...]

The specific *ayans* we are referring to rose primarily in the eighteenth century because of a scarcity of personnel necessary to administer the state lands and to collect taxes for the government. It seems that there were two sources for the rise of the *ayans*. First, there were the old communal leaders known as *ayans* or *esraf* among Muslims, and *corbaci* among the

Source: Kemal H. Karpat, "The Stages of Ottoman History: A Structural Comparative Approach," in *The Ottoman State and Its Place in World History*, edited by Kemal H. Karpat (Leiden: E. J. Brill, 1974), 90–93.

non-Muslims, or *multezims* in Egypt. These it was claimed, were elected (this election has not been fully ascertained) by the population in their respective districts and town quarters, and were responsible for local administration, order, and security. Second, there were enterprising individuals rising from every social stratum, including peasants and rank-and-file soldiers who achieved social preeminence by taking advantage of the opportunities in land administration and the tax collection. The function of the *ayans* expanded. On behalf of the state they assumed administrative roles in leasing state lands to villages and peasants, and signed the *tapu*, the lease deed which later acquired the meaning of property title. [...] The same *ayans* also assumed important roles on as assessors of taxes on individual villagers as well as tax collectors. Eventually they auctioned the tax and became tax farmers. Moreover, as the *ayans'* local influence increased, they emerged as key elements in the administration of towns and even small regions. Consequently, the government saw it as practical to bureaucratize this natural social growth by recognizing it as an institution, the *ayanlik*. It began issuing *berat*, title deeds to those whom it recognized as such. Many of the *ayans*, however, functioned without the government's *berat* in open defiance of the established traditions of authority.

It is interesting to note that the *ayans* associated many of the functions performed previously by the *sipahis* with regard to land administration and tax collection. But unlike the *sipahis* of the past who was appointed by the government, the *ayan* rose from society at large, often by relying upon his own initiative, and established a leadership position based upon his own wealth and influence in the community. [...]

The *ayans'* power increased rapidy. Chief *ayans*, referred to also as *derebeys*, or lords of the valley, who were backed by lesser *ayans*, assumed extensive power. They became the rulers of extensive territories and successfully defied the central government. The reign of

Selim III (1789–1807) consisted of an incessant struggle against the *ayans* of Anatolia and the Balkans. The institution of *ayanlik* was formally abolished in 1786, but the government became unable to gather taxes or even to draft soldiers and reestablished it in 1790. Thus, it became apparent to the *ayans* that their social position, if not legalized, was in danger, while the sultan and the upper bureaucracy realized that the *ayans*, who had economic power and exercised influence in the local communities, threatened their own authority. The conflict was solved first in favor of the *ayans*, who under the leadership of Mustafa Pasa, the *ayan* of Ruscuk, were instrumental in bringing Mahmud II to the throne in 1808. The same year they secured from the new sultan the *Sened-i Ittifak*, or the Pact of Alliance. This pact, signed by the Porte and the chief *ayans*, legalized the *ayans'* property rights, accorded inheritance rights to their sons, and freed them from official government interference in local administration.

The period under discussion, as well as the rise of the *ayans*, cannot be understood without taking into account the gradual liberalization and intensification of trade, the changes in the modes of production, the expansion of market economy, the accumulation of capital in private hands, and the search for investment outlets in agriculture, as clearly demonstrated by the frantic efforts by Turkish businessmen inhabiting the Danube towns to invest in the Wallachian lands.

Thus, the rise of the *ayans* and of their future allies, the commercial groups in towns, their defense of individual property, freedom of trade, and even of a primitive form of capitalism, and eventually their opposition to absolutism (Ziya Gökalp, the ideologue of Turkish nationalism pointed out this fact), heralded probably the most fundamental stage of transformation in Ottoman history. This is, in fact, the period in which the economic and social seeds of modern nationalism were sown.

The Meiji Revolution and Japan's Modernization

Kuwabara Takeo is a leader of the school of Japanese scholars who contend that the Japanese transformation of the late nineteenth century was truly revolutionary. In this article, his approach is to investigate the French Revolution and the Meiji Ishin comparatively. He concludes that, while one effect of the Ishin was to "westernize" Japan, it was the geographic, cultural, and social factors within Japan rather than outside influences that were most important to defining and shaping the revolution.

>> 53. The Meiji Revolution and Japan's Modernization

KUWABARA TAKEO [1985]

Basically, I see the Meiji Ishin as follows: The Japanese people, who had cut themselves off from contact with the world and preserved their independence through national seclusion, had created and disseminated throughout the country a sophisticated culture during 250 years of peace. However, in the mid nineteenth century they realized that international power relations were such that opening the country was unavoidable, and they boldly and voluntarily began to introduce Western civilization into Japan. The Meiji Restoration was a cultural revolution carried out in order to create a modern state. [...]

How did this country, which alone lay outside the West, manage to modernize itself? Many interrelated factors made this possible, some of which are: (1) geographical conditions; (2) national independence; (3) a stable society fostered by ethnic homogeneity and prolonged national seclusion; (4) a highly developed feudal society; (5) 250 years of peace; (6) the spread of education; (7) well-developed national unity; (8) absence of a "philosophy"; (9) adaptability; (10) the powerlessness of religion; and (11) thorough abolition of the traditional system of social strata. [...]

1. Japan was the country that was most distant as the Western powers set out upon the subjugation of the world. Moreover, it is an island country, and the Korea Strait is too wide to swim. It was relatively easy to sustain the policy of seclusion.

2. My second point is connected to point 1. Japan is one of few countries in the world never invaded by another people, and a rare example of a country that never underwent colonization. Unlike in a colonized country, in which rebellion naturally emerges against the modernization brought in by the aggressor nation, the Meiji cultural revolution was carried out entirely on internal initiative. [...]

3. This and the points that follow are all conditions resulting from national seclusion. Scholars are still divided over how to evaluate the seclusion policy. Although it worked to disadvantage in that Japan lagged behind somewhat in world progress, it was advantageous in that the country's unique culture flourished under its protective wing. [...]

4. Feudal institutions are, of course, not suitable to contemporary times, but it is a stage that must be gone through in order to modernize. The case of India sufficiently proves this, I think. Division of labour became well advanced in the latter stages of the Tokugawa period, and a bureaucratic system with few equals in the world took shape.

5. No other country in pre-modern times enjoyed 250 years of peace. This good fortune,

Source: Kuwabara Takeo, "The Meiji Revolution and Japan's Modernization," in *Meiji Ishin: Restoration and Revolution,* edited by Nagai Michio and Miguel Urrutia (Tokyo: The United Nations University, 1985), 21, 25–28.

despite the undeniable stagnation that gripped society, allowed the culture to mature with peculiar refinement.

6. […] The literacy rate in Japan at the time of the Meiji Restoration was 43 per cent for men and 15 per cent for women. There are no surveys of literacy in France at the time of the Revolution, but it is said that the number of people who could sign their own names on their marriage licenses was 47 per cent for men and 27 per cent for women, so literacy must have been even lower than these figures. […]

7. Among European states, France is a relatively well unified nation, but at the time of the French Revolution methods of agriculture as well as the legal system were different in the northern and southern parts of the country. National unity was greater in Japan at the time of the Restoration, and communication was facilitated because all citizens spoke the same language.

8. Nakae Chomin went so far as to say that Japan from ancient times, and even to the present, had no philosophy. Perhaps he thought so because, despite the prolonged civil war in the Sengoku period (fifteenth and sixteenth centuries), on the whole civil strife in its history was minimal. Especially in the stable society of the Tokugawa period, there seemed little need for ideological struggle. […]

9. Professor Sakuta Keiichi, sociologist, asserts that "There is a long tradition in Japanese society of acceptance of circumstances as destiny and accommodation to given situations," and this is adaptability. Just as the *shishi*, committed to the slogan "revere the emperor, expel the barbarians," switched later, in the Bakumatsu period, to support for opening the ports, the tendency to alter one's views in response to different situations is strong. This may make the Japanese appear unprincipled, but I believe that this adaptability helped to nurture a progressive, dynamic industrialism in contrast to the conservatism of the spirit of agriculture.

10. Confrontation is avoided in Japanese society, but there were bloody religious wars in Japan's medieval period, and times when one provincial ruler would expel another and take over his lands. Then in the Tokugawa period the central government drove out Christianity and forced the various Buddhist sects to submit to its authority. That is why the power of religion to support those of traditionalist or conservative thinking who resisted modernization was so negligible. In this respect Japan was quite different from other countries in Asia.

11. I believe that Japan achieved the abolition of the status system more thoroughly than any other country. There are many ways in which the class system lingers on even today in advanced countries such as England and France. In this respect, however, the Meiji Restoration was truly revolutionary. It strengthened mobility within society and encouraged the release of nationalist energy.

The Different Experiences of China and Japan in the Mid-Nineteenth Century

Shibahara Takuji is one of a number of scholars who have looked at the fates of Japan and China during the nineteenth century in comparative perspective. Whereas Japan underwent the Meiji Ishin and emerged an industrializing power, China during this period experienced growing European, American, and later Japanese commercial imperialism and became economically dependent for a time on the industrialized states. Takuji argues that part of the reason for Japan's apparent success can be found in its different treatment by Americans and Europeans, who focused on exploiting the far greater wealth of China, thus allowing Japan to shape its own modernization process.

>> 54. Japan's Modernization from the Perspective of International Relations

SHIBAHARA TAKUJI [1985]

Many of the historical problems relating to Japan's modernization, as is true of the efforts of other non-Western nations in the modernization process, were closely connected with the pressures exerted by the Western powers. In this respect, the study of the international environment is indispensable to an understanding of the Meiji Restoration.

The arrival in 1853 of the American fleet led by Commodore Perry was the first incidence of foreign pressure backed up by armed force. However, the impact of the West upon Japan was multi-faceted. One aspect was the forced opening of ports to "free trade" and the resultant social and economic changes (including the collapse of the existing industrial and market structure and the restructuring that accompanied incorporation into the world market). A second aspect involved the political, diplomatic, and military pressures exerted upon Japan by the West under the unequal treaties (conventional tariffs, the right to build foreign settlements, consular jurisdiction, unilateral most-favoured-nation treatment and other clauses). Third, as diplomatic and commercial relations grew closer, industrial technology and modern science were brought into the country, and Western values, civilization and culture, as well as aspects of its political systems, gained increasing influence. Just how these aspects of the Western impact affected Japan varied according to the relations—sometimes co-operative, sometimes antagonistic and competitive—between the Western powers themselves (Great Britain, France, the United States, and Russia) and to Japan's economic, political and diplomatic capacity to respond to that impact. [...]

In the latter half of the nineteenth century, how did Japan succeed in industrializing and in modernizing its social institutions when China was unable to do so? Among Japanese scholars, two interpretations of this question predominate. One is that by the mid nineteenth century Japan had already achieved many of the conditions required for modernization. The other is that the level of economic and political subordination of China by the West was greater than that of Japan, and that Japan, therefore, had a greater chance of pursuing its own independent development. [...]

From the end of the eighteenth century, China was drawn into the triangular trade between Britain, India, and China, although the Chinese participation was conducted only at Canton [Guangzhou] and under government control. Britain launched two wars against China, the First Opium War in 1840–1842 and the Second Opium War in 1856–1858, motivated by its push to expand the export of opium to China and open up markets in China for the output of its rapidly growing cotton industry. China was forced to yield by this gunboat policy, and signed the treaties at Nanking [Nanjing] (1842), Tientsin [Tianjin] (1858), and Peking [Beijing] (1860), handed over Hong Kong [Xianggang] and Kowloon [Jiulong] to Britain, and opened a total of 14 ports. It was also forced to pay huge indemnities. Beginning in 1844, the United States and France acquired the same special treaty rights as Britain.

The Western powers' attitude towards Japan, however, was somewhat different. The United States, though it had taken the initiative in forcing Japan to open its doors, was interested in the country mainly as a supply and fuelling stop for ships on the way to China and as a place of refuge for shipwrecked mariners. It was not so much interested in the Japanese trade per se. What convinced the shogunate that it must sign the Ansei commercial treaties (with the US, Britain, France, Russia, and the Netherlands) in 1858, beginning with the Harris Treaty (the United States–Japan Treaty of Amity and Commerce), was the formidable

Source: Shibahara Takuji, "Japan's Modernization from the Perspective of International Relations," in *Meiji Ishin: Restoration and Revolution,* edited by Nagai Michio and Miguel Urrutia (Tokyo: The United Nations University, 1985), 61–62, 64–65.

military superiority of the British as demonstrated by their victory in the Second Opium War, as well as the rumour that Japan would also be forced to agree to diplomatic and commercial relations by the invincible British fleet. Thus, it was not long after Japan's doors were opened that Great Britain, the world's empire and the world's workshop, took the lead among the Western powers in commercial and diplomatic affairs with this country.

A comparison of the treaties between the Western powers and China and Japan show that they included, for both countries, such major unequal provisions as the permanent stationing of ministers and consuls of the foreign powers with privileges relating to their status, low tariff rates, conventional customs duties, the establishment of foreign settlements, and consular jurisdiction, as well as the unilateral most-favoured-nation clause. Provisions unique to the treaties with China included the legalization of the opium trade, the right of foreign merchants to engage in commercial activities inside China, permission to propagate Christianity, and the placement of a foreigner as Inspector-General of Customs to supervise maritime customs affairs in China (on the pretext of ensuring that the indemnities would be paid). These differences, as well as the cession of Hong Kong [Xianggang] and Kowloon [Jiulong] and the large indemnities extracted from China, show without a doubt that Britain and the other Western powers exerted greater political and military pressure upon China through the priority given to the Chinese market. Clearly the Western powers treated China more harshly than they did Japan.

The Meiji Charter Oath

The Charter Oath of the Meiji administration contained five central policy statements. The oath called for a legislative body, collaboration between classes, basic economic freedoms, the embracing of international law, and openness to foreign ideas. Interestingly, we have four drafts of this statement. The first two were written by the samurai scholars Yuri Kimimasa and Fukuoka Takachika. The third draft, on which the final form was based, was written by Kido Kōin. In its final form the draft was published in 1868.

>> 55. Drafts of the Charter Oath

[1868]

Three Drafts of the Charter Oath, 1868
(a) Draft by Yuri Kimimasa

General Outline on Legislative Matters

1. It is requested that a system be established under which common people may be permitted to pursue their respective callings so that there may be no discontent.
2. It is necessary for the samurai and common people to unite in carrying out vigorously the administration of economic and financial affairs (*keirin*).
3. Knowledge shall be sought throughout the world so as to widen and strengthen the foundations of imperial rule.
4. The term of office held by qualified men [selected by the *han*] (*kōshi*) must be limited. Thereafter they must yield their positions to talented men.
5. All matters of state must be decided by open discussion (*kōron*) [with the participation of all factions on *han* concerned] and must not be discussed privately.

The intent of the [proposed] League of the *Daimyō* (*Shokō Kaimei*) may be announced along the lines discussed above [It is further

Source: "Drafts of the Charter Oath", in *Sources of Japanese History,* vol. 2 edited by David John Lu, (New York: McGraw-Hill, 1974), 35–36.

recommended that] general amnesty be announced concurrently.

(b) Amended Draft by Fukuoka Takachika

A Compact

1. An assembly consisting of *daimyō* shall be established, and all matters of state shall be decided by open discussion.
2. It is requested that a system be established under which not only the civil and military officials, but also the common people may be permitted to pursue their respective callings so that there may be no discontent.
3. The high and low shall all unite in carrying out vigorously the administration of economic and financial affairs.
4. Knowledge shall be sought throughout the world so as to broaden and strengthen the foundations of imperial rule.
5. The term of office of those appointed [by the imperial government] must be limited. Thereafter they must yield their positions to talented men.

The above may be announced as the intents. When the League [of the *Daimyō*] is formed, it is suggested that general amnesty be announced concurrently.

(c) Draft by Kido Kōin

Oath

1. An assembly consisting of *daimyō* shall be established, and all matters of state shall be decided by open discussion.
2. The high and low shall all unite in carrying out the administration of economic and financial affairs.
3. It is requested that a system be established under which not only the civil and military

officials, but also the common people may be permitted to pursue their respective callings so that there may be no discontent.

4. Evil practices of the past shall be discarded and [all our actions] shall follow the accepted practices of the world.
5. Knowledge shall be sought throughout the world so as to broaden and strengthen the foundations of imperial rule.

Excerpts from the Document on the Form of Government (Seitaisho), 1868

1. In determining the national policy and establishing a new system of government and regulations, the text of the Charter Oath shall become the guide.

   (1) A deliberative assembly shall be convoked on a broad basis, and all matters of state shall be decided by open discussion.
   (2) The high and low shall all unite in carrying out vigorously the administration of economic and financial affairs.
   (3) It is necessary to have a system under which not only the civil and military officials, but also the common people may be permitted to pursue their respective callings so that there may be no discontent.
   (4) Evil practices of the past shall be discarded and [all our actions] shall follow the just way of the world [i.e., international law].
   (5) Knowledge shall be sought throughout the world so as to broaden and strengthen the foundations of imperial rule.

The intent of this document is not to go contrary to the conditions set forth in the above oath.

>> Mastering the Material

1. What diplomatic innovations does Naff suggest Selim III undertook? Why does he believe they were unsuccessful?

2. Evaluate the 1799 Anglo-Turkish treaty of alliance (Reading 51). Naff suggests that Selim III was not a competent diplomat. Does this treaty seem uneven to you? How well did Selim's negotiators do in winning concessions from the British?

3. Who are the Ottoman *a'yan*? How did they challenge the government of Selim III?

4. Selim III's central "modernizing" reform was to strengthen the army. Do you think this was the result of pressure from the West or from the *a'yan*? Which was more dangerous to Selim, the prospect of military defeat more or that of a bourgeois revolution?

5. What internal factors does Kuwabara Takeo suggest led to Japan's successful modernization through and beyond the Meiji Ishin?

6. Takeo focuses to some degree on Japanese cultural attributes as formative factors in the Meiji Ishin. Do you agree that national cultures can help or hinder attempts to modernize?

7. Compare Shibahara Takuji's and Kuwabara Takeo's arguments. Which is more convincing? Why?

8. Consider the four drafts of the Charter Oath of 1686. How do they differ from each other? What do they have in common?

9. Kuwabara Takeo suggests that the Meiji Ishin was a true revolution. What is a true revolution? Do the drafts of the Charter Oath seem to support this assertion or refute it?

>> Making Connections

1. Look at the map at the beginning of Part 3. Why was the Ottoman Empire an important ally for Britain in the late-eighteenth and nineteenth centuries? What was Britain trying to protect?

2. Kuwabara Takeo explicitly compares Japan during the late Tokugawa period to France just prior to the French Revolution. Why do you think he makes this comparison?

3. Some scholars believe that the Meiji Ishin was a "bourgeois" revolution in that it served the needs of nonaristocratic entrepreneurs. Consider the excerpts from Takeo's article and the Charter Oath. Is there any evidence in either of them that it was or was not a bourgeois revolution?

4. Having read about revolutions and reforms around the world in the early modern era, do you agree that there was a global bourgeois revolution during this period? When? How do each of the revolutions discussed in Part 2 fit into this model, or why do they not?

Part 2 Conclusion

What is a revolution? The answer, unfortunately, cannot be quickly found in a dictionary. "Revolution" is a term applied to a set of events or trends either by the people who study it or by participants. Often, the participants have a vested interest in promoting a change as revolutionary, which means that they will use the term even if the actual change it describes is small. On the other hand, participants in a major transformation often do not realize how important and dramatic are the events in which they are involved, and only later do scholars look back and recognize them as revolutionary.

In fact, the term *revolution* is often misleading, because it is misunderstood to indicate drastic and rapid change that occurs because of an immediate, localized challenge facing a society. In fact, revolutionary change is more often rooted in long-term and global trends. It is the contribution of world historians to retell the stories of revolutions in a way that recognizes the connections between moments of revolutionary change and global enduring trends.

The sources in Part 2, while often individually concentrating on singular events, together paint a picture of an era of global readjustment in the seventeenth, eighteenth, and nineteenth centuries. This is the first world history lesson of the age of revolutions: They are all connected. Following the establishment of the Columbian Exchange, societies everywhere began to adjust to the new global realities of connectedness and exchange. At the heart of these transformations was the rise of trade, which buoyed with it merchant classes not just in Europe, but everywhere, although not always to the same degree. The increase of commerce raised the wealth of traders, and with them investors and producers. These groups, with their new wealth, also became consumers, fueling the global economy through their desire for new goods. This bourgeoisie could be found on the coast of western Africa, in the Ottoman Empire, and in the ports of China. However, they became particularly powerful where wealth was being concentrated—in the cities and to some degree the countryside of northwestern Europe and its American colonies. Even in these regions, the bourgeois classes found themselves constrained by the existing powerful landowning classes of the feudality: the aristocrats. It was their struggle to overturn this older class that in many ways characterizes the French and American (U.S.) revolutions. The bourgeoisie, however, were not uniformly fighting for rights for everyone. In fact, many were left out of these revolutions to varying degrees: women, the lower classes, and non-Europeans. Thus the Haitian Revolution was a complex rebellion both by the Haitian bourgeoisie in favor of the French Revolution and the enslaved classes against bourgeois plantation owners. Latin American revolutions of the nineteenth century were equally complex, with bourgeois creoles and lower-class slaves and indigenous groups fighting both with and against each other.

The success of the bourgeoisie in winning the gains they wanted in the French and American revolutions—and more gradually in Britain and other northwestern European states—helped these states to enjoy economic, technological, and military gains in the eighteenth and nineteenth centuries. In other parts of the world, local governments and populations recognized this and adjusted to the new realities of a changing world. They employed a variety of strategies, of which the most important was defensive modernization: the attempt to emulate European states' military and industrial revolutions within the context of their own cultural and political systems. This endeavor was carried out with varying success. Some states, such as Japan and to a degree the Ottoman Empire, were relatively successful. Others, such as China, were torn apart by the process. Yet it must be seen that in all of these states, European or not, the same struggle was occurring, the struggle to adjust to a changing global situation.

World history also teaches us a second lesson about revolutions by dispelling the myth of invention. By rooting revolutions in global history, we see more clearly that revolutions are often the result of slow and gradual change, and that some of the causes of that change can be found outside a society. Both the role of diffusion and the incremental, step-by-step nature of revolutions can be seen in the industrial revolution in Britain, for example. The transformations in social organization and the invention of new processes and machines in Britain was not the work of a few "scientists." Instead, it was the result of the efforts of a long line of investors, tinkerers and craftspeople, farmers, and even government regulators. Each small change—the building of a canal, the development of a new type of gear, the growing of a new crop that added calories to the diet of workers—made possible further changes, but there was not a "revolutionary moment."

Moreover, many of the important factors that contributed to the growth of industry in Britain were global rather than local. Resources poured in from overseas, both from the colonies and from independent countries. These regions also provided markets for British goods. Financiers invested the money they made from slave-worked plantations in the Americas into buying land locally for wool production, in the process displacing farmers who subsequently became factory workers. New crops from the Americas helped to feed them. New techniques were learned from France, the United States, and many other countries. In every way, the Industrial Revolution in Britain was a result of Britain's location in an increasingly global economy. The location of other countries and regions was different. As a resource-producing colony, Haiti was not in a position to become an industrial power, locked as it was into a dependant position. By contrast, Japan's political and economic independence put its government in a position to industrialize, if much later than Britain.

The revolutions of the period 1600–1870 were about local issues, but they were also ultimately about global issues as well. No state or population could survive in isolation, but rather they all had to try to survive and thrive in an increasingly interconnected world. This meant that people increasingly learned lessons from each other, tried to gain access to resources abroad, and struggled to grasp opportunities for change while at the same time defending closely held traditions. Thus the many revolutions of this period were, in fact, part of world history as much as the history of each region.

Further Reading

Revolutions in world history have most often been studied purely in national context, and many attempts to link or compare regions have been rapidly criticized. One relatively successful model of interlinked early modern revolutions in Europe and Asia is Jack Goldstone, *Revolution and Rebellion in the Early Modern World* (Berkeley: University of California Press, 1993). The connections between the Haitian and French revolutions have been explored by several scholars. An immensely readable analysis of this sort is Laurent Dubois, *Avengers of the New World* (Massachusetts: Belknap Press, 2005). The intellectual developments of the enlightenment are placed in global perspective in Geoffrey C. Gunn, *First Globalization* (Lanham: Rowman and Littlefield, 2003). David Bender similarly locates the American Revolution and early U.S. political development in a global setting in *A Nation Among Nations* (New York: Hill and Wang, 2006).

Terms to Know

master narrative   *(p. 76)*

ancien regime   *(p. 76)*

aristocratic   *(p. 79)*

Glorious Revolution
(p. 79)

Enlightenment   *(p. 80)*

liberalism   *(p. 80)*

mercantilism   *(p. 80)*

responsive commercialism
(p. 81)

dependency cycle   *(p. 86)*

creoles   *(p. 95)*

nationalism   *(p. 95)*

popular sovereignty
(p. 95)

third estate   *(p. 97)*

peninsulares   *(p. 105)*

biological regime
(p. 119)

agricultural revolution
(p. 120)

underdevelopment
(p. 126)

defensive modernization
(p. 133)

Part 3

Debating the New Imperialism, 1850–1914

European empires in most cases receded during the period of revolutions in the Americas. The only exception was the British Empire, whose losses in North America were counterbalanced by gains in the mid-nineteenth century in India and Oceania. Yet in the half-century that began in the 1870s European empires grew again, subjugating once more many of the free states and independent populations of the world. The newly conquered colonies encompassed much of the world's landmass: parts of Asia, almost the entirety of Africa, portions of the Middle East, the islands of the Pacific, and the great expanse of Australia. Taken together with the settlement of the vast North American interior by the United States, the extension of the Russian empire into eastern Asia, and Japanese occupation of Korea in the same period, this imperialist expansion surpassed in scope even the fifteenth- to seventeenth-century European conquest of American peoples. Even parts of the world that were not conquerors or conquered were unable to avoid the effects of this process. Great empires like those of the Ottomans (central Asia, eastern Europe, and north Africa) and Qing (central and East Asia) as well as the young Latin American states, for example, in this period became the subjects of commercial and military competition between the maritime empires of Britain, France, Germany, Japan, and the United States.

Almost immediately, this late-nineteenth-century expansionism came to be known as the **new imperialism,** a phrase coined by the British anti-imperialist John Hobson. If in some ways this new phase echoed the earlier creation of the Portuguese and Spanish overseas empires, it was also a truly unique phenomenon. The new imperialism reflected a new understanding of the world among segments of the populations of Europe, the United States, and Japan. These groups came to believe that their countries had a right and even a duty to conquer or control the affairs of societies on other sides of the globe. Nor were the new imperial societies merely *willing* to create new empires. They were also *able* to do so. In a departure from earlier eras, late-nineteenth-century European states, along with the United States and Japan, possessed a significant military advantage over African and Asian peoples. Only very rarely were imperial armies of conquest—armed with industrial technology—defeated in this period. Other technological advances, such as steamboats, telegraphs, and new medicines, allowed the conquerors to administer the vast areas they took over. The process of establishing full colonial rule by force—ironically called **pacification** although it was anything but peaceful—took a number of decades and in some areas extended beyond the First World War.

The new colonialism was substantially more extensive than the Spanish and Portuguese empires of earlier centuries. The territory conquered and directly administered was far greater than the earlier establishment of chains of European forts and ports in the Americas and along the coastlines of Asia and Africa. Economic integration, too, was more complete. The new colonies fed, for the first time, a global economy indisputably centered in Europe instead of Asia. The world's newly industrialized imperial societies fed on the raw materials of their new colonies and produced consumer goods for sale in the colonies on a massive scale. Culturally, as well, the new overseas empires entailed the creation of a web of relationships that on a new scale, starting with the movement of largely Christian missionaries from Europe and the United States to the new colonies.

If this period marked the height of European supremacy it also revealed the shifting fortunes of power. Most obviously, several of the imperial powers of the late nineteenth centuries were not the same European states who had established themselves overseas in previous centuries. Spain, Portugal, and the Netherlands were largely replaced by Germany and Italy, newly unified states built from minor princedoms. Even more significantly, the industrialized expansionist states of Japan and the United States were able to compete quite well with the European powers. The United States was a collection of former European colonies turned imperial contender. Japan, by contrast, had never been conquered. Its rise to prominence showed that the much-debated European superiority was perhaps not so exceptional after all.

Japan and the United States occupy an ambivalent position in the story of the new imperialism. On the one hand, they were imperial powers themselves. On the other hand, they are extreme examples of the nineteenth-century challenge to Europeans by groups outside of Europe. Some American, Asian, and African merchants, for example, were able to manipulate the competition between rival firms from competing European states whose industries relied on the raw materials they provided. These merchants attempted to dictate the prices they were paid and the conditions under which they would sell goods to companies from the industrialized nations. Similarly, there were numerous instances of rulers and decision makers in African and Asian states negotiating for favorable relationship terms with imperial agents. Arguably, it was these challenges to the commercial and political pursuits of the industrialized states that caused them to respond by annexing these regions outright where possible. Once conquered, however, colonized people still tried to resist, negotiate with, and subvert the will of the **metropole,** or imperial state, that ruled them.

The maneuvering and bargaining between imperial and local merchants and rulers demonstrates that political and commercial flows both immediately preceding and during the new imperialism were **reciprocal,** or two-way rather than merely one-way. Similarly, the cultural relationship between conquerors and conquered both before and after the wars of colonial expansion was characterized by exchange rather than domination. The inhabitants of the colonies impacted the religions, architectures, arts, ideas, foods, and lifestyles of the colonizers in ways that were perhaps more subtle and hidden than the impact of European culture on the colonies, but significant nevertheless. This global, reciprocal view of the new imperialism is matched by a long view of world history that sees various regions enjoying different advantages at different times. For example, it is important to realize that China and India, once the major producers of quality goods in the world, by the late nineteenth century became dominated by European states and Japan. India, with its vast population and sophisticated organization, was conquered by tiny Britain. China was torn apart by rival world powers and its own internal disorders. Yet 100 years later, in the year 2005, China and India have reemerged as the second and third largest economies in the world in terms of **gross domestic product,** while Britain has become a second-rate economic power at best. This is not to suggest that the new imperialism did have a lasting legacy. Colonial rule and economic exploitation had a negative impact on many of the conquered regions of the world, and many academics who study sub-Saharan Africa and southeast Asia blame the oppression of colonial rule for much of those regions' current problems.

In Part 3, we ask two principal questions. The first is: Why did the new imperialism emerge? In the preceding century (1770–1870), European overseas empires had shrunk rather than expanded as Caribbean and American colonies achieved their independence. The British empire alone had expanded, pushed by settlers and corporations more than the imperial government. Why, suddenly, did Britain find itself challenged by expanding European empires, Japan, and the United States in the 1870s? A number of answers have been suggested that should be familiar to us from previous debates: changing economic realities, shifting cultural norms, geopolitical and military competition between antagonistic states, and a sense of moral mission. Most of these theories suggest that the *motive* for building these new empires was a result of changes within the imperial powers themselves. However, several theorists argue that in fact it was the growing dependence of these states on other regions of the world for markets and raw materials that set off the great colonial race.

The second question is: How were the imperialist powers able to conquer regions that previously had been too inaccessible, or too powerfully defended, to fall to the sword of maritime imperialists? Here the obvious answer is some sort of technological gap created by the industrial and scientific changes of the previous two centuries in Europe. However, the debate over the significance of these changes, and the inability of the conquered states to resist, goes on. Many historians contend that the gap was limited, and that the invaders *still* were too weak to rule their new territories without some local help. They also argue that the gap was short lived. In just a half-century or so these colonies would begin fighting for their independence, utilizing new weapons and strategies that successfully defeated the great imperial armies.

Part 3 Timeline

1873	Depression in Europe and the United States begins, fueled by industrial overproduction and competition for global markets.
1874	Following the collapse of the Fante Confederation, a western African movement for self-rule, Great Britain annexes the Gold Coast Colony and Protectorate.
1874	Sir Andrew Clarke forces the rulers of Malaya to sign the "Pangkor Agreement," transferring a wide variety of powers to the British.
1882	Having defeated a nationalist uprising, Britain installs a "Debt Administration" in Egypt.
1884	European governments and corporations meeting at the Berlin Conference agree on a process for claiming and annexing territories in Africa.
1885	Dadabai Naoroji participates in the founding of the Indian Congress Party.
1896	The Ndebele Uprising begins in Rhodesia.
1898	Spanish-American war makes the United States a force in the Pacific and leads to U.S. occupation of the Philippines.
1898	The battle of Omdurman, in the Sudan.
1905	Having gradually conquered much of western Africa, France creates the civilian-ruled super-colony of French West Africa.
1910	Japan formally occupies Korea.

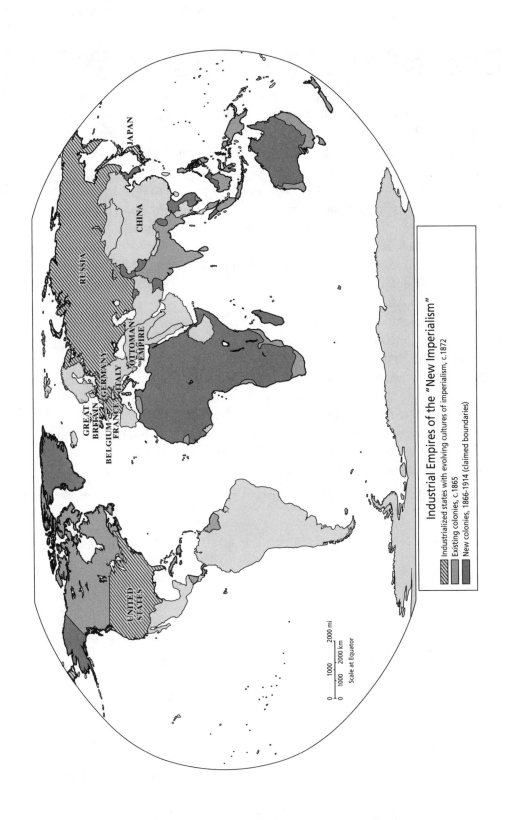

Industrial Empires of the "New Imperialism"

Industrialized states with evolving cultures of imperialism, c.1872

Existing colonies, c.1865

New colonies, 1866–1914 (claimed boundaries)

RUSSIA

JAPAN

CHINA

GREAT
BRITAIN

GERMANY

BELGIUM

FRANCE

ITALY

OTTOMAN
EMPIRE

UNITED
STATES

0   1000   2000 mi
0   1000   2000 km
Scale at Equator

Chapter 12

Strategic Explanations

When scholars first began to study the origins of the new imperialism and of modern colonialism, they searched for causes *within* the societies of the imperialist powers. This seemed perfectly logical. After all, it was these states—primarily the United States, Japan, Britain, France, Germany, and Italy—who had undertaken the great projects of conquering and ruling new, vast overseas empires. However, while some sociologists and historians continue today to investigate each society individually, other historians and a number of political scientists are concentrating on the interaction *among* the emerging imperial powers in the late nineteenth century. Their main observation is that the new imperialism was a competitive process. They argue that the synchronization of imperialist projects proved that each state was reacting to the perceived imperial aspirations of the other states. Factors that seemed internal to each imperialist society in the late nineteenth century—the growth of patriotism, the desire for national prestige, the sense of mission to "civilize" or convert to Christianity people in other regions—are reinterpreted as evidence of the growing tension between the great states. Understanding this competitive friction between industrialized states, they argue, is the key to comprehending the new imperialism. In the late nineteenth century, competition between the industrial powers was on the rise. Europe had been relatively peaceful since the 1815 Treaty of Vienna that ended the Napoleonic wars, but behind the scene tension was building. Eventually, this simmering hostility would culminate in the First World War, but for now it found release in imperial expansion.

The rivalry between the great powers was partly economic: competition for both raw materials to feed factories and markets in which to sell the goods they produced. Other sources of antagonism, however, were strategic in nature. For more than sixty years Britain had been the only country able to truly project its military force around the world, but as an island with a relatively small population it was increasingly challenged by the emerging industrialized armies within Europe; especially those of Germany, France, and Russia. Europe's relative harmony was shattered in the 1870s by a series of wars involving these states, the most important being the Franco-Prussian War of 1870–1871, in which the emerging state of Germany defeated France. Most of the conflicts, however, were played out outside of Europe. In southwest Asia (the Middle East), for example, Russia and Britain vied for dominance. For the British, the region was a vital link in the trade route to India and China, while for Russia it was a portal onto the Mediterranean and Indian Ocean. Open conflict erupted in the Crimean War 1854–1856, the result of which did nothing to settle the issue. In the Pacific, as well, Britain's commercial dominance was being challenged by both the United States and Japan.

Before the 1880s, however, emerging rivalries between the great powers did not generally result in territorial acquisition overseas. It was the emergence of Germany as an imperial power that changed this. Initially, the German populace had little interest in overseas empires, and calls for the development of an overseas empire came from only a very limited **colonial lobby;** a small group of patriots, military men, and merchants who pushed the German government to occupy new territories. In fact, throughout the early years of the German state its Chancellor, Otto von Bismarck, was firmly focused on European affairs. His sudden interest in acquiring colonies in 1883 has long been the subject of scholarly debate. Some theorists argue that his imperial policy was merely an extension of his European policy; that he hoped to use Germany's colonies as either a threat or a bargaining chip to force Britain to support Germany in any future war against France. Other political historians believe German politics were the key to Bismarck's reversal. The colonial lobby included a number of important businessmen, and Bismarck may have hoped to win their support for his domestic projects by giving in to their demands for colonies. Germany's King, Wilhelm II, appears to have viewed colonies merely as a way to raise his own prestige and to earn Germany "a place in the sun" alongside more established European powers such as Britain and France. All of these theories are expressed especially well in the work of A. J. P. Taylor, an early proponent of strategic interpretations of the new imperialism.

Of all the European states France was most frightened by the strengthening of its German neighbor. Successive French administrations responded to the German threat by expanding their own colonial possessions. In part, they hoped the conquest of new colonies would help France to regain the prestige lost by its defeat in the Franco-Prussian war. More tangibly, the populations of colonies were seen as potential recruits to help redress the imbalance between the vast German army and the smaller French forces. As Prime Minister Jules Ferry made clear in his 1881 speech to the *Chambre des Deputies,* the French parliament, the colonies were both symbol and source of national strength, and colonialism was seen as a strategic, economic, and moral necessity.

Like Germany, the United States and Japan were both relatively new powers attempting to compete with the established European powers both commercially and strategically. Few Americans in the late nineteenth century still believed that European intervention in the Americas was a threat to the United States, but many believed that a strong navy was necessary to protect American companies overseas as well as to guard the United States' ocean borders. To American imperialists like Admiral Alfred Thayer Mahan, the only way to secure these objectives was through the possession of ports and islands in both oceans. Mahan's *The Influence of Seapower upon History* helped convince politicians like President Theodore Roosevelt to annex Caribbean and Pacific positions. In important articles like the

"Effects of Asiatic Conditions upon International Policies," he also called for the United States to exercise military might and political influence on China and southeast Asia.

Japan's path to imperialism also reflected the interplay of strategy and economics. Japan's motivations were somewhat different. Unlike the United States, Japan was a small island with few resources, and even in the early phases of industrialization some of its leaders had considered occupying and colonizing the Korean peninsula to get at raw materials. However, Japanese politicians and military men also recognized that until Japan had completed its industrialization they were still vulnerable to the more established European powers. Ôkubo Toshimichi was one scholar-statesman who supported a strategy of gradual expansion. His opinion on the proposed invasion of Korea, embodied in the letter that is the final source for this chapter, shows an awareness that while Japan had the potential to become a great imperialist power, she might also still become the victim of imperialism herself.

European Rivalry and German Imperialism

One of the most stunning manifestations of the new imperialism was the process by which Europeans conquered almost the entirety of Africa. In previous centuries, the strength of African armies and states and the challenging nature of African environments had limited Europeans inroads into the continent. As late as the 1870s, Europeans controlled only a few coastal positions in Africa, as well as a large expanse in the southern tip of the continent. The vast majority of the continent remained independent. Yet in the last two decades of the nineteenth century almost the entirety of the African landmass was conquered or claimed by Europeans. Arguably, this reversal of fortunes was enabled by the growing technological superiority of Europeans in the fields of medicine, transport, communication, and armaments, as discussed later in this unit. However, the question remains why Europeans would suddenly develop the will to conquer regions in which they had previously expressed little interest at all. European powers even struggled for control of the Sahara Desert, a region that cost far more to administer than it ever produced for its conquerors! This 'scramble for Africa' was in many ways catalyzed by the colonial aspirations of the new state of Germany, which suddenly began to build itself an Empire in 1884–1885, forcing Britain and France especially to respond. Why Germany would want an empire, however, has always been something of a mystery: Economically and politically it was a purely European power, and there seems little reason for its Chancellor, Bismarck, to have supported imperialism. In this analysis, the well known British historian A.J.P. Taylor argues that Germany's annexation of territories in Africa, and also the Pacific, was part of a plot to secure Germany's power in Europe by increasing tensions between the two great existing European imperial states, Britain and France. Taylor also refutes competing theories that Bismarck conversion to an imperialist position was caused by internal politics or economic considerations. Taylor's article, however, is not the last word on German imperialism and competing theories have resurfaced in the decades following Taylor's scholarship.

>> 56. Germany's First Bid for Colonies 1884–1885: A Move in Bismarck's European Policy

A. J. P. TAYLOR [1938]

In these years of "the scramble for Africa" there was suddenly added to the old colonial rivals, France and England, a power which had hitherto confined itself strictly to the European continent. The German colonial empire, or rather the formulation of its theoretical claims, was virtually the work of a single year: the Cameroons were established in July 1884, German South-West Africa in August, New Guinea in December 1884, and German East Africa was begun in May 1885 (though its frontiers were not settled until 1890); Samoa was added in 1899; otherwise—apart from some minor adjustments of the Cameroons frontier at the expense of France after the second Moroccan crisis (1911)—the German colonial empire was complete. The success of Germany, as previously of Prussia, had been due to freedom from all concern in non-German questions. [...]

It is therefore surprising that Germany should have deliberately pushed her way into the hornets' nest of colonial conflicts. The explanation of this German outburst of colonial activity has usually been found in the rising enthusiasm for colonies, and it is true that there was in Germany a certain amount of colonial agitation. [...]

[Yet] [T]o imagine that Bismarck was influenced by public opinion, or that he was swayed by fear of "a crushing parliamentary defeat" is to transfer to Germany the conceptions of constitutional government as practised in England or France. [...] Nor is it conceivable that Bismarck was suddenly converted, after years of scepticism, to a belief in the value of colonies. [...]

It is the purpose of the following chapters to discover an explanation of Bismarck's colonial policy by fitting it into the structure of contemporary European politics. His colonial policy alone seems meaningless and irrational; but when to the relations of England and Germany are added those of Germany and France, and those of France and England, Bismarck's policy in 1884 and 1885 becomes as purposeful as at any other time in his career. Such an examination shows that Bismarck quarrelled with England in order to draw closer to France; and ·that the method of quarrel was the deliberately provocative claim to ownerless lands, in which the German government had hitherto shown no interest. These lands had a certain negative value to Great Britain, in that they adjoined existing British colonies or lay near British strategic routes; but their value was not such as to provoke the English government into a war. Moreover, they were of no concern to any other power, and claims to them would not cause any international complications, such as would have been occasioned by German demands in China or Persia.

Jules Ferry's Defense of French Colonialism

Jules Ferry was a French politician who came to prominence following the defeat of France in the 1870–1871 war with Prussia. As Prime Minister, he was a committed imperialist, arguing that France could only compete with the growing power of Germany by establishing an overseas empire. The speech excerpted here was given during his second term as Prime Minister and at the height of French expansionism. It is notable for tying together three motives expressed by proponents of imperialism: geo-politics, economics,

Source: A. J. P. Taylor, *Germany's First Bid for Colonies, 1884–1885: A Move in Bismarck's European Policy* (London: Macmillan, 1938), 3–6.

and a moral mission. It is therefore a fitting first primary source for this unit. However, it must be noted that Ferry was primarily concerned with meeting France's strategic needs. He hoped that the new colonies in Africa, South-East Asia, and the Pacific Islands would help provide the funding, manpower, global reach, and strategic resources necessary to win the next war with Germany. This conception eventually came to fruition in World War I, in which France's colonies provided soldiers, laborers, and raw materials for the war effort.

>> 57. Speech Before the French Chamber of Deputies, March 28, 1884

JULES FERRY [1884]

The policy of colonial expansion is a political and economic system...that can be connected to three sets of ideas: economic ideas; the most far-reaching ideas of civilization; and ideas of a political and patriotic sort.

In the area of economics, I am placing before you, with the support of some statistics, the considerations that justify the policy of colonial expansion, as seen from the perspective of a need, felt more and more urgently by the industrialized population of Europe and especially the people of our rich and hardworking country of France: the need for outlets [for exports]. Is this a fantasy? Is this a concern [that can wait] for the future? Or is this not a pressing need, one may say a crying need, of our industrial population? I merely express in a general way what each one of you can see for himself in the various parts of France. Yes, what our major industries [textiles, etc.], irrevocably steered by the treaties of 1860[1] into exports, lack more and more are outlets. Why? Because next door Germany is setting up trade barriers; because across the ocean the United States of America have become protectionists, and extreme protectionists at that; because not only are these great markets...shrinking, becoming more and more difficult of access, but these great states are beginning to pour into our own markets products not seen there before. This is true not only for our agriculture, which has been so sorely tried...and for which competition is no longer limited to the circle of large European states....Today, as you know, competition, the law of supply and demand, freedom of trade, the effects of speculation, all radiate in a circle that reaches to the ends of the earth....That is a great complication, a great economic difficulty;...an extremely serious problem. It is so serious, gentlemen, so acute, that the least informed persons must already glimpse, foresee, and take precautions against the time when the great South American market that has, in a manner of speaking, belonged to us forever will be disputed and perhaps taken away from us by North American products. Nothing is more serious; there can be no graver social problem; and these matters are linked intimately to colonial policy.

Gentlemen, we must speak more loudly and more honestly! We must say openly that indeed the higher races have a right over the lower races....

I repeat, that the superior races have a right because they have a duty. They have the duty to civilize the inferior races....In the history of earlier centuries these duties, gentlemen, have often been misunderstood; and certainly when the Spanish soldiers and explorers introduced

---

Source: Jules Ferry, "Speech Before the French Chamber of Deputies, March 28, 1884," originally collected in *Discours et Opinions de Jules Ferry,* edited by Paul Robiquet (Paris: Armand Colin & Cie., 1897), -1. 5, 199–201, 210–211, 215–218.

slavery into Central America, they did not fulfill their duty as men of a higher race.... But, in our time, I maintain that European nations acquit themselves with generosity, with grandeur, and with sincerity of this superior civilizing duty.

I say that French colonial policy, the policy of colonial expansion, the policy that has taken us under the Empire [the Second Empire, of Napoleon 1111, to Saigon, to Indochina [Vietnam], that has led us to Tunisia, to Madagascar—I say that this policy of colonial expansion was inspired by...the fact that a navy such as ours cannot do without safe harbors, defenses, supply centers on the high seas.... Are you unaware of this? Look at a map of the world.

Gentlemen, these are considerations that merit the full attention of patriots. The conditions of naval warfare have greatly changed.... At present, as you know, a warship, however perfect its design, cannot carry more than two weeks' supply of coal; and a vessel without coal is a wreck on the high seas, abandoned to the first occupier. Hence the need to have places of supply, shelters, ports for defense and provisioning.... And that is why we needed Tunisia; that is why we needed Saigon and Indochina; that is why we need Madagascar...and why we shall never leave them!...Gentlemen, in Europe such as it is today, in this competition of the many rivals we see rising up around us, some by military or naval improvements, others by the prodigious development of a constantly growing population; in a Europe, or rather in a universe thus constituted, a policy of withdrawal or abstention is simply the high road to decadence! In our time nations are great only through the activity they deploy; it is not by spreading the peaceable light of their institutions...that they are great, in the present day.

Spreading light without acting, without taking part in the affairs of the world, keeping out of all European alliances and seeing as a trap, an adventure, all expansion into Africa or the Orient—for a great nation to live this way, believe me, is to abdicate and, in less time than you may think, to sink from the first rank to the third and fourth.

The United States' Naval Power in the Pacific

Alfred Mahan, born to a military family, was a leading proponent of American imperialism from the 1880s until his death on the eve of World War II. A naval captain and later a Rear Admiral, Thayer was also an accomplished theorist and an 'anglo' nationalist who believed that the United States and Great Britain had a destiny to control the world together. Mahan believed that the United States' security and the economic prosperity of the nation could only be achieved through the development of a large navy capable of overcoming European navies in pitched battles. Such a fleet necessitated the possession of ports around the world which could serve as safe harbors and re-supply stations for American ships. Mahan expressed this argument in a two-volume history of sea power as well as in a number of influential articles. This article, for example, was in response to the Boxer Rebellion in China, a popular turn-of-the-century uprising rooted largely in resentment against treaty conditions imposed by overseas imperial powers. In response, Japan, the United States, and European nations sent forces to China that eventually suppressed the rebellion. Mahan acknowledged that these events had temporarily united the imperial powers, but believed that the effect was temporary, and urged the United States to protect its own interests against the resurgence of competition with rival states.

>> 58. Effects of Asiatic Conditions upon International Policies

ALFRED THAYER MAHAN [1900]

In the general progress of events it has come to pass, in this closing year of a century, that the commerce of the world,—which implies as a main incident the utilization of the Sea, the chief medium of commerce,—has become the prize for which all the great states of the world are in competition. Some possibly do not expect ever to be leaders, but all either wish a greater share than they now have, or at the least to preserve their present proportion. This includes not only the power to produce,—chiefly an internal question,—but the power to exchange freely throughout as large a section of the world's population as can be reached. In this competition the most of states are, as a matter of policy unwilling to trust entirely to the operation of what we may call, not quite accurately, "natural forces." The race as hitherto run, or the particular conditions of the more favored nations,—the United States for example, so richly dowered with the raw material of wealth, and with energy to use it,—have resulted in giving some a start which puts the remainder at a disadvantage, if the issue is left to purely commercial causes; to superiority in quantity or quality of production, for instance, or to greater ability of management, either in intelligence or economy. Issues determined in this manner are more solid, but they require longer time than impatience wishes to concede; hence the desire to hasten prosperity by extending territorial control, and reserving to one's self commercial preferences in the regions mastered. This result may be reached either by direct annexation or by preponderant political influence. Both these mean, ultimately,

physical force, exerted or potential; and this generates opposing force, averse from allowing its own people to be deprived by such means. Thus competition becomes conflict, the instrument of which is not commercial emulation but military power—on land or on sea.

In Europe and America, territorial occupancy is now politically fixed and guaranteed, so far as broad lines are concerned. Any changes of boundaries now possible, if effected, would produce no material result in universal commercial conditions. Australasia also is occupied, and the political dependence of the islands of the sea has been determined by arrangements between civilized states, more or less artificial, but internationally final. The huge continent of Africa, with exceptions small and inconsequential relatively to its area, is in the same condition. Its commercial relations, therefore, will be prescribed by states whose established right to do so will not be contested. Moreover, in the regard of Commerce, the fewness and backwardness of its inhabitants as yet make Africa a field of minor importance.

There remains, therefore, Asia. In the north and south of that great continent, also, we find political control fairly settled in the hands of European powers; the principal holders being Great Britain and Russia. Between the two, however, there is a broad belt, loosely defined by parallels 30 deg. and 40 deg. north latitude, in which commercial possibilities are very great, owing to natural resources and numbers of population; while political tenure, despite long prescription, is uncertain through political incapacity or racial disorder. Upon these districts, as is notorious, the ambitions or apprehensions of foreign states are fixed; for in their possibilities of development and the uncertainty of their future is necessarily involved the welfare of other peoples, bordering upon them or dealing with them. [...]

Source: Alfred Thayer Mahan, "Effects of Asiatic Conditions upon International Policies," *North American Review*, 171 (November 1900): 612–613.

Debating Japanese Intervention in Korea

Ōkubo Toshimichi was one architect of the Meiji Restoration in Japan. As one of the Meiji Emperor's key supporters, he was a proponent of industrial modernization and the adaption of some European technological and political concepts. He also foresaw that the island of Japan would not be able to industrialize without access to natural resources on the Asian mainland, and generally supported calls for Japanese expansion into Korea. However, Toschimichi worried about moving too fast. A Korean expedition would be expensive, and he had noted that states that bankrupted themselves elsewhere—like Egypt and Mughal India—had become easy prey for Britain and other expansionist states. Japan, he felt, had to be constantly aware of its relationship with the great powers in the Pacific—specifically Britain and the United States—at least until it had completed its industrialization and military modernization. In this 1873 opinion, Toschimichi carefully laid out his reasoning for a gradual, rather than rapid, strategy toward Korea.

>> 59. Opinion against the Korean Expedition

ŌKUBO TOSHIMICHI [1873]

Ōkubo Toshimichi's Opinion Against Korean Expedition, October 1873. In order to govern the country and protect the people it is necessary to have a flexible policy and to watch [the world situation]; always watching the situation we go forward or retreat. If the situation is bad we simply stop. The reasons *why I say that it is too early to send a mission to Korea are as follows*:

1. ... The basis of our government is not yet firmly established. We have made remarkable progress in abolishing the *han*, etc., and if we look at the central part of Japan, everything seems accomplished, but if we look at the countryside, many people who oppose this will be seen. We have established a fortress and have good military equipment, so they dare not rise up against us. But if we reveal some weak point, they will be quick to take advantage. There is no special problem now, but we must look to the future. With the restoration many new laws have been promulgated, but people are not yet at ease and

they fear our government. In the last two years there have been many misunderstandings and these led to uprisings. It is a truly difficult situation. This is one reason why I am opposed to making war on Korea.

2. Today government expenditures are tremendous, and income is below expense. Thus if we open fire and send several tens of thousands of men abroad we will incur enormous expense. This will require heavy taxes or foreign loans or the issuance of paper notes and will lead to higher prices, social unrest and uprisings. Already we have 5,000,000 [yen] in foreign loans; even this is difficult to pay.

3. Our government has started to stimulate industries, but it will be several years before we get results.... If we now begin an unnecessary war, spend a huge amount of money, shed blood, and worsen the daily life of people, all these government works will break like a bubble and lose several decades of time. We will regret it.

4. Regarding the foreign trade situation, each year there is a one million yen deficit... and our gold reserve decreases. Thus our international credit worsens, leading to inflation and our people's livelihood becoming hard. Also the export

Source: Ōkubo Toshimichi, "Opinion against the Korean Expedition," in *Sources of Japanese History*, vol. 2, edited by David John Lu (New York: McGraw-Hill, 1973), 52–53.

of our products faces difficulties. If we open fire without thinking of our economic and military power, our soldiers will have a bad time and their parents will be in difficulty; they will cease to work well and our national productivity will decrease. Such things as weapons must be purchased from foreign countries; our foreign trade deficit will become worse and worse.

5. In regard to the diplomatic situation, the most important countries for us are Russia and Britain....Relations with them are uncertain. I fear that Russia will interfere unless we secure our independence. If we open fire on Korea, Russia will fish out both the clam and the bird and get a fisherman's profit. Thus we should not begin a war in Korea now.

6. In regard to the Asian situation, Britain is especially powerful, watching with a tiger's eye. Our foreign loans depend on Britain. If there is trouble and we become poor, Britain will surely interfere in our internal affairs on that pretext. Look at India . . . observe carefully the process by which India became a colony. We must build our industry, our exports, etc. It is our most urgent business.

7. The Japanese treaties with Europe and America are not equal. This is harmful for our independence. Therefore we must do our best to revise them, or England and France will send armies on the pretext of an insecure internal situation.... The first thing is to revise the treaties, the Korean business after that.

Conclusion. As I have said above we must not hurry to begin war. Of course, we cannot overlook the arrogant attitude of Korea, but we have no clear reason to attack Korea. Now it is argued, send the envoy and depending on his reception open fire or not. But we may be sure from experience that his reception will be cold, so this automatically means open fire. Thus we must decide about sending an army before we send the envoy. If there is war we must have more than 100,000 soldiers, laborers, ships, etc. It will cost many times 10,000 yen. Even though we are victorious, the expense will be far beyond the profit. Also after the victory there will be uprisings over there. Even though we get all kinds of goods in Korea, they will amount to less than the expense. Also it is said that neither China nor Russia will intervene, but there is no proof. It is said that we cannot endure Korean arrogance, but this is an insufficient reason and it would be very bad to open fire without thinking of our security and our people's welfare. Therefore I oppose....

>> Mastering the Material

1. Ferry's defense of maritime colonialism can be seen to rest upon either strategic or economic motives, or both. Which do you see occurring most in this text. Is it possible to separate strategy from economics?

2. How does Ferry's argument for overseas colonies concur with the writing of naval strategists like A. T. Mayhan?

3. Why does the navy, rather than the army, receive such attention in the thinking of the proponents of the new imperialism?

4. What, according to A. J. P. Taylor, was the strategic reason for Germany's sudden annexation of colonies in Africa in 1884?

5. Ōkubo Toshimichi presents Japanese imperialism as a case of conquer or be conquered. To what degree does this explanation justify the new imperialism generally?

>> Making Connections

1. In the fifteenth century, the Ming Emperors came to the decision to focus on agrarian reform rather than building fleets and a maritime empire. In the nineteenth century, the Meiji administration of Japan came to the opposite conclusion. What differing circumstances led to these diverging choices?

2. What changes in Europe, and especially in the way Europeans viewed their world intellectually, in the period preceding the new imperialism and discussed in Part 2, can be seen to have influenced the things Ferry says in this chapter?

3. The United States had once been a collection of colonies, and had fought for its own independence. Why were Americans like A. T. Mahan now willing to propose that the United States take away the independence of other regions and form its own colonies? What had changed?

4. Consider Japan's participation in the new imperialism in light of the ideas put forward in the four drafts of the Charter Oath. Is there a contradiction between the egalitarian ideals of this oath and the building of a colonial empire? How do you think Toschimichi would have justified Japanese imperialism despite these ideals?

5. Consider the wide range of arguments put forward in Part 1 to explain the rise of sixteenth century European maritime empires. Do you think it is convincing to argue that the new imperialism of the nineteenth century, which affected much of the world, had its origins solely in the strategic relationship between the five or six industrialized powers that became the most extensive colonizers? Why or why not?

Chapter 13

Economic Explanations

Among the most common explanations for modern colonialism is that it was planned and carried out to make money. Britain, industrializing all alone in the early nineteenth-century, had been able to make vast profits through aggressively pursuing policies of free trade. British factories could produce goods more efficiently and British shipping could transport them more cheaply than those of any other state. However, by the 1870s the Industrial Revolution was largely complete in western Europe and the United States. The industries of these states, and later Japan, increasingly competed with longer-established British banks and corporations. As competition grew fierce, industrialists and financiers began to urge their governments to assist them in securing a share of global trade. This pressure arguably caused colonialism, as the great powers annexed colonies in order to deny them to their rivals. Each colony not only provided resources to the metropole but also represented a pool of inexpensive labor. Perhaps most important, they were markets for the goods produced by European factories. In many parts of the world, cheap mass-produced European goods began to replace locally produced products.

The economic importance of colonies should not be underestimated, and not only to factory owners. Some economic historians believe that colonial enterprises gradually became the principal income generators for important groups of investors who have been given the title imperial capitalists. Vladimir Lenin, a leading Marxist scholar before he became the first premier of the Soviet Union, contended that imperialism was simply a scheme by financiers and bourgeois investors to make ever more profit. **Marxist** thinkers, basing their work on the writings of the political philosopher Karl Marx, view capitalism as a fundamentally unjust system in which the bourgeoisie exploits the working classes in search of maximized profits. They therefore view all of history through the lens of struggles between different socioeconomic classes. Marxist theory forms the foundation for communism, a political theory that advocates public, rather than private, ownership of assets and means of production. In his 1916 pamphlet *Imperialism: The Highest Stage of Capitalism,* Lenin applied Marxist theory to imperialism. He argued that the new imperialism was the consequence of capitalist competition in Europe. Because of increasing competition between industrialized European states (and the eastern seaboard of the United States), Lenin suggested, capitalists had begun to run out of possibilities for profit at home. Thus they began to look for markets abroad and found them in Africa and Asia. Needing to protect these investments, they then called upon their state governments to take formal control of overseas regions.

A number of economic historians continue to embrace Lenin's argument that it was economic crisis in the industrialized states that caused the new imperialism. By 1873, the competing industrialized powers were producing a glut of industrial goods, and the result was a massive worldwide depression. In the United States and Europe, especially, banks and manufacturing companies began to fail, prompting mass unemployment. Politicians in the industrialized nations blamed this problem on their competitors in order to shift blame from themselves—in Britain, for example, German and American industry were depicted as the causes of the depression. In this interpretation the annexation of colonial markets as dumping grounds for industrial goods was carried by politicians as a way to divert the workers' anger.

However, two historians—Peter Cain and Anthony Hopkins—have given Lenin's theory a modern twist. Focusing on the British Empire, Cain and Hopkins suggest that it was a specific and very wealthy class of money owners, the Gentlemanly Capitalists, who guided the expansion of the British Empire from a one-square-mile financial district in London known as the "City." They suggest that these stockbrokers and investors were the driving force behind the new imperialism for Britain. The two historians first explored this theory in their article "Gentlemanly Capitalism and British Expansion Overseas II: New Imperialism, 1850–1945," and later expanded it in a two-volume text that helped revive British imperial studies in the late 1990s: *British Imperialism: 1688–2000.*

Thus the expansion of colonialism caused the governments of the competing imperial powers to spend large amounts of money in conquering and ruling colonies, arguably to the benefit of only a very few industrialists and financiers. This inequity drew criticism from anti-imperialists both in the metropole and the colonies. John Hobson, a leading critic of Britain's new colonial expansion, argued in his seminal 1898 study *Imperialism* that the British government should concentrate on social programs within Britain rather than expansion overseas. Another critique came from the Indian intellectual Dadabhai Naoroji. Naoroji wrote extensively on the economic impact of British rule in India and used his 1880 memorandum "On the Moral Poverty in India and Native Thoughts on the Present British Indian Policy" to point out the many costs of colonial rule to the Indian people. Together, these two critics illustrate that if there were economic winners in the race for new colonies, they made their money at great cost to the people of both the colonizing states and the colonized.

V. I. Lenin Connects Capitalism and Imperialism

V. I. Lenin was a witness to the new imperialism, and he viewed it as merely an extension of the historic class struggle between capitalists and workers. In 1916, he spent about six months in Switzerland reading and writing about imperialism. He devised a theory that brought together Marxist interpretations of history and his own observations of the imperialism and colonialism he was witnessing. Lenin argued that the powerful capitalists were no longer just the factory owners, but also the financiers: investors and stockbrokers. These individuals had grouped together in cartels, or monopolies, to exploit the resources first of the industrial European states and later much of the rest of the world. These monopolies, he asserted, then divided the world up between themselves. They were interested both in regions where it was proven a profit could be made and in regions that potentially could be profitable, and in order to pro-tect their investments they convinced their governments to agree to formally take over the parts of the world they claimed. Economic history is often difficult to read, Marxist economic history even more so, and this excerpt is perhaps the most difficult primary source in this whole volume. However, it is so important to understanding economic histories of imperialism that it is worth the effort.

>> 60. Imperialism: The Highest Stage of Capitalism

VLADIMIR ILLYICH LENIN [1916]

Under the old capitalism, when free competition prevailed, the export of *goods* was the most typi-cal feature. Under modern capitalism, when monopolies prevail, the export of *capital* has become the typical feature. [...]

As long as capitalism remains what it is, sur-plus capital will never be utilised for the purpose of raising the standard of living of the masses in a given country, for this would mean a decline in profits for the capitalists; it will be used for the purpose of increasing those profits by exporting capital abroad to the backward countries. [...]

[T]he characteristic feature of this period is the final partition of the globe—not in the sense that a *new* partition is impossible—on the contrary, new partitions are possible and inevitable—but in the sense that the colonial policy of the capitalist coun-tries has *completed* the seizure of the unoccupied territories on our planet. [...]

The principal feature of modern capitalism is the domination of monopolist combines of the big capitalists. These monopolies are most firmly established when *all* the sources of raw materials are controlled by the one group. And we have seen with what zeal the international capitalist combines exert every effort to make it impossible

for their rivals to compete with them; for exam-ple, by buying up mineral lands, oil fields, etc. Colonial possession alone gives complete guaran-tee of success to the monopolies against all the risks of the struggle with competitors, including the risk that the latter will defend themselves by means of a law establishing a state monopoly. The more capitalism is developed, the more the need for raw materials is felt, the more bitter competi-tion becomes, and the more feverishly the hunt for raw materials proceeds throughout the whole world, the more desperate becomes the struggle for the acquisition of colonies. [...]

Finance capital is not only interested in the already known sources of raw materials; it is also interested in potenial sources of raw materials, because present-day technical development is extremely rapid, and because land which is use-less today may be made fertile tomorrow if new methods are applied (to devise these new meth-ods a big bank can equip a whole expedition of engineers, agricultural experts, etc.), and large amounts of capital are invested. This also applies to prospecting for minerals, to new methods of working up and utilising raw materials, etc., etc. Hence, the inevitable striving of finance capital to extend its economic territory and even its territory in general. In the same way that the trusts capitalise their property by estimating it at two or three times its value, taking into account

Source: Vladimir Illyich Lenin, *Imperialism: The Highest Stage of Capitalism* (New York: International Publishers, 1939), 62–63, 76–77, 82–84, 88–89. First published in 1916.

its "potential" (and not present) returns, and the further results of monopoly, so finance capital strives to seize the largest possible amount of land of all kinds and in any place it can, and by any means, counting on the possibilities of finding raw materials there, and fearing to be left behind in the insensate struggle for the last available scraps of undivided territory, or for the repartition of that which has been already divided.

The British capitalists are exerting every effort to develop cotton growing in *their* colony, Egypt (in 1904, out of 2,300,000 hectares of land under cultivation, 600,000 or more than one-fourth, were devoted to cotton, growing); the Russians are doing the same in *their* colony, Turkestan; and they are doing so because in this way they will be in a better position to defeat their foreign competitors, to monopolize the sources of raw materials and from a more economical and profitable textile trust in which *all* the processes of cotton production and manufacturing will be "combined" and concentrated in the hands of a single owner.

The necessity of exporting capital also gives an impetus to the conquest of colonies, for in the colonial market it is easier to eliminate competition, to make sure of orders, to strengthen the necessary "connections," etc. [...]

If it were necessary to give the briefest possible definition of imperialism we should have to say that imperialism is the monopoly stage of capitalism. Such a definition would include what is most important, for, on the one hand, finance capital is the bank capital of a few big monopolist banks, merged with the capital of the monopolist combines of manufacturers; and, on the other hand, the division of the world is the transition from a colonial policy which has extended without hindrance to territories unoccupied by any capitalist power, to a colonial policy of monopolistic possession of the territory of the world which has been completely divided up. [...]

Imperialism is capitalism in the stage of development in which the dominance of monopolies and finance capital has established itself; in which the export of capital has acquired pronounced importance; in which the division of the world among the international trusts has begun; in which the division of all territories of the globe among the great capitalist powers has been completed.

Gentlemanly Capitalism

Cain and Hopkins' revision of theories of economic history is linked to Lenin's analysis in several ways. The first is the concentration upon a similar class of people within industrialized societies, specifically Britain. Cain and Hopkins sometimes refer to these groups as the "service sector" or "Gentlemanly Capitalists," but they are largely the same financial capitalists identified by Lenin. Utilizing a wide array of evidence, the two historians suggest that these stockbrokers and investors worked in partnership with the British government in this period to establish a "financial empire," in which the government and military often did their bidding. This included not only negotiations and gunboat diplomacy to protect British investors' money abroad, but also sometimes outright annexation of regions they believed they needed to control to protect their finances. In this excerpt, the two authors explore the ways in which they operated in the European-settled colonies of Canada, South Africa, and Oceania; in the still-independent states of Latin America, China, and the Ottoman Empire; and in the African colonies of exploitation. Cain and Hopkins' work has been criticized by scholars who suggest that they have ignored other groups important to the process, such as colonial settlers, factory owners, naval officers, career bureaucrats, and the indigenous peoples of the colonies.

>> 61. Gentlemanly Capitalism and British Expansion Overseas II: New Imperialism, 1850–1945

P. J. CAIN AND A. G. HOPKINS [1987]

The growth of the service sector, including the financial institutions centred upon London, was the chief influence upon Britain's presence overseas after 1850. This influence was particularly marked between 1850 and 1914—a period of rapid expansion—but was also felt strongly in less advantageous conditions after World War I. After 1850, investment abroad was no longer confined to entrepôts and coastlines; and railway companies (many with headquarters in the City) began to develop the interior of continents which had hitherto proved impenetrable. While provincial industrialists worried about foreign competition, the City of London extended its institutional frame across the globe to act as banker and carrier to the world's commerce and trade. [...]

The financial agents of gentlemanly capitalism and its ideological supports were found mainly in the newly settled world, where, in some circumstances, Britain's role was so dominant that it is reasonable to speak of the relationship as being one economic imperialism. [...] Parts of Latin America, notably Argentina and Uruguay and, to a lesser extent, Brazil, were similarly placed, the rhythm of their economic life being dependent upon the ebb and flow of London funds. [...]

In [...] alien environments, penetration depended more obviously upon the success of informal political influence. The degree of power exercised by Britain in any particular area was itself a function of her relationship with other great powers and of the resilience of the indigenous culture. In both China and the Middle East great power rivalry and the hostility of the local ruling élites imposed severe constraints on Britain's effective authority. These constraints, in turn, affected the supply of capital a nervous and suspicious City would provide, and further limited the British presence. The outcome was a complex and sometimes uneasy partnership between bankers and government. The banks were inclined, for purely commercial reasons, to strike up cosmopolitan alliances which could embarrass their political patrons; and they often used state support as a way of limiting competition from their foreign rivals. Governments occasionally forced their financial backers into international schemes against their will, pushed them further than their commercial instincts would have taken them, and sometimes abandoned them when the diplomatic climate changed. But whether the ultimate objectives of policy were strategic or diplomatic, as in Persia, or economic, as in China, financiers and governments needed each other's support. Bankers could not raise funds profitably or use them effectively on these uncertain frontiers without the backing of the state. Governments could not hope to create the infrastructures which would provide the conditions for spontaneous flows of capital and trade, and enhance Britian's power and prestige, without the means provided by the money brokers and their connexions in the City. [...]

Elsewhere, the barriers to penetration were lower. Egypt's rulers co-operated readily with foreign interests, and Britain was able to expand her influence there largely unhampered by diplomatic constraints. The Boer republics were less willing modernizers, but their smallness and isolation from other great-power influences made access to them relatively easy. In both cases economic penetration generated development crises which in turn led to British intervention. The occupation of Egypt in 1882 and the advances in South Africa in the 1890s cannot be reduced to conspiracies of bondholders or mineowners. But Britain's merciless insistence on debt repayment did bring down her Egyptian allies, whose plight

Source: P. J. Cain, and A. G. Hopkins, "Gentlemanly Capitalism and British Expansion Overseas II: New Imperialism, 1850–1945," *The Economic History Review* 40 (1987): 10–13.

was regarded as evidence that "orientals" were incapable of self-government. Similarly, the costly decision to bring the Boer republics under control can only be understood in the context of the need to defend Britain's substantial financial and commercial stake in South Africa. [...] The hostility displayed towards Egyptian and Boer nationalism stemmed largely from the fact that both disputed the rules of the game—rules devised by gentlemanly capitalists in London and regarded as being vital to Britain's economic advance abroad and to her political security.

A Liberal Interpretation of the Economic Origins of Imperialism

John Hobson was an economic historian in Britain and another witness to the new imperialism. At first something of a supporter, Hobson came to be a critic of British colonial expansion for its effects not only on overseas populations but on Britain as well. A believer that government economic policy should be imbued with a sense of moral responsibility, Hobson was a liberal critic of empire, although he would later be cited by more radical socialist thinkers like Lenin. In the first five paragraphs of this excerpt, Hobson outlines the economic justification given by proponents of imperialism. He then refutes them by arguing that empire was a waste of money that could otherwise have been spent on social programs for Britain's citizens. The inhabitants of countries such as Denmark and Sweden, he argues, enjoyed a better standard of living as a result of not investing in empire.

>> 62. Imperialism: A Study

JOHN A. HOBSON [1902]

No mere array of facts and figures adduced to illustrate the economic nature of the new Imperialism will suffice to dispel the popular delusion that the use of national force to secure new markets by annexing fresh tracts of territory is a sound and a necessary policy for an advanced industrial country like Great Britain. [...]

It is open to Imperialists to argue thus: "We must have markets for our growing manufactures, we must have new outlets for the investment of our surplus capital and for the energies of the adventurous surplus of our population: such expansion is a necessity of life to a nation with our great and growing powers of production. An ever larger share of our population is devoted to the manufacturers and commerce of towns, and is thus dependent for life and work upon food and raw materials from foreign lands. In order to buy and pay for these things we must sell our goods abroad. During the first three-quarters of the nineteenth century we could do so without difficulty by a natural expansion of commerce with continental nations and our colonies, all of which were far behind us in the main arts of manufacture and the carrying trades. So long as England held a virtual monopoly of the world markets for certain important classes of manufactured goods, Imperialism was unnecessary. After 1870 this manufacturing and trading supremacy was greatly impaired: other nations, especially Germany, the United States, and Belgium, advanced with great rapidity, and while they have not crushed or even stayed the increase of our external trade, their competition made it more and more difficult to dispose of the full surplus of our manufacturers at

Source: John A. Hobson, *Imperialism: A Study* (London: George Allen & Unwin, 1954), 71–72, 77–78, 80–81, 92–93. First published in 1902.

a profit. The encroachments made by these nations upon our old markets, even in our own possessions, made it most urgent that we should take energetic means to secure new markets. These new markets had to lie in hitherto undeveloped countries, chiefly in the tropics, where vast populations lived capable of growing economic needs which our manufacturers and merchants could supply. Our rivals were seizing and annexing territories for similar purposes, and when they had annexed them closed them to our trade. The diplomacy and the arms of Great Britain had to be used in order to compel the owners of the new markets to deal with us: and experience showed that the safest means of securing and developing such markets is by establishing 'protectorates' or by annexation. [...]

[In the United States, for example]...[I]t was this sudden demand for foreign markets for manufactures and for investments which was avowedly responsible for the adoption of Imperialism as a political policy. [...] They needed Imperialism because they desired to use the public resources of their country to find profitable employment for their capital which otherwise would be superfluous. [...]

Every improvement of methods of production, every concentration of ownership and control, seems to accentuate the tendency. As one nation after another enters the machine economy and adopts advanced industrial methods, it becomes more difficult for its manufacturers, merchants, and financiers to dispose profitably of their economic resources, and they are tempted more and more to use their Governments in order to secure for their particular use some distant undeveloped country by annexation and protection.

The process, we may be told, is inevitable, and so it seems upon a superficial inspection. Everywhere appear excessive powers of production, excessive capital in search of investment. It is admitted by all business men that the growth of the powers of production in their country exceeds the growth in consumption, that more goods can be produced than can be sold at a profit, and that more capital exists than can find remunerative investment.

It is this economic condition of affairs that forms the taproot of Imperialism. If the consuming public in this country raised its standard of consumption to keep pace with every rise of productive powers, there could be no excess of goods or capital clamorous to use Imperialism in order to find markets. [...]

Everywhere the issue of quantitative *versus* qualitative growth comes up. This is the entire issue of empire. A people limited in number and energy and in the land they occupy have the choice of improving to the utmost the political and economic management of their own land, confining themselves to such accessions of territory as are justified by the most economical disposition of a growing population; or they may proceed, like the slovenly farmer, to spread their power and energy over the whole earth, tempted by the speculative value or the quick profits of some new market, or else by mere greed of territorial acquisition, and ignoring the political and economic wastes and risks involved by this imperial career. It must be clearly understood that this is essentially a choice of alternatives; a full simultaneous application of intensive and extensive cultivation is impossible. A nation may either, following the example of Denmark or Switzerland, put brains into agriculture, develop a finely varied system of public education, general and technical, apply the ripest science to its special manufacturing industries, and so support in progressive comfort and character a considerable population upon a strictly limited area; or it may, like Great Britain, neglect its agriculture, allowing its lands to go out of cultivation and its population to grow up in towns, fall behind other nations in its methods of education and in the capacity of adapting to its uses the latest scientific knowledge, in order that it may squander its pecuniary and military resources in forcing bad markets and finding speculative fields of investment in distant corners of the earth, adding millions of square miles and of unassimilable population to the area of the Empire.

The driving forces of class interest which stimulate and support this false economy we have explained. No remedy will serve which permits the future operation of these forces. It is idle to attack Imperialism or Militarism as political expedients or policies unless the axe is laid at the economic root of the tree, and the classes for whose interest Imperialism works are shorn of the surplus revenues which seek this outlet.

British Misrule and the Impoverishment of India

As an intellectual, Dadabhai Naoroji was the result of crosscurrents of thought given birth by the new imperialism. Very much a scholar in the Indian tradition, he was also western-educated and came to understand British rule in India in its own terms. Using the language of British officialdom, he was able to build the case that the British were misruling India. Focusing sometimes on economics and sometimes on moral issues, Naoroji brought the argument for reform of British rule to the British parliament and people. Back in India, he helped form the Indian National Congress, which would later fight for India's independence. Naoroji also heavily influenced a number of later anticolonial leaders. In this article he depicts the British administration and British companies as parasites, taking away the profits of the Indians' hard work for their own benefit. He seeks to refute a particular claim of the British, that India's poverty was a result of its overpopulation, by suggesting that India had become impoverished because the food and resources to feed its dense population were being diverted to enrich Britain.

>> 63. Memorandum No. 2 on the Moral Poverty in India and Native Thoughts on the Present British Indian Policy

DADABHAI NAOROJI [1880]

[British theorists] talk, and so far truly, of the increase by British peace, but they quite forget the destruction by the British drain. They talk of the pitiless operations of economic laws, but somehow they forgot that there is no such thing in India as the natural operation of economic laws. It is not the pitiless operations of economic laws, but it is the thoughtless and pitiless action of the British policy; it is the pitiless eating of India's substance in India, and the further pitiless drain in England; in short, it is the pitiless *perversion* of economic laws by the sad bleeding to which India is subjected, that is destroying India. Why blame poor Nature when the fault lies at your own door? Let natural and economic laws have their full and fair day, and India will become another England, with manifold greater benefit to England herself than at present.

As long as the English do not allow the country to produce what it can produce, as long as the people are not allowed to enjoy what they can produce, as long as the English are the very party of their trial, they have no right, and are not competent, to give an opinion whether the country is over-populated or not. In fact, it is absurd to talk of over-population—*i.e.*, the country's incapability,

Source: Dadabhai Naoroji, "Memorandum No. 2 on the Moral Poverty in India and Native Thoughts on the Present British Indian Policy," 16 November, 1880, in *Voices of Indian Freedom Movement,* edited by J. C. Johari (New Delhi: Akashdeep Publishing, 1993), 100–101.

by its food or other produce, to supply the means of support to its people—if the country is unceasingly and forcibly deprived of its means or capital. Let the country keep what it produces for only then can any right judgment be formed whether it is over-populated or not. Let England first hold hands off India's wealth, and then there will be disinterestedness in, and respect for her judgment. The present cant of the excuse of over-population is adding a distressful insult to agonising injury. To all of over-population at present is just as reasonable as to cut off a man's hands, and then to taunt him that he was not able to maintain himself or move his hands.

>> Mastering the Material

1. Who were the "gentlemen capitalists"? What, according to Cain and Hopkins, was their role in the formulation of the British Empire?

2. Hobson, Naoroji, and Lenin were all opponents of imperialism. On what basis does each argue against imperialism? To what degree do you think they would agree with each other?

3. Dadabai Naoroji was a trained mathematician. How did he mobilize his expertise to argue against British rule of India?

>> Making Connections

1. In Reading 57, Jules Ferry argues that empire was necessary for the economic prosperity of the metropole. How do the readings in this chapter elaborate on or refute this argument?

2. Several scholars cited in Parts 1 and 2 argued that capitalism helped western Europeans and European settlers get ahead of other regions and peoples of the world in the early modern era. Do you think Lenin would agree with this assessment? Why or why not?

Chapter 14

Moral Explanations

So far in Part 3 we have explored the geopolitical and economic origins of the new imperialism. At their most basic, these causative factors are easily definable and quite understandable. The search for money and power are often put forth as the rational causes of many of the great transformative events in world history: war, exploration, and the building of states to name but a few. But, as we have also seen, the race to acquire formal colonies and informal influence in the era of the new imperialism was not always rational. What possible economic motives, for example, can explain the competition of Britain, France, and at times Italy to dominate the Sahara desert? Of what strategic use were Pacific Islands to Germany, a continental European power? Certainly political and economic considerations were important causes of the new imperialism, but are they enough of an explanation? Or was the new imperialism based partly on abstract, difficult-to-understand values and cultural norms rather than purely concrete, pragmatic considerations? Did the colonizing powers believe that imperialism was a virtuous undertaking, that they had a privilege, a right, or even a duty to acquire colonies overseas?

This question brings us right to the heart of a great contradiction. Following an era of enlightenment and political revolutions, the states that were colonizing the world were arguably the most democratic large-scale societies on the planet. The United States, Britain, France, Germany, Belgium, Italy, and Japan all had at least limited representative government and large numbers of voters—even if women, the poor, and certain ethnic groups were often excluded from the electoral process. Within these countries powerful groups espoused ideas of humanitarianism, philanthropy, and tolerance. Yet these same nation-states, which were extending many rights to their own citizens for the first time in their histories, concurrently undertook to oppress much of the rest of the world through an imperialism that was almost always coercive, usually violent, and at times even genocidal in its treatment of local populations. How did the leaders and inhabitants of the imperial powers reconcile their much-vaunted moral ethics with the realities of colonialism?

A number of theories have been advanced to explain how even leading liberals, religious figures, and humanists became allied to the cause of imperialism. They generally involve the notion of a **civilizing mission.** Many western Europeans and American intellectuals of this period, whether secular or religious, depict imperialism as a service to the colonized. They argue that colonialism brought with it the three Cs: civilization, commerce, and Christianity. Therefore, it improved the lives of those they depicted as savages. This idea is expressed in Rudyard Kipling's famous poem about the American occupation of the Philippines, *The White Man's Burden,* written in 1899.

Many social and cultural elements within industrialized nations came together in the 1890s to promote this vision of imperialism as a service, and each has its roots in the changing worldviews in Europe, Japan, and the United States in previous periods. Evangelical Protestantism and the Catholic response of the counter-reformation, for example, intellectually and financially prepared religious members of society to become overseas missionaries and to accept the mission of converting others to Christianity. Similarly, notions of humanism led both religious and secular individuals to believe in a mission to help other humans in other ways. In some parts of the world, for example, imperialism went hand in hand with the British-led campaign against slavery. Simultaneously, however, a peculiar mixture of developing scientific concepts such as evolutionary biology and the growing military superiority of industrialized armies and navies led imperialist philosophers to develop the idea that industrialized nations had a "right" to conquer weaker regions. The idea of natural selection, developed by Charles Darwin to describe biological processes but later twisted by supporters of imperialism, was used to justify the horrors of conquest and rule. Thus science was often misused to defend racism, and racism to excuse colonialism. Another intellectual precursor of imperialism was nationalism. Although nationalism in Europe, Japan, and the United States may have begun as a movement to liberate the people of a nation from the tyranny of despotic rulers, quite quickly some began to reinterpret it as a race to establish national superiority.

The moral justifications for imperialism took slightly different forms in each of the different imperialist states, two of which are highlighted in this unit. British notions were especially tinted by evangelical Protestantism, by notions of liberalism, by ideas of hierarchy taken from their own class-bound society, and by their relationship with India, a colony of long standing. British supporters of imperialism therefore often spoke of their Christian duty toward colonized peoples. This idea pervaded British society as early as the 1790s, when Protestant missionary societies such as the Baptist Missionary Society, the London Missionary Society, and the Wesleyan Methodist Missionary Society proliferated. These groups campaigned not only for the spreading of the Gospel but also for the abolition of slavery and the suppression of cultural practices that they disliked. They promoted colonialism because they felt that British rule would not only speed the conversion of non-Christians but also bring "civilization" to other regions of the world. Many of these societies published texts for British men, women, and children not only to prepare them to become missionaries but also to convince them of the righteousness of colonialism. Most evangelical attention was focused on men, but women, too, were given roles. At first their prescribed function was merely to support their husbands, but over time, as Frances Elizabeth Davies writes in "The Missionary's Bride," the wives' lifestyles and prayers were also considered important in ministering to and converting especially the women of the colonies.

The racialism of the imperial worldview also led colonial agents to classify the peoples of the world according to assumed traits. Some Nepalese populations, for example, were considered by the British to be useful as soldiers and were therefore described as hearty and masculine, but most peoples of India were depicted as effemi-nate and inefficient. This hierarchical perspective was submerged in an overall view of the west as dynamic and on the rise and the east as stagnant and on the decline. This worldview, which has been given the overall name **orientalism,** is well represented here by the writings of the Earl of Cromer, first British Governor of Egypt following its annexation in 1882. Cromer's assertions that Britain had saved Egypt from its own decadence and misrule were, however, aptly parried by Egyptian nationalists such as Aḥmad Luṭfī al-Sayyid.

French notions of the imperial mission were slightly different. During the early years of the new imperialism many of France's leaders genuinely saw themselves as carrying out the mission of the French Revolution—to spread freedom, enlight-enment, and French civilization around the world. Even in France, their efforts had been coercive—many dissident groups and ethnic minorities such as the Breton had been "civilized" at sword point. Overseas, as historian Alice Conklin suggests in her book *A Mission to Civilize,* French colonial officials hoped that they could increase the strength and economy of France and at the same time bring French culture and social practices, which they felt were superior, to the people of West Africa and elsewhere.

In some cases, the moral imperative for empire sounds quite convincing. The British did, in fact, largely end the export of slaves from Africa to Arabia by annexing much of the region. The French did largely end ritual sacrifices in some regions of cen-tral Africa. However, there are at least four problems with the civilizing mission. The first is that it assumes that the imperial power had moral superiority over the popula-tions they conquered. The very fact that the great powers felt they had the right to go out and militarily conquer independent peoples casts doubt on that assertion. The second problem is that moral duty, humanitarianism, and the Christian mission were often just window dressing used by greedy leaders to convince the people of their countries to support imperialism. An additional problem was that even when Africans or Asians abandoned their own cultures, became western educated and joined European or American Christian churches, they were still usually not accepted as equals. Finally, no matter how nice the theory sounded, in practice imperialism required force and resulted in oppression and death. The first known incidents of genocide and concentration camps in the modern world, for example, were in Spanish Cuba, British South Africa, and German South–West Africa.

The White Man's Burden

Rudyard Kipling was in many ways the laureate of British and American colonial-ism. Born in India but educated in Britain, Kipling worked as a reporter before turn-ing to write books, articles, and poems that dealt with colonialism and extolled the virtues of Anglo (British and American) colonizers. As this poem commemorating the American occupation of the Philippines shows, he believed deeply in the civilizing mission.

>> 64. The White Man's Burden

RUDYARD KIPLING [1899]

Take up the White Man's burden—
Send forth the best ye breed—
Go send your sons to exile
To serve your captives' need
To wait in heavy harness
On fluttered folk and wild—
Your new-caught, sullen peoples,
Half devil and half child

Take up the White Man's burden
In patience to abide
To veil the threat of terror
And check the show of pride;
By open speech and simple
An hundred times made plain
To seek another's profit
And work another's gain

Take up the White Man's burden—
And reap his old reward:
The blame of those ye better
The hate of those ye guard—
The cry of hosts ye humour
(Ah slowly) to the light:
"Why brought ye us from bondage,
Our loved Egyptian night?"

Take up the White Man's burden—
Have done with childish days—
The lightly proffered laurel,
The easy, ungrudged praise.
Comes now, to search your
    manhood
Through all the thankless years,
Cold-edged with dear-bought
    wisdom,
The judgment of your peers!

The Missionary's Bride

One of the key features of imperialism was the constant barrage of information, propaganda, and opinion about empire both in the metropole and the colonies. There is a great debate as to why the proponents of imperialism kept up such a flood of texts, posters, music, hymns, and papers. Some scholars argue that it was because public support for empire was weak and had to be constantly propped up. Others argue just the opposite, that this volume of writing proves that interest in empire was very high. Among the key opinion makers were missionary societies, and their propaganda paved the way for the new imperialism. After the mid-nineteenth century, missionary societies began to favor sending married couples overseas instead of single men. In part, this reflected the growing notion in British society that men operating in the public sphere needed the support of women who managed the home and that missionary families would be good models for potential converts. It also reflected the slowly dawning realization that female missionaries would be better able to convert women in the colonies. Some of the most active promoters of female missionary service were women who had grown up in missionary households, like Frances Elizabeth Davies, the daughter of a New Zealand pastor.

Source: Rudyard Kipling, *The White Man's Burden*, Widely published from 1899.

>> 65. The Missionary's Bride

FRANCES ELIZABETH DAVIES [1845]

With orange blossoms bind her brows,
And twine among her hair
Roses, as white as sunlit snows,
But jewels place not there.
No gems of vanity should speak,
Nor fashion's glittering prize,
While meekness blushes on the cheek,
And faith lights up the eyes.
There should be nought of human pride,
About the missionary's bride.

Around her form no ribbons gay,
Nor gaudy silks should shine;
But India's muslins float and play,
In chastely pure design.
About her lip, and eye, and cheek,
A gentle smile should be;
Religion's high resolve to speak,
From earthly passion free;
For holy hope should e'er abide
About a missionary's bride.

Tears at the bridal of are shed,
That bind the worldling's vow;
But ne'er when Christian labourers wed;
Then lady, weep not thou!
What though a long farewell to take,
Be sorrow evermore; a
For every earthly tie we break
Tenfold doth God restore.
Go forth, then! at thy husband's side,
A worthy missionary's bride.

'Tis true thou leavest country—all,
To cross the bounding sea,
But many a heathen voice shall call,
On Jesus, taught by thee.
Besides full many a sufferer's bed,
Thy pious prayers shall rise,
And many a tiny infant's head,
Be lifted toward the skies;
While kindred souls, by grace allied,
Shall bless the missionary's bride.

Then look not back, so fondly still,
On friendship's cherish'd claim,
Strive, humbly strive, thy post to fill,
Exalt thy matron name.
Nor murmuring sigh, nor anxious care,
Should that blest lot afford—
The precious privilege to share,
The service of the Lord.
Then be thou strong, in God confide!
He'll help the missionary's bride.

Chase, chase away the gushing tear,
Although thou far may'st roam,
There watcheth One thy soul to cheer,
And bless thy distant home.
Although thou never more may'st see
Each long remember'd place,
Thy love and labours still shall be
Before thy Father's face;
While sin and death shall ne'er divide
From Christ the missionary's bride.

Source: Frances Elizabeth Davies, "The Missionary's Bride," *Evangelical Magazine*, vol. 23 (1845): 536.

An "Orientalist" Perspective on Egypt

Evelyn Baring, First Earl of Cromer, was the British Consul-General who came to administer Egypt in 1883. Egypt had formerly been subject to the Ottoman Empire, but in the early part of the century had become largely autonomous under a khedive, or hereditary governor. However, the Egyptian khedives fell into debt to British and French bankers, and in the late 1870s the two states began to enforce a "debt administration" that placed their agents in positions of authority in the Egyptian government. In 1881 a group of nationalist reformers led by Egyptian army officers rebelled, hoping to eliminate European control over Egypt's finances. Because Egypt (with its Suez Canal) was a vital trade link in the route to India, the British Crown responded by landing an expeditionary force that rapidly defeated the nationalists. It could be argued that the principal goals of the British action were strategic (to control the canal) or economic (to force Egypt to pay back debts at ruinously high rates of interest). The British justification of the time was that rioting in Alexandria was threatening the Christian and European population there. In his memoirs, however, the Earl of Cromer argued that Britain's actions were partially aimed at reversing years of misrule, and thus that Britain's actions were merely the assumption of its moral duty to guide the Egyptian people. These excerpts from those memoirs are a good example of the orientalist perspective.

>> 66. Modern Egypt

EVELYN BARING CROMER [1908]

I was for some while in Egypt before I fully realised how little I understood my subject; and I found, to the last day of my residence in the country, that I was constantly learning something new. No casual visitor can hope to obtain much real insight into the true state of native opinion. Divergence of religion and habits of thought; in my own case ignorance of the vernacular language; the reticence of Orientals when speaking to any one in authority; their tendency to agree with any one to whom they may be talking; the want of mental symmetry and precision, which is the chief distinguishing feature between the illogical and picturesque East and the logical West, and which lends such peculiar interest to the study of Eastern life and politics; the fact that religion enters to a greater extent than in Europe into the social life and laws and customs of the people; and the further fact that the European and the Oriental, reasoning from the same premises, will often arrive at diametrically opposite conclusions. [...]

The Englishman had planted his foot on the banks of the Nile, and sat in the seats of the faithful. He came not as a conqueror, but in the familiar garb of a saviour of society. The mere assumption of this part, whether by a nation or by an individual, is calculated to arouse some degree of suspicion. The world is apt to think that the saviour is not improbably looking more to his own interests than to the salvation of society, and experience has proved that the suspicion is not infrequently well founded. Yet assuredly the Englishman could in this case produce a valid title to justify his assumption of the part which had been thrust upon him. His advent was hailed with delight by the lawful rulers of Egypt and by the mass of the Egyptian people. The greater portion of Europe also looked upon his action without disfavour, if not with positive approval. [...]

Source: Evelyn Baring Cromer, *Modern Egypt* (London: MacMillan and Co., 1907–1908), vol. I, 7 and vol. II, 123–125, 569–571.

[O]ne of the first qualifications necessary in order to play the part of a saviour of society is that the saviour should believe in himself and in his mission. This the Englishman did. He was convinced that his mission was to save Egyptian society, and, moreover, that he was able to save it. [...]

He adopted a middle course. He compromised. [...] He would assert his native genius by working a system, which, according to every canon of political thought, was unworkable. He would not annex Egypt, but he would do as much good to the country as if he had annexed it. He would not interfere with the liberty of action of the Khedivial Government, but in practice he would insist on the Khedive and the Egyptian Ministers conforming to his views. He would in theory be one of many Powers exercising equal rights, but in practice he would wield a paramount influence. He would occupy a portion of the Ottoman dominions with British troops, and at the same time he would do nothing to infringe the legitimate rights of the Sultan. He would not break his promise to the Frenchman, but he would wrap it in a napkin to be produced on some more convenient occasion. In a word, he would act with all the practical common sense, the scorn for theory, and the total absence of any fixed plan based on logical reasoning, which are the distinguishing features of his race. [...]

[N]o effort should be spared to render the native Egyptians capable of eventually taking their share in the government of a really autonomous community. Much has already been done in this direction, and it may be confidently anticipated, now that the finances of the country are established on a sound footing and the most pressing demands necessary to ensure material prosperity have been met, that intellectual, and perhaps moral progress will proceed more rapidly during the next quarter of a century than during that which has now terminated. [...]

Lastly, it should never be forgotten that, in default of community of race, religion, language, and habits of thought, which ordinarily constitute the main bonds of union between the rulers and the ruled, we must endeavour to forge such artificial bonds between the Englishman and the Egyptian as the circumstances of the case render available.

One of the most important of these bonds must always be the exhibition of reasonable and disciplined sympathy for the Egyptians, not merely by the British Government, but by every individual Englishman engaged in the work of Egyptian administration. This sympathy is a quality, the possession or absence of which is displayed by Englishmen in very various degrees when they are brought in contact with Asiatic or African races. Some go to the extreme of almost brutal antipathy, whilst others display their ill-regulated sympathy in forms which are exaggerated and even mischievous. The Egyptians rightly resent the conduct of the one class, and ridicule that of the other. A middle course, based on accurate information and on a careful study of Egyptian facts and of the Egyptian character, will be found more productive of result than either extreme.

Another bond may, to some extent, be forged by appealing to the person or the pocket. A proper system of justice and of police can protect, the former. Material interests can be served by various means, the most effective of which is to keep taxation low. Do not let us, however, imagine that, under any circumstances, we can ever create a feeling of loyalty in the breasts of the Egyptians akin to that felt by a self-governing people for indigenous rulers if, besides being indigenous, they are also beneficent. Neither by the display, sympathy, nor by good government, can we forge bonds which will be other than brittle. Sir Herbert Edwards, writing to Lord Lawrence a few years after the annexation of the Punjab, said: "We are not *liked* anywhere.... The people hailed us as deliverers from Sikh maladministration, and we were popular so long as we were plaistering wounds. But the patient is well now, and he finds the doctor a bore. There is no getting over the fact that we are not Mohammedans, that we neither eat, drink, nor intermarry with them."

The present situation in Egypt is very similar to that which existed in the Punjab when Sir Herbert Edwards wrote these lines. The want of gratitude displayed by a nation to its alien benefactors is almost as old as history itself. In whatever degree ingratitude may exist, it would be unjust to blame the Egyptians for following the dictates of human nature. In any case, whatever be the moral harvest we may reap, we must continue to do our duty, and our duty has been indicated to us by the Apostle St. Paul. We must not be "weary in well-doing."

An Egyptian Rejoinder

Egyptian nationalism, as a movement against British rule and for Egyptian independence, stretches back to deep in the period of the new imperialism and was in many ways a model for later independence movements in other parts of Africa and the Arab community. The first major nationalist party in Egypt was the Wafd, formed in 1918, and it was joined in 1922 by the Liberal Constitutional Party. Aḥmad Luṭfī al-Sayyid, a leading Liberal Constitutionalist, can be said to have experienced Britain's moral missionism first-hand. He was schooled in institutions modeled after those in Britain, including the School of Law in Cairo, and much of his work builds on British texts for keys to Egyptian independence. He was convinced that Egypt had to both adopt some Western ideas, especially in law and the sciences, and celebrate its unique history. As editor of the newspaper Al-Jarida, *Luṭfī al-Sayyid responded to Cromer's last report on his tenure of rule in Egypt, in which the Consul-General had expressed dismay at ongoing Egyptian "ineptitude." Note that in some ways Luṭfī al-Sayyid's evaluation is quite balanced, but at times it reflects his fervent nationalism.*

>> 67. Lord Cromer before History

AHMAD LUṬFĪ AL-SAYYID [1907]

What is the total result of [Lord Cromer's] policy? The result is that if we look at it through English eyes, we can only praise it. But if we look at it as any Egyptian must who seeks the welfare of his country, we cannot drum up the slightest praise for his political accomplishments in Egypt. He has deprived Egypt of the political life for which every living nation yearns. If we cannot but acknowledge that Lord Cromer extended the sphere of personal freedom, we cannot deny that he did just the opposite with respect to the Egyptian officials in the government. He divested them of freedom, authority, and influence, and handed these over to the English officials, and therefore many gifted young Egyptians began to shun the government service. There is no greater proof of this than the current drastic need of the government for officials and employees. We do not think that the ineptitude that Lord Cromer mentions in his report is anything but the reflex of defective education and the poor treatment meted out to officials and employees in the government. Perhaps he thought that the abandonment of decent education was in accord with the best interests of Great Britain, for Lord Cromer seeks the interest of his country above all else in everything–which is the manner in which a zealous patriot will behave toward his fatherland. [...] And cut to the same

Source: Aḥmad Luṭfī al-Sayyid, "Lord Cromer before History," *Al-Jarida,* 13 April 1907, in *The Evolution of Egyptian National Image,* edited by Charles Wendell (Berkeley: University of California Press, 1972), 300–301.

pattern are every act, every agreement, every step, and every measure adopted by this great English statesman.

Perhaps it would have been within the power of Lord Cromer to obtain even more advantages for his country than he did, had he also put his mind to winning the affection of the Egyptians as whose friend he described himself, to establishing the foundations of a kind of public education that would be productive and serviceable to the nation, and to expelling those who opposed this from the educational system. And if he had relied

on competent Egyptians to effect his reforms, and had trained them for good administration by allowing them freedom of action; and if he had refrained from simply eliminating true Egyptian nationality by his remarks about creating an "internationalist" nationality for Egypt, there is no doubt that he would have won the friendship of the Egyptian nation for his country, and for himself praise from the Egyptians equaling their praise for his work in enlarging the domain of personal freedom, and inculcating respect for justice and equality among all classes of the nation.

A Civilizing Mission

Historian of France Alice Conklin has looked at notions of a moral imperative during the Third Republic period of French history, which coincided with the new imperialism. In her book A Mission to Civilize, *Conklin acknowledges two rival scholarly interpretations of the moral mission* (mission civilisatrice) *described by French proponents of colonialism: The first was that the French truly believed they had a duty to bring the light of their most advanced civilization to peoples elsewhere, and the second was that it was merely a cover for the pillaging of colonies for France's benefit. She argues that many of the leaders and agents of French imperialism truly believed they were bringing benefits to the* indigenous *peoples of the colonies, and undertook projects whose purported goal was to aid just those people. They failed to see, she argued, that the civilizing mission was inherently racist, in contrast to France's stated commitment to universal equality.*

>> 68. A Mission to Civilize: The Republican Idea of Empire in France and West Africa, 1895–1930

ALICE CONKLIN [1997]

Civilization is a particularly French concept; the French invented the term in the eighteenth century and have celebrated the achievements of their own ever since. At no point in modern history, however, did the French make more claims for their civilization than during the "new" imperialism of the Third Republic. Of course all European powers at the end

of the nineteenth century claimed to be carrying out the work of civilization in their overseas territories; but only in republican France was this claim elevated to the realm of official imperial doctrine. From about 1870, when France began to enlarge its holdings in Africa and Indochina, French publicists, and subsequently politicians, declared that their government alone among the Western states had a special mission to civilize the indigenous peoples now coming under its control—what the French called their *mission civilisatrice.*

This idea of a secular *mission civilisatrice* did not originate under the Third Republic; it nevertheless

Source: Alice Conklin, *A Mission to Civilize: The Republican Idea of Empire in France and West Africa 1895–1930* (Stanford: Stanford University Press, 1997), 1–2, 248–249, 256.

acquired a particularly strong resonance after the return of democratic institutions in France, as the new regime struggled to reconcile its aggressive imperialism with its republican ideals. The notion of a civilizing mission rested upon certain fundamental assumptions about the superiority of French culture and the perfectibility of humankind. It implied that France's colonial subjects were too primitive to rule themselves, but were capable of being uplifted. It intimated that the French were particularly suited, by temperament and by virtue of both their revolutionary past and their current industrial strength, to carry out this task. Last but not least, it assumed that the Third Republic had a duty and a right to remake "primitive" cultures along lines inspired by the cultural, political, and economic development of France.

The ideology of the civilizing mission could not but strike a responsive chord in a nation now publicly committed to institutionalizing the universal principles of 1789. At the end of the nineteenth century, few French citizens doubted that the French were materially and morally superior to—and that they lived in greater freedom than—the rest of the earth's inhabitants. Many may have scoffed at the idea that the Republic's empire was actually bestowing these blessings upon those ostensibly still oppressed. But no one questioned the premise of French superiority upon which the empire rested, or even that the civilizing mission could in fact be accomplished. Such convictions were part of what it meant to be French and republican in this period, and had a profound impact upon the way in which the French ran their colonies. [...]

As heirs to the universalizing impulses of 1789, French republican policy-makers never questioned that Africans had to learn to feel French, though they insisted that their subjects evolve within their own cultures. The conviction that democratic France had a special obligation to improve the lives of all Africans, and not just those of an indigenous elite, was also widely held. Moral improvement would occur through a selective extension of the rights of man to Africans: the abolition of slavery, "feudal" tyranny, and barbaric custom first, and then the gradual initiation into representative government. Modern science and technology would develop Africa's human and natural resources and raise the standard of living. And in exchange for their largesse, French administrators had no qualms imposing on their *sujets* many of the obligations of *citoyens*: taxes of course, but also conscription, so that Africans, too, might defend the motherland. [...]

While racism was always present between 1895 and 1930, it came shrouded first in emancipationist rhetoric and subsequently in scientific "respect" for traditional cultures. Both claims made it difficult for many liberals to see how inconsistent the very notion of a civilizing mission was with the Republic's universalist commitments. If the empire endured as long as it did, it was in part because French racism often worked hand-in-glove with more progressive values. As the French today struggle to build a genuinely pluralistic society, there are still lessons to be learned from the civilizing delusions of their recent past.

>> Mastering the Material

1. Analyze Rudyard Kipling's *The White Man's Burden*. What does he suggest that burden was? How does he depict white (European and American) people? How does he depict colonized peoples?

2. Compare Davies' *The Missionary's Bride* to Kipling's *The White Man's Burden*. Both suggest a duty and a sacrifice for Europeans or Anglo-Americans serving overseas, but one focuses on women and the other is more focused on men. How are these two sources different? In what ways are they similar? What do you conclude from this?

3. Some critics, even in the late nineteenth century, suggested Britain took control of Egypt for purely selfish reasons. How does Cromer reply to these allegations, and how convincing do you find him?

4. On what basis does Luṭfī Al-Sayyid criticize Cromer? Does he entirely refute the British "civilizing mission," or does he give Cromer credit in some areas?

5. What does Conklin argue was particular to the *French* notion of a civilizing mission?

>> Making Connections

1. Could eighteenth- and nineteenth-century changes in France, as discussed in Part 2, have formed the foundation for the *mission civilisatrice* discussed by Alice Conklin? If so, how do you explain the way in which the liberating ideology of nationalism became an excuse for the conquest of others?

2. Consider the primary and secondary sources in this chapter together with sources from other chapters in Part 3. To what degree do you accept the argument, put forward by Cromer and discussed by Conklin, that there truly was a sense of a moral mission behind the new imperialism? How important was morality as a motivating factor compared with strategic and economic concerns (Chapters 12 and 13)?

Chapter 15

Technological Explanations

"Whatever happens we have got / the Maxim gun and they have not." Thus wrote the British poet Hillaire Beloc following news of the 1898 battle of Omdurman, in which 11,000 Sudanese were killed at the cost of only 20 members of the British expeditionary force in Sudan. The Sudanese were followers of the Khalifa Abdullahi ibn Muhammad al-Ta'ashi, whose title means "successor." The Khalifa was a Muslim revivalist who claimed to have been anointed to lead the faithful against evil in the form of British and Egyptian occupational forces. His troops were armed with firearms, but these were little match for the cannon-bearing river gunboats, field artillery, and early machine guns (the Maxim) of the British forces.

As discussed in Part 1, western Europeans debatably had little military advantage over Asians and Africans in the first period of colonial expansion, 1450–1650. Most Old World societies possessed iron and horses, resistance to European diseases. Many Asian and North African armies were armed with comparable muskets and often superior cannon to the Spanish and Portuguese. By about the middle of the nineteenth century, however, this had changed. A **weapons gap** had opened up between industrialized and nonindustrialized societies that encompassed not only firearms but also tactics and training. In *The World and the West* the celebrated historian Phillip Curtin lists the key nineteenth-century innovations in industrial weaponry: the development of bolt-action and magazine-fed rifles with longer range, better speed, and greater accuracy than muskets. He also identifies developments in artillery, naval and especially shore-bombardment vessels, and machine guns. This weapons gap, he suggests, did not last long. It began to fade as early as the first decades of the twentieth century as non-European states began to develop the strategies and weapons of guerilla warfare that would help bring the era of formal colonialism to an end just over half a century later.

Nevertheless, at least for the brief period of the late nineteenth century a weapons gap existed that facilitated the conquest of colonies worldwide. Nor was this the only technological disparity between the imperial powers and the rest of the world. Dynamite and rifles were complemented by combustion and steam engines for ships, cars, and later airplanes. These gave industrial armies greater mobility, protection, and firepower. Communications were also revolutionized, first by the telegraph and subsequently the radio. These inventions allowed individual colonial officials to make reports and call for aid almost instantaneously, facilitating the administration of far-flung empires. Finally, innovations in medicine allowed Europeans and North Americans for the first time to survive in areas of Latin America, Asia, and Africa where they had no immunity to local and especially tropical diseases. Sometimes medical discoveries came from unexpected sources: Cinchona bark was known to healers in Peru as a medicine. Introduced to Europeans, it soon saw action as a malaria prophylactic in Africa and Asia.

The debate over the nature and extent of the European military advantage remains lively. The battle of Omdurman, recounted in this chapter by eyewitness and future British Prime Minister Winston Churchill, was a decisive victory for Britain and representative of a whole range of battles that helped build the new empires of the late nineteenth century. However, not every such battle resulted in a victory for imperial invaders. The British expeditionary force at Omdurman, for example, was avenging the defeat of an earlier British-Egyptian force at the battle of Khartoum. Only a few years after Omdurman, Italy suffered a crushing defeat at the hands of Ethiopian soldiers armed with Western weapons just next door at the battle of Adowa. At the other end of the continent, a British column was similarly annihilated in 1879 by a Zulu force at Isandhlwana.

In general, however, the industrialized powers tended to have the upper hand in these mass engagements. It was only when defenders turned to guerilla tactics that imperial armies usually became confounded. Such tactics are perhaps best known for its role in the late twentieth century struggles that ended colonial rule in many parts of Africa and Asia, but as Ndansi Kumalo points out in Reading 70, they were also adopted in late nineteenth century revolts such as the 1896 Ndebele Rebellion in southern Africa. By the mid-twentieth century the weapons gap was closed not only by the tactical innovations of guerilla armies but also by the flow of technology brought about by the expansion of the great empires into new territories. The final source in this chapter is an excerpt from *The Tentacles of Progress,* by one of the leading historians of technology and the new imperialism, Daniel Headrick. In this book Headrick depicts the flow of technology between metropole and colony *after* the initial conquests. He argues that almost immediately following the imposition of colonialism technology began to flow and the knowledge gap to disappear, partly because of imperial investment in the colonies, but also largely because the colonized peoples sought ways to gain access to the innovations they did not possess. In this way he depicts the transfer of technology in the new imperialism as a story in which the colonized peoples, as well as the colonizers, were agents of change.

It is commonly accepted that the technology of industrialized states like Japan, the United States, the western European countries, and to some extent Russia enabled them to conquer vast tracts of land overseas and as well as in their own backyards. But it is also possible to argue that the new industrial technology was a *cause* of the new imperialism. This argument is linked to strategic and economic interpretations of the new imperialism. As industrial powers began to compete economically, their new factories required products and markets around the world. As they began to compete strategically around the world, their steamships, telegraphs, and radios needed ports from which to be stationed, to be fed coal, and to transmit to passing fleets. In this way imperialism and technological innovation were intrinsically intertwined.

Winston Churchill Witnesses the Battle of Omdurman

Winston Churchill, future Prime Minister of Great Britain, reveled in the adventure of expeditions to Africa and Asia as a soldier and war correspondent for the Fourth Hussar cavalry regiment. His experiences fighting in India, South Africa, and the Sudan greatly influenced his support for the empire throughout his political career. In this account of the Battle of Omdurman, Churchill recounts the impact of modern weapons such as gunboats, artillery, carbine rifles, searchlights, and Maxim machine guns that defeated the large Sudanese army of the Khalifa, an army that had some years previously defeated a less well-prepared British-Egyptian force. While the tone of celebration is a bit discomfiting, this is an accurate portrayal of the effectiveness of modern technology, even against an opponent armed with guns.

>> 69. The River War: An Historical Account of the Reconquest of the Soudan

WINSTON S. CHURCHILL [c. 1898]

The Dervish centre, had come within range. But it was not the British and Egyptian army that began the battle. If there was one arm in which the Arabs were beyond all comparison inferior to their adversaries, it was in guns. [...] Great clouds of smoke appeared all along the front of the British and Soudanese brigades. One after another four batteries opened on the enemy at a range of about 3,000 yards. The sound of the cannonade rolled up to us on the ridge, and was reechoed by the hills. Above the heads of the moving masses shells began to burst, dotting the air with smoke-balls and the ground with bodies. But they were nearly two miles away, and the distance rendered me unsympathetic. I had a nearer tragedy to witness. I looked back to the 'White Flags'; they were nearly over the crest. In another minute they would become visible to the batteries. Did they realise what would come to meet them? They were in a dense mass, 2,800 yards from the 32nd Field Battery and the gunboats. The ranges were known. It was a matter of

machinery. The more distant slaughter passed unnoticed, as the mind was fascinated by the impending horror. I could see it coming. In a few seconds swift destruction would rush on these brave men. They topped the crest and drew out into full view of the whole army. Their white banners made them conspicuous above all. As they saw the camp of their enemies, they discharged their rifles with a great roar of musketry and quickened their pace. [...] For a moment the white flags advanced in regular order, and the whole division crossed the crest and were exposed. Forthwith the gunboats, the 32nd British Field Battery, and other guns from the *zeriba* opened on them. I was but 400 yards away, and with excellent glasses could almost see the faces of the Dervishes who met the fearful fire. About twenty shells struck them in the first minute. Some burst high in the air, others exactly in their faces. Others, again, plunged into the sand and, exploding, dashed clouds of red dust, splinters, and bullets amid their ranks. The white banners toppled over in all directions. Yet they rose again immediately, as other men pressed forward to die for the Mahdi's sacred cause and in the defense of the successor of the True Prophet of the Only God. It was a terrible sight,

Source: Winston S. Churchill, *The River War: An Historical Account of the Reconquest of the Soudan*, vol. 2 (London: Longmans, Green, and Co., 1899), 114–119.

for as yet they had not hurt us at all, and it seemed an unfair advantage to strike thus cruelly when they could not reply. Nevertheless I watched the effect of the fire most carefully from a close and convenient position. About five men on the average fell to every shell: and there were many shells. Under their influence the mass of the 'White Flags' dissolved into thin lines of spearmen and skirmishers, and came on in altered formation and diminished numbers, but with unabated enthusiasm. And now, the whole attack being thoroughly exposed, it became the duty of the cavalry to clear the front as quickly as possible, and leave the further conduct of the debate to the infantry and the Maxim guns. All the patrols trotted or cantered back to their squadrons, and the regiment retired swiftly into the *zeriba,* while the shells from the gunboats screamed overhead and the whole length of the position began to burst into flame and smoke. Now was it long before the tremendous banging of the artillery was swelled by the roar of musketry. [...]

Now it was the turn of the infantry. The long line of bayonets had been drawn up even before the sun had completely risen. The officers and men had watched the light grow in the plain, and had scanned the distant hills and nearer ridge with eager, anxious eyes. [...] Battalion by battalion— the Guards first at 2,700 yards, then the Seaforths at 2,000 yards, and the others following according to the taste and fancy of their commanding officers—the British division began to fire. As the range shortened Maxwell's Soudanese brigade,

and a moment later MacDonald's, joined in the fusillade, until by 6.45 more than 12,000 infantry were engaged in that mechanical scattering of death which the polite nations of the earth have brought to such monstrous perfection.

They fired steadily and stolidly, without hurry or excitement, for the enemy were far away and the officers careful. Besides, the soldiers were interested in the work and took great pains. But presently the mere physical act became tedious. The tiny figures seen over the slide of the back-sight seemed a little larger, but also fewer at each successive volley. The rifles grew hot—so hot that they had to be changed for those of the reserve companies. The Maxim guns exhausted all the water in their jackets, and several had to be refreshed from the water-bottles of the Cameron Highlanders before they could go on with their deadly work. The empty cartridge-cases, tinkling to the ground, formed small but growing heaps beside each man. And all the time out on the plain on the other side bullets were shearing through flesh, smashing and splintering bone; blood spouted from terrible wounds; valiant men were struggling on through a hell of whistling metal, exploding shells, and spurting dust—suffering, despairing, dying. Such was the first phase of the battle of Omdurman.

The Khalifa's plan to attack appears to have been complex and ingenious. It was, however, based on an extraordinary miscalculation of the power of modern weapons; with the exception of this cardinal error, it is not necessary to criticise it.

Guerilla Tactics during the Ndebele Rebellion

Many of the battles of the late nineteenth century were uneven victories, in which the industrial powers used their technology to overpower the less potent armies of states in sub-Saharan Africa, the Middle East, and Asia. However, even in the midst of their defeat the conquered peoples were learning skills that would later enable them to fight for independence. In the face of the overwhelming firepower of the imperial powers, the solution gradually developed by many societies was guerilla warfare. A good example of this is the Ndebele Rebellion of 1896. The Ndebele had initially been subjugated in 1893 by the hired guns and settlers of Cecil Rhodes' South Africa Company, which expanded northward in search of gold mines. They were confined to a small reservation, insufficient for their food needs, in order to force them to become cheap labor for British settlers. In 1896–1897, they rose up in a rebellion that succeeded at first, forcing the settlers to send for British reinforcements to put down the insurrection. Even after the arrival of imperial troops, the rebellion's success forced the British to come to the bargaining table. Ndansi Kumalo, one of the rebels, told his story to the scholar Margery Perham, a critic of colonialism, in 1932 when he was brought to Britain to play the role of the Ndebele King Logenbula in the 1833 film Rhodes of Africa. *In this excerpt Kumalo describes a key strategy in guerilla warfare: the ambush.*

>> 70. The Story of Ndansi Kumalo of the Matabele Tribe, Southern Rhodesia

NDANSI KUMALO [1932]

I fought in the rebellion. We used to look out for valleys where the white men were likely to approach. We took cover behind rocks and trees and tried to ambush them. We were forced by the nature of our weapons not to expose ourselves. I had a gun, a breech-loader. They—the white men—fought us with big guns and Maxims and rifles.

I remember a fight in the Matoppos when we charged the white men. There were some hundreds of us; the white men also were many. We charged them at close quarters: we thought we had a good chance to kill them but the Maxims were too much for us. We drove them off at the first charge, but they returned and formed up again. We made a second charge, but they were too strong for us. I cannot say how many white people were killed, but we think it was a quite a lot. I do not know if I killed any of them, but I know I killed one of their horses. I remember how, when one of their scouts fell wounded, two of his companions raced out and took him away. Many of our people were killed in this fight: I saw four of my cousins shot. One was shot in the jaw and the whole of his face was blown away—like this—and he died. One was hit between the eyes; another here, in the shoulder; another had part of his ear shot off. We made many charges but each time we were beaten off, until at last the white men packed up and retreated. But for the Maxims, it would have been different.

The Diffusion of Technology during the Age of Empires

Daniel Headrick has written widely on the role of technology in global history. In an early book, The Tools of Empire, *Headrick investigated the way in which imperial powers used technology in their colonial conquests. In this subsequent volume,* The Tentacles of Progress, *Headrick continues the narrative by looking at the impact of colonial expansion and imperialism upon technology globally. For Headrick, the scramble for colonies of the new imperialism is a point of departure from which to view later periods in world history.*

Source: Ndansi Kumalo, "The Story of Ndansi Kumalo of the Matabele Tribe, Southern Rhodesla," in *Ten Africans*, edited by Margery Perham (London: Faber and Faber, 1963), 72–73.

>> 71. The Tentacles of Progress: Technology Transfer in the Age of Imperialism, 1850–1940

DANIEL HEADRICK [1988]

This era, the "new imperialism," coincides with the creation of modern underdeveloped economies in Asia and Africa. While these two processes have often been linked, their relationship remains unclear. A consideration of the technologies involved can shed some light on this question. [...]

In the relationships between technological change and European imperialism, we can begin by distinguishing five interactions. The first of these concerns the penetration of Asia and Africa by Europeans and the conquest of colonial empires. What distinguishes the new imperialism from its many predecessors is that it was so swift, thorough, and cheap. In a few years, roughly the half-century before 1914, the major Western powers conquered Africa, Oceania, and large parts of Asia, and they did so at a very small cost in European men and money.

This sudden scramble for territories aroused much interest, not only among contemporaries, but also later among historians and political theorists. Their interest has focused mainly on the motivations of the imperialists and their involvement with Western politics and economics. Yet there is no reason to believe that late in nineteenth-century imperialists were any more strongly motivated than their predecessors. The reason for their sudden success was a shift in technology, similar in the development of oceangoing ships some four centuries earlier. Until the nineteenth century relations between Europe, on the one hand, and Asia and Africa, on the other, were determined by their technological balance. At sea, Europeans were almost invincible, as they had been for centuries. Their efforts to penetrate inland, however, were restrained by their numerical inferiority in Asia and their vulnerability to disease in Africa.

In 1800, after three centuries of lurking offshore, Europeans could claim only a few footholds in Asia and Africa, mainly harbors and islands.

The new ability of Europeans in the nineteenth century to conquer other continents stemmed from a relatively few inventions. The first was the application of steam and iron to riverboats, starting in the 1820s. By the 1860s iron-hulled steamships appeared regularly in Asian and African waters. Constant improvements in firearms, from muskets to machine guns, gave small European-led units an overwhelming advantage over their African and Asian enemies. Quinine prophylaxis reduced the death rate among Europeans in the tropics, especially in Africa. Steamships, railways, and telegraphs allowed Europeans to control their newly acquired colonies efficiently. With these tools, Europeans brought about the shift in global relations we call the new imperialism. [...]

Whatever the motives of the imperialists— the long-standing debate on this question is still going strong—the territories they added to the Western empires were soon incorporated into the world economy. This incorporation, in fact, predated the scramble and included territories that were never officially annexed; for that reason, it has been called the "imperialism of free trade." Hence the second of our five interactions is the impact of an expanding Western economy on world trade. In the nineteenth century, the industrialization of the Western nations stimulated a growing demand for the products of the tropics. Falling transport costs made it increasingly worthwhile to ship cheap bulky commodities. New industries in the West required new raw materials from the tropics: cotton and indigo for cloth, palm oil to grease machinery, copper and gutta-percha for electric and telegraph lines, tin for canned goods, and rubber for clothing and automobiles. In addition, an affluent and demanding Western clientele consumed

Source: Daniel Headrick, *The Tentacles of Progress: Technology Transfer in the Age of Imperialism, 1850–1940* (Oxford: Oxford University Press, 1988), 4–8.

increasing amounts of sugar, tea, coffee, cocoa, and other tropical goods. [...]

Once in control of an area, Western colonialists were not content to administer their new subjects and tax the existing economy, as previous conquerors had done. Instead, they strove to increase production and lower the costs of tropical products by applying Western industrial and scientific methods. Thus our third interaction is a massive transfer of technology from the West to Africa and Asia. This transfer stimulated a growth in tropical production and in international trade. Meanwhile, greater security, more regular food supplies and growing demand for labor in turn stimulated the growth of tropical populations. The transfer did not, however, diversify the tropical economies, nor did it significantly raise per capita incomes. In other words, the tropical economies grew, but did not develop.

The fourth consequence of technological change was cultural as well as economic. Colonized people were not mere objects at the hands of the colonizers. The invasion of their countries by a technologically more advanced culture awakened not only the well-known movements for national independence, but also a desire to obtain more Western products and share in the benefits of Western technology. The Western invasion created new desires among tropical consumers. Railways and telegraphs built by the Europeans for their own benefit were soon flooded with Asian and African customers. In the twentieth century, motor vehicles, televisions, and modern weapons have become irresistible but barely affordable temptations for the people of poor countries. Along with the demand for devices has arisen a parallel demand for technological knowledge. Thus Western technology flowed to Asia and Africa, first pushed upon the colonies by Europeans and later pulled the awakening demands of Asians and Africans. It reversed the age-old pattern of world trade in which the Western peoples craved the goods of the East, but had little but bullion to offer in exchange. Starting in the mid-nineteenth century, Asia and Africa imported ever-increasing quantities of manufactured goods from the West.

Meanwhile, other Western innovations, stimulated by war, politics, and science, have had a fifth, and more ominous, impact on the tropics. Almost all the technological changes which affected the relations between the West and the tropics originated in the West or from the work of Western scientists and engineers; they were developed for the benefit of the West, or of some section of Western society, with scant regard for their long-range impact on the tropics. The Western talent for technological innovation could easily turn against the tropics. Already in the nineteenth century, Westerners had shown a propensity for finding substitutes for goods in short supply. During the Napoleonic Wars, beet sugar replaced cane sugar on the European continent; by the turn of the century it had all but ruined the economy of the West Indies. In the second half of the nineteenth century, aniline dyes replaced indigo and other natural colorings; iron and steel ships ruined the teak shipbuilding industries of South Asia; and petroleum replaced palm oil in the lubrication of machinery.

>> Mastering the Material

1. Read Churchill's account of the battle of Omdurman closely. To what do you attribute British success in this battle? Was the Khalifa's army competently led? Were the British generals exceptionally brilliant? How great was the difference in the armament of the two sides?

2. If there was a Western advantage in technology in the era of the new imperialism, what was it? What were its limits? Was the answer merely the "Maxim gun" as Kumalo and

Churchill seem to suggest? The inventions put forward by Headrick? Something more extensive and general?

3. According to Headrick, how did the new imperialism act to help technology spread across the globe? Who were the agents of this diffusion? What were its limits?

>> Making Connections

1. What was the "role" of technology in the new imperialism? Did it cause the sudden scramble for colonies, as Headrick suggests, or merely enable it to happen? Is it as important a causative factor as strategic, idealistic, or economic considerations (Chapters 12, 13, and 14)?

Chapter 16

The Answer Is in the Periphery

The great majority of scholars who have sought to explain the new imperialism have focused on trends within and among the major industrial and imperial powers—the United States, Japan, Britain, France, Germany, and to a lesser extent Russia and Italy. Since these were the states and societies that sent armies, bureaucrats, and missionaries abroad in a process that culminated in the occupation of Africa and much of southeast and southern Asia in this period, it seems obvious that anyone seeking an explanation for this process must search within these "metropolitan" settings for its origins. Indeed, Part 3 has explored several sets of theories that suggest the new imperialism was the result of competition for global geopolitical dominance or economic advantage between these great states. Similarly, scholars have seen the origins of this sudden expansionism in moral and technological developments within industrialized societies in the late nineteenth century.

These metropole-centered constructions of the new imperialism depict the rest of the world, outside of the great powers, as part of a **periphery.** In these models, the periphery can only respond to actions taken by the imperial metropole. Plans for military campaigns or diplomatic moves are formulated in London, Paris, or Washington and then carried out in western Africa, Indochina, or the Philippines. Schemes to annex new territories are engineered in metropolitan government ministries and then carried out in the colonies. However, some historians who in the last half-century have really begun to look closely at the history of colonized regions of the world have found that this model does not really describe the unfolding of colonial conquest, annexation, and occupation. In many cases, they argue, both underpinning trends and important causative events in the creation of a colony actually took place locally. Hundreds of individual case studies, put together, suggest to these scholars that there was no great colonial plan to the new imperialism. Instead, the colonial secretariats and foreign offices in the capitals of the great imperial powers were often merely reacting to events abroad, rather than initiating them.

This model, in which the imperial periphery is seen as the center of the action, is an explicit critique of all previous interpretations. Its proponents suggest that imperial governments were too far distant to really control events. Rather than focusing on imperial bureaucracies, they explore the interaction between different groups of people in each of the areas that became colonies for evidence of the unfolding of colonialism. One of the earliest scholarly works to embed this interpretation within a wider analysis was Ronald Robinson and John Gallagher's *Africa and the Victorians.* These two authors developed a theory that British participation in the scramble for African colonies was not merely a response to imperialist rumblings to France and Germany, but also to nationalist groups forming in Africa that threatened the profitability and livelihood of British bankers, merchants, and settlers. Although Robinson and Gallagher focused their attention on southern Africa and Egypt, examples from western Africa like the antagonism of British officials toward the Fante Confederation suggest that developing senses of identity and the growing strength of some states in the periphery were seen by agents of the great powers as a threat.

By contrast, in some case studies some scholars have suggested that the colonization process was at least partly motivated by the need to prop up weak imperial trading partners and allies in the periphery. One example is Malaysia, where a late-nineteenth-century conflict between various Malay and Chinese factions negatively impacted British merchants involved in the local tin-mining industry. These merchants agitated for British imperial forces and bureaucrats to step in and take over local affairs in order to safeguard their interests. The process gradually culminated in the establishment of a formal colony. However, the assumption of British control over Malaysia as described in the account by Sir Frank Swettenham in Reading 75 was not ordered from London. Instead, it was a local British official who responded to the merchants' entreaties and decided to take matters into his own hands. The noted Atlantic and world historian Philip Curtin has identified this process as **man-on-the-spotism:** a progression toward colonial acquisition that starts with imperial agents in the periphery, the metropole being informed only after events are concluded.

But there are limits to theories that stress events in the periphery. Without the emergence of a nationalist–imperialist sentiment in the metropole, for example, it seems unlikely conquest or annexation would have been attempted by men-on-the-spot. Similarly, only colonial secretariats in the metropole could sanction the actions of agents abroad. Finally, there is a great deal of evidence that imperial governments did plan and order the establishment of new colonies in at least some cases. Nevertheless, the work of scholars like Curtin, Robinson, and Gallagher helps us to reinterpret the new imperialism as the result of global, rather than merely Western, factors.

African Incitements to British Imperialism?

Ronald Robinson and John Gallagher are often celebrated as leading proponents of the strategic view of the new imperialism. Their most important work on the subject, Africa and the Victorians, *focuses on the "official mind" of British planners in the era of the race for African colonies, which they entitle the "late Victorian" period. Yet Robinson and Gallagher were also among the earliest historians of the British Empire to acknowledge events in Africa as causes of colonial expansion. In* Africa and the Victorians, *the authors look closely at two principal transformations in Africa that changed the equation used by British officials to calculate the costs of colonialism, convincing the British government to annex much of the continent. The first of these was the rise of a constitutionalist movement in Egypt, which gained power at the expense of the Khedive, an ally of the British. This movement enjoyed broad-based support in Egypt from liberal reformers, Muslim conservatives, anti-European landlords, and disgruntled army officers—all of whom had reasons to resent British influence. The second was the increasing independence of European settlers in southern Africa—especially Dutch-speaking white settlers, or Afrikaners—who threatened Britain's control over potentially rich regions and also clashed with English speakers who subsequently appealed to Britain for support.*

>> 72. Africa and the Victorians:
The Climax of Imperialism in the Dark Continent

RONALD ROBINSON AND JOHN GALLAGHER
WITH ALICE DENNY [1961]

It cannot be taken for granted that positive impulses from European society or the European economy were alone in starting up imperial rivalries. The collapse of African governments under the strain of previous Western influences may have played a part, even a predominant part in the process. The British advances may have been the culmination of the destructive workings of earlier exercises of informal empire over the coastal *régimes*. Hence crises in Africa, no less than imperial ambitions and international rivalries in Europe, have to be taken into account. Allowance has also to be made for the diversity of interest and circumstances in the different regions of Africa. It seems unlikely that the motives in regions as dissimilar as Egypt, the Niger and south Africa can be fitted easily into a single, simple formula of 'imperialism'.

Another factor must be included. Victorian expansion by the Eighteen eighties has long historical roots and world-wide ramifications. Its manifold workings tended sometimes to build up, and sometimes to break down the societies drawn under its influence. While in some countries, British agencies helped to create vortices of disorder and nationalist reaction, in others they helped local communities to grow until they became expansive in their own right. In these ways the processes of expansion were soon receding out of metropolitan control.

Some satellites tended to break up; others were beginning to throw off galaxies of their own. It is not unlikely that both these tendencies helped to drag British ministries into African empire. Lastly, it is quite possible that they did not acquire a new empire for its intrinsic value, but because Africa's relationship to their total strategy in Europe, the Mediterranean, or the East had altered. [...]

At the first level of analysis, the decisive motive behind late-Victorian strategy in Africa was to protect the all-important stakes in India and the East.

An essentially negative objective, it had been attained hitherto without large African possessions. Mere influence and co-operation with other Powers had been enough to safeguard strategic points in north Africa; while in south Africa control of coastal regions had sufficed. The ambition of late-Victorian ministers reached no higher than to uphold these mid-Victorian systems of security in Egypt and south Africa. They were distinguished from their predecessors only in this: that their security by influence was breaking down. In attempting to restore it by intervention and diplomacy, they incidentally marked out the ground on which a vastly extended African empire was later to arise. Nearly all the interventions appear to have been consequences, direct or indirect, of internal Egyptian or south African crises which endangered British influence and security in the world. Such an interpretation alone seems to fit the actual calculations of policy. Ministers felt frankly that they were making the best of a bad job. They were doing no more than protecting old interests in worsening circumstances. To many, the

---

Source: Ronald Robinson and John Gallagher with Alice Denny, *Africa and the Victorians: The Climax of Imperialism in the Dark Continent* (New York: St. Martin's Press, 1961), 18, 464–465, 467–468.

flare-up of European rivalry in Africa seemed unreasonable and even absurd; yet most of them felt driven to take part because of tantalising circumstances beyond their control. They went forward as a measure of precaution, or as a way back to the saner mid-Victorian systems of informal influence. Gloomily, they were fumbling to adjust their old strategy to a changing Africa. And the necessity arose much more from altered circumstances in Africa than from any revolution in the nature, strength or direction of British expansion.

Hence the question of motive should be formulated afresh. It is no longer the winning of a new empire in Africa which has to be explained. The question is simpler: Why could the late-Victorian after 1880 no longer rely upon influence to protect traditional interests? What forced them in the end into imperial solutions? The answer is to be found first in the nationalist crises in Africa itself, which were the work of intensifying European influences during previous decades; and only secondarily in the interlocking of these crises in Africa with rivalries in Europe. Together the two drove British step by step to regain by territorial claims and occupation that security which could no longer be had by influence alone. The compelling conditions for British advances in tropical Africa were first called into being, not by the German victory of 1871, nor by Leopold's interest in the Congo, nor by the petty rivalry of missionaries and merchants, nor by a rising imperialist spirit, nor even by the French occupation of Tunis in 1881 — but by the collapse of the Khedival *régimes* in Egypt. [...]

By 1882 the Egyptian Khedivate had corroded and cracked after decades of European paramountcy. But economic expansion was certainly not the sufficient cause of the occupation. Hitherto, commerce and investment had gone on without the help of outright political control. The thrusts of the industrial economy into Egypt had come to a stop with Ismail's bankruptcy, and little new enterprise was to accompany British control. Although the expanding economy had helped to make a revolutionary situation in Egypt, it was not the moving interest behind the British invasion. Nor does it seem that Anglo-French rivalry or the state of the European balance precipitated the invasion. It was rather the internal nationalist reaction against a decaying government which split Britain from France and switched European rivalries into Africa. [...]

The causes of imperial expansion in southern Africa were altogether different. It was essentially unconnected with the contemporary crisis in Egypt and its consequences in tropical Africa; it moved on a different time-scale, and the impulses behind it were separate. Unlike Egypt and tropical Africa, south Africa was to a great extent insulated from the rivalries of European Powers. Unlike them also, it was being rapidly developed by British commercial interests. The crisis which faced British governments was produced by colonial growth, and not by the decay of a native government. It arose from internal conflicts among the colonists, rather than from rivalries among the Powers. But the south African and Egyptian crises were alike in this: neither was precipitated by drastic changes in the local purposes of British expansion; but in both, the ate-Victorians strained to keep up their supreme influence against a nationalist threat, and they were drawn at last into re-conquering paramountcy by occupation.

The Constitution of the Fante Confederation and the Response of the British Administrator

Robinson and Gallagher, and a number of other scholars of the 1960s, recognized the role of Egyptians and Afrikaners in the expanded colonialism of the 1870s through the 1900s. It took longer for scholars to focus their attention on the indigenous inhabitants of sub-Saharan Africa. Yet evidence increasingly shows that groups of western Africans were increasingly challenging the imperial powers in the prelude to the race for new colonies. African merchants, for example, were developing strategies to force corporations based in France, Germany, and Britain to compete for their business. Moreover, in many African states strong and expansive state structures were developing as a response to pressure from European powers. One example of this process was the nationalist movement known as the Fante Confederation. Formulated in 1867, the Fante Confederation was a response to a British–Dutch plan to divide control of trade along the Gold Coast of western Africa with the purpose of taxing local merchants and producers. The inhabitants of the Gold Coast responded by banding together, in the case of the Fante people by formally unifying their small states into a single confederation over a period of four years. The new state was not explicitly anti-British. Indeed, many of the Confederation's leaders wanted to model their state upon Britain. However, it did challenge the authority of the British officials in the region and it did undermine their projects to tax local commerce. The Confederation was partly successful in that it drove away the Dutch. The British administrator, however, responded to the publication of the Fante Constitution by arresting all of the Confederation's leadership on which he could lay his hands. His actions were illegal, as Britain had no established sovereignty over the Fante states, but they were also effective. The Confederation fell apart and by 1874 Britain had established a colony in the region.

>> 73. "Constitution of the New Fantee Confederacy" and a Letter from Administrator Salmon

[1871]

Constitution of the New Fantee Confederacy

To all whom it may concern:

WHEREAS we, the undersigned kings and chiefs of Fanti, have taken into consideration the deplorable state of our peoples and subjects in the interior of the Gold Coast, and whereas we are of opinion that unity and concord among ourselves would conduce to our mutual well-being, and promote and advance the social and political condition of our peoples and subjects, who are in a state of degradation, without the means of education and of carrying on proper industry, we, the said kings and chiefs, after having duly discussed and considered the subject at meetings held at Mankessim on the 16th day of October last and following days, have unanimously resolved and agreed upon the articles hereinafter named.

Article 1. That we, the kings and chiefs of Fanti here present, form ourselves into a committee with the view of effecting unity of purpose and of action between the kings and chiefs of the Fanti territory.

Article 2. That we, the kings and chiefs here assembled, now form ourselves into a compact body for the purpose of more effectually bringing about certain improvements (hereafter to be considered) in the country.

Article 3. That this compact body shall be recognised under the title and designation of the "Fanti Confederation."

Article 4. That there shall be elected a president, vice-president, secretary... under secretary, treasurer, and assistant treasurer.

Source: "Constitution of the New Fantee Confederacy," November 1871, reproduced in Parliamentary Papers XLIX of 1873, House of Commons printed series 11/3637, 3–8; and letter of 10 December 1871 in same, 3.

Article 5. That the president be elected from the body of kings, and be proclaimed king-president of the Fanti Confederation.

Article 6. That the vice-president, secretary and under secretary, treasurer, and assistant treasurer, who shall constitute the ministry, be men of education and position.

Article 7. That it be competent to the Fanti Confederation thus constituted to receive into its body politc any other king or kings, chief or chiefs, who may not now be present.

Article 8. That it be the object of the Confederation—

Section 1. To promote friendly intercourse between all the kings and chiefs of Fanti, and to unite them for offensive and defensive purposes against their common enemy.

Section 2. To direct the labors of the Confederation towards the improvement of the country at large.

Section 3. To make good and substantial roads throughout all the interior districts included in the Confederation.

Section 4. To erect school-houses and establish schools for the education of all children within the Confederation, and to obtain the service of efficient schoolmasters.

Section 5. To promote agricultural and industrial pursuits, and to endeavour to introduce such new plants as may hereafter become sources of profitable commerce to the country.

Section 6. To develop and facilitate the working of the mineral and other resources of the country.

Government House, Cape Coast,
Sir,   10 December 1871,

I have the honour to inform your Excellency that, respecting the so-called Confederation, all the parties except Gharty, claiming to hold office under it, have been arrested and allowed out on bail, but not to leave Cape Coast. The two kings are expected here in a few days; they are very slow in their movements; they were afraid of being arrested and sent to Sierra Leone, but I assured their friends that all I wanted was some guarantee that the affair should end, not to be revived. [...]

4. The law of the matter is clear. The authority of the protecting power respecting life and death, the levying of taxes, and the making of treaties with foreign powers, and the supremacy of its courts, is well established by custom and precedent, and could not be departed from without dire confusion resulting.

5. I consider that the cases should be tried in the Judicial Assessor's Court, to show more fully to all the illegality of the proceeding, but not for the sake of punishing those concerned this time.

I have, &c.
(signed) *C.S. Salmon,*
Acting Administrator.

Man-on-the-Spotism

Trained as an Africanist, Philip Curtin was a pioneer of the study of the Atlantic Ocean as a historical zone, and more recently has become an important world historian. In this section of his recent book The World and the West *Curtin focuses on the colonial agent outside of the metropole as initiators of colonialism. He argues that bureaucrats and politicians in London, Paris, and other imperial capitals were usually too concerned with domestic and European considerations to push colonialism. On the other hand, the citizens of imperial nations resident in Africa, the Middle East, and Asia—merchants and settlers, colonial officials and missionaries—had to respond quickly to local issues that threatened their personal well-being and chances for promotion and success. As a result, these 'men-on-the-spot' often acted quickly to undertake military or diplomatic action in periods of crisis, and only later applied for official recognition of their actions.*

>> 74. The World and the West: The European Challenge and the Overseas Response in the Age of Empire

PHILIP D. CURTIN [2000]

In the Anglo-Burma War of 1852 and the British encroachment in Malaya later in the century, the impetus for empire building came from the periphery, not the imperial center. A similar tendency could be traced in patterns of French expansion into West Africa or Dutch expansion in Southeast Asia. It was, indeed, so common a tendency that the phenomenon has been identified as "man-on-the-spotism."

Some of its sources are clear enough. Peripheral policy makers interpreted their task as one maximizing the power and advantage of themselves and their fellow countrymen within that narrow local range. If, for example, a particular project would cost more than the local budget would bear, it was always possible to ask the center for more money, justifying the request as furthering the common good. It was also possible to make commitments that the center would be forced to honor in the longer run, even though it would have refused if permission had been asked for in advance.

Policy makers at the center, on the other hand, were closer to the taxpayers' representatives and others concerned about a wider range of costs and responsibilities. From the central point of view, it was necessary to balance the demands from different parts of the world and from various agencies within the central government. French cabinets after the 1870s had to balance the claims of revenge against Germany against those of expansion in Africa, Indo-China, or elsewhere. They also had to balance the demands of the Ministry of the Navy, which controlled most overseas colonies, against those of the War Ministry, with its principal responsibility in Europe and North Africa, to say nothing of the broader international concerns of the Ministry of Foreign Affairs. British imperial affairs were divided and balanced in much the same way between the Colonial Office, which ruled over most colonies, the India Office, which ruled India, and the Foreign Office, which was in charge of Egypt, the Anglo-Egyptian Sudan, and a few other territories. These multiple balancing acts increased the central tendency to say "no," or at least to set limits on requests that came to it from the periphery.

Men-on-the-spot were also those most likely to encounter cross-cultural confrontation. Whether they were merchants, missionaries, or administrators, they had to deal with people, within the imperial frontiers or beyond, who were culturally different from themselves, with different values and different ways of conducting business. Dealing with those beyond the frontiers was more difficult because it required compromise with the "barbarians" at every turn. If, on the other hand, the outsiders were within the empire and a colonial government could make the rules, compromise might still be necessary, but the dominant political authorities would at least be those that shared one's own culture and values.

Source: Philip D. Curtin, *The World and the West: The European Challenge and the Overseas Response in the Age of Empire* (Cambridge: Cambridge University Press, 2000), 48–50.

In the 1800s, men-on-the-spot had two additional incentives to expand. The weapons gap based on industrialization lowered the price tag of any use of force against non-Europeans. Men-on-the-spot were therefore in a position to relieve their cross-cultural frustrations more cheaply than ever before. In addition, that same industrialization in Europe tended to bring about new economic and social dislocations overseas. The preindustrial resources of public administration were often inadequate. Europeans had newly developed reasons to think they could handle the problems.

Malay tin mining is only one instance of a worldwide process. European industrial demand for goods from overseas encouraged non-Europeans to meet the demand, and that very process brought about disruptive changes, which, as in this instance, were bad for trade and damaging to a cheap source of tin. In other instances as well, it appeared to Europeans that more efficient government was required than the "natives" could furnish, and they saw no prospect for improvement except in European hands. Europeans in general were influenced by the new pride in the new organizational power of European governments, and this pride was itself a major source of the cultural chauvinism and racism that was so marked in European thought in the late 1800s. On the periphery, the frustrations of trying to deal with people with a different way of life were more severe, and consciousness of the organizational and industrial power of Europe gave men-on-the-spot a heightened sense of the value of empire, combined with the promise of victory at a decreasing price.

British Intervention in Malaysia

Although the Portuguese had conquered the important port of Malacca in the early sixteenth century, most of Malaysia and indeed almost all of southeast Asia remained independent of European domination until the era of the new imperialism. The British were the leading imperial power on the Malay peninsula by the 1870s, controlling trading posts in Penang, Malacca, and Singapore. The Dutch and Portuguese colonies in southeast Asia were in decline; the United States and Japan were wary of interfering in the region for fear of aggravating Britain; and the French government had only just begun to seriously intervene in nearby Vietnam. None of these other powers threatened British domination of the region, or British merchant's controls over the local tin-mining industry. Therefore it was not strategic or economic concerns that drove Britain to force local rulers to sign the Pangkor Agreement of 1874, confirming a British "Resident" in Malaysia who would gradually come to exercise colonial authority.

There are several theories as to the actual cause of Britain's sudden intervention, but most scholars agree that local events were most important. In the early 1870s, conflict between various Malaysian rulers and also immigrant Chinese factions over who should be chosen as the Sultan of the state of Pêrak threatened the stability of the tin industry, causing British merchants in the area to call for their government to step in. Some scholars, however, stress the role of the senior British colonial official in the area, Sir Andrew Clarke, who was empowered to deal with any emergencies by his superior in London, the Secretary of State for the Colonies Lord Kimberley. As this account by a fellow administrator suggests, Clarke forced the Malay rulers to sign the Pangkor Agreement on his own authority, without first seeking the advice of Kimberley or his successor Lord Carnarvon in London.

>> 75. British Malaya: An Account of the Origin and Progress of British Influence in Malaya

FRANK SWETTENHAM [1906]

Lord Kimberley's instructions were as wide as could be wished, and they contained a valuable and definite suggestion; but they invited the Governor to report his proposals, and Sir Andrew Clarke, a man of energy and decision, ready to take any responsibility, decided that this was no time for talking; the situation demanded immediate action, and he would take it, reporting what he had done, not what he proposed to do. Naturally the Governor did not come to this conclusion until he had gone thoroughly into the case, taken the advice of all those who had any knowledge of Malay and Chinese affairs, and felt confident that he could carry his plan to a successful issue.

At that time there was, in Singapore, a very remarkable and able officer in charge of Chinese affairs, Mr. W. A. Pickering (afterwards created C. M. G for his many public services), and he was sent to Pinang to endeavour to persuade the heads of the Chinese factions, then warring in Lârut, to agree to accept the Governor's settlement of their differences. In this duty Mr. Pickering was entirely successful, and, as soon as he had telegraphed the result of his negotiations, the Governor started from Singapore in the colonial yacht for the island of Pangkor lying off the coast of the Dindings, near the mouth of the Pêrak River. The Governor sent ahead, or took with him, Mr. Bradell, the Attorney-General; Major McNair, R.A., the Colonial Engineer; Colonel Dunlop, R.A., the Inspector-General of

Police; and Mr. A. M Skinner of the Secretariat, the party reaching Pangkor on 13 January. Meanwhile, by the Governor's instructions, I went from Pinang to Lârut on board H.M.S *Avon* to tell the Chinese that their friends in Pinang had agreed to suspend hostilities, and to invite the Mantri, and any other chiefs who could be got at, to meet Sir Andrew at the rendezvous on 15 January. By that date it had been possible to collect at Pangkor, Raja Abdullah, his relative Raja Idris (the present Sultan of Pêrak), and the chiefs who were his adherents, also the Raja Bĕndahâra, the Mantri, the Tĕmĕnggong, and the Dato Sâgor; but Raja Ismail and Raja Yusuf were too far away, and made no effort to attend. Mr. Pickering and the heads of the Chinese factions were also present.

After some days of discussion an instrument was drawn up in English and Malay, and was signed and sealed on 20 January, 1874. It is known as the Pangkor Engagement, or Treaty, and provides, amongst other things, for the recognition of Raja Abdullah as Sultan of Pêrak, and the grant of the title of Ex-Sultan to Ismail, who is to hand over the regalia to Sultan Abdullah.

The two most important clauses are as follows:

Clause VI. "That the Sultan receive and provide a suitable residence for a British officer, to be called Resident, who shall be accredited to his Court, and whose advice must be asked and acted upon in all questions other than those touching Malay religion and custom."

Clause X. "That the collection and control of all revenues and the general administration of the Country be regulated under the advice of these Residents."

Source: Frank Swettenham, *British Malaya: An Account of the Origin and Progress of British Influence in Malaya* (London: G. Allen and Unwin, 1948), 175–177. First published in 1906.

>> Mastering the Material

1. According to Robinson and Gallagher, what was the main reason for Britain's participation in the scramble for African colonies?

2. Philip Curtin introduces us to 'men-on-the-spot' and their motivations. In what way did men-on-the-spot make policy on their own, without consulting the Colonial Office in Britain, in the cases of the Fante Confederation and the Malay Peninsula?

3. In what ways does Swettenham's narrative of the development of British control over Malaysia illustrate Curtin's theory?

4. Having read the two clauses of the Pangkor Agreement highlighted by Swettenham, do you think the British Resident came to act more as an "advisor" or a colonial ruler in subsequent decades?

>> Making Connections

1. How does Robinson and Gallagher's theory of "local crises" modify, augment, or contradict the "strategic" theories for the colonization of Africa put forth in Chapter 12?

2. Why do you think Administrator Salmon moved to quash the Fante Confederation, an act that led to the establishment of the British Gold Coast Colony? Were the reasons strategic or economic? Were there moral factors? Does this document lead you to question accounts of the new imperialism that suggest large overarching themes as the principal factors in the establishment of colonies?

Part 3 Conclusion

Imperialism and colonialism are fundamentally global stories, as is obvious from the debate over their origins. Initially, of course, scholars did not recognize that the new imperialism of the late nineteenth century originated out of a changing global background. Instead, contemporary observers contextualized colonialization in either national or at most "great power" levels. Some argued that it was changes internal to each society that produced the new empires—internal politics, the growth of new industries, and the development of nationalism that encompassed both racism and at the same time a sense of national destiny or duty. Most, however, recognized that these were traits that were shared among the new imperial states and made certain connections between them. They saw that nationalism was logically connected to economic competition between states, and that industrialization in many individual countries when taken together produced these commercial rivalries. Finally, they saw imperialism as the turning of this moral, intellectual, economic, and military competition outward into the world.

What most twentieth-century scholars failed to see, however, was the way in which this story was larger than just Europe and the United States and Japan. They failed to see how European economies had to respond not only to their industrialized competitors but also to merchants in Africa and Asia, who took advantage of this competition to try to drive down prices. They missed the way in which the governments of small states tried to play the imperial powers against each other in order to gain access to arms and technology. In short, they continued to believe in a story that was played out on a European rather than a global level. Most historians and their peers in other disciplines now recognize this globality, just as they recognize that there was not a single thematic explanation for the new imperialism. Economics, culture, political and military factors, and technological change all played a role.

The global story of the new imperialism does not end with the conquest of colonies and the spread of influence. The new empires built from this late-nineteenth and early twentieth-century race were very global indeed. Many stretched across multiple continents and traversed wide seas. In each of these empires, the connection between metropole and capital on the one hand and colonies and protectorates on the other made for great changes. These changes did not just take place in the periphery, but also at the imperial center. The experience of ruling Haiti between 1917 and 1935 transformed the culture of the United States just as it did that of Haiti. The same is true of other empires. Connected by strands of law, policy, the movement of people, and trade, colony and metropole slowly grew to reflect each other and to become increasingly integrated. This process was not always positive. As Part 4 will show, the brutality of colonial rule helped to contribute to the viciousness of the First World War and later the horrors of the Holocaust. Nevertheless, for better or for worse, empires connected the globe in myriad ways and helped to shape the world we live in today.

Further Reading

The period of the new or high imperialism has received a great deal of attention in the last few decades from scholars who argue that the modern world was shaped by imperial processes. Perhaps the most famous of these texts is Edward W. Said, *Orientalism* (New York: Vintage Books, 1978), in which the author looks at the ways in which the ideas of the "west" and the "east" emerged out of imperialism and colonialism both in this period and somewhat earlier. A somewhat more straightforward theoretical overview of the experience of colonialism is Jurgen Osterhammel (Princeton: Markus Weiner, 1997). Imperialism as an ideology and practice is similarly explored by several authors. Probably the most complete analyses are D. K. Fieldhouse, *Colonialism 1870–1845* (Basingstoke: Macmillian, 1988) and the somewhat more theoretical Wolfgang J. Mommsen, *Theories of Imperialism,* translated by P. S. Falla (New York: Random House, 1980).

Terms to Know

new imperialism *(p. 150)*

pacification *(p. 150)*

metropole *(p. 151)*

reciprocal *(p. 151)*

gross domestic product
  (p. 152)

colonial lobby *(p. 156)*

Marxism *(p. 165)*

civilizing mission *(p. 174)*

orientalism *(p. 176)*

weapons gap *(p. 185)*

periphery *(p. 193)*

man-on-the-spotism
  (p. 194)

Part 4

Debating Global Wars, 1914–1945

In July 1914, Europe erupted into war as the imperial, industrialized powers of France, Britain, Germany, Russia, Italy, the Ottoman Empire, and the Austro-Hungarian Empire mobilized against each other in two grand alliances. This four-year conflict, which we call the First World War, soon absorbed most of the smaller states of Europe and dragged in the United States, certain Latin American states, and Japan as belligerents as well. The war was fought not only in Europe but also in Africa and Asia. Naval confrontations took place off the Pacific and Caribbean coasts of the Americas and in the Indian Ocean. The populations of colonies around the world were mobilized as soldiers and laborers for imperial war efforts. The exhausted antagonists lowered their weapons following the surrender of Germany in 1918, but the armistice they signed did not bring lasting peace as hoped; it merely signaled a decade-long lull in the fighting. Conflict resurfaced in Asia first with Japanese aggression against China, but by 1939 much of the globe was engulfed in the Second World War. Open conflict subsided again in 1945 but was replaced almost immediately with the "cold war" between the Soviet-led Warsaw Pact on the one hand and NATO, led by the United States, on the other.

Scholars have often depicted the period 1914–1945 as a benchmark in world history. Many argue that the world wars fundamentally shifted the balance of global power away from western Europe to the United States and the Soviet Union. Others suggest that by exhausting the great European states the wars set the stage for the collapse of their empires. Yet if the wars of the first half of the twentieth century resulted in great transformations, they were also characterized by great continuities. Many of the ideas and trends that had distinguished the age of revolutions and the new imperialism reached their apogee in the war period. The enlightenment ideal of nationhood, expressed as unbridled patriotism, drove the great powers to hostilities and at the same time stirred ethnic minorities toward rebellion. Nationalism would eventually mutate into the extremist ideologies that drove the Second World War: ultranationalism, militarism, fascism, and Nazism. Imperialism also contributed to strained relations between the industrialized states. Imperialism was based on competition, and not always of the friendly sort, and colonies were sources of manpower and strategic materials for the war effort. Industrialization, too, played a role by making longer, bloodier wars possible by enabling states to mobilize their entire economies and populations. And in the end, the two wars proved the growing importance of globalization. In both wars, it was the powers with the greatest global reach—specifically Britain, the Soviet Union, and the United States—that emerged victorious.

How did this transformational period of conflict begin? What were its causes? These questions are much debated, especially for the First World War (1914–1918). The earliest attempts at an answer to these questions examined the aspirations of each of the antagonists. Austro-Hungary was desperately trying to contain ethnic separatism within the Balkan provinces of its multinational empire. Russia hoped that war fever would divert its populace from domestic crises, but equally important were its strategic objectives in the Balkans and its hopes for a window onto the Mediterranean Sea. The Ottomans aspired to regain their won Balkan empire at the expense of Russia. The young state of Germany, under Kaiser Wilhelm II, had bold global and European ambitions that have led some historians to assign it most of the blame for the war. France, smarting from an earlier defeat at the hands of a German coalition, hoped to regain lost pride and territory. Britain had a global empire to protect and a hearty nationalist lobby pushing for war. The entry of Japan, Italy, and the United States into the war can be variously ascribed to opportunism, nationalism, and self-defense. Some states, like Belgium, had little choice but to resist armed incursions.

Yet underpinning these national objectives were shared trends that were both global and European. Nationalism and imperialism stoked the fires of any potential conflict, and the European system of alliances arguably determined that any war between two powers would immediately be transformed into a general conflict. Moreover, the requirements of industry and manpower, along with the ideologies of the time, called for offensive strategies that left little hope for a pullback from the brink of war. All of this has led some scholars to declare the First World War inevitable.

Not all who have studied the origins of the war agree, however. At several points in the two decades preceding 1914 Europe had been close to general war and yet its diplomats had found a way out. Perhaps the blame for the war can be put on a few incompetent or war-mongering monarchs, diplomats, politicians, and radicals. After all, it was an unexpected event—the assassination of an Austrian Archduke in Sarajevo—that sparked the war, and some have suggested that its origins are to be found not in larger trends but in the posturing and diplomatic fumbling immediately following this assassination. It took only a few swaggering kings and generals to commit much of Europe to war, and these great states then dragged in the rest of the world, however unwillingly.

The First World War lasted more than four years, and ended not with a bang, but a whimper. The defeat of Germany, Austria-Hungary, and the Ottomans was caused principally by exhaustion and Britain's successful maritime blockade. Germany's army had, in fact, proven the most competent of all the combatants and cannot be said to have been decisively defeated in battle. Yet the victorious powers, and especially France, demanded enormous reparations from the German government and forced it to agree to humiliating territorial and military limitations. These extreme measures ensured that the First World War was not, as its contemporaries had hoped, the "war to end all wars."

The heavy financial burden imposed on Germany coincided with not one but two global depressions, from 1919 to 1924 and from 1929 to 1939. An exhausted United States withdrew into isolationism, with many of its leaders pledging never again to get involved in a European war. In Russia, the costs of the war had sparked the **Bolshevik** Revolution, leaders of which had replaced the tsarist monarchy with a Marxist (communist) administration led by Vladimir Ilyich Lenin and renamed the state the Union of Soviet Socialist Republics. Arguably, it was fear of a similar revolution in their own societies that drove the middle classes of some European states to seek refuge in the lies of dogmatic and militaristic super-nationalist parties, such as the Nazis in Germany and the Fascists in Italy. In Asia, Japanese militarism was similarly flexing its muscles. Most interpretations of the origins of the Second World War focus on the ambitions of these aggressive powers, especially the Nazi party of Adolf Hitler. Throughout the 1930s, Germany, Italy, and Japan snatched up nearby states and regions in pursuit of strategic resources, territory, and ideological goals.

Why were these militarist powers not headed off by Russia, Britain, the United States, and France? At the end of the First World War a sense of internationalism had emerged from the exhaustion of nationalist warfare. Its greatest achievement was the development of the League of Nations, which its supporters hoped would peacefully resolve future conflicts. Communist Russia, too, was theoretically internationalist. Moreover, the militarism of Japan and Germany was dangerous to the security of the Soviet Union, squeezed as it was between them. Yet over time the League proved powerless to stop military adventurism. In 1935 it proved helpless to protect one of its own members, Abyssinia (Ethiopia), from attack by the Fascist armies of Italy. In part the League had been undermined by the failure of the United States to ever become a member. Mistrust between the liberal powers of Britain and France on the one hand and the communist leadership of the Soviet Union on the other also contributed to its failure. Each side regarded the other principally as a likely enemy, rather than a potential ally. Thus, in the end, both liberal and communist internationalism failed to stop the growth of the military juggernauts of Germany, Italy, and Japan. Scholars now debate whether or not Britain and France might have avoided war by taking a tougher line against Japanese campaigns in China, German remilitarization, and Italy's aggression in Abyssinia.

Yet there is an even darker episode of the Second World War than the slaughter of industrial warfare. As the Nazis spread across Europe they implemented a **genocide** against Europe's Jewish population as well as other ethnic minorities, such as the Gypsy population. This systematic plan to exterminate entire ethnic, national, and religious groups resulted in the murder of 15 to 25 million innocent men, women, and children. Known today as the Holocaust, it was termed by some of its participants the "final solution." Yet as horrible as it was, the Holocaust was debatably not an isolated event. Some scholars have argued instead that it was the culmination of a combination of trends in modernization: ultra-nationalism, the industrialization of killing, and pseudo-scientific notions of race. In fact, the early twentieth century was characterized by the **racialization** of enemy combatants and civilians alike. This was the process by which enemy civilians were depicted as racially inferior and even non-human, and therefore suitable for abuse or extermination. Three outstanding examples are the German genocide against the Herero peoples of southwestern Africa at the turn of the century, the massacre of Armenians in Turkey just prior to the First World War, and the Japanese military's patterns of rape and murder in China in the 1930s and 1940s. Even in the United States, the internment of Japanese-Americans fits into a pattern of racialization of the enemy, although it was not genocidal. As for the Holocaust, the objectives and mechanisms of each of these events is a matter of often-impassioned debate, but together they suggest an increasingly brutal and racist side to modernity.

However, some scholars reject this view of the Holocaust as merely representative of wider trends. They argue that the Nazi's actions were uniquely premeditated, planned by the party early in their rise to power, and implemented systematically before and during the war. This is often known as the **intentionalist** model of Holocaust studies.

As illustrated by the debate over the origins of the Holocaust, the war era aptly demonstrates the convergence of two great processes that define global history in the modern world: nationalism and globalization. These trends helped to shape the world wars and the Holocaust, and they also characterized the conflicts' outcomes. One could argue that the two world wars were disruptive events that marked a real break in world history. One could also argue that they merely marked new stages in the development of a modernity that was increasingly bringing the world together and tearing it apart at the same time.

Part 4 Timeline

1882	The Triple Alliance between Germany, Austria-Hungary, and Italy is signed. Italy will later leave the alliance.
1907	Britain and Russia resolve many of their differences, setting the stage for a British, Russian, and French alliance.
1911	The Second Moroccan Crisis (Agadir) drives Britain and Germany apart.
1913	The Second Balkan War.
1914	Following the assassination of the Archduke Ferdinand, the First World War begins in Europe and globally.
1914	Ottoman authorities order the expulsion of a large proportion of the Armenian population of the Ottoman Empire, an act that culminates in the deaths of millions of civilians.
1918	Germany and the Central Powers surrender, ending the First World War.
1929	The Great Depression begins.
1935	The Nuremburg Race laws are passed in Germany, placing numerous restrictions on the Jewish population.
1937	Japanese forces, having captured the Chinese city of Nanking, commit numerous atrocities.
1939	Nazi-Soviet nonaggression pact signed.
1939	Nazi Germany under Adolf Hitler invades Poland, causing Britain and France to declare war on Germany.
1940	Following a German sneak attack, the Soviet Union joins the war.
1941	Following a Japanese sneak attack, the United States joins the war.
1942	At the Wannsee Conference, Nazi leaders plan the extermination of Europe's Jewish population.
1945	The Second World War ends in the defeat of the Fascist powers and their allies.

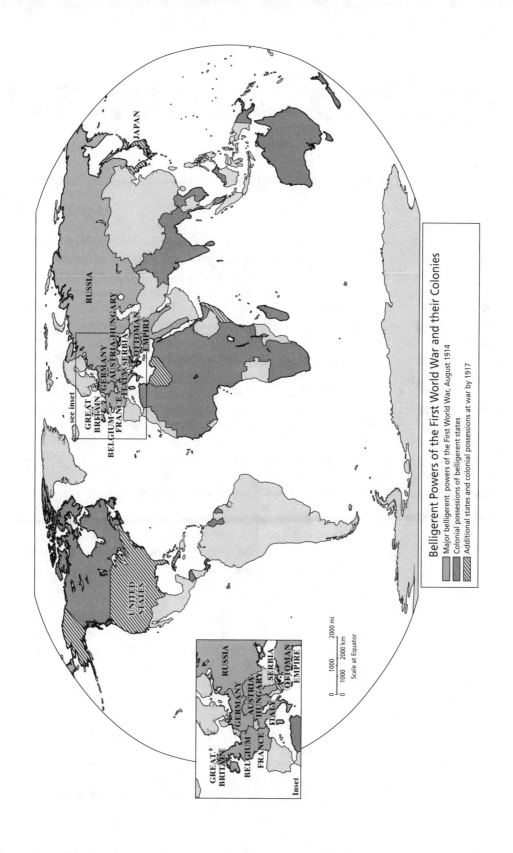

Belligerent Powers of the First World War and their Colonies

Major belligerent powers of the First World War, August 1914

Colonial possessions of belligerent states

Additional states and colonial possessions at war by 1917

JAPAN

RUSSIA

GREAT BRITAIN
GERMANY
AUSTRIA-HUNGARY
BELGIUM SERBIA
FRANCE ITALY OTTOMAN
EMPIRE

see inset

UNITED STATES

0   1000   2000 mi
0 1000 2000 km
Scale at Equator

RUSSIA

GREAT BRITAIN
GERMANY
AUSTRIA-HUNGARY
BELGIUM SERBIA
FRANCE ITALY OTTOMAN
EMPIRE

Inset

209

Chapter 17

The "Long Fuse" of the First World War

The First World War has one of the longest and deepest scholarly pedigrees of any event in modern world history. Even in the run-up to the war, the belligerent states were very aware of the advantage of casting blame on their opponents. The German government, for example, fabricated evidence in 1914 of French intentions to invade Germany, Switzerland, and Belgium as a justification for their own invasion of France. Similarly, the French and British governments manufactured evidence of German "atrocities" in Belgium in order to sway public opinion in the United States. Following the German surrender, France and its allies revived the question of "war guilt." The Treaty of Versailles (sometimes referred to as the Treaty of Paris) that ended the war forced Germany to accept almost the entire blame for the conflict. This blame game, which is discussed fully in the next chapter, began to fade in the 1950s, to be replaced with a more evenhanded, thematic evaluation of the causes of the conflict.

This transition to a thematic analysis was demonstrated by the 1951 conclusions of a group of important French and German scholars. At a meeting to discuss the ways in which textbooks in each country should deal with the war, this group of historians came to a general agreement that, basically, everyone was to blame:

> *The documents do not permit attributing a premeditated desire for a European war on the part of any government or people in 1914. Distrust was at a peak and ruling circles were dominated by the idea that war was inevitable. Each one accused the other of aggressive intentions; each accepted the risk of war and saw its hope of security in the alliance system and the development of armament.*

These new and more profound studies of the origins of the war were somewhat fatalistic. Historians began to argue that Europe had for some decades been heading toward a "great" war that would inevitably involve all of the world's major military powers. They began to identify what they saw as underpinning factors behind the conflict: the growth of industrial militarization, the instability of the alliance system, the general acceptance of the risks of war, imperialism, and nationalism. They argued that these factors created a "long fuse" that burned slowly, propelling the states of Europe toward conflict over a period of decades, and they pointed out that in the fifteen years preceding 1914 general hostilities were only barely avoided several times.

Seemingly at the heart of this slide over the brink were the great European alliances. By the late nineteenth century, two such alliances had coalesced. The earliest was the Austro-Hungarian and German Triple Alliance with Italy as a junior power in

1882. Although Italy switched sides in 1914, the alliance between Austria-Hungary and Germany established them as the **Central Powers** of the First World War, so termed because of their location at the center of Europe. This alliance directly threatened France and Russia, who signed the **Franco-Russian Entente** in 1894, thus forming a rival coalition.

While these alliances were coalescing, the greatest global power of them all— Great Britain—remained aloof in "splendid isolation," as did three other important states: the United States, the Ottoman Empire, and Japan. As antagonism between the two alliances intensified, France, Germany, and Russia competed to win over these uncommitted states, and especially Britain. Yet as an island nation with no territorial aims in Europe Britain was vulnerable only in its connection to the empire. Britain's economy, especially, was reliant on its commerce with India, the crown jewel of colonies. Thus around the turn of the century the major belligerents plotted to black-mail, threaten, or cajole Britain into committing to one alliance or another by playing the imperial card. Germany and France threatened one of Britain's great imperial chokepoints, the Suez Canal in Egypt, by annexing colonies along the upper Nile. Germany also tried to create a crisis by threatening Morocco, at the other entrance to Britain's Mediterranean route to India. This attempt—the famous Agadir crisis of 1911—ultimately backfired and drove Britain, Russia, and France closer to each other. The Entente powers capitalized on this trend by making concessions to Britain in both northern Africa and Asia. Thus they secured closer relations with Britain, even as Kaiser Wilhelm II of Germany antagonized the British by building a fleet to rival the British navy. Britain's entry into the Franco-Russian coalition in 1907 transformed it into the **Triple Entente.** However, the imperial maneuvering had unintended conse-quences. Each "spark" of imperial conflict also drove Europe inexorably toward war, as the much-admired war historian James Joll argues in this chapter.

Meanwhile, military and industrial techniques that would make World War I a more horrible and destructive type of warfare were being developed and practiced in the colonies. British officials watched with approval as airplanes bombed striking workers in southern Africa, and German colonial soldiers used machine guns and starvation as weapons against rebels in nearby southwestern Africa and Tanganyika. At home, imperialism also helped to foster militaristic cultures of nationalism and superiority. John H. Morrow, Jr., a leading historian of World War I, has argued in *The Great War: An Imperial History* that psychologically, socially, and intellectually imperialism cultivated the happy rush to war:

> *Once the Europeans divided themselves into "races", into superior and inferior peoples, what was to prevent the extension of the brutal attitudes towards "colored peoples" to other Europeans for the sake of progress and survival?*

The origins of extreme nationalism within imperialism is a theme that we will return to when we look at the Second World War. Yet imperialism was, arguably, merely one facet of the nationalist worldviews that were fast coming to characterize European societies in the mid-nineteenth century. In this textbook we have traced European nationalism from its earliest emergence as a political force in the eighteenth century. By the early twentieth century it had mutated from an ideology of political emancipation to one that embraced extreme racism, jingoism, chauvinism, and militarism. Early twentieth-century nationalism within the great powers fed on the socioeconomic phenomena of that period. The same economic rivalry for overseas markets and resources that had driven the new imperialism also fed nationalism. So did the rise of poverty among industrial workers. Politicians, eager to find someone to blame for the plight of the impoverished masses, vilified neighboring or rival states. They hoped in this way to defuse the appeal of socialist and communist parties that blamed the upper classes for the impoverishment of workers. Aggressive foreign policies thus became useful tools for distracting the people from domestic problems. There was also the underlying tension of history. France yearned to reclaim Alsace and Lorraine, lost in 1871 to Germany. The Ottoman Turks hoped to reclaim their place in the Balkans. Germany, a relatively new state, hoped to claim a "place in the sun" alongside older powers like Britain.

Yet at the same time, a different strain of nationalism continued to promise emancipation for ethnic minorities living within the great states of Europe who were beginning to conceive of themselves as nations for the first time. Liberation movements emerged, especially among the Austro-Hungarian Empire's Czechs, Slavic peoples like the Serbs, and Poles, some of whom looked to Slavic Russia for aid. The multiethnic Ottoman Empire was similarly beginning to come apart. It was Serbian nationalism at the end of an assassin's gun barrel, of course, that sparked the war. Bernadotte E. Schmitt, an influential scholar of this period, argues that it was these strands of nationalism, first and foremost, that led Europe and then much of the world to war.

Nationalism was undoubtedly one of the principal causes of the "cult of the offensive" that accelerated the march to war and made general conflict an inevitable outcome of diplomatic posturing in 1914. There had been few major wars between industrialized European powers prior to the First World War, and European military staffs had drawn the wrong conclusions from those that had occurred. Following the French defeat by the Prussians and other German states in 1870–1871, for example, observers had come to the conclusion that France's defeat had been the result of an absence of *élan,* or aggressive spirit. This, of course, was entirely the wrong conclusion. Germany had won because of its superior industrial and military organization and infrastructure. A closer analysis of the trench conditions and horror of the American Civil War also would have revealed this. Yet Europeans, absorbed by concept of national pride, refused to contemplate developing patient or defensive strategy. As Stephen van Evera shows in his article "The Cult of the Offensive and the Origins of the First World War," this offensive spirit doomed Europe to rush to war rather than taking time to consider its implications.

That this very rapid mobilization and commitment of armies came to dominate the pace of diplomatic efforts and eventually to lead to war is illustrated by a memorandum written by General Helmuth von Moltke to German Chancellor Theobald von Bethmann Hollweg. Von Moltke had inherited a plan of attack that forced Germany to attack the heavily industrialized France first, hopefully to knock her out of the war before her ally Russia could mobilize. This plan forced Germany to declare war on France despite the fact that the initial crisis lay in the east, in the Balkan states. The rigidity of the German plan thus turned a Balkan conflict into a general war. Yet, as von Moltke's letter shows, Germany's commitment to a general mobilization was partly a result of its fear of French and Russian mobilization.

Imperialism, nationalism, and the nature of industrialized warfare were arguably underpinning causes of the First World War. Yet not all scholars see a direct line between these trends and the outbreak of the war. Nor do they agree that these factors necessarily led to the transition from a European war to a truly global conflict. In the next chapter, scholars will point to internal issues unique to some of the belligerents, the actions of individual activists and politicians, and the events of a single month—July 1914—as alternate explanations for these transformations.

Imperial Rivalries

In The Origins of the First World War, *noted war historian James Joll discusses a wide range of causes of this war. These included local crises, the alliance system, and development of war industries. Joll fits imperialism into this spectrum of causes, arguing that the ongoing conflict over influence and colonies worldwide increased tension between the European great powers. In his interpretation, it was imperial crises that ultimately drove the great empires into two antagonistic alliances. While nationalism and events internal to Europe may have provoked the war, he suggests these imperial considerations helped shape it. Joll focuses especially on Germany. He argues that the German development of an oceangoing navy and German threats to British imperial security drove Britain to end its former hostilities with France and Russia. The reconciliation of these three powers eventually brought Britain into the war on the side of her allies and turned a European conflict into a truly global war.*

>> 76. The Origins of the First World War

JAMES JOLL [1984]

The outbreak of war in 1914 was not caused by immediate imperialist rivalries; and Germany's aspirations for colonial territory might well have been achieved by agreement with Britain if the Germans had been prepared to abate their claims to naval hegemony and world power. Nevertheless weak independent states such as Morocco and the Ottoman Empire itself were a constant temptation to imperialist or would-be imperialist powers, so that Franco-German rivalry in Morocco and Italian ambitions in Tripoli could produce crises in 1911 which added to the instability of the international system. By 1914, however, specifically colonial conflicts in North Africa or the Middle East were subordinated to a wider pattern of international ambitions and apprehensions. The crisis over Morocco was solved by a compromise colonial agreement between France and Germany which left neither side wholly satisfied, but the importance of the crisis lay less in the specific redistribution of African territory than in the general exacerbation of mutual suspicion between

Source: James Joll, *The Origins of the First World War* (New York: Longman, 1984), 164–167.

France and Germany and the intensification of the arms race, supported by a new wave of nationalist propaganda on both sides of the frontier. By 1914 the psychological consequences of a generation of imperialism were more important than the actual territorial gains or losses.

The older imperial rivalries had not disappeared, but they had been pushed into second place by the new alignment caused especially by German ambitions to take a place among the world powers. A mass of detailed disagreements still troubled relations between Britain and France in spite of the *Entente Cordiale*—arguments, for example, over the international status of Tangier or economic interests in Syria; and these were to become worse once the war had started and the possibility of a partition of the Ottoman Empire revived old suspicions and aroused new ambitions. Yet again and again both in London and Paris the need for mutual support against Germany led, if not to a solution of these differences, at least to an agreement to overlook them temporarily. British relations with Russia were more difficult. Although the Anglo-Russian agreement of 1907 appeared to resolve the conflicting claims on the borders of the two empires—in Afghanistan and Tibet and Persia—local rivalries and old distrust that went back for generations still caused problems. The agreement had been criticized in both countries, particularly because the recognition of British and Russian spheres of influence in Persia coincided with a revolution there in which both sides tried to win British or Russian support. [...] Yet in spite of moments of tension, as when in 1908 the Russian commander of the Shah's Cossack Brigade ordered his troops to surround the British legation in Tehran, Grey and the Foreign Office consistently sacrificed local interests in Persia and the Far East to a wider cause of maintaining the *entente* with Russia. [...]

Britain's relationship with India was central to the idea of empire and had been the key to British foreign policy for more than a century. [...]

With the agreement with Russia in 1907, one of the main threats to India's external security seemed to have been removed—even if the government of India and the soldiers were rather reluctant to recognize the fact. [...]

The immediate motives which led governments to decide to go to war in 1914 were not directly imperialist and the crisis they faced was a crisis in Europe, but earlier imperialist policies had contributed to the frame of mind in which decisions were taken. For Russia the lure of Constantinople and the Straits was a main motive in her Balkan policy, to which Asian ambitions were temporarily subordinated. For Germany vague aspirations to world hegemony had contributed to the decision to construct a navy which was inevitably seen by Britain as a challenge. England who, as the German ambassador in London remarked, 'has the best colonies and doesn't need a war with us to acquire more', had nevertheless come to accept the British Empire as something that had to be preserved at any cost. The French, by accepting the need urged by the *parti colonial* to gain control of Morocco had added a colonial dimension to their resentment against Germany in Europe, while the Germans by deliberately provoking the Agadir crisis contributed to the growth of nationalist agitation in both countries and the acceleration of the arms race, and thus added to the growing international tension in 1912–14, tension in the growth of which the collapse of Ottoman rule in Europe under the impact of Italian imperialism and Balkan nationalism had also played a major part.

Anglo-Russian Reconciliation

Throughout the nineteenth century, Britain and Russia were imperial adversaries. Their two expanding empires—Russia's land-based Asian empire and Britain's global maritime empire—overlapped at strategic points like Afghanistan, Tibet, and Persia. Russia's Tsar's were interested in adding each of these to their empire, whereas Britain fought to keep them independent but within its sphere of influence. Faced with the growing power and imperial ambitions of Germany in the decade prior to the First World War, however, the governments of both Russia and Britain moved to reconcile and in late 1907 signed the first of a number of agreements. This British Memorandum respecting the 1907 agreement circulated by the Foreign Office in early 1908 is a key document for understanding the creation of the French-British-Russian Triple Entente. It reflects the British understanding of the advantages of the treaty with Russia. The treaty defined spheres of influence in different parts of Persia (Iran), limited Russian involvement in Afghanistan and Tibet, and pledged the British government not to formally annex Tibet. It was signed without first consulting with either the rulers or people of these territories.

>> 77. Memorandum Respecting the Anglo-Russian Convention

[1907]

Persia

Foreign office, January 29, 1908
Confidential. (9180.)

The limits of the British sphere of influence in Persia as defined by Article II (^{2}) were inspired by the desire of His Majesty's Government to secure their really vital interest in the safeguarding of the strategical position on the Indian frontier. This was indicated by the late Government in 1908 as a triangle of territory including Seistan, Kerman, and Bunder Abbas so as to render it impossible to construct a Russian railway to Bunder Abbas or any port east of that place, the Admiralty considering that, with our practical possession of the Mussendim promontory, all danger from a Russian port in the Persian Gulf would be obviated. It was held that, if the Government of India could obtain this and nothing more by the payment of 500,000*l.* to the Persian Government, a good bargain would have been made, as it might save India from largely increased naval contributions and military expenditure in the future. This view was accepted by the Viceroy.

The recognition by Persia of the British sphere of influence in South-East Persia would have had no binding effect upon Russia, but the Russian Government have now formally recognized this sphere of influence, and no payment in money has been made for it.

The creation of a Russian and British sphere of influence is in reality only a self-denying Ordinance, by which each Government pledge themselves not to seek for concessions in the other's sphere. Other Powers are at liberty, as formerly to seek concessions all over Persia, and British trade will be carried on in the Russian and neutral zones on the same terms as hitherto and as the trade of other foreign countries, the sole restriction on British enterprise being that British Concessions cannot be sought in the Russian zone. [...]

Afghanistan

We have now for the first time obtained from Russia, in writing and in the form of a definite Treaty engagement,(^{3}) assurances on the following

---

Source: "Memorandum Respecting the Anglo-Russian Convention," in *British Documents on the Origins of the War 1898–1914*, edited by G. P. Gooch and Harold Temperley (London: H. M. Stationery Office, 1929), 612–614, 616.

three points, which had hitherto been only verbal and, as the Russian Government stated, not binding indefinitely upon them:—

1. That the Russian Government consider Afghanistan as outside the sphere of Russian influence.
2. That all their political relations with Afghanistan shall be conducted through the intermediary of His Majesty's Government.
3. That they will not send any Agents into Afghanistan. [...]

The [need of the] consent of the Ameer to an Agreement relating to Afghanistan was recognized by the late Government, since in the proposals submitted by Lord Lansdowne to the Russian Ambassador the following sentence occurs:—

"It will be necessary that His Majesty's Government should obtain the approval of the Ameer of Afghanistan before any Arrangement dealing with this question is concluded."

Moreover, the Ameer is bound to follow our advice in his foreign relations. To have consulted him about the questions of direct communication and commercial arrangements before signing the Agreement with Russia would have made him a third party to the negotiations. To have omitted Article V would have involved allowing the Russian Government at once to give effect to the arrangements as to frontier communications and trade, but this would have been impossible without the Ameer's consent.

The dilemma was to get the Ameer's consent before or after signature. It was decided for the above reasons to get it after signature. We have no reason to doubt that the Ameer will give his consent. He was on tour when the Treaty was signed. He wrote on the 29th September that he could not deal with so important a subject until he was back at his capital. This attitude was reasonable. He returned to Cabul on the 25th November. In view of the time which Orientals take over correspondence, and the importance of the subject, which necessitated consultation with his advisers, it is no matter of surprise that he has not yet replied.

Thibet

The provisions of the Agreement relating to Thibet ([4]) do not go beyond the assurances given in 1904 by Lord Lansdowne to the Russian Ambassador.

The position is that, in return for agreeing to embody the assurances of the late Government in a formal document, we have obtained similar assurances from Russia; and that in addition, we actually get formal Russian consent to the maintenance of a preferential position for Great Britain in Thibet over all other foreign countries in regard to frontier and commercial matters. [...]

With regard to the Anglo-Russian Convention as a whole, it may be generally stated that it has successfully removed causes of friction between Great Britain and Russia in Asia, and has enabled the two Powers to co-operate usefully together in Persia in maintaining a peaceful policy which it would quite recently have been difficult to secure had no such Convention existed. The removal of all causes of discord in Asia will no doubt contribute to more harmonious relations between the two Powers in Europe.

Nationalism and the Origins of the First World War

Bernadotte Schmitt is acknowledged as one of the senior historians of the First World War. In this pamphlet, Schmitt rejects the argument that "the war had grown out of economic jealousies and rival imperialism." While admitting that colonial tensions and commercial rivalries could at times be quite sharp, he points out that the Great Powers were also major trading partners, and that they had managed to partition Africa peacefully just a few decades previously. The real culprit, he argues, was nationalist tensions both among minorities within states and between the Great Powers.

>> 78. The Origins of the First World War

BERNADOTTE E. SCHMITT [1958]

The primary cause of the war was the conflict between political frontiers and the distribution of peoples, the denial of what is commonly called the right of self-determination (although this term was not ordinarily used before 1914). In 1914, from the Rhine eastwards, political frontiers, as determined by the Congress of Vienna a century before and by the wars of the nineteenth century, everywhere cut across well-recognized lines of nationality. To begin with, Germany held Alsace-Lorraine, taken from France in 1871, where the majority of the population resented having been annexed to Germany, disliked German rule, and wished to return to France. Austria-Hungary contained eleven different racial groups, nine of which were kept in greater or less submission by a ruling clique of the other two (Germans, Magyars). In the Balkans, racial and political frontiers rarely coincided. Finally, the western portion of the Russian Empire was made up of non-Russian regions represented today Finland, the Baltic States, and Poland. Poland was the most notorious case, for it was still divided between the Austrian, German and Russian empires which had partitioned it in the eighteenth century.

So Germany was faced with the problem of French, Danish and Polish minorities, and Austria-Hungary consisted chiefly of minorities. Some minorities were treated more harshly than others, but everywhere they were growing increasingly restless and demanding change. In some cases minorities were able to look across their own frontiers to free kinsmen who, it was hoped, would one day free them from the oppression (as they saw it) under which they suffered. The Yugoslavs in both Austria and Hungary, denied relief by their Habsburg rulers, turned for help to Serbia under King Peter Karageorgevich, and the Romanians of Transylvania, in southeastern Hungary, gazed longingly across the Carpathians at independent Romania under its Hohenzollern king. Neither Yugoslavs nor Romanians had in the past been united, but if the nineteenth century had seen the unification of Italians and Germans, why should not the twentieth century witness the joining together of Yugoslavs or Romanians? The Poles, too, dreamed of reunion, even if before 1914 there seemed no prospect of it.

More than any other circumstance, this conflict between existing governments and their unhappy minorities was responsible for the catastrophe of 1914. Germany understood perfectly well that the annexation of Alsace-Lorraine could be maintained only by the sword, and France knew equally well that the provinces could be regained only by the sword. The multi-national Habsburg state depended more and more on force, less and less on the loyalty of its peoples. The partition of Poland was maintained only by force. Since the astonishing victories of Prussia in the wars against Denmark, Austria and France were attributed to its conscript armies, it was not surprising

Source: Bernadotte E. Schmitt, *The Origins of the First World War* (Pamphlet of the Historical Association, 1958), 6–7.

that the new German Empire established in 1871 continued to recruit its armies by universal service. Inevitably, Germany's neighbours adopted the same system. Not only that, but every increase in strength, every improvement in the weapons of war made by one country, had to be met by all. From 1872 to 1913, this rigorous competition in the building up of armies went on, every government spending as much money as it could persuade its people to pay or its national economy would support (Germany bore this cost easily, but for Italy the burden was ruinous), without, however, any corresponding increase in security being felt.

The Cult of the Offensive

Bernadotte Schmitt attributes the growth of great armies and aggressive strategies to the nationalist spirit of the times, and a number of other scholars have picked up on this theme. In this extract, Stephen van Evera shows how the idea of an offensive spirit, or élan, shaped military strategy. As van Evera explains, military leaders as well as politicians across Europe believed that victory belonged to the army that took the offensive. Such ideological orthodoxy left little time for diplomacy once the mobilization of armies had begun, and helped to shorten the gap between the murder of Archduke Ferdinand in Sarajevo and the commitment of all of the Great Powers to war. It also led to massive casualty rates as nineteenth-century mass-attack strategy went up against twentieth-century weaponry. Finally, as van Evera notes, the cult of the offensive ensured that any Balkan conflict would become a general war. On the one hand, the Russians calculated that they needed to mobilize quickly against not only Austria but Germany. On the other, the German General Staff came to believe that an early knock-out blow would have to be aimed not at Russia, but at France, which had the capacity to mobilize faster than her less industrialized Russian ally. Thus was born the Schlieffen plan, in which Germany would preempt a French offensive by attacking through Belgium deep toward Paris. This, unfortunately, guaranteed that Britain would come into the war, not only because Belgium was ostensibly neutral but also because a German fleet based in Belgium could truly threaten the British coastline.

>> 79. The Cult of the Offensive and the Origins of the First World War

Stephen van Evera [1991]

The gulf between myth and the realities of warfare has never been greater than in the years before World War I. Despite the large and growing advantage which defenders gained against attackers as a result of the invention of rifled and repeating small arms, the machine gun, barbed wire, and the development of railroads, Europeans increasingly believed that attackers would hold the advantage on the battlefield and that wars would be short and decisive,—a "brief storm" in the words of the

Source: Stephen van Evera, "The Cult of the Offensive and the Origins of the First World War," in *Military Strategy and the Origins of the First World War*, edited by Steven E. Miller (Princeton: Princeton University Press, 1991), 58–59, 61, 85–86, 92–93.

German Chancellor, Bethmann Hollweg. They largely overlooked the lesson of the American Civil War, the Russo-Turkish War of 1877–78, the Boer War and the Russo-Japanese War, which had demonstrated the power of the new defensive technologies. Instead, Europeans embraced a set of political and military myths which obscured both the defender's advantages and the obstacles an aggressor would confront. This mindset helped to mold the offensive military doctrines which every European power adopted during the period 1892–1913.

In Germany the military glorified the offense in strident terms, and inculcated German society with similar views. General Alfred von Schlieffen, author of the 1914 German war plan, declared that "Attack is the best defense," while the popular publicist Friedrich von Bernhardi proclaimed that "the offensive mode of action is by far superior to the defensive mode," and that "the superiority of offensive warfare under modern conditions is greater than formerly German Chief of Staff General Helmuth von Molfker also endorsed "the principle that the offensive is the best defense," while General August von Keim, founder of the Army League, argued that "Germany ought to be armed for attack," since "the offensive is the only way of insuring victory." These assumptions guided the Schlieffen Plan, which envisaged rapid and decisive attacks on Belgium, France, and Russia. [. . .]

British and French officers suggested that superior morale on the attacking side could overcome superior defensive firepower, and that this superiority in morale could be achieved simply by assuming the role of attacker, since offense was a morale-building activity. One French officer contended that "the offensive doubles the energy of the troops" and "concentrates the thoughts of the commander on a single objective," while British officers declared that "Modern [war] conditions have enormously increased the value of moral quality," and "the moral attributes [are] the primary causes of all great success." In short, mind would prevail over matter; morale would triumph over machine guns. [. . .]

The spreading of World War I outward from the Balkans is often ascribed to the scope and rigidity of the Russian and German plans for mobilization, which required that Russia must also mobilize armies against Germany when it mobilized against Austria-Hungary, and that Germany also attack France and Belgium if it fought Russia. [. . .]

The scope and character of these plans in turn reflected the assumption that the offense was strong. In an offense-dominant world Russia would have been prudent to mobilize against Germany if it mobilized against Austria-Hungary; and Germany probably would have been prudent to attack Belgium and France at the start of any Russo-German war. Thus the troublesome railroad schedules of 1914 reflected the offense-dominant world in which the schedulers believed they lived. Had they known that the defense was powerful, they would have been drawn towards flexible plans for limited deployment on single frontiers; and had such planning prevailed, the war might have been confined to Eastern Europe or the Balkans.

Moreover, the "inflexibility" of the war plans may have reflected the same offensive assumptions which determined their shape. Russian and German soldiers understandably developed only options which they believed prudent to exercise, while omitting plans which they believed would be dangerous to implement. These judgments in turn reflected their own and their adversaries' offensive ideas. Options were few because these offensive ideas seemed to narrow the range of prudent choice.

Lastly, the assumption of offense-dominance gave preset plans greater influence over the conduct of the July crisis, by raising the cost of improvisation if statesmen insisted on adjusting plans at the last minute. Russian statesmen were told that an improvised partial mobilization would place Russia in a "extremely dangerous situation," and German civilians were warned against improvisation in similar terms. This in turn reflected the size of the "windows" which improvised partial mobilizations would open for the adversary on the frontier which the partial mobilization left unguarded, which in turn reflected the assumption that the offense was strong (since if defenses were strong a bungled mobilization would create less opportunity for others to exploit). Thus the cult of the offensive gave planners greater power to bind statesmen to the plans they had prepared. [...]

"Mobilization meant war" in 1914 because mobilization meant war to Germany: the German war plan mandated that special units of the German standing army would attack Belgium and Luxemburg immediately after mobilization was ordered, and long before it was completed. (In fact Germany invaded Luxemburg on August 1, the same day on which it ordered full mobilization.) Thus Germany had no pure "mobilization" plan, but rather had a "mobilization and attack" plan under which mobilizing and attacking would be undertaken simultaneously. As a result, Europe would cascade into war if any European state mobilized in a manner which eventually forced German mobilization.

This melding of mobilization and attack in Germany reflected two decisions to which I have already alluded. First, Germans believed that they would lose their chance for victory and create a grave danger for themselves if they gave the Entente time to mobilize its superior numbers. In German eyes, German defenses would be too weak to defeat this superiority. As one German apologist later argued, "Germany could never with success have warded off numerically far superior opponents by means of a defensive war against a mobilized Europe" had it mobilized and stood in place. Hence it was "essential for the Central Powers to begin hostilities as soon as possible" following mobilization. Likewise, during the July crisis, Jagow explained that Germany must attack in response to Russian mobilization because "we are obliged to act as fast as possible before Russia has the time to mobilize her army.

A German General's Perspective on the Causes of the First World War

Historians often try to look at wars from the perspective of a commanding general. One of the most important military leaders in 1914 was German Army Chief of Staff Helmuth von Moltke. Von Moltke was a committed nationalist and a somewhat more experienced soldier than the commanding officers of the armies of the other Great Powers. He had inherited Schlieffen's plan to attack France first, but weakened it (perhaps mortally) by removing several divisions to the east out of fear that Russian armies would hit Germany before France could be knocked out of the war. In this selection—a letter written to his superior Chancellor Theobald von Bethman Hollweg on the morning following Austria-Hungary's declaration of war against Serbia—von Moltke blames Serbia and Russia for provoking German mobilization. It is a document that demonstrates the seemingly inevitable spread of war as each state reacted to its rivals as well as giving the perspective of a general serving his country.

>> 80. Letter to Theobald von Bethman Hollweg

HELMUTH VON MOLTKE [1914]

BERLIN, *July 29, 1914.*

Summary of the Political Situation

It goes without saying that no nation of Europe would regard the conflict between Austria and Serbia with any interest except that of humanity, if there did not lie within it the danger of general political complications that today already threaten to unchain a world war. For more than five years Serbia has been the cause of a European tension which has been pressing with simply intolerable weight on the political and economic existence of nations. With a patience approaching weakness, Austria has up to the present borne the continuous provocations and the political machinations aimed at the disruption of her own national stability by a people which proceeded from regicide at home to the murder of princes in a neighboring land. It was only after the last despicable crime that she took to extreme measures, in order to burn out with a glowing iron a cancer that has constantly threatened to poison the body of Europe. One would think that all Europe would be grateful to her. All Europe would have drawn a breath of relief if this mischief-maker could have been properly chastised, and peace and order thereby have been restored to the Balkans; but Russia placed herself at the side of this criminal nation. It was only then that the Austro-Serbian affair became the thunder-cloud which may at any moment break over Europe.

Austria has declared to the European cabinets that she intends neither to make any territorial acquisitions at Serbia's expense nor to infringe upon her status as a nation; that she only wants to force her unruly neighbor to accept the conditions that she considers necessary if they are to continue to exist side by side, and which Serbia, as experience has proved, would never live up to, despite solemn assurances, unless compelled by force. The Austro-Serbian affair is a purely private quarrel in which, as has been said, nobody in Europe would have a profound interest and which would in no way threaten the peace of Europe but, on the contrary, would establish it more firmly, if Russia had not injected herself into it. This was what first gave the matter its menacing aspect.

Austria has only mobilized a portion of her armed forces, eight army corps, against Serbia—just enough with which to be able to put through her punitive expedition. As against this, Russia has made all preparations to enable her to mobilize the army corps of the military districts of Kiev, Odessa and Moscow, twelve army corps in all, within the briefest period, and is providing for similar preparatory measures in the north also, along the German border and the Baltic Sea. She announces that she intends to mobilize when Austria advances into Serbia, as she cannot permit the destruction of Serbia by Austria, though Austria has explained that she intends nothing of the sort.

What must and will the further consequences be? If Austria advances into Serbia she will have to face not only the Serbian army but also the vastly superior strength of Russia; thus she can not enter upon a war with Serbia without securing herself against an attack by Russia. That means that she will be forced to mobilize the other half of her Army, for she can not possibly surrender at discretion to a Russia all prepared for war. At the moment, however, in which Austria mobilizes her whole Army, the collision between herself and Russia will become inevitable. But that, for Germany, is the *casus foederis*. If Germany is not to be false to her word and permit her ally to suffer annihilation at the

---

Source: Helmuth Von Moltke to Bethman Hollweg, July 29, 1914, Document 349 in *Outbreak of the World War: German Documents Collected by Karl Kautsky,* edited by Max Montgelas and Walther Schücking (New York: Oxford University Press, 1924), 306–307.

hands of Russian superiority, she, too, must mobilize. And that would bring about the mobilization of the rest of Russia's military districts as a result. But then Russia will be able to say: I am being attacked by Germany. She will then assure herself of the support of France, which, according to the compact of alliance, is obliged to take part in the war, should her ally, Russia, be attacked. Thus the Franco-Russian alliance, so often held up to praise as a purely defensive compact, created only in order to meet the aggressive plans of Germany, will become active, and the mutual butchery of the civilized nations of Europe will begin.

>> Mastering the Material

1. According to Joll, how did imperialism and colonialism contribute to the outbreak of the First World War?

2. Why, according to the sources, did Britain choose to ally itself with Russia and France? What was the significance of the Anglo-Russian Convention of 1907 to this process?

3. In what way does von Moltke's letter and the theory put forward by van Evera support the notion that once mobilization was underway war was inevitable? Do you agree with this conclusion?

4. Are you convinced by Schmitt's arguments that the key underlying cause of the First World War was nationalist aspirations and tensions? Why or why not?

>> Making Connections

1. Historians like John H. Morrow have suggested that the First World War was partly caused by a sense of national superiority that had been growing for centuries within each of the large European states. Proponents of this view argue that at first this sentiment was expressed as racism toward colonized people, but that in the twentieth century it came to be aimed against rival European powers. Other theorists reject this premise as far-fetched. Consider the sixteenth-century sources on cultural superiority in Chapter 3 and the sense of moral superiority evident in the nineteenth-century sources in Chapter 14. To what degree, do you think, could the ideas reflected in these sources be connected to the outbreak of the First World War?

Chapter 18

The Joyful Leap to War

As we saw in the last chapter, scholars have sought the causes of the First World War in a number of long-term, underlying trends in European and world history. Yet the fact remains that the war crisis ultimately materialized from the actions of a single individual, the Bosnian Serb Gavrilo Princip, who on 28 June 1914 shot Archduke Franz Ferdinand, the nephew of Emperor Franz Joseph I of Austria-Hungary. It is generally accepted that Princip was acting alone. Admittedly the Serbian secret service had provided Princip with his weapon, but there is no evidence that they thought he would use it to assassinate the archduke. Nevertheless, the Austro-Hungarian Dual Monarchy declared war on Serbia on 28 July 1914. Russia mobilized its troops the next day, and on 1 August 1914 Germany declared war on Russia—the first Great Powers to open hostilities with another. Two days later, as set down in the Schlieffen plan, Germany invaded Belgium, bringing France and Britain into the war.

Why did events spiral out of control so quickly? Was the war in fact an avoidable misadventure, rather than the inevitable result of great trends it has been made out to be? Some researchers have sought the war's origins not in the preceding decades but in the fateful days of July 1914. The events of this month—between the murder of Franz Ferdinand and the German declaration of war—have been studied through a microscope by a chain of scholars like Immanuel Geiss, Samuel R. Williamson Jr., and Russel van Wyk. Within this group of historians, some researchers have come to view the war as an avoidable tragedy whose cause was the miscalculation and indeed negligence of key administrators, politicians, and diplomats. One such scholar is the British historian Clive Ponting, who insists that the immediate crisis in the Balkans be seen as more than just the spark that lit the war, but as its principal cause.

Ponting also rejects a second conventional interpretation of the war: that Germany was largely to blame. Mainstream theories of German guilt date back to the end of the war. As part of the 1919–1920 peace conference process, the victorious powers—especially France and Britain—commissioned a report on responsibility for the war. The conclusions of this "Report Presented to the Preliminary Peace Conference," excerpted in Reading 82, neatly placed total responsibility for the war on Germany and its allies. Although this position came to be challenged in the 1950s, it reemerged a decade later through the influential work of the great German war historian Fritz Fischer. Fischer's 1961 text, translated into English as *Germany's Aims in the First World War,* allocated the majority of guilt for the war to the aggressive German policy of *Weltpolitik,* or global politics. According to Fischer, the German decision makers almost single-handedly incited the war through their forceful pursuit of a belligerent policy. Not surprisingly, critics of Fischer's work emerged rapidly. The arguments of both sides are evenhandedly evaluated in James Joll's 1966 article "The 1914 Debate Continues: Fritz Fischer and His Critics." As Joll points out, many reputable scholars have rejected the notion of German war guilt. Other scholars have gone further, blaming Russia and France for the war. Yet the notion of German culpability endures, in part due to the legacy of the *Second* World War.

The blame game is entirely European in focus, but the First World War was unprecedented in its global impact. Not only were ostensibly neutral industrialized states rapidly sucked in to the maelstrom, but so too were states on the fringes of the zone of conflict. The Ottomans were first, anxious to defend their interests in the Balkans against Russia. Britain had already begun to depart from its "splendid isolation," wooed by Russia and aggravated by German construction of a grand fleet. It was finally provoked by the German invasion of Belgium to declare war. The entry of Britain committed to war not only the British Isles themselves but moreover its far-flung empire in Oceania, the Caribbean, Canada, Africa, and southern Asia. These colonies contributed more than two million combatants, the largest contingents coming from India, Canada, Australia, New Zealand, and South Africa. Laborers from across the empire were also put to work. The French similarly mobilized their entire empire. Yet many colonized peoples felt little motivation to fight for their overlords. Thus the imperial powers turned to involuntary conscription of their colonial subjects, as Joe Lunn demonstrates in his work on Senegalese soldiers conscripted to the French army.

In the United States, as well, most people were initially against entering the war. As late as April 1917, President Woodrow Wilson faced significant opposition among the general population and in the Senate when he proposed declaring war on Germany. His case was aided, however, by German policies such as unrestricted submarine warfare and by the famous Zimmerman telegram urging the Mexican government to enter the conflict on the side of the Central Powers. Once the United States entered the war, it exerted a gravitational pull upon its neighbors, and a number of Latin American states subsequently also committed to the cause of the Entente.

The Third Balkan War

Clive Ponting is one of the leading proponents of the "Third Balkan War" theory of the origins of the 1914–1918 world war. Thus he looks for the causes of the war in the area in which it began, the Balkan states. Under Serbia's leadership, a coalition of Balkan states had defeated the Ottoman Turks in 1912 in what was known as the First Balkan War. However, the coalition broke up and in June 1913 Bulgaria attacked Serbia. Ponting suggests that the events of July 1914 were merely a sequel to these two confrontations and that they escalated out of control because of the immediate decisions of a few leaders in Russia, Serbia, and Austria-Hungary. The conflict widened in the thirteen days following Austria-Hungary's ultimatum to Serbia because diplomacy could not catch up with events, and thus a general war broke out despite the fact that no European government really wanted one.

>> 81. Thirteen Days: The Road to the First World War

CLIVE PONTING [2002]

Over the last eighty years scholars have looked for deep, fundamental causes in the European power structure that made the outbreak of war almost inevitable. [...] The common picture is of a Europe reaching boiling point as heat was applied by a number of factors resulting in an inevitable explosion in the summer of 1914. The assassination of Franz Ferdinand was seen as no more than the action that lit the fuse that set off the conflagration.

This book rejects such explanations. It does not deny that the tensions were there, but it does deny that they were inevitably going to cause a European war. Europe had been divided into two alliance structures since the mid-1890s but this had not led to war. Economic and imperial rivalries around the globe were settled by negotiation and Europe was not engaged in a major arms race. On average, defence spending was at the level found in peacetime Europe throughout the twentieth century. Europe did face a large number of diplomatic disputes in the period between 1905 and 1913—Morocco in 1905–6, Bosnia–Herzegovina in 1908–9, Agadir in 1911 and the vast range of problems stemming from the Balkan Wars of 1912–13—but the crucial point is that they were all settled through diplomacy. The key question that has to be answered is why the crisis produced by the assassinations at Sarajevo was not resolved by diplomatic means. [...]

This book argues that the First World War only occurred because of the situation in the Balkans. It was the outcome of the two Balkan wars between 1912 and 1913, the changes they precipitated in the strategic balance in the region, together with the struggle for influence between Austria–Hungary and Russia, that led to war. In this respect what began as the 'Third Balkan War'

rapidly escalated into a European conflict. The primary responsibility for war therefore lies with three states. First, Serbia, where there was an aggressive, ideologically motivated nationalism, entrenched under the extremists who brought the Karadjordjevic dynasty to the throne in the bloody 1903 coup. The extreme nationalists were never reconciled to the Austro-Hungarian annexation of Bosnia–Herzogovina in 1908 which they saw as part of historic Serbia, even though the majority of the population of the provinces were not Serbs. The assassinations at Sarajevo were directed, funded and organised by factions within the Serbian administration. They were carried out by extreme Serb nationalist terrorists. The second state which must bear primary responsibility for the war is Austria–Hungary. It viewed the expansion of Serbia in 1912–13 as a fundamental threat. It was not simply the Serbian desire to gain Bosnia–Herzegovina that made it an enemy of Austria–Hungary. The mere existence of a Serb national state acted as a potential disintegrating force within the multinational Habsburg empire and tended to encourage other minority populations, not just Serbs, to look outside the empire for support in establishing their own national states. It was the determination of the government in Vienna to use the assassinations as an excuse to permanently cripple Serbia through military conquest and dismemberment, and throughout the July crisis to reject any diplomatic settlement, that was a fundamental cause of the outbreak of the war. The third state was Russia. It had been expanding westwards for more than two hundred years and saw the Balkans as an important area which should form part of its sphere of influence, even though the attempt to bring this about inevitably brought it into conflict with Austria–Hungary. Russia supported Serbia simply because it was an enemy of Austria–Hungary, although some elements in the Russian government also saw such actions as support for another

Source: Clive Ponting, *Thirteen Days: The Road to the First World War* (London: Chatto & Windus, 2002), ix-xii.

Slav and Orthodox state. It was the Russian decision not to allow Austria–Hungary to impose a diplomatic humiliation on Serbia, let alone defeat it in a local war, that ensured the outbreak of a European war. [...]

The thirteen-day crisis led to the outbreak of the First World War, something that no power in Europe wanted. That war ended the old European order for ever. The instability the war produced led to the establishment of Communism in Russia and the rise of Fascism and Nazism. After only a short pause, the second round of what had become a European civil war began in 1939. That in its turn led to the collapse of the European empires across the globe and the eclipse of Europe by the United States and, to some extent, the Soviet Union. It was the assassinations at Sarajevo and the thirteen-day diplomatic crisis in 1914 that were to shape much of European history for the rest of the twentieth century.

Placing the Blame on Germany

Ponting's argument represents a relatively evenhanded approach, apportioning the blame to both the Central Powers and the Entente. Not all commentators or scholars have reached such unbiased conclusions, however. In the immediate aftermath of the war, a committee appointed by the victorious powers—The United States, France, Great Britain, Italy, Japan, Belgium, Greece, Poland, Romania, and Serbia—was commissioned to write a report on the causes of the war. No representatives from the defeated states participated, and thus it is no surprise that the committee came to place the entirety of the blame on Germany and Austria-Hungary (here simply called Austria) and their allies. Although many of the facts presented in this report are correct, the committee neither took into consideration any long-term causes of the war nor attempted a balanced approach. As a result, the reader is left feeling that the war was hatched by a conspiracy of Austrian and Germany leaders who saw in Princip's assassination of the archduke a pretext to carry out their aggressive plans against their neighbors.

>> 82. Report Presented to the Preliminary Peace Conference

CARNEGIE ENDOWMENT FOR INTERNATIONAL PEACE [1924]

On the question of the responsibility of the authors of the war, the Commission, after having examined a number of official documents relating to the origin of the World War, and to the violations of neutrality and of frontiers which accompanied its inception, has determined that the responsibility for it lies wholly upon the Powers which declared war in pursuance of a policy of aggression, the concealment of which gives to the origin of this war the character of a dark conspiracy against the peace of Europe.

This responsibility rests first on Germany and Austria, secondly on Turkey and Bulgaria. The responsibility is made all the graver by reason of the violation by Germany and Austria of the neutrality of Belgium and Luxemburg, which they themselves had guaranteed. It is increased, with regard to both France and Serbia, by the violation of their frontiers before the declaration of war.

Source: Carnegie Endowment for International Peace, "Report Presented to the Preliminary Peace Conference," *German White Book Concerning the Responsibility of the Authors of the War* (New York: Oxford University Press, 1924), 15–18.

Many months before the crisis of 1914 the German Emperor had ceased to pose as the champion pf peace. Naturally believing in the overwhelming superiority of his Army, he openly showed his enmity towards France. General von Moltke said to the King of the Belgians: "This time the matter must be settled." In vain the King protested. The Emperor and his Chief of Staff remained no less fixed in their attitude.

On the 28th of June, 1914, occurred the assassination at Sarajevo of the heir-apparent of Austria. "It is the act of a little group of madmen," said Francis Joseph. The act, committed as it was by a subject of Austria–Hungary on Austro-Hungarian territory, could in no wise compromise Serbia, which very correctly expressed its condolences and stopped public rejoicings in Belgrade. If the Government of Vienna thought that there was any Serbian complicity, Serbia was ready to seek out the guilty parties. But this attitude failed to satisfy Austria and still less Germany, who, after their first astonishment had passed, saw in this royal and national misfortune a pretext to initiate war.

At Potsdam a "decisive consultation" took place on the 5th of July, 1914. Vienna and Berlin decided upon this plan: "Vienna will send to Belgrade a very emphatic ultimatum with a very short limit of time."

The Bavarian Minister, von Lerchenfeld, said in a confidential dispatch dated the 18th of July, 1914, the facts stated in which have never been officially denied: "It is clear that Serbia can not accept the demands, which are inconsistent with the dignity of an independent state." Count Lerchenfeld reveals in this report that, at the time it was made, the ultimatum to Serbia had been jointly decided upon by the Governments of Berlin and Vienna; that they were waiting to send it until President Poincaré and Mr. Viviani should have left for St. Petersburg; and that no illusions were cherished, either at Berlin or Vienna, as to the consequences which this threatening measure would involve. It was perfectly well known that war would be the result.

The Bavarian Minister explains, moreover, that the only fear of the Berlin Government was that Austria-Hungary might hesitate and draw back at the last minute, and that on the other hand Serbia, on the advice of France and Great Britain, might yield to the pressure put upon her. Now, "the Berlin Government considers that war is necessary." Therefore, it gave full powers to Count Berchtold, who instructed the Ballplatz on the 18th of July, 1914, to negotiate with Bulgaria to induce her to enter into an alliance and to participate in the war. [...]

Contrary to the expectation of Austria-Hungary and Germany, Serbia yielded. She agreed to all the requirements of the ultimatum, subject to the single reservation that, in the judicial inquiry which she would commence for the purpose of seeking out the guilty parties, the participation of Austrian officials would be kept within the limits assigned by international law. "If the Austro-Hungarian Government is not satisfied with this," Serbia declared she was ready "to submit to the decision of the Hague Tribunal.

"A quarter of an hour before the expiration of the time limit," at 5:45 on the 25th, Mr. Pashitch, the Serbian Minister for Foreign Affairs, delivered this reply to Baron Giesl, the Austro-Hungarian Minister.

On Mr. Pashitch's return to his own office he found awaiting him a letter from Baron Giesl saying that he was not satisfied with the reply. At 6:30 the latter had left Belgrade, and even before he had arrived at Vienna, the Austro-Hungarian Government had handed his passports to Mr. Yovanovitch, the Serbian Minister, and had prepared thirty-three mobilization proclamations, which were published on the following morning in the Budepesti Kozlöni, the official gazette of the Hungarian Government. [...]

As early as the 21st of July German mobilization had commenced by the recall of a certain number of classes of the reserve, then of German officers in Switzerland, and finally of the Metz garrison on the 25th of July. On the 26th of July the German Fleet was called back from Norway.

The Entente did not relax its conciliatory efforts, but the German Government systematically brought all its attempts to nought. When Austria consented for the first time on the 31st of July to discuss the contents of the Serbian note with the Russian Government and the Austro-Hungarian Ambassador received orders to "converse" with the Russian Minister of Foreign Affairs, Germany made any negotiation impossible by sending her ultimatum to Russia. Prince Lichnowsky wrote that "a hint from Berlin would have been enough to decide Count Berchtold to content himself with a diplomatic success and to declare that he was satisfied with the Serbian reply, but this hint was not given. *On the contrary they went forward towards war.*"

On the 1st August the German Emperor addressed a telegram to the King of England containing the following sentence: "The troops on my frontier are, at this moment, being kept back by telegraphic and telephonic orders from crossing the French frontier." Now, war was not declared till two days after that date, and as the German mobilization orders were issued on that same day, the 1st of August, it follows that, as a matter of fact, the German Army had been mobilized and concentrated in pursuance of previous orders.

Debating German Aggression

Fritz Fischer's controversial book was entitled, in German, Griff nach der Weltmacht, *or* Grasping at World Power. *When translated into English it was given the far less emotional title* Germany's Aims in the First World War. *The text was published in 1961, at much the same time as A. J. P. Taylor's* Origins of the Second World War, *which we will discuss in Chapter 19. Both books suggested that modern Germany had an underlying aggressive tendency that connected the First and Second World Wars. Fischer's work was also important because it suggested that Germany's leaders alone could be blamed for transforming the Balkan conflict into a general European war. This argument ran directly counter to the mainstream of scholarship in this period, which had begun to focus on underlying trends shared by the Great Powers. Fischer, in fact, was so highly critical of the German military and government that German scholars and politicians almost universally rejected his thesis. Most vehement response was to Fischer's description of the German Chancellor, Theobald von Bethman Hollweg, as a belligerent architect of war whose expansionist goals were similar to those of Adolf Hitler in the next war. Fischer's account of the actions of von Bethman Hollweg and his colleagues in July and August 1914 was assailed by German historians, of whom the most important was arguably Gerhart Ritter. James Joll was one of the few contemporary historians to impartially assess both Fischer's thesis and Ritter's criticism.*

>> 83. The 1914 Debate Continues. Fritz Fischer and His Critics

JAMES JOLL [1996]

Fischer's main thesis—perhaps over-emphasized by the title "Grasping at Word Power"—is that Germany was ready to resort to war in order to establish herself as a "*Weltmacht,*" a Great Power,

that is, which could take its place along with the other world powers, who had established their position in the world before Germany had achieved national unity. This idea of achieving true great power status in a world balance of power—a concept which Professor Ludwig Dehio, although he has criticized some of Fischer's conclusions, had previously examined and developed in some interesting essays—was

Source: James Joll, "The 1914 Debate Continues. Fritz Fischer and His Critics," *Past and Present* 34 (1996): 102–109.

easily turned into a plan for organizing the world, or part of it, in such a way that it should be dominated by Germany and serve German economic, cultural, or strategic interests. Professor Fischer demonstrates, by a detailed examination of the documents, first that the German government, if they did not actually want war in 1914, were at any rate prepared to face the risk of it in pursuit of their general aims, and that they systematically encouraged their Austrian allies to provoke war with Serbia even when they saw that it could not be localized; and, secondly, that, as soon as the war had started, they developed plans, which they had already previously discussed, for large-scale territorial annexations and for the establishment of a German-controlled new order in Europe. [...]

The most striking section of Fischer's book—and it has led many of his critics to overlook the interesting elaboration of his themes in later chapters—is the early part in which he deals with the crisis of 1914 and with the formulation of German aims in the first weeks of the war, when it still looked as if a speedy victory over the French, as foreseen by the German military planners, might be possible. In the discussion of this section of the book, some of Professor Fischer's original intentions have perhaps been forgotten and misunderstood. He is anxious to show that Germany's plans for war and her aims once the war had begun were the product of the social and economic situation in Germany, so that the presuppositions of Germany's leaders and the pressures to which they were subjected were such that, in a sense, the personalities and decisions of individuals were of little importance and their choices in fact strictly limited by the political, social, economic, and ideological climate within which they were operating. The critics of Fischer's views, however, have tended to concentrate on the personalities of the men whose actions were crucial to German policy in the months of July and August 1914—the Kaiser, Bethmann-Hollweg (the Imperial Chancellor), Jagow (the State Secretary of the Foreign Ministry), and Helmuth von Moltke (the Chief of the General Staff). In particular, it is the new

view of Bethmann-Hollweg's character and purposes as it emerges from the documents Professor Fischer has discovered that has upset people most. Indeed, it has, in spite of Professor Fischer's expressed intentions, turned the discussion largely into one about personalities. Once this is so, then the interpretation of documents necessarily depends on the interpretation of character; for the way in which one reads the documents is determined by one's general view of the nature and motives of the writer of the document, and divergent views of a man's character will result in differing interpretations of what he writes.

In professor Fischer's view, Bethmann's pre-war policy had been based on the assumption that British neutrality in the war—a war which, on this view, he regarded as inevitable—could best be secured by making sure that the outbreak of war appeared to have been provoked deliberately by Russia or by France. Thus, when, at the end of 1912, the German Government was collaborating with the British to keep the Balkan War localized but when, at the same time, they were preparing for new military and naval increases, Bethmann wrote that a war with Russia in the Balkans would certainly involve France, but that it was "from many indications at least doubtful whether England would actively intervene if Russia and France appear directly as provoking the war". For Professor Fischer this is evidence of the continuity of Bethmann's policies, and he suggests that the Chancellor in 1912, as in 1914, was less concerned with pursuing peace than with dividing Britain from France and Russia and with keeping Britain neutral by making sure that France and Russia appeared to be in the wrong. This is one of several points at which Professor Gerhard Ritter, the most formidable of Fischer's critics, to whom we shall return later, challenges Fisher's interpretation and accuses him of misreading the documents. He says that Bethmann in this particular report was making a purely tactical point intended to calm down the Kaiser, who was always ready to fly into a rage with the British, and to try and make him resist the proposed naval increases, which to the British appeared as German provocation. If one reads the report in question dispassionately, it can, it seems to me, be taken *either* way, and one's interpretation is not conditioned by the document itself, or even entirely by the circumstances in which it was drafted, but rather by one's view of Bethmann's character and policies as a whole. A historian's view of a man's aims and motives is formed to a large extent by the documents, but it necessarily also influences the way he reads them; and it is unrealistic to expect Professor Fischer, who, on his reading of the evidence, has formed one opinion of Bethmann's political personality, to agree with Professor Ritter, who, from the same evidence, has come to a radically different conclusion. Each, when interpreting a particular document, is looking for support for a view already formed through reading many other pieces of evidence.

Let us look, however, at Fischer's general view of Bethmann and his policy. For Fischer, Bethmann is a typical product of the forces which dominated German life at the beginning of the century, a period in which Fischer (following Ludwig Dehio) sees the Germans convinced of their own strength—politically, militarily, and industrially—and wanting desperately to be a world power, to have a vaguely defined and obscurely conceived World Mission which would, in the world balance of power, make up for the disadvantage under which Germany suffered because of coming too late as a united nation on to the world scene. Bethmann was, Fischer shows convincingly, already before the war in touch with people who were specifically thinking in terms of a German-dominated *Mitteleuropa,* and to a large extent shared their thinking. And, although he hoped for the possibility of achieving *Weltmacht ohne Krieg,* he was ready to accept the idea of war and to base his policy on the necessity of ensuring, if it came, that it was under conditions as favorable to Germany as possible. According to Fischer, Bethmann overestimated Germany's strength, and above all maintained up to the final crisis an unfounded belief in the probability of Britain's

neutrality. It is in the light of these general assumptions about Bethmann that Fischer interprets his conduct of affairs in the crisis of July 1914 and in the early weeks of the war.

It is here that the importance of Bethmann's memorandum of 9 September 1914, lies, and it certainly forces us to reconsider the conventional picture of Bethmann as the liberal statesman (who reminded Lord Haldane of Abraham Lincoln), striving in vain to maintain peace against the machinations of the militarists. The memorandum was sent by Bethmann from the G.H.Q. in Coblenz to his deputy, Clemens Delbrück, the State Secretary of the Interior, in Berlin, just at the moment when the French counter-attack on the Marne was going to transform the course of the war, but before the outcome of the battle was known, so that the Germans still seemed to be faced with the problems that would confront them on achieving victory in the West. Bethmann laid down that the aim of the forthcoming peace settlement must be

> *the security of the German Empire in the West and in the East for the foreseeable future. To this end, France must be so weakened that she cannot rise again as a great power, Russia must be pushed as far as possible from the German frontier, and her rule over non-Russian subject peoples must be broken.*

Professor Fischer makes two important points about this document. First, he shows in the subsequent chapters of his book that it in fact contains the minimum aims which some German leaders consistently attempted to pursue throughout the war: the reduction of France to a second class power by territorial annexations, the establishment of some form of long-term control over Belgium, the spread of German power eastwards, either by direct annexation or by the creation of a German satellite state in Poland, and the weakening of Russia by the encouragement of subversive movements of all kinds, while at the same time Germany would lay the basis of a new colonial empire by the acquisition of large areas of Central Africa. Secondly, Professor Fischer shows that this programme has strong similarities both with the ideas of a number of leading German industrialists for establishing a German-dominated, economically unified *Mitteleuropa,* and even with the more outspokenly annexationist demands of the Pan-German League, which had been drafted shortly before. [...]

Since it is Fischer's account of the period July-September 1914 on which his critics have largely concentrated, it is worth looking at what they say on this point. [...]

The most respected and the most formidable of the older generation of German historians, professor Gerhard Ritter, has not only suggested that Fischer misinterprets documents but has also implied that he has a political purpose in doing this. [...]

It is worth comparing the general picture which emerges from Ritter's book with that which is to be found in Fischer's *Griff nach der Weltmacht,* as this illustrates the difference of interpretation which underlies the current controversy. Owing to the publicity given to the argument—the fact that it was prominently featured in the popular weekly *Der Spiegel,* for example—and the personal bitterness which some of Fischer's critics injected into it, it is hard not to feel obliged to take sides with one or the other party. But perhaps this would be a mistake, and it may be that each book illuminates one aspect of German behavior in 1914, and that it is because German society and

German ideology in the twentieth-century were so ambivalent that they are hard to understand and lend themselves to different interpretations, not one of which is wholly adequate to explain the facts. For Professor Ritter, the German leaders, and especially Bethmann and Moltke, are the helpless and often anguished victims of circumstances, carried into war against their will by the inexorable unfolding of military plans which they did not devise and whose political consequences had never been properly foreseen. [...]

There is no doubt that Bethmann was wracked by doubts, hesitations, and fears. There is equally no doubt that Helmuth von Moltke, the *Feldherr wider Willen,* was so haunted by his own inadequacy and so broken by his physical and neurotic weaknesses that he virtually collapsed as soon as war started. Even the Kaiser, although I think Fischer is right in taking his violent racist outbursts seriously, had his moments of lucidity, responsibility, and anxiety. It is quite true, as Professor Ritter emphasizes both in *Staatskunst und Kriegshandwerk* and in his study of the Schlieffen Plan, that the military plans had irrevocable political consequences with which their authors had not been very much concerned and which their successors, and especially those responsible for foreign relations in 1914—principally Bethmann and Jagow—had to face. And yet, in the light of the new evidence produced by Fischer, it is hard to accept the picture of Germany's leaders as helpless victims of a fate they were trying to avoid.

The Conscription of Colonial Soldiers

The First World War started in Europe, but it quickly spread to encompass much of the world through the participation of overseas colonies. Some warfare did take place in colonies in Africa, the Pacific, and the Arabian Peninsula, but more significantly the empires drew on colonial manpower to replace the vast numbers of their own soldiers rapidly killed by the new industrialized warfare of machine guns and poison gas. Britain recruited more than 2 million soldiers from its vast empire, including many settlers of British extraction from Canada, South Africa, New Zealand, and Australia. The largest contingent, however, was the almost 700,000 Indian combatants and probably 400,000 laborers who were drafted along with smaller contingents from Africa, Burma, and other colonies. Germany, cut off from its empire by the British navy, nevertheless relied on colonial troops to defend each colony. Russia's army was filled out by troops from Siberia, Kazakhstan, and other parts of its expanding Asian Empire, and the Ottoman and Austro-Hungarian armies comprised literally dozens of nationalities. France also relied deeply on the indigenous peoples of its overseas colonies for manpower. Northern Africans, southeast Asians, and western Africans formed independent units that fought in France as well as in Africa. One of the largest national groups was the 135,000 Senegalese recruits. In this excerpt from his important work on Senegalese soldiers in the First World War, Africanist Joe Lunn analyzes the methods of recruitment, and the resistance of, Senegalese men.

>> 84. Memoirs of the Maelstrom: A Senegalese Oral History of the First World War

JOE LUNN [1999]

Senegalese Recruitment Methods

The methods used by the French to impose the new "tax in blood," as well as the range of African responses to it, vividly illuminate the impact of the wartime recruitment drives on the Senegalese. Aside from a mere handful of often reluctant "volunteers," the vast majority of Africans recruited between 1914 and 1917 had "no choice" in the matter of their induction. Young men were raised by the colonial authorities by a variety of means that reflected the largely improvised nature of the recruitment system. On occasion in areas near army garrisons, French officers, accompanied by military escorts, enlisted Africans directly. Such instances were, however, extremely rare. Much more commonly, the colonial administration relied, as it did when exacting other demands, on an array of African intermediaries to impose its will. As a result, most Senegalese were recruited in one of three other ways: though their village chief's compliance with the dictates of their *chef de canton*; through the admonitions of their marabouts;

or by outright capture, through armed raids by either the retainers of the cantonal chiefs or by other African recruiting "agents" working directly for the French.

In the villages, the local chiefs filled the quotas expected of them by a variety of means. "Lotteries" were sometimes held in the early days of recruitment, with the unlucky winners being reluctantly sacrificed to satisfy the obligations of the collective unit. Elsewhere, and usually when only a few recruits were as yet demanded from a village, domestic slaves, the "very poor," or alternatively one of the chief's sons might be sent. But as the wartime calls for men grew, other expedients were devised. Frequently, the ultimate burden of decision was shifted from the village chiefs to the heads of compounds, who were each periodically required to designate "one son per family" to present before the Recruiting Commissions. Finally, but only restrictedly and usually belatedly, "lists" of all those of "the age to enter the army" in the village were compiled for use by the *chefs de canton* to determine who was eligible to present to the French.

Among the Mourides, [religious order] whose disciples were often beyond the pale of chiefly authority and who, at least initially, were deemed of doubtful military utility by the French because of their sullen spiritual detachment, a similar but

---

Source: Joe Lunn, *Memoirs of the Maelstrom: A Senegalese Oral History of the First World War* (Portsmouth: Heinemann, 1999), 39–41, 43.

nevertheless distinctive system was employed. Complying with the instructions of Amadu Bamba [founder and heart of the order] (who, like the Tidjaniya leader Malik Sy, eventually bowed to French pressure in 1915 and agreed to sanction recruitment), marabouts fulfilled the function of the *chefs de canton*. These men, including Ibra Fall, a former *ceddo* [warrior] convert and one of Bamba's most prominent followers, in turn provided recruits in the designated numbers from among their *Talibe* [followers].

Finally, in areas where recruitment proved exceptionally difficult, especially on the fringes of colonial authority [...] "surprise" raids equated with "man hunts" were conducted by auxiliaries of the French in an effort to capture young men. Sometimes composed of the retainers of the *chefs de canton* (*dag* in Wolof) or, alternatively, of other locally recruited "agents" [...], these men, or more often those they served in the former case, normally received a "gift" of up to 25 francs for each "recruit" they caught. The unfortunates they seized were frequently bound, linked with "ropes around their necks," and marched in coffles to points of assembly for presentation to the French Recruiting Commissions. [...]

Senegalese reactions to the exactions imposed on them in the face of such dire premonitions varied. A handful, motivated either by the French bounties or other personal considerations, willingly enlisted. Others, and especially those who were "ordered" by their Mouride marabouts to enter the army, accepted their fate without opposition, which was interpreted as the "will of Allah." After receiving the benediction of Amadu Bamba—with his compelling admonition to: "Go...and come back!"—they complied with differing degrees of enthusiasm to the temporal demands made on them by their marabouts and the French. The overwhelming majority of those who acceded to the wishes of the colonial authorities, however, did so only with greatest reluctance and the most profound misgivings. Knowing themselves to be powerless to "resist the *Tubabs*" and not "dar[ing] to refuse" their commands, most of the Senegalese

rural collectives responded to the harsh realities they confronted by grudgingly sacrificing those deemed most expendable. [...]

Nevertheless, in the face of such daunting sacrifices, not all Senegalese complied with the French requisitions of young men. Their resistance to the recruitment policy assumed two forms: avoidance of the French demands or, when this proved impossible, defiance of them. Avoidance of the draft might be accomplished by one of several means. For the wealthy or well connected, it was sometimes possible to obtain exemption from the army through the patronage of a French employer, by bribing a *chef de canton,* securing a replacement, or through the lucky expedient of having an obliging kinsman act as interpreter when the recruits were being selected. A second possibility was to fail the French medical examination and thus be designated unfit. The use of herbal concoctions designed to create the illusions of illness—*paftan* leaves crushed into powder were used to discolor eyes, while *palme de cajou* combined with grain created swollen sores when applied to the face and feet—was widespread throughout Senegal, and resort to such measures sometimes fooled the French doctors.

By far, however, the most common way of attempting to avoid enlistment was through flight. Indeed, it is probably true for every soldier recruited in rural Senegal between 1914 and 1917, another potential inductee fled the colony to seek refuge in foreign territories. Resource to this option appears to have been determined to a major extent by the relative proximity of an individual to sanctuary. In the more densely populated areas of central Senegal, where recruitment levies were heaviest, this course of action was more difficult to accomplish. There were few nearby havens and the countryside was continually combed by chiefly retainers searching for fugitives. Moreover, flight farther afield often entailed separation from kinsmen as well as enhanced risk of capture. In the more sparsely inhabited regions of the Fleuve and eastern Senegal, flight from the village to the comparative safety of the countryside was more common.

There, potential recruits temporarily sought refuge in the "bush" until the Recruitment Commissions had exacted their tolls or, alternatively, crossed over into Mauritania, where the French exercised but scant control. Finally, in those areas such as Saloum, Niani-Ouli, and the Casamance, which bordered on either British Gambia or Portuguese Guinea where recruits were not being levied, avoidance assumed the dimensions of a major exodus.

Woodrow Wilson Justifies the U.S. Entry into the War

Unlike Africa and the Middle East, the Americas had no German or Ottoman colonies, and, aside from Canada, only a few Caribbean islands and slivers of South America remained in the possession of Britain and France. The states of North and South America therefore remained neutral well into the war. However, in many countries descendents of German, French, and British settlers agitated for their governments to enter the war during the period 1914–1917. The greatest prize, of course, was the United States. The U.S. president, Woodrow Wilson, had been elected on a platform of neutrality. In April 1917, however, he reversed his stance and called for the United States to enter the war on the side of the Entente powers of Britain, France, and Russia. What had changed? There are several theories. In the piece below, Wilson himself cited Germany's declaration of unrestricted submarine warfare against ships from the (largely neutral) countries of the Americas traveling to Europe. Anger at German submarine attacks had grown especially out of the May 1915 sinking of the American ocean liner Lusitania, and Wilson cited this incident in his justifications for war. In another part of the speech Wilson also implied that the United States had a duty to rescue the democracies of Europe—Britain and France—against the monarchies of Germany and Austria-Hungary. Wilson's critics, including Senator George W. Norris, countered these arguments. Norris pointed out that Britain was stopping American shipments to Germany and, if perhaps not as destructive to human life as unrestricted submarine warfare, this was equally unlawful. Other critics noted that Britain and France were allied with one of the most oppressive European regimes: Russia. Wilson carried the day and the United States entered the war, but opponents continued to allege that the United States entered the war either at the behest of bankers who had loaned money to the Entente powers or because of agitation by Anglo-Americans and Franco-Americans.

>> 85. Address to Congress

WOODROW WILSON [1917]

On the third of February last I officially laid before you the extraordinary announcement of the Imperial German Government that on and after the first day of February it was its purpose to put aside all restraints of law or of humanity and use its submarines to sink every vessel that sought to approach either the ports of the Great Britain and Ireland or the western coasts of Europe or any of the ports controlled by the enemies of Germany within the Mediterranean. That had seemed to be the object of the German submarine warfare

---

Source: Woodrow Wilson, "Address to Congress," April 2, 1917, in *Source Records of the Great War*, vol. V, V. edited by Charles F. Horne (Indianapolis: The American Legion, 1931), 108–111.

earlier in the war, but since April of last year the Imperial Government had somewhat restrained the commanders of its undersea craft in conformity with its promise then given to us that passenger boats should not be sunk and that due warning would be given to all other vessels which its submarines might seek to destroy, when no resistance was offered or escape attempted, and care taken that their crews were given at least a fair chance to save their lives in their open boats. The precautions taken were meager and haphazard enough, as was proved in distressing instance after instance in the progress of the cruel and unmanly business, but a certain degree or restraint was observed. The new policy has swept every restriction aside. Vessels of every kind, whatever their flag, their character, their cargo, their destination, their errand, have been ruthlessly sent to the bottom without warning and without thought of help or mercy for those on board, the vessels of friendly neutrals along with those of belligerents. Even hospital ships and ships carrying relief to the sorely bereaved and stricken people of Belgium, though the latter were provided with safe conduct through the proscribed areas by the German Government itself and were distinguished by unmistakable marks of identity, have been sunk with the same reckless lack of compassion or of principle.

I was for a little while unable to believe that such things would in fact be done by any Government that had hitherto subscribed to humane practices of civilized nations. International law had its origin in the attempt to set up some law which would be respected and observed upon the seas, where no nation had right of dominion and where lay the free highways of the world. By painful stage after stage has that law been built up, with meager enough results, indeed, after all was accomplished that could be accomplished, but always with a clear view, at least, of what the heart and conscience of mankind demanded. This minimum of right the German Government has swept aside, under the plea of retaliation and necessity and because it had no weapons which it could use at sea except these which it is impossible to employ as it is employing them without throwing to the wind all scruples of humanity or of respect for the understanding that were supposed to underlie the intercourse of the world. I am not now thinking of the loss of property involved, immense and serious as that is, but only of the wanton and wholesale destruction of the lives of non-combatants, men, women and children, engaged in pursuits which have always, even in the darkest periods of modern history, been deemed innocent and legitimate. Property can be paid for; the lives of peaceful and innocent people cannot be. The present German submarine warfare against commerce is a warfare against mankind.

It is a war against all nations. American ships have been sunk, American lives taken, in ways which it has stirred us very deeply to learn of, but the ships and people of other neutral and friendly nations have been sunk and overwhelmed in the waters in the same way. There has been no discrimination. The challenge is to all mankind. Each nation must decide for itself how it will meet it. The choice we make for ourselves must be made with a moderation of counsel and a temperateness of judgment befitting our character and our motives as a nation. We must put excited feeling away. Our motive will not be revenge or the victorious assertion of the physical might of the nation, but only the vindication of right, of human right, of which we are only a single champion. [...]

With a profound sense of the solemn and even tragical character of the step I am taking and of the grave responsibilities which it involves, but in unhesitating obedience to what I deem my constitutional duty, I advise that the Congress declare the recent course of the Imperial German Government to be in fact nothing less than war against the Government and people of the United States; that it formally accept the status of belligerent which has thus been thrust upon it; and that it take immediate steps not only to put the country in a more thorough state of defense, but also to exert all its power and employ all its resources to bring the Government of the German Empire to terms and end the war.

What this will involve is clear. It will involve the utmost practicable coöperation in counsel and action with the governments now at war with Germany, and, as incident to that, the extension to those governments of the most liberal financial credits, in order that our resources may so far as possible be added to theirs. It will involve the organization and mobilization of all the material resources of the country to supply the materials of war and serve the incidental needs of the nation in the most abundant and yet the most economical and efficient way possible. It will involve the immediate full equipment of the navy in all respects but particularly in supplying it with the best means of dealing with the enemy's submarines. It will involve the immediate addition to the armed forces of the United States already provided for by law in case of war of at least five hundred thousand men, who should, in my opinion, be chosen upon the principle of universal liability to service, and also the authorization of subsequent additional increments of equal force so soon as they may be needed and can be handled in training. It will involve also, of course, the granting of adequate credits to the Government, sustained, I hope, so far as they can equitably be sustained by the present generation, by well-conceived taxation.

The Zimmermann Telegram

Woodrow Wilson severed diplomatic relations with Germany around New Year's Day, 1917, in response to Germany's decision to commence unrestricted submarine warfare. Although this was not a declaration of war, Germany's Foreign Minister Arthur Zimmermann instructed his ambassador to Mexico, Heinrich von Eckerhardt, to offer Mexico an alliance in case the United States did declare war. Mexico's reward was to be part of the territory Mexico had lost to the United States during the nineteenth century. Unfortunately for Zimmermann, British intelligence intercepted the document and turned it over to Wilson's government in February. It was published by the press and became an important piece of propaganda for pro-war politicians and ultimately played a part in Wilson's decision to ask Congress to declare war on Germany.

>> 86. Decoded Telegram January 8, 1917

ARTHUR ZIMMERMANN [1917]

TELEGRAM RECEIVED

From 2nd from London # 5747

"We intend to begin on the first of February unrestricted submarine warfare. We shall endeavor in spite of this to keep the United States of America neutral. In the event of this not succeeding, we make Mexico a proposal of alliance on the following basis: make war together, make peace together, generous financial support and an understanding on our part that Mexico is to reconquer the lost territory in Texas, New Mexico, and Arizona. The settlement in detail is left to you. You will inform the President of the above most secretly as soon as the outbreak of war with the United States of America is certain and add the suggestion that he should, on his own initiative, invite Japan to immediate adherence and at the same time mediate between Japan and ourselves. Please call the President's attention to the fact that the ruthless employment of our submarines now offers the prospect of compelling England in a few months to make peace."

Signed, ZIMMERMANN

Source: Arthur Zimmermann, decoded telegram January 8, 1917, provided to U.S. Department of State, Decimal File 862.20212/69 (1910–1929), General Records of the Department of State, Record Group 59.

>> Mastering the Material

1. Do you think the "Report Presented to the Preliminary Peace Conference" was an objective assessment of the causes of the First World War? Why or why not? What does this tell us about how we should read official documents as historical sources?

2. According to Joe Lunn, how were Senegalese men recruited to become soldiers to fight for France in the First World War?

3. Why did the "Third Balkan War" become the "First World War"? What were the processes and mechanisms that led to the spread of conflict between 1914 and 1917, first across Europe and then around the world?

4. According to President Woodrow Wilson, on what issues did the United States enter the First World War? How does the Zimmermann telegram support or refute his argument?

>> Making Connections

1. Consider James Joll's assessment of the work of Fritz Fischer and his critics. Does his analysis seem evenhanded and objective? Based on the sources in this chapter and Chapter 17, what do *you* think of Fischer's theory?

2. Was the recruiting of Senegalese troops for the French army in 1917 a type of enslavement? Compare the evidence presented by Joe Lunn to Ottobah Cuguano's depiction of the Atlantic slave trade (Reading 48, Chapter 10).

3. In general, do you believe that the First World War was more a product of deep, underpinning trends in Europe in the decades leading up to the conflict, or a product of the decisions and actions of a few leaders in 1914?

4. Was the First World War inevitable?

Chapter 19

The Rise of Fascism and Militarism

The beginning of the Second World War is traditionally dated to 1 September 1939, the date of the German invasion of Poland that led Britain and France to declare war on Nazi Germany. Yet this periodization is problematic. Two of the largest players—the United States and the Union of Soviet Socialist Republics (Soviet Union), did not become engaged until 1941. More important, the invasion of Poland was not the beginning, but rather the culmination, of almost a decade of aggression on the part of the three principal **Axis Powers**—Italy, Germany, and Japan.

Most mainstream analyses of the origins of this war hold these three Axis states entirely responsible. This conclusion was reached by most scholars writing in the days following the victory of the **Allied Powers**—led by Britain, and including the Soviet Union, China, France, and the United States—and it is an interpretation that has largely withstood the test of time because it is backed up by substantial evidence. For example, Japan's aggression against China in 1931 was entirely unprovoked, although Japanese military officers attempted to manufacture evidence of a Chinese plot—the famous Manchurian incident. Italy similarly invaded peaceful Abyssinia (Ethiopia) without provocation in October 1935. Nazi Germany, remilitarized in the 1930s, intervened in the civil war in Spain and then proceeded to occupy Austria on 12 March 1938, to menace and eventually occupy Czechoslovakia in the same year, and finally to invade Poland and other neutral European states in a wide arc stretching from Scandinavia to the Balkans. The Soviet Union was brought into the war by a German sneak attack in the summer of 1941, the United States by a Japanese sneak attack in December of the same year. Admittedly, a few historians have constructed theories that Josef Stalin, the Premier of the Soviet Union, or Franklin D. Roosevelt, the President of the United States, manufactured the conflict for their own benefit, but none have been convincing.

However, a number of debates do remain. The first centers on the causes of Axis aggression. Scholars have asked why these three states adopted such highly militaristic postures and policies. Were they seeking to settle unresolved problems of international diplomacy, or to distract attention from internal woes? Was their belligerency indicative of political and social defects, or a result of the flawed peace settlement of the First World War? Or should causes be sought deeper in their national histories? The traditional approach has been to search for characteristics shared by Japan, Germany, and Italy. Political analysts, for example, suggest that all three states shared political doctrines that are collectively termed **fascism.** The term is derived from the name of the Italian political party that, under Benito Mussolini, first embraced its underlying principles. Fascism as an ideology views human existence as a constant struggle between different nations or nationalities. It calls for the subordination of the individual to the power of the state. Only in this way can the nation thrive. Thus fascism is both a rejection of the enlightenment ideals of liberalness and an extreme form of nationalism informed by contemporary notions of race and racialism. Fascism also rejects the ideas of communism, which promoted class solidarity instead of national unity. It embraces action and conflict, and rejects pacifism. Perhaps the most definitive statement of fascist principals is Mussolini's 1923 "Definition of Fascism."

The political doctrine of fascism spread rapidly but unevenly through Europe during the interwar period. The Soviet Union, with its own brand of state (communist) totalitarianism, was immune. In northern and western Europe, functioning parliamentary governments also managed to keep fascist parties out of power. However, in a number of central and southern European states fascist agitators seized power in the 1930s. Spain and Hungary were two examples, but the greatest of the fascist movements was Adolf Hitler's National Socialist (Nazi) party in Germany. This party came to power legitimately on 30 January 1933, but subsequently solidified their rule through arson, assassination, and oppression. The origins of the Nazis are still debated, as is the degree of complicity of the German people in supporting such a violent, racialist party. Although the Nazis never won a majority of the electorate before elections were suspended in 1933, they were the largest political party in the German *Reichstag,* or parliament, in that year.

A number of theories have been proposed to account for the support the Nazis enjoyed. The first was the middle classes' fear of the emergence of communism during the chaotic years following the First World War. Other scholars suggest that Germans were culturally predisposed to accept authoritarian governments. Two interlinked causes that are generally well accepted are poverty and nationalism. The Treaty of Versailles that ended the First World War was especially harsh in its treatment of Germany. The German army was restricted, and its outlaying provinces and empire were dismembered. Germany was forced to give up 13 percent of its territory to Denmark, Luxembourg, Belgium, Poland, and Lithuania. Perhaps most damaging were the financial indemnities, outlined in Articles 231–235 of the peace treaty. These articles not only embodied Germany's "guilt" but also chained it to a postwar cycle of poverty. The result was a period of enormous inflation and impoverishment of the German working and middle classes between 1918–1924. American loans stabilized the situation briefly. However, it worsened again during the Great Depression of 1929–1933, a period that not coincidentally coincided with the Nazi party's seizure of power. Economic realities, expressed in bankruptcies and unemployment, helped to turn the populace away from centrist parties and to build popular support for the Nazis.

Once in power, the Nazis set themselves to the task of transforming Germany from a defeated if democratizing state to a totalitarian world power. The three core principles of Hitler's foreign policy were the removal of the restrictions put on Germany at the end of the First World War, the rebuilding of a German Empire, and the acquisition of **lebensraum,** or living space, to the detriment of non-Germans. Yet there is some debate among scholars as to whether or not Hitler intended to provoke a world war to gain these objectives. The conventional view is that Hitler had a plan to pursue a war of global domination that he followed in stages. This theory is called **intentionalism.** But in 1961 an important British historian, A. J. P. Taylor, questioned this notion in his controversial book *The Origins of the Second World War.* Taylor suggested that Hitler was an opportunist, not a plotter. In this revisionist view, Hitler hoped France and Britain would allow him to swallow up small states in eastern Europe and was surprised when they reacted in defense of Poland. A synthesis of these two views is provided by Alan Bullock in "Hitler and the Origins of the Second World War." Bullock suggests that Hitler was both a plotter and an opportunist. One of the most important sources that inform this debate is the "Hossbach Memorandum," an account of a prewar conference between Hitler and his principal advisors.

Can war-era Japan also be described as a fascist power like Mussolini's Italy and Hitler's Germany? Although it was clearly militarist, not all scholars accept that Japan was truly fascist. In fact, a number of scholars have come to interpret Japanese actions in the 1930s as an incoherent set of responses to regional challenges, rather than planned aggression. Certainly Japan, like Germany, suffered deeply during the Great Depression. In fact, Japan's troubles were especially pronounced since the Japanese islands themselves possessed few strategic resources. Japan thus looked abroad, and especially to China, for mineral and organic raw materials. Japanese expansion, however, was blocked at every turn: France, the Netherlands, and Britain controlled much of southeast Asia; northeast Asia was in the hands of the Soviet Union; and the China, with the backing of the United States, refused to provide Japan with strategic minerals. This has led some scholars to suggest that Japan's belligerency was the result of a lack of alternatives, rather than fascist fanaticism. Alliance with Germany and Italy was merely convenient because all three powers faced the same opponents. James Crowley's *Japan's Quest for Autonomy* is a good example of this interpretation. Yet not all scholars accept this view. Some of Crowley's opponents point to overtly fascist official documents, like the August 1, 1941 booklet *The Way of Subjects,* which clearly laid out a justification for the war based on totalitarian, nationalist principles.

Benito Mussolini's Definition of Fascism

Benito Mussolini, an Italian former socialist, was the first fascist leader to seize power in a European state. Although his party had only been formed in 1919, it won widespread support during the parliamentary elections of 1922. His elevation was completed in October 1922 when he marched at the head of an army of supporters to Rome and was invited by King Victor Emmanuel II to become prime minister. In a process that foreshadowed Adolf Hitler's consolidation of power in Germany a decade later, Mussolini used threats and violence to eliminate his rivals and to rule supreme. As Duce, or leader, of Italy he then formalized the doctrine of fascism to express his political goals and ideology. This contribution to a political dictionary stands as one of the foremost definitions of fascism by one of its practitioners.

>> 87. Definition of Fascism

BENITO MUSSOLINI [1923]

3. Above all, Fascism, in so far as it considers and observes the future and the development of humanity quite apart from the political considerations of the moment, believes neither in the possibility nor in the utility of perpetual peace. It thus repudiates the doctrine of Pacifism—born of a renunciation of the struggle and an act of cowardice in the face of sacrifice. War alone brings up to their highest tension all human energies and puts the stamp of nobility upon the peoples who have the courage to meet it. All other trials are substitutes, which never really put a man in front of himself in the alternative of life and death. [...]

4. The "demographic" policy of the regime follows from these premises. Even the Fascist does in fact love his neighbour, but this "neighbour" is not for him a vague and ill-defined concept; love for one's neighbour does not exclude necessary educational severities, and still less differentiations and distances. Fascism rejects universal concord, and, since it lives in the community of civilized peoples, it keeps them vigilantly and suspiciously before its eyes, it follows their states of mind and the changes in their interests and it does not let itself be deceived by temporary and fallacious appearances.

5. Such a conception of life makes Fascism the precise negation of that doctrine which formed the basis of the so-called Scientific or Marxian Socialism: the doctrine of historical Materialism, according to which the history of human civilizations can be explained only as the struggle of interest between the different social groups and as arising out of change in the means and instruments of production. [...] Fascism believes, now and always, in holiness and in heroism, that is in acts in which no economic motive—remote or immediate—plays a part. With this negation of historical materialism, according to which men would be only by-products of history, who appear and disappear on the surface of the waves while in the depths the real directive forces are at work there is also denied the immutable and irreparable "class struggle," which is the natural product of this economic conception of history and above all it is denied that the class struggle can be the primary agent of social changes. Socialism, being thus wounded in these two primary tenets of its doctrine, nothing of it is left save the sentimental aspiration—old as humanity—towards a social order in which the suffering and the pains of the humblest folk could be alleviated. [...]

6. After Socialism, Fascism attacks the whole complex of democratic ideologies and rejects them both in their theoretical premises and in their applications or practical manifestations. Fascism denies that the majority, through the mere fact of being a majority, can rule human societies; it denies that this majority can govern by means of a periodical consultation; it affirms the irremediable, fruitful and beneficent inequality of men, who cannot be leveled by such a mechanical and extrinsic fact as universal suffrage. [...]

10. The keystone of Fascist doctrine is the conception of the State, of its essence, of its tasks, of its ends. For Fascism the State is an absolute before which individuals and groups are relative. Individuals and groups are "thinkable" in so far as they are within the State. [...] The State, as conceived by Fascism and as it acts, is a spiritual and moral fact because it makes concrete the political, juridical, economic organization of the nation and such an organization is, in its origin and in its development, a manifestation of the spirit. The State is the guarantor of internal and external security, but it is also the guardian and the transmitter of the spirit of the people as it has been elaborated through the centuries in language, custom, faith. The State is not only present, it is also past, and above all future. It is the State which, transcending the brief limit of individual lives, represents the immanent conscience of the nation. The forms in which States express themselves change, but the necessity of the State remains.

Source: Benito Mussolini, "Definition of Fascism," in *The Social and Political Doctrines of Contemporary Europe*, edited and translated by Michael Oakenshott (Cambridge: Cambridge University Press, 1939), 170–172, 175–176.

"War Guilt" and "Reparations" Clauses of the Versailles Peace Treaty

The victors in the First World War forced Germany, as part of the peace agreements of 1918–1919, to accept the blame for starting the war. The resulting peace treaty not only dismembered Austria-Hungary and parts of Germany, but at the insistence of France forced Germany to pay her enemies' war costs. The final bill presented to Germany was over six and a half billion British pounds, an unprecedented amount. The key clauses that promulgated this process were Articles 231–235 of the Treaty of Versailles.

>> 88. The Treaty of Versailles

[1919]

Article 231

The Allied and Associated Governments affirm and Germany accepts the responsibility of Germany and her Allies for causing all the loss and damage to which the Allied and Associated Governments and their nationals have been subjected as a consequence of the war imposed upon them by the aggression of Germany and her allies. [...]

Article 232

The Allied and Associated Governments recognize that the resources of Germany are not adequate, after taking into account permanent diminutions of such resources which will result from other provisions of the present Treaty, to make complete reparation for all such loss and damage.

The Allied and Associated Governments, however, require, and Germany undertakes, that she will make compensation for all damage done to the civilian population of the Allied and Associated Powers and to their property during the period of the belligerency of each as an Allied or Associated Power against Germany by such aggression by land, by sea and from the air, and in general all damage as defined in Annex I hereto. [...]

Article 234

The Reparation Commission shall after May 1, 1921, from time to time, consider the resources and capacity of Germany, and, after giving her representatives a just opportunity to be heard, shall have discretion to extend the date, and to modify the form of payments, such as are to be provided for in accordance with Article 233; but not to cancel any part, except with the specific authority of the several Governments represented upon the Commission.

Article 235

In order to enable the Allied and Associated Powers to proceed at once to the restoration of their industrial and economic life, pending the full determination of their claims, Germany shall pay in such instalments and in such manner (whether in gold, commodities, ships, securities or otherwise) as the Reparation Commission may fix, during 1919, 1920 and the first four months of 1921, the equivalent of 20,000,000,000 gold marks. Out of this sum the expenses of the armies of occupation subsequent to the Armistice of November 11, 1918, shall first be met, and such supplies of food and raw materials as may be judged by the Governments of the Principal Allied and Associated Powers to be essential to enable Germany to meet her obligations for

Source: The Treaty of Versailles, Papers Relating to the Foreign Relations of the United States: The Paris Peace Conference, vol. XIII (Washington, D.C.: Government Printing Office, 1947), 413, 425, 438.

reparation may also, with the approval of the said Governments, be paid for out of the above sum. The balance shall be reckoned towards liquidation of the amounts due for reparation. Germany shall further deposit bonds as prescribed in paragraph 12 (c) of Annex II hereto.

Unemployment and Bankruptcy Figures for Germany

In the interwar period, Germany struggled not only to pay reparations but also the debts it had incurred during the war. Moreover, a global depression that began with the U.S. stock market crash in 1929 significantly affected Germans. Its impact was reflected not only in unemployment, which is a measure of the impoverishment of the working class, but also in bankruptcies, which helps measure the impact on the business-owning classes. The result was an increasing polarization as many Germans abandoned the established political parties and joined revolutionary parties—either the Communists or the Nazis. In the end, powerful German businesses and politicians who did not ideologically sympathize with the Nazis came to embrace them as the only force capable of resisting a communist revolution.

>> 89. The Nazi Years: A Documentary History

[1969]

Unemployment in Germany, 1928–1932

Year	Number
1928	1,862,000
1929	2,850,000
1930	3,217,000
1931	4,886,000
1932	6,042,000

Bankruptcies in Germany, 1928–1932

Year	Number
1928	10,595
1929	13,180
1930	15,486
1931	19,254
1932	14,138

Hitler, Fanatic and Opportunist

Following the defeat of Nazi Germany in 1945, as after the victory of the Entente power at the end of the First World War, blame for the conflict was placed squarely the German leadership. Indeed, the case against the Nazi leadership, and especially Adolf Hitler, was so strong that this view was not significantly challenged until the early 1960s. A. J. P. Taylor's revisionist The Origins of the Second World War, *in which he argued that Hitler's foreign policy was opportunistic and pragmatic, rather than fanatically aggressive, therefore caused a stir among scholars. Yet few historians accepted this argument at face value, and*

Source: The Nazi Years: A Documentary History, edited by Joachim Remak (Englewood Cliffs: Prentice-Hall, 1969), 24.

many rejected it out of hand. One who contemplated it seriously was Alan Bullock, who responded with this well-considered article in which he suggests that Hitler was both fanatic and opportunist. In these excerpts, Bullock addresses two foreign policy affairs: the Hossbach Memorandum, which is Reading 91, and the 1938 Czechoslovakia affair, which is discussed further in Chapter 20.

>> 90. Hitler and the Origins of the Second World War

ALAN BULLOCK [1997]

There are two contrasted versions of Hitler's foreign policy which for convenience's sake I will call the fanatic and the opportunist.

The first fastens upon Hitler's racist views and his insistence that the future of the German people could be secured, neither by economic development nor by overseas colonization, not even by the restoration of Germany's 1914 frontiers, but only by the conquest of living space (*Lebensraum*) in Eastern Europe. Here the scattered populations of Germans living outside the Reich could be concentrated, together with the surplus population of the homeland, and a Germanic empire established, racially homogeneous, economically self-sufficient, and militarily impregnable. Such *Lebensraum* could only be obtained at the expense of Russia and the states bordering on her and could only be won and cleared of its existing population by force, a view which coincided with Hitler's belief in struggle as the law of life, and war as the test of a people's racial superiority. [...]

The alternative version treats Hitler's talk of *Lebensraum* and racist empire in the East as an expression of the fantasy side of his personality and fastens on the opportunism of Hitler's actual conduct of foreign policy. In practice—so this version runs—Hitler was an astute and cynical politician who took advantage of the mistakes and illusions of others to extend German power along lines entirely familiar from the previous century of German history. So little did he take

his own professions seriously that he actually concluded a pact with the Bolsheviks whom he had denounced, and when Hitler belatedly began to put his so-called programme into practice, it marked the point at which he lost the capacity to distinguish between fantasy and reality and, with it, the opportunist's touch which had been responsible for his long run of successes. Thereafter he suffered nothing but one disaster after another. [...]

It is a mistake, however, I believe, to treat these two contrasting views as alternatives, for if that is done, then, whichever alternative is adopted, a great deal of evidence has to be ignored. The truth is, I submit, that they have to be combined and that Hitler can only be understood if it is realized that he was at once both fanatical *and* cynical; unyielding in his assertion of will-power *and* cunning in calculation; convinced of his role as a man of destiny *and* prepared to use all the actor's arts in playing it. To leave out either side, the irrational or the calculating, is to fail to grasp the combination which marks Hitler out from all his imitators.

The same argument, I believe, applies to Hitler's foreign policy which combined consistency of aim with complete opportunism in method and tactics. This is, after all, a classical receipt for success in foreign affairs. It was precisely because he knew where he wanted to go that Hitler could afford to be opportunistic and saw how to take advantage of the mistakes and fears of others. Consistency of aim Hitler's part has been confused with a time-table, blueprint, or plan of action fixed in advance, as if it were pinned up on the wall of the General Staff offices

Source: Alan Bullock, *Hitler and the Origins of the Second World War* (London: Proceedings of the British Academy, 1997), 260–263, 275–276.

and ticked off as one item succeeded another. Nothing of the sort. Hitler frequently improvised, kept his options open to the last possible moment, and was never sure until he got there which of several courses of action he would choose. But this does not alter the fact that his moves followed a logical (though not a predetermined) course—in contrast to Mussolini, an opportunist who snatched eagerly at any chance that was going but never succeeded in combining even his successes into a coherent policy. [...]

So far as the events of 1938 go, there seem to be two possible answers to the question, what was in Hitler's mind?

The first is that his object was to destroy the Czech State by the sort of blitzkrieg for which he had rearmed Germany and which he was to carry out a year later against Poland. This was to come at the end of a six months' political, diplomatic, and propaganda campaign designed to isolate and undermine the Czechs, and to manoeuvre the Western Powers into abandoning them to their fate rather than risk a European war. The evidence for this view consists in the series of secret directives and the military preparations to which they led, plus Hitler's declaration on several occasions to the generals and his other collaborators that he meant to settle the matter by force, with 1 October as D-day. On this view, he was only prevented from carrying out his attack by the intervention of Chamberlain which, however great the cost to the Czechs, prevented war or at least postponed it for a year.

The other view is that Hitler never intended to go to war, that his objective was from the beginning a political settlement such as was offered to him at Munich, that his military preparations were not intended seriously but were designed as threats to increase the pressure.

The choice between these two alternatives, however—*either* the one *or* the other—seems to me unreal. The obvious course for Hitler to pursue was to keep both possibilities open to the very last possible moment, the more so since they did not conflict. The more seriously the military preparations were carried out, the more effective was the pressure in favour of a political settlement if at the last moment he decided not to take the risks involved in a military operation. If we adopt this view, then we remove all the difficulties in interpreting the evidence which are created either by attempting to pin Hitler down on any particular declaration and say *now,* at this point, he had decided on war—or by the dogmatic assumption that Hitler *never* seriously contemplated the use of force, with the consequent need to dismiss his military directives as bluff.

The Hossbach Memorandum

Researchers consider a November 1937 memorandum written by Hitler's adjutant Friedrich Hossbach to be among the principal evidence against the German leader. Hossbach's memorandum is his account of a speech given by Hitler to his military council. It is a damning indictment, as it clearly shows intent not only to provoke an incident over Czechoslovakia but to commit to war against France. Yet some scholars have argued that it should not be read literally. Taylor, for example, suggests that Hitler's intent was to convince his senior officers—most of them not committed Nazis— to support the Nazi party's program for increasing expenses on armaments. Others suggest that Hossbach may have exaggerated what his Führer, or leader, actually said. Nevertheless, the document was prescient. Much of what Hitler had predicted actually came to pass, prompting many historians to accept the memorandum as evidence that his aggressive foreign policy was planned.

>> 91. Memorandum

COLONEL COUNT FRIEDRICH
HOSSBACH [1937]

The Führer then continued:

The aim of German policy was to make secure and to preserve the racial community [*Volksmasse*] and to enlarge it. It was therefore a question of space.

The German racial community comprised over 85 million people and, because of their number and the narrow limits of habitable space in Europe, constituted a tightly packed racial core such as was not to be met in any other country and such as implied the right to a greater living space than in the case of other peoples. If, territorially speaking, there existed no political result corresponding to this German racial core, that was a consequence of centuries of historical development, and in the continuance of these political conditions lay the greatest danger to the preservation of the German race at its present peak. To arrest the decline of Germanism [*Deutschtum*] in Austria and Czechoslovakia was as little possible as to maintain the present level in Germany itself. Instead of increase, sterility was setting in, and in its train disorders of a social character must arise in course of time, since political and ideological ideas remain effective only so long as they furnish the basis for the realization of the essential vital demands of a people. Germany's future was therefore wholly conditional upon the solving of the need for space, and such a solution could be sought, of course, only for a foreseeable period of about one to three generations. [...]

Germany's problem could only be solved by means of force and this was never without attendant risk. [...]

Our relative strength would decrease in relation to the rearmament which would by then have been carried out by the rest of the world. If we did not act by 1943–45, any year could, in consequence of a lack of reserves, produce the food crisis, to cope with which the necessary foreign exchange was not available, and this must be regarded as a "waning point of the regime." Besides, the world was expecting our attack and was increasing its countermeasures from year to year. It was while the rest of the world was still preparing its defenses [*sich abriegele*] that we were obliged to take the offensive.

Nobody knew today what the situation would be in the years 1943–45. One thing only was certain, that we could not wait longer.

On the one hand there was the great *Wehrmacht*, and the necessity of maintaining it at its present level, the aging of the movement and of its leaders; and on the other, the prospect of a lowering of the standard of living and of a limitation of the birth rate, which left no choice but to act. If the Führer was still living, it was his unalterable resolve to solve Germany's problem of space at the latest by 1943–45. [...]

For the improvement of our politico-military position our first objective, in the event of our being embroiled in war, must be to overthrow Czechoslovakia and Austria simultaneously in order to remove the threat to our flank in any possible operation against the West. In a conflict with France it was hardly to be regarded as likely that the Czechs would declare war on us on the very same day as France. The desire to join in the war would, however, increase among the Czechs in proportion to any weakening on our part and then her participation could clearly take the form of an attack toward Silesia, toward the north or toward the west. [...]

Actually, the Führer believed that almost certainly Britain, and probably France as well, had already tacitly written off the Czechs and were reconciled to the fact that this question would be cleared up in due course by Germany.

Source: Colonel Count Friedrich Hossbach, Memorandum, translated in *Documents on German Foreign Policy, 1918–1945,* (Washington, D.C.: Government Printing Office, 1949), 29–30, 34–35.

The Way of Subjects

Japan's close alliance with Germany and Italy began, in 1936, as an agreement to oppose communist Russia, which spanned much of the vast area between the European fascist powers and Japan. It was formalized on September 27, 1940, in the Tripartate Pact, which pledged the three states to support each other in case of war. The treaty was consummated in December 1941, when Germany and Italy declared war on the United States following Japan's sneak attack on Pearl Harbor. Many commentators at the time and scholars since have argued that the three were natural ideological allies, espousing similar racialist, nationalist ideals. This has led many to label Japan a fascist state, and to suggest that Japan's entry into the war was part of a planned process guided by the notions of Japanese imperialism and a right to rule. These theorists see the Japanese invasion of Manchuria (in northeastern China) in 1931 and the establishment of the puppet state of Manchukuo as the first step in the plan to spread Japanese imperial domination across Asia. When the United States, China, and others objected to this process Japan withdrew from the League of Nations, and in 1937 the Japanese army resumed its invasion of China. Japan declared war against Britain in 1940, and occupied much of British, Dutch, and French southeast Asia before finally launching the sneak attack against the United States in December 1941. Just months prior to that bombing of the U.S. fleet at Pearl Harbor, the Japanese Ministry of Education issued this pamphlet, "The Way of Subjects." In it, the authors suggested that Japan was besieged by Western notions of liberalism, which must be rejected in favor of loyalty to the Emperor and state. This, they predicted, would culminate in the fulfillment of "Japan's mission": the creation of an Asian empire.

>> 92. The Way of Subjects

GOVERNMENT OF JAPAN [1941]

Preamble

The way of the subjects of the Emperor issues from the polity of the Emperor, and is to guard and maintain the Imperial Throne coexistent with the Heavens and the Earth. This is not in the sphere of the abstract, but a way of daily practices based on history. The life and activities of the nation are all attuned to the task of giving great firmness to the foundation of the Empire.

In retrospection, this country has been widely seeking knowledge in the world since the Meiji Restoration, thereby fostering and maintaining the prosperity of the state. With the influx of European and American culture into this country, however, individualism, liberalism, utilitarianism, and materialism began to assert themselves, with the result that the traditional character of the country was much impaired and the virtuous habits and customs bequeathed by our ancestors were affected unfavorably. [...]

If this situation is left unremedied, it will be difficult to eradicate the evils of European and American thought that are deeply penetrating various strata of the national life of Japan, and to achieve the unprecedentedly great tasks by establishing a structure of national solidarity of guarding and maintaining the prosperity of the Imperial Throne. Herein lies an urgent need of discarding the self-centered and utilitarian ideas and of elevating and practicing the way of the

---

Source: Government of Japan, "The Way of Subjects," in *Tokyo Record*, translated by Otto D. Tolischus (New York: Reynal and Hitchcock, 1943), 405–406, 408, 419, 426–427.

subjects of the Emperor based on state services as the primary requisite.

An old order that has been placing world humanity under individualism, liberalism, and materialism for several hundred years since the early period of the modern epoch of history is now crumbling. A new order is now in the making amid unprecedented world changes. An outline of the modern history of the world must be looked over to give clearness to significance of the new world order. [...]

The thoughts that have formed the foundation of the Western civilization since the early period of the modern age are individualism, liberalism, materialism, and so on. These thoughts regard the strong preying on the weak as reasonable, unstintedly promote epicurean desires, seek a highly expanded material life, and stimulate the competition for acquiring colonies and securing trade, thereby leading the world to a veritable hell of fighting and bloodshed through complicated causes and effects. The self-destruction in the shape of the World War finally followed. It was only natural that cries were raised even among men of those countries after the war that the Occidental civilization was crumbling. A vigorous movement was started by Britain, France, and the United States to maintain the status quo by all means. Simultaneously, a movement aiming at social revolution through class conflict on the basis of thoroughgoing materialism like Communism also was developed with unremitting vigor. On the other hand, Nazism and Fascism arose with great force. The basic theories of these new racial principles and the totalitarianism in Germany and Italy are to remove and improve the evils of individualism and liberalism.

That these principles show great concern for Oriental culture and spirit is a noteworthy fact that suggests the future of the Occidental civilization and the creation of a new culture. Thus, the orientation of world history has made the collapse of the world of the old order an assured conclusion. Japan has hereby opened the start for the construction of a new world order based on moral principles. [...]

The cardinal objective of strengthening the total war organism is solely to help the Imperial Throne, and this can be attained by all the people fulfilling their duty as subjects through their respective standpoints. The Soviet Union has world domination through Communism as its objective, and for this that country follows the policy of using compulsory rights through class dictatorship. [...]

The great duty of the Japanese people to guard and maintain the Imperial Throne has lasted to the present since the Empire-founding and will last forever and ever. To serve the Emperor is its key point. Our lives will become sincere and true when they are offered to the Emperor and the state. Our own private life is fulfillment of the way of the subjects; in other words, it is not private, but public, insofar as it is held by the subjects supporting the Throne. [...]

Japan is the fountain source of the Yamato race, Manchukuo its reservoir, and East Asia is its paddy field.

A Pragmatic Explanation for Japanese Belligerence

Documents such as "The Way of Subjects" certainly seem to suggest that Japan adhered to a certain type of fascism, at least after 1937, when militarists gained power and Prince Fumimaro Konoe was elevated to the post of Prime Minister of the Japanese government. Konoe proclaimed a new, Japanese-led "order" in eastern Asia, ordered the 1937 invasion of central China, and has been seen as a belligerent promoter of Japanese expansionism. Yet James Crowley and others have suggested that ideology was not the driving force in Japanese aggression before, or even during, the Konoe regime. Crowley depicts Japan as an imperial power like those of Europe, but blocked from access to overseas resources by Britain, France, Russia, and the United States. The actions of the Japanese government, Crowley argues, were pragmatic decisions taken in the interest of national security.

>> 93. Japan's Quest for Autonomy: National Security and Foreign Policy, 1930–1938

JAMES B. CROWLEY [1966]

Whatever faults or consequences one attributes to the security and foreign policies of the Imperial government during the1930's, they were formulated by responsible political and military leaders. It seems equally evident that an inordinate emphasis on the subject of "national defense" served to rationalize aggression and authoritarianism as the best ways to overcome the challenges posed by the demands of total war and two strategic enemies endowed with plentiful natural resources. It is not easy to dismiss this obsession with national security, this compulsion to acquire a status of military and economic parity with the United States and the Soviet Union. Neither of these powers was prepared to support firmly Japan's treaty rights in Manchuria, let alone to encourage additional economic privileges in China or new rights in the South Seas. Perhaps it is not amiss to view the diplomatic, economic, and military circumstances prevailing in Japan in the age of the great depression as reminiscent of a Greek tragedy. The element of hubris—a burning desire for full equality which, in effect, meant naval and military superiority in East Asia—had, in the past, been a commendable virtue. This, combined with the good fortune of past decades—the regionalization of sea power, the impotence of Ch'ing and Republican China, and the weakness of Tsarist and Communist Russia—had yielded an empire and the status of a world power. Subsequent developments—the China and naval policies of the American government, the surging tide of Chinese nationalism, the maturing power of the Soviet Union, and the demands of total war—were less auspicious. Without an intense racial and national pride, perhaps these new issues would not have been viewed as they were. Still, this racial and national pride had been crucial in the notable achievements of Meiji and Taishō Japan; and, judging by the painful manner in which European powers have been compelled to adjust to the phenomenon of nationalism in colonial areas and to the overwhelming might of the Soviet Union and the United States, it is difficult to castigate Japan's leaders for their unwillingness to abandon the quest for parity with their strategic enemies, or to moderate their special claims in Manchuria. [...]

As were his immediate predecessors in the office of premier, [Prince] Konoe too was ensnared in a painful tangle of geographical, technological, diplomatic, and military circumstances. None of the major actors in East Asia—Nationalist China, the Soviet Union, the United States, and Japan—had been disposed to perpetuate the *status quo* embodied in the Washington Conference treaties; and, after 1931, none of the other powers were prepared to endorse Japan's continental policies, first in Manchuria, later in North China and Inner Mongolia. Throughout the twentieth century, Japan's hegemony in Northeast Asia had been confirmed by her military strength and by alliances with the maritime powers. When they were confronted by a formidable group of critics in the 1930's, it is not surprising that Japan's political and military leaders steadfastly adhered to the traditional aspiration of the empire, hegemony in Northeast Asia, or that this gave rise to a quest for political and military autonomy.

Source: James B. Crowley, *Japan's Quest for Autonomy: National Security and Foreign Policy, 1930–1938* (Princeton: Princeton University Press, 1966), 394–395, 397.

>> Mastering the Material

1. From the readings in this chapter, what do you gather are the principal tenets of fascism as a doctrine and ideology?

2. Compare and contrast Mussolini's *Definition of Fascism* and "The Way of Subjects," issued by the Japanese government. What are the similarities between these two ideologies? What are the differences? Do you think "The Way of Subjects" shows that Japan was under a fascist regime like that of Italy and Germany? Why or why not?

3. How do the economic figures (bankruptcies and unemployment) and Treaty of Versailles clauses on war guilt and reparations contribute to our understanding of the rise of Nazism in Germany?

4. How is the Hossbach Memorandum used as evidence by Bullock in the scholarly debate on Hitler's intentions?

5. Before reading this chapter, had you heard of the Japanese role in the Second World War? Was your understanding of this role more like Crowley's account of Japanese intentions or like "The Way of Subjects"? Have you changed your opinion?

6. To what degree, do you think, did Japan and Germany go to war for ideological reasons? To what degree was their decision to go to war a pragmatic one based on regional and global considerations? To what degree did they fall into war by mistake? How are the readings in Part 4 useful as evidence for this question?

>> Making Connections

1. Both Mussolini's *Definition of Fascism* and the Japanese document "The Way of Subjects" define their respective government's ideology partly through their opposition to Western capitalist liberalism, as exemplified by the governments of the United States, France, and Britain. What are the principal differences between fascist militarism and capitalist liberalism?

2. Modern European states exhibited both imperialism and nationalism during the late-nineteenth to early twentieth-century period. To what degree do you think these ideologies are linked? To what degree were they causes of the Second World War?

Chapter 20

Appeasement and Isolationism

In 1935, the British Empire spanned the globe, protected by the mightiest navy in the world. The United States possessed the world's greatest industrial economy, even if it was still recovering from six years of depression. The Soviet Union (Union of Soviet Socialist Republics) could call upon the vast manpower and mineral resources of the world's most extensive territorial state. The French army was the most highly regarded anywhere on the face of the globe. Yet these states—which would eventually become the principal Allied Powers—stood by while the militarist Axis Powers of Japan, Germany, and Italy swallowed up neutral, independent states in Europe, Africa, and Asia. France and Britain eventually committed to a European conflict following the September 1939 invasion of Poland, but the Soviet Union and the United States could not be stimulated until they were personally attacked—the former by Germany in the summer of 1941, the latter by Japan six months later.

In hindsight, the pacifism and gullibility of the Allies may seem reprehensible, but only a very few reputable scholars have argued that they were leading causes of the Second World War. Among these few is the German historian Ernst Topitsch who has argued that the Soviet Premier, Joseph Stalin, goaded Hitler into war against Britain and France. In a similar line of analysis, U.S. historian Paul Schroeder has suggested that the American President, Franklin Delano Roosevelt, pushed Japan into war through his unwillingness to compromise. But these theories have attracted few supporters and many critics.

A more convincing claim is that Britain, France, the United States, and the Soviet Union bear some responsibility not because of their actions, but because of their inaction—their lethargy during the years when the Axis Powers were growing in strength. Their inaction was perhaps understandable. In the wake of the horrors of the First World War, their citizenry feared another global conflict and urged their governments to create institutions to peacefully resolve future conflicts. The most important of these, created at the Paris Peace Conference in 1919, was the League of Nations. By 1926, Britain, Italy, France, Japan, and Germany were all permanent members, as were forty-four other states. The League even enjoyed some successes in resolving disputes between member nations in the Balkans and Scandinavia as well as in negotiating a settlement between Turkey and Iraq over the disputed territory of Mosul. However, it was hamstrung by the nonparticipation of the United States and the Soviet Union. Moreover, while the League enjoyed great popular support in its member states, some governments viewed it merely as a policy forum. Thus they refrained from really committing to its core principles.

This was never more evident than when, in the 1930s, the three Axis states began to pursue aggressive policies against member states. The United States protested Japan's 1931 invasion of Manchuria, but the League of Nations failed to act, although China was a member. In 1935, Mussolini's Italian armies invaded Abyssinia—the African state it had failed to conquer in the 1890s. Efforts to impose economic sanctions against Italy fizzled because France and Britain feared alienating Mussolini. The Abyssinian (Ethiopian) Emperor Haile Selassie's emotional appeal to the League of Nations was ignored. Adolf Hitler watched these events closely and interpreted them as indicating weakness in the two great western European democracies. Along with Mussolini, in 1936 Hitler began supporting Fascist rebels in Spain. In the same year, in direct violation of the Treaty of Versailles, he sent troops into the demilitarized Rhineland of western Germany. When Britain and France failed to react to these provocations, he laid plans for an occupation of Austria, which he considered to be an ethnic German state. He eventually carried this plan out in March 1938. Many Austrians welcomed him, but others did not. Emboldened by his successes, he demanded that Czechoslovakia hand over to Germany the slice of its territory known as the Sudetenland. The Czechoslovakian President, Eduard Benes, anticipated that his British and French allies would leap to his aid, but British Prime Minister Neville Chamberlain instead told him in no uncertain terms that the Czechs should submit to the German demands. Chamberlain agreed not to oppose Hitler's claims at a series of conferences in Munich beginning September 29, and returned home convinced he had preserved peace, as he told British Parliament on October 3, 1938.

There is much debate over the Chamberlain administration's practice of giving in to Hitler's early demands—a policy known as **appeasement.** John Wheeler-Bennett's *Munich: Prologue to Tragedy* represents the mainstream thinking of immediate postwar analysis, which saw appeasement as a weak, short-sighted, and selfish policy. D. C. Watt's *How War Came,* on the other hand, is an example of a revisionist trend that emerged among British historians in the late-1960s. The revisionists' work suggested that appeasement was a logical policy given the realities of Britain's military and economic situation. Some even go so far as to suggest that appeasement bought Britain the time necessary to re-arm for the war that finally broke out in September 1939.

On 15 March, 1939, Hitler broke the pact he had signed with Chamberlain in Munich and annexed the rest of Czechoslovakia. Even Chamberlain realized from this act that Hitler was preparing to embark on a wider war of conquest. Consequently, Britain and France together guaranteed the sovereignty of Poland. When Hitler invaded that state in September of that year, France and Britain declared war on Nazi Germany. The United States and the Soviet Union, however, did not. In the case of the United States, the First World War coupled with the effects of the Great Depression had culminated in a policy of **isolationism.** Although

President Roosevelt gave moral and eventually material support to Britain, the United States remained officially neutral. Arnold A. Offner argues in his article "The United States and National Socialist Germany" that Roosevelt truly hoped for a peaceful resolution to the conflict.

The position of the communist government of the Soviet Union is more complex. The natural antipathy between Nazi and Marxist Soviet ideology is clearly represented in Soviet Foreign Minister Maxim Litvinov's speech of December 29, 1939. Yet neither was the Soviet Union an ideological ally of Britain and France. While fearing German expansionism, Premier Stalin also mistrusted the anticommunist western European parliamentary democracies. In 1939, he chose to sign a treaty of nonaggression with Nazi Germany, and subsequently was rewarded with a piece of Poland. When, in the summer of 1941, the Soviets themselves became victims of Nazi aggression Stalin appears to have been genuinely surprised. The Soviet attitude toward Hitler has been subjected to several lines of analysis. Most Soviet-era Russian historians suggest that the Soviet Union had initially wanted an alliance with France and Britain but were put off by Chamberlain's decision to appease Hitler. Some modern revisionists suggest that Stalin hoped Britain, France, and Germany would destroy each other and the Soviets could mop up afterward. Still a third group of scholars suggests that Stalin, like Britain, was unready for war. Which of these explanations is sufficient to account for the Soviet–German treaty?

Britain's appeasement policy, the collapse of the authority of the League of Nations, the pact with the Soviet Union, and the United States' isolationism all signaled Hitler, Mussolini, and the Japanese that their continued aggression would be unopposed. Some scholars have suggested that if the antifascist states had taken a stand earlier, the Second World War would have been averted. Others, however, argue that an earlier war might have favored the Axis states, and that the time lag gave the Allies, Britain, especially crucial time to re-arm. The debate remains unresolved.

Haile Selassie's Appeal to the League Assembly

The appeal of the Emperor of Abyssinia (Ethiopia) to the League of Nations, is a poignant example of the League's failure to protect its members from aggression. Ethiopia, a League member state, was one of only two African states to survive the late-nineteenth century scramble for colonies, largely by defeating an Italian army in 1896. In 1935 Italian Fascist forces returned to conquer the state and add it to the Italian empire Mussolini had promised to create. The Ethiopian army was unable to defend the state, and thus Selassie traveled to Geneva to speak before the League Assembly in April 1936. Italian diplomats delayed Selassie's speech until the end of June, by which time his forces had collapsed.

>> 94. Speech to the League of Nations Assembly

EMPEROR HAILE SELASSIE [1936]

I, Haile Selassie I, Emperor of Ethiopia, am here today to claim that justice which is due to my people and the assistance promised it eight months ago, when fifty nations asserted that aggression had been committed in violation of international treaties. None other than the Emperor can address the appeal of the Ethiopian people to those fifty nations.

There is no precedent for the head of a State himself speaking in this Assembly, but there is also no precedent for a people being the victim of such injustice and of being at present threatened by abandonment to an aggressor.

Also there has never before been an example of any government proceeding with the systematic extermination of a nation by barbarous means in violation of the most solemn promises, made to all the nations of the earth, that there should be no resort to a war of conquest and that there should not be used against innocent human beings terrible poison and harmful gases....

I pray to Almighty God that He shall spare the nations the terrible sufferings that have just been inflicted on my people and of which the chiefs who accompany me here have been the horrified witnesses.

It is my duty here to inform the governments assembled at Geneva—responsible as they are for the lives of men, women, and children—of the deadly peril which threatens them by describing to them the fate which has been suffered by Ethiopia. It is not only upon the warriors that the Italian Government has made war. It has, above all attacked populations far removed from hostilities in order to terrorize and exterminate them.

[Here Selassie reviews bombing, air operations, poison gas sprayed from planes, poisoning of water, etc.;
Reviews war and League discussions;
Reminds the fifty-two nations which, in October, 1935, assured him, that the aggressor would not triumph, of their promise of support; and
States that he had faith in collective security, so did not prepare, for war as did Italy. –True of the small countries of Europe also.]

I was defending the cause of all small people who are threatened with aggression....

I assert that the problem submitted to the Assembly today is much wider than merely a question of settlement of Italian aggression; it is collective security, it is the very existence of the League. It is the confidence that each State is to place in international treaties. It is the value of promises to small States that their integrity and independence shall be respected and insured. It is the principle of equality of States on the one hand, or otherwise the obligation made upon small powers to accept the bonds of vassalship. In a word, it is international morality that is at stake.

Apart from the Kingdom of the Lord, there is not on this earth any nation that is superior to any other. Should it happen that a strong government finds that it may, with impunity, destroy a small people, then the hour strikes for that weak people to appeal to the League to give its judgment in all freedom. God and history will remember your judgment.

Placed by the aggressor face to face with an accomplished fact, are the States going to set up the terrible precedent of bowing before force? Your Assembly doubtless has before it proposals for reform of the covenant and rendering more effective the guarantee of collective security. Is it the covenant that needs reform?

Source: Originally printed in the *New York Times,* 30 June 1936, as well as a number of other newspapers. Later reprinted in *Fighting for Freedom,* edited by H. A. Hansen, J. G. Herndon, and W. B. Langsdorf, (Philadelphia: John Winston, 1947), 61–63.

What undertakings can be of any value if the will to keep them is lacking? It is international morality which is at stake, and not the articles of the covenant.

Of the powers who have promised to guarantee the collective security of small States and who raise the threat that they may one day suffer the fate of Ethiopia, I ask: What measures do you intend to take? Representatives of the world, I have come to Geneva to discharge in your midst the most painful of duties for the head of a State. What reply have I to take back to my people?

Neville Chamberlain Defends the Policy of Appeasement

The British Prime Minister in the period immediately leading up to the Second World War was Neville Chamberlain. Elected to office May 29, 1937, Chamberlain was an efficient administrator but was often accused of arrogance and disregarding public opinion. Ironically, most of the British public supported him in his decision to sacrifice part of Czechoslovakia to Hitler's war machine rather than defend the small, eastern European state. Chamberlain's predecessors, after all, had followed similar policies in regard to Spain and Abyssinia. But even during the height of the Czechoslovakian crisis, following initial meetings in Munich, Chamberlain came under attack in Parliament from opponents of appeasement (he refers to them here as "My right Hon. Friends"). In this speech, given October 3, 1938, he defends the policy and his agreements with Hitler, whom he praises as a statesman. He also warns, however, that Britain must re-arm in the face of Germany's growing power.

>> 95. Parliamentary Debates: House of Commons [1938]

I would like to say a few words in respect of the various other participants, besides ourselves, in the Munich Agreement. After everything that has been said about the German Chancellor to-day and in the past, I do feel that the House ought to recognise the difficulty for a man in that position to take back such emphatic declarations as he had already made amidst the enthusiastic cheers of his supporters, and to recognise that in consenting, even though it were only at the last moment, to discuss with the representatives of other Powers those things which he had declared he had already decided once for all, was a real and a substantial contribution on his part. With regard to Signor Mussolini, his contribution was certainly notable and perhaps decisive. It was on his suggestion that the final stages of mobilisation were postponed for 24 hours to give us an opportunity of discussing the situation, and I wish to say that at the Conference itself both he and the Italian Foreign Secretary, Count Ciano, were most helpful in the discussion. It was they who very early in the proceedings, produced the Memorandum which M. Daladier and I were able to accept as a basis of discussion. I think that Europe and the world have reason to be grateful to the head of the Italian Government for his work in contributing to a peaceful solution. [...]

Source: Parliamentary Debates: House of Commons, Fifth Series–Volume 339, 3 October 1938 (London: His Majesty's Stationary Office, 1938), 47–50.

In my view the strongest force of all, one which grew and took fresh shapes and forms every day was the force not of any one individual, but was that unmistakable sense of unanimity among the peoples of the world that war somehow must be averted. The peoples of the British Empire were at one with those of Germany, of France and of Italy, and their anxiety, their intense desire for peace, pervaded the whole atmosphere of the conference, and I believe that that, and not threats, made possible the concessions that were made. I know the House will want to hear what I am sure it does not doubt, that throughout these discussions the Dominions, the Governments of the Dominions, have been kept in the closest touch with the march of events by telegraph and by personal contact, and I would like to say how greatly I was encouraged on each of the journeys I made to Germany by the knowledge that I went with the good wishes of the Governments of the Dominions. They shared all our anxieties and all our hopes. They rejoiced with us that peace was preserved, and with us they look forward to further efforts to consolidate what has been done.

Ever since I assumed my present office my main purpose has been to work for the pacification of Europe, for the removal of those suspicions and those animosities which have so long poisoned the air. The path which leads to appeasement is long and bristles with obstacles. The question of Czechoslovakia is the latest and perhaps the most dangerous. Now that we have got past it, I feel that it may be possible to make further progress along the road to sanity.

My right hon. Friend has alluded in somewhat bitter terms to my conversation last Friday morning with Herr Hitler. I do not know why that conversation should give rise to suspicion, still less to criticism. I entered into no pact. I made no new commitments. There is no secret understanding. Our conversation was hostile to no other nation. The objects of that conversation, for which I asked, was to try to extend a little further the personal contact which I had established

with Herr Hitler and which I believe to be essential in modern diplomacy. We had a friendly and entirely non-committal conversation, carried on, on my part, largely with a view to seeing whether there could be points in common between the head of a democratic Government and the ruler of a totalitarian State. We see the result in the declaration which has been published, in which my right hon. Friend finds so much ground for suspicion. What does it say?

There are three paragraphs. The first says that we agree

"in recognising that the question of Anglo-German relations is of the first importance for the two countries and for Europe."

Does anyone deny that? The second is an expression of opinion only. It says that:

"We regard the agreement signed last night and the Anglo-German Naval Agreement as symbolic of the desire of the two peoples never to go to war with one another again."

Once more I ask, does anyone doubt that that is the desire of the two peoples? What is the last paragraph?

"We are resolved that the method of consultation shall be the method adopted to deal with any other questions that may concern our two countries, and we are determined to continue our efforts to remove possible sources of difference and thus to contribute to assure the peace of Europe."

Who will stand up and condemn that sentence?

I believe there are many who will feel with me that such a declaration, signed by the German Chancellor and myself, is something more than a pious expression of opinion. In our relations with other countries everything depends upon there being sincerity and good will on both sides. I believe that there is sincerity and good will on both sides in this declaration. That is why to me its significance goes far beyond its actual words. If there is one lesson which we should learn from the events of these last weeks it is this, that lasting peace is not to be obtained by sitting still and waiting for it to come. It requires active, positive efforts to achieve it. No doubt I shall have plenty of critics who will say that I am guilty of facile optimism, and that I should disbelieve every word that is uttered by rulers of other great States in Europe. I am too much of a realist to believe that we are going to achieve our paradise in a day. We have only laid the foundations of peace. The superstructure is not even begun.

For a long period now we have been engaged in this country in a great programme of rearmament, which is daily increasing in pace and in volume. Let no one think that because we have signed this agreement between these four Powers at Munich we can afford to relax our efforts in regard to that programme at this moment. Disarmament on the part of this country can never be unilateral again. We have tried that once, and we very nearly brought ourselves to disaster. If disarmament is to come it must come by steps, and it must come by the agreement and the active co-operation of other countries. Until we know that we have obtained that co-operation and until we have agreed upon the actual steps to be taken, we here must remain on guard.

A Post-War Scholar Attacks Appeasement

The British scholar John Wheeler-Bennett was an early detractor of appeasement, writing the accusatory text Munich: Prologue to Tragedy *in 1948, only three years after the end of the war. Wheeler-Bennett is by no means the harshest of Chamberlain's critics, and acknowledges that Chamberlain was to some degree a victim of circumstances beyond his control. However, he argues, the choice to appease Hitler was a major error that had impact on Britain's relationship with the Soviet Union and the United States, and that incited Hitler to attack Poland in the belief that Britain would never intervene. He also contends that appeasement was a morally reprehensible policy.*

>> 96. Munich: Prologue to Tragedy

JOHN W. WHEELER-BENNETT [1948]

Let us say of the Munich Agreement that it was inescapable that, faced with the lack of preparedness in Britain's armaments and defences, with the lack of unity at home and in the Commonwealth, with the collapse of French morale, and with the uncertainty of Russia's capacity to fight, Mr. Chamberlain had no alternative to do other than he did; let us pay tribute to his persistence in carrying out a policy which he honestly believed to be right. Let us accept and admit all these things, but in so doing let us not omit the shame and humiliation which were ours; let us not forget that, in order to save our own skins—that because we were too weak to protect ourselves—we were forced to sacrifice a small Power to slavery. It is of no avail to say that we saved Czechoslovakia from that fate which was later suffered by our ally Poland, that, but for Munich, Bohemia and Moravia would have been devastated as were the provinces of Cracow and Lodz and Warsaw. In reality it was the Czechs who saved us, for, had President Benes elected to fight with Russian support and thus precipitate an Eastern European war, it is impossible to believe that Britain and France could have

Source: John W. Wheeler-Bennett, *Munich: Prologue to Tragedy* (London: Macmillan, 1966), 433, 435–437. Originally printed in 1948.

kept aloof, however reluctantly they might have been dragged into participation. [...]

Should we have fought in October 1938? On this point the military authorities on the highest level are divided. There are those who believe that, considering our lack of preparation, that Germany was from two to three years ahead of us in armaments, that France was in little better state than ourselves and Russia an unknown quantity, we were not only more than justified in not fighting in 1938, but were guilty, in Lord Trenchard's phrase, of "sheer audacity in going to war in 1939". Others maintain that, although our essential weakness must be admitted, it would have been better to have fought in 1938, since war with Germany was inevitable, with the military forces of Czechoslovakia and Russia on our side than later when Germany had been able to destroy the one and neutralize the other. They point out, in addition, that the German defences in the West were not completed in 1938 and that, in obtaining at Munich the necessary time for this, Germany profited more from the breathing-space than did Britain and France, since for her it represented a year's work at full speed, and to them only seven months' work at a varying tempo.

It is true that the interval between September 1938 and September 1939 enabled Mr. Chamberlain to meet the Polish crisis with the support of a united Britain and a united Commonwealth, and that the British Government no longer felt that it was useless to go to war if the immediate object of their assistance was to be at once overwhelmed by Germany. This had been the argument employed with Czechoslovakia in 1938, but by 1939 it had been realized that Hitler must be fought and beaten even with the certainty of initial reverses.

Yet it is equally true that if, in 1939, it was the hope of British statesmanship to avoid war, the chances of so doing had been materially diminished by the events of 1938, since Hitler can hardly be blamed for thinking that those Powers who had

abandoned an unassailably strong moral and political position in respect of Czechoslovakia, would not proceed to extremes in the case of Poland. Just as Mr. Chamberlain had failed to comprehend the depths of German infamy, so, in his turn, Hitler underestimated the capacity of the British for illogical virtue.

In the United States of America great harm was done to British prestige by the policy of Munich, harm of which the full degree was not to be realized until after the outbreak of the Second World War. France and Britain lost more friends in America, and the forces of Isolationism gained more recruits, by reason of the Munich Agreement than by almost any other event in the years between the wars. Though there was no great body of American opinion which would have favoured intervention on the side of Britain had she gone to war in 1938, the fact remains that the hands of those who bitterly opposed the granting of American aid in 1939–41 were substantially strengthened by the suspicion and mistrust of British policy which was engendered by her surrender at Munich, and the protagonists of the "all-aid-short-or-war" movement before Pearl Harbour numbered among them many former friends of Britain, who openly proclaimed that their motives were opposition to Hitler and not friendship for Britain. [...]

There remains the enigma of Russia, ever a sphinx, ever a mystery. Had Britain and France made in 1938 the advances to Moscow which they made a year later, would the result have been different? That Russia was prepared to fight at the time of Munich is more than a strong probability; it is only the effectiveness and capacity of her intervention which are in doubt. [...]

But, above all, the salient point of the story of Munich is not so much its immediate importance as its significance as an analysis of a case-history in the disease of political myopia which afflicted the leaders and the peoples of the world in the years between the wars. For the problem posed then is the same which confronts us now—and remains unsolved. It is not, fundamentally, a political or a technical problem; it is psychological and spiritual. Can we, with the experience of two world wars behind us, admit, both consciously and subconsciously, the essential truth that peace is one and indivisible; that, in our efforts "to seek peace and ensue it", we must realize that a threat to the peace of any country is a threat to ourselves—and must be recognized as such?

A Revisionist View of Appeasement

D. C. Watt is a revisionist scholar of appeasement. Revisionists argue that Chamberlain and his cabinet ministers were forced to consider the challenge of Hitler in terms of increasing threats to the British Empire in all regions of the world as well as British domestic attitudes, economy, and military preparedness. Some revisionists merely argue that these factors justify the decision to appease Hitler in Czechoslovakia, even if that policy was ultimately wrongheaded. Others actually argue that appeasement was necessary to give Britain time to prepare for war. In this excerpt of his book How War Came, *Watt gives us some idea of the important issues that influenced the decisions of Chamberlain and the British cabinet in October 1938.*

>> 97. How War Came: The Immediate Origins of the Second World War, 1938–1939

DONALD CAMERON WATT [1989]

Behind the disagreements within the Cabinet, and much of Whitehall, there were four elements which all held in common. The first was the memory of the four ghastly years, 1914–18. These years had seen the decimation—and more—of a generation of Britons. The losses of the war were remembered every year, on November 11, at 11 a.m. when, irrespective of the day of the week or the press of business, all activity stopped for two minutes. Those losses were, in most cases, intensely personal. Sons, husbands, lovers, fathers, school friends, neighbours, work-mates, all were missed and mourned. The daily lists of dead and wounded in the newspapers, the terror aroused by the appearance of a post office delivery man with a telegram the empty faces of those who returned, these memories were mingled with fears of a new war which would begin with death and destruction by bombs and poison gas rained from the sky. To these were added the memories and myths of the lost golden days of Edwardian greatness, vanished along with the financial supremacy that had been sold for American arms to outweigh German industrial superiority. A new war might well bring about defeat through bankruptcy.

To these worries were added those of 1931, memories of the vulnerability of sterling to short-term financial panic. In 1937 and 1938 Britain was still buying much more from abroad than she sold, even allowing for all the invisible items of trade, financial services, earnings from shipping, insurance and so on. All of these depended on a revival of world trade, as did the re-employment of those thrown out of work by the collapse of Britain's own primary industries, and the key to this was a rise in demand for the basic commodities—wheat, sugar, coal, rubber, sisal, tin

Source: Donald Cameron Watt, *How War Came: The Immediate Origins of the Second World War, 1938–1939* (London: Heinemann, 1989), 81–82.

and so on—upon which depended the well-being of Britain's colonial empire. An increase in world trade depended on an end to the closed economies of America and Germany, and to subsidized exports where prices were manipulated by devaluation or exchange control.

Third in the list was a common consciousness of the disparity between Britain's commitments and the resources available to defend them. Rearmament was essential in order to end the vulnerability, especially to air attack, which made British diplomatic pressure for peace, British efforts to defuse potential crises, not credible to those who had to be deterred. British power could never be adequate to face concurrent wars in Europe, the Mediterranean and the Far East. Britain needed fewer enemies; she needed, too, a measure of disarmament or arms control, especially in the air. But rearmament which weakened Britain's capacity to fight and win a long war was unwise. The dilemma lay in the need for rearmament to be visible and impressive, if it was to deter war. As war became seemingly more imminent, so the fears of bankruptcy, the gloomy prognostications of the Treasury, were progressively set aside. By December 1940, they had come true. Lend-lease provided the remedy; but in 1938 lend-lease was unimaginable.

The last, in these days of moral relativism, and in a world which, for better or worse, has ceased to uphold the moral values of nineteenth-century Europe, is the most difficult to explain. Chamberlain, the majority of British opinion with him, believed that peace was the normal state of relations between nations, and that that peace depended upon the observance by those nations of a number of rules and conventions of international behaviour, of which keeping one's word, and respect for the rights and interests of other nations were the most important. Not that these rules, like those of football, for instance, were not sometimes violated; but the adoption of a course of behaviour which ignored or flouted them could only be taken as criminal, marking the violator as one who was totally determined on war and conquest. Whatever the inner debates in Whitehall might have turned on, such violation was, after all, the reason which took Britain united into the war against Germany in 1914. It was this feeling which had so incensed, and which had been so exploited by, the Sovietophobes of the period 1917–30. Peace was a moral issue, it was true. But the defence of 'civilization'; the codeword for this complex of beliefs and attitudes, could, as a matter of hard necessity, override the avoidance of war.

Roosevelt and the Nazi Threat

John Wheeler-Bennett and other critics of appeasement argue that Chamberlain's policies had the effect of tilting the United States back toward isolationism. In fact, however, appeasement was only one factor in a complex relationship between the United States and Nazi Germany. Arnold Offner argues that the principal goal of the Roosevelt administration was in fact to preserve peace in Europe, but that especially after 1937 the President and his advisors came to consider Hitler and the Nazis a great threat to that peace. Eventually, this concern led Roosevelt to commit material and moral aid to Britain by becoming, as he declared in a December 29, 1940 speech, the "Arsenal of Democracy." However, the United States remained unwilling to commit to war throughout this period, and at least until summer 1940 Roosevelt still believed in a negotiated solution and therefore offered little real support to Britain and France.

>> 98. The United States and National Socialist Germany

ARNOLD A. OFFNER [1983]

From spring 1933 onwards Roosevelt received a steady stream of reports from business and diplomatic observers (many favourably disposed toward Germany) that Hitler had so extinguished personal liberty and brought to a frenzy nationalistic and militaristic passions that Germany, 'a nation which loves to be led, is again marching', and that the likelihood of war was at least 50 per cent. Ambassador Dodd's reports in 1934–5 on the 'extensive military preparation' in Germany led him to conclude that German annexations and predominance over 'the whole of Europe' was virtually inevitable, and that Germany's 'fixed purpose' was war within two or three years. By early 1935 Ambassador Long reported that he and every European leader (including Mussolini) expected war with Germany shortly, and that there was no escape from 'a real cataclysm'. Likewise Bullitt reported that he now agreed with Roosevelt's hunch that war would come first in Europe—not Asia—and that Hitler would advance down the Danube, or perhaps into the Ukraine, and that nothing could stop the 'horrible' march of events. Ambassador Cudahy stressed repeatedly that war was inevitable unless the Hitler government was 'overthrown and this war preparation brought to a stop'. By November 1936 Ambassador Davis concluded that it was impossible to achieve any arms agreement because no national leader believed that Germany, Italy, or Japan would honour it, and that 'it is not possible to reason with Dictators like Hitler and Mussolini, who had a

Frankenstein that forces them to keep on the move'.

Within this context the American response—frequently ambiguous and ambivalent—to the challenge of National Socialist Germany emerges. The Americans believed that post-1919 Europe needed political and economic reordering, including redress of German political and economic grievances. But the Americans' jaundiced view of the British and French meant pursuit of any diplomatic initiative at arm's length—and occasionally at cross purposes—while fear and loathing of National Socialism meant uncertainty as to whether Germany ought to be appeased faster or resisted sooner. Without choosing between alternatives, the Roosevelt administration in 1936 set out to preserve peace in Europe, which it believed to be in the same state as in 1914; 'at the mercy of an incident'. Thus Ambassador Bingham wrote from London that whereas Germany's unilateral revision of the Treaty of Versailles had brought political equality, Europe was dividing into two armed camps and that inevitably the United States would again be drawn into a European war. 'Therefore, the question arises as to what we can do in our own interest to aid an appeasement in Europe'. Moral leadership was ineffective, direct involvement in political settlements domestically unacceptable. Consequently, recourse had to be to traditional American faith in the peaceful effect of arms limitation, increased equality of access to markets and materials, and reduced trade barriers. [...]

Throughout the ensuing German-Czech crisis American policy remained of two minds. Roosevelt worried that negotiations would only postpone the 'inevitable conflict' and that the British and French would abandon Czechoslovakia and 'wash the blood from

Source: Arnold A. Offner, "The United States and National Socialist Germany," in *The Fascist Challenge and the Policy of Appeasement,* edited by Wolfgang J. Mommsen and Lothar Kettenacker (London: Goerge Allen & Unwin, 1983), 417–421.

their Judas Iscariot hands'. He also told the British that if Hitler got his way now he would press further territorial demands until war came. Yet the President said he did not want to encourage the Czechs to 'vain resistance', and he was prepared to attend a conference to reorganise 'all unsatisfactory frontiers on rational lines'. Roosevelt's cables to the heads of state on 26 September 'originally contained a definite hint of treaty revision' to induce Germany to request the President's good offices, but Hull watered it down. The Welles–Berle draft of Roosevelt's appeal to Hitler the next day suggested parallel political and economic conferences, but was then made less explicit. After the Munich Conference Welles said that there was now more opportunity than at any time in the last twenty years to establish an international order based upon law and justice, and Roosevelt wrote that he rejoiced that war had been averted. But soon he said that 'peace by fear has no higher or more enduring quality than peace by the sword'; or as Berle put it: 'A German government which was not heavily armed would be less of a threat to the outside world.'

By January 1939 Roosevelt was telling the Senate Military Affairs Committee in private that Germany, Italy and Japan sought 'world domination' and that America's first line of defence in the Atlantic included the 'continued, independent existence' of eighteen nations stretching from the Baltic through the Balkans to Turkey and Persia. The German occupation of Bohemia and Moravia in March 1939 and Italy's invasion of Albania in April led Berle to record that 'no one here has any illusions that the German Napoleonic machine will not extend itself indefinitely; and I suppose this is the year', while the State Department divided narrowly against breaking relations with Germany. Secretary of Agriculture Henry Wallace opposed an appeal to Hitler or Mussolini because 'the two madmen respect force and force alone', and it would only be 'delivering a sermon to a mad dog', Even

Hull warned a group of Congressmen that the coming struggle was not going to be 'another goddamn piddling dispute over a boundary line' but a global contest against nations 'practicing a philosophy of barbarism'. None the less, on 14 April Roosevelt proposed to Hitler and Mussolini ten-year non-aggression pacts in return for parallel political and economic appeasement conferences. The notes the President scrawled for use in conversation with the Italian Ambassador revealed FDR's mixed motives, or impulses: 'Muss. holds key to peace', Hitler was in 'bad shape' and needed war (and Italy, although he would 'cast her aside') as a 'way out'. Italy, he thought, should serve its best interests and 'sit around the table and work it out' and thereby 'save peace – save dom. of Europe by Germany''.

As the crisis over Poland developed. Americans believed that the Germans were 'beginning to beat the tom-toms for a final work up to a war psychology', and while 'readjustments in Central Europe are necessary', the Germans could not be allowed to dominate the Atlantic, and an unchecked German–Italian combination would leave the United States to confront 'imperialist schemes in South and Central America, not on a paper basis, as we do now, but backed up by an extremely strong naval and military force'. The Nazi–Soviet pact of 22 August created a 'bloc running from the Pacific clear to the Rhine', the 'combined Soviet–Nazi allies now have all Europe' and would partition Poland. The British, Welles felt, 'will sell out the Chinese completely…in return for an Anglo-Japanese understanding'. Roosevelt appealed to Berlin and Warsaw on 24 August for negotiations, but this was to do what had not been done in 1914: 'put the bee on Germany'.

The start of war produced many mediation calls, but Roosevelt turned these aside primarily because, as Hull said, the United States would not act to consolidate a regime of 'force and aggression'. The Soviet attack on Poland gave dark reality to Berle's 'nightmare': Hitler and Stalin 'able to rule from Manchuria to the Rhine...and nothing to stop the combined Russian–German force at any point...Europe is gone'. Roosevelt worried that the Germans intended to 'keep on going while the going was good', including 'into Persia or towards India'. Then there would be 'a drive at the west. The real objective would be to get into the Atlantic.' The ensuing Soviet 'dreadful rape of Finland' to use Roosevelt's words, left the Americans wondering what horrors would come next.

Despite the dark prospect—or perhaps because of it—Roosevelt inclined towards a negotiated settlement. The State Department believed that it might propose the principles of peace, and soon organised committees to consider postwar political, arms limitation and economic problems. Columnist Walter Lippmann expressed a public hope that the British and French, unencumbered as in the First World War by secret deals or territorial ambitions, could offer Germany 'a revision of the Versailles system', including colonies. Then in November and December the young, independent German emissary. Adam von Trott zu Solz, pressed State Department officials to urge

the Allies to offer a 'peace of reconciliation'. Finally there persisted hope, as Assistant Secretary Long summarised it, that the Germans might be tempted to 'retire' Hitler in favour of Goering: 'He is a practical man and not a psychopath like Hitler. The western Powers could deal with him.'

By December 1939 Roosevelt was hinting that he would make peace in the spring. He said he did not have the 1918 notion to make a century of peace, but he also feared a 'patched up temporizing peace which would blow up in our faces in a year or two'. Some observers, he said, felt the Russians and Germans would war, others felt that they would divide Europe and reach to Asia and Africa, and imperil the Americas. In January 1940 Roosevelt decided to send Welles to Europe on a mission that reflected the full ambiguity of American appeasement in the 1930s: at best Welles would achieve a negotiated settlement; perhaps he might divide Italy from Germany and postpone the spring offensives; at worst, the American people would start to think about the 'ultimate results in Europe and the Far East' and develop that needed 'deep sense of world crisis'.

Soviet Policy and the Nazi Threat

The Soviet Union had been born of the October 1917 Communist revolution. As well as transforming Russian society, the revolution ended Russian involvement in the First World War. The Bolshevik, Communist party that came to power was ostensibly internationalist in its outlook. But by the 1930s, under Josef Stalin, the Soviet Union's communist government was highly concerned with its continued existence as a state. Although enormous in size, the Soviet Union had few friends and, after the 1932 elections in Germany, was perched between hostile governments in both Germany and Japan. Hitler's rise to power in that year was highly problematic to the Soviets, especially as Hitler had explicitly claimed Soviet territory as German "living space." In this excerpt from a speech before the Central Executive Committee, Soviet People's Commissar for Foreign Affairs Maxim Litvinov spells out these dangers, but also proposes that the Soviet Union follow a pragmatic policy of peace to reach an agreement with the Nazis—a policy that was ultimately pursued. It is likely that Litvinov's speech was previously approved by Stalin and reflected Stalin's thinking.

>> 99. Address to the Central Executive Committee of the Soviet Union

MAXIM LITVINOV [1933]

Our relations with Germany during the last year have become, it may be said, unrecognizable.

In Germany speeches and declarations were made, and acts took place, which were not only not in consonance with our former relations, but rather gave one cause to think that these relations had been transformed into their very opposite. The causes for this have been as follows: With the change of Government in Germany which took place in 1932, a political leader obtained office and subsequently took the helm who, at the time of our very best relations with Germany, openly opposed these relations and advocated a *rapprochement* with the West for a joint attack upon the Soviet Union.

He organized a new political club where this idea was propagated, and he worked zealously for its realization. On coming to power he made an attempt, true unsuccessful, to realize this idea formally. Subsequently, a *coup d'état* occurred in Germany which brought a new party into power which propagated the most extreme anti-Soviet ideas. The founder of this party developed in detail his conception of the foreign policy of Germany in a literary work.

According to this conception, Germany had to reconquer not only everything she had lost by the Versailles Treaty, not only had she to conquer lands where there were German minorities, but by fire and sword she had to carve a way for herself for expansion eastwards, without stopping at the frontiers of the Soviet Union, and subject to her will the peoples of the U.S.S.R. . . . .

There have been, in addition, not a few anti-Soviet negotiations and proposals with the above ideas at their base entered into by people, not indeed occupying State posts, but, nevertheless, in very responsible positions. . . . All this is what has made our former relations with Germany unrecognizable.

I considered it necessary to say this openly since, on the German side, attempts are often made to ascribe to us the initiative for the change in our relations and to explain it as the result of our displeasure at the present régime which persecutes Communists, and others. We, of course, have our own opinion about the German régime. We, of course, sympathize with the sufferings of our German comrades, but we Marxists are the last who can be reproached with allowing our feelings to dictate our policy.

The whole world knows that we can and do maintain good relations with capitalist States of any régime, including the Fascist. We do not interfere in the internal affairs of Germany, as we do not interfere in that of other countries, and our relations with her are conditioned not by her internal but by her external policy. . . . .

I am asked by representatives of the German Government what exactly is it that we want from Germany and what she must do to set our doubts at rest regarding her loyalty. To this I generally reply, let her not do what she is doing. Let the German Government look into what her numerous agents and emissaries are doing, and let her tell them that they should not do it.

But we also make the following declaration: We desire to have with Germany, as with other States, the best of relations. Nothing but good can result from such relations, both for the Soviet Union and Germany. We on our side are not striving to expand either on the west, or on the east, or in any other direction. We have no feelings of hostility towards the German people and are not preparing to attack either their territory or their rights, and whatever we may do we shall never encourage other States to make such attacks.

Source: Maxim Litvinov, Address to the Central Executive Committee of the Soviet Union, 29 December 1933, in *Documentary Background of World War II, 1931 to 1941,* edited by James W. Gantenbein (New York: Columbia University Press, 1948), 544–545.

We should be glad if Germany could say the same to us and if there were no facts which could contradict them. We would desire to be assured that such declarations referred, not only to the present moment, but also to that time when she will have stronger forces for realizing those aggressive ideas which her present leaders preached before their rise to power, and which some of them preach even now.

>> Mastering the Material

1. Why do you think Haile Selassie's speech failed to convince the League of Nations to intervene in the Italian invasion of Abyssinia?

2. How did Chamberlain defend the Munich agreement before Parliament? Do you think he truly trusted Hitler, or was he just buying time?

3. Do you agree with Wheeler-Bennett that appeasement was morally reprehensible, or do you think, given the situation in which Britain found itself in the fall of 1938, that it was a morally defensible policy?

4. What does Watt suggest were the underpinning reasons that Chamberlain and his cabinet chose to follow a policy of appeasement?

5. Compare and contrast Watt's four "common elements" to Chamberlain's own speech and Wheeler-Bennet's comments. Why do *you* think Chamberlain chose to follow a policy of appeasement?

6. According to Offner, what was Roosevelt's reaction to the Munich agreement in September–October 1938?

7. Offner suggests that American officials increasingly saw Hitler and the Nazis as "mad dogs" in the period 1937–1939. Why then did Roosevelt try to end the war through negotiations, rather than committing to the side of Britain and France at this time?

8. Litvinov's speech illustrates the antagonism between Soviet and Nazi ideologies, yet the two powers signed a treaty of nonaggression in August 1939 that enabled Hitler to safely invade Poland. How do you explain this?

>> Making Connections

1. Looking at the readings in this chapter in conjunction with those in Chapter 19, to what degree were the policies of Britain, the Soviet Union, and the United States to blame for the origin of the war? To what degree can we place the blame solely upon Japan, Germany, and Italy?

2. Why do you think most scholarly accounts of the Second World War to date focus upon the policies of the great states, rather than underpinning social, political, cultural, or economic causes, as in the case of the First World War?

Chapter 21

The Holocaust

One of the principal features of Second World War–era hypernationalist fascist ideology was the vilification of those who were considered "outside" the nation. As we have seen, fascist doctrine portrayed the struggle between nations as the central feature of world history. Even within the nation, fascism called for the elimination of members of other political parties, especially social democrats and communists. These ideological principles were often expressed physically through violence against ethnic minorities as well as political dissidents. Italian atrocities in Libya, the execution of anarchists and socialists by Spanish fascists, and the massacre of Chinese and other civilian populations by Japanese troops were all justified by racialism and the notion of war as part of a struggle between nations rather than merely armies.

However, it is the murder of 15 to 25 million political prisoners, ethnic minorities, and especially Jewish Europeans by the Nazis that stands out as the most extreme, brutal, and chilling manifestation of the fascist doctrines of aggression, nationalism, racialism, and totalitarianism. From the beginning of his political career, Hitler had espoused **anti-Semitic** (prejudiced against Jews) ideas, and Nazi state-sanctioned persecution of the Jewish minority in Germany began soon after they seized power. Laws implemented in 1933–1934 restricted Jews from owning land, editing newspapers, practicing law, and participating in public life. The 1935 Nuremberg race laws forbade Jews from marrying non-Jews. On 9 November 1938, the Nazis organized the coordinated attack on Jewish homes and businesses known as *Kristallnacht,* or "the night of broken glass." During the same period, the Nazi party established concentration camps for homosexuals, political opponents, and accused criminals. Soon Jews, Gypsies, and other ethnic minorities were being confined in these camps.

Initially some Nazi rhetoric called for the relocation or isolation of ethnic populations, but by early 1942 a decision was made to commit genocide: the extermination of the entire Jewish population. The German conquest of much of Europe in 1940 and 1941 had brought most of the world's Jewish population under Nazi control. Europe's Jews were first isolated in urban ghettoes and subsequently shipped to large concentration camps in Germany and the conquered territories. In the conquered territories of the Soviet Union, special squads called *Einsatzgruppen* followed the combat troops and murdered Soviet Jews as well as political figures and military officers. In December 1941 poison gas was first used to efficiently murder large groups of civilians at concentration camps in Poland. Eventually, six million Jews would be murdered in this **Holocaust,** most in these camps.

The discovery of the Nazi genocide by the allied armies was so shocking that it provoked intense debate by scholars who sought to understand how such a terrible process could have happened. Two main lines of analysis characterize this debate. The first seeks to understand whether the Holocaust was planned by the Nazis from the beginning or whether it developed gradually over time. The second interrogates the causes of the Holocaust: Was it a product of unique Nazi ideologies? of a propensity for racialism and violence in German society? Or was it simply the culmination of the nationalism and industrial modernization that had helped produce the First and Second World Wars?

The dominant interpretation immediately following the war was the intentionalist reading of the evidence. As in the debate over the origins of the war, the intentionalists studying the Holocaust argued that Hitler's role was central, and that Hitler and the Nazis had plotted the campaign against the Jews in the same way as they had planned the war itself. Intentionalists like Lucy Dawidowicz, in *The Holocaust and the Historians,* suggest that the Holocaust was something uniquely German, a result of the **Sonderweg,** or "special path" of Germany. Leading proponents of the *Sonderweg* include Fritz Fischer, who connected the two wars and the Holocaust by suggesting that German aggression was the result of a unique path of development. Germany, Fischer and others argued, had failed to develop strong institutions of democracy in the nineteenth and early twentieth century, instead evolving a peculiar alliance of industrialists and authoritarians that led Germany on the path to war and genocide.

Beginning in the 1960s, new interpretations emerged that competed with the intentionalist school. We tend to call this approach **structuralism,** because its proponents argue that the institutions and processes of Nazi governance and society created the Holocaust through an ad-hoc process. Although the structuralists agree that anti-Semitism in Germany dated back some centuries, they contend that there was no plan for genocide before the war broke out. Instead, the "final solution" to exterminate the Jews developed gradually during the war years. One of the most important structuralist articles, Christian Gerlach's "The Wannsee Conference, the Fate of German Jews, and Hitler's Decision in Principle to Exterminate All European Jews" illustrates this process. Gerlach's article discusses a single event: the Conference of Nazi leaders at Wannsee in January 1941, a record of which serves as source 102 in this chapter. In the article, Gerlach advances the assertion that that Nazi policy toward Jewish populations was at first haphazard. It was in the conquered regions of Russia that German soldiers were first ordered to shoot Jews as if they were partisans. By December 1941 this policy was extended across eastern Europe. The Conference at Wannsee in the same month was arguably the moment at which the Nazi party leadership decided to implement a structured and extensive policy of methodically exterminating the Jewish populations of Europe.

Another challenge to the intentionalists came from historians who disputed the uniqueness of the Holocaust. Scholars of colonialism, especially Hannah Arendt in her seminal work *The Origins of Totalitariansm,* point to connections between the Holocaust and military operations in German overseas colonies before the First World War. In these colonies, racialized scientific research and the mass killing of anti-colonial rebels were sanctioned by administrative policy. Nor were these atrocities limited to German colonies. Arendt was followed by Swedish author Sven Lindqvist, who shows in his book *Exterminate All the Brutes* how colonial administrations around the world pioneered such strategies and policies as concentration camps, manmade famines, the execution of women and children, and arguably genocide. For Lindqvist the Holocaust, while unique in Europe, simply mirrored the nineteenth- and twentieth-century hunting to near-extermination of indigenous populations in Australia, the ethnic cleansing of the Armenian population of Turkey, and the development of relocation and concentration camps in Cuba and South Africa. Yet it remains debatable whether the Holocaust was merely a change of scenery. Never before had genocide been carried out in such a planned and extensive fashion. In many ways, the Holocaust was symptomatic of the nationalism and industrial modernization of the twentieth century. In other ways, as Dawidowicz argues, it was probably unique in human history.

An Intentionalist Perspective on the Holocaust

Lucy Dawidowicz is a modern proponent of the intentionalist school of Holocaust studies. In this introductory section from her historiographical survey of Holocaust studies, Dawidowicz makes three connected arguments. The first is that the Holocaust was interlinked with Nazi war plans. The second is that the Nazis had planned to eliminate the Jews even before the war. Finally, she says that the murder of Jews was a unique event in world history.

>> 100. The Holocaust and the Historians

LUCY S. DAWIDOWICZ [1981]

While planning and conducting the military war to gain *Lebensraum*—"living space" for the German people—and mastery over the whole European continent, Germany simultaneously planned and carried out a systematic program of mass murder. The National Socialists regarded this mass murder as nothing less than an ideological war and its prosecution was synergized with the conventional military war. The High Command of the German Armed Forces conducted the military war, while the SS, the dreaded armed police force of the National

Socialist movement, conducted the ideological war. Both wars were concurrent undertakings, strategically and operationally meshed. The success of the mass-murder offensive was made possible by the SS's parasitic dependence upon Germany's military establishment and its national wartime resources, and the operations of the military war provided the cover for the mass murder.

The mass murder represented itself as a holy war to annihilate Germany's "mortal enemy." The mortal enemy—*Todfeind* was Hitler's word—consisted of the Jews, who were, according to the doctrines of National Socialism, the chief antagonists to the German "Aryans." In Nazi ideology the Jew was the primal adversary,

Source: Lucy S. Dawidowicz, *The Holocaust and the Historians* (Cambridge: Harvard University Press, 1981), 8–9, 11–15.

the biological archenemy of the German people, whose physical presence, it was alleged, threatened the purity and even the very existence of the "Aryan" race. No other people, nation, or "race" held that status. [...]

The Jews: A Special Case

The fate of the Jews under National Socialism was unique. They obsessed Hitler all his life and their presence in Germany, their very existence, preoccupied the policymakers of the German dictatorship. The *Judenfrage*—the question of the Jews—riveted all Germany. The age-old heritage of anti-Semitism, compounded of Christian prejudices, economic rivalries, and social envy, was fanned by Nazi racism. Every German city, town, and village applied itself to the Jews and the Jewish question with rampant violence and meticulous legalism.

Once the National Socialists came to power, they incorporated their racist beliefs into law, in a short time enacting a major corpus of anti-Jewish legislation. The laws established legal definitions of the Jews and then, step by step, deprived the Jews of their rights, their property, and their livelihoods. In time, the Jews became segregated and ostracized from German society and were deprived of the protection of the law—even such as it was in Nazi Germany.

But National Socialist Germany had a still more radical objective with regard to the Jews: total annihilation. The war which Hitler unleashed in September 1939 was intended to achieve that objective while the Germans also pursued their aggressive expansionism against the nations of Europe.

The German dictatorship devised two strategies to conduct its war of annihilation against the Jews: mass shooting and mass gassing. Special-duty troops of the SS's Security Service and Security Police, called *Einsatzgruppen,* were assigned to each of the German armies invading the Soviet Union. Following hard upon the armed forces and dependent upon them for basic services, the Einsatzgruppen were given the task of rounding up the Jews and killing them. The procedures used everywhere behind the Russian front were crude and primitive. (To talk of harnessing modern technology to mass murder is nonsense.) The Jews were loaded on trucks or forced to march to some desolate area with antitank trenches already dug or natural ravines. Otherwise, the Jews were ordered to dig what would become their own mass graves. Then they were machine-gunned at the rim of the trench or pit into which their bodies toppled. The International Military Tribunal at Nuremberg estimated that the Einsatzgruppen murdered about 2 million Jews.

To systematize the murder of the rest of the European Jews the National Socialist state built six installations with large-scale gassing facilities and with crematoria for the disposal of the bodies. These were all located on Polish territory: Oświęcim (better known by its German name, Auschwitz), Belzec, Chelmno, Majdanek, Sobibór, and Treblinka. The technology applied here—discharging poison gas through showerhead vents in sealed chambers—was barely more sophisticated than the brute violence of the Einsatzgruppen. The logistics, however, were impressive, and in the three years during which these killing installations operated, about 3.5 million Jews from every country of Europe were murdered there. (Approximately 1.5 million non-Jews were gassed in these camps, most at Auschwitz.)

Of the 9 million Jews who lived in the countries of Europe that fell under German rule during the war, about 6 million—that is, two-thirds of all European Jews—were murdered. Their numbers and concentration in Eastern Europe and their uninterrupted cultural traditions there for a thousand years had rendered them the most vital Jewish community, whose creativity sustained Jews throughout the world. Though the Soviet Union suffered greater losses than the Jews in absolute figures, no other people anywhere lost the main body of its population and the fountainhead of its cultural resources. No other people were chosen for total extinction.

The deaths of the 6 million European Jews were not a by-product of the war. The Jews did not die as a consequence of the indiscriminate reach of bombs or gunfire or of the unselective fallout of deadly weapons. Nor were they the victims of the cruel and brutal expediency that actuated the Nazis to kill the Soviet prisoners of war and the Polish elite. Those murders were intended as means to practical ends: they were meant to protect and to consolidate the position of the Germans as undisputed masters over Europe. The murder of the Jews and the destruction of Jewish communal existence were, in contrast, ends in themselves, ultimate goals to which the National Socialist state had dedicated itself.

To refer to the murder of the 6 million Jews as distinctive, as unique, is not an attempt to magnify the catastrophe that befell them nor to beg tears and pity for them. It is not intended to minimize the deaths of the millions of non-Jews that the Germans brought about, or to underplay the immeasurable and unendurable suffering of Russians, Poles, Gypsies, and other victims of the German murder machine. To speak of the singularity of the murder of the 6 million European Jews is not to deny the incontestable fact that the gas chambers extinguished without discrimination all human life. The murder of the 6 million Jews stands apart from the deaths of the other millions, not because of any distinctive fate that the individual victims endured, but because of the differentiative intent of the murderers and the unique effect of the murders. [...]

The Holocaust Universalized: Metaphor and Analogy

The murder of the 6 million Jews, in its unparalleled scope, devastating effect, and incomprehensible intent, overtook the capacity of man's imagination to conceive of evil. The killing camps, an empire of death with their bulging gas chambers and smoke-belching crematoria operated by the SS Death's Head Division, eclipsed man's visions of hell. The names of these death factories—and especially the name of Auschwitz—replaced Dante's Nine Circles of Hell as the quintessential epitome of evil, for they were located not in the literary reaches of the medieval religious imagination, but in the political reality of twentieth-century Europe.

A Structuralist Interpretation of the Wannsee Conference

Structuralists have responded to intentionalists with evidence that the decision to exterminate Jews was made only late in the war, probably after the United States entered. Up until that date, they argue, treatment of Jews was uneven and most decisions were made at a local level rather than directed from the top. The German historian Christian Gerlach made this argument minutely in this 1998 article, first printed in German the previous year. Gerlach suggests that the Hitler ordered a "final solution"—genocide against the Jews—in mid-December 1941. Before that date, while some Jewish populations had been exterminated, others had experienced deportation to work camps, were forced into ghettoes, or in some cases merely faced significant discrimination. Hitler's decision, Gerlach argues, was promulgated by a January conference in Wannsee, outside of Berlin. Although initially scheduled to organize deportations, the conferees instead developed a blueprint for genocide.

>> 101. The Wannsee Conference, the Fate of German Jews, and Hitler's Decision in Principle to Exterminate All European Jews

CHRISTIAN GERLACH [1998]

In the following essay I will attempt to show that, despite all the attention paid to it, the significance of the Wannsee Conference of January 20, 1942, has not been fully appreciated. First, it was a precondition not just for the execution of the "eastern Jews" but also for the extermination of German and western European Jews. Second, it was closely connected with Hitler's fundamental decision to proceed with the liquidation of *all* Jews living in Europe. In my opinion, Hitler made this decision in early December 1941. At least that is when he first made it public, with clear and calamitous consequences. It was not a solitary decision. Hitler was reacting to political impulses and initiatives that originated from within the administration and from inside the party apparatus. In order to show this clearly, I will first examine the course of events through the end of 1941. By that time, a liquidation of the Jews had already begun in the German-occupied areas of the Soviet Union and in some other parts of eastern Europe. As of the autumn of 1941, however, when the mass deportations of Jews from the German Reich began, a decision to exterminate them had not yet been made. That becomes evident from the different kinds of treatment the German Jewish deportees received when they arrived at their various destinations.

It was in this context that the Wannsee meeting was originally conceived. At this stage, its purpose—as I will show ill the second section of this article—was to resolve existing differences between governmental and party functionaries as to the future treatment of German Jews and, presumably, of Jews from the remainder of western Europe as well. In particular, one of its aims was to work out a viable definition of who was to be treated as a Jew. But the conference had to be postponed, and Hitler's fundamental decision to liquidate all European Jews [...] altered the context in which the meeting was eventually to take place. [...]

The Wannsee Conference was a meeting between representatives from the RSHA and state secretaries and other officials from the ministerial bureaucracy. Its purpose was to discuss the "Final Solution of the Jewish Question." It took place on January 20, 1942. It had originally been scheduled to occur on December 9, 1941. Initial invitations to participate had gone out on November 29. [...]

The decision to "exterminate the Jews in Europe" must have been made after December 7 and before December 14, 1941.

It is well known that Hitler in an infamous speech to the Reichstag on January 30, 1939, had spoken as follows: "If the world of international financial Jewry, both in and outside of Europe, should succeed in plunging the nations into another *world war,* the result will not be the Bolshevization of the world and thus a victory for Judaism. The result will be the extermination of the Jewish race in Europe." Hitler announced his declaration of war against the United States in the Reichstag on December 11, 1941. For Germany, that made the war a world war. Thus the situation Hitler had envisioned in 1939 had come about. With complete logical consistency—consistent within the framework of his antisemitic worldview—Hitler then proclaimed his decision to exterminate all Jews in Europe. He did not, to be sure, include this announcement in his Reichstag speech of December 11, a speech

Source: Christian Gerlach, "The Wannsee Conference, the Fate of German Jews, and Hitler's Decision in Principle to Exterminate All European Jews," *The Journal of Modern History* 70 (1998): 760–761, 764, 784–785, 793–794, 808–809, 811–812.

broadcast on radio. In that speech he claimed only that Jewish war agitators were behind Roosevelt. But on the following afternoon, December 12, 1941, Hitler addressed a meeting of the most important sectional leaders of the National Socialist Party (the *Reichsleiter*) and of regional party leaders (the *Gauleiter*). According to Goebbels's notes on this meeting of the *Reichsleiter* and *Gauleiter,* Hitler spoke as follows:

Regarding the Jewish question, the Führer is determined to clear the table. He warned the Jews that if they were to cause another world war, it would lead to their own destruction. Those were not empty words. Now the world war has come. The destruction of the Jews must be its necessary consequence. We cannot be sentimental about it. It is not for us to feel sympathy for the Jews. We should have sympathy rather with our own German people. If the German people have to sacrifice 160,000 victims in yet another campaign in the east, then those responsible for this bloody conflict will have to pay for it with their lives.

There were other occasions, too, both before and after December 1941, when Hitler made reference to his infamous "prophecy." But he never before did so as clearly, as unambiguously, or in such a matter-of-fact way as recorded here by Goebbels. What Hitler said was not intended metaphorically or as propaganda—that is the meaning of Goebbels's phrase, "Those were not empty words." Above all, Hitler had now spoken of the beginning of total annihilation. [...]

On December 8, 1941, one day before it was originally scheduled to take place, the Wannsee Conference was postponed indefinitely. [...]

Heydrich opened the meeting with a long presentation. He reviewed Göring's commission to "prepare a Final Solution for the Jewish Question in Europe." He emphasized that overall responsibility and authority were his. He expressed his desire that all their efforts should proceed, after appropriate consultation, in parallel. Finally, he summarized the progress of antisemitic policies, emphasizing developments since 1939: the stage of forced individual emigration and, "with appropriate prior approval by the Führer," the stage of collective "evacuation of the Jews to the east."

He then went on to outline his plan for a "Final Solution," involving the mass murder of Jews from all the countries of Europe, including allied, neutral, and hostile nations. Some of the Jews would first be employed for forced labor. [...]

In the final analysis, what really matters is that the suggestion that there never was a central decision made by Hitler regarding the extermination of the European Jews cannot be sustained. Equally unsupportable is the thesis that the final decision was not made until May or June of 1942. The fundamental decision announced in December of 1941 is a crucial missing piece of the decision-making process leading up to the liquidation of the Jews. Hitler's decision put the planning for these crimes on a new basis. But it relieved no one of responsibility. Its result was that the various existing ideas, proposals, and initiatives for extermination projects at the regional levels received support and legitimation. They received new impetus and became systematized. Significantly, only four days before the Führer's decision, and independent of it, the first extermination camp at Chelmno had begun its grisly work. [...]

In order to understand the decision-making process that led to the destruction of the European Jews it may be useful to refer to the concept of the utopian. The National Socialists, with Hitler foremost among them, certainly entertained ideas about eliminating the Jews and indicated a willingness to put these ideas into practice well before 1941. But there is a difference between having ideas or intentions to exterminate a people and the actual implementation of those ideas and intentions. The initial schemes for a "Final Solution" involved various plans for a forced migration. They were markedly destructive in character, with features such as slow annihilation through brutal living conditions and limits on reproduction. In a way, however, these plans were also utopian, principally because none of them, however seriously pursued, had any practical chance of being realized. This was as true of the Madagascar plan as it was of the 1939–40 plan to deport Jews to the Lublin district. Destructive elements grew more pronounced in the plan to deport European Jews to conquered regions of the Soviet Union following a successful conclusion of the war there. Exactly how to go about exterminating the Jews became imaginable only little by little, even though a widespread readiness to do so had long existed. What was decisive for the actual realization of mass murder plans were the intermediate steps between the utopian emigration and extermination schemes, on the one hand, and liquidation programs that could be practically implemented, on the other. The scheme proposed at the outset of 1941 to reduce some thirty million individuals in the Soviet Union to starvation in order to guarantee food supplies to the European areas controlled by Germany proved to be impractical. It was replaced in the fall of 1941 by programs for eliminating groups of specific individuals, like the millions of Soviet war prisoners who were "incapable of work." For the antisemitic efforts, the steps undertaken in December 1941 marked an ominous turn toward the practical implementation of concrete measures for racial genocide.

Although these monstrous developments could certainly not be called normal politics, and although Hitler intervened directly, in one sense this life or death decision regarding the fate of the Jews living in Europe came to pass in a manner very much like any other "normal" political decision. The Führer did not make the decision alone; he made it only after some time had passed; and, in a specific situation and for a specific set of reasons, he gave his approval to initiatives that had arisen from the administrative and party apparatus. As with many evolving policies, the demands for the extermination of the European Jews came from many sources. Before they could all be acted upon in some systematic manner, however, the National Socialist system required a leadership decision by Hitler.

Protocol of the Wannsee Conference, 20 January 1942

The Wannsee Conference was presided over by SS-Lieutenant General Reinhard Heydrich, Chief of the Security Police and Security Service. The minutes were recorded by SS Lt-Colonel Adolf Eichmann. Both were important architects of the Holocaust and were later convicted of crimes against humanity. Much of the conference was taken up with the details of the mechanics of moving an estimated 11 million people throughout the Nazi empire, and with a debate over how to deal with mischlinge, *or part-Jews. At Eichmann's 1961 trial, however, he made it clear that the core topic of discussion was the genocide of the Jewish population: "they, in very direct words—not the words I had to use in the Protocol, but in very direct words—called things as they were, with no attempt to disguise them." The decision to commit genocide is hidden in the Protocol but can be ascertained through certain phrases such as "they would have to be dealt with appropriately" and the "final solution."*

>> 102. Protocol of the Wannsee Conference

ADOLF EICHMANN [1942]

II. The meeting opened with the announcement by the Chief of the Security Police and the SD, SS *Obergruppenführer* Heydrich, of his appointment by the Reich Marshall as Plenipotentiary for the Preparation of the Final Solution of the European Jewish Question. He noted that this Conference had been called in order to obtain clarity on questions of principle. The Reich Marshal's request for a draft plan concerning the organizational, practical and economic aspects of the final solution of the European Jewish question required prior joint consideration by all central agencies directly involved in these questions, with a view to maintaining parallel policy lines.

Responsibility for the handling of the final solution of the Jewish question, he said, would lie centrally with the *Reichsführer* SS and the Chief of the German Police (Chief of the Security Police and the SD), without regard to geographic boundaries.

The Chief of the Security Police and the SD then gave a brief review of the struggle conducted up to now against this foe.

The most important elements are:
a) Forcing the Jews out of the various areas of life (*Lebensgebiete*) of the German people.
b) Forcing the Jews out of the living space (*Lebensraum*) of the German people.

In pursuit of these aims, the accelerated emigration of the Jews from the area of the Reich, as the only possible provisional solution, was pressed forward and carried out according to plan.

On instructions by the Reich Marshal, a Reich Central Office for Jewish Emigration was set up in January 1939, and its direction entrusted to the Chief of the Security Police and the SD. Its tasks were, in particular:
a) To take all measures for the *preparation* of increased emigration of the Jews;
b) To *direct* the flow of emigration;
c) To speed up emigration in *individual* cases.

The aim of this task was to cleanse the German living space of Jews in a legal manner. [...]

III. Emigration has now been replaced by evacuation of the Jews to the East, as a further possible solution, with the appropriate prior authorization by the Führer.

However, this operation should be regarded only as a provisional option; but it is already supplying practical experience of great significance in view of the coming final solution of the Jewish question.

In the course of this final solution of the European Jewish question approximately 11 million Jews may be taken into consideration. [...]

Under appropriate direction the Jews are to be utilized for work in the East in an expedient manner in the course of the final solution. In large (labor) columns, with the sexes separated, Jews capable of work will be moved into these areas as they build roads, during which a large proportion will no doubt drop out through natural reduction. The remnant that eventually remains will require suitable treatment; because it will without doubt represent the most [physically] resistant part, it consists of a natural selection that could, on its release, become the germcell of a new Jewish revival. (Witness the experience of history.)

Europe is to be combed through from West to East in the course of the practical implementation of the final solution. The area of the Reich, including the Protectorate of Bohemia and Moravia, will have to be handled in advance, if

Source: Adolf Eichmann, "Protocol of the Wannsee Conference," 20 January 1942, translated by Lea Ben Dor in *Documents on the Holocaust,* edited by Yitzhak Arad, Yisrael Gutman, and Abraham Margaliot (Jerusalem: Ktav Publishing House, 1981), 250–251, 253, 256–257, 260–261.

only because of the housing problem and other socio-political needs.

The evacuated Jews will first be taken, group by group, to so-called transit ghettos, in order to be transported further east from there. [...]

IV. In the implementation of the plan for the final solution, the Nuremberg Laws are to form the basis, as it were; a precondition for the total clearing up of the problem will also require solutions for the question of mixed marriages and *Mischlinge.* [...]

SS *Gruppenführer* Hofmann is of the opinion that extensive use must be made of sterilization, as the *Mischling,* given the choice of evacuation or sterilization, would prefer to accept sterilization.

Secretary of State Dr. Stuckart noted that in this form the practical aspects of the possible solutions proposed above for the settling of the problems of mixed marriages and *Mischlinge* would entail endless administrative work. In order to take the biological realities into account, at any rate, Secretary of State Dr. Stuckart proposed a move in the direction of compulsory sterilization.

To simplify the problem of the *Mischlinge* further possibilities should be considered, with the aim that the Legislator should rule something like: "These marriages are dissolved."

As to the question of the effect of the evacuation of the Jews on the economy, Secretary of State Neumann stated that Jews employed in essential war industries could not be evacuated for the present, as long as no replacements were available.

SS *Obergruppenführer* Heydrich pointed out that those Jews would not be evacuated in any case, in accordance with the directives approved by him for the implementation of the current evacuation *Aktion.*

Secretary of State Dr. Bühler put on record that the Government-General would welcome it if the final solution of this problem *was begun in the Government-General,* as, on the one hand, the question of transport there played no major role and considerations of labor supply would not hinder the course of this *Aktion.* Jews must be removed as fast as possible from the Government-General, because it was there in particular that the Jew as carrier of epidemics spelled a great danger, and, at the same time, he caused constant disorder in the economic structure of the country by his continuous black-market dealings. Furthermore, of the approximately $2^1/_2$ million Jews under consideration, the majority were in any case *unfit for work.*

Secretary of State Dr. Bühler further states that the solution of the Jewish question in the Government-General was primarily the responsibility of the Chief of the Security Police and the SD and that his work would have the support of the authorities of the Government-General. He had only one request: that the Jewish question in this area be solved as quickly as possible.

In conclusion, there was a discussion of the various possible forms which the solution might take, and here both *Gauleiter* Dr. Meyer and Secretary of state Dr. Bühler were of the opinion that certain preparatory work for the final solution should be carried out locally in the area concerned, but that, in doing so, alarm among the population must be avoided.

The conference concluded with the request of the Chief of the Security Police and the SD to the participants at the conference to give him the necessary support in carrying out the tasks of the [final] solution.

The Colonial Origins of Genocide?

Sven Lindqvist's part-travelogue, part-bibliographical Exterminate All the Brutes *is an exploration of the relationship between imperialism and the Holocaust. It is a personal journey to understand the final words of the anti-hero Kurtz in Joseph Conrad's famous novel on imperialism,* Heart of Darkness. *In the book, Lindqvist seeks to understand the origins of the racialism that accompanied the new imperialism and that he argues culminated in the genocide of the Second World War. Lindqvist suggests that this slaughter of civilians was made possible by more than a century of European (and American and Japanese) ideology that the extermination of other "races" was appropriate.*

>> 103. Exterminate All the Brutes

SVEN LINDQVIST [1992]

A battle over the living past is going on at present in Germany. This *Historikerstreit,* as they call it, concerns the question: Is the Nazi extermination of the Jews unique or not?

The German historian Ernst Nolte has called "the so-called extermination of the Jews by the Third Reich" "a reaction or a distorted copy and not an original action." The original was, according to Nolte, the extermination of the Kulaks in the Soviet Union and Stalin's purges in the 1930s. They were what Hitler copied.

The idea that the extermination of the Kulaks *caused* the extermination of the Jews seems to have been abandoned, and many people emphasize that all historical events are unique and not copies of each other. But they can be compared. Thus both likenesses and differences arise between the extermination of the Jews and other mass murders, from the massacre of the Armenians at the beginning of the 1900s to the more recent atrocities of Pol Pot.

But in this debate no one mentions the German extermination of the Herero people in southwest Africa during Hitler's childhood. No one mentions the corresponding genocide by the French, the British, or the Americans. No one points out that during Hitler's childhood, a major element in the European view of mankind was the conviction that "inferior races" were by nature condemned to extinction: the true compassion of the superior races consisted in helping them on the way.

All German historians participating in this debate seem to look in the same direction. None looks to the west. But Hitler did. What Hitler wished to create when he sought *Lebensraum* in the east was a continental equivalent of the British Empire. It was in the British and other western European peoples that he found the models, of which the extermination of the Jews is, in Nolte's words, "a distorted copy." [...]

On the night of September 18, 1941, Hitler painted for his collaborators a rosy future in which the Ukraine and the Volga basin had become the bread basket of Europe. There, German industry would exchange grain for cheap utility goods. "We'll send to the Ukraine kerchiefs, glass beads, and other things colonial peoples like."

Of course, he was joking. But to understand Hitler's campaign to the east it is important to realize that he considered he was fighting a colonial war. For wars of that kind, special rules applied—those already laid down in *Politik* (1898) by the German extreme right's most beloved political scientist, Heinrich von Treitschke: "International law becomes phrases if its standards are also applied to barbaric people. To punish a Negro tribe, villages must be burned, and without setting examples of that kind, nothing can be achieved. If the German Reich in such cases applied international law, it would not be humanity or justice but shameful weakness."

Treitschke was only putting into words the practice European states had long applied and which Hitler now used against his future "colonial peoples" in the east. [...]

Source: Sven Lindqvist, *Exterminate All the Brutes* (New York: The New Press, 1996), 10, 157–160. Originally published in Swedish in 1992.

"Many of the most horrendous of Nazi actions (especially the massacre of the Jews)… had comparatively little to do with the imperialist parts of the Nazi program," writes Woodruff D. Smith in *The Ideological Origins of Nazi Imperialism* (1986).

Smith is a great specialist in this field, but in my opinion he is wrong. Imperialist expansion gave the Nazis the practical opportunity and economic reasons to exterminate the Jews. The extermination project's theoretical framework, the *Lebensraum* theory, is part of imperialist tradition. To the same tradition belongs the historical model of extermination of Jews: genocide in the colonies.

When the mass murder of Jews began, there were only a quarter of a million Jews left in Germany. The rest had either fled or been banished. The great Jewish populations were in Poland and Russia. Hitler had the practical possibility of eradicating them only by attacking and capturing these areas.

The main intention behind the conquest was not to murder Jews, just as the Americans did not advance westward in order to murder Indians. The intention was to expand Germany's own *Lebensraum*. The Russian Jews lived in just those areas Hitler was after, making up 10 percent of the total population there and up to 40 percent of the urban population.

To faithful Nazis, the killing of Jews was a way of implementing the most central point of the party program. For those less faithful, it was a practical way of reducing the consumption of food and making room for the future German settlement. German bureaucracy spoke of "de-Jewishing" (*Entjudung*) as a way of clearing out "superfluous eaters" (*überzähligen Essern*) and in that way creating a "balance between population and food supply."

Hitler himself was driven throughout his political career by a fanatical anti-Semitism with roots in a tradition of over a thousand years, which had often led to killing and even to mass murder of Jews. But the step from mass murder to genocide was not taken until the anti-Semitic tradition met the tradition of genocide arising during Europe's expansion in America, Australia, Africa, and Asia.

According to the *Lebensraum* theory, the Jews were a landless people, like the stunted hunting people of the African interior. They belonged to an even lower race than Russians and Poles, a race which could not lay claim to the right to live. It was only natural that such lower races (whether Tasmanians, Indians, or Jews) should be exterminated if they were in the way. The other Western master races had done just that.

The Nazis gave the Jews a star on their coats and crowded them into "reserves"—just as the Indians, the Hereros, the Bushmen, the Amandabele, and all the other children of the stars had been crowded together. They died on their own when the food supply to the reserves was cut off. It was a sad rule that low-standing people died out on contact with highly cultivated people. If they did not die fast enough, then it was merciful to shorten their suffering. They were going to die anyhow.

Order Establishing Concentration Camps in the South African War

Although the Nazis developed the first scientific extermination camps, they did not invent the concentration camp. That dishonor is shared by the Spanish forces in Cuba and the British Army in South Africa. The South African War of 1899 and 1902 was fought largely between the British Army and the descendents of Dutch settlers

(Boers) who had established two states in the interior of southern Africa. Large numbers of Africans were also involved as auxiliaries and in some cases soldiers. During the first year of the war, irregular Boer forces proved highly successful in fighting a guerilla campaign against the British Army. They were helped by numerous households that fed, accommodated, and acted as informants for the Boer columns, or Komandos. In response, the British commander Lord Kitchener ordered the imprisoning of thousands of civilians—both Boer and in some cases Africans—in concentration camps. Although these camps were technically intended to relocate, rather than exterminate, the civilians, disease and malnutrition killed tens of thousands of internees during the war. Were these colonial concentration camps the forerunners of Nazi extermination camps? Note that Kitchener uses the word "Kaffir," an intensely derogatory term, to refer to Africans.

>> 104. Circular Memorandum N. 29

LORD KITCHENER [1900]

AG Circular Memorandum No. 29
21 December 1900

The General Officer Commanding in Chief is desirous that all possible measures be taken to stop the present guerrilla warfare.

Of the various measures suggested for the accomplishment of this object, one, which has been strongly recommended and has been successfully tried on a small scale, is the removal of all men women and children and natives from the districts which the enemy's bands persistently occupy. This course has been pointed out by surrendered burgers, who are anxious to finish the war, as the most effective method of limiting the endurance of the guerrillas as the men and women left on the farms, if disloyal, willingly supply burgers, if loyal dare not refuse to do so. Moreover seeing the unprotected state of women now living out in the Districts, this course is desirable to ensure their not being molested by natives.

Lord Kitchener desires that General Officers will, according to the means at their disposal, follow this system in the Districts which they now occupy or traverse.

The women and children brought in should be kept near the railway for supply purposes, and should be divided into two categories; 1st Refugees and the families of neutrals, non-combatants and surrendered burgers. 2nd. Those whose husbands, fathers or sons are on commando. The preference in accommodation, etc, should, of course, be given to the first class. The Ordnance will supply the necessary tents and the District Commissioner will look after the food on the scale now in use.

It should be clearly explained to burgers in the field that if they voluntarily surrender they will be allowed to live with their families in the camp until it is safe for them to return to their homes.

With regard to natives it is not intended to clear the Kaffir locations, but only such Kaffirs and their stock as are on Boer farms. Every endeavour should be made to cause as little loss to the natives removed and to give them protection when brought in. They will be available for any works undertaken, for which they will receive pay at native rates.

Source: *The National Archives of South Africa,* The Military Governor of Pretoria (MGP) Vol. 258. Circular Memorandum N. 29, 21 December 1900. Document provided by Dr. Stowell Kessler.

>> Mastering the Material

1. On what points do Dawidowicz and Gerlach disagree? With whom do you agree more?

2. How does Gerlach interpret the Wannsee Conference minutes? Do you agree with his interpretation?

3. What is the significance of the timing of the Wannsee Conference?

4. Sven Lindqvist argues that the Holocaust was not an isolated incident or the result of a specifically German path. What then were its origins? Would Dawidowicz agree?

5. Read closely the order establishing concentration camps in the South African War. It does not seem to call for anything more than the relocation of civilians for their own safety and security. Yet scholars argue that tens of thousands of these civilians—black and white—died in the South African concentration camps. Now compare this order to the phrasing of the Protocol of the Wannsee Conference. Are there similarities between the two documents?

>> Making Connections

1. What is the relationship between the intentionalist school of Holocaust studies (here represented by Dawidowicz), and the intentionalist interpretation of the origins of the Second World War (Chapter 19)?

2. Having read the debate about the role of Germany in the First World War (Chapter 17), the Second World War (Chapter 19), and the Holocaust, do you believe there was a German *Sonderweg,* or special path? Was Germany in the twentieth century more inclined toward autocracy and aggression than other European or world states?

3. Look back at Churchill's account of the Battle of Omdurman (Chapter 15) and Sepulveda's *Democrates Secundus* (Chapter 2). Were imperial attitudes toward colonized peoples precedents for the Holocaust? Is Lindqvist's argument that the two were connected convincing, or does the evidence you have read so far suggest that he is stretching the point?

Part 4 Conclusion

What was the Holocaust? To many historians, it seems clear that it was something special, the manifestation of a purely German path toward modernization that resulted from the unique conditions of the Second World War. To others, it was merely one more in a long line of horrors that resulted from modernity. Their list often begins with the deaths of millions of indigenous Americans in the sixteenth century and millions of Africans during the era of the Atlantic slave trade, includes the violence of colonialism, and culminates not in the Second World War but with more recent genocides in Rwanda and Cambodia. Probably most researchers position themselves somewhere in between, recognizing earlier mass deaths but also seeing the Holocaust as a particular moment at which racialism, violence, and industrialized modernity collided in a way that profoundly affected the world.

Nor is the Holocaust the only legacy of the three decades between the murder of the Archduke Ferdinand in 1914 and the moment the guns fell silent in East Asia in 1945. This era was one of violence and warfare and often extreme racism and nationalism. Admittedly, those are not the only stories to be told. Outside of war human beings as always enjoyed day-to-day lives, struggled to overcome major challenges, and interacted with each other in many ways. Nevertheless, the experiences of the First and Second World Wars were central to the lives of most people who lived through this period, and these experiences in many ways shaped the world we live in now. While the current generations of historians are focusing less and less on military history, they are also increasingly suggesting that warfare is important in the ways in which it shapes society and culture. Thus, for example, some suggest that the horrors of the First World War helped to condition societies for the violence of the Holocaust.

Together, the First and Second World Wars and the period between them transformed the world. In this period, the primacy of the European global empires was shattered, and thus in the wake of the wars colonies worldwide achieved their independence. This era also saw the birth of global communism, first in the Soviet Union in 1917 and then in China following the Second World War. On the cultural front, the breakdown of normalcy during the war years helped to create the opportunity for movements for social equality and equal rights in many countries. Internationally, attempts to avoid repeating the terrors of the two wars also brought hope to the world in the form of the League of Nations and later the United Nations. Although neither turned out to be perfect, these were steps in the direction of global peace.

It is this attempt to avoid repeating the destruction from the two world wars that brings us to study their origins. History does not repeat itself, and acting like it does can be very dangerous. For example, the Western democracies appeased Nazi Germany in the 1930s in order to avoid repeating the rush to war that characterized the opening rounds of the First World War. Nevertheless, certain patterns can be discerned in the two world wars that are worth noting in their complexity. For example, isolationism is often a mistake in the face of aggressive nationalism. On the other hand, belligerence is seldom a better response. Instead, perhaps, governments should usually employ diplomatic engagement and a variety of strategies in between avoidance and militaristic aggressiveness. Equally important, this era shows that violence and genocide cannot just be ignored, even if they are happening "to someone else," for they are symptoms of a disease that can easily be turned upon any enemy.

This begs the question why the terrible suffering of the Second World War, experienced worldwide, did not end genocide and warfare forever. Rather, the late twentieth century was characterized by quite high levels warfare in the contexts of the Cold War and struggles for independence. At least part of the answer is that the conclusion of the Second World War, like that of the First World War, was imperfect. It is with this point in mind that we begin the last part of this book.

Further Reading

Aside from the sometimes controversial sources used in this part there are several concise surveys of the origins of the two world wars. A useful example is Frank McDonough, *The Origins of the First and Second World Wars* (Cambridge: Cambridge University Press, 1997). Perhaps the most widespread debate was that surrounding A. J. P. Taylor's discussion of Germany's role in both wars. G. Martel edited a compilation of that controversy's most important articles entitled *The Origins of the Second World War Reconsidered* (Routledge: London, 1986). An important source for understanding both the wars and the Holocaust is the work of the German-American journalist and political philosopher Hannah Arendt, who first connected the violence and genocide of the Second World War to its colonial roots in *The Origins of Totalitarianism* (New York: Shocken, 1951). There are many books that focus on the European great powers and the origins of both conflicts, but an early investigation of the transcontinental development of the war is G. Baer, *Test Case: Italy, Ethiopia, and the League of Nations* (Stanford: Hoover Institute, 1977).

Terms to Know

Bolshevik *(p. 206)*

genocide *(p. 207)*

racialization *(p. 207)*

intentionalists *(p. 208)*

Central Power (First World War) *(p. 211)*

Franco-Russian Entente (First World War) *(p. 211)*

Triple Entente (First World War) *(p. 211)*

Axis Power (Second World War) *(p. 238)*

Allied Powers (Second World War) *(p. 238)*

fascism *(p. 238)*

lebensraum *(p. 239)*

intentionalism *(p. 240)*

appeasement *(p. 252)*

isolationism *(p. 252)*

anti-Semitism *(p. 266)*

Holocaust *(p. 266)*

structuralism *(p. 267)*

Sonderweg *(p. 267)*

Part 5

Debating Globalization, Nationalism, and Modernity, 1945–Present

The post-war period is as yet only barely the domain of historians. There is simply too little historical distance between the end of the Second World War and today. Thus the task of historians seeking to understand recent events frequently overlaps the work of sociologists, political scientists, and economists. The greatest contribution historians can make at present is to set events like the Cold War, the collapse of the great European overseas empires, and the current global security situation within a long view of the human past. That, in fact, is the intent of many of the contributors in Part 5

It is possible for studies of recent history to be guilty of **presentism:** viewing all of history through the filter of current events. Often, theorists seeking to explain how the world around them came into being come to very different conclusions. For example, some political philosophers suggest that over the past 500 years the world has been steadily moving toward a system of capitalist, democratic nation-states such as those that developed first in western Europe. Yet both within the academic community and in the world at large this master narrative of history is increasingly being subjected to wide criticism. Some critics argue that in this era of great global connectivity we must acknowledge that there are many alternatives to the western models of capitalism and the nation-state that have equal or at least roughly equivalent value. Other commentators contend that the nation-state is reaching not its apex but its end because there is less need for borders and state governments in an increasingly globalized world. Others suggest that the politico-economic revitalization of China, India, and other nonwestern powers is fostering a competing set of ideologies and structures to the western nation-state. Defenders of the nation-state and capitalism, however, argue that challengers like India and China are in fact nation-states and that their rise to prominence has come at least in part from their embrace of capitalism.

Historians tend to suggest that both the international struggle and the global cooperation that characterizes recent years should be seen through the lens of the past. Therefore, in its focus on the last half-century Part 5 spotlights three trends that span many periods. The first is the process of globalization. Although this term only became popular in the 1990s, many world historians accept that the global interconnection of human societies has been an important trend for perhaps several millennia. Certainly one of the most important events in this process was the sustained reconnection of the New World American continents and the Old World continents of Africa, Asia, and Europe in the late fifteenth century. It is hard to attach a value judgment to this episode in world history. Empires and world wars were to follow, but so did a great web of learning that fostered a flowering of ideas across the world. Similarly, it is difficult to judge whether the acceleration of globalization in the post-war era has been positive or negative. International relations in the last five decades may have featured the Cold War and the underdevelopment of large sections of the world, but they also helped to produce decolonization, the United Nations, and the World Health Organization.

It is similarly difficult to attach a value to nationalism. In a selection excerpted in the Part 1 of this book, Joseph Strayer suggests that it was the evolution of the sustained, centralized European state in the thirteenth and fourteenth centuries that led to the modern nation-state and to nationalism. An alternate date often given for the formation of the nation-state system in Europe is the Treaty of Westphalia in 1648 that ended the Thirty Years War. Other important events in the evolution of nationalism explored in this text were the French and American revolutions, which have been interpreted as first bringing to fruition the idea of the *people* as the nation. Nationalism can have positive repercussions: In Haiti it was a vehicle for slaves to rebel against their owners. Yet it can also be very negative. Ultranationalism leads not only to war, but to fascism and eventually to genocide, as it did during the Second World War. After that experience, in many parts of the world nationalism has been regarded with great suspicion, and the United Nations and other great global institutions and agreements were brought into being by a wave of popular internationalism. Yet in the same period nationalism was embraced in over a hundred former colonies around the globe as a tool to bring about independence. In the modern day, many activists consider the nation-state and national identity to be among citizens' last defenses against corporate globalization, while others decry it as a tool of oppression and hatred.

Both nationalism and globalization in the post-war era have been heavily influenced by modernization and modernity. Modernity, as introduced in earlier chapters, is another term that is difficult to define. What it means to be "modern" is contested among many different groups. Because modernity is often associated with industrialization and capitalism, for some time the idea that **modernization** meant "to be like western Europe and the United States" predominated. Nationalists in many parts of the world prior to the Second World War, for example, believed that the only way to compete with the industrialized West was to become like them: to build industry, to welcome capitalism, and even to embrace **secularism.** Yet in the post-war period the strategy of mimicking the West was questioned by some of the new generation of nationalists who sought to overthrow the colonial empires. In many parts of the developing world debates emerged as to what form their newly independent states should take, and some leaders turned their back on what they saw as predatory capitalism and foreign ideas. In seeking to build national independence, some thinkers and statesmen celebrated local roots and encouraged the rejection of Western influences. They either rejected the idea of modernization entirely or sought to decouple it from westernization and suggest that there were alternate pathways to modernity.

In Part 5 we look at four topics that are sometimes seen as being discrete from each other: the Cold War, decolonization, the political economy of the world, and global conflict. They are tied together by the shared concepts of nationalism, globalization, and modernity. They are also all examples of history being used to shape as well as to explain the modern world. In each case, rebels, politicians, and scholars put history to work to explain their perspectives on the present and to justify strategies for the future.

Working with sources that address these topics can be difficult. In previous parts, we have seen how writers—both scholars and others—attach value judgments to historical actors and events, depicting them as good or evil, negative or positive. For historians, it is harder to be objective about the recent past than long-gone events. Many historians believe that subjectivity is unavoidable and even acceptable, so long as the author discloses his or her bias to the reader. Almost all, however, agree that the historian's primary task is not to judge the morality of their subjects but to seek to understand what happened and why. The difficulty of achieving this type of objectivity complicates the efforts of the historian working in the contemporary period.

Part 5 Timeline

1947	India achieves its independence.
1948–1949	The Soviet Union blockades West Berlin, and the United States and its allies respond by initiating an airlift of food and supplies into the city.
1950–1953	The Korean War.
1954	The Viet Minh defeat French forces at Dien Bien Phu, leading to a partition of Vietnam into two sections.
1957	Ghana becomes the first sub-Saharan African colony to win its independence.
1957	The European Economic Community (EEC) is formed. It will later evolve into the European Union.
1959	Communist nationalist leader Fidel Castro seizes power in Cuba from U.S.–supported dictator Fulgencio Batista.
1960	The United Nations passes a resolution calling for an end to colonialism.
1962–1990	Nelson Mandela, a leader in the struggle for majority rule in South Africa, is imprisoned.
1965	The first United States marine combat units arrive in Vietnam.
1988–1990	Protest movements in eastern Europe lead to collapse of the Warsaw Pact and later the Soviet Union.
1993–1994	The United States, Mexico, and Canada sign the North American Free Trade Agreement (NAFTA).
2001	Terrorists launch attacks on the World Trade Center in New York and the Pentagon in Washington, D.C.

Chapter 22

Perspectives on Decolonization

Decolonization in Part 5 refers to the transfer of political sovereignty from the formal European, American, and Japanese empires to national governments, especially in the Caribbean, Africa, Asia, and Oceania during the post-war period. In some cases, independence came rapidly and was clearly linked to the events of the Second World War. The defeated powers, especially Italy and Japan, were forced almost immediately to relinquish their claims to their colonies in North Africa and the Pacific. France's colonies in the eastern Mediterranean were able to exploit the German occupation of France during the war by building institutions of self-government to replace the French colonial apparatus. Yet the repercussions of the war on colonial institutions and colonized peoples were far more widespread. Not only France but also Britain, Belgium, and the Netherlands were devastated by the conflict and found it difficult to reestablish their economic and military power. The war's principal victors—the United States, the Soviet Union, and China—adopted anti-imperial stances for a variety of reasons; some altruistic, others self-serving. The international institutions such as the United Nations set up at the end of the war quickly became fora for decolonization (Reading 110). The former colonies that most swiftly won their independence, notably India in 1947 and Ghana in 1957, rapidly became sponsors of anti-imperial movements in neighboring and even distant states. This "demonstration effect" is described by the political scientist David Abernethy in one of the most important survey works on empire in recent decades, *The Dynamics of Global Dominance,* Reading 109.

In most cases the emergence of sovereign nation-states was rapid; by 1961 two-thirds of the world's colonized states had achieved their independence. In other cases, the transition was slow and bloody, as in Algeria, Vietnam, and southern Africa. In these regions armed rebellions were made possible in part by the closing of the weapons gap. In the 1960s and 1970s cheap, mass-produced personal weapons like the AK-47 and rocket-propelled grenades finally gave guerilla forces the tools to oppose European armies, and during these eras local insurgents gradually overcame imperial forces across the globe. Many observers, witnessing the seemingly unstoppable retreat of empires, came to see decolonization as inevitable, the result of global processes brought about by the events of the Second World War and by the realities of its conclusion.

Yet some theorists reject global explanations for this process, arguing that such interpretations inevitably exaggerate the importance of great power politics rather than events within the colonies. Instead of the term *decolonization,* these revisionists embrace the terms *independence* and *liberation.* Scholars as well as veterans of the liberation struggle have argued that the end of formal empires was the result of an upsurge of **emancipatory nationalism** within the colonies. Independence, they suggest, was not a gift from the imperial powers, or even the United States and the Soviet Union, but rather a prize won through political agitation, organization, and in some cases armed revolt. In this interpretation, decolonization is seen as the culmination of a long tradition of internal resistance. These revisionists argue that action and organization against colonialism occurred throughout the colonial era. The movements of the post-war period succeeded only because they achieved a greater level of unity than earlier efforts. Political parties that emerged within the colonies in the 1940s and 1950s were highly organized, often well funded, led by charismatic individuals who appealed to the entire populace rather than specific classes or ethnicities. Moreover, while their ideas and strategies were specifically relevant to their own people, leaders like Mohandas K. Gandhi of India (Reading 106) and Nelson Mandela of South Africa (Reading 108) were united in their rejections of colonial oppression based on categories of race, gender, and ethnicity. With the backing of the great mass of their own populations, and often help from other former colonies, they overwhelmed the world's great empires and forced them to disband.

Studies that investigate the development of emancipatory nationalism tend to be more regionally focused than those that look at the global context of decolonization, yet they can be equally revealing. A superior example is Jean Suret-Canale and A. Adu Boahen's survey of the struggle for political sovereignty in "West Africa 1945–1965." These two authors highlight the role played by political parties such as the Convention People's Party in the British Gold Coast Colony (modern day Ghana). The CPP surpassed its predecessor, the elitist United Gold Coast Convention, by becoming a populist party that drew support from many sectors of the population. Its grassroots strategy was largely formulated by Kwame Nkrumah, who acted first as the UGCC party secretary, then as the leader of the CPP, and later as Ghana's first Prime Minister. Nkrumah detailed the organization and tactics of the party in his retrospective *I Speak of Freedom*.

As these sources demonstrate, a core feature of the debate over decolonization is the relative importance of the global context of the mid-twentieth century versus that of nationalist movements and parties. Supporters of a more global understanding cite the cumulative impact of the First World War, the Great Depression, and especially the Second World War. These events caused damage and economic distress within the colonies. Submarine warfare and industrial decline deprived colonized peoples of markets for their goods and cheap mass-produced products. Both civilians and soldiers were killed in outright warfare in the colonies. Imperial powers made promises to the populaces of their colonies in order to gain their support during times of crisis, but subsequently broke those promises. Moreover, in experiencing economic depression and conflict, colonized people gained a new sense of their importance and of the fallibility of the colonial system of economic dependency and racial hierarchy. All of these factors coincided in the early twentieth century to provide a global context for independence movements. On the other hand, proponents of a more nationalist view of liberation struggles suggest that after the war Europeans tried to intensify colonialism, rather than abandon it. That this intensification failed was due to the growing anger and sense of self-worth among colonized people that was the result of a long process rather than immediate events.

More recently, modernization has joined globalization and nationalism as an explanation for decolonization. Scholars suggest, for example, that nationalism was a Western concept born of the Enlightenment and that its adoption or adaptation by colonized peoples represented their attempt to catch up with the industrialized West. They point to evidence that many anticolonial leaders were trained in the West, or in Western-style universities, where they read Hobson, Lenin, and other European and American scholars. Generally, in fact, the leaders of both political liberation movements and insurgencies were drawn from the most westernized and modernized class of colonized people. Critics of this view generally admit that European writing and political thought was influential, but argue that independence leaders built their own unique ideologies and strategies upon this base. New concepts spanned the range from local self-reliance and a rejection of the global economic system in the case of Julius Nyrere's Tankanyika, to broad notions of racial unity like Senegalese President Leopold Senghor's *negritude* and the pan-African movement, to concepts of the unity of oppressed peoples like that of the Afro-Asian Solidarity Movement led by Egypt's Anwar al-Sadat.

In addressing these debates, it is important to note again that we define decolonization as a *political* process for the purposes of this part. Admittedly, the struggle for independence was accompanied by a great intellectual birth and a philosophy of the decolonization of the mind. It also prompted attempts to escape from the economic dominance of the industrialized states. These efforts, however, were not as successful as the fight to overthrow imperial political dominion. More important, they were significant struggles in their own right and cannot merely be discussed as adjuncts of the political struggle.

Nationalism in West Africa

While a few historians have dealt with decolonization thematically across regions, in many cases the heart of the story lies within each colony. It is regional specialists who have contributed most to historians' understandings of this process. Jean Suret-Canale, a leading scholar of French Africa, collaborated with the acclaimed Ghanaian historian A. Adu Boahen in producing one of the most complete short syntheses of this process in the French and British colonies of West Africa. Their work appeared in the superb General History of Africa *commissioned by the United Nations Educational, Scientific, and Cultural Organization and edited mainly by African scholars. In this excerpt, the two authors stress the development of highly organized West African political parties as the central process in the political organization that defeated colonialism, although they also acknowledge the importance of the Second World War, long-term historical trends, and the pan-African movement. Although this selection focuses on the British Gold Coast Colony (Ghana), important parties were developing concurrently in French West Africa and other British colonies in the region.*

>> 105. West Africa 1945–1960

JEAN SURET-CANALE AND A. ADU BOAHEN
[1993]

As has been amply demonstrated [...] African nationalist or anti-colonial activities started from the very beginning of the imposition of the colonial system on Africa and grew in intensity and complexity with the years. African nationalism or anti-colonialism reached its xenophobic height during the decade following the end of the Second World War due to a number of factors. The first of them [...] was the impact of the war itself and the disappointment generated by the British government's attitude to the Atlantic Charter.

The second factor, which not only greatly stimulated but also radicalized nationalist activities in British West Africa in particular, was the Pan-African Congress which was held in Manchester in 1945. [...] Though there have been many pan-African congresses since 1900, this one was unique and epoch-making in a number of ways. To begin with, it was the first of these congresses in which Africans, such as Kwame Nkrumah of Ghana, played a leading role in its planning and running, and in which a far greater number of Africans attended. [...] Secondly, it was this congress that for the first time not only called for 'complete and absolute independence' and a unified Africa with a socialist economy but also outlined the strategies to be applied. [...]

However, the factor that made the greatest contribution to the great upsurge of nationalism was the sense of anger, disappointment, and frustration generated by the deteriorating economic and social conditions as well as the inadequate reforms introduced by the colonial powers in general and the British in particular after the war. [...]

A whole host of political parties emerged in Africa in general and in British West Africa in particular during the first decade after the end of

the Second World War. These included the United Gold Coast Convention (UGCC), the Convention People's Party (CPP) and the Northern People's Party formed in Ghana in 1947, 1949 and 1954 respectively; the National Council for Nigerian Citizens (NCNC), the Action Group (AG) and the Northern People's Congress (NPC) in Nigeria in 1944, 1950 and 1951 respectively; the National Council of Sierra Leone (NCSL) and the Sierra Leone People's Party (SLPP) in 1950 and 1951 respectively; and finally the United Party and the People's Progressive Party (PPP) in the Gambia in 1951 and 1959 respectively. It was under the leadership of these parties that the battle for independence was won. The question then is why did these post-Second-World-War political parties and movements succeed while those in the period before failed.

The first answer is the nature of the parties, associations and clubs of the post-war period. Unlike those of the pre-war period, these parties were not élitist parties confined only to the educated élite and to the urban centres but they were, by-and-large, mass parties with following in the urban as well as the rural areas. They had the support, to varying degrees, of the ex-servicemen, the trade union congresses, students, women's organizations, farmers, traders, traditional rulers, and so on. Because of this support, these post-war parties could not be ignored or written off by the colonial authorities as the former parties were. The role of the trade unions, to be discussed below, should be emphasized here, for whereas in Ghana the Trades Union Congress (TUC) gave its full support to the CPP and played a leading role in its campaigning, in Nigeria and the other colonies either because of its weakness or its divisions reflecting the regional divisions, the TUC was not a major participant. Secondly, unlike the former groups, these parties were not run on a part-time basis but were well-organized parties

Source: Jean Suret-Canale and A. Adu Boahen, "West Africa 1945–1960," in *The UNESCO General History of Africa VIII: Africa since 1935,* edited by Ali A. Mazrui (Berkeley: University of California Press, 1999), 165–169. Originally published in 1993.

with offices, slogans and modern equipment such as propaganda vans, loudspeakers and presses—and, above all, they had full-time officers at national, regional and local levels. They were able therefore to put their views across and extend them to the remotest parts of their regions or countries with a consequent increase in their membership and strength. Thirdly, unlike the former parties, some of the parties were ready to use any strategies, peaceful or violent, constitutional or unconstitutional, local and international to achieve their ends. The peaceful and constitutional strategies included mass rallies, newspaper campaigns, participation in the many elections, some of which were insisted on by the colonial powers, and appeals to international bodies such as the United Nations Organization and anticolonial governments such as the United States of America and Soviet Union. The violent and unconstitutional methods included boycotts, strikes, looting and attacks on colonial institutions and commercial establishments. Fourthly, most of the leaders of these parties were extremely charismatic and demagogic, which enabled them to capture and hold a mass following—the greatest of them being Kwame Nkrumah of Ghana and Azikiwe and Awolowo of Nigeria. Finally, and the most important, of all, their objectives and slogans were very radical because they both reflected and provided blueprints for the resolution of social issues and were therefore very irresistible for the masses; the call was for 'Self-government now' or 'Self-government step-by-step'—but not, as in the 1930s, for a reform of colonialism. Of all the parties that emerged in British West Africa, if not in the whole of Africa, there was none that was better-organized, better-disciplined, more dynamic and radical and enjoyed more charismatic and demagogic leadership than the Convention People's Party of Ghana—thanks principally to its founder and leader, Kwame Nkrumah. It was obviously this unique status of the CPP that partly explains not only why it gained the ascendancy in Ghana but also why Ghana was the first British colony south of the Sahara to win the battle for independence.

Mohandas Gandhi's *Hind Swaraj* and "Message to Chinese Women"

India's struggle for independence, which it finally achieved in 1947, made it a model for anticolonial movements worldwide. The campaign against British rule can be said to date as far back as the Indian Mutiny of 1857, but it had mainly gathered steam after 1916 under the guidance of Mohandas Gandhi. Gandhi was both a Western-trained lawyer and a deeply spiritual Hindu theologian and philosopher. He led an independence movement that affirmed Indian culture as the tool for creating an independent state. Along with rejecting Western industrialization, Gandhi embraced nonviolence (ahimsa), *wide notions of faith from many religious communities, and a search for truth and simplicity. He stretched the anticolonial movement to encompass not merely elite men, but all Indians regardless of social status, gender, religion, or ethnicity. In 1910, Gandhi wrote* Hind Swaraj, *which called for self-rule for India. The book was not merely a rejection of modern Western principles and imperial rule, but also an assertion of south Asian culture. Among the most important values it put forth was that of passive resistance, which Gandhi believed could be used to defeat colonialism. This value was then put into practice in a series of passive resistance campaigns that effectively turned global public opinion against the British government of India. The movement was successful in part because it embraced all members of society, and Gandhi especially believed that women could be effective nonviolent resistors, as he made clear in a 1947 address to Chinese women. India achieved its independence in 1947, but Gandhi was tragically assassinated on 30 January, 1948. Mohandas Gandhi is often known as the Mahatma, or "great soul."*

>> 106. Hind Swaraj, or Indian Home Rule [1910] and Message to Chinese Women

MOHANDAS GANDHI [1947]

PASSIVE RESISTANCE

Reader: It is necessary to understand this passive resistance more fully. It will be better, therefore, if you enlarge upon it.

Editor: Passive resistance is a method of securing rights by personal suffering, it is the reverse of resistance by arms. When I refuse to do a thing that is repugnant to my conscience, I use soul-force. For instance, the Government of the day has passed a law which is applicable to me. I do not like it. If by using violence I, force the Government to repeal the law, I am employing what may be termed body-force. If I do not obey the law and accept the penalty for its breach, I use soul-force. It involves sacrifice of self.

Everybody admits that sacrifice of self is infinitely superior to sacrifice of others. Moreover, if this kind of force is used in a cause that is unjust, only the person using it suffers. He does not make others suffer for his mistakes. Men have before now done many things which were subsequently found to have been wrong. No man can claim that he is absolutely in the right or that a particular thing is wrong because he thinks so, but it is wrong for him so long as that is his deliberate judgment. It is therefore meet that he should not do that which he knows to be wrong, and suffer the consequence whatever it may be. This is the key to the use of soul-force.

Reader: You would then disregard laws. This is rank disloyalty. We have always been considered a law abiding nation. You seem to be going even beyond the extremists. They say that we must obey the laws that have been pressed but that if the laws be had, we must drive out the law givers even by force.

Editor: Whether I go beyond them or whether I do not is a matter of no consequence to either of us. We simply want to find out what is right and to act accordingly. The real meaning of the statement that we are a law-abiding, nation is that we are passive resisters. When we do not like certain laws, we do not break the heads of lawgivers but we suffer and do not submit to the laws. That we should obey laws whether good or bad is a newfangled nation. There was no such thing in former days. The people disregarded those laws they did not like and suffered the penalties for their breach. It is contrary to our manhood if we obey laws repugnant to our conscience. Such teaching is opposed to a religion and means slavery. If the Government were to ask us to go about without any clothing, should we do so? If I were a passive resister, I would say to them that I would have nothing to do with their law. But we have so forgotten ourselves and become so compliant that we do not mind degrading law.

A man who has realized his manhood, who fears only God, will fear no one else. Man made laws are not necessarily binding on him. Even the Government does not expect any such things from us. They do not say: "You must do such and such a thing," but they say: "If you do not do it, we will punish you." We are sunk so low that we fancy that it is our duty and our religion to do what the law lays down. If man will only realize that it is

Source: Mohandas Gandhi, *Hind Swaraj*, or *Indian Home Rule* (Madras: G. A. Natesan, 1921), Chapter XVII. First published in 1910. And "Message to Chinese Women," *Bihar Pacchi Dilhi*, 18 July 1947, 354.

unmanly to obey laws that are unjust, no man's tyranny will enslave him. This is the key to self-rule or home-rule. [. . .]

To use brute force, to use gunpowder, is contrary to passive resistance, for it means that we want our opponent to do by force that which we desire but he does not. And if such a use of force is justifiable surely he is entitled to do likewise by us. And so we should never come to an agreement. We may simply fancy, like the blind horse moving in a circle round a mill, that we are making progress. Those who believe that they are not bound to obey laws which are repugnant to their conscience have only the remedy of passive resistance open to them. Any other must lead to disaster.

Reader: From what you say I deduce that passive resistance is a splendid weapon of the weak, but that when they are strong they may take up arms.

Editor: This is gross ignorance. Passive resistance, that is, soul-force, is matchless. It is superior to the force of arms. How, then, can it be considered only a weapon of the weak? Physical-force men are strangers to the courage that is requisite in a passive resister. Do you believe that a coward can ever disobey a law that he dislikes? Extremists are considered to be advocates of brute force. Why do they, then, talk about obeying laws? I do not blame them. They can say nothing else. When they succeed in driving out the English and they themselves become governors, they will want you and me to obey their laws. And that is a fitting thing for their constitution. But a passive resister will say he will not obey a law that is against his conscience, even though he may be blown to pieces at the mouth of a cannon.

What do you think? Wherein is courage required in blowing others to pieces from behind a cannon, or with a smiling face to approach a cannon and be blown to pieces? Who is the true warrior be, who keeps death always as a bosom-friend, or he who controls the death of others? Believe me that a man devoid of courage and manhood can never be a passive resister.

This however, I will admit: that even a man weak in body is capable of offering this resistance. One man can offer it just as well as millions. Both men and women can indulge in it. It does not require the training of an army; it needs no jiujitsu. Control over the mind is alone necessary, and when that is attained, man is free like the king of the forest and his very glance withers the enemy.

Passive resistance is an all-sided sword, it can be used anyhow; it blesses him who uses it and him against whom it is used. Without drawing a drop of blood it produces far reaching results. It never rusts and cannot be stolen. Competition between passive resisters does not exhaust. The sword of passive resistance does not require a scabbard. It is strange indeed that you should consider such a weapon to be a weapon merely of the weak.

Reader: You have said that passive resistance is a specialty of India. Have cannons never been used in India?

Editor: Evidently, in your opinion, India means its few princes. To me it means its teeming millions on whom depends the existence of its princes and our own.

Kings will always use their kingly weapons. To use force is bred in them. They want to command, but those who have to obey commands do not want guns: and these are in a majority throughout the world. They have to learn either body-force or soul-force. Where they learn the former, both the rulers and the ruled become like so many madmen: but where they learn soul-force, the commands of the rulers do not go beyond the point of their swords, for true men disregard unjust commands. Peasants have never been subdued by the sword, and never will be. They do not know the use of sword and they are not frightened by the use of it by others. That nation is great which rests its head upon death as its pillow. Those who defy death are free from all fear. For those who are laboring under the delusive charms of brute-force, this picture is not overdrawn. The fact is that, in India the nation at large has generally used passive resistance in all departments of life. We cease to co-operate with our rulers when they displease us. This is passive resistance.

I remember an instance when, in a small principality, the villagers were offended by some command issued by the prince. The former immediately began vacating the village. The prince became nervous, apologized to his subjects and withdrew his command. Many such instances can be found in India. Real home rule is possible only where passive resistance is the guiding force of the people. Any other rule is foreign rule.

Message to Chinese Women

If only the women of the world would come together they could display such heroic nonviolence as to kick away the atom bomb like a mere ball. Women have been so gifted by God. If an ancestral treasure lying buried in a corner of the house unknown to the members of the family were suddenly discovered, what a celebration it would occasion. Similarly, women's marvelous power is lying dormant. If the women of Asia wake up, they will dazzle the world. My experiment in non-violence would be instantly successful if I could secure women's help.

Kwame Nkrumah on Organizing a National Political Movement

Kwame Nkrumah was one of the leading anticolonial leaders of the period of decolonization. Nkrumah was formally educated in colonial schools in the Gold Coast Colony (as Ghana was then known) and later at Lincoln University in Pennsylvania. In the United States, he became increasingly politicized and consequently helped to convene the 1945 Pan-African Congress in the United Kingdom. Even after he later became Prime Minister of Ghana, he remained committed to the Pan-African Congress and assisted anticolonial leaders from around Africa, especially Sekou Touré of Guinea. Nkrumah returned to the Gold Coast in December 1947 to take up the post of General Secretary of the United Gold Coast Convention, which mainly represented urban professionals and enjoyed relatively little support in many regions of the colony. This excerpt from his autobiographical and ideological book I Speak of Freedom *takes up his story at the point of his return to the colony. Although far from objective, it reveals the work he and others undertook to create popular appeal for the movement, including speaking tours, organizing chapters around the country, editing newspapers, and spending time in jail. One significant event was his ejection from the UGCC. The UGCC leadership found many of his ideas too radical, and the colonial administration suspected Nkrumah of communist tendencies. Thus he was forced to form his own party, the Convention People's Party. Due in large part to Nkrumah's populist strategies, the CPP eventually took power in the Gold Coast and ushered it into independence as the state of Ghana in 1957.*

>> 107. I Speak of Freedom: A Statement of African Ideology

KWAME NKRUMAH [1961]

In December 1947 I returned to my country after twelve years in America and the United Kingdom. I had been asked to become general secretary of the United Gold Coast Convention, a political organization set up to secure independence 'in the shortest possible time'. The U.G.C.C. was slow to make much impression on the country as a whole, probably because it was composed mainly of business and professional men, especially lawyers. My task as general secretary was to widen the

Source: Kwame Nkrumah, *I Speak of Freedom: A Statement of African Ideology* (New York: Praeger, 1961), 1, 6–7, 9–13, 15–16, 18–19, 22.

membership and to turn the U.G.C.C. into an active, popular movement. [...]

The work of the U.G.C.C., combined with the growing economic tension in February 1948 led to a state of affairs which was highly inflammable. Sure enough, at the end of the month an event occurred which proved to be a decisive step in the struggle for independence.

Saturday, 28 February 1948 is still clear in my mind. I was addressing a meeting in Saltpond when news reached me of rioting in Accra. Police had opened fire on a body of ex-servicemen as they demonstrated at Christiansborg Castle crossroads, about 300 yards from the Castle itself, where the Governor lived. They were unarmed and two were shot down. Pandemonium followed. Angry crowds rushed through the streets of Accra looting and destroying as they went, smashing cars and setting shops alight. For a time the police were powerless. [...]

The police were jittery; it was a time of repression and arrest. On Tuesday, 9 March *The West African Monitor* came out with great gaps in its columns and a heavy black headline reading THE MONITOR RAIDED BY POLICE. Many other newspapers shared the same fate. Rumours that the police were looking for the leaders of the U.G.C.C. reached me. I laid low for a while in the house of two women supporters and spent the time planning the development of the Convention People's Party.

It was not long, however, before the police caught me. I was arrested during the night at Cape Coast. The police also arrested the other leaders, Danquah, Ofori Atta, Akuffo Addo, Ako Adjei, and Obetsebi Lamptey. We were known as the Big Six and we were taken off to be detained in various parts of the country. I was taken to Kumasi and then to a lonely part of the Northern Territories. [...]

As the summer went on, dissatisfaction grew. The Watson Commission had brought no immediate relief, though a constitutional committee was to be set up later on. The ordinary people in the country were getting restive. It was at this time that serious differences arose between myself and the Working Committee of the U.G.C.C. [...]

On the very day on which I ceased to be general secretary the first issue of my paper, *The Accra Evening News,* appeared with its famous fighting motto: WE PREFER SELF GOVERNMENT WITH DANGER TO SERVITUDE IN TRANQUILLITY. Through the columns of this paper I was able to reach a wide circle of readers. Day after day, in various ways, I hammered home the message of full self-government, not in the shortest possible time, but now, NOW. [...]

Demand for the *Evening News* rose by leaps and bounds. I now had another means of reaching the people. My pen, as well as my voice, had entered the campaign. At this time the phrase SELF GOVERNMENT NOW began to appear on walls and buildings up and down the country. Stirring headlines kept the issue in readers' minds. The theme of self-government was never allowed to grow cold. *The West African Monitor,* using another motto SERVICE NOT SERVITUDE, published many inspiring articles in the last months of 1948. [...]

Although the *Evening News* took up much of my time, I continued to address large meetings in many parts of the country. About this time there was a particularly successful gathering at Sekondi. The subject of my talk was 'The True National'. I described such a man as morally strong, skilled in action, honest, free from bribery and corruption. He should have compassion and firm determination. [...]

At the end of my talk I launched a 1,000,000 shillings appeal fund in aid of the Ghana College. [...]

One of my most successful speeches was made at this time. The occasion was a meeting of the Youth Study Group in Accra. Over three thousand people attended and I spoke to them for well over an hour. I briefly traced the history of the Gold Coast since Europeans first came to the country. Then I went on to the question of a new constitution. It must, I said, provide for universal adult suffrage, a national assembly and a board of ministers collectively responsible to the national assembly. [...]

The youth of the country were already organised. The Youth Study Group which I founded had grown into a nationalist youth movement known as the C.Y.O. (Committee on Youth Organization). All youth organizations, clubs and societies were invited to affiliate with the C.Y.O. Applications poured in, and soon members of the Working Committee of the U.G.C.C. began to object. They feared the growing strength of the youth movement with its programme of 'Self Government Now'. They saw in it a threat to their own power, particularly as most of the members of the C.Y.O. came from the less privileged section of the people. […]

On 12 June came the split with the U.G.C.C. and the founding of my own party, the Convention People's Party. […]

All over the country, people hurried to join my Party. […]

Branches of the C.P.P. were opened in more and more places. Women as well as men flocked to our meetings. I travelled vast distances to explain our policy and to introduce the new Party. […]

The political and social revolution in Ghana may be said to have started at midnight on 8 January 1950, when Positive Action began. It was clear by then that the government had no inten-tion of calling a constituent assembly to let the people decide for themselves whether they would adopt the Coussey Report or not. The economic life of the country was paralysed and trouble was unavoidable. The story of my subsequent arrest and imprisonment has been told in my Autobiography. It is sufficient here to say that during the fourteen months I spent in James Fort prison, the campaign for Independence never stopped. My supporters outside, led by Komla Gbedemah, kept in touch with me and I was able to get messages smuggled out to them.

In the General Election of February 1951 the C.P.P. won the majority of seats in the Assembly. I was elected for Accra Central with the largest poll ever recorded. The Governor ordered my release, and I left James Fort as the elected leader of the first African-dominated government of the Gold Coast. Thousands of people crowded round the car, singing the C.P.P. song, waving and cheer-ing. As our slow procession wound its way into Horse Road, men, women and children stood on roof-tops and leaned from windows. Every inch of the way, the crowds seemed to grow larger.

Nelson Mandela's Rivonia Manifesto

Strictly speaking, the anticolonial movement in South Africa was fighting not for political independence but for majority rule. The descendents of European settlers had left the British Empire to create an independent republic in 1961, but they reserved political rights in this state for themselves alone. The African majority of the population labored under policies of apartheid *(separateness), which denied them not only political representation but also the rights to freedom of movement, to ownership of businesses, to equal education, to fair trials, and to live permanently outside of urban "townships" and rural* Bantustans *(reservations). This oppressive system was opposed by a series of resistance movements, the most long-lived of which was the African National Congress. The precepts of the ANC were and remain equal-ity, democracy, and multiracial cooperation. In 1961 the South African government arrested a number of ANC leaders in a house in the suburb of Rivonia, including the young lawyer Nelson Mandela. Released briefly, he was later reincarcerated in 1962. Mandela was allowed to make a statement prior to sentencing, excerpted here. He believed at the time that he would be executed and spoke of his willingness to give his life for ideals that were neither Western nor communist, but rather informed by both and at the same time uniquely African. In fact, Mandela was sentenced to prison for*

27 years. His release was part of the crumbling of the apartheid system following massive uprisings of African youths and subsequent international sanctions against the apartheid government. In 1994 Mandela was elected the first president of a democratic South Africa and guided the implementation of a constitution that celebrated the ANC's democratic and egalitarian ideals.

>> 108. Statement from the Dock at the Rivonia Trial, Pretoria Supreme Court

Nelson Mandela [1964]

I have always regarded myself, in the first place, as an African patriot. After all, I was born in Umtata, forty-six years ago. My guardian was my cousin, who was the acting paramount chief of Tembuland, and I am related both to the present paramount chief of Tembuland, Sabata Dalindyebo, and to Kaizer Matanzima, the Chief Minister of the Transkei.

Today I am attracted by the idea of a classless society, an attraction which springs in part from Marxist reading and, in part, from my admiration of the structure and organization of early African societies in this country. The land, then the main means of production, belonged to the tribe. There were no rich or poor and there was no exploitation.

It is true, as I have already stated, that I have been influenced by Marxist thought. But this is also true of many of the leaders of the new independent States. Such widely different persons as Gandhi, Nehru, Nkrumah, and Nasser all acknowledge this fact. We all accept the need for some form of socialism to enable our people to catch up with the advanced countries of this world and to overcome their legacy of extreme poverty. But this does not mean we are Marxists.

Indeed, for my own part, I believe that it is open to debate whether the Communist Party has any specific role to play at this particular stage of our political struggle. The basic task at the present moment is the removal of race discrimination and the attainment of democratic rights on the basis of the Freedom Charter. In so far as that Party furthers this task, I welcome its assistance. I realize that it is one of the means by which people of all races can be drawn into our struggle.

From my reading of Marxist literature and from conversations with Marxists, I have gained the impression that communists regard the parliamentary system of the West as undemocratic and reactionary. But, on the contrary, I am an admirer of such a system.

The Magna Carta, the Petition of Rights, and the Bill of Rights are documents which are held in veneration by democrats throughout the world.

I have great respect for British political institutions, and for the country's system of justice. I regard the British Parliament as the most democratic institution in the world, and the independence and impartiality of its judiciary never fail to arouse my admiration.

The American Congress, that country's doctrine of separation of powers, as well as the independence of its judiciary, arouses in me similar sentiments.

I have been influenced in my thinking by both West and East. All this has led me to feel that in my search for a political formula, I should be absolutely impartial and objective. I should tie myself to no particular system of society other than of socialism. I must leave myself free to borrow the best from the West and from the East...

Africans want to be paid a living wage. Africans want to perform work which they

---

Source: Nelson Mandela, "Statement from the Dock at the Rivonia Trial," Pretoria Supreme Court, 20 April 1964.

are capable of doing, and not work which the Government declares them to be capable of. Africans want to be allowed to live where they obtain work, and not be endorsed out of an area because they were not born there. Africans want to be allowed to own land in places where they work, and not to be obliged to live in rented houses which they can never call their own. Africans want to be part of the general population, and not confined to living in their own ghettoes. African men want to have their wives and children to live with them where they work, and not be forced into an unnatural existence in men's hostels. African women want to be with their menfolk and not be left permanently widowed in the Reserves. Africans want to be allowed out after eleven o'clock at night and not to be confined to their rooms like little children. Africans want to be allowed to travel in their own country and to seek work where they want to and not where the Labour Bureau tells them to. Africans want a just share in the whole of South Africa; they want security and a stake in society.

Above all, we want equal political rights, because without them our disabilities will be permanent. I know this sounds revolutionary to the whites in this country, because the majority of voters will be Africans. This makes the white man fear democracy.

But this fear cannot be allowed to stand in the way of the only solution which will guarantee racial harmony and freedom for all. It is not true that the enfranchisement of all will result in racial domination. Political division, based on colour, is entirely artificial and, when it disappears, so will the domination of one colour group by another. The ANC has spent half a century fighting against racialism. When it triumphs it will not change that policy.

This then is what the ANC is fighting. Their struggle is a truly national one. It is a struggle of the African people, inspired by their own suffering and their own experience. It is a struggle for the right to live.

During my lifetime I have dedicated myself to this struggle of the African people. I have fought against white domination, and I have fought against black domination. I have cherished the ideal of a democratic and free society in which all persons live together in harmony and with equal opportunities. It is an ideal which I hope to live for and to achieve. But if needs be, it is an ideal for which I am prepared to die.

The International Context of Decolonization

Only a few scholars have seriously attempted a book-length analysis of all European overseas empires in the entire modern period. Political scientist David Abernethy is one of these, and his text The Dynamics of Global Dominance *is an inclusive and highly theoretical look at empires from a social science perspective. In his text, Abernethy sometimes abandons chronology to pursue a theme, as in his investigation of decolonization. For example, he identifies two similar periods of imperial decline—the late eighteenth/early nineteenth century, during which colonies in the Americas established their independence, and the post-war period. Interestingly, he weaves them together in his investigation of three proposed causes of the collapse of empires: nationalism, structural problems within colonial systems, and changing international contexts. In these brief selections Abernethy focuses on two important types of global changes during both of these periods. The first is the impact of widespread war on the empire. The second is the effect of liberation in some colonies on other, especially neighboring, colonial possessions.*

>> 109. The Dynamics of Global Dominance: European Overseas Empires, 1415–1980

DAVID ABERNETHY [2000]

What turned precariously poised relationships into unsustainable ones were crises impacting several empires at the same time, crises whose course and outcome no one metropole could control. Since the mid–eighteenth century four wars were fought to determine which states would dominate world affairs: the Seven Years' War (1756–63), the Napoleonic Wars (intermittently between 1799 and 1815), and World Wars I (1914–18) and II (1939–45). Each of these struggles became a catalyst for imperial decline, suddenly and dramatically reinforcing from outside the boundaries of empire trends that had quietly evolved within those boundaries. Wars altered power relations in one or more of the following ways: (1) they lowered metropolitan capacity to retain overseas possessions, (2) they diminished metropolitan will to retain them, (3) they increased colonial capacity for autonomy, and (4) they intensified colonial will for autonomy. The most important was the fourth. [...]

The capacity of metropoles to govern colonies was severely impaired in wartime. In several cases metropoles were invaded and became temporarily unable to govern themselves, much less others: Portugal, Spain, and Holland in the wars of [the eighteenth and early nineteenth centuries], Belgium in World War I, and France, Belgium, and Holland in World War II. England's blockade of continental ports during the revolutionary and Napoleonic Wars prevented France and, at times, Holland and Spain from linking up with their overseas possessions. Naval warfare frayed and sometimes severed shipping ties connecting far-flung empires. The usual trade flows were disrupted, and administrators did not circulate

between metropoles and colonies as they did in peacetime. Japan's invasion of Southeast Asia removed metropolitan officials from top decision-making posts.

In contrast, many colonies were economically stimulated and politically empowered by war. Transport and communications lines were improved to facilitate movement of war-related matériel and troops. Areas not invaded or directly involved in fighting had opportunities to develop, particularly if their exports helped the war effort and were in great demand. Some colonies adopted economic policies consistent with their own interests. With commercial ties to Spain cut off during the Napoleonic Wars, Spanish American colonies could violate mercantilist policies with impunity, and trade with Britain and the United States flourished. Industrialization in India accelerated in World War I, increasing economic self-reliance while assisting the war effort. Young men who had never held a rifle were recruited to fight. Their training and experiences prepared them for post-war nationalist activities, whether as soldiers or political activists. Of vital importance in the Indonesian struggle against Holland after World War II were young soldiers trained by the Japanese. [...]

The timing of hegemonic wars makes the timing of decolonization phases more understandable. But wars by themselves cannot account for the magnitude and temporal compression of these phases. New-state formation had a transformative effect in its own right on the interstate system. [There exist] numerous instances of the impact independence in one territory had on the drive for independence elsewhere. If anything, changes at the international level played an even more important part in decolonization than suggested thus far. Once war-related independence movements succeeded, demonstration effects sustained and even

Source: David Abernethy, *The Dynamics of Global Dominance: European Overseas Empires, 1415–1980* (New Haven: Yale University Press, 2000), 345, 348, 357–358.

accelerated the momentum for change in territories not so directly affected by war.

Independence of the United States and India had far-reaching observation effects, emboldening people elsewhere to act once they could point to real examples of political change. Leaders of other [eighteenth and early nineteenth centuries] movements were impressed, among other things, that Americans were willing to fight for freedom. Many [twentieth century] nationalists were impressed by the peaceful mass mobilization techniques pioneered by Gandhi demonstrates and adopted them in their own work. [...]

Observation effects crossed imperial lines. What BNA colonists achieved was noted in Haiti and Spanish America; what India did was noted in Indonesia and Indochina. Francophone Africans noted Ghana's independence; residents of Leopoldville in the Belgian Congo heard of General de Gaulle's independence offer, made across the river in Brazzaville. If postwar crises were intra-imperial, pitting colonies against their metropoles, observation effects had wide-ranging impacts on two or more empires.

The direct influence effect also crossed imperial lines. Haitians assisted Bolívar when he was in dire straits. U.S. citizens supported Spanish American liberation struggles, and the Monroe Doctrine formally committed the U.S. government to oppose Spanish reconquest efforts. Guerrilla fighters in Portugal's African colonies received help from Algeria and other former French colonies, the former Belgian Congo, and Tanzania. These interventions helped nationalist movements struggling under highly repressive regimes.

There were no international organizations in [the early nineteenth century] to bring diplomatic pressures from many sources to bear, either to limit or prevent vertical violence. The presence of international organizations in [the twentieth century] added the indirect influence option. The United Nations was very important both in accelerating new-state formation and in limiting the violence associated with power transfers. The U.N. Charter embodied principles of national self-determination articulated earlier by President Wilson and the Atlantic Charter, ensuring efforts to apply them universally. In this setting defenders of overseas empires were placed ideologically and morally on the defensive. As each new state entered the United Nations, the organization became even more a forum for anticolonial lobbying. It hastened the Dutch departure from Indonesia [...]. The trusteeship system subtly but surely forced Belgium and France to abandon adamant opposition to independence in their sub-Saharan possessions. Another international structure, the Commonwealth, pressured Britain to move its colonies more rapidly toward self-government and to intervene to end the Rhodesian civil war.

The United Nations' Declaration on the Granting of Independence

Some of the founders of the United Nations, particularly Britain's Winston Churchill, initially conceived of it as a way for the world's major powers to maintain peace and global security as well as their own strategic positions through diplomacy and negotiation. Yet as decolonization proceeded and more and more new states were created, decolonization became a focus of debates in the UN General Assembly. This process was pushed along by India, which achieved independence in 1948, and by the communist administration of the People's Republic of China, which came to power in 1949. Other newly independent states, like Ghana, also led the call for independence for their neighbors. The process was self-catalyzing. Each new independent state tipped the balance toward the anticolonial bloc within the General Assembly. An important milestone in the process was the Declaration on the Granting of Independence to Colonial Countries and Peoples, passed December 1960.

>> 110. Declaration on the Granting of Independence to Colonial Countries and Peoples

UNITED NATIONS GENERAL ASSEMBLY
[1961]

The General Assembly,

Mindful of the determination proclaimed by the peoples of the world in the Charter of the United Nations to reaffirm faith in fundamental human rights, in the dignity and worth of the human person, in the equal rights of men and women and of nations large and small and to promote social progress and better standards of life in larger freedom,

Conscious of the need for the creation of conditions of stability and well-being and peaceful and friendly relations based on respect for the principles of equal rights and self-determination of all peoples, and of universal respect for, and observance of, human rights and fundamental freedoms for all without distinction as to race, sex, language or religion,

Recognizing the passionate yearning for freedom in all dependent peoples and the decisive role of such peoples in the attainment of their independence,

Aware of the increasing conflicts resulting from the denial of or impediments in the way of the freedom of such peoples, which constitute a serious threat to world peace,

Considering the important role of the United Nations in assisting the movement for independence in Trust and Non-Self-Governing Territories,

Recognizing that the peoples of the world ardently desire the end of colonialism in all its manifestations,

Convinced that the continued existence of colonialism prevents the development of international economic cooperation, impedes the social, cultural and economic development of dependent peoples and militates against the United Nations ideal of universal peace,

Affirming that peoples may, for their own ends, freely dispose of their natural wealth and resources without prejudice to any obligations arising out of international economic co-operation, based upon the principle of mutual benefit, and international law,

Believing that the process of liberation is irresistible and irreversible and that, in order to avoid serious crises, an end must be put to colonialism and all practices of segregation and discrimination associated therewith,

Welcoming the emergence in recent years of a large number of dependent territories into freedom and independence, and recognizing the increasingly powerful trends towards freedom in such territories which have not yet attained independence,

Convinced that all peoples have an inalienable right to complete freedom, the exercise of their sovereignty and the integrity of their national territory,

Solemnly proclaims the necessity of bringing to a speedy and unconditional end colonialism in all its forms and manifestations;

And to this end
Declares that:

1. The subjection of peoples to alien subjugation, domination and exploitation constitutes a denial of fundamental human rights, is

Source: United Nations General Assembly, "Declaration on the Granting of Independence to Colonial Countries and Peoples," *Official Records of the General Assembly,* Fifteenth Session, Supplement 16 (A/4684) (New York, 1961), 66–67.

contrary to the Charter of the United Nations and is an impediment to the promotion of world peace and co-operation.

2. All peoples have the right to self-determination; by virtue of that right they freely determine their political status and freely pursue their economic, social and cultural development.

3. Inadequacy of political, economic, social or educational preparedness should never serve as a pretext for delaying independence.

4. All armed action or repressive measures of all kinds directed against dependent peoples shall cease in order to enable them to exercise peacefully and freely their right to complete independence, and the integrity of their national territory shall be respected.

5. Immediate steps shall be taken, in Trust and Non-Self-Governing Territories or all other territories which have not yet attained independence, to transfer all powers to the peoples of those territories, without any conditions or reservations, in accordance with their freely expressed will and desire, without any distinction as to race, creed or colour, in order to enable them to enjoy complete independence and freedom.

6. Any attempt aimed at the partial or total disruption of the national unity and the territorial integrity of a country is incompatible with the purposes and principles of the Charter of the United Nations.

7. All States shall observe faithfully and strictly the provisions of the Charter of the United Nations, the Universal Declaration of Human Rights and the present Declaration on the basis of equality, noninterference in the internal affairs of all States, and respect for the sovereign rights of all peoples and their territorial integrity.

947th plenary meeting,
14 December 1960.

>> Mastering the Material

1. How does Nkrumah's account of the years 1947–1949 in the Gold Coast complement or contradict Jean Suret-Canale and A. Adu Boahen's arguments?

2. What are the uses and limitations of a source like Nkrumah's *I Speak of Freedom* for a scholar?

3. Mohandas Gandhi and Nelson Mandela were both lawyers. So were many other leaders of nationalist and anticolonial movements in the colonies. Why do you think this may have been so?

4. Consider the readings from Mandela, Nkrumah, and Gandhi together. Each source details some of the strategies, mechanisms, and ideologies of anticolonial movements in different parts of the world. What do these sources tell us about these movements? Were they mere copies of Western nationalism? Were they based on theories of racial or class struggle? Were they unique to their own local situations? Why do you think they were successful in ending imperial political domination of their states?

5. What is the International Demonstration Effect? Why do you think it might have been even more important during the decolonization period of 1945 to 1980 than during the earlier period of imperial decline from 1776 to 1830?

6. The imperial powers all had seats in the United Nations General Assembly, and two—Britain and France—even held permanent seats on the Security Council. Yet in

December 1960 a declaration passed the General Assembly calling for the end to colonialism worldwide. Why do you think such a resolution was not passed earlier, and what changes enabled it to be passed in 1960?

7. The United Nations was not a sovereign power and could not force the imperial powers to decolonize. Of what importance, then, was the Declaration on the Granting of Independence to Colonial Countries and Peoples?

>> Making Connections

1. The age of the new imperialism began around 1875, with much of Africa and large parts of the Asian continent conquered by 1900 (India somewhat earlier). For the great mass of these regions, independence was achieved between about 1948 and 1965. Was this a long time, historically speaking? What factors might have influenced the length of time it took for colonies to achieve their independence?

2. In Part 3, we saw many arguments put forward by proponents of colonies. They contended that colonies were necessary for strategic, economic, and even moral reasons. Yet barely a half-century later the empires fell apart. What had changed? Should we look for answers in the decline of Britain, France, Belgium, the Netherlands, Italy, Portugal, and Japan? Should we look to changes within the colonies? Or should we point to some other factors, such as the changing position of the United States and the Soviet Union?

3. Consider the nationalism described by Jean Suret-Canale and A. Adu Boahen. What relationship does the nationalism of decolonization bear to the nationalism of the American and French revolutions (Part 2)? To the nationalism of fascism in pre-war Italy and Japan (Chapter 19)?

Chapter 23

Perspectives on the Cold War

The eclipsing of the European imperial powers by the United States and the Soviet Union was an important stimulus for decolonization. However, while the two superpowers were both interested in pulling down the formal European empires, in most other respects the two quickly became global adversaries. This superpower rivalry manifested itself as a political, ideological, and economic conflict known as the Cold War. Some scholars, like Paul Kennedy, argue that the Cold War was merely a continuation of the great alliance politics that had characterized Europe in previous periods. Following the defeat of Germany and Italy and the decline of Britain and France to second-rate powers, the United States and the Soviet Union merely came to assume the leadership of coalescing alliances. In many ways, Russia had been the leading power on the eastern edge of Europe since before the Napoleonic period, and perhaps the United States simply assumed the position in the west previously occupied by the Great Britain.

Other theorists see the post-war antagonism between the United States and the Soviet Union as an unprecedented type of conflict. The Cold War was set in an era in which events in distant parts of the world communicated much more quickly and were more inextricably linked than in previous eras. As a result, the superpower conflict of the post-war era was an international and indeed global struggle to an even greater degree than the Seven Years War and the two world wars. The Soviet Union with its **Warsaw Pact** allies and the United States with its **NATO (North Atlantic Treaty Organization)** allies never actually engaged in open, formal conflict—hence the term "cold" war. Nevertheless, they sponsored and sustained guerilla operations in Central America, coups and civil wars in Africa, and armed insurrections in southeast Asia. Almost all of the military clashes of the post-war era had some Cold War connection. Nor was the NATO–Warsaw Pact antagonism solely a factor in military affairs. It also had a profound impact on global commerce and economics, cultural development, and political organization.

Most scholars agree that the Cold War was more than simply a great power rivalry. It was also a clash between two rival political ideologies and socioeconomic systems. American free-market capitalism with its emphasis on consumerism was substantively different from Soviet state-directed socialism. American liberal democracy with its focus on individual rights contrasted with Soviet communism with its ideology of collective rights. Both strategies purported to serve the needs of their people, but were very different approaches to doing so.

During the Second World War the two states had managed to bury their differences and to operate as allies. Yet even in the last months of the war their relations had begun to deteriorate. By early 1946, each side was accusing the other of greed and fraud. The Soviet Union, having suffered as many as 20 million casualties in the war, felt the need to build a communist buffer zone in Eastern Europe and the Balkans to protect itself from future attacks. However, the Western allies were suspicious of this Soviet activity, which prompted British Prime Minister Winston Churchill's famous remark that an "iron curtain" had fallen across Europe. Friction also emerged in other points around the world. Tension over great power interests in Iran and the surfacing of a Soviet spy operation in Canada drove the Truman administration in Washington to request its senior diplomat in Moscow, George F. Kennan, to report on Soviet intentions. On February 23, Kennan wrote a telegram in which he argued that Soviet mistrust of the West was based on both the broad sweep of Russian history and Soviet psychology. He predicted that the Soviets would become increasingly aggressive and urged Truman to adopt a proactively aggressive policy. Meanwhile, the Soviets were coming to a similar conclusion about the United States. On September 27 of the same year the leading Soviet diplomat in the United States, Nikolai Novikov, wrote a telegram to his superiors arguing that the United States was committed to world supremacy and that the Soviet Union must respond with a firm stance. Documents such as these have been interpreted in various ways. Some scholars regard them as proof that the ideological and geopolitical clash between the Soviet Union and United States was inevitable. Others see them as a sad example of misunderstanding and missed signals leading to an otherwise avoidable conflict.

Much of the scholarly analysis of the Cold War period that was produced *during* the conflict focused on assigning blame rather than searching for underlying trends. In its early stages scholarship on both sides was hijacked to the political needs of the state. In the United States, for example, a nationalist school emerged that faulted the Soviet Union for grabbing territory in southern and eastern Europe at the end of the Second World War, and accused it of unilaterally building up its military. Theorists of this school portrayed the Soviets as expansionists and accused them of supporting worldwide communist revolutions. In the Soviet Union, on the other hand, the main line of scholarly and political writing depicted the United States as an inherently imperialist power that relentlessly sought new markets for its business interests and that sought to dominate the world. That these interpretations were influenced by the official policies that developed in the wake of the Kennan and Novikov telegrams is quite evident.

Yet the story of the Cold War is much broader than the policies of the two superpowers. Through its policy of **containment,** the United States drew ideologically or opportunistically allied states into a great circle around the Soviet Union, a circle that stretched from Britain in western Europe to Japan on the eastern edge of Asia as well as numerous countries in the Americas. The Soviets, meanwhile, sought to escape this containment, perhaps most aggressively by establishing an alliance with Fidel Castro in Cuba, just off the coast of Florida. The communist victory in mainland China in 1949 added another element to the conflict, although China quickly established its own foreign policy rather than adhering to that of the Soviet Union.

However, even if the many diplomatic and military clashes around the world must be seen as having a Cold War component, they were also intensely localized in their causes and in how they unfolded. A case in point was the conflict in Vietnam. The Vietnamese wars of independence were part of the process of decolonization. Since the establishment of the French colony of Indochina, including Vietnam, in the late nineteenth century, numerous nationalist groups had briefly flourished. The Japanese occupation of Indochina during the Second World War was initially welcomed by some Vietnamese, but many saw it as merely an alternative form of exploitation and opposed Japanese forces. Among these was Ho Chi Minh, a committed nationalist who had lived in Paris but had also been trained in Moscow. During the war, Ho had fought with the Chinese before returning to Vietnam to coordinate the insurrection against Japan as the head of the communist-dominated nationalist movement, the Viet Minh. At the end of the war, the Viet Minh opposed the return of French control, and fought an ongoing insurrection that culminated in the victory of Dien Bien Phu in 1954. This defeat drove France to the bargaining table. As part of the agreement that resulted, the French left the country and Vietnam was divided into two states, with a communist government in the north and a Western-oriented government in the south. As the Cold War intensified, the United States gradually came to intervene in support of the South Vietnamese government and in pursuit of their own perceived national interests in the region. Rather than viewing the conflict in terms of nationalist aspirations, the United States government took the stance that it was part of the struggle between Western democracy and capitalism on the one hand and communism and Marxism on the other.

There is no doubt that Ho Chi Minh was a communist, and the United States administrations of the 1960s and 1970s appear to have truly judged that the conflict in Vietnam was a war to stop communism. Yet some biographers argue that Ho Chi Minh was first and foremost a nationalist, and that he was forced to embrace communism by French and later American opposition to his nationalist goals. They point out that the 1945 Vietnamese Declaration of Independence, largely written by Ho Chi Minh, cites the Declaration of Independence of the United States and the French Declaration of the Rights of Man and the Citizen. Detractors of this theory contend that Ho Chi Minh was a committed communist. These scholars point to Ho Chi Minh's early socialist writings (prior to the Second World War). They also assert that even if Ho Chi Minh's motives were those of national liberation, Soviet and at times Chinese support for the Viet Minh was very real and probably inspired by wider geopolitical motivations. Those who defend American intervention, like veteran and author James Webb, argue that the United States interceded to defend the independent state of South Vietnam against aggression from the north.

An American Perspective on Soviet Cold War Strategy

George Frost Kennan was the charge d'affaires at the U.S. Embassy in Moscow when he was asked to explain the increasingly confrontational Soviet stance toward the United States. Much of the telegram he sent in response comprises a historical and psychological analysis of the Soviet government and Russian people. However, Kennan went beyond mere interpretation and proposed that the United States respond by implementing a forceful policy of "containment." His proposal was well received by President Harry S Truman, and the telegram was distributed to newspapers and publications as well as being largely adopted by the Truman administration as a policy statement.

>> 111. Long Telegram

GEORGE F. KENNAN [1946]

At bottom of Kremlin's neurotic view of world affairs is *the* traditional and instictive Russian sense of insecurity. Originally, this was *the* insecurity of a peaceful agricultural people trying to live on *a* vast exposed plain in *the* neighborhood of fierce nomadic peoples. To this was added, as Russia came into contact with *the* economically advanced West, fear of more competent, more powerful, more highly organized societies in that area. But this latter type of insecurity was one which afflicted rather Russian rulers than Russian people, for Russian rulers have invariably sensed that their rule was relatively archaic in form, fragile and artificial in its psychological foundation, unable to stand comparison or contact with *the* political systems of Western countries. [...]

Soviet leaders are driven [by] necessities of their own past and present position to put forward a dogma which [depicts the] outside world as evil, hostile and menacing, but as bearing within itself germs of *a* creeping disease and destined to be wracked with growing internal convulsions until it is given *a* final coup de grace by *the* rising power of socialism and yields to *a* new and better world. This thesis provides justification for that increase of military and police power of *the* Russian state, for that isolation of *the* Russian population from *the* outside world, and for that fluid and constant pressure to extend *the* limits of Russian police power which are together the natural and instinctive urges of Russian rulers. [...]

It should not be thought from [the] above that Soviet party line is necessarily disingenuous and insincere on *the* part of all those who put it forward. Many of them are too ignorant of *the* outside world and mentally too dependent to question [their] self-hypnotism, and [many] have no difficulty making themselves believe what they find it comforting and convenient to believe. Finally we have the unsolved mystery as to who, if anyone, in this great land actually receives accurate and unbiased information about *the* outside world. In *the* atmosphere of oriental secretiveness and conspiracy which pervades this Government, *the* possibilities for distorting or poisoning sources and currents of information are infinite. The very disrespect of Russians for objective truth—indeed, their disbelief in its existence—leads them to view all stated facts as instruments for furtherance of one ulterior purpose or another. [...]

In summary, we have here a political force committed fanatically to the belief that with *the* US there can be no permanent modus vivendi, that it is desirable and necessary that the internal harmony of our society be disrupted, our traditional way of life be destroyed, the international authority of our state be broken, if Soviet power is to be secure. This political force has complete power of disposition over *the* energies of one of *the* world's greatest peoples and *the* resources of *the* world's richest national

---

Source: George F. Kennan, "Long Telegram," in *Debating the Origins of the Cold War: American and Russian Perspectives,* edited by Ralph B. Levering, Vladimir O. Pechatnov, Verena Botzenhart-Viehe, and C. Earl Edmondson (Lanham: Rowman and Littlefield Publishers, 2002), 69–71.

territory, and is borne along by deep and powerful currents of Russian nationalism. In addition, it has an elaborate and far flung apparatus for exertion of its influence in other countries, an apparatus of amazing flexibility and versatility, managed by people whose experience and skill in underground methods are presumably without parallel in history. Finally, it is seemingly inaccessible to considerations of reality in its basic reactions.

A Soviet Perspective on American Cold War Strategy

The Novikov telegram closely parallels the Kennan telegram of eight months earlier. It too was written by a senior diplomat in a foreign capital. It was also commissioned for a similar purpose and was similarly structured. Nikolai Novikov, the senior Soviet diplomat in Washington, believed that there could be no easy peace with the United States, which in his view was "striving for world supremacy." He argued that the Truman administration was intent on weakening the Soviet Union and pointed to a perceived U.S. military buildup as evidence. In many ways, this telegram depicts a typical Marxist interpretation of history and politics, by arguing that the objectives of the United States were primarily commercial and economic. The telegram remained classified until 1990.

>> 112. Telegram

Nikolai Novikov [1946]

[All underlining replicates that of Foreign Minister Vyacheslav Molotov.]

U.S. Foreign Policy in the Postwar Period.

The foreign policy of the United States, which reflects the imperialist tendencies of American monopolistic capital, is characterized in the postwar period by a striving for world supremacy. This is the real meaning of the many statements by President Truman and other representatives of American ruling circles: that the United States has the right to lead the world. All the forces of American diplomacy—the army, the air force, the navy, industry, and science—are enlisted in the service of this foreign policy. For this purpose broad plans for expansion have been developed and are being implemented through diplomacy and the establishment of a system of naval and air bases stretching far beyond the boundaries of the United States, through the arms race, and through the creation of ever newer types of weapons. [...]

The USSR's international position is currently stronger than it was in the prewar period. Thanks to the historical victories of Soviet weapons, the Soviet armed forces are located on the territory of Germany and other formerly hostile countries, thus guaranteeing that these countries will not be used again for an attack on the USSR....

Such a situation in Eastern and Southeastern Europe cannot help but be regarded by the American imperialists as an obstacle in the path of the expansionist policy of the United States. [...]

Obvious indications of the U.S. effort to establish world dominance are also to be found in the increase in military potential in peacetime and in the establishment of a large number of

Source: Nikolai Novikov, "Telegram" in *Debating the Origins of the Cold War: American and Russian Perspectives,* edited by Ralph B. Levering, Vladimir O. Pechatnov, Verena Botzenhart-Viehe, and C. Earl Edmondson (Lanham: Rowman and Littlefield Publishers, 2002), 160–163.

naval and air bases both in the United States and beyond its borders.

In the summer of 1946, for the first time in the history of the country, Congress passed a law on the establishment of a peacetime army, not on a volunteer basis but on the basis of universal military service. The size of the army, which is supposed to amount to about one million persons as of July 1, 1947, was also increased significantly. The size of the navy at the conclusion of the war decreased quite insignificantly in comparison with wartime. At the present time, the American navy occupies first place in the world, leaving England's navy far behind, to say nothing of those of other countries....

The establishment of American bases on islands that are often 10,000 to 12,000 kilometers from the territory of the United States and are on the other side of the Atlantic and Pacific oceans clearly indicates the offensive nature of the strategic concepts of the commands of the U.S. army and navy....

All of these facts show clearly that a decisive role in the realization of plans for world dominance by the United States is played by its armed forces. [...]

The "hard-line" policy with regard to the USSR announced by Byrnes after the rapprochement of the reactionary Democrats with the Republicans is at present the main obstacle on the road to cooperation of the Great Powers. It consists mainly of the fact that in the postwar period the United States no longer follows a policy of strengthening cooperation among the Big Three (or Four) but rather has striven to undermine the unity of these countries. The objective has been to impose the will of other countries on the Soviet Union....

The present policy of the American government with regard to the USSR is also directed at limiting or dislodging the influence of the Soviet Union from neighboring countries. In implementing this policy in former enemy or Allied countries adjacent to the USSR, the United States attempts, at various international conferences or directly in these countries themselves, to support reactionary forces with the purpose of creating obstacles to the process of democratization of these countries. In so doing, it also attempts to secure positions for the penetration of American capital into their economics. Such a policy is intended to weaken and overthrow the democratic governments in power there, which are friendly toward the USSR, and replace them in the future with new governments that would obediently carry out a policy dictated from the United States. In this policy, the United States receives full support from English diplomacy.

Declaration of Independence of the Democratic Republic of Viet Nam

Ho Chi Minh (born Nguyen Sinh Cuong) declared independence for Vietnam on September 2, 1945 — the same day Japan surrendered to the Allied forces. Ho Chi Minh and his colleagues were hoping to gain support for the idea of an independent Vietnam, especially from Britain and the United States. The document therefore seems designed to appeal to a Western audience, as well as to the half-million Vietnamese who witnessed its proclamation in Ba Dinh Square at the center of Hanoi. The nationalists who wrote the document focused on the notion of liberty, the Vietnamese contribution to the struggle against Japan, and the oppression of Japanese and French imperialism. To their disappointment, the United States government came to view their struggle against the return of the French more as a communist uprising than an anticolonial insurrection.

>> 113. Declaration of Independence of the Democratic Republic of Viet Nam

HO CHI MINH [1945]

"All men are created equal. They are endowed by their Creator with certain unalienable Rights; among these are Life, Liberty and the pursuit of Happiness."

This immortal statement appeared in the Declaration of Independence of the United States of America in 1776. In a broader sense, it means: All the peoples on the earth are equal from birth, all the peoples have a right to live and to be happy and free.

The Declaration of the Rights of Man and the Citizen, made at the time of the French Revolution, in 1791, also states: "All men are born free and with equal rights, and must always remain free and have equal rights."

Those are undeniable truths.

Nevertheless, for more than eighty years, the French imperialists, abusing the standard of Liberty, Equality and Fraternity, have violated our Fatherland and oppressed our fellow-citizens. They have acted contrary to the ideals of humanity and justice.

Politically, they have deprived our people of every democratic liberty.

They have enforced inhuman laws; they have set up three different political regimes in the North, the Centre and the South of Viet Nam in order to wreck our country's oneness and prevent our people from being united.

They have built more prisons than schools. They have mercilessly massacred our patriots. They have drowned our uprisings in seas of blood.

They have fettered public opinion and practised obscurantism.

They have weakened our race with opium and alcohol.

In the field of economics, they have sucked us dry, driven our people to destitution and devastated our land.

They have robbed us of our ricefields, our mines, our forests and our natural resources. They have monopolized the issue of bank-notes and the import and export trade.

They have invented numerous unjustifiable taxes and reduced our people, especially our peasantry, to extreme poverty.

They have made it impossible for our national bourgeoisie to prosper; they have mercilessly exploited our workers.

In the autumn of 1940, when the Japanese fascists invaded Indochina to establish new bases against the Allies, the French colonialists went down on their bended knees and opened the doors of our country to welcome Japanese in. [...]

When the Japanese surrendered to the Allies, our entire people rose to gain power and founded the Democratic Republic of Viet Nam.

The truth is that we have wrested our independence from the Japanese, not from the French.

The French have fled, the Japanese have capitulated, Emperor Bao Dai has abdicated. Our people have broken the chains which have fettered them for nearly a century and have won independence for Viet Nam. At the same time they have overthrown the centuries-old monarchic regime and established a democratic republican regime.

We, the Provisional Government of the new Viet Nam, representing the entire Vietnamese people, hereby declare that from now on we break off all relations of a colonial character with France; cancel all treaties signed by France on Viet Nam, and abolish all privileges held by France in our country.

The entire Vietnamese people are of one mind in their determination to oppose all wicked schemes by the French colonialists.

Source: Ho Chi Minh, "Declaration of Independence of the Democratic Republic of Viet Nam," in *Ho Chi Minh: Selected Writings 1920–1969* (Hanoi: Foreign Languages Publishing House, 1977), 53–56.

We are convinced that the Allies, which at the Teheran and San Francisco Conferences upheld the principle of equality among the nations, cannot fail to recognize the right of the Vietnamese people to independence.

A people who have courageously opposed French enslavement for more than eighty years, a people who have resolutely sided with the Allies against the fascists during these last years, such a people must be free, such a people must be independent.

For these reasons, we, the Provisional Government of the Democratic Republic of Viet Nam, solemnly make this declaration to the world:

Viet Nam has the right to enjoy freedom and independence and in fact has become a free and independent country. The entire Vietnamese people are determined to mobilize all their physical and mental strength, to sacrifice their lives and property in order to safeguard their freedom and independence.

A U.S. Veteran's Interpretation of the Origins of the Vietnam War

Before his election to the U.S. Congress as the Junior Senator from Virginia in November 2006, James Webb was most celebrated as the author of novels and nonfiction texts, many of which address the experience of being a United States Marine. Webb served, in Vietnam and elsewhere, between 1968 and 1972, and was awarded the Navy Cross, the Silver Star Medal, two Bronze Star Medals, and two Purple Hearts. He subsequently became a lawyer as well as an author and went into government service. In 1987 he became Secretary of the Navy for the Republican President of the United States, Ronald Reagan. As he is now a Democratic Senator, he is one of the few major political figures in the United States to have served both large political parties.

Webb has written a number of articles that address the experience of the United States in the Vietnam war. In Why We Fought and Why We Would Do it Again, *Webb gives a different perspective on modern Vietnamese history and the origins of the Vietnam conflict than that described in the Vietnamese Declaration of Independence. A veteran of this conflict himself, Webb defends American actions and asserts that the United States forces in Indochina fought effectively and justifiably in defense of South Vietnam's sovereignty.*

>> 114. Why We Fought and Why We Would Do It Again

JAMES WEBB [2003]

Forty years ago, Asia was at a vital crossroads, moving into an uncertain future dominated by three different historical trends. The first involved the aftermath of the carnage and destruction of World War II, which left scars on every country in the region and dramatically changed Japan's role in East Asian affairs. The second was the sudden, regionwide end of European colonialism, which created governmental vacuums in every second-tier country except Thailand and, to a lesser extent, the Philippines. The third was the emergence of communism as a powerful tool of expansionism by

Source: James Webb, *Why We Fought and Why We Would Do It Again,* September 2003, http://www.jameswebb.com/articles/variouspubs/amlegionwhywefought.htm.

military force, its doctrine and strategies emanating principally from the birthplace of the Communist International: the Soviet Union.

Europe's withdrawal from the region dramatically played into the hands of communist revolutionary movements, especially in the wake of the communist takeover of China in 1949. Unlike in Europe, these countries had never known Western-style democracy. In 1950, the partitioned country of Korea exploded into war when the communist North invaded South Korea, with the Chinese Army joining the effort six months later. Communist insurgencies erupted throughout Indochina. In Malaysia, the British led a 10-year anti-guerrilla campaign against China-backed revolutionaries. A similar insurgency in Indonesia brought about a communist coup attempt, also sponsored by the Chinese, which was put down in 1965.

The situation inside Vietnam was the most complicated. First, for a variety of reasons the French had not withdrawn from their long-term colony after World War II, making it easy for insurgents to rally the nationalistic Vietnamese to their side. Second, the charismatic, Soviet-trained communist leader Ho Chi Minh had quickly consolidated his anti-French power base just after the war by assassinating the leadership of competing political groups that were both anti-French and anti-communist. Third, once the Korean War armistice was signed in 1953, the Chinese had shifted large amounts of sophisticated weaponry to Ho Chi Minh's army. The Viet Minh's sudden acquisition of larger-caliber weapons and field artillery such as the 105-millimeter Howitzer abruptly changed the nature of the war and contributed heavily to the French humiliation at Dien Bien Phu.

Fourth, further war became inevitable when U.S.-led backers of the incipient South Vietnamese democracy called off a 1956 election agreed upon after Vietnam was divided in 1954. In geopolitical terms, this failure to go forward with elections was prudent, since it was clear a totalitarian state had emerged in the north. President Eisenhower's frequently quoted admonition that Ho Chi Minh would get 75 percent of the vote was not predicated on the communist leader's popularity but on the impossibility of getting a fair vote in communist-controlled North Vietnam. But in propaganda terms, it solidified Ho Chi Minh's standing and in many eyes justified the renewed warfare he would begin in the south two years later.

In 1958, the communists unleashed a terrorist campaign in the south. Within two years, their northern-trained squads were assassinating an average of 11 government officials a day. President Kennedy referred to this campaign in 1961 when he decided to increase the number of American soldiers operating inside South Vietnam. "We have talked about and read stories of 7,000 to 15,000 guerrillas operating in Vietnam, killing 2,000 civil officers a year and 2,000 police officers a year—4,000 total," Kennedy said. "How we fight that kind of problem, which is going to be with us all through this decade, seems to me to be one of the great problems now before the United States."

Among the local populace, the communist assassination squads were the "stick," threatening to kill anyone who officially affiliated with the South Vietnamese government. Along with the assassination squads came the "carrot," a highly trained political cadre that also infiltrated South Vietnam from the north. The cadre helped the people prepare defenses in their villages, took rice from farmers as taxes and recruited Viet Cong soldiers from the local young population. Spreading out into key areas—such as those provinces just below the demilitarized zone, those bordering Laos and Cambodia, and those with future access routes to key cities—the communists gained strong footholds.

The communists began spreading out from their enclaves, fighting on three levels simultaneously. First, they continued their terror campaign, assassinating local leaders, police officers, teachers and others who declared support for the South Vietnamese government. Second, they waged an effective small-unit guerrilla war that was designed to disrupt commerce, destroy morale and clasp local communities to their cause. And finally, beginning in late 1964, they introduced conventional forces from the north, capable of facing, if not defeating, main force infantry units—including the Americans—on the battlefield. Their gamble was that once the United States began fighting on a larger scale— as it did in March 1965—its people would not support a long war of attrition. As Ho Chi Minh famously put it, "For every one of yours we kill, you will kill 10 of ours. But in the end it is you who will grow tired."

Ho Chi Minh was right. The infamous "body counts" were continuously disparaged by the media and the antiwar movement. Hanoi removed the doubt in 1995, when on the 20th anniversary of the fall of Saigon officials admitted having lost 1.1 million combat soldiers dead, with another 300,000 "still missing."

Communist losses of 1.4 million dead compared to America's losses of 58,000 and South Vietnam's 245,000 stand as stark evidence that eliminates many myths about the war. The communists, and particularly the North Vietnamese, were excellent and determined soldiers. But the "wily, elusive guerrillas" that the media loved to portray were not exclusively wily, elusive or even guerrillas when one considers that their combat deaths were four times those of their enemies, combined. And an American military that located itself halfway around the world to take on a determined enemy on the terrain of the enemy's choosing was hardly the incompetent, demoralized and confused force that so many antiwar professors, journalists and filmmakers love to portray.

Why Did We Fight? The United States recognized South Vietnam as a political entity separate from North Vietnam, just as it recognized West Germany as separate from communist-controlled East Germany and just as it continues to recognize South Korea from communist-controlled North Korea. As signatories of the Southeast Asian Treaty Organization, we pledged to defend South Vietnam from external aggression. South Vietnam was invaded by the north, just as certainly, although with more sophistication, as South Korea was invaded by North Korea. The extent to which the North Vietnamese, as well as antiwar Americans, went to deny this reality by pretending the war was fought only by Viet Cong soldiers from the south is, historically, one of the clearest examples of their disingenuous conduct. . . .

>> Mastering the Material

1. Analyze the Kennan and Novikov telegrams as sources. Are they statements of fact, or opinions? Why were they so well received by their own governments? What do they tell us about their authors? Do you think these individuals were effective diplomats?

2. The Kennan and Novikov telegrams could be used as evidence of either a real ideological divide between the United States and the Soviet Union in 1946 or a series of misunderstandings that led to confrontation. Which analysis do you think is more correct? Why?

3. Reread the Vietnamese Declaration of Independence carefully. Why do you think it was written? What was its intended audience? How do you know?

4. James Webb explains the United States' entry into the Vietnam war from the perspective of a veteran and later policy maker. Do you think the threat of a communist Vietnam seemed very real to policy makers in the United States at the time? Why or why not?

5. Consider the two readings on the Vietnam War together. Do you think it was a mistake for the United States' goverment not to recognize an independent Vietnam in 1945, or not? Why do you think they did not do so?

>> Making Connections

1. Do you think the Cold War was merely a continuation of "great-power" politics such as led to the new imperialism and the First World War? Why or why not?

2. Both Kwame Nkrumah (Chapter 22) and Ho Chi Minh were nationalists who came to embrace socialism and, in the case of Ho Chi Minh, communism. Many other independence leaders did as well. How do you explain this tendency?

3. Just as Vladimir Lenin saw imperialism in largely economic terms (Chapter 13), Nikolai Novikov depicted U.S. foreign policy as serving the aims of capitalism. This reflects the Marxist interpretation of history that places primacy on economic causality. In your opinion, is this an accurate depiction of history?

4. James P. Harrison brings up the legacy of appeasement—the Munich effect (Chapter 20)—to help explain American involvement in Vietnam. What does he mean by this? How might the events the Munich appeasement of 1938 have contributed to the thinking of American policy makers in the 1960s?

5. To what degree does the Vietnamese Declaration of Independence reflect "enlightenment" values (Chapters 7 and 8)?

6. Compare and contrast the Vietnamese Declaration of Independence to the Haitian Declaration of Independence (Chapter 9). How are they different, and why? Are there ways in which they are very similar?

7. During the Rivonia trial, Nelson Mandela (Chapter 22) was accused of being a communist/Marxist. He responded by writing "I have been influenced by Marxist thought. But this is true of many of the leaders of the new independent states. Such widely different persons as Gandhi, Nehru, Nkrumah, and Nasser all acknowledge this fact." Why do you think so many leaders of independence movements, such as these individuals and Ho Chi Minh, were heavily influenced by communism? To what degree was it merely in order to win the support of the Soviet Union in the context of the Cold War? To what degree was it because of ideological similarities between anticolonial and Marxist ideologies (Chapter 13)?

Chapter 24

Perspectives on Globalization

The term **globalization** became widely popularized in the 1990s as a label for the evident interconnectedness of human societies. Arguably, globalization was not entirely new. Indeed, an underlying principle of world history is that connections between societies were important in shaping the human experience even in the distant past. However, globalization had never been as apparent a key factor in daily life as in the past fifty years. In the post-war era, populations have shared information, goods, and money more than ever before, and isolation from the world seems increasingly less achievable.

In Part 5, we have already explored two post-war global political processes: the Cold War and decolonization. Globalization also manifested itself in this period in the environment: the impact of pollution produced in one region upon other regions, for example. Culture, similarly, flowed across state boundaries almost without impediment. Contemporary observers identified the globalization of American and Japanese fashion, food, and technology first, but the process was far more complex and reciprocal.

The most easily observable aspect of globalization in the past half-century, however, has been the increasing integration of the world's economies. The ongoing amalgamation of global production and markets since the uniting of the Old and New Worlds in the fifteenth century culminated in the post-war period in a world economy that seemed to transcend borders. Admittedly, it is still sometimes useful to speak of economies in national terms. Thus many economic historians point out that for much of the post-war period the United States' economy seemed preeminent, even while the United States was being challenged politically and militarily by the Soviet Union. Yet the resurrection of European and Japanese industrialization and the subsequent emergence of China, India, and southeast Asia as leading global producers drew some scholars to conclude that the global post-war economy really had many centers, rather than just one. More disturbingly, scholars as early as the 1960s began to describe and then to criticize the limited role allowed to the economies of Africa, parts of Asia, Latin America, and other formerly colonized regions by the global market. They argued that even though these states had liberated themselves politically from imperial domination, they remained "economically colonized" because their economies were merely producers of raw materials and consumers of finished products. Thus they were dependent on companies owned largely by shareholders in wealthy countries, who kept most of the profits out of the hands of the populations of more impoverished states. As dissidents began to label this aspect of the global economy **neocolonialism,** regional dissatisfaction began to coalesce into opposition to globalization. Although these movements were initially confined to intellectuals by the 1990s, they had become widely popular in some parts of the world, especially among low-waged workers, farmers, and the unemployed. Often described as antiglobalization, these protestors tend to focus their anger on certain aspects of the global economy rather than interrelatedness itself.

This concept of exploitation is central to the debate over economic globalization. Specifically, scholars have struggled to determine whether globalization is a deliberate and guided process in which a few wealthy groups and individuals have sought to dominate the world economy or merely an unguided process that has unfolded in response to global trends and events. Ironically, this debate has sometimes been expressed in terms of national identity. Detractors have depicted globalization as especially serving the needs of the United States. Yet other theorists have argued that placing the United States at the center of globalization is **ahistorical:** It lacks an acknowledgement of the phenomenon's historical roots and the path it wove through many periods of history. One of the principal arguments of such theorists is that the process by which economies have become integrated goes back far beyond the creation of the United States, at least to the fifteenth century age of exploration and exploitation and perhaps as far back as the Bronze Age in Eurasia and North Africa (3000 B.C.E.). Nevertheless, there can be little doubt that in the post-war period the United States played a leading role in globalization in the post-war era. To what extent did the U.S. government shape this latest phase of economic integration? That is the question addressed by David Reynolds in his article "American Globalism: Mass, Motion, and the Multiplier Effect."

Neither Reynolds nor the well-known leftist economic historian Andre Gunder Frank sees globalization as the project of a particular state alone. Yet Frank has argued in his influential economic history *Capitalism and Underdevelopment in Latin America* that global economic integration has largely had a negative impact on the populations of some states and regions. Much of the pioneering work on underdevelopment focused on Latin America. Scholars based at Latin American universities initiated the argument that their states' resources, like those of many other regions, were largely expropriated by wealthy groups in Europe and the United States. To these theorists, twentieth-century economic globalization was merely a continuation of exploitation of the populations of these regions.

While some attention has been focused on the idea of globalization as the project of states and governments, other observers suggest instead that globalization is in fact rendering the state increasingly irrelevant. The principal forces trying to shape and influence globalization, they argue, are international corporations, global lobbies, transnational ideological affiliations including terrorist groups, and organizations such as the World Bank and the United Nations. This is the understanding of globalization embraced by Keith Suter, who argues in *Global Order and Global Disorder* that the post-war period is in fact the cusp of a new era in world history, one in which the nation-state will become outmoded. Suter thus argues that we are in a crisis moment in world history, in which the future system of global organization remains to be defined. This debate is taken up in Chapter 25 as well.

Not all who foresee the replacement of states by multinational entities are optimistic about the future. Among the critics of globalization is the Zapatista leader Subcomandante Marcos in Chiapas, Mexico. Subcomandante Marcos' original identity is not fully determined, although the Mexican government has identified him as a former academic at the Metropolitan Autonomous University in Mexico City. Marcos is a leader of the Zapatista uprising, a major challenge to the Mexican state by indigenous peoples in the south of the country. Yet he also plays a greater role in embracing citizens of other states whom he believes have been oppressed and sidelined by globalization. In the late 1990s, Marcos defined the struggle to shape globalization as the Fourth World War. He argued that the current model of what he calls "neoliberal" (capitalist) globalization is a continuity of colonialism and serves only the economic purposes of a few wealthy individuals. Marcos' writings represent an important strand in the ideology of an increasingly international antiglobalization movement. Another strand comes from activists like Medha Paktar who use non-violent resistance as a tool to protect villagers from development in places like India. Ironically, by organizing across societies and regions this loosely aligned set of factions is itself becoming increasingly globalized.

An American Century?

The issue of globalization seems a natural fit with the discipline of world history. The two really converged in the late 1990s, as economists responded to historians' reinterpreting the history of the world with a view to the issue of global interrelationships by adding a historical dimension to their work on economic globalization. One result was the edited volume Globalization in World History, *which linked the post-war integration with earlier eras of globalization. The culminating chapter of the book is David Reynolds' "American Globalism: Mass, Motion, and the Multiplier Effect." In it, Reynolds responds to two important scholars. The first, Henry Luce, wrote in 1941 about the coming "American Century": the post-war U.S. dominance of global finance. The second, Francis Fukuyama, has written recently about what he asserts is the triumph of the American capitalist, nation-state system. Reynolds assesses these claims through two questions. First, to what degree was post-war globalization an American-led phenomenon? Second, to what extent was it something new rather than merely the reproduction of earlier globalizations? His conclusions are very balanced*

>> 115. American Globalism: Mass, Motion, and the Multiplier Effect

DAVID REYNOLDS [2002]

In February 1941 Henry R. Luce, the owner of *Time* and *Life* magazines, published what became a celebrated essay entitled 'The American Century'. In it he claimed that humanity constituted 'for the first time in history one world, fundamentally indivisible'. Luce also insisted that the twentieth century would and should be 'the American Century', defined by the country's wealth, power and values in four fundamental respects. Only the United States, said Luce, could determine whether 'a system of free economic

Source: David Reynolds, "American Globalism: Mass, Motion, and the Multiplier Effect," in *Globalization in World History,* edited by A. G. Hopkins (London: Pimlico, 2002), 243–244, 252, 255, 257–258.

enterprise' would prevail globally. He also argued that America must act as the main source and trainer of skilled labour. Third, it was the country's duty to be 'the Good Samaritan of the entire world', feeding the hungry and helping the destitute. Above all, Luce argued, the United States should serve not merely as a 'sanctuary' for 'the ideals of Freedom and Justice' in an era of war but also 'the powerhouse' from which those ideals 'spread throughout the world'.

Sixty years on, many Americans would probably say that Luce's agenda has been amply realized. The twentieth century seems indeed to have been the American century. Having 'won' the Cold War and watched the collapse of the Soviet Union, having witnessed the collapse of communism across Eastern Europe and its slow but apparently inexorable metamorphosis within 'Red China', the United States was left as the sole superpower. America was also the centre of the Internet revolution and the internationalization of financial markets. Its consumer values of 'fast music, fast computers and fast food' were apparently carrying all before them, 'pressing nations into one homogeneous theme park, one McWorld'. The most celebrated exponent of American triumphalism, Francis Fukuyama, argued that the 'unabashed victory of economic and political liberalism' in the Cold War signalled 'the end point of mankind's ideological evolution and the universalization of Western liberal democracy as the final form of human government'. [...]

Globalization became a cult concept of the 1990s. Pundits filled up the column inches; academics generated weighty tomes. [...]

American globalism *was* historically distinctive, not so much because of some intrinsic American virtues but because of its interaction with the historical novelty of modern mass technologies. [...]

Much of the explanation for the extent and intensity of American globalism lies in the distinctiveness of modern technologies and the pre-eminence of the United States in exploiting them. My shorthands for this process are mass, motion and the multiplier effect. Mass has two referents. One is the truism that the twentieth century is in various ways 'the age of the masses', especially in democratic politics, consumer economies and popular culture. The other referent is the 'mass' of the United States itself as a very large and very prosperous state that also enjoyed, in the twentieth century, remarkable stability. America's mass was the crucible of 'massification'. And that mass was mobilized internationally through the multiplier effect of modern technology. This has enabled America to ratchet up its power, wealth and cultural influence to a historically unprecedented degree. [...]

But the world was not a blank slate for Americans to write on. Mobilization provoked opposition: that is a familiar, though important, point. More interesting are the ways in which America's international impact varied according to national circumstances—the global modified by the local.

In the arena of power, the Vietnam War is a classic example of what has been called the impotence of omnipotence. Despite committing 500,000 troops, sustaining 50,000 deaths and dropping a larger tonnage of bombs than it did in the whole of World War II, the United States could not avert a communist takeover of South Vietnam. Some of its impotence was self-induced (the domestic backlash against US involvement), some of it a consequence of Cold-War confrontation (the desire to avoid direct conflict with the Russians and the Chinese). Nevertheless, the outcome of that war was a reminder that the size of a country's GDP or the magnitude of its nuclear arsenal did not automatically determine international outcomes. [...]

In various ways [...] it is simplistic to imply that the world is being Americanized. Moreover, as in earlier epochs of US history, America's own identity is not fixed: the international is also still being used to define the national. In the 'unipolar' era of the 1990s, some pundits discerned new threats to replace that of Soviet-directed communism. Near the top of the list was a supposed monolith called militant Islam. Samuel Huntington enlarged this anxiety into a general argument that 'the fault lines between civilizations will be the battlelines of the future'. On closer examination, however, many of the most ruinous recent wars have occurred *within* rather than *between* his putative civilizations (Vietnam–Cambodia, Iran–Iraq or Hutu–Tutsi). As John Gray has remarked, Huntington's vision 'tells us more about contemporary American anxieties than it does about the late modern world'. [...]

What, then, should we make of Henry Luce's assertions about the American Century? [...] Americans did not invent globalization, nor did they simply stamp the modern world in their own image. [...]

[But] American-led globalization has been historically distinct. This is because of the unusual bulk and coherence of the United States as a very large yet functionally effective polity and economy and because that mass was mobilized globally through the unprecedentedly large multiplier effect of modern technologies. The twentieth century was neither the end of history nor the beginning of globalization. But it was conspicuously American.

Transnationality

Globalization is sometimes interpreted as consigning borders to irrelevancy. In fact, scholars have probably paid too much attention to borders throughout history as zones of exclusion, portraying great differences between the people, ideas, and products on each side. Instead, borders are often zones of interaction: places where ideas, people, and things are exchanged. Australian social scientist Keith Suter and others argue that the ongoing integration of the world is further diminishing the importance of borders. Suter contends that the role of nation-states and state governments is fading at a faster pace than at any time in the previous four centuries. However, even he admits that it remains unclear what type of geopolitical system will replace the network of nation-states that has characterized the modern era.

>> 116. Global Order and Global Disorder: Globalization and the Nation-State

KEITH SUTER [2003]

The current world order is ending, but there is no clear replacement for it. The old order has been based on nation-states, or countries, with centralized national governments. The old order has worn well but now it is wearing out.

The process of globalization, which is now the most important factor in world politics, is undermining the traditional order and leading to world disorder.

Globalization is defined in this book as the process by which the nation-state is eroding as the basic unit of world politics. The term includes the declining power of national governments and the reduced significance of national boundaries. [...]

Source: Keith Suter, *Global Order and Global Disorder: Globalization and the Nation-State* (Westport: Praeger, 2003), 1, 17, 31, 67, 115.

The nation-state is the basic component of the old world order. The old world order is also called the Westphalian System, and it is named after the Westphalian peace process of 1648. The Westphalian System has worn well. But it is now wearing out.

No one in Europe in 1648 suddenly realized that he or she was now living in a new era. Everyday life remained harsh. There were plagues and poverty; that the peace at the end of the Thirty Years War would last was not guaranteed. Some of the components of the Westphalian System were in place before the key year of 1648, and many of them would arrive later.

Within the context of the globalization process, the world is moving into a post-Westphalian era, with the new process creeping up on nation-states. It is not possible suddenly to declare that the Westphalian System has ended and that a new global system has taken its place. People living through such a momentous global change are the least equipped to detect the full extent of that change; later historians will have to do that. All that can now be done is identify some of the features of the change. [...]

The Westphalian System is running into problems. The nation-state [...] is being assailed in three ways. First, the high point of the Westphalian System was a two-level world, nation-states and their colonies. The era of the Europeanization of the globe has now ended. While almost all the colonies have become independent, many are having problems coping with the nation-state system, including the concept of self-determination. Meanwhile, other nation-states are also having problems coping with the legacy of empire, such as compensation for indigenous peoples.

Second, the present craft of diplomacy, which evolved in the early stages of the Westphalian System to accommodate the clique of nation-states, cannot easily absorb a far larger number of nation-states of differing sizes. Yet the legal principle of the sovereign equality of nation-states assures that, in theory at least, all states have to be accorded equal status.

Finally, the era of conventional warfare arrived with the nation-states system. For three centuries, the main mode of fighting was conventional and international warfare. That mode of warfare is being replaced by a new era in which warfare is guerrilla and internal. Instead of military forces enabling one state to attack or defend another, the forces are having to be used to maintain national governments in power and to put down dissident secessionist movements. Despite secession being such a major factor for the Westphalian System, there is a lack of both consistent international law and government practice about it. Meanwhile, the attacks of September 11, 2001, have been a reminder of the international community's failure to deal with "terrorism." [...]

Nation-states are having to share their power with three groups of global actors: transnational corporations; international, or more accurately intergovernmental, organizations such as the United Nations; and nongovernmental organizations (NGOs). This chapter looks at the new global actors.

The process of globalization, which is causing so many problems for national governments, is also having an impact on the study of international relations. The late Susan Strange, of the University of London, commented in 1992 that the standard texts in international relations subscribed to the dominant realist school of thought; this thinking held that the central issue in international society was war among nation-states, and the prime task was the maintenance of order in the relations among those states. This traditional view of international relations also held that the object of study was the behavior of states towards other states and whether the outcome of the various behaviors meant that the states were better or worse off, less or more powerful, or less or more secure. Although transnational corporations may be mentioned in passing, they were seen as adjuncts to or instruments of state policy. However, Strange argued that transnational corporations should now be put at center stage because their corporate strategies in choosing host countries as partners were already having a great and increasing influence on the development of the global political economy. [...]

The Westphalian System is similar to the view that gave the world Newtonian physics and the industrial revolution. That worldview is based on categorization, strict divisions, and neat arrangements whether these are of scientific theories, machines, or national boundaries.

But the earth's biosphere is inter-related, fluid and messy. It is a world of complex systems, with everything connected to everything else. Canadian scientists Ranjit Kumar and Barbara Murck pointed out that in order to understand the world, humans divide it up into concepts, pieces, categories, and disciplines. But the world itself is a single whole. There are no clear dividing lines between chemistry and physics, between land and sea, between Iran and Iraq, between human beings and nature— except lines made in the human mind. Even when people do recognize the world's complex interconnections, they are often surprised by these interdependencies as well as causes and effects very far apart in place or time. A drought in Canada affects wheat prices in Ghana. Pesticides applied to agricultural fields may show up in ground water 10 years later, causing cancer 30 years after that. Many of these connections are traceable and knowable, if people look for them. However, if humans are not used to crossing conceptual categories and seeing interrelationships, they will not manage things very well and will sometimes be unpleasantly surprised.

This chapter argues that the world is becoming functionally more homogenous but politically more heterogeneous. In other words, factors such as technology, finance, and communications are overriding nation-state borders, while people within those borders are ceasing to have the national uniformity required by the Westphalian System. The previous chapter argued that there are signs of both global order and disorder. While signs of both also run throughout this chapter, the notion of disorder has predominance.

Underdevelopment in Latin America

Following his seminal 1966 article "The Development of Underdevelopment," Andre Gunder Frank published an analysis of the predatory role of global economics in Brazil and Chile entitled Capitalism and Underdevelopment in Latin America. *Frank was born in Germany, and after his family fled Adolf Hitler he lived, studied, and worked in Switzerland and the United States before settling in Chile. There he contributed to the reforms of the socialist Chilean government of Salvador Allende. Frank saw the Allende reforms as an attempt to undo the ravages of underdevelopment, and he became a leading member of a global and largely Marxist group of scholars who were at that time seeking to explain underdevelopment. Frank's underlying argument was that monopolistic companies based in the industrialized nations (which he terms metropolitans), working in some cases in alliance with portions of the Latin American bourgeoisie, were purposefully holding back economic and industrial development in Latin America. In the following selections from* Capitalism and Underdevelopment, *Frank undertakes a chronologically extended analysis of the origins of Latin American dependency before focusing on the recent past. As we know from previous chapters, following the publication of this book Frank went on to work on a global scale and made his mark as an important leftist world historian before dying in 2005.*

>> 117. Capitalism and Underdevelopment in Latin America: Historical Studies of Chile and Brazil

ANDRE GUNDER FRANK [1967]

The very conquest and colonization of Latin America were acts of what today we would call foreign finance or aid. Christopher Columbus, the discoverer of America, had declared: "The best thing in the world is gold…it can even send souls to heaven…." Cortés, the conquerer of Mexico, added: "The Spaniards are troubled with a disease of the heart for which gold is the specific remedy." The Franciscan Friars confirmed: "Where there is no silver, religion does not enter." That is, the voyages of discovery and Spanish investment in Latin America, much of it with Dutch and Italian merchant capital, were part of the mercantile capitalist expansion and an attempt to tap colonial satellite natural and human resources—mostly precious metals and labor—so as to plow the proceeds into metropolitan development and consumption. […]

The Portuguese in Brazil and later the Dutch, English, and French in the Caribbean did not find a happy combination of silver, labor, and civilization; and therefore they had to create a colonial economy through foreign finance. Indirectly, it was the previous Spanish-American bonanza that made this finance possible, if not necessary, by concentrating income and raising the prices of sugar and other products in Europe. The metropolitan countries erected plantation economies in these tropical lands, putting African Negroes to work producing Latin American sugar for European tables. […]

It is clear, then, that from the beginning the real flow of foreign finance has been heavily from Latin America to the metropolis. This means that Latin America has had resources or investment capital of its own but that much of it has been transferred abroad through foreign trade and finance, and invested there instead of in Latin America. This transfer of capital out of Latin America, rather than its supposed nonexistence there, has evidently been the first cause of Latin America's need for more investment capital, such as that invested by foreigners. […]

The economic and political ascendancy of Great Britain and the political independence of Latin America after the Napoleonic Wars left three major interest groups to decide the future of Latin America through their tripartite struggle: (1) The Latin American agricultural, mining, and commercial interests who sought to maintain the underdevelopment-generating, export-economy structure—and only wanted to dislodge their Iberian rivals from their privileged positions in it; (2) the industrial and other interest groups from the aforementioned and other interior regions, who sought to defend their budding but still weak development-generating economies from more free trade and foreign finance, which was threatening to force them out of existence; and (3) the victorious and industrializing British whose Foreign Secretary Lord Canning noted in 1824: "Spanish America is free; and if we do not mismanage our affairs sadly, she is English." The battle lines were drawn, with the traditional Latin American import-export and the metropolitan industrial-merchant bourgeoisies in natural alliance against the weak Latin American provincial and industrial nationalists. The outcome was practically predetermined by the past historical process of capitalist development, which had stacked the cards this way.

In 1824, in accord with Canning's guideline remarks, Britain began—mostly through Baring Brothers—to make massive loans to various Latin American governments who had begun life with debts incurred for the expenses of the wars of independence and even debts inherited from their colonial predecessors. The loans, of course, were granted to pave the way for trade with Britain,

Source: Andre Gunder Frank, *Capitalism and Underdevelopment in Latin America: Historical Studies of Chile and Brazil* (New York: Monthly Review Press, 1967), 281–286, 294–296, 299, 304–306, 312.

and in some cases they were accompanied by investments in mining and other activities. But the time was not yet ripe.

Reviewing this episode, Rosa Luxemburg asks with Tugan-Baranowski, whom she quotes: "But from where did the South American countries take the means to buy twice as many commodities in 1825 as in 1821? The British themselves supplied these means. The loans floated on the London stock exchange served as payment for imported goods." [...]

The significance and "profitability" of imperialist foreign finance lies not in the net earnings of foreign investment, however calculated, but in their place in capitalist development and underdevelopment. Imperialist finance directed a large net flow of capital from the poor underdeveloped Latin American countries to the rich developed ones of the metropolis even at the height of Lenin's "capital export" imperialism; Cairncross (1953: 180) estimates Britain's export of capital at £ 2,400 million and the income from its investments at £ 4,100 million between 1870 and 1913. Latin America supplied the metropolis with needed industrial raw materials and cheap food for their workers at terms of trade ever more favorable to the metropolis—which helped to stem the rise of metropolitan wages, and to provide foreign markets for capital equipment and consumer goods—thus helping to maintain high monopoly prices and profits in the metropolis while exerting further downward pressure on real wages. [...]

Indeed, in Latin America imperialism went further. It not only availed itself of the state to invade agriculture; it took over nearly all economic and political institutions to incorporate the entire economy into the imperialist system. The latifundia grew at a pace and to proportions unknown in all previous history, especially in Argentina, Uruguay, Brazil, Cuba, Mexico, and Central America. With the aid of the Latin American governments, foreigners came to own—usually for next to nothing—immense tracts of land. And where they did not get the land, they got its products anyway; because the metropolis also took over and monopolized the merchandising of agricultural and most other products. The

metropolis took over Latin American mines and expanded their output, sometimes exhausting irreplaceable resources, such, as the Chilean nitrates, in a few years. To get these raw materials out of Latin America and to get its equipment and goods in, the metropolis stimulated the construction of ports and railroads and, to service all this, public utilities. The railroad network and electric grid, far from being grid-like, was ray-like and connected the hinterland of each country and sometimes of several countries with the port of entry and exit, which was in turn connected to the metropolis. Today, four score years later, much of this export-import pattern still remains, in part because the railroad right-of-way is still laid out that way and, more important, because the metropolitan-oriented urban, economic, and political development which nineteenth-century imperialism generated in Latin America gave rise to vested interests who, with metropolitan support, managed to maintain and expand this development of Latin American underdevelopment during the twentieth century.

Implanted in the colonial epoch and deepened in the free trade era, the structure of underdevelopment was consolidated in Latin America by nineteenth-century imperialist trade and finance. [...]

With World War I the world capitalist system began a new stage of its development. This was not so much the shift of the metropolitan center from Europe to the United States, as the associated transformation of what had been industrial and then financial capitalism into monopoly capitalism. Beginning typically in the United States but then arising also in Europe and Japan, the simple industrial firm or financial house of old was replaced by the nationally-based but world-embracing and really international giant monopoly corporation, which, is a multi-industry, mass assembly-line producer of standardized products—and now of new technology as well—and is its own worldwide purchasing agent, salesman, financier, and often de facto government in many satellite countries and increasingly in many metropolitan ones as well. [...]

By 1950, 300 American corporations accounted for more than 90 percent of American direct investment holdings in Latin America and since then "the degree of concentration has been consolidated still more." [...]

In Latin America, the international monopoly corporation uses technology to compete with and eliminate or absorb local rivals, who lack the funds or suppliers to buy, or cannot get import licenses for similar equipment. [...]

This monopoly-capitalist foreign finance, beyond supplying the profits with which more and more of the Latin American economy is bought up by the metropolitan monopolies, of course generates an ever larger remission of profits by these foreign firms and flow of capital from Latin America to the United States. [...]

Since the international corporations evade taxes and exchange restrictions by regular overpricing the home office sales to their Latin American subsidiaries, and underpricing its purchases from them, part of their profits are hidden under the cost items; and the real remission of profits from investments in, and therewith of capital from, Latin America to the metropolis is higher than that registered by either the metropolitan or the Latin American governments. [...]

Neo-imperialist monopoly capitalism has rapidly and effectively penetrated and incorporated the Latin American economy, polity, society, and culture. Like colonial and imperialist development before it, only more so, this neo-imperialist penetration of Latin America has found old Latin American interest groups and created new ones that are allied and subservient to metropolitan interests and policy. They increasingly monopolize the Latin American economy and share among them the spoils of exploiting the people of Latin America (and to a lesser extent the people of the metropolis).

Subcomandante Marcos on the "The Fourth World War"

Keith Suter is generally seen as a proponent of globalization, partly as a means of eradicating conflict between nation-states. Yet opinion remains divided on the usefulness of eliminating national identity and the nation-state. One critic is the Mexican dissident Subcomandante Marcos who, in this excerpted speech, builds on Andre Gunder Frank's definition of globalization as a "neoliberal" project intended to serve the needs of the wealthy by creating a single global market. An important component of this process, Marcos argues, is breaking down people's culture and identities in order to turn them into faceless producers and consumers. Marcos associates the struggle to preserve national and ethnic identities with resistance to oppression based on gender, sexual orientation, and ethnicity. In his view, globalization is a conspiracy against which all oppressed people must struggle. That is the meaning of the "Fourth World War."

>> 118. The Fourth World War

SUBCOMANDANTE MARCOS [2001]

The Third World War, or the Cold War, lasted from 1946 (or, if you wish, from the bombing of Hiroshima in 1945) until 1985–1990. It was a large world war made up of many local wars. [...]

The result, as we all know, was the defeat and destruction of the USSR, and the victory of the US, around which the great majority of countries have now come together. This is when what we call the "Fourth World War" broke out. And here a problem arose. The product of the previous war should have been a unipolar

Source: Subcomandante Marcos, "The Fourth World War," *In Motion Magazine* (November 2001).

world—one single nation which dominated a world where there were no rivals—but, in order to make itself effective, this unipolar world would have to reach what is known as "globalization." The world must be conceived as a large conquered territory with an enemy destroyed. It was necessary to administer this new world, and, therefore, to globalize it. They turned, then, to information technology, which, in the development of humanity, is as important as the invention of the steam engine. Computers allow one to be anywhere simultaneously. There are no longer any borders or constraints of time or geography. It is thanks to computers that the process of globalization began. Separations, differences, Nation States, all eroded, and the world became what is called, realistically, the global village.

The concept on which globalization is based is what we call "neoliberalism," a new religion which is going to permit this process to be carried out. With this Fourth World War, once again, territories are being conquered, enemies are being destroyed and the conquest of these territories is being administered.

The problem is, what territories are being conquered and reorganized, and who is the enemy? Given that the previous enemy has disappeared, we are saying that humanity is now the enemy. The Fourth World War is destroying humanity as globalization is universalizing the market, and everything human which opposes the logic of the market is an enemy and must be destroyed. In this sense, we are all the enemy to be vanquished: indigenous, non-indigenous, human rights observers, teachers, intellectuals, artists. Anyone who believes themselves to be free and is not. [...]

The first obstacle is the Nation States: they must be attacked and destroyed. Everything which makes a State "national" must be destroyed: language, culture, economy, its political life and its social fabric. If national languages are no longer of use, they must be destroyed, and a new language must be promoted. Contrary to what one might think, it is not English, but computers. All languages must be made the same,

translated into computer language, even English. All cultural aspects that make a French person French, an Italian Italian, a Dane Danish, a Mexican Mexican, must be destroyed, because they are barriers which prevent them from entering the globalized market. It is no longer a question of making one market for the French, and another for the English or the Italians. There must be one single market, in which the same person can consume the same product in any part of the world, and where the same person acts like a citizen of the world, and no longer as a citizen of a Nation State. [...]

If the social fabric is broken, the old relationships of solidarity which make coexistence possible in a Nation State also break down. That is why campaigns against homosexuals and lesbians, against immigrants, or the campaigns of xenophobia, are encouraged. Everything which previously maintained a certain equilibrium has to be broken at the point at which this world war attacks a Nation State and transforms it into something else.

It is about homogenizing, of making everyone equal, and of hegemonizing a lifestyle. It is global life. Its greatest diversion should be the computer, its work should be the computer, its value as a human being should be the number of credit cards, one's purchasing capacity, one's productive capacity. The case of the teachers is quite clear. The one who has the most knowledge or who is the wisest is no longer valuable. Now the one who produces the most research is valuable, and that is how his salary, his grants, his place in the university, are decided.

This has a lot to do with the United States model. It also so happens, however, that this Fourth World War produces an opposite effect, which we call "fragmentation." The world is, paradoxically, not becoming one, it is breaking up into many pieces. Although it is assumed that the citizen is being made equal, differences as differences are emerging: homosexuals and lesbians, young people, immigrants. Nation States are functioning as a large State, the anonymous State-land-society which divides us into many pieces.

Interview with Medha Patkar

Not all critics of globalization are militants like Subcommandante Marcos. Medha Patkar is a social worker who became the leader of a movement to stop the building of a dam that threatened to flood numerous villages in India. Paktar utilizes Gandhian strategies of noncompliance and nonviolent resistance like hunger strikes, community education, and peaceful marches against police brutality and imprisonment. In this interview, Paktar explains to Robert Jensen her opposition to unquestioned "development" and globalization. She argues that not all industrialization and development is positive, but rather that it must be managed to meet peoples needs. She also suggests that since the challenges facing her community are global, so too must be the solutions. Although she has her critics, Paktar has won great recognition and many prizes.

>> 119. Interview with Medha Patkar

ROBERT JENSEN [2004]

....Do you see these issues as fundamentally international in scope?

Development issues cannot be contained within national boundaries. In India, even though there is hardly any land to relocate people onto, the projects are on the fast track, and those decisions are being made not just in Delhi and Bombay but also in Washington and Geneva. When there are more and more such projects going forward, the people's sovereignty over natural resources and human rights are by passed. It's essential that we reach the global centers of power to fight not just centralized planning, but privatization-based planning. We have fought that at the local and national level. We have to ally with friends across the world to know the companies and challenge the companies; we need joint plans and action.

What role can people in the United States play?

We have to challenge these forces, conveying to them that we who resist are not just in nooks and corners of the world. We are together. A decade ago no one could have imagined we would be in

Seattle [protest of the World Trade Organization in 1999] or Prague [protest of the International Monetary Fund and World Bank in 2000] in such numbers. But it can't be just a one-time demonstration in the street, but continuous strategizing and action on multiple fronts that can challenge these forces, which are otherwise very arrogant and secretive. People in the United States can have a confrontational dialogue with U.S. companies, and convey to them our views. It's important for us to get information about these companies—about lawsuits against them in the United States, for example, or about those companies' interests—so that we know what companies are being ushered in by our government and then we can mobilize people in India more effectively.

The development paradigm can be better challenged if we join hands. Otherwise, it is seen as the poor and displaced people raising questions for their own interests. There has to be a micro-to-macro linkage to put ourselves forward as political actors.

For example, the World Bank is going into water and hydropower, not only through large dams, but also in the inter-river basin transfer projects and even some large dams in the northeast of India. This is threatening the water rights of many communities. This interlinking of rivers

Source: Robert Jensen, "Interview with Medha Patkar," *ZMag* 17 (April 2004).

will lead to privatization of our rivers. Groups in the United States can help us by challenging the institutions there that are involved.

Some say "You want to keep people poor" or "You romanticize peasant life." You've heard those criticisms. What is wrong with their development paradigm? What is your vision of sustainable development?

We've made it very clear that we are not against development per se, if that is defined as a change that is desirable and acceptable within our value framework. Our framework is not an individualist one. It is the framework of the Indian constitution, values of equity and justice. Sustainability has to mean justice to the population beyond one generation. That can come only if the priorities are set right. Our priority is the basic need fulfillment of every individual and that cannot happen unless the planning process is really democratic. Equitable and sustainable development presumes that the natural resources will be used. But in the choice of technologies and the priorities of goals and objectives, the preference should be given to the most needy sections, not to those who already have.

If you have to submerge the land in an agricultural area, you are not only displacing people, but also affecting the core of the economy, and hence that decision needs to be taken carefully, to avoid displacement as much as possible. The government does not have the alternative land to rehabilitate people. If we don't give priority to community needs and instead focus on taking water to distant populations, then we invariably encroach on community rights.

How should development go forward?

We must have decentralized management of resources, whether it is water, land, forest, or fish. Rights should be granted first to the smallest unit of population and the benefits should first take care of that unit, moving upward. That doesn't mean that no exogenous source of water should be used. The same can be said of minerals. Unless you grant rights to the people living on the land under which you find mineral resources, you deprive the local population of that resource.

Our view of development is supportive of labor-intensive technologies that would not create unemployment, but would create livelihood opportunities for people when the resources are used. We are for technology that will not spoil, pollute, and destroy our natural resources, which still are rich enough and still in the hands of rural communities, which are simple-living, non-consumerist communities. The choice of technology is invariably related to the kind of living standard and lifestyle one visualizes as a part of development. Simple living, which would bring in more equity and justice across the world, among countries and within countries, is what we value. Technologies can bring some comforts, but we shouldn't go to the other extreme of not using the human body and human power.

The process has to be decentralized and democratic, which is more than simply allowing people to participate in some consultations—it's allowing people to have the first right to their resources and to say yes or no to a plan proposed by some outside agency.

>> Mastering the Material

1. To what extent was the post-war era a period of American dominance? To what extent has modern globalization taken place under American leadership?

2. What conclusions does Reynolds draw from the United States' inability to prevent a communist takeover of South Vietnam? Do you agree? Was the Vietnam War really about America's attempts to dominate global political-economy? How does this fit in interpretations that stress the impact of anticolonial ideology and the Cold War?

3. Do you agree with Keith Suter that the political, social, and economic significance of the nation-state is declining rapidly? Evaluate the evidence Suter brings to bear on this subject. Is it convincing?

4. What is Andre Gunder Frank's core argument as to the causes of Latin American under-development?

5. Andre Gunder Frank and Subcomandante Marcos are both critics of some aspects of globalization in Latin America. Describe their respective criticisms. Are there commonalities in their analyses?

6. Define the Fourth World War in the perspective of Subcomandante Marcos. Do you agree that such a war is in progress? Do you agree with his use of the term *world war* to describe the struggle he is addressing?

7. Is Medha Patkar a critic or a supporter of globalization? Can globalization have both good and bad aspects? Is it all a matter of perspective? Should critics of globalization turn their backs on the world and try to work locally, or should they try to harness globalization to their own needs?

>> Making Connections

1. Is post-war globalization merely the latest phase of a long path toward closer global interrelationships? Was the settlement and exploitation of the Americas by Europeans part of this process (Part 1)? Can the apparent connections between revolutions in the seventeenth through mid-nineteenth centuries be linked to this process (Part 2)? What role was played by the new imperialism (Part 3)? By the world wars and the post-war settlements (Part 4 and Chapters 22 and 23)?

2. Keith Suter has proposed that the establishment of the Westphalian System in 1648 was the key event in the making of the modern world because it created a nation-state system in Europe that came to be widely adopted and adapted globally. Other scholars have responded that the advent of the Columbian Exchange (the linking of Eurasia, Africa, and the Americas in a sustained relationship) was more significant because it tied most of the world's landmasses together. Which do you think is more accurate? Why?

3. To what extent are there similarities between Andre Gunder Frank's long-view analysis of underdevelopment in Latin America and the excerpt from Walter Rodney's *How Europe Underdeveloped Africa* (Reading 47)? Do you think that European imperialism and colonialism are largely to blame for the impoverishment of much of Africa's and Latin America's populations?

4. Consider the notion of development as discussed by Medha Patkar. Do you think big projects and technology have moved humans forward toward better lives over time? Have we used our innovateness to progress, or have there always been prices to pay and people to suffer for each advance?

Chapter 25

Perspectives on Civilizations and Struggles

Within the discipline of history the term *civilization* is frequently used to describe human developments and societies right up until approximately 1500 C.E. but less so in the early modern and modern periods covered by this volume. Users of both volumes of this text will find a discussion of the term and several sources relating to it in the introduction to Volume I. There are many explanations for this terminological divide. The first is that the gradual integration of global societies that followed the sustained connection of the Old and New Worlds made it impossible to conceive of societies in different parts of the globe as isolated "civilizations." A second argument is that as the nation-state has come to dominate the world politically in the modern era, so it has come to dominate the discipline of history as the accepted unit of study. However, in the following decade the fragmentation of the Soviet Union and emerging conflicts between extremist religious and nationalist groups brought some theorists back to the concept of civilizational struggle. Although some attention has been focused by these academics and pundits on China and Russia, the greatest emphasis of civilizationist discourse has been aimed at the rift between "Islam and the West."

A number of long-standing issues characterize the recent relationships between population groups and nation-states in the West (generally defined as industrialized societies with a dominant European and largely Judeo-Christian heritage) and the Islamic world (variously defined as all Muslims globally or just those Asian and African states with Muslim majorities). The ongoing Israeli-Palestinian conflict, pressure over the price of petroleum products, ideological differences, the legacies of colonialism, and globalization have all created tensions between states that are reflected in popular culture. Before the 1990s, these points of antagonism were to some degree pushed into the background by the Cold War. However, they regained their urgency following the Iraqi attack on the small oil-producing state of Kuwait in August of 1990. In response to this invasion, a coalition led by the United States was formed with the participation of both western and predominantly Muslim states. The coalition's forces defeated the Iraqi army in 1991, but their victory was incomplete and the conflict merely entered a long and uneasy lull punctuated by the September 11, 2001, terrorist attacks on the World Trade Centers in New York and the Pentagon in Washington, D.C. The bombers were militants loyal to Al-Qaida, a terrorist network with an expansionist and evangelical view of Islam defined by the concept of a civilizational struggle with the West. Al-Qaida's support came in part from the ideologically rigid Afghani Taliban party, but the organization had also established cells in many parts of the world including western European states and the United States. The affiliated groups organized around local issues as well as global religious and ideological struggles.

In the United States as well, perceived Muslim–Western animosity was defined as a struggle between civilizations. One of the most widely read civilizational interpretations was Benjamin J. Barber's March 1992 article "Jihad vs. McWorld." Barber's argument—that two great worldviews were struggling for supremacy—presaged that of Samuel P. Huntington, a political scientist who had served several White House administrations. Huntington elaborated on Barber's model in his article "The Clash of Civilizations?", which begins with the premise that the system of nation-states is declining in significance. Its replacement, Huntington contended, is a system of competition and conflict between several great civilizations, not only Western and Islamic but also Hindu, Japanese, Confucian, Slavic-Orthodox, Latin American, and (possibly) African. Most of the wars and tension in the world, he suggested, was the result of stress along the faultlines between these civilizations. Writing in 1993, Huntington predicted ongoing clashes between Islam and the West.

The notion of a clash of civilizations has become important enough that it informs important political opinions, especially in the United States. Huntington's work both supports and undermines the doctrine of the administration of President George W. Bush. This president has proposed that the "democratic" world, led by the United States, has a duty and a responsibility to replicate the democratic, capitalist system around the world. In his speeches he suggests that the global conflict is not a fight between "Western" and "Islamic" population but rather between good and evil. Yet by implication, it is the American system that is good and the Islamic system that is bad. The concept of a campaign to replace a broken, backward, or even evil system with superior American values is supported by the work of some Western historians of the Islamic world. A number of widely circulating texts in the United States suggest that the Islamic political world is dominated by shabby dictators and ideological militants and that Islam is a "civilization" that has been in decline for centuries. Yet Huntington himself does not accept this bipolar interpretation, urging instead a more complex understanding of a variety (at least seven or eight) of different conceptions of what is good and what is bad, one for each civilization.

Civilizationalism has drawn a great deal of criticism. Some detractors have focused their criticism on the very notion of cohesive civilizations. They assert that there is as much tension to be found *within* the purported civilizations as *among* them. Others suggest that attempts to draw lines between civilizations ignore the heterogeneous nature of many states, which have multi-ethnic populations that in many cases manage to live together quite peacefully. One of the most important of Huntington's critics was the Palestinian scholar Edward Said, who argued in a 2001 article that Islam and the West are entirely inseparable from each other. In critiquing Huntington, Said also attacks the "distortion" of both science and religion by those who seek to polarize the global population. Said's comments intersect in places with the writings of the Kuwaiti-born Imam Feisal Abdul Rauf, who serves at a mosque in New York City. In a 2004 paper entitled "Why Multiculturalism?" Imam Abdul Rauf exhorts both dominant groups in the United States and Europe on the one hand and Muslims on the other to embrae a tolerant and multi-ethnic worldview and dialogue through shared religious and spiritual values. His paper is partly a history of Islam from a particular perspective, and partly a call for conversation across religious and cultural boundaries.

The Clash of Civilizations?

The importance of Samuel P. Huntington's 1993 article "The Clash of Civilizations?" can be judged from the response it drew. In the months and years following its publication, dozens of members of the political, religious, and scholarly communities published critiques, some of them furious. Huntington responded by expanding the study in book form. Some observers have called his analysis of global affairs prescient for its predictions of Western–Islamic clash and a revival of the Gulf War. Others have criticized it heavily. Even Huntington's definition of a civilization as a cultural entity based on a sense of belonging is controversial. Certainly, however, both the article and the book have informed the decisions of policy makers in the United States and possibly elsewhere.

>> 120. The Clash of Civilizations?

SAMUEL P. HUNTINGTON [1993]

World politics is entering a new phase, and intellectuals have not hesitated to proliferate visions of what it will be—the end of history, the return of traditional rivalries between nation states, and the decline of the nation state from the conflicting pulls of tribalism and globalism, among others. Each of these visions catches aspects of the emerging reality. Yet they all miss a crucial, indeed a central, aspect of what global politics is likely to be in the coming years.

It is my hypothesis that the fundamental source of conflict in this new world will not be primarily ideological or primarily economic. The great divisions among humankind and the dominating source of conflict will be cultural. Nation states will remain the most powerful actors in world *affairs,* but the principal conflicts of global politics will occur between nations and groups of different civilizations. The clash of civilizations will dominate global politics. The fault lines between civilizations will be the battle lines of the future. [...]

What do we mean when we talk of a civilization? A civilization is a cultural entity. Villages, regions, ethnic groups, nationalities, religious groups, all have distinct cultures at different levels of cultural heterogeneity. The culture of a village in southern Italy may be different from that of a village in northern Italy, but both will share in a common Italian culture that distinguishes them from German villages. European communities, in turn, will share cultural features that distinguish them from Arab or Chinese communities. Arabs, Chinese and Westerners, however, are not part of any broader cultural entity. They constitute civilizations. A civilization is thus the highest cultural grouping of people and the broadest level of cultural identity people have short of that which distinguishes humans from other species. It is defined both by common objective elements, such as language, history, religion, customs, institutions, and by the subjective self-identification of people. People have levels of identity: a resident of Rome may define himself with varying degrees of intensity as a Roman, an Italian, a Catholic, a Christian, a European, a Westerner. The civilization to which he belongs is the broadest level of identification with which he intensely identifies. People can and do

---

Source: Samuel P. Huntington, "The Clash of Civilizations?" *Foreign Affairs* 72 (Summer 1993) 22–36.

redefine their identities and, as a result, the composition and boundaries of civilizations change. [...]

Civilization identity will be increasingly important in the future, and the world will be shaped in large measure by the interactions among seven or eight major civilizations. These include Western, Confucian, Japanese, Islamic, Hindu, Slavic-Orthodox, Latin American and possibly African civilization. The most important conflicts of the future will occur along the cultural fault lines separating these civilizations from one another. [...]

The clash of civilizations occurs at two levels. At the micro-level, adjacent groups along the fault lines between civilizations struggle, often violently, over the control of territory and each other. At the macro-level, states from different civilizations compete for relative military and economic power, struggle over the control of international institutions and third parties, and competitively promote their particular political and religious values. [...]

The fault lines between civilizations are replacing the political and ideological boundaries of the Cold War as the flash points for crisis and bloodshed. The Cold War began when the Iron Curtain divided Europe politically and ideologically. The Cold War ended with the end of the Iron Curtain. As the ideological division of Europe has disappeared, the cultural division of Europe between Western Christianity, on the one hand, and Orthodox Christianity and Islam, on the other, has reemerged. [...]

Conflict along the fault line between Western and Islamic civilizations has been going on for 1,300 years. After the founding of Islam, the Arab and Moorish surge west and north only ended at Tours in 732. From the eleventh to the thirteenth century the Crusaders attempted with temporary success to bring Christianity and Christian rule to the Holy Land. From the fourteenth to the seventeenth century, the Ottoman Turks reversed the balance, extended their sway over the Middle East and the Balkans, captured Constantinople, and twice laid siege to Vienna. In the nineteenth and early twentieth centuries as Ottoman power declined Britain, France, and Italy established Western control over most of North Africa and the Middle East.

After World War II, the West, in turn, began to retreat; the colonial empires disappeared; first Arab nationalism and then Islamic fundamentalism manifested themselves; the West became heavily dependent on the Persian Gulf countries for its energy; the oil-rich Muslim countries became money-rich and, when they wished to, weapons-rich. Several wars occurred between Arabs and Israel (created by the West). France fought a bloody and ruthless war in Algeria for most of the 1950s; British and French forces invaded Egypt in 1956; American forces went into Lebanon in 1958; subsequently American forces returned to Lebanon, attacked Libya, and engaged in various military encounters with Iran; Arab and Islamic terrorists, supported by at least three Middle Eastern governments, employed the weapon of the weak and bombed Western planes and installations and seized Western hostages. This warfare between Arabs and the West culminated in 1990, when the United States sent a massive army to the Persian Gulf to defend some Arab countries against aggression by another. In its aftermath NATO planning is increasingly directed to potential threats and instability along its "southern tier."

This centuries-old military interaction between the West and Islam is unlikely to decline. It could become more virulent. The Gulf War left some Arabs feeling proud that Saddam Hussein had attacked Israel and stood up to the West. It also left many feeling humiliated and resentful of the West's military presence in the Persian Gulf, the West's overwhelming military dominance, and their apparent inability to shape their own destiny. Many Arab countries, in addition to the oil exporters, are reaching levels of economic and social development where autocratic forms of government become inappropriate and efforts to introduce democracy become stronger. Some openings in Arab political systems have already occurred. The principal beneficiaries of these openings have been Islamist movements. In the Arab world, in short, Western democracy strengthens anti-Western political forces. This may be a passing phenomenon, but it surely complicates relations between Islamic countries and the West.

Those relations are also complicated by demography. The spectacular population growth in Arab countries, particularly in North Africa, has led to increased migration to Western Europe. The movement within Western Europe toward minimizing internal boundaries has sharpened political sensitivities with respect to this development. In Italy, France and Germany, racism is increasingly open, and political reactions and violence against Arab and Turkish migrants have become more intense and more widespread since 1990. On both sides the interaction between Islam and the West is seen as a clash of civilizations. The West's "next confrontation," observes M. J. Akbar, an Indian Muslim author, "is definitely going to come from the Muslim world. It is in the sweep of the Islamic nations from the Meghreb to Pakistan that the struggle for a new world order will begin." [...]

[I]n the Gulf War one Arab state invaded another and then fought a coalition of Arab, Western and other states. While only a few Muslim governments overtly supported Saddam Hussein, many Arab elites privately cheered him on, and he was highly popular among large sections of the Arab publics. Islamic fundamentalist movements universally supported Iraq rather than the Western-backed governments of Kuwait and Saudi Arabia. Forswearing Arab nationalism, Saddam Hussein explicitly invoked an Islamic appeal. He and his supporters attempted to define the war as a war between civilizations. "It is not the world against Iraq," as Safar Al-Hawaii, dean of Islamic Studies at the Umm Al-Qura University in Mecca, put it in a widely circulated tape. "It is the West against Islam." Ignoring the rivalry between Iran and Iraq, the chief Iranian religious leader, Ayatollah Ali Khamenei, called for a holy war against the West: "The struggle against American aggression, greed, plans and policies will be counted as a jihad, and anybody who is killed on that path is a martyr." "This is a war," King Hussein of Jordan argued, "against all Arabs and all Muslims and not against Iraq alone."

The rallying of substantial sections of Arab elites and publics behind Saddam Hussein called those Arab governments in the anti-Iraq coalition to moderate their activities and temper their public statements. Arab governments opposed or distanced themselves from subsequent Western efforts to apply pressure on Iraq, including enforcement of a no-fly zone in the summer of 1992 and the bombing of Iraq in January 1993. The Western-Soviet-Turkish-Arab anti-Iraq coalition of 1990 had by 1993 become a coalition of almost only the West and Kuwait against Iraq.

Edward Said Critiques the "Clash of Civilizations" Thesis

Edward Said, who passed away in 2003, was probably best known for the theory of orientalism discussed in Part 3 of this text. His work on the ways in which early modern and colonial-era Europeans depicted Muslims as "different" and "the other" combined with his background as a Christian-born Arab in Palestine to lead him into political activism in the 1970s, mostly in support of an independent Palestinian state. Throughout his career, Said took controversial and nuanced stances. He was a secular individual who criticized what he saw as religious extremism. He was a Palestinian activist who sometimes condemned the Palestinian Authority. He was a supporter of the Israeli-Palestinian peace process who nevertheless opposed some concessions demanded by Israel. Most important, Said believed that Islamic and Western identities were historically bound together and remained inextricably connected even after the events of September 11, 2001.

>> 121. The Clash of Ignorance

EDWARD W. SAID [2001]

The challenge for Western policy-makers, says Huntington, is to make sure that the West gets stronger and fends off all the others, Islam in particular. More troubling is Huntington's assumption that his perspective, which is to survey the entire world from a perch outside all ordinary attachments and hidden loyalties, is the correct one, as if everyone else were scurrying around looking for the answers that he has already found. In fact, Huntington is an ideologist, someone who wants to make "civilizations" and "identities" into what they are not: shut-down, sealed-off entities that have been purged of the myriad currents and countercurrents that animate human history, and that over centuries have made it possible for that history not only to contain wars of religion and imperial conquest but also to be one of exchange, cross-fertilization and sharing. This far less visible history is ignored in the rush to highlight the ludicrously compressed and constricted warfare that "the clash of civilizations" argues is the reality. When he published his book by the same title in 1996, Huntington tried to give his argument a little more subtlety and many, many more footnotes; all he did, however, was confuse himself and demonstrate what a clumsy writer and inelegant thinker he was.

The basic paradigm of West versus the rest (the cold war opposition reformulated) remained untouched, and this is what has persisted, often insidiously and implicitly, in discussion since the terrible events of September 11. The carefully planned and horrendous, pathologically motivated suicide attack and mass slaughter by a small group of deranged militants has been turned into proof of Huntington's thesis. Instead of seeing it for what it is—the capture of big ideas (I use the word loosely) by a tiny band of crazed fanatics for criminal purposes. [...]

[There is a] problem with unedifying labels like Islam and the West: They mislead and confuse the mind, which is trying to make sense of a disorderly reality that won't be pigeonholed or strapped down as easily as all that. I remember interrupting a man who, after a lecture I had given at a West Bank university in 1994, rose from the audience and started to attack my ideas as "Western," as opposed to the strict Islamic ones he espoused. "Why are you wearing a suit and tie?" was the first retort that came to mind. "They're Western too." He sat down with an embarrassed smile on his face, but I recalled the incident when information on the September 11 terrorists started to come in: how they had mastered all the technical details required to inflict their homicidal evil on the World Trade Center, the Pentagon and the aircraft they had commandeered. Where does one draw the line between "Western" technology and, as Berlusconi declared, "Islam's" inability to be a part of "modernity"?

One cannot easily do so, of course. How finally inadequate are the labels, generalizations and cultural assertions. At some level, for instance, primitive passions and sophisticated know-how converge in ways that give the lie to a fortified boundary not only between "West" and "Islam" but also between past and present, us and them, to say nothing of the very concepts of identity and nationality about which there is unending disagreement and debate. A unilateral decision made to draw lines in the sand, to undertake crusades, to oppose their evil with our good, to extirpate terrorism and, in Paul Wolfowitz's nihilistic vocabulary, to end nations entirely, doesn't make the supposed entities any easier to see; rather, it speaks to how much simpler it is to make bellicose statements for the purpose of

Source: Edward W. Said, "The Clash of Ignorance," *The Nation* 22 (October 2001).

mobilizing collective passions than to reflect, examine, sort out what it is we are dealing with in reality, the interconnectedness of innumerable lives, "ours' as well as "theirs." [...]

[T]here are closer ties between apparently warring civilizations than most of us would like to believe; both Freud and Nietzsche showed how the traffic across carefully maintained, even policed boundaries moves with often terrifying ease. But then such fluid ideas, full of ambiguity and skepticism about notions that we hold on to, scarcely furnish us with suitable, practical guidelines for situations such as the one we face now. Hence the altogether more reassuring battle orders (a crusade, good versus evil, freedom against fear, etc.) drawn out of Huntington's alleged opposition between Islam and the West, from which official discourse drew its vocabulary in the first days after the September 11 attacks. There's since been a noticeable de-escalation in that discourse, but to judge from the steady amount of hate speech and actions, plus reports of law enforcement efforts directed against Arabs, Muslims and Indians all over the country, the paradigm stays on.

One further reason for its persistence is the increased presence of Muslims all over Europe and the United States. Think of the populations today of France, Italy, Germany, Spain, Britain, America, even Sweden, and you must concede that Islam is no longer on the fringes of the West but at its center. But what is so threatening about that presence? Buried in the collective culture are memories of the first great Arab-Islamic conquests, which began in the seventh century and which, as the celebrated Belgian historian Henri Pirenne wrote in his landmark book *Mohammed and Charlemagne* (1939), shattered once and for all the ancient unity of the Mediterranean, destroyed the Christian-Roman synthesis and gave rise to a new civilization dominated by northern powers (Germany and Carolingian France) whose mission, he seemed to be saying, is to resume defense of the "West" against its historical-cultural enemies. What Pirenne left

out, alas, is that in the creation of this new line of defense the West drew on the humanism, science, philosophy, sociology and historiography of Islam, which had already interposed itself between Charlemagne's world and classical antiquity. Islam is inside from the start, as even Dante, great enemy of Mohammed, had to concede when he placed the Prophet at the very heart of his *Inferno*.

Then there is the persisting legacy of monotheism itself, the Abrahamic religions, as Louis Massignon aptly called them. Beginning with Judaism and Christianity, each is a successor haunted by what came before; for Muslims, Islam fulfills and ends the line of prophecy. There is still no decent history or demystification of the many-sided contest among these three followers—not one of them by any means a monolithic, unified camp—of the most jealous of all gods, even though the bloody modern convergence on Palestine furnishes a rich secular instance of what has been so tragically irreconcilable about them. Not surprisingly, then, Muslims and Christians speak readily of crusades and *jihads,* both of them eliding the Judaic presence with often sublime insouciance. Such an agenda, says Eqbal Ahmad, is "very reassuring to the men and women who are stranded in the middle of the ford, between the deep waters of tradition and modernity."

But we are all swimming in those waters, Westerners and Muslims and others alike. And since the waters are part of the ocean of history, trying to plow or divide them with barriers is futile. These are tense times, but it is better to think in terms of powerful and powerless communities, the secular politics of reason and ignorance, and universal principles of justice and injustice, than to wander off in search of vast abstractions that may give momentary satisfaction but little self-knowledge or informed analysis. "The Clash of Civilizations" thesis is a gimmick like "The War of the Worlds," better for reinforcing defensive self-pride than for critical understanding of the bewildering interdependence of our time.

George W. Bush on the Struggle between "Good" and "Evil"

The presidency of George W. Bush has not yet really become the domain of historians. Nor is it clear what this president's historical legacy will be. Yet President Bush himself has closely defined his conception of the role of the United States in the world. In this speech to graduating cadets at West Point, the United States Army Academy, he refers to it historically (concerning the Cold War), in terms of the present, and with an eye to the future. By the end of this speech, Bush formally refutes the notion of a clash of civilizations, preferring instead to portray the global security situation as a struggle between good and evil.

>> 122. Graduation Speech at the United States Military Academy

GEORGE W. BUSH [2002]

West Point is guided by tradition, and in honor of the "Golden Children of the Corps," —(applause)— [...] History has [...] issued its call to your generation. In your last year, America was attacked by a ruthless and resourceful enemy. You graduate from this Academy in a time of war, taking your place in an American military that is powerful and is honorable. Our war on terror is only begun, but in Afghanistan it was begun well. (Applause.)

I am proud of the men and women who have fought on my orders. America is profoundly grateful for all who serve the cause of freedom, and for all who have given their lives in its defense. This nation respects and trusts our military, and we are confident in your victories to come. (Applause.)

This war will take many turns we cannot predict. Yet I am certain of this: Wherever we carry it, the American flag will stand not only for our power, but for freedom. (Applause.) Our nation's cause has always been larger than our nation's defense. We fight, as we always fight, for a just peace—a peace that favors human liberty. We will defend the peace against threats from terrorists and tyrants. We will preserve the peace by building good relations among the great powers. And we will extend the peace by encouraging free and open societies on every continent.

Building this just peace is America's opportunity, and America's duty. From this day forward, it is your challenge, as well, and we will meet this challenge together. (Applause.) You will wear the uniform of a great and unique country. America has no empire to extend or utopia to establish. We wish for others only what we wish for ourselves— safety from violence, the rewards of liberty, and the hope for a better life. [...]

(Applause.) Moral truth is the same in every culture, in every time, and in every place. Targeting innocent civilians for murder is always and everywhere wrong. (Applause.) Brutality against women is always and everywhere wrong. (Applause.) There can be no neutrality between justice and cruelty, between the innocent and the guilty. We are in a conflict between good and evil, and America will call evil by its name. (Applause.) By confronting evil and lawless regimes, we do not create a problem, we reveal a problem. And we will lead the world in opposing it. (Applause.)

Source: George W. Bush, Graduation Speech at the United States Military Academy, White House, Office of the Press Secretary, June 1, 2002. Permanent URL http://www.whitehouse.gov/news/releases/2002/06/print/20020601-3.html.

As we defend the peace, we also have an historic opportunity to preserve the peace. We have our best chance since the rise of the nation state in the 17th century to build a world where the great powers compete in peace instead of prepare for war. The history of the last century, in particular, was dominated by a series of destructive national rivalries that left battlefields and graveyards across the Earth. Germany fought France, the Axis fought the Allies, and then the East fought the West, in proxy wars and tense standoffs, against a backdrop of nuclear Armageddon.

Competition between great nations is inevitable, but armed conflict in our world is not. More and more, civilized nations find ourselves on the same side—united by common dangers of terrorist violence and chaos. America has, and intends to keep, military strengths beyond challenge—(applause)—thereby, making the destabilizing arms races of other eras pointless, and limiting rivalries to trade and other pursuits of peace.

Today the great powers are also increasingly united by common values, instead of divided by conflicting ideologies. The United States, Japan and our Pacific friends, and now all of Europe, share a deep commitment to human freedom, embodied in strong alliances such as NATO. And the tide of liberty is rising in many other nations.

Generations of West Point officers planned and practiced for battles with Soviet Russia. I've just returned from a new Russia, now a country reaching toward democracy, and our partner in the war against terror. (Applause.) Even in China, leaders are discovering that economic freedom is the only lasting source of national wealth. In time, they will find that social and political freedom is the only true source of national greatness. (Applause.)

When the great powers share common values, we are better able to confront serious regional conflicts together, better able to cooperate in preventing the spread of violence or economic chaos. In the past, great power rivals took sides in difficult regional problems, making divisions deeper and more complicated. Today, from the Middle East to South Asia, we are gathering broad international coalitions to increase the pressure for peace. We must build strong and great power relations when times are good; to help manage crisis when times are bad. America needs partners to preserve the peace, and we will work with every nation that shares this noble goal. (Applause.)

And finally, America stands for more than the absence of war. We have a great opportunity to extend a just peace, by replacing poverty, repression, and resentment around the world with hope of a better day. Through most of history, poverty was persistent, inescapable, and almost universal. In the last few decades, we've seen nations from Chile to South Korea build modern economies and freer societies, lifting millions of people out of despair and want. And there's no mystery to this achievement.

The 20th century ended with a single surviving model of human progress, based on nonnegotiable demands of human dignity, the rule of law, limits on the power of the state, respect for women and private property and free speech and equal justice and religious tolerance. America cannot impose this vision—yet we can support and reward governments that make the right choices for their own people. In our development aid, in our diplomatic efforts, in our international broadcasting, and in our educational assistance, the United States will promote moderation and tolerance and human rights. And we will defend the peace that makes all progress possible.

When it comes to the common rights and needs of men and women, there is no clash of civilizations. The requirements of freedom apply fully to Africa and Latin America and the entire Islamic world. The peoples of the Islamic nations want and deserve the same freedoms and opportunities as people in every nation. And their governments should listen to their hopes. (Applause.)

Why Multiculturalism?

Imam Feisal Abdul Rauf is a cleric who was born in Kuwait, then educated in Egypt, Malaysia, and the United Kingdom, and who now lives and works in the United States. Among other works, he has written What's Right with Islam Is What's Right for America, *in which he expresses his love both for Islam and for his adopted country, and argues that their systems of morality overlap extensively. Imam Feisal Abdul Rauf explains the current conflict between the United States and many Muslims in historical terms, the result of many of the ideologies and events that characterize the development of the modern world including colonialism, capitalism, and racism. These trends tended to negate the multiculturalism of premodern societies. He argues that reclaiming this multiculturalism is the key to a peaceful future, and he proposes steps that Muslims, especially, can take to eliminate civilizational conflict and achieve multiculturalism again.*

>> 123. Why Multiculturalism?

IMAM FEISAL ABDUL RAUF [2004]

[article presented by Imam Feisal Abdul Rauf at the Prato Multicultural conference in Prato, Italy, on September 2004]

Among the questions facing humanity today are, what kind of world do we want to live in, for ourselves, our children and grandchildren? What kind of global social contract is appropriate to the human condition, both nationally and internationally in a globalised world? And what do our religious faith traditions, and in my case Islam, teach us in this regard?

We have two choices before us: we can either opt for a monocultural world or a multicultural one. Monoculturalism careens humanity towards a 'Clash of Civilizations' conflict-paradigm, whereas if we want social and global harmony I don't see any alternative than striving towards a multicultural society. [...]

Fortunately for the world, the West in the last half-century finally evolved away from two pernicious by-products of monoculturalism,

identity-paradigms that governed Europe for more than half a millennium. They are:

1. The *racist* paradigm, euphemistically phrased as the "White Man's Burden," that led to a Western triumphalism that aggressively proselytized the rest of the world into adopting Western culture and religion. The British, for example, sought to create a race of 'brown Englishmen' in India. The French Francophiled their North- and West-African colonies (Algeria, Morocco and Senegal) while the Spanish completely displaced Central and South American native cultures with their own Hispanic culture and Catholic religion. It was this attitude that fueled the discriminatory "White Australia" immigration policy until the mid-20th century and sanctioned other policies that permitted the horrible treatment of Australian aborigines. It also explains the American genocide of the Native American Indians and slavery of the black race, behavior neither countenanced by any religion nor by the American Declaration of Independence.

Source: Imam Feisal Abdul Rauf, "Why Multiculturalism?" White Paper Presented at the Prato Multicultural Conference, September 2004.

2. The *nation-state* paradigm, which aggressively sought to homogenize human identities within a geographic boundary. When race was not different, ethnic, linguistic or religious minorities were oppressed and treated as outsiders, alien to the dominant culture. Where once wars were conducted by a warrior class or by soldiers, wars between nation-states drew whole populations into participating in national wars, broadening the conflict to include non-combatants. Pogroms against Jews in East Europe, the treatment of the Irish Catholics by the Protestants, and the ejection of Jews and Muslims from the Iberian Peninsula are examples of what happens when societies shift from a multicultural social contract to a monocultural one.

These two paradigms ineluctably ushered a 'Clash of Civilizations' that reached its most explosive apogee in the two World Wars of the 20th century and with the Nazi regime, which sought to establish a purified white Aryan race and gave us the holocaust. Monoculturalism weakened the European powers and almost destroyed the human race.

How the Muslim World Lost Its Multiculturalism

Until the 20th century, the Muslim world operated under a multicultural paradigm, understood as flowing from Islamic theology, law and historical precedent. Until the First World War, Istanbul, capital of the Ottoman caliphate since 1453, was almost half Greek, with many cities and regions of modern Turkey populated by Greek majorities. Smyrna, the modern Izmir, for example, was two-thirds Greek until 1922. 400,000 Greeks lived in Alexandria, Egypt until the mid-1950s. Today it has less than 3% of this figure. Armenians, Jews, Kurds, Arabs, Turks, and Persians, reflecting the full variety of Jewish, Christian and Muslim interpretations: Shia and Sunni with all the varieties of legal schools of interpretation, lived and worked in intimate proximity with each other, as did Hindus and Muslims in South Asia. Today the

head Patriarch of the Greek Orthodox Church is still based in Istanbul.

Starting with WW1, the Muslim world, under the colonial influence of the West and legitimately enamored of many Western ideas that catalyzed Western prosperity, uncritically adopted these two pernicious paradigms. The result was the rise of triumphalist nation-state identities around ethnicity and religion. Monoculturalist societies began to emerge around hardening ethnic and religious identification. Arab nationalism was one, fueled by the British in the late-19th century as a means of breaking up the Ottoman Empire. Traditional Islamic systems of rule came to an end, systems that had hitherto ruled over multicultural groups of peoples, including the Islamic nation, the ummah, based upon workable concepts of a multi-ethnic, multi-religious and multi-lingual society not defined by geography.

Geographically homogeneous ethnic nations were born, seeding ethnic conflicts that continue to this day. The end of the Ottoman caliphate and empire, and its transformation into a Turkish nation-state meant that this new social contract had no space for Greeks, who felt forced to leave in large numbers to Greece, while Armenians and Kurds suffered atrocities Islamic law forbids. Pakistan and Israel were examples of geographies carved to accommodate religious nationalisms that philosophically had no space for Hindus and Gentiles as equals, violations of the very religious ethical principles of Islam and Judaism. And when Arab nationalism failed to progress society, Islamic nationalism readily filled the vacuum, a concept completely alien to the traditional notions of Islamic thought, theology or legal and historical precedent.

An Islamic version of the White Man's Burden evolved in the 20th century: a "Muslim's burden" that sought both to defend the "House of Islam" from what was perceived as militant secularism and militant Jewish nationalism. It also sought to aggressively proselytize non-Muslims towards Islam, just as in the past European religious groups tried to convert Muslims to Christianity, or at the very least neutralize or secularize them.

One unfortunate result of this was that the historical embrace and protection by Muslims of the varieties of Christian churches in their midst, Christian communities whose histories trace back continuously to the time of Jesus Christ, have withered, and non-Muslim communities increasingly feel under attack by an Islamic militancy that was never allowed such prominence in the 14 centuries since the rise of Islam in Arabia.

The precedent established by the Caliph Umar b. Al-Khattab's in 638 CE, graciously honoring the Orthodox patriarch in Jerusalem, granting Christians protection, and inviting seventy Jewish families to immigrate to Jerusalem from Tiberius to re-establish a Jewish community in the City of David, is hardly on the radar screen of many young Muslims today. Gripped by their Islamic fervor, they are often taken aback when reminded of this important legal precedent that shaped interfaith relations between Muslims and non-Muslims, and of its Quranic basis in injunctions like "there shall be no compulsion in religion," and "tell the infidels, 'to you your religion, to me mine.'" These principles are firmly enshrined in Islamic law and historical precedent, which require Muslims to honor and protect those who frequently remember God's names and hymn His praises in "cloisters, synagogues, churches and mosques."

The Prophet's intention of creating an Islamic identity, or ummah, was to replace the tribalism of the *jahiliyyah* period, which fueled constant conflict, with a notion of identity based on human God-given values mandated by the above-mentioned verses [and others] which urge humanity to live by the second commandment of the Abrahamic faith traditions: *to love thy neighbor as thyself,* to treat others as you would want yourself to be treated.

The larger question is, what is the basis of our human identity, as Europeans or non-Europeans, as religious or not, as black, white, yellow or brown races? Can we create layers of identity nested in a larger sense of identity, starting from the individual all the way to a globalised human one? Our religious traditions teach us that every human being is created in the Divine image—the Quran states that God breathed a bit of His Spirit into the clay of Adam, thereby enlivening him. Does this not mean then that we must see ourselves in the faces of others? And that we are—and must live as—one consciousness?

>> Mastering the Material

1. Samuel P. Huntington wrote his article "The Clash of Civilizations?" in 1993. Do the events of September 11, 2001, and after prove his analysis to have been correct? Why or why not?

2. On what basis does Edward Said critique Huntington? What are his major arguments? Do you agree with his evaluation of the clash of civilizations thesis?

3. Historians seek to understand the context and experiences of authors in assessing their arguments. John Gray argues, for example, that Huntington's classification of civilizations is "an artifact of American multiculturalism." What does he mean by this?

4. Read President George W. Bush's speech very closely. Most political observers have described him as an idealist, but others believe that his view of the world stems from his political realism. Which label do you think better applies to him? Why?

5. President Bush argues that there is no clash of civilizations, but rather a struggle between good and evil. Is this analysis more or less convincing than that of Huntington? Or is neither convincing?

6. How does Imam Feisal Abdul Rauf suggest that Islam is inherently multicultural? Does this interpretation conflict with, modify, or support the notion of a fundamental rift between civilizations?

7. Edward Said, on the other hand, suggests that religious fundamentalism within many religions is partly the cause of the current conflict. To what degree do you think he is correct?

>> Making Connections

1. Samuel P. Huntington defines seven or eight major civilizations and argues that civilizational identity "is increasingly important in the future." Yet some critics have denied that civilizations exist in the modern world at all. Look at the list of civilizations listed by Huntington. Are these, indeed, cohesive and distinctive groups in modern world history?

2. Huntington suggests that the relationship between Islam and the West has historically been one of antagonism. Imam Feisal Abdul Rauf similarly notes a troubled history of relations but seems to suggest that the relationship was not always—and is not fundamentally—antagonistic. Evaluate, to the degree that you are able, the accuracy of these arguments.

3. Imam Feisal Abdul Rauf suggests that imperialism and colonialism are important contributing factors to distrust between some Muslims and the West. Assess this argument in light of the ideologies and impact of the new imperialism (Part 3, Chapters 20 and 21).

4. Compare and contrast the notions of a clash of civilizations as presented by Huntington and of a Fourth World War as presented by Subcomandante Marcos (Reading 118). Do you think that current threats to global security are more a product of economic, political, or ideological differences, or are there more significant underlying causes?

5. In the introduction to Volume I of this series, there is a discussion of the evolution of the term *civilization*. Compare the sources there to those presented here (the Huntington source is reproduced in both places). Consider: What does the late twentieth and early twenty-first century use of "civilization" tell us about the way we view the human past? What does it tell us about the world in which we ourselves live?

Part 5 Conclusion

The First and Second World Wars helped to transform societies—and the relationships among them—across the globe. The terrors of these conflicts also changed the way we viewed history. In their wake historians began to question many of the closely held beliefs of the prewar era. The Holocaust, the Armenian genocide, and other terrible episodes led them to question the established view of the last 500 years as a march toward enlightenment, industrialization, and a specific kind of modernity: capitalism, rationality, and the nation-state. Barbarism was no longer solely the domain of the distant past but rather very much a feature of the present. Nor, in light of decades of warfare, fascism, and genocide in Europe could it be argued that the West was uniquely civilized in contrast to the rest of the world.

It was in part this renewed questioning of the West-centered historical master narrative of progress that contributed to the development of world history. Another contributing factor, however, was the new range of voices being heard within and around the community of historians. Perhaps most important, the newly independent states in Asia, Africa, and the Caribbean gave birth to historians who, freed from colonial interference, began to fight for a place for their own societies in global history. Similarly, within the United States and other powerful countries long-silenced groups, fighting for their own liberation and equality, also began to question their absence from the historical record. These included women, ethnic minorities, and the disabled. These groups fought for recognition of the fact that, while they had been left out of scholarly histories, they had nevertheless contributed mightily to the history of the human experience.

The wave of new histories written by a growing range of historians contributed to world history in several ways. The first major contribution was to add to the historical record less biased histories of many nations and regions, which together painted a picture of a shared human experience. The research they conducted and the stories they told made clear the many similarities and connections between societies, and thus suggested that while the societies and states that humans construct are each unique, they also share many attributes. Perhaps, in fact, they are so linked together that none can be considered in isolation.

A second contribution of the post-war generations of historians has been the growing acceptance of the many different perspectives both of historians and of the people they study. The job of the historian today is in part to explore and reveal the perspectives of the past, yet to recognize that no one perspective automatically invalidates others. History is the unfolding of relationships among people who have internal reasons for making decisions, reasons that we cannot simply depict as truth.

These new ideas of how history happens and what the historians task is are intimately related to the breakup of the great European empires, the end of Western intellectual dominance, and the societal shifts of the post-war period. Historians, after all, do not work in a vacuum. Their perspectives on the past are heavily influenced by the present in which they live. Equally, their work leads us to question our interpretations not just of history but also of the world in which we live. Is the rise of Chinese industry today merely a return to the centuries prior to 1800 when China was the world's greatest manufacturing power? Is the unipolar American-dominated world a brief anomaly in a longer history of states balanced against each other? Is the world becoming more peaceful as democracies engage each other diplomatically, or more insecure as terrorists armed with weapons of mass destruction face off with militarized governments? For now, these are questions for prognosticators—economists, political analysts, or maybe astrologers. But historians, as always, will have the last word.

Final Questions

1   To what degree are diffusion and exchange, rather than invention, the more or less important factors in understanding the human experience of the last 500 years? Give examples.

2   Has the world become more "globalized" or more "fragmented" during the early modern and modern eras? Defend your answer.

3   In a narrative, trace nationalism from its origins to the modern era. What causes nationalism? Is it possible to evaluate nationalism as good or bad? Is nationalism becoming more or less important in the modern era? Give examples.

4   Consider the notion of the "rise of the West." What is your understanding of the terms *rise* and *West*? What type of dominance did the West actually have, and to what degree? Some scholars have argued that the west "rose" by 1492, others put the date at 1850. What do you think? Is the West's period of dominance over? Did it ever exist?

5   To what degree is it possible for historians to uncover the truth, to understand finally and fully the causes of major world events?

6   Define world history.

Further Reading

Historians' contributions to studies of the post–1945 world have become more common as history has become more interdisciplinary. Similarly, scholars based in other disciplines have become increasingly aware of the need to historicize current events. A number of different interpretations of global affairs have emerged. One important debate centers around the processes of globalization, especially whether their cumulative impact is negative or positive. An accessible survey of this topic is Manfred B. Steger, *Globalization: A Very Short Introduction* (Oxford: Oxford University Press, 2003). A critical text that alternately defines globalism as a new sort of imperialism is Michael Hardt and Antonio Negri, *Empire* (Massachusetts: Harvard University Press, 2001). Other scholars have looked at global trends today in terms of the ongoing impact of formal imperialism and colonialism from earlier eras. An important if somewhat older contribution of this sort is Franz Fanon, *The Wretched of the Earth* (New York: Grove Press, 1965). Still other contemporary studies focus on the Cold War as the context for many recent developments. One superior example is Odd Arne Westad, *The Global Cold War* (Cambridge: Cambridge University Press, 2005).

Terms to Know

presentism *(p. 282)*

modernization   *(p. 283)*

secularism   *(p. 283)*

decolonization   *(p. 285)*

emancipatory
nationalism   *(p. 286)*

Warsaw Pact   *(p. 302)*

NATO (North Atlantic Treaty Organization) *(p. 302)*

containment   *(p. 303)*

globalization   *(p. 313)*

neocolonialism   *(p. 313)*

ahistorical   *(p. 314)*

Credits

Page 13: *Reports on the Discovery of Peru*, translated and edited by C.R. Markham, Cambridge: the Hakluyt Society, 1872, 52–56. p. 15: From GUNS, GERMS AND STEEL: THE FATES OF HUMAN SOCIETIES by Jared Diamond. Copyright © 1997 by Jared Diamond. Used by permission of W. W. Norton & Company, Inc. Page 16: McNeill, J.R., "The World According to Jared Diamond", *The History Teacher*, 34 (2), 2001. Page 18: "A Conversation with Christopher Ehret", *World History Connected*, 2 (1), 2004, permanent URL http://worldhistoryconnected.press.uiuc.edu/2.1/ehret.html. Page 23: Huan, Ma *Ying-Yai Sheng-Lan* or, *The Overall Survey of the Ocean's Shores*, edited by Feng Ch'eng Chun and J.V.G. Mills, Cambridge: Hakluyt Society, 1970, 179–180. Page 24: Chang, Kuei-Sheng, "The Maritime Scene in China at the Dawn of Great European Discoveries," *Journal of the American Oriental Society*, 94 (3), 1974, 347–359. Page 26: Bing, Li Ung, *Outlines in Chinese History*, Shanghai: The Commercial Press, 1914, pp. 232–240. Page 27: POMERANZ, KENNETH; *THE GREAT DIVERGENCE*. © 2000 Princeton University Press. Reprinted by permission of the Princeton University Press. Page 30: Pages 113–120 from THE SPANISH TRADITION IN AMERICA, EDITED by CHARLES GIBSON. Compilation, Introduction, Notes, and Translations by the editor copyright © 1968 by Charles Gibson. Reprinted by permission or HarperCollins Publishers. Page 33: From LATIN AMERICAN CIVILIZATION: HISTORY AND SOCIETY 1492 TO THE PRESENT, 7E by BENJAMIN KEEN. Copyright © 1999 by Westview Press, A Member of the Perseus Books Group. Reprinted by permission of Westview Press, a member of Perseus Books, L.L.C. Page 34: From THE WEALTH AND POVERTY OF NATIONS: WHY SOME ARE SO RICH AND SOME SO POOR by David S. Landes. Copyright © 1998 by David S. Landes. Used by permission of W. W. Norton & Company, Inc. Page 36: Reprinted with permission from The New York Review of Books. Copyright ©1998 NYREV, Inc. Page 41: Nicolo Barbaro, *Diary of the Siege of Constantinople 1453*, translated by John Melville-Jones, New York: Exposition Press, 1969,1, 30–31, 62–64. Page 43: "A Malay Account of the Conquest of Malacca, translated by C.C. Brown, *Journal of the Malayan Branch Royal Asiatic Society*, 25, 1952, 167–169. Page 44: Correa, Gaspar, *The Three Voyages of Vasco de Gama and his Viceroyalrty*, translated by Henry E.J. Stanley, New York: Cambridge: Hakluyt Society, 1869, 367–372. Page 45: Marshall, P.J., "Western Arms in Maritime Asia in the Early Phases of Expansion," *Modern Asian Studies*, 14, 1980, 13–28. Reprinted with the permission of Cambridge University Press. Page 46: Thornton, John K., "The Art of War in Angola, 1575–1680," *Comparative Studies in Society and History*, 30, 1988, 360–378. Reprinted with the permission of Cambridge University Press. Page 51: STRAYER, JOSEPH R.; *ON THE MEDIEVAL ORIGINS OF THE MODERN STATE*. © 1970 Princeton University Press, 1998 renewed PUP. Reprinted by permission of the Princeton University Press. Page 52: From THE RISE AND FALL OF THE GREAT POWERS by Paul Kennedy copyright © 1987 by Paul Kennedy. Used by permission of Random House, Inc. Page 54: "Letters Patent from Henry VI to the Lord Lieutenant," in THE EMPIRE OF THE BRETAIGNES, 1175–1688: THE FOUNDATIONS OF A COLONIAL SYSTEM OF GOVERNMENT, Frederick Madden with David Fieldhouse, Editors. Copyright © 1985 by Frederick Madden and David Fieldhouse. Reproduced with permission of Greenwood Publishing Group, Inc. Westport, CT. Page 55: Lieberman, Victor, "Transcending East-West Dichotomies: State and Culture Formation in Six Ostensibly Disparate Areas," *Modern Asian Studies*, 31 (1997), pp.463–546. Reprinted with the permission of Cambridge University Press. Page 57: de Mendoza, Juan Gonzalez, *The History of the Great and Mighty Kingdom of China and the Situation Thereof*, translated by R. Parke and edited by Sir George T. Staunton, London: Hakluyt Society, 1854, 66–67. I have further edited the translation. Page 58: From Yang-ming Ch'uan-shu, 26:1b-5a, in William Theodore de Bary, Wing-tsit Chan, and Burton Watson, compilers, *Sources of Chinese Tradition*, New York: Columbia University Press, 1960, pp.572–574. Page 63: Reyolds, Robert L.. EUROPE EMERGES. ©1961. Reprinted by permission of The University of Wisconsin Press. Page 65: Stark, Rodney, "How Christianity (and Capitalism) Led to Science," *The Chronicle of Higher Education*, 2 December, 2005. Page 67: In Richards, Gertrude (ed), *Florentine Merchants in the Age of Medici*, Cambridge, MA: Harvard University Press, 1932, pp.236–240. Page 69: Labib, Subhi Y., "Capitalism in Medieval Islam," *The Journal of Economic History*, 29, 1969, 76–96. Reprinted with the permission of Cambridge University Press. Page 71: Ibn Hajar al-'Asqalani, from Levtzion, N. and J.F.P. Hopkins, *Corpus of Early Arabic Sources for West African History*, Cambridge: Cambridge University Press, 1981, 357–358. Reprinted with the permission of Cambridge University Press. Page 83: Smith, Adam, *An Inquiry into the Nature and Causes of the Wealth of Nations*, Everyman's Library, London: Dent & Sons, 1904, Vol. II, Book IV, Chapter VII, Part III, 1776. Page 87: POMERANZ, KENNETH; *THE GREAT DIVERGENCE*. © 2000 Princeton University Press. Reprinted by permission of the Princeton University Press. Page 89: O'Brien, Patrick, "European Economic Development: The Contribution of the Periphery," *The Economic History Review*, New Series, 35, 1982, pp.1–18. Page 91: In *News and Rumor in Renaissance Europe: The Fugger Newsletters*, Matthews, George T., ed, New York: Capricorn Books, 1959, pp. 64–71. Page 97: Sieyès, Emmanuel, "Qu'est-ce que le tiers état?" translated and reproduced in Stewart, John Hall, *A Documentary Survey of the French Revolution*, New York: Macmillan, 1951, pp. 43–44. Page 99: Reprinted by permission of the publisher from NATIONALISM: FIVE ROADS TO MODERNITY by Liah Greenfield, pp. 154–155, 184–186, Cambridge, Mass.: Harvard University Press, Copyright © 1992 by Liah Greenfield. Page 101: Breen, T.H. "'Baubles of Britain" The American and Consumer Revolutions of the Eighteenth Century.'" *Past and Present*, 119 (1988), pp.73–77, 97–99, 103–104. Reprinted by permission of Oxford University Press. Page 103: *Declaration and Resolves of the First Continental Congress*, October 14, 1774. Page 106: Anderson, Benedict, *Imagined Communities: Reflections on the Origin and Spread of Nationalism*, New York: Verso, 1983, pp.56–58, 62, 64–65. Page 110: Palmer, R.R., "The World Revolution of the West: 1763–1801," *Political Science Quarterly*, 69 (1954), pp.1–10. Reprinted by permission from *Political Science Quarterly*, 69 (March 1954): 1–14. Page 111: De Tocqueville, Alexis, *L'ancien régime et la revolution*, Translated by M.W. Patterson, Oxford: Basil Blackwell, 1856?, pp.155–157. Page 113: Knight, Franklin W., "The Haitian Revolution," *American Historical Review*, 105 (2000), pp.106, 109–114. Page 114: In Rainsford, Marcus, *An Historical account of the Black empire of Hayti: Comprehending a View of the Principal Transactions in the Revolution of Saint-Domingo; with its Ancient and Modern State*, James Cundee: London, 1805, pp.439–441. Page 116: Lynch, John, "The Origins of Spanish American Independence" in Bethell, Leslie, (ed) *The Independence of Latin America*, Cambridge: Cambridge University Press, 1987, pp.43–47. Reprinted with the permission of Cambridge University Press. Page 122: Mathias, Peter, *The First Industrial Nation: An Economic History of Britain 1700–1914*, New York: Methuen, 1969, pp.7–14. Reprinted with the permission of Routledge. Page 124: From CAPITALISM AND SLAVERY by Eric Williams. Copyright © 1944 by the University of North Carolina Press, renewed 1972 by Eric Williams. New introduction by Colin A. Palmer © 1994 by the University of North Carolina Press. Used by permission of the publisher. Page 125: In *The Novels and Miscellaneous Works of Daniel Defoe*, vol. XVII, Oxford: D.A. Talboys, 1841, pp.248–253. Page 127: Rodney, Walter, *How Europe Underdeveloped Africal*, Washington: Howard University press, 1981, originally published 1972. Page 128: Cugoano, Ottobah, *Thoughts and Sentiments on the Evil of Slavery*, London: Dawsons, 1969, pp.26–27, 94–96. Originally published 1787. Page 130: Testimony of Elizabeth Bentley, Commission for Inquiry Into the Employment of Children in Factories. Second Report. 1833. Testimony of Abina Mansah, in the case of Regina v Quamina Eddoo, Gold Coast, 1876. Page 136: Naff, Thomas, "Reform and the Conduct of Ottoman Diplomacy in the Reign of Selim III, 1789–1807", in *Journal of the American Oriental Society*, 83 (1963)", pp. 295, 310–311, 315. Page 138: In Hurewitz, J.C., ed., *Documents of Near East Diplomatic History*, New York: Columbia University, 1951. Page 139: Karpat, Kemal H., "The Stages of Ottoman History: A Structural Comparative Approach," in Karpat, Kemal H., ed., *The Ottoman State and its Place in World History*, Leiden: E.J. Brill, 1974, pp.90–93. Page 141: Takeo, Kuwabara, "The Meiji Revolution and Japan's Modernization," in *Meiji Ishin: Restoration and Revolution*, Michio, Nagai and Miguel Urrutia, eds., Tokyo: The United Nations University, 1985, pp. 21, 25–28. Page 143: Takuji, Shibahara, "Japan's Modernization from the Perspective of International Relations," in *Meiji Ishin: Restoration and Revolution*, Michio, Nagai and Miguel Urrutia, eds., Tokyo: The United Nations University, 1985, pp. 61–65. Page 144: In Lu, David John, *Sources of Japanese History*, volume 2, New York: McGraw-Hill, 1973, pp. 35–36. Page 158: Taylor, A.J.P., *Germany's First Bid for Colonies*, London: Macmillan, 1938, 3–7. Page 159: Ferry, Jules, "Speech Before the French Chamber of Deputies, March 28, 1884," Originally collected in , Discours et Opinions de Jules Ferry, edited by Paul Robiquet, Paris: Armand Colin & Cie., 1897, vol. 5, pp. 199–201, 210–11, 215–18. Page 161: Mahan, Alfred Thayer, "Effects of Asiatic Conditions upon International Policies," *North American Review*, 171 (November 1900), 612–613. Page 162: Ôkubo Toschimichi, Opinion Against Korean Expedition, October 1873, in Lu, David John, *Sources of Japanese History*, volume 2, New York: McGraw-Hill, 1973, pp.52–53. Page 167: Lenin, Vladimir Illyich, Imperialism: The Highest Phase of Capitalism, New York: International Publishers, 1939, pp. 62–63, 76–77, 83–84, 88–89. First published 1916. Page 169: Cain, P.J. and A.G. Hopkins, "Gentlemanly Capitalism and British Expansion Overseas II: New Imperialism, 1850–1945," *The*

Economic History Review, 40 (1987), 10–13. Page 170: Hobson, John A., Imperialism: A Study, London: George Allen & Unwin, 1954, pp.71–93. First published 1902. Page 172: Naoroji, Dadabhai, "Memorandum No.2 on The Moral Poverty in India and Native Thoughts on the Present British Indian Policy," 16 November, 1880, in Johari, J.C., (editor), *Voices of Indian Freedom Movement*, New Delhi: Akashdeep Publishing, 1993, 100–102. Page 177: Kipling, Rudyard, "The White Man's Burden," widely published from 1899 onwards. Page 178: Davies, Frances Elizagbeth, "The Missionary's Bride," in *Evangelical Magazine*, Volume 23 (1845) 536. 'Blackburn-house, Liverpool, 29 August, 1845. Page 179: Cromer, Evelyn Baring, *Modern Egypt*, London: MacMillan and Co, 1908, Vol. I, xvii-xviii, 7 and Vol. II, 568–570. Page 181: Lutfi al-Sayyid, Ahmad, "Lord Cromer before History," *Al-Jarida*, 13 April 1907, in Wendell, Charles, *The Evolution of Egyptian National Image*, Berkeley: University of California Press, 1972, 300–301. Reprinted by permission of the Regents of the University of California. Page 182: Excerpts from Conklin, Alice L. A MISSION TO CIVILIZE: THE REPUBLICAN IDEA OF EMPIRE IN FRANCE AND WEST AFRICA, 1895–1930. Copyright © 1997 by the Board of Trustees of the Leland Stanford Junior University. All rights reserved. Used with permission of the Stanford University Press, www.sup.org. Page 187: Churchill, Winston S., *The River War: An Historical Account of The Reconquest of the Soudan*, 2 Vols., London: Longmans, Green, 1899, pp. 82–164. Page 189: Margery Perham, *Ten Africans*, London: Faber and Faber Ltd., 1963, 73–74. Page 190: From THE TENTACLES OF PROGRESS: TECHNOLOGY TRANSFER IN THE AGE OF IMPERIALISM, 1850–1940 by Daniel R. Headrick, copyright © 1988 by Oxford University Press, Inc. Used by permission of Oxford University Press, Inc. Page 195: Robinson, Ronald and John Gallagher with Alice Denny, *Africa and the Victorians: The Climax of Imperialism in the Dark Continent*, New York: St. Martins Press, 1961, 18, 464–465, 467–468. Reproduced with the permission of Palgrave MacMillan. Page 197: "Constitution of the New Fantee Confederacy," November 1871, reproduced in Parliamentary Papers XLIX of 1873, House of Commons printed series 11/3637, 3–8; and letter of 10 December 1871 in same, 3. Page 199: Curtin, Philip D., *The World and the West: The European Challenge and the Overseas Response in the Age of Empire*, Cambridge: Cambridge University Press, 2000, 48–50. Page 201: Swettenham, Frank, *British Malaya: An Account of the Origin and Progress of British Influence in Malaya*, London G. Allen and Unwin, 1948, 175–177. First published 1906. Page 213: Stewart, John Hall, DOCUMENTARY SURVEY OF THE FRENCH REVOLUTION, 1st Edition, © 1951, pp. 43–44. Reprinted by permission of Pearson Education, Inc., Upper Saddle River, NJ. Page 215: "Memorandum respecting the Anglo-Russian Convention", in Gooch, G.P and Harold Temperley, editors, *British Documents on the Origins of the War 1898–1914*, London: H.M. Stationery Office, 1929, 612–616. Page 217: Schmitt, Bernadotte E., *The Origins of the First World War*, Pamphlet of the Historical Association, 1958, pp.6–7. Permission to reprint granted by The Historical Association. Page 218: Van Evera, Stephen, *The Cult of the Offensive and the Origins of the First World War*, in Steven E. Miller, ed., *Military Strategy and the Origins of the First World War*, Princeton: Princeton University Press, 1991, pp.58–60, 85. Page 221: Von Moltke to Bethman Hollweg, July 29, 1914, document 349 in Karl Kautsky, collector, *Outbreak of the World War: German Documents collected by Karl Kautsky*, New York: Oxford University Press, 1924. Page 225: Ponting, Clive, *Thirteen Days: The Road to the First World War*, London: Chatto & Windus, 2002, ix-xii. Page 226: Carnegie Endowment for International Peace, *German White Book Concerning the Responsibility of the Authors of the War*, New York: Oxford University Press, 1924. Page 228: Joll, James, "The 1914 Debate Continues: Fritz Fischer and His Critics." Past and Present, 34 (1996), pp. 100–113. Reprinted by permission of Oxford University Press. Page 232: Reprinted by permission from *Memoirs of the Maelstrom* by Joe Lunn. Copyright © 1999 by Joe Lunn. Published by Heinemann, a division of Reed Elsevier, Inc., Portsmouth, NH. All rights reserved. Page 234: In Horne, Charles F., ed., *Source Records of the Great War*, Volume V, Indianapolis: The American Legion, 1931, pp.107–111. Page 236: Decoded telegram provided to US Department of State, Decimal File 862.20212/69 (1910–1929), General Records of the Department of State, Record Group 59. Page 241: Translated and printed in Oakeshott, Michael, *The Social and Political Doctrines of Contemporary Europe*, Cambridge: Cambridge University Press, 1939, pp. 168–179. Reprinted with the permission of Cambridge University Press. Page 242: In *Papers Relating to the Foreign Relations of the United States: The Paris Peace Conference*, Vol. XIII, Washington: Government Printing Office, 1947, pp. 413, 425,489. Page 243: In Joachim Remak, ed, *The Nazi Years: A Documentary History*, Englewood Cliffs: Prentice-Hall , 1969, p. 24. Page 244: Bullock, Alan, *Hitler and the Origins of the Second World War*, London: Proceedings of the British Academy, 1967, pp 260–263, 270–272, 275–276. © The British Academy 1968. Reproduced by permission from *Proceedings from the British Academy* 53; 1967. Page 246: Translated in *Documents on German Foreign Policy, 1918–1947*, Washington: Government Printing Office, 1949, pp. 29–39. Page 247: Excerpts from "The Way of the Subjects" in TOKYO RECORD, copyright © 1943 by Ollo D. Tolischus and renewed 1970 by Naya G. Tolischus, reprinted by permission of Harcourt, Inc. Page 249: CROWLEY, JAMES B.: *JAPAN'S QUEST FOR AUTONOMY*. ©Princeton University Pres, 1994 renewed PUP. Reprinted by permission of the Princeton University Press. Page 254: Haile Selassie's Appeal to the League Assembly, originally printed in the *New York Times*, 30 April 1936, p. 8, as well as a number of other newspapers. It was later reprinted in Harold A. Hansen et. al., eds., *Fighting for freedom*, Philadelphia: John Winston, 1947. Page 255: *Parliamentary Debates: House of Commons, Fifth Series-Volume 339*, London: His Majesty's Stationary Office, 1938, pp.47–50. Page 257: Wheeler-Bennett, John W., *Munich: Prologue to Tragedy*, London: Macmillan, 1966, pp.433–437. First printed 1948. Reproduced with the permission of Palgrave Macmillan. Page 259: Reproduced from *How War Came* by Donald Cameron Watt (Copyright © Donald Cameron Watt 1989) by permission of PFD on behalf of Professor Donald Cameron Watt. Page 261: Offner, Arnold A., "The United States and National Socialist Germany," in Wolfgang J. Mommsen and Lothar Kettenacker, eds., *The Fascist Challenge and the Policy of Appeasement*, London: George Allen & Unwin, 1983, 417–421. Page 264: Address by Maxim Litvinov, 29 December 1933, from *Documentary Background of World War II 1931 to 1941*, edited by James W. Gantenbein. Copyright © 1948 Columbia University Press. Reprinted with permission of the publisher. Page 268: Reprinted by permission of the publisher from THE HOLOCAUST AND THE HISTORIANS by Lucy S. Dawidowicz, pp. 8–9, 11–14, 15, Cambridge, Mass.: Harvard University Press, Copyright © 1981 by Lucy S. Dawidowicz. Page 271: Gerlach, Christian, "The Wannsee Conference, the Fate of the Jews, and Hitler's Decision in Principle to Exterminate all the European Jews", *The Journal of Modern History*, 1998, (70) pp.759–812, translated by Stephen Duffy. Page 274: This translation in Arad, Yitzhak, Yisrael Gutman, and Abraham Margaliot, (eds.), *Documents on the Holocaust*, Jerusalem: Ktav Publishing House, 1981, pp. 249–261, translated by Lea Ben Dor. Page 276: Copyright © 1996 Exterminate All the Brutes by Sven Lindqvist. Reprinted by the permission of the New Press. www.thenewpress.com. Page 278: *The National Archives of South Africa*, The Military Governor of Pretoria (MGP) Vol. 258. Circular Memorandum N. 29, 21 December 1900. My thanks to Dr. Stowell Kessler for providing this document. Page 288: Suret-Canale, Jean and A. Adu Boahen, "West Africa 1945–1960," in Mazrui, Ali, (ed), *Unesco General History of Africa VIII: Africa since 1935*, Berkeley: University of California Press, 1999, pp. 165–169. Originally published in 1993. Page 290: Gandhi, Mohandas, *Hind Swaraj, or Indian Home Rule*, Madras: G.A. Natesan, 1921, Chapter XVII. First published 1910. And "Message to Chinese Women," *Bihar Pacchi Dilhi*, 18 July 1947, 354.. Page 292: Nkrumah, Kwame, *I Speak of Freedom: A Statement of African Ideology*, New York: Praeger, 1961, pp1, 6–7, 9–13, 15–16, 18–19, 22. Page 295: Mandela, Nelson, "statement from the dock at the Rivonia trial," Pretoria Supreme Court, 20 April 1964. Page 297: David Abernethy, *The Dynamics of Global Dominance: European Overseas Empires, 1415–1980*, New Haven: Yale University Press, 2000, pp. 345, 348, 357–358. Page 299: "Declaration on the granting of independence to colonial countries and peoples," *Official Records of the General Assembly*, Fifteenth Session, Supplement 2 (A/4684), New York, 1961, pp.66–67. Page 305: In Ralph B. Levering, Vladimir O. Pechatnov, Verena Botzenhart-Vieha, and C. Earl Edmondson, *Debating the Origins of the Cold War: American and Russian Perspectives:*, Lanham: Rowman and Littlefield Publishers, 2002, pp.69–71. Page 306: In Ralph B. Levering, Vladimir O. Pechatnov, Verena Botzenhart-Vieha, and C. Earl Edmondson, Debating the Origins of the Cold War: American and Russian Perspectives:, Lanham: Rowman and Littlefield Publishers, 2002, pp.160–163. Page 308: Ho Chi Minh: Selected Writings 1920–1969, Hanoi: Foreign Languages Publishing House, 1977, pp. 53–56. Page 309: Webb, James, "Why We Fought and Why We Would Do it Again," September 2003, http://www.jameswebb.com/articles/variouspubs/amlegionwhywefought.htm. Page 315: From "Amarican Globalism" by David Reynolds from Globalization In World History edited by A G Hopkins, published by Pimlico. *Reprinted by permission of the Random House Group*. Page 317: *Globalization and the Nation State* by Keith Suter. Copyright © by Keith Suter. Reproduced with permission of Greenwood Publishing Group, Inc., Westport, CT. Page 320: Frank, Andre Gunder, *Capitalism and Underdevelopment in Latin America: Historical Studies of Chile and Brazil*, pp. 281–286, 294–296, 304–306, 312. Copyright © by Monthly Review Press. Reprinted by permission of Monthly Review Foundation. Page 322: Subcommandante Marcos, "The Fourth World War," *In Motion Magazine*, November 11, 2001, Permanent URL: http://www.inmotionmagazine.com/auto/fourth.html. Page 324: Robert Jensen, "Interview with Medha Patkar," *ZMag* 17 (April 2004). Page 329: Huntington, Samuel P., "The Clash of Civilizations?" Reprinted by permission of *Foreign Affairs*, Summer 1993 (72), pp.22–36. Copyright © 1993 by the Council on Foreign Relations, Inc. Page 332: Said, Edward W., "The Clash of Ignorance," *The Nation*, 22 October 2001. Page 334: White House, Office of the Press Secretary, June 1, 2002. Permanent URL http://www.whitehouse.gov/news/releases/2002/06/print/20020601–3.html. Page 336: Abdul Rauf, Imam Feisal, "Why Multiculturalism," Article presented at the Prato Multicultural conference, Prato, Italy, September 2004.